PC WORLD
DOS 6
Command Reference
& Problem Solver

*For Dilip
Hope this
supports your
efforts.*

PC WORLD
DOS 6
Command Reference & Problem Solver

by John Socha and Devra Hall

IDG BOOKS

IDG Books Worldwide, Inc.
An International Data Group Company

San Mateo, California ♦ Indianapolis, Indiana ♦ Boston, Massachusetts

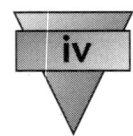

DOS 6 Command Reference and Problem Solver

Published by
IDG Books Worldwide, Inc.
An International Data Group Company
155 Bovet Road, Suite 310
San Mateo, CA 94402

Text and art copyright ©1993 by IDG Books Worldwide. All rights reserved. No part of this book may be reproduced or transmitted in any form, by any means (electronic, photocopying, recording, or otherwise) without the prior written permission of the publisher.

Library of Congress Catalog Card No.: 93-61071

ISBN   1-56884-055-1

Printed in the United States of America

10 9 8 7 6 5 4 3 2 1

Distributed in the United States by IDG Books Worldwide, Inc.

Distributed in Canada by Macmillan of Canada, a Division of Canada Publishing Corporation; by Computer and Technical Books in Miami, Florida, for South America and the Caribbean; by Longman Singapore in Singapore, Malaysia, Thailand, and Korea; by Toppan Co. Ltd. in Japan; by Asia Computerworld in Hong Kong; by Woodslane Pty. Ltd. in Australia and New Zealand; and by Transword Publishers Ltd. in the U.K. and Europe.

For information on where to purchase IDG Books outside the U.S., contact Christina Turner at 415-312-0633.

For information on translations, contact Marc Jeffrey Mikulich, Foreign Rights Manager, at IDG Books Worldwide; FAX NUMBER 415-358-1260.

For sales inquiries and special prices for bulk quantities, write to the address above or call IDG Books Worldwide at 415-312-0650.

Limit of Liability/Disclaimer of Warranty: The author and publisher have used their best efforts in preparing this book. IDG Books Worldwide, Inc., International Data Group, Inc., PC World, and the author make no representation or warranties with respect to the accuracy or completeness of the contents of this book and specifically disclaim any implied warranties or merchantability or fitness for any particular purpose and shall in no event be liable for any loss of profit or any other commercial damage, including but not limited to special, incidental, consequential, or other damages.

Trademarks: Microsoft and MS-DOS are registered trademarks and Microsoft Windows is a trademark of Microsoft Corporation. All brand names and product names used in this book are trademarks, registered trademarks, or trade names of their respective holders. IDG Books Worldwide is not associated with any product or vendor mentioned in this book. PC World is a registered trademark of PCW Communications, Inc.

About the Authors

John Socha

John Socha is the president of Socha Computing, Inc., the developer of *Imaginaria*, the multimedia screen saver published by Claris Corporation. He is also the creator of the bestselling *Norton Commander*, which has sold hundreds of thousands of copies.

John has also authored and coauthored a number of books: *PC World DOS 6 Handbook* (with Clint Hicks and Devra Hall, IDG Books, 1993), *DOS 6.0 Power Tools* (with John M. Goodman), *Assembly Language for the PC* (with Peter Norton, Brady Books, 1993; formerly titled: *Peter Norton's Assembly Language Book*), and *Learn Programming and Visual Basic 2 with John Socha* (Sybex, 1992).

In the early days of the IBM PC, he wrote a column for the long defunct magazine, *Softalk for the IBM PC*, where he published such programs as ScreenSave (the first screen blanker for PCs), KbdBuffer (extends the keyboard buffer), and Whereis (the first find program). After the demise of *Softalk*, John concentrated on finishing his PhD in physics and writing a commercial program that became the *Norton Commander*.

Later, John worked for several years at Peter Norton Computing, where he continued to develop the *Norton Commander* through version 3.0. He was also the first director of research and development at Peter Norton Computing, which is now a division of Symantec Corp. John started Socha Computing, Inc. in 1992 to develop first-rate Windows products to be published by other companies.

John grew up in Wisconsin, earned a B.S. Degree in Electrical Engineering from the University of Wisconsin – Madison and an M.S. and PhD in Applied Physics from Cornell University. He now lives on Lake Washington in Bellevue, Washington.

Devra Hall

Devra Hall is coauthor of the bestselling *PC World DOS 6 Handbook* and director of corporate communications for Looking Glass Software, Inc. a Los Angeles-based firm that develops multimedia software tools.

Devra has been working with computers for more than 20 years. Starting as a programmer, she worked her way to mainframe systems design before transitioning to the world of PCs in the early 1980s.

By the mid-1980s, Devra widened her career path to include corporate computer consulting, entertainment industry public relations, journalism, and university teaching.

In the last few years, Devra has done extensive research in the field of interactive multimedia in education (she has a Master's Degree in Educational Technology and Media), wrote countless on-line help applications for a variety of software, and was a member of the creative team that produced the *Illuminated Books and Manuscripts* for IBM.

Devra continues her virtual journey through this earthly dimension as an author, educator, multimedia designer, and corporate communicator, living in Glendale, California.

About IDG Books Worldwide

Welcome to the world of IDG Books Worldwide.

IDG Books Worldwide, Inc., is a division of International Data Group, the world's largest publisher of computer-related information and the leading global provider of information services on information technology. IDG publishes over 194 computer publications in 62 countries. Forty million people read one or more IDG publications each month.

If you use personal computers, IDG Books is committed to publishing quality books that meet your needs. We rely on our extensive network of publications, including such leading periodicals as *Macworld, InfoWorld, PC World, Computerworld, Publish, Network World*, and *SunWorld*, to help us make informed and timely decisions in creating useful computer books that meet your needs.

Every IDG book strives to bring extra value and skill-building instruction to the reader. Our books are written by experts, with the backing of IDG periodicals, and with careful thought devoted to issues such as audience, interior design, use of icons, and illustrations. Our editorial staff is a careful mix of high-tech journalists and experienced book people. Our close contact with the makers of computer products helps ensure accuracy and thorough coverage. Our heavy use of personal computers at every step in production means we can deliver books in the most timely manner.

We are delivering books of high quality at competitive prices on topics customers want. At IDG, we believe in quality, and we have been delivering quality for over 25 years. You'll find no better book on a subject than an IDG book.

John Kilcullen
President and C.E.O.
IDG Books Worldwide, Inc.

IDG Books Worldwide, Inc. is a division of International Data Group. The officers are Patrick J. McGovern, Founder and Board Chairman; Walter Boyd, President. International Data Group's publications include: **ARGENTINA's** Computerworld Argentina, InfoWorld Argentina; **ASIA's** Computerworld Hong Kong, PC World Hong Kong, Computerworld Southeast Asia, PC World Singapore, Computerworld Malaysia, PC World Malaysia; **AUSTRALIA's** Computerworld Australia, Australian PC World, Australian Macworld, Network World, Reseller, IDG Sources; **AUSTRIA's** Computerwelt Oesterreich, PC Test; **BRAZIL's** Computerworld, Mundo IBM, Mundo Unix, PC World, Publish; **BULGARIA's** Computerworld Bulgaria, Ediworld, PC & Mac World Bulgaria; **CANADA's** Direct Access, Graduate Computerworld, InfoCanada, Network World Canada; **CHILE's** Computerworld, Informatica; **COLOMBIA's** Computerworld Colombia; **CZECH REPUBLIC's** Computerworld, Elektronika, PC World; **DENMARK's** CAD/CAM WORLD, Communications World, Computerworld Danmark, LOTUS World, Macintosh Produktkatalog, Macworld Danmark, PC World Produktguide, Windows World; **EQUADOR's** PC World; **EGYPT's** Computerworld (CW) Middle East, PC World Middle East; **FINLAND's** MikroPC, Tietoviikko, Tietoverkko; **FRANCE's** Distributique, GOLDEN MAC, InfoPC, Languages & Systems, Le Guide du Monde Informatique, Le Monde Informatique, Telecoms & Reseaux; **GERMANY's** Computerwoche, Computerwoche Focus, Computerwoche Extra, Computerwoche Karriere, Information Management, Macwelt, Netzwelt, PC Welt, PC Woche, Publish, Unit; **HUNGARY's** Alaplap, Computerworld SZT, PC World; **INDIA's** Computers & Communications; **ISRAEL's** Computerworld Israel, PC World Israel; **ITALY's** Computerworld Italia, Lotus Magazine, Macworld Italia, Networking Italia, PC World Italia; **JAPAN's** Computerworld Japan, Macworld Japan, SunWorld Japan, Windows World; **KENYA's** East African Computer News; **KOREA's** Computerworld Korea, Macworld Korea, PC World Korea; **MEXICO's** Compu Edicion, Compu Manufactura, Computacion/Punto de Venta, Computerworld Mexico, MacWorld, Mundo Unix, PC World, Windows; **THE NETHERLAND'S** Computer! Totaal, LAN Magazine, MacWorld; **NEW ZEALAND's** Computer Listings, Computerworld New Zealand, New Zealand PC World; **NIGERIA's** PC World Africa; **NORWAY's** Computerworld Norge, C/World, Lotusworld Norge, Macworld Norge, Networld, PC World Ekspress, PC World Norge, PC World's Product Guide, Publish World, Student Data, Unix World, Windowsworld, IDG Direct Response; **PANAMA's** PC World; **PERU's** Computerworld Peru, PC World; **PEOPLES REPUBLIC OF CHINA's** China Computerworld, PC World China, Electronics International, China Network World; **IDG HIGH TECH BEIJING's** New Product World; **IDG SHENZHEN's** Computer News Digest; **PHILLIPPINES'** Computerworld, PC World; **POLAND's** Computerworld Poland, PC World/Komputer; **PORTUGAL's** Cerebro/PC World, Correio Informatico/Computerworld, MacIn; **ROMANIA's** PC World; **RUSSIA's** Computerworld-Moscow, Mir-PC, Sety; **SLOVENIA's** Monitor Magazine; **SOUTH AFRICA's** Computing S.A.; **SPAIN's** Amiga World, Computerworld Espana, Communicaciones World, Macworld Espana, NeXTWORLD, PC World Espana, Publish, Sunworld; **SWEDEN's** Attack, ComputerSweden, Corporate Computing, Lokala Natverk/LAN, Lotus World, MAC&PC, Macworld, Mikrodatorn, PC World, Publishing & Design (CAP), Datalngenjoren, Maxi Data, Windows World; **SWITZERLAND's** Computerworld Schweiz, Macworld Schweiz, PC & Workstation; **TAIWAN's** Computerworld Taiwan, Global Computer Express, PC World Taiwan; **THAILAND's** Thai Computerworld; **TURKEY's** Computerworld Monitor, Macworld Turkiye, PC World Turkiye; **UNITED KINGDOM's** Lotus Magazine, Macworld, Sunworld; **UNITED STATES'** AmigaWorld, Cable in the Classroom, CD Review, CIO, Computerworld, Desktop Video World, DOS Resource Guide, Electronic News, Federal Computer Week, Federal Integrator, GamePro, IDG Books, InfoWorld, InfoWorld Direct, Laser Event, Macworld, Multimedia World, Network World, NeXTWORLD, PC Games, PC Letter, PC World Publish, Sumeria, SunWorld, SWATPro, Video Event; **VENEZUELA's** Computerworld Venezuela, MicroComputerworld Venezuela; **VIETNAM's** PC World Vietnam

Dedication

JS — To Michele, for putting up with too many books.

DH — To FRED, a source of never-ending challenges.

Acknowledgments

We'd like to thank the people at IDG Books who transformed our manuscript into this book: Stuart Stuple, our project editor who masterminded its completion; Mary Bednarek and Diane Steele, for managing the editorial process; Beth Jenkins and Mary Breidenbach, for guiding the book through the production process; Marian Bernstein, for a wonderful cover; and Corbin Collins, for his outstanding editorial work.

The publisher would like to give special thanks to Patrick J. McGovern, without whom this book would not have been possible.

Credits

Publisher
David Solomon

Managing Editor
Mary Bednarek

Acquisitions Editor
Janna Custer

Production Manager
Beth Jenkins

Senior Editors
Sandy Blackthorn
Diane Graves Steele

Production Coordinator
Cindy L. Phipps

Acquisitions Assistant
Megg Bonar

Editorial Assistant
Patricia R. Reynolds

Project Editor
Stuart J. Stuple

Editor
Corbin Collins

Technical Reviewer
Stuart J. Stuple

Production Staff
Beth Jenkins
Mary Breidenbach

Proofreader
Charles A. Hutchinson

Indexer
Steve Rath

Book Design
Mary Breidenbach

Contents at a Glance

Introduction 1

Part I: Problem Solver 7

Chapter 1: Installing MS-DOS 6 9
Chapter 2: Startup Process 23
Chapter 3: SmartDrive 35
Chapter 4: DoubleSpace 43
Chapter 5: Memory Management 63
Chapter 6: The DOS 6 Utility Programs 77

Part II: Command Reference 89

Index 499

Table of Contents

Introduction 1
    The MS-DOS 6.2 upgrade 2
    What's in this book? 3
    Conventions we use 4
        Commands 4
        Syntax lines 4
        Icons 5
    How to use this book 5

Part I: Problem Solver 7

Chapter 1: Installing MS-DOS 6 9

Problems with the Setup Program 10
    Is your video display unreadable? 10
        If the lines on your screen are truncated, or (even worse) if they are totally unintelligible, your problems may be caused by incompatible hardware settings.
    Are your upgrade disks defective? 11
        There is always a chance that one or more of your installation disks is defective. Your disk is probably defective if during the copy process you receive one or more error messages such as Data error reading or General failure reading.
    Are you receiving repeated prompts to insert the same disk or
    warnings that your Uninstall disk is not correct? 11
        Sometimes memory-resident programs interfere with the Setup program's capability to read a Setup or Uninstall disk. Some disk-caching programs can also cause this problem. There are a few possible remedies.
        Installing Setup from your hard drive 11
        Installing MS-DOS 6 manually 12

Problems with Disk Space and Partitions 12
    You are using a compression program and were sure that you would have
    enough space to install MS-DOS 6, but your system said "not!" 12
        The MS-DOS files, not including any of the utility programs, require 4.2MB of free disk space. Your system reports 6MB free on your compressed drive, so you shouldn't have a problem, right? Not necessarily. It depends on the ratio by which the program files can be compressed.

You'd like to install the utility programs, or at least some of them, but you're not sure how much space each one requires. 13

The MS-DOS files, not including any of the utility programs, require 4.2MB of free disk space. During the installation process, you are asked to specify whether or not you want to include the Backup, Undelete, or Anti-Virus utility programs in the installation, and, if so, whether you want the DOS version, Windows version, or both.

Is there any way to make MS-DOS 6 take up less space? 14

Hard disk space is prime real estate, and even if you are planning to use DoubleSpace, you may want to keep as much disk space as possible free for other uses. There are a few adjustments you can make to save a little space.

Installing MS-DOS 6 program files individually 15

You get the message `Your computer uses a disk compression program.` 16

If this message appears when you run Setup, you may say "Yes, thank you. I know that. So what?" What it doesn't tell you, however, is that because of it you will not be able to create an Uninstall disk. That also means that you will not be able to restore your previous DOS version once you run Setup.

You get the message `Your computer uses SuperStor disk compression.` 17

When Setup gives you a very specific message, such as this one about the SuperStor product from AddStor, Inc., it means that you need to fix the problem using tools from the third-party vendor (AddStor) rather than Microsoft.

You get the message `Too Many Primary Partitions or Incompatible Primary DOS Partition.` 17

These messages generally indicate that DOS is either unable to figure out which partition to use during installation or is unable to take control of the primary partition. You need to reconfigure your hard drive using the FDISK command.

Repartitioning your hard drive with FDISK 17

You get the message `Incompatible hard disk or device driver.` 18

This message usually appears if your computer has a Novell, Priam, Everex, UNIX, XENIX, or Vfeature Deluxe partition; or if your computer has a SyQuest or Bernoulli drive.

You get the message `Incompatible partition.` 19

If you have an incompatible partition, such as a SpeedStor Bootall partition, Setup cannot automatically update your system. You can try installing MS-DOS 6 manually or, alternatively, you can delete the incompatible partition and create a new DOS partition. If that doesn't work, you may need to contact Microsoft or the manufacturer of the software that created the incompatible partition.

Hardware and Third-Party Software Considerations 19

Can you use DOS 6 on your IBM PS/1? 19

Yes, you can. You should not have any problem installing MS-DOS 6 on an IBM PS/1 computer.

Can you use DOS 6 on your Tandy? 20

Yes, you can. You should not have any problem installing MS-DOS 6 on most models of the Tandy computer.

Converting from DR DOS to MS-DOS 6. 20

You should not have any problem converting from DR DOS to MS-DOS 6. However, you need to take some preliminary steps in preparation for running MS-DOS Setup.

Problems Running MS-DOS after Setup Is Finished 21
   How can you determine where the problem exists? 21
The way to narrow down the potential problem area is to execute individual startup commands while bypassing the others. Because you were able to run the Setup program successfully, you can now use the F8 and F5 keys to bypass portions of the startup process.

Chapter 2: Startup Process 23

Interactive Startup Techniques 23
   You've heard the term interactive startup, but you're not sure what it is or what it's for. 23
The main purpose of any interactive startup is to find the root of a system problem that may be caused by a command in your CONFIG.SYS or AUTOEXEC.BAT file. The term interactive startup, as applied to MS-DOS, can be confusing. Not only are there a few different interactive startup methods, but you can approach startup problem-solving in two distinct ways: constructive or deconstructive.

   Your computer hangs. Is the problem caused by something in one of your startup files? How can you find out? 25
If you're installing a new device or experiencing a problem communicating with a system device, the cause is probably in a startup file. If a device works with one program but not another, the problem is probably not in the a startup file. If you're not sure that this is where the problem lies, you can test your theory by bypassing both your CONFIG.SYS and AUTOEXEC.BAT files entirely. This is the interactive startup method sometimes referred to as a clean start, and it forces the system to start up with a minimum configuration.

   You know you have a problem in either your CONFIG.SYS or AUTOEXEC.BAT file. What can you do to track it down? 25
In order to determine which command is causing your problems, you need to isolate the commands. For example, if you suspect the problem is a device driver that you just added, be aware that you may have another device driver that conflicts (even though it had been working fine). Try loading just the new driver (with memory management if appropriate) to see if it works alone.

     Interacting with the CONFIG.SYS file 25
     Interacting with the AUTOEXEC.BAT file 26

   Do you really have to confirm or bypass each and every startup command individually, one at a time? 26
When you're using an interactive startup to isolate problems in your CONFIG.SYS or AUTOEXEC.BAT files, you may have to restart repeatedly until you find the problem line. Whether you're using the construction or deconstruction approach (both are described at the beginning of this section), you can tell the system to run all the remaining commands in the startup file without prompting you further for individual line confirmation. Similarly, you can also tell the system to bypass all the remaining commands.

   Can you use an interactive startup method when using multiple configurations? 26
No problem here. You just begin a little differently.

Multiple Configurations 27
Your system boots up with the default configuration, bypassing your startup menu. What's wrong? 28
After going to all the trouble of creating multiple configurations, you find that your startup menu fails to appear. Chances are good that it's just an errant blank space or special character that's in the way.

You defined pretty menu colors, but after startup the colors revert to the default screen colors. What happened? 28
After going to all the trouble of looking up which numbers represent which colors and setting your color scheme to suit your taste, you find that the colors vanish as soon as you've made your menu selection.

You are using multiple configuration submenus and would like to find a way to go back to a previous menu. 28
There's nothing worse then selecting a menu option accidentally, or just changing your mind, and then finding out that it's too late; you can't get back to the prior menu. Luckily, that need not ever happen to you. You can include menu options to return to the prior menu or just memorize the secret keystroke.

Is there any way to create blank lines between menu options? How about clearing the screen? 29
These two questions appeared several times in the MS-DOS forum on CompuServe. Some menu creators thought if they could double-space the options on the screen, it would cut down on the number of times people accidentally selected a wrong menu. The desire to clear the screen was an aesthetic one, but remember that the screen clears automatically when you select a submenu.

CONFIG.SYS and AUTOEXEC.BAT Commands 30
How does DoubleSpace interact with your CONFIG.SYS file? Does this have anything to do with the assignment of drive letters for other uses? 30
When you run DoubleSpace for the first time, the setup program adds a DEVICE command to your CONFIG.SYS file to load the DBLSPACE.SYS device driver. Even though DoubleSpace does this for you, there are a few things you should know in the event that you are making any changes to your CONFIG.SYS file.

Do you really need to set the FILES line in your CONFIG.SYS file? 30
Your computer uses RAM for all kinds of things, such as storing information about files (their contents as well as bookkeeping data). You may be surprised to learn that the amount of RAM dedicated to keeping track of files is under your control via the FILES and BUFFERS commands.

Why would you run SMARTDRV from your CONFIG.SYS file? 31
If you are familiar with earlier versions of MS-DOS, you may be thinking that SMARTDRV belongs in your CONFIG.SYS file. That used to be true, but beginning with MS-DOS 6.0, the SMARTDRV.EXE command, run from the AUTOEXEC.BAT file, replaced the SMARTDRV.SYS device driver. Okay, no problem. But now to add to the confusion, you've heard that you can (and in some cases should) still run SmartDrive from your CONFIG.SYS file.

What's the difference between using BUFFERS and SMARTDRV? 32
If you're confused about the difference between the BUFFERS command and SmartDrive, you're not alone. Both commands share a common purpose: to speed up disk access.

How many buffers should you allocate? 32
The number of buffers you allocate depends on two things: the size of your hard disk and whether you plan to use a disk-caching utility, such as SMARTDRV. Generally, if you're operating a cache, you don't need very many buffers.

What's the most effective way to organize the paths to
your various programs? 33
A long path may require an increase in environment variable space. Windows users can get around this pretty easily, and DOS users can too, but they have to work a little harder at it.

What can you do if you get a startup message saying
Error: Unable to control A20 line? 34
The A20 line controls whether the high memory area (HMA) is available or not. It is a hardware component of systems with 286 or higher processors that allows programs to access the first 64K of extended memory. If DOS cannot control the A20 line, then it is also unable to access the HMA. Sometimes HIMEM.SYS cannot determine how to control the A20 line, and you must help.

Chapter 3: SmartDrive 35

Disk Caching: Basic Concepts 35
You've heard a lot about the benefits of caching and the dangers
of write caching? What do these terms mean? 35
The whole point of caching is to speed up communication between your relatively slow hard disk and the faster processing power of your system. Because there are two times when the system accesses the disk (to read and to write data), there are two kinds of disk caching. Caching during the read part of the access is a common and proven technology. Microsoft introduced write caching to SmartDrive with DOS 6.0 and, as with many new products, there were some problems.

What does the phrase flush the cache mean, and is it important? 36
This term is used in conjunction with write-behind caching.

Can you use Read Only caching on one drive and Read and
Write on another? 36
If you are reading extremely critical data from one disk and never want to risk losing that data (no matter how small the risk), you might want to set the cache to Read Only. But meanwhile you're writing less critical information to another disk and would like to have the benefit of the Read and Write cache on that drive.

Preventing File Corruption 36
What is the problem with SmartDrive, and should you use it? 36
The problem is write-behind caching — not so much the concept (it does indeed improve performance), but the fact that it was incorporated into MS-DOS 6 as the default setting, and the fact that unsuspecting users were unaware that the return of a DOS prompt did not necessarily mean that the cache had been flushed.

What SmartDrive precautions can you take if you are using MS-DOS 6.0? ... 37
The version of SmartDrive included with MS-DOS 6.0 can be used in a safe and problem-free manner. The key is understanding fully how SmartDrive works. Once you understand its actions, you can use the SmartDrive switch settings to control its actions to suit your work needs.

What's different about SmartDrive in MS-DOS 6.2,
and how does it prevent file corruption? 37
In order to help users who may experience problems caused by turning off the machine with the write cache filled, Microsoft has a new SmartDrive version that is more conservative. They do not consider this to be a "bug fix," but the default settings are safer. The tradeoff is slightly slower disk-write performance, so if you prefer speed over vigilance, you can still use the switch settings to suit your own preferences.

Commonly Asked SmartDrive Questions 38
How can you see the current status of SmartDrive on your system? 38
If you want to know the size of your cache and what type of cache is running on each drive, you can run the SMARTDRV command from the DOS prompt.

How can you determine whether you need to use SmartDrive's
DOUBLE_BUFFER feature? 39
If you want some advice on whether or not you should use the DOUBLE_BUFFER feature, you can run the SMARTDRV command from the DOS prompt. The status chart displayed also indicates for each drive whether double buffering is advisable.

How can you tell if your cache is really effective? 39
In order to evaluate the effectiveness of your cache, you want to know the size of the data elements as well as how often the cache saves your system from having to read from the disk.

Will changing the cache size, element size, or both increase SmartDrive's
performance? 40
Computer users are forever in search of better and faster means for accomplishing their tasks. When used optimally, disk caching can achieve noticeable speed benefits.

What size should the cache be? 40
Whereas disk caching can achieve noticeable speed benefits, determining the optimal cache size for your system configuration and work habits may be a matter of trial and error. But you can follow some general principles.

What does the Windows SmartMonitor hit rate really measure,
and can you alter it? 41
Hit rate is the percentage of data that SmartDrive is able to deliver to a program without reading the disk again. The Cache Hit Rate area in the lower right-hand portion of the window displays a histogram showing the performance history of the SmartDrive cache. And here's how it works.

Does sequence matter when you specify SMARTDRV parameters? 41
Generally, you can place command parameters and switches in any order you want. In the case of SmartDrive, however, the placement of the ElementSize switch (/E) has repercussions.

Does SmartDrive really cache DoubleSpace drives? 42
DoubleSpace drives are really just files, and SmartDrive does not cache files. Nevertheless, when you run SMARTDRV from the DOS prompt, the Disk Caching Status chart shows YES under read cache for both your DoubleSpace and host drives. And if you've enabled write caching, it shows YES under write cache, too. How can that be?

Chapter 4: Double Space 43

Understanding How DoubleSpace Works 43
What is disk compression? 43
Disk compression programs combine data compression algorithms with more effective disk-storage management techniques to make more effective use of your system's disk space.

Data compression 43
More effective storage management 44

Table of Contents

How much can I really gain by using DoubleSpace? 46

Commercial compression programs talk about doubling your disk space, and even Microsoft calls the MS-DOS 6 program DoubleSpace. In reality, however, doubling is usually a figure of speech. The precise compression ratio varies from file to file. Some files have a lot of replaceable parts, making ratios of even 4:1 quite possible. Other files have very few, if any, extra parts, and the ratio can be as low as 1:1, meaning no space savings at all.

What's the difference between creating a CVF and compressing the current drive? 46

It is easy to become confused when Microsoft refers to creating a compressed volume file (CVF) as something different from compressing the current drive. After all, to compress a drive — any drive — DoubleSpace creates a CVF.

Compressing the current drive 46
Creating an empty CVF 46

You want to specify how much space you want left uncompressed when DoubleSpace compresses the current drive. 47

When you run DoubleSpace, the program gives you a choice between Express or Custom Setup. The Express option turns all control over to the Setup program and compresses your current drive.

How does DoubleSpace assign drive letters? 47

The assignment of drive letters depends first on whether you are compressing the existing drive or creating a new empty compressed volume file. If you're compressing the existing drive, the drive letter assignment also depends on whether DoubleSpace detects Novell Netware in memory.

You want to change the drive letter that DoubleSpace has already assigned to the new host drive. 48

If you have devices, such as a RAM drive or CD-ROM, and you run DoubleSpace to compress the existing drive during a time when those devices are not loaded, you may find that you need to change the drive letter that was assigned by DoubleSpace.

Can't find your compressed drive? 48

The importance of the Mount and Unmount commands in the Drive menu becomes clear when you remember that a compressed drive is not a real drive at all but a file masquerading as a drive. The Mount command creates the connection between a CVF and a drive letter; the Unmount command severs this connection.

You're running MS-DOS 6.0 and you want to use compressed floppy disks without running DoubleSpace Setup on your system. 49

When you run DoubleSpace Setup, the Setup program creates a DBLSPACE.INI file (among others) and places the DBLSPACE.BIN file in the root directory of the startup drive so that it loads automatically upon bootup. In order to use DoubleSpace compressed floppy disks, DoubleSpace must be loaded, and the INI file must be available, but you do not need to run Setup. Instead, you can create your own INI file and copy the BIN file to the root.

You haven't created any compressed volume files on your hard drive but you get a message saying `There are no more drive letters reserved for DoubleSpace to use...` **What should you do?** 50

This message appears whenever you try to mount a compressed floppy disk, and DoubleSpace cannot find the required DBLSPACE.BIN and DBLSPACE.INI files. If you have never run DoubleSpace to create a CVF on your hard drive, then these files do not exist yet. You have two choices.

PC World DOS 6 Command Reference and Problem Solver

Optimizing DoubleSpace 50
    You want to adjust the estimated compression ratio to reflect more
    accurate projections of available free space. 50

DoubleSpace has two compression ratios: one for data already stored in your compressed volume file and the other for projecting free space. The first number is the average of all the compression ratios used when storing the files, and its value changes each time a file is added, modified, or deleted from the CVF. The second number is the ratio that DoubleSpace uses to estimate how much free space you have on a compressed volume. Initially, DoubleSpace uses 2:1 as the ratio for its estimated projection of available space, and this value remains constant unless you choose to alter it.

    Is there a way to automatically match the estimated free space
    ratio with the actual ratio used with existing files? 51

Yes. You can make the computer do all the work for you. After all, isn't that what the computer is for? You can bypass the menus and selection screens by using the Ratio switch with the DoubleSpace command.

    Do you need all that uncompressed free space on the host drive? 52

When DoubleSpace compresses a drive, it leaves about 2MB of uncompressed space for the host drive. This is where DoubleSpace then places your system files. If you're a Windows user and have a permanent swapfile, DoubleSpace also places it on the host drive.

    How do you adjust the size of the host drive and compressed
    volume file (CVF)? 52

Changing the size of a CVF means changing the amount of free space on the host drive. (Remember: the CVF is just a file on the host.) In order to increase the size of the CVF, you must use uncompressed free space from the host drive. Conversely, when you decrease the size of a CVF, you increase the amount of uncompressed free space available on the host drive. Space reappropriated from a compressed volume file must be contiguous, so you really should run the DoubleSpace defragment command first.

    Should you use DEFRAG or DBLSPACE /DEF? 53

If you are confused by the abbreviated use of the word defragment in two separate commands, you are not alone. Although the function of both the DEFRAG and the DBLSPACE /DEF commands is to use contiguous disk sectors, the goal of DEFRAG is to create contiguous sectors of related data on the disk, whereas the DBLSPACE /DEF command's goal is to create contiguous sectors of free space at the end of the compressed volume file.

        DEFRAG *53*
        DBLSPACE /DEF *53*

    What can you do if you see this error message: `DoubleSpace cannot`
    `defragment because an unknown error occurred`? 54

If you see this message, chances are that you're running a screen saver program. The solution is easy.

    How can you detect bad sectors in a DoubleSpace volume? 54

If you get a `Data error reading drive X` *or* `Sector not found reading drive X` *message, or if you cannot mount your host drive, you probably have a bad sector in your compressed volume file. (If you are running MS-DOS 6.2, see the 6.2 icon following this problem/answer segment.)*

    How can you repair bad sectors in a DoubleSpace volume? 55

The easiest way to repair bad sectors in a DoubleSpace volume is to upgrade to DOS 6.2 and use the ScanDisk utility. Or, if you already own a third-party surface scan utility such as Norton Disk Doctor (one of Symantec's Norton Utilities) or DiskFix from Central Point Software, you can use that. If you do not want to upgrade to MS-DOS 6.2 and you don't have any third-party utilities, you can use DOS 6 to reformat the disk.

Table of Contents

  Using ScanDisk *55*
  Using a third-party surface scan utility *56*
  Using MS-DOS 6 programs *56*
 You want to know how to handle Windows swapfiles when using
 DoubleSpace compression. 56
  A permanent swapfile cannot reside on a compressed volume, but if you try to move it there, you do not get an error message. A temporary swapfile, on the other hand, is just a file and can reside anywhere. Nevertheless, it doesn't make much sense to place a temporary swapfile on a compressed drive because the purpose of a swapfile is to gain speed, and the DoubleSpace compression routines just slow it down.

Converting to DoubleSpace 57
 You want to convert to DoubleSpace from third-party
 compression software. 57
  Well, convert may be a misnomer here, unless you can find a conversion utility program for the third-party software in question (such as the Stacker conversion utility provided by Microsoft). However, there is a workaround.
 How to use the Stacker Conversion disk. 58
  The Stacker Conversion program is quite straightforward. The only problem we've heard about is a syntax error message, which is presumed to relate to path problems. The solution is simple.

Removing DoubleSpace 58
 How can you remove DoubleSpace from your system? 59
  The Delete command on the DoubleSpace Drive menu allows you to delete an entire CVF, files and all. However, just as with Format, DoubleSpace will not allow you to delete your setup drive. So, if you've compressed your startup drive — and most of us have — you need another option.

DoubleSpace Incompatibilities 59
 You are a gamester and think DoubleSpace may be causing
 you problems. 60
  Indeed, some games don't work well when run from a compressed drive. Here's what we know so far.
 You use one or more financial and/or spreadsheet programs and think that
 DoubleSpace may be causing you problems. 60
  Quite a few money-management and spreadsheet programs also seem to misbehave when run from a compressed drive. Here's what we know so far.
 What other programs have been identified as incompatible with
 DoubleSpace? 61
  A few other programs have been reported as having difficulty when run from a compressed drive. Here's what we know so far.

Chapter 5: Memory Management 63

Understanding Memory Types 63
What's the difference between RAM and ROM, EMS and XMA, HMA and UMB? 63
Computer terminology generates a lot of alphabet soup. Unfortunately, a lot of that alphabet soup is necessary for understanding the solutions to your problems. Here are some definitions.

You want to stop EMM386 from allocating expanded memory. 64
EMM386.EXE has two functions: It converts some of your extended memory into expanded memory and it can convert some extended memory into UMBs, which are useful for loading other device drivers and programs into upper memory. If you do not use any programs that need expanded memory, you can prevent EMM386 from using extended memory (XMS) to simulate expanded memory (EMS) and have more extended memory available for use by programs that need it (such as Windows).

Getting the Most out of Memory 65
You know you've got it (after all you paid for it) but you can't seem to access your expanded or extended memory. 65
In order to take advantage of expanded and/or extended memory, you must load the memory management drivers — HIMEM.SYS and EMM386.EXE.

You have extended memory available, but what you need is more conventional memory. Is there a way to move DOS to the extended region? 65
If you have determined that your programs need more conventional memory and you have extended memory to spare, you can load DOS into the High Memory Area (HMA).

You don't have any special memory but would like to get the most from what you have. 66
Without any expanded or extended memory, your best bet is to make use of the FILES and BUFFERS commands.

Your system seems to run slowly, especially when accessing the disk or running certain programs. 66
If you're using a word processor, for example, and just typing away, chances are that you perceive your system as being fast, if you think about it at all. However, if you're using a database program, for example, and are doing a lot of searching to retrieve information, your system may seem to be moving rather slowly. This is because disk access, whether reading from or writing to disk, takes time. You may only be dealing with nanoseconds here, but there are ways to speed up this process.

You receive an `Out of memory` message, possibly when running one of the Microsoft utility programs. 67
This message usually appears when a program cannot access enough conventional memory. However, if you are running a Windows-based program at the time, the program is more likely looking for extended memory. In either event, because memory is such an important part of your system, you should make sure you're getting the most from what you have.

What does Error: `Unknown command "/l:0;1"` mean? 67
This error occurs when LOADHIGH switches are not recognized by third-party shells (also known as command interpreters). With MS-DOS 6, the LOADHIGH command supports the use of the /L and /S switches to control the loading of programs into UMBs. MemMaker makes the most use of these switches in optimizing memory usage. Unfortunately, they are generally not compatible with third-party command interpreters such as 4DOS and NDOS.

Table of Contents

You want to make more effective use of upper memory (UMBs) when
loading drivers and TSRs, without using MemMaker. What can you do? 67
*When the CONFIG.SYS file executes, the system reads through the file once and then on the second
read loads all the device drivers in the same sequence as they appear in the file. You can do two
things to optimize placement: either rearrange the sequence of command lines in your CONFIG.SYS
file or indicate the specific upper memory region in which to load each driver.*

What can you do if you receive a message about `Insufficient
memory for UMBs or virtual HMA`? 70
*You see this message if, for example, you try to set up an HMA (High Memory Area) and a full
UMA (Upper Memory Area) with only 1MB of RAM. You're 64K short.*

You tried to free up XMS memory by loading everything in
conventional memory but still find 1088K of XMS unaccounted for. 71
Chances are that you're loading SMARTDRV in your AUTOEXEC.BAT.

Running MemMaker 71

Should you use MemMaker? 71
*MemMaker optimizes memory usage. In this context, optimize means that the program examines
your CONFIG.SYS and AUTOEXEC.BAT files and figures out where in memory to load the drivers
and TSR programs for maximum efficiency. There are some restrictions in using MemMaker, and if
you're a Windows user, other considerations come into play as well.*

Can you use MemMaker to optimize memory usage on a
diskless workstation? 72
MemMaker requires a hard disk drive and cannot be run on a diskless workstation.

When MemMaker's Custom Setup asks whether or not to Optimize
upper memory for use with Windows, what should you reply? 72
*Optimizing upper memory for use with Windows benefits DOS-based programs that are run from
Windows.*

How can you use MemMaker with multiple configurations? 72
*The use of multiple configurations introduces some problems for MemMaker. MemMaker is
designed to optimize a single configuration, providing the best integrated fit for the programs and
device drivers loaded in your CONFIG.SYS and AUTOEXEC.BAT files. Basically, MemMaker works
like an electronic puzzle solver, arranging the pieces to fill the available spaces in upper memory.*

What does it mean if your MemMaker memory adjustments
do not match? 73
*When MemMaker is finished, it displays a screen showing before and after figures for conventional
memory and upper memory usage. Usually these differences match so that if you gain 50K in conventional memory, you lose 50K in upper memory. Occasionally, though, these figures do not match.*

What should you do if the MemMaker optimization process
never finishes? 73
*The last step in MemMaker's optimization process is to reboot your system using the updated
CONFIG.SYS and AUTOEXEC.BAT files to ensure that everything works properly. If, right after the
Starting MS-DOS message, a screen appears saying that the computer was restarted before
MemMaker had finished optimizing, chances are that you are executing a batch file from inside the
AUTOEXEC.BAT file. A second possibility is that another program file (perhaps a TSR program) is
in conflict with MemMaker and is causing it to freeze up before finishing.*

PC World DOS 6 Command Reference and Problem Solver

What if MemMaker fails to restart and then provides no
choice to undo changes? 74

When MemMaker detects a restart before it has completed optimization, a screen appears listing possible reasons for the problem and providing instructions for continuing or aborting the process. You usually have the option of undoing any changes that MemMaker made. Even if MemMaker fails to give you this option, or if later after quitting MemMaker you decide that you want to undo MemMaker changes, you still can.

You want to undo changes made by MemMaker but you can't
because you are running third-party compression software. 74

MemMaker is not able to restore the original CONFIG.SYS and AUTOEXEC.BAT files on systems using third-party compression software such as Stacker or SuperStor. When MemMaker fails, it still gives you the undo option but is unable to carry it out because the compressed drive is no longer mounted.

How can you remove all traces of an aborted MemMaker process? 75

When MemMaker does not finish properly, it leaves the MemMaker command in the AUTOEXEC.BAT file and the CHKSTATE.SYS line in the CONFIG.SYS file. The CHKSTATE.SYS device line in your CONFIG.SYS file is the telltale trace that alerts DOS to the fact that the optimization process is not finished. Also left behind are the MEMMAKER.STS files on your boot drive.

What can you do if MemMaker hangs with a SCSI hard drive? 75

SmartDrive has a double-buffering feature that is designed to assist devices, such as small computer system interface (SCSI) devices, that may have problems communicating with the memory provided when running EMM386 or Windows 386 enhanced mode. The MemMaker program can hang if a SCSI device driver loads into memory before SmartDrive's double-buffer driver.

What can you do if MemMaker conflicts with your ability to
access CMOS setup? 76

This problem can occur when you use the aggressive scan option in MemMaker's Custom Setup. When MemMaker scans aggressively, it includes the area between F000 and F7FF (960K through 992K), which is usually reserved for ROM BIOS. Some computers, however, don't start properly when this area is used for UMBs.

Why does MemMaker change the FCB line, and what's an FCB anyway? 76

The FCBs command is similar to the FILES command, except for older version programs. It looks like something where the first number is the number of files that FCBs can open at any one time, and the second number is the number of files opened that MS-DOS cannot automatically close.

Chapter 6: The DOS 6 Utility Programs 77

Installing and Running the MS-DOS 6 Utility Programs 77

Can you install the optional utility programs later,
after DOS 6 is already installed? 77

The answer is yes. If you did not choose to install the Backup, Undelete, and Anti-Virus programs when you installed DOS 6, you can still do so quite easily.

Can you install both the DOS and Windows versions of
one or more of the MS-DOS 6 utility programs? 78

MS-DOS 6 includes three utility programs: Backup, Anti-Virus, and Undelete. And each program has two versions: one for DOS and another for Windows.

Can I run the DOS version of a utility program from Windows? 78

The answer to this question is both yes and no.

Table of Contents

Questions about the Backup Utility Program 78
Your computer failed the Backup compatibility test.
What's wrong and what can you do now? 78
Reasons for test failure range from a lack of free disk space to incompatible hardware to software conflicts. In this section we list several possible causes and suggest a few ways to fix the most common problems.

You experience problems with the compatibility test when running Backup with Windows in 386 Enhanced Mode but not with Backup for DOS. 79
In addition to the simple problems and solutions described in the previous question, there is a much more complex issue associated with Microsoft Backup for Windows: third-party virtual device drivers. This problem can only occur when running Windows in 386 Enhanced Mode.

No matter what you try, your system continues to fail the
compatibility test. What should you do now? 80
If the compatibility test continues to fail, you will not be able to select backup destinations, such as your floppy disk drive, from the Backup To dialog box. You should, however, be able to specify the desired destination manually by selecting MS-DOS Path from the dialog box and then entering the desired drive and path. This manual method was designed to provide the maximum possible compatibility with other systems.

Can I use DoubleSpace diskettes with Backup? 80
The answer to this question is no, but there is an alternative.

You get the `DMA Buffer Size Too Small` error message. 81
If the direct memory access (DMA) buffer used by EMM386.EXE is too small, the Backup compatibility test program issues this message.

How can you be sure that Backup creates reliable file copies? 81
The whole point of backing up the files on your hard drive is to protect your data. In case of hard drive failure, you should be able to reconstruct as much of your data as possible. This means that your backup disks must be reliable.

    Verify Backup Data option *81*
    Use Error Correction on Diskettes option *82*

You get the `Unable to open component file` error message. 82
If you choose to back up your files to a directory on your hard drive or to some drive other than a floppy drive, the Backup program creates a component file in a directory called FUL. (The component file has a 001 filename extension.) If this file is moved, you will be unable to restore your files.

Questions about the Anti-Virus Utility Program 82
How can you update the viral signatures file, and where
can you find the information? 83
Detection of a virus and curing a virus by cleaning it off your drive are two separate functions. You can update the viral signatures that MSAV or MWAV recognizes by adding new information to the signature file, and you can update the Anti-Virus program so that it can remove new viruses as well.

When you upgrade your software, you get a lot of Anti-Virus
warnings. What's the problem? 83
When you upgrade software, changes are often made to the program files. The Anti-Virus program may detect these changes and think they indicate virus activity. You can reduce the occurrence of these messages by taking the following steps.

PC World DOS 6 Command Reference and Problem Solver

You removed a virus and now the program won't run. 83

It is possible that when a virus is detected, the damage to the program file is irreparable. Usually the Anti-Virus program knows this and warns you with the File was destroyed by the virus message. Sometimes, however, Anti-Virus may not detect the damage or might possibly cause the damage itself during the removal process.

You can't display the VSafe Warning Options screen using Alt-V. 84

Alt-V is the default key combination to bring up the Warning Options screen used with the DOS version of the Anti-Virus program. It only works with the DOS version and must be loaded into memory.

Questions about the Undelete Utility Program 84

What's the difference between the various conditions of a deleted file? 84

The Undelete utility program uses five different conditions to indicate the likelihood of a successful restoration.

You are using Sentry protection but still can't undelete certain files. 85

Depending on the settings for Sentry protection, the file(s) that you want to undelete may not have been protected at all, their protection time may have expired, or they may have been overwritten by more recently deleted files.

You want to UNDELETE a directory. 86

Undelete protection in MS-DOS 6 is quite powerful, but not all of its features are available in both the DOS and Windows versions.

Part II: Command Reference 91

Index 499

Reader Response Card ....back of book

Introduction

With a book called the *DOS 6 Command Reference and Problem Solver*, you might be wondering if MS-DOS 6 is worth the potential problems. Absolutely! MS-DOS 6 provides many new features — including a number of powerful, useful, and easy-to-use utilities — to meet a variety of user needs. The purpose of this book is to help you surmount some of the more obscure problems (and some not so obscure) you might encounter with MS-DOS 6.

While problems with MS-DOS 6 were reported by users and the media, many (but not all) of these difficulties turned out to be the result of people not understanding all the ins and outs of the new MS-DOS (and why should you?), rather than the result of errors in the product. Nevertheless, as Microsoft acknowledges, any difficulty experienced by a user is a problem, whether or not it is a program bug. We address the most commonly reported difficulties and incompatibilities in the *Problem Solver* portion of the book.

We also discuss the newest version of MS-DOS — MS-DOS 6.2 — released by Microsoft to address some of the concerns voiced by users of version 6.0. Version 6.2 contains some changes in default settings to err on the side of safety instead of speed (speed was favored in version 6.0), and a number of enhancements and new features, including a brand new utility: ScanDisk. We point out the improvements and leave it to you to decide whether the upgrade is for you.

Most of the problems reported by the press about MS-DOS 6.0 were associated with the new disk compression program, DoubleSpace. DoubleSpace uses a set of special techniques to fit more data onto your disks. As with any new technology, some people have been frightened by the unknown. We think that the dangers of DoubleSpace have been greatly exaggerated, but we are also happy to see that Microsoft has addressed some of these concerns with the inclusion of the DoubleGuard technology in MS-DOS 6.2.

Many of the problems encountered by users of MS-DOS 6.0 were not caused by DoubleSpace, as originally believed, but rather by the default settings in the new version of SmartDrive. In our Problem Solver section on SmartDrive, we show you how to avoid the problems caused by these settings, and then we tell you how MS-DOS 6.2 resolved the problem issues.

This is not to say, however, that DoubleSpace doesn't have any problems of its own. A number of memory-collision problems have been reported, collisions between DoubleSpace's use of memory and the use of memory by other programs running on a DoubleSpace compressed drive. We talk about those in the Problem Solver section on DoubleSpace. But wait — we're getting ahead of ourselves.

The MS-DOS 6.2 upgrade

What's new and what's worth the money? MS-DOS 6.2 contains a number of enhancements and new features:

The **SmartDrive** default settings have been altered for more conservative use of its caching features. The initial default is now a read-only cache. If you opt for a read-and-write cache, the default setting tells SmartDrive not to return a DOS prompt to the screen until after it writes the cached data to disk. This lessens the chance of your turning off your computer too soon and accidentally losing data that was still in the cache. In addition, SmartDrive is now able to cache CD-ROM drives, and new switches have been added to allow the user more control. We discuss these new settings and switches extensively in both the *Problem Solver* and *Command Reference* portions of this book.

DoubleSpace has two new options: **AutoMount**, to save you from having to manually mount a compressed volume file, and **Uncompress**, to remove a DoubleSpace drive from your system. In addition, the new **DoubleGuard** feature helps to protect your data on compressed drives by verifying data integrity before writing to disk. Also, if DoubleGuard detects memory corruption, it shuts down your system. Finally, DoubleSpace is easier to configure because of new switches you can use to update your INI file.

ScanDisk is the new utility for detecting, diagnosing, and repairing disk errors on both uncompressed and DoubleSpace compressed drives. Microsoft intends for this utility to replace the older CHKDSK (CheckDisk) command. We detail the use of this utility in the *Command Reference*.

New enhancements to the **Interactive Startup** routine include the ability to "step through" your AUTOEXEC.BAT file, confirming or bypassing individual command lines. Plus, new function key commands enable you to carry out or bypass all remaining commands in the file. An additional **Clean Start** option has also been added, allowing you to boot up without loading DoubleSpace.

Unless run from a batch file or a DOS shell, **MOVE**, **COPY**, and **XCOPY** now prompt the user for confirmation before overwriting an existing file. This enhancement is designed to protect you from accidentally writing over a file of the same name.

Additional enhancements include a new parameter for **HIMEM.SYS** that tests for unreliable memory chips during startup; **DEFRAG**'s ability to handle more files and larger drives; the addition of commas (,) to the numeric output of the **DIR**, **MEM**, **CHKDSK**, and **FORMAT** commands; and **DISKCOPY**'s use of the hard drive for temporary storage. This last enhancement makes it possible for the program to ask you whether you want more than one copy of a disk and puts an end to the nuisance of disk-swapping (first the source, then the target, then the source again, then the target again, and so on) when you copy disks from drive A to drive A.

Introduction

What's in this book?

This book is divided into two main parts: the *Problem Solver*, six chapters in which we present information in a question-and-answer or statement-and-resolution format, and the *Command Reference*, where we describe each command in alphabetical order.

The *Problem Solver* details a variety of problems that you might encounter when installing or using MS-DOS 6. Each problem is described in detail and, when appropriate, instructions are given for determining whether the problem affects your system. In every case we try to provide complete and easy-to-follow instructions about fixing or avoiding the problem.

Chapter 1 is "Installing MS-DOS 6." In this chapter we talk about problems that you may have with the installation process — problems ranging from defective Setup Disks to lack of space, incompatible partitions, and compression conversions. We even talk about the compatibility of some third-party hardware and software products.

Chapter 2, "Startup Process," covers interactive startup methods for diagnosing system problems, multiple configurations, and problems with various command lines in your CONFIG.SYS and AUTOEXEC.BAT files.

Chapter 3, "SmartDrive," shows you how to prevent the file-corruption problems experienced by some users. We also explain the basic concepts of disk caching and show you how to evaluate the effectiveness of your cache settings.

Chapter 4, "DoubleSpace," deals exclusively with DoubleSpace issues. In this chapter we not only explain how DoubleSpace works to save your space, but we also talk about converting from other compression programs, optimizing DoubleSpace, and removing compressed drives from your system. We explain the meaning of some error messages and alert you to some of the programs that do not function well on DoubleSpace drives.

Chapter 5, "Memory Management," focuses on helping you sort out the different types of memory and then showing you how to make the most of each megabyte. Issues of memory optimization lead to a discussion of MemMaker, in which we address questions about its benefits and limitations, error messages, use with multiple configurations, and more.

Chapter 6, "The DOS 6 Utility Programs," covers questions about installing and running the MS-DOS 6 utility programs with individual sections devoted to each utility: Backup, Anti-Virus, and Undelete.

The *Command Reference* portion of the book covers every command known to MS-DOS, from version 3.3 through 6.2. Presented one at a time in alphabetical sequence. We believe that this is the most comprehensive and clearest command reference on the market. Not only do we explain when and why you might want to use each command, but we describe how each command works, show you the acceptable command syntax, and provide notes on its secret features with examples of how you might use it on your own system.

Conventions we use

Take a moment to learn some of the conventions that we use in this book. These consistent elements are intended to help you navigate the material and to clarify our meaning.

Commands

You'll find that commands are easy to spot. When we're showing you how to do something, a command generally appears on its own line in monospace, lowercase type, prefaced by a prompt (such as C:\>). We use **bold lettering** to indicate the portion that you would type. For example:

```
C:\>dir
```

Even when referred to in text, you'll find the commands are still easy to spot. When we talk about a MS-DOS program, such as SmartDrive, we spell out the program name using Microsoft's style for capitalization. When we want to refer to the command itself, such as SMARTDRV, we use all capital letters. This is true whether or not we use a phrase such as *the SMARTDRV command* or use the command alone.

Information that you would enter into a file you'll see in monospace type without a prompt. We use this style most often when we're talking about statements that belong in your AUTOEXEC.BAT or CONFIG.SYS files. For example, a sample PATH statement would be indicated like so:

```
path=c:\dos;c:\windows;c:\;c:\utils;
```

Syntax lines

In the *Command Reference* portion of this book, when we show you the syntax for a command, we generally separate it from the text.

If you're a beginning DOS user, you might be wondering what the heck a syntax line is. Simply put, it's the structure that you use for a command. We put the parts of the command that you would type exactly as they appear in bold type (such as the word *copy* in the following example). We use placeholders for all the things that you must supply when you actually use the command. The placeholders, or *parameters*, are indicated with italics (as in the words *source* and *target* in the example). Syntax lines are like diagrams of sentences, but instead of noun-verb-object, you see something like the following:

copy *source* [*target*]

The brackets are a convention commonly used in the computer world to indicate parts of the command that are optional. When you want to include them and you substitute the particulars, you don't actually type the brackets.

Introduction

Icons

We use this icon in the *Problem Solver* to indicate that the subject in the text beside the icon is new to MS-DOS 6.2.

We use this icon occasionally in the *Problem Solver* to identify an important point or a side discussion of particular interest.

This icon shows cross-references to identical or related topics addressed elsewhere in the book. It might point to a *Command Reference* entry containing more detail or to another *Problem Solver* section containing related information. We also use it to point out other resources that might help you solve the problem.

We use this icon in the *Problem Solver* to remind you of certain facts that have some bearing on what actions you may choose to take.

This icon, used throughout the *Problem Solver*, highlights telephone numbers for technical support at some of the companies mentioned.

You will find this icon only in the *Command Reference*. It means that the subject of the text beside the icon is new to MS-DOS 6.0.

You will find this icon only in the *Command Reference*. It means that the subject of the text beside the icon is new to MS-DOS 6.2.

This icon, used only in the *Command Reference,* indicates that a change worth noting was made to the command in version 6.0.

This icon, used only in the *Command Reference,* indicates that a change worth noting was made to the command in version 6.2.

Used only in the *Command Reference,* this icon highlights commands that are no longer available in version 6.0.

Used only in the *Command Reference,* this icon highlights commands that are no longer available in version 6.2.

How to use this book

We don't expect you to read this book from cover to cover. The *Problem Solver* portion of the book is designed to help you solve specific problems that you may have using MS-DOS. Each chapter in the *Problem Solver* is broken down into sections, and each section begins with a brief description of the topics covered. You can see a list of the questions and statements for each section in the Table of Contents. If you are in search of specific information about a command, such as how to use a particular switch, you can look up the command directly in the *Command Reference* portion of the book. Of course, you can also look at the Index to find all the references to a particular command.

Part I: Problem Solver

Chapter 1: Installing MS-DOS 6
Chapter 2: Startup Process
Chapter 3: SmartDrive
Chapter 4: DoubleSpace
Chapter 5: Memory Management
Chapter 6: The DOS Utility Programs

Chapter 1
Installing MS-DOS 6

In general, you want to use the MS-DOS 6.0 Setup program to install DOS on your hard disk. Setup first scans your computer and identifies its system components and then creates an OLD_DOS_1 directory, where it stores some DOS files from the DOS version you're currently running. (Each time you install, a new OLD_DOS directory is created. The second would be OLD_DOS_2.)

You need to have a floppy disk available (two disks if they're only 360K) for uninstall information. The Setup program places some of the old DOS files, along with a copy of your CONFIG.SYS and AUTOEXEC.BAT files, on this Uninstall disk. The rest of the DOS files from the older version are placed in the OLD_DOS_1 directory we just mentioned.

You can delete the OLD_DOS_1 directory later (using the DELOLDOS or DELTREE command), but once you do, you cannot uninstall MS-DOS 6.0 to return to your previous DOS version.

There are two separate ways to get MS-DOS 6.2 and the one you need depends upon what you are currently using. The MS-DOS 6.2 Upgrade works as describe here and is intended for most people. The other way is to use the MS-DOS 6.2 StepUp, but you can only use that approach if you have already upgraded to MS-DOS 6.0. If you have the full version of MS-DOS 6.0 and the MS-DOS 6.2 StepUp, you should use the Setup program from MS-DOS 6.0 to install new programs (or to re-install if necessary) and then run the MS-DOS 6.2 StepUp to bring your system up-to-date.

You should run the Setup program from the disk drive containing the new MS-DOS files, so switch to whichever floppy drive you plan to use (in our example, drive A). At the prompt, type

    A:\>**setup**

and press Enter to begin. For the first couple of minutes, DOS checks out your system configuration and generates a pre-installation report using MSD (the Microsoft Diagnostics program). The MSD report comes in handy if for some reason you run into a problem during installation and have to call on technical support — but that scenario is unusual. MSD is a program that is installed as part of DOS 6. Often, when you call technical support (whether Microsoft's or another vendor's), you are asked for information from this report.

You can solve a lot of problems by understanding how flexible the MS-DOS 6 Setup program is. The SETUP command has switches that you can use to tailor the installation process to your specific needs. For example, if you've already installed DOS 6 and you just want to install one or more of the optional programs (Anti-Virus, Undelete, and Backup), use the /E switch. You can see the following list of SETUP switches and explanations on your own screen by typing **SETUP /?** from the floppy disk drive:

Part I: Problem Solver

```
Installs MS-DOS 6 or optional programs.

SETUP [/B] [/E] [/F] [/G [/H]] [/I] [/M] [/Q] [/U]

/B   Displays Setup screens in monochrome instead of color.
/E   Installs Windows and MS-DOS optional programs.
/F   Installs a minimal MS-DOS 6 system on a floppy disk.
/G   Does not create the Uninstall Disk and does not prompt
     you when you need to update your network.
/H   Uses default Setup options.
/I   Turns off hardware detection.
/M   Installs a minimal MS-DOS 6 system.
/Q   Copies MS-DOS files to a hard disk.
/U   Installs MS-DOS even if Setup detects disk partitions that
     might be incompatible with MS-DOS 6.
```

If you don't want to take advantage of the DOS Uninstall capability (which means you don't have to have the disk space for storing the old versions of the DOS files in OLD_DOS_1), you can use the /G switch to bypass the prompt to create an Uninstall disk. The /F switch allows you to install a minimal DOS system on a floppy disk.

If you have any installation problems at all, they usually fall into one of three categories: problems with the Setup program; problems with disk-space management; or problems with hardware compatibility or third-party software.

Problems with the Setup Program

Problems with the Setup program itself are infrequent. However, problems caused by equipment conflicts such as incompatible equipment, defective disks, memory-resident programs, or disk-caching programs can interfere with the setup process.

Is your video display unreadable?

If the lines on your screen are truncated, or (even worse) if they are totally unintelligible, your problems may be caused by incompatible hardware settings.

If you are running an earlier DOS version, try running the Setup program with the /I switch to disable the automatic hardware detection. Type

    A:\>**setup /i**

The Setup program then prompts you to identify your hardware configuration.

If this does not resolve your problem, or if you are experiencing this problem with an operating system other than MS-DOS, you can try installing DOS 6.0 manually. This procedure involves booting up from the floppy drive (using either the Setup Disk or another startup disk), using the SYS command to transfer the system files from the floppy to your hard drive, and running the Setup program from your drive C using the /U and /Q switches. The /U switch tells Setup to bypass hard-disk detection, and the /Q switch tells Setup to copy the MS-DOS 6 files directly to your hard drive.

For more detailed, step-by-step instructions on the procedure for manually installing MS-DOS 6, see pages 196-197 of your *Microsoft MS-DOS 6 User's Guide*.

Chapter 1: Installing MS-DOS 6

Are your upgrade disks defective?

There is always a chance that one or more of your installation disks is defective. Your disk is probably defective if during the copy process you receive one or more error messages such as Data error reading *or* General failure reading.

To find out if this is the case, we recommend using what we call *the null test*. The null test attempts to read files from the floppy disk in question and copy them to the null device. (The null device, or *bit bucket,* is used for testing the readability of a disk without creating a new file. *Null* means *nothing,* and anything you write to this device just disappears, as if written to nowhere.)

Insert the suspected disk into your floppy drive. Then, from your hard disk drive, type

    `C:\>`**`copy a:\*.* nul`**

If you do not receive any error messages, then your disk is probably fine, and you should look elsewhere for the problem.

If your disks are defective, you can order replacement disks by calling Microsoft Consumer Sales at 800-426-9400.

Are you receiving repeated prompts to insert the same disk or warnings that your Uninstall disk is not correct?

Sometimes memory-resident programs interfere with the Setup program's capability to read a Setup or Uninstall disk. Some disk-caching programs can also cause this problem. There are a few possible remedies.

First, try removing all memory-resident and disk-caching programs from your CONFIG.SYS and AUTOEXEC.BAT files, rebooting your computer, and running Setup again.

You do not have to actually delete these programs. Instead, you can insert REM followed by a space at the beginning of each line containing a memory-resident or disk-caching program in your CONFIG.SYS and AUTOEXEC.BAT files. REM stands for *remark,* and DOS bypasses any commands on a remark line.

If that doesn't do the trick, you can try placing all of the Setup files onto your hard drive and running Setup from there. We call this "Installing Setup from your hard drive," and we'll explain the steps in just a moment.

As a last resort, you may have to do what Microsoft refers to as a "Installing MS-DOS manually." The *manual* part of this process refers to the fact that you must copy the MS-DOS system files yourself, using the SYS command. We describe this process right after the explanation for installing setup from your hard drive.

Installing Setup from your hard drive

Create a SETUP directory on your hard drive:

    `C:\>`**`md setup`**

Copy all of the files from each installation disk to your new SETUP directory:

    `C:\SETUP>`**`copy a:\*.*`**

Part I: Problem Solver

Then run Setup from the SETUP directory:

```
C:\SETUP>setup
```

If all goes well, you can then remove the SETUP directory, and its files, after you've successfully installed MS-DOS 6.

Installing MS-DOS 6 manually

Start your system using the floppy drive (using either the Setup Disk or another startup disk). You must start your system with the system disk in drive A.

If you do not already have a DOS directory on your system, create one:

```
A:\>md c:\dos
```

Use the command

```
A:\>sys c:
```

to install the system files onto your hard drive. This copies the hidden system files and COMMAND.COM into your root directory.

You should then change to drive C and move to the DOS directory:

```
A:\>c:
C:\>cd \dos
```

Run SETUP from your drive C using the /U and /Q switches:

```
C:\DOS>a:setup /q/u
```

The /U switch tells Setup to bypass hard-disk detection, and the /Q switch tells Setup to copy the MS-DOS 6 files directly to your hard drive. You should now be able to reboot your system using your hard disk.

For more detailed, step-by-step instructions on the procedure for manually installing MS-DOS 6, see pages 196-197 of your *Microsoft MS-DOS 6 User's Guide*.

Problems with Disk Space and Partitions

You obviously need enough hard disk space to install the essential DOS files, but how much space is enough? If you think that you have plenty of space because you are using a disk compression program (such as Stacker), think again. Ironically, chances are that if you are using a compression program, you can find yourself in short supply of space when installing program files. You need to have some uncompressed space available (for installing the system files), but the real potential for running into space problems depends on the compression ratio applied to the MS-DOS program files. And then there's also the possibility that your disk partitions may not be compatible.

 **You are using a compression program and were sure that you would have enough space to install MS-DOS 6, but your system said "***not!***"**

The MS-DOS files, not including any of the utility programs, require 4.2MB of free disk space. Your system reports 6MB free on your compressed drive, so you shouldn't have a problem, right? Not necessarily. It depends on the ratio by which the program files can be compressed.

Every compression program uses an estimate when projecting how much free space is available in a compressed volume. Usually that estimate is 2:1, meaning that 2MB of data can be compressed and stored in 1MB of real space. Regardless of the estimate, however, the compression ratio depends on the type of file and its contents.

For example, when compressing a text file, a compression program replaces repetitive groups of letters (such as "ing" or "ight") with a single character. Compression programs can usually compress graphic files by a much larger ratio — sometimes 4:1 or better. This is possible because graphic files, which are composed of pixels instead of characters, generally have more repetitive patterns of pixels. At the other end of the spectrum are executable files. These files contain programming code and don't usually leave much room for compression.

So, the moral of this story is that if you need 4.2MB free to install MS-DOS 6, and your compression program uses an estimated compression ratio of 2:1, do whatever you can to free up some more space until your compressed drive reports 8MB or more of free space.

You'd like to install the utility programs, or at least some of them, but you're not sure how much space each one requires.

The MS-DOS files, not including any of the utility programs, require 4.2MB of free disk space. During the installation process, you are asked to specify whether or not you want to include the Backup, Undelete, or Anti-Virus utility programs in the installation, and, if so, whether you want the DOS version, Windows version, or both.

When using SETUP (without any switches) to install MS-DOS 6, you don't have any control over how much space is appropriated for the regular MS-DOS files. You can, however, control the installation of the new MS-DOS 6 utilities files. The screen used for making your selections is shown in Figure 1-1.

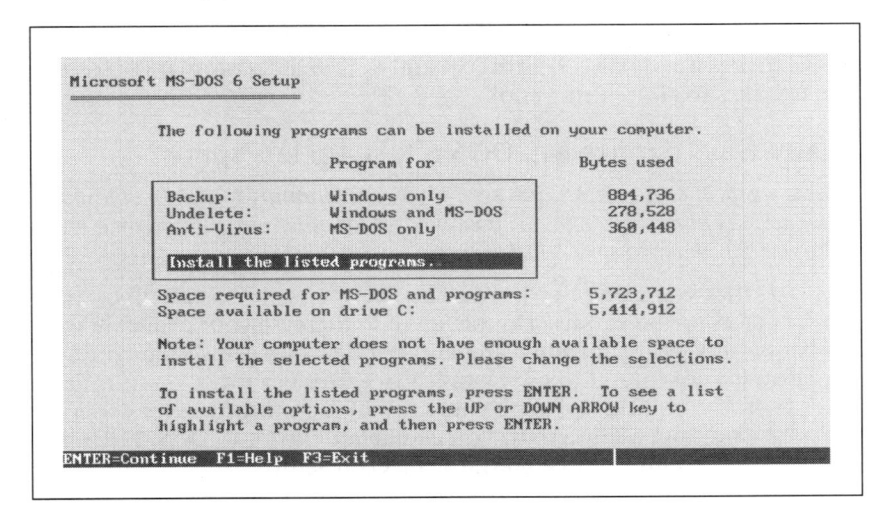

Figure 1-1: Utility programs selection screen for Microsoft MS-DOS 6 Setup.

Whether or not the utility program files are essential is up to you. Each of them is described in the *Command Reference*. You may prefer to use utility programs from other vendors.

Table 1-1 shows you the additional space requirements for adding in the utility programs.

Table 1-1: Space Requirements for Backup, Undelete, and Anti-Virus Programs

Program	DOS version	Windows version	Both versions
Backup	901,120	884,736	1,765,856
Undelete	32,768	278,528	278,528
Anti-Virus	360,448	786,432	1,032,192

Referring again to Figure 1-1, you can see that it shows you how much space is required for installing DOS and your selected utility programs as well as how much space is available on your drive C. If not enough room is available (as is the case in the example in Figure 1-1), a note suggesting that you change your selections also appears. (When enough space exists on the drive, this message disappears.)

If you don't have the necessary 4.2MB of space, you have a few options. The first, and simplest, is to back up some of your seldom-if-ever-used program and data files and then delete them from your system. You could also use the CHKDSK command to recover any lost allocation units that might be using up disk space unnecessarily. And yet another option is to instruct Setup to perform a minimum installation (see the next question).

ScanDisk replaces the CHKDSK command in MS-DOS 6.2.

For details on using the BACKUP, CHKDSK and SCANDISK commands, see the *Command Reference* section of this book.

Is there any way to make MS-DOS 6 take up less space?

Hard disk space is prime real estate, and even if you are planning to use DoubleSpace, you may want to keep as much disk space as possible free for other uses. There are a few adjustments you can make to save a little space.

First, make sure that you really need to free up the space now. Remember that once you install MS-DOS 6, you can use DoubleSpace to increase your available hard disk space. (Of course, if you are already using another disk compression technology or for some reason do not intend to use DoubleSpace, this is a moot point.) Also, don't forget that MS-DOS 6 will be replacing your current DOS directory (or other operating system software), not adding to it. You can delete the OLD_DOS_1 directory after you have successfully completed the MS-DOS 6 Setup.

Chapter 1: Installing MS-DOS 6

If you need more free space, you might consider installing only a minimum MS-DOS 6 system instead of the full system. To run only a minimum install, use the /M switch with Setup, like so:

    A:\>**setup /m**

This upgrades your system to MS-DOS 6, but installs only the DOS system files. Also, even though Setup creates a DOS directory for the new version, the program does not place any files in the directory during the minimum install. Furthermore, you will no longer have your CONFIG.SYS or AUTOEXEC.BAT files, so you will not have access to extended memory, your mouse, or any other devices that would have been installed from your startup files. To add in any of the external MS-DOS commands, see the section "Installing MS-DOS 6 program files individually."

Finally, you have two other options, both of which involve selecting only those MS-DOS files that you want to use. The first method is to use Setup to install all of the MS-DOS 6 program files and then selectively delete those that you don't want to keep on your system. We suggest that you go through the list of files and if you don't recognize the command — or think you won't have a need for the command — delete it. Of course, before you delete it, be sure you understand its function. If you don't recognize the command or aren't sure, we suggest that you look it up in the *Command Reference* section of this book. It's a great way to learn about new commands and possibly free up some disk space at the same time.

The second method is to install the desired MS-DOS 6 program files one at a time. This method is much more time consuming. First, you need to boot up from the MS-DOS 6 Setup Disk 1 and use the SYS command to transfer the new system files over to the root directory of your hard drive, as described in the section "Installing MS-DOS 6 manually" earlier in this chapter. But then, instead of running the Setup program, you would install each program file individually, as described in the following section "Installing MS-DOS 6 program files individually."

Installing MS-DOS 6 program files individually

Most of the files on the Setup Disks are compressed, so you need to use the EXPAND command to decompress them. If you have MS-DOS 4 or an earlier MS-DOS version, you probably need to copy the EXPAND.EXE file from Setup Disk 1 to your hard drive. (The EXPAND command itself is not compressed!)

You can easily tell which files are compressed and which are not. Compressed files have file extensions ending with an underscore character (_). For example, in alphabetical sequence, the first two compressed files on Setup Disk 1 are 8514.VI_ and ANSI.SY_.

In order to use EXPAND, you have to know what the full extension should be when decompressed. For example, 8514.VI_ is 8514.VID, and ANSI.SY_ is ANSI.SYS (see Table 1-2). To expand a compressed file (ANSI.SY_) from your MS-DOS 6 floppy disk and place the decompressed file (ANSI.SYS) in your DOS directory on your hard drive, type

    C:\>**expand a:\ansi.sy_ c:\dos\ansi.sys**

Part I: Problem Solver

Table 1-2 lists all the compressed file extensions and their uncompressed counterparts. There are only two exceptions, and they pertain to Setup Disk 3 only.

Table 1-2: Compressed and Expanded Filename Extensions for the MS-DOS 6 Setup Disks

Compressed extension	Expanded extension
38_	386
BI_	BIN
CO_	COM
CP_	CPI
DL_	DLL
EX_	EXE
GR_	GRB (except for Disk 3)
	GRP (for Disk 3 only)
HL_	HLP
IC_	ICE
IN_	INI (except for Disk 3)
	INF (for Disk 3 only)
LS_	LST
OV_	OVL
PR_	PRO
SY_	SYS
VI_	VID

NOTE: PACKING.LST is the name of a file on Setup Disk 1 that contains a list of the complete filenames for all of the files on each of the Setup Disks.

You get the message `Your computer uses a disk compression program.`

If this message appears when you run Setup, you may say "Yes, thank you. I know that. So what?" What it doesn't tell you, however, is that because of it you will not be able to create an Uninstall disk. That also means that you will not be able to restore your previous DOS version once you run Setup.

This is not a bad thing. After all, you don't want to run your old DOS version — that's why you're upgrading. Nevertheless, you might want to take some precautions.

We suggest that you back up your data files before running Setup. This is good advice whether or not you are using a disk compression program. We also suggest that you create a startup or boot disk for your earlier DOS version. This way, if anything should go wrong during setup, you can always reboot the old version from the floppy disk. You probably won't need it, but as the old cliché goes, *better safe than sorry*.

You get the message `Your computer uses SuperStor disk compression.`

When Setup gives you a very specific message, such as this one about the SuperStor product from AddStor, Inc., it means that you need to fix the problem using tools from the third-party vendor (AddStor) rather than Microsoft.

The SuperStor installation disk contains the ADD2SWP.EXE file. Place that disk in your floppy drive and type

```
C:\>a:add2swp c:
```

Then follow the directions displayed on your screen. When the ADD2SWP program is finished, reboot your computer and run Setup again.

You get the message `Too Many Primary Partitions or Incompatible Primary DOS Partition.`

These messages generally indicate that DOS is either unable to figure out which partition to use during installation or is unable to take control of the primary partition. You need to reconfigure your hard drive using the FDISK command.

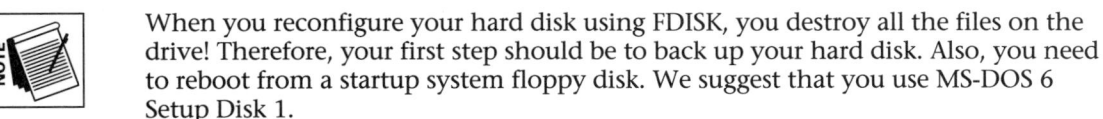

When you reconfigure your hard disk using FDISK, you destroy all the files on the drive! Therefore, your first step should be to back up your hard disk. Also, you need to reboot from a startup system floppy disk. We suggest that you use MS-DOS 6 Setup Disk 1.

Next, use the FDISK command right from the Setup Disk (it's not compressed) to repartition your hard disk as described in the following section "Repartitioning your hard drive with FDISK." Then use the FORMAT command, also right from the Setup Disk, to format your hard disk. When the formatting is complete, you should be able to run the Setup program without any trouble. And after you're done installing MS-DOS 6, you can restore your files from the backup disks, tape, or cartridge. (The RESTORE program will be in your DOS directory and will work to restore the backup files created with your earlier DOS version of the Backup program.)

Repartitioning your hard drive with FDISK

Warning: If the hard disk that you want to modify has any important data at all on it, *back it up before you attempt to use FDISK. Repeat: back it up!* After you finish with FDISK, you can restore all the data to the disk.

In order to repartition your hard disk, you need to delete existing partitions and then create a new primary partition.

Part I: Problem Solver

With the drive fully backed up, you need to restart your computer using a DOS system floppy disk (startup disk). When you've rebooted from the system disk, type

    A:\>**fdisk**

The FDISK Options screen appears. Select option 3 to bring up the Delete DOS Partition or Logical DOS Drive screen. From that screen, select option 4 to bring up the Delete Non-DOS Partition screen, or option 1 to Delete Primary DOS Partition if you have too many primary partitions. Choose the appropriate partition number and press Enter. When prompted for confirmation, press Y to confirm.

When that's done, press Esc to get back to the FDISK Options screen and select option 1 to bring up the Create DOS Partition or Logical DOS Drive screen. Select option 1 again to create a primary DOS partition. When you are asked whether you want to use the entire disk as the primary DOS partition, answer Y unless you plan to create an extended partition.

Finally, press Esc again to return to the FDISK Options screen and select option 2 to bring up the Set Active Partition screen. If the partition you just created is the only partition with system files, it is already active. If not, be sure to set your Primary DOS partition as the active partition.

Pages 204-216 of your *Microsoft MS-DOS 6 User's Guide* contain detailed instructions for each of these steps, plus instructions for creating and deleting primary MS-DOS partitions, extended MS-DOS partitions, and logical drives. For a more in-depth explanation of this subject, the *PC World DOS 6 Handbook* (Chapter 16) is another excellent source of step-by-step information. For details on using the FORMAT, BACKUP, and RESTORE commands, see the *Command Reference* portion of this book.

You get the message Incompatible hard disk or device driver.

This message usually appears if your computer has a Novell, Priam, Everex, UNIX, XENIX, or Vfeature Deluxe partition; or if your computer has a SyQuest or Bernoulli drive.

In some cases, you can simply run Setup using the /u switch to tell Setup to bypass hard-disk detection. This is true if your hard disk has **Novell** partitions, or **UNIX** or **XENIX** partitions in addition to a standard DOS partition.

If you have **Priam** or **Everex** partitions, or if you choose your operating system from a screen that includes choices for **UNIX** or **XENIX** when you boot up, you should try bypassing the Setup program and installing the MS-DOS 6 system files manually. (See "Installing MS-DOS 6 manually" earlier in this chapter.) When you run the Setup program, use the /U and /Q switches to install the rest of the files. The /U switch tells Setup to bypass hard-disk detection, and the /Q switch tells Setup to copy the MS-DOS 6 files directly to your hard drive.

For more detailed, step-by-step instructions on the procedure for manually installing MS-DOS 6, see pages 196-197 of your *Microsoft MS-DOS 6 User's Guide*.

If you have a **Vfeature Deluxe** partition, contact Golden Bow Systems about the availability of an upgrade. If one is not available, use FDISK to repartition your disk. (See "Repartitioning your hard drive with FDISK" earlier in this chapter.)

Chapter 1: Installing MS-DOS 6

The problem with **SyQuest** removable hard disks is caused by the DEVICE=SYQ55.SYS statement in your CONFIG.SYS file. Just remark out that line (by placing REM followed by a space at the beginning of the line) and reboot before running Setup. Then, when Setup is finished, you can remove the REM statement to change your CONFIG.SYS file back to normal.

The REM command also helps solve the problem caused by using a disk-caching program for your **Bernoulli** drive. Use REM to disable the command line that installs your disk-caching program. Then run Setup and re-enable the line again after Setup is finished.

If the `Incompatible hard disk or device driver` message appears, and you do not have one of the above-mentioned drives or partitions, you probably have an incompatible partition and need to delete it from your hard drive using the same FDISK procedure that we described in "Repartitioning your hard drive with FDISK" earlier in this chapter. If possible, you should check with the manufacturer to see whether they offer an upgrade or an alternative solution.

You get the message `Incompatible partition`.

If you have an incompatible partition, such as a SpeedStor Bootall partition, Setup cannot automatically update your system. You can try installing MS-DOS 6 manually or, alternatively, you can delete the incompatible partition and create a new DOS partition. If that doesn't work, you may need to contact Microsoft or the manufacturer of the software that created the incompatible partition.

You will not be able to use the Setup program but you may install MS-DOS 6 system files manually. See "Installing MS-DOS 6 manually" earlier in this chapter. If you want to repartition your hard disk, see "Repartitioning your hard drive with FDISK" earlier in this chapter.

You can reach Microsoft Product Support Services for MS-DOS 6 on weekdays between 6 a.m. and 6 p.m. Pacific time by calling 206-646-5104.

Hardware and Third-Party Software Considerations

You can install MS-DOS 6 on a number of different hardware platforms, including IBM's PS/1 and several Tandy models. You may also convert to MS-DOS 6 from other operating systems such as DR DOS.

Can you use DOS 6 on your IBM PS/1?

Yes, you can. You should not have any problem installing MS-DOS 6 on an IBM PS/1 computer.

You will, however, have to make one change to the PS/1 startup procedure so that it recognizes system files from the disk instead of only those stored on the ROM chip (ROM stands for read-only memory). To do this you need to select Your Software from the System menu and change the settings in the CUSTOMIZ file.

For detailed instructions, see pages 203-204 in your *Microsoft MS-DOS 6 User's Guide*.

Part I: Problem Solver

Can you use DOS 6 on your Tandy?

Yes, you can. You should not have any problem installing MS-DOS 6 on most models of the Tandy computer.

However, if you have a Tandy model that uses ROMDOS, you need to disable the ROMDOS before installing the MS-DOS 6 upgrade. The Tandy models in question include 1000HX, 1000SL, 1000SL2, 1000TL, 1000TL2, 1000TL3, 2500XL, and 2500XL2.

The methods for disabling ROMDOS vary from model to model, so you need to contact Tandy Technical Support at 817-878-6875 for specific instructions.

Converting from DR DOS to MS-DOS 6.

You should not have any problem converting from DR DOS to MS-DOS 6. However, you need to take some preliminary steps in preparation for running MS-DOS Setup.

1. Remove all instances of the DR DOS CHAIN command and any conditional commands (such as ? and GOTO) from your CONFIG.SYS and AUTOEXEC.BAT files. Be sure to adjust the sequence of the remaining commands as needed.

2. If your DR DOS directory, CONFIG.SYS, AUTOEXEC.BAT, and/or any system files are password protected, use the DR DOS PASSWORD command to disable the password protection. Also, disable any other security features used by your system.

3. If you are using DELWATCH, purge deleted files and disable delete watch protection.

These steps should prevent Setup from delivering messages such as `Your computer is using an incompatible delete-protection program` or `Your computer uses password protection`. If either of these messages appears, you probably skipped a step or overlooked a line in your CONFIG.SYS or AUTOEXEC.BAT files.

If you are using disk compression, but your startup drive (drive C) is not compressed, you see the following MS-DOS message:

```
Your CONFIG.SYS file contains commands that are not valid MS-DOS commands
```

This is not a problem. Choose the Modify original files option.

If you are using DR DOS disk compression, and your startup drive (drive C) is compressed, you need to copy your AUTOEXEC.BAT file from your compressed drive to your uncompressed drive and combine the CONFIG.SYS file from your compressed drive with the DCONFIG.SYS file on your uncompressed drive.

Choose Continue when the `Because you are currently using the DR DOS operating system` message appears. If, after Setup is complete, MS-DOS displays `Unrecognized command` messages, you need to remove those commands from your CONFIG.SYS and AUTOEXEC.BAT files. You may also need to add DEVICE=HIMEM.SYS to the beginning of your CONFIG.SYS file. Then reboot.

You can find more detailed instructions in section 1.10 of the README.TXT file on the MS-DOS 6.0 Setup Disk 1 and in section 1.12 of the README.TXT file on the MS-DOS 6.2 Setup Disk 1. We find it easiest to open readme files using the MS-DOS Edit program that came into being with MS-DOS 5. In this case you type

    C:\>**edit a:\readme.txt**

and when the Edit program appears with the README.TXT file loaded, use the Search option from the Edit menu to search for 1.10. If you don't have EDIT, you can use any ASCII text editor or copy the EDIT and QBASIC files onto your hard disk from Setup Disk 2.

Problems Running MS-DOS after Setup Is Finished

If MS-DOS does not start after running Setup successfully, the problem usually falls into one or four areas: 1) the EMM386 memory manager; 2) a conflicting memory-resident program or device driver in your CONFIG.SYS or AUTOEXEC.BAT files; 3) some other command line in your AUTOEXEC.BAT file; or 4) some other command line in your CONFIG.SYS file.

How can you determine where the problem exists?

The way to narrow down the potential problem area is to execute individual startup commands while bypassing the others. Because you were able to run the Setup program successfully, you can now use the F8 and F5 keys to bypass portions of the startup process.

When you boot up your computer, pressing F8 as soon as you see the `Starting MS-DOS...` message on your screen signals MS-DOS 6 to prompt you for confirmation before executing each command in your CONFIG.SYS file and again before running the AUTOEXEC.BAT file.

To see whether the EMM386 memory manager is causing the problem, press Y to confirm all the CONFIG.SYS command lines except for the one that loads the EMM386 memory manager. When you are prompted to confirm the EMM386 command line, press N. That command line should look something like this:

    DEVICE=C:\DOS\EMM386.EXE

When prompted to confirm running the AUTOEXEC.BAT file, press Y. If your computer starts up okay, the problem was probably with the memory manager, and you might want to try running MemMaker.

If your computer still doesn't start up, the next most likely cause is a conflicting memory-resident program or device driver. This time press F5 as soon as you see the `Starting MS-DOS...` message on your screen, signaling MS-DOS 6 to bypass both the CONFIG.SYS and AUTOEXEC.BAT files altogether. If your computer does not start this time, you need to contact Microsoft Product Support Services.

If your computer starts up okay, then the problem is inside either your AUTOEXEC.BAT or CONFIG.SYS file. Restart your computer one more time and use F8 again. This time confirm every command line by pressing Y, but when prompted to confirm running the AUTOEXEC.BAT file, press N. If your computer starts okay, then the problem is most likely in the AUTOEXEC.BAT file. If your computer does not start up okay, there is a problem with one or more of the command lines in your CONFIG.SYS file.

We talk more about problem diagnosis and the interactive startup process in the next chapter. You can also find more detailed, step-by-step instructions for finding the problem command line on pages 197-203 of your *Microsoft MS-DOS 6 User's Guide*.

Chapter 2
Startup Process

When you turn on your computer, the BIOS (Basic Input Output System) program that resides on a chip reads three hidden files that tell it how to start up MS-DOS. During this time you see a message on your screen:

```
Starting MS-DOS...
```

Then, if you have any DoubleSpace drives, the system loads DBLSPACE.BIN. The next step in the startup process is the execution of the CONFIG.SYS file containing DOS options and commands to load device drivers and memory-resident programs into memory. The process concludes with the execution of the AUTOEXEC.BAT file containing a series of commands that you want to run once, and only once, each time you start your computer.

When you, the user, have the opportunity to interact with DOS during the execution of the CONFIG.SYS and AUTOEXEC.BAT files, we call that *interactive startup*. The first part of this section illustrates the use of the interactive startup techniques to isolate system problems. The second section deals with problems related to the multiple configurations feature introduced with MS-DOS 6.0. And the third section covers other problems relating to command lines in your CONFIG.SYS and AUTOEXEC.BAT files.

Interactive Startup Techniques

MS-DOS 6.0 introduced two methods for interactive startup that are useful for isolating any commands that might be causing trouble during the startup process. Then Microsoft added two more interactive startup options with the MS-DOS 6.2 upgrade.

> **You've heard the term *interactive startup*, but you're not sure what it is or what it's for.**
>
> *The main purpose of any interactive startup is to find the root of a system problem that may be caused by a command in your CONFIG.SYS or AUTOEXEC.BAT file. The term interactive startup, as applied to MS-DOS, can be confusing. Not only are there a few different interactive startup methods, but you can approach startup problem-solving in two distinct ways: constructive or deconstructive.*
>
> The *constructive* approach refers to constructing your startup files one line at a time. Each time you run an interactive startup you confirm one command more than the previous run. If the startup is successful, then you do it again, confirming yet another command. If a startup attempt fails, or if you experience a system problem, then you know that the last command you confirmed is somehow the cause of your problem.

The *deconstructive* approach works in just the opposite way. You eliminate one command line at a time. If you still experience the problem, then the line you bypassed was not the cause of the problem. If your problem disappears, then the line you bypassed was the cause of the problem.

Table 2-1 is a list of interactive startup methods and the keys used for selection. (We provide more detailed instructions for using these methods in the problems following this one.)

Table 2-1: Interactive Startup Methods

Key	Response to prompt (if any)	Startup method
F5		Bypass both the CONFIG.SYS and AUTOEXEC.BAT files entirely. This is sometimes referred to as a clean start.
F8	N	Interact with the CONFIG.SYS file commands and then (by responding No to the prompt) bypass the AUTOEXEC.BAT file entirely.
	Y (MS-DOS 6.0 only)	Interact with the CONFIG.SYS file commands and then (by responding Yes to the prompt) run the AUTOEXEC.BAT file in its entirety.
	Y (MS-DOS 6.2 only)	Interact with the CONFIG.SYS file commands and then (by responding Yes to the prompt) interact with the AUTOEXEC.BAT commands as well.
Ctrl-F5 (For use on DOS 6.2 systems with one or more DoubleSpace drives.)		Bypass the loading of DBLSPACE.BIN into memory in addition to bypassing the CONFIG.SYS and AUTOEXEC.BAT files entirely.
Ctrl-F8 (For use on DOS 6.2 systems with one or more DoubleSpace drives.)	N	Bypass the loading of DBLSPACE.BIN into memory, interact with the CONFIG.SYS file, and bypass the AUTOEXEC.BAT file entirely.
	Y	Bypass the loading of DBLSPACE.BIN into memory and interact with both the CONFIG.SYS and AUTOEXEC.BAT commands.

Chapter 2: Startup Process

Your computer hangs. Is the problem caused by something in one of your startup files? How can you find out?

If you're installing a new device or experiencing a problem communicating with a system device, the cause is probably in a startup file. If a device works with one program but not another, the problem is probably not in the a startup file. If you're not sure that this is where the problem lies, you can test your theory by bypassing both your CONFIG.SYS and AUTOEXEC.BAT files entirely. This is the interactive startup method sometimes referred to as a clean start, and it forces the system to start up with a minimum configuration.

To signal your system to completely bypass both the CONFIG.SYS and AUTOEXEC.BAT files, boot up your computer and press F5 as soon as you see the following text:

```
Starting MS-DOS...
```

When you use this minimal approach, your installable device drivers are not loaded, and you are mouseless. You don't have access to expanded or extended memory, your prompt shows only the drive (C>, A>, and so on), and no PATH statement is in effect (in fact none of the environment variables are set), so every command you enter has to include the full path to the command.

If you can successfully boot your system this way and experience no other problems, then the problem you experienced earlier was most likely caused by a command in your AUTOEXEC.BAT or CONFIG.SYS file. Now you need to determine which command line is the source of your troubles (see next problem).

You know you have a problem in either your CONFIG.SYS or AUTOEXEC.BAT file. What can you do to track it down?

In order to determine which command is causing your problems, you need to isolate the commands. For example, if you suspect the problem is a device driver that you just added, be aware that you may have another device driver that conflicts (even though it had been working fine). Try loading just the new driver (with memory management if appropriate) to see if it works alone.

Interactive startup enables you to confirm or bypass each individual command in the CONFIG.SYS file and then to choose whether or not to bypass the AUTOEXEC.BAT file. If you choose to run the AUTOEXEC.BAT file, MS-DOS 6.0 simply runs the file in its entirety, whereas MS-DOS 6.2 allows you to confirm or bypass each individual command in the AUTOEXEC.BAT file.

Interacting with the CONFIG.SYS file

To confirm each and every CONFIG.SYS file command, you must signal the system to prompt you for a yes or no response before DOS executes each line. Using this approach gives you the opportunity to bypass one or more individual lines without skipping the rest of the commands.

To signal the system, boot up your computer and press F8 as soon as it displays the following text:

```
Starting MS-DOS...
```

DOS displays each command line one at a time. For example, if the first command in your CONFIG.SYS file is a BREAK command, the first thing you see is something like the following:

```
break=on [y, n]?
```

Press either Y or N, causing the system to either execute or bypass the line and then display the next line

```
files=30 [y, n]?
```

until, after the final command, DOS displays

```
process autoexec.bat [y, n]?
```

and you choose whether or not you want to run the AUTOEXEC.BAT file.

Interacting with the AUTOEXEC.BAT file

If you are running MS-DOS 6.2 and you select Y when asked whether to process the AUTOEXEC.BAT file, each individual command line appears for you to confirm or bypass, just as described previously for the CONFIG.SYS file commands.

Do you really have to confirm or bypass each and every startup command individually, one at a time?

When you're using an interactive startup to isolate problems in your CONFIG.SYS or AUTOEXEC.BAT files, you may have to restart repeatedly until you find the problem line. Whether you're using the construction or deconstruction approach (both are described at the beginning of this section), you can tell the system to run all the remaining commands in the startup file without prompting you further for individual line confirmation. Similarly, you can also tell the system to bypass all the remaining commands.

At any time during the interactive startup, you can respond with F5 or Esc instead of Y to confirm or N to bypass. If you use F5, the system bypasses all the remaining commands. Esc tells the system to stop the interactive process and carry out all the remaining commands.

Can you use an interactive startup method when using multiple configurations?

No problem here. You just begin a little differently.

In order to employ an interactive startup method when using multiple configurations, you wait until the startup menu appears. At the bottom of your screen you will see the following line:

```
F5=Bypass startup files    F8=Confirm each CONFIG.SYS line [N]
```

Pressing F5 immediately bypasses the running of both files. Pressing F8 toggles the value shown on the screen between N and Y. When you select your item from the menu, you are prompted for command confirmations only if the value at the bottom was Y when you made your selection. Note that the prompt line is slightly different for MS-DOS 6.2.

Multiple Configurations

In order to address some of the common problems and questions regarding multiple configurations, a brief review of the requirements for defining them is in order.

You must define a menu using MENUITEM for each configuration choice. You can also set a default choice using MENUDEFAULT and select colors for the menu text and background using MENUCOLOR. You can use the SUBMENU command to have one menu bring up another menu.

Each section in the file is called a *block,* and each block begins with a *header* (a header is a name between square brackets). The three types of blocks are menu blocks, configuration blocks, and common blocks. Menu blocks contain the menu information (either as MENUITEM or SUBMENU commands), whereas configuration and common blocks contain the actual CONFIG.SYS commands. The commands in a configuration block apply only to that configuration; the commands in a common block apply to all configurations.

The first step in defining blocks is to define the startup menu. This menu block begins with the header [MENU] and is followed by one or more MENUITEM or SUBMENU commands. Each MENUITEM command contains the name of a configuration and an optional text description.

You may also use the MENUDEFAULT command to appoint a default configuration so that if a choice is not made by the user in a specified amount of time, startup proceeds using the default configuration.

Another nifty command that you may use in the menu block is MENUCOLOR, which, you guessed it, enables you to select colors for the menu text and background (in that order).

A typical menu block might look something like this:

```
[menu]
menuitem=dos, DOS-based programs
menuitem=windows, Startup for Windows
menuitem=network, Start the network
submenu=individuals, Individual users
menudefault=dos, 30
menucolor=15,1
```

This sets up four menu items: DOS-based programs, Startup for Windows, Start the network, and Individual users. The final menu item, Individual users, will actually display a submenu. The startup menu will be bright white (15) on blue (1) and will default to the DOS-based programs menu after 30 seconds.

Part I: Problem Solver

Some of the most common questions and problems with multiple configuration involve the use of menus. (The other most common problems involve the use of MemMaker with multiple configurations, and we address that issue in Chapter 5, "Memory Management.")

Your system boots up with the default configuration, bypassing your startup menu. What's wrong?

After going to all the trouble of creating multiple configurations, you find that your startup menu fails to appear. Chances are good that it's just an errant blank space or special character that's in the way.

The menu block containing the definition for the startup menu must be called [MENU]. The configuration name, or value for each MENUITEM command, must be one word (of any length), and special characters are not allowed.

In our example, we have three configuration names: DOS, WINDOWS, and NETWORK. Whatever names you choose, the header of each configuration block to follow must be identical to the value given in the MENUITEM command here (in our example, [DOS], [WINDOWS] and [NETWORK]). If a configuration name does not match the header, or if any special characters appear in a header, the default configuration will be applied. The same is true for the submenu name, INDIVIDUALS, which must match the header for the associated menu block.

You defined pretty menu colors, but after startup the colors revert to the default screen colors. What happened?

After going to all the trouble of looking up which numbers represent which colors and setting your color scheme to suit your taste, you find that the colors vanish as soon as you've made your menu selection.

Once you select a menu option, the startup process takes control of all screen output and resets your screen colors. Unfortunately, there is nothing you can do.

You are using multiple configuration submenus and would like to find a way to go back to a previous menu.

There's nothing worse then selecting a menu option accidentally, or just changing your mind, and then finding out that it's too late; you can't get back to the prior menu. Luckily, that need not ever happen to you. You can include menu options to return to the prior menu or just memorize the secret keystroke.

If you are already using submenus, then you know that SUBMENU is used instead of MENUITEM to bring up a different menu. There is no rule against creating a submenu option to take you back to a parent menu. In our example at the beginning of this section on multiple configurations, our startup menu block was called MENU, and we referred to a submenu called INDIVIDUALS. In our INDIVIDUALS submenu, we want to set up individual configurations for Jack and Jill, as well as create a menu option for returning to the startup menu. That menu block would look something like this:

Chapter 2: Startup Process

```
[individuals]
menuitem=Jack, Jack's preferred settings
menuitem-Jill, Jill's preferred settings
submenu=Menu, Return to main menu
```

Ah yes, the secret keystroke. It's the Backspace key. If you do not want to go to the trouble of adding submenu lines, you can simply press Backspace to return to the prior menu.

Is there any way to create blank lines between menu options? How about clearing the screen?

These two questions appeared several times in the MS-DOS forum on CompuServe. Some menu creators thought if they could double-space the options on the screen, it would cut down on the number of times people accidentally selected a wrong menu. The desire to clear the screen was an aesthetic one, but remember that the screen clears automatically when you select a submenu.

Multiple configuration menus were not intended to have blank lines between the options, so this question kind of stumped the Microsoft Technical Support people on the CompuServe forum. If it's something you really want, however, we can offer a work-around as a possible solution for you, one that you may have thought of already.

If you're thinking that you could simply create a MENUITEM entry with no text description, something like

```
menuitem=dummy1,
```

you can, provided that you create a dummy menu block for the empty option. Applying this idea to our earlier sample, the MENU block would then look something like this:

```
[menu]
menuitem=dos, Setting for DOS-based programs
menuitem=dummy1,
menuitem=windows, Setting and startup for Windows
menuitem=dummy2,
menuitem=network, Start the network
```

The end result on the screen, however, may be confusing to users. The system assigns numbers to all MENUITEM entries, even to the dummy ones, so in this case you see five numbered options, two of which appear to be missing their descriptions.

Clearing the screen is a simple problem to handle. The solution is easy because you can use the CLS command in one of your common blocks. (Common blocks have the header [COMMON] and contain commands that apply to all the configurations.) The only tricky part is determining the common block into which you want to place the CLS command. Because we don't know what's in your CONFIG.SYS file, we can't really help you make this determination. Just remember that your blocks are processed in sequence, bypassing only those blocks that relate to the specific configurations other than the one you selected from the menu. To start with a blank screen after startup, place the CLS command at the end of your AUTOEXEC.BAT file.

CONFIG.SYS and AUTOEXEC.BAT Commands

Most of the answers to questions about how CONFIG.SYS or AUTOEXEC.BAT file commands operate can be found in other *Problem Solver* chapters (this is particularly true for DoubleSpace and SmartDrive). But a few questions remain. In this section, we look at those DoubleSpace and SmartDrive issues that are specific to the configuration process, as well as some problems relating to FILES, BUFFERS, RAMDRIVE.SYS, HIMEM.SYS, and the use of environment variable space by the PATH command.

How does DoubleSpace interact with your CONFIG.SYS file? Does this have anything to do with the assignment of drive letters for other uses?

When you run DoubleSpace for the first time, the setup program adds a DEVICE command to your CONFIG.SYS file to load the DBLSPACE.SYS device driver. Even though DoubleSpace does this for you, there are a few things you should know in the event that you are making any changes to your CONFIG.SYS file.

DBLSPACE.BIN, a hidden system file in the root directory of your startup drive, enables the DoubleSpace program to access your CVFs. The BIN file loads into the top of conventional memory during boot up and prior to the execution of the CONFIG.SYS file. Then, when your system runs your CONFIG.SYS file, it loads the DBLSPACE.SYS device driver, which in turn moves the BIN file to its final location in memory.

By altering the position of the device line, you can control the placement of DBLSPACE.BIN in memory. For example, if you want to make more effective use of memory, you might resequence your device drivers to load by size, largest first.

For more details, see "You want to make more effective use of upper memory..." in Chapter 5, "Memory Management."

If you use a RAM drive, you want to make sure that RAMDRIVE.SYS precedes DBLSPACE.SYS. A RAMDRIVE command should always come before loading DoubleSpace drives so that it can always get the same drive letter designation each time you boot up. If DBLSPACE loads before a RAM drive is created, the RAM drive may have to take a different letter each time it's loaded.

Of course, HIMEM.SYS has to be loaded to have access to upper memory, so it has to come before RAMDRIVE. The proper sequence is HIMEM.SYS, RAMDRIVE.SYS, and then DBLSPACE.SYS.

Do you really need to set the FILES line in your CONFIG.SYS file?

Your computer uses RAM for all kinds of things, such as storing information about files (their contents as well as bookkeeping data). You may be surprised to learn that the amount of RAM dedicated to keeping track of files is under your control via the FILES and BUFFERS commands.

The FILES command tells MS-DOS how much space to set aside to handle files. This sets a limit on how many files you can have open at a single time. The smaller the number you specify, the less RAM MS-DOS uses. The lower limit is eight open files, which may not be enough for some applications; the upper limit is 255.

Consider a word processor, where you can have the application itself open as well as two documents, a spelling checker, a printer driver, and so on. Then add in the temporary files created by the word processor. MS-DOS documentation suggests 20 as a typical number of files to set as open; however, you may want to set the number lower. For example, if you want to set your system to allow only 10 files open at a time, include the line

```
FILES=10
```

in your CONFIG.SYS file. If you don't use the FILES command, DOS lets you have only eight files open.

We suggest that you keep FILES=20, unless you're a Windows user, in which case we suggest FILES=30. Because FILES has very little impact on RAM use, we believe that it's better to have too many rather than too few openable files.

Why would you run SMARTDRV from your CONFIG.SYS file?

If you are familiar with earlier versions of MS-DOS, you may be thinking that SMARTDRV belongs in your CONFIG.SYS file. That used to be true, but beginning with MS-DOS 6.0, the SMARTDRV.EXE command, run from the AUTOEXEC.BAT file, replaced the SMARTDRV.SYS device driver. Okay, no problem. But now to add to the confusion, you've heard that you can (and in some cases should) still run SmartDrive from your CONFIG.SYS file.

If you want to use SmartDrive's double-buffering feature, you need to load SMARTDRV.EXE with a device line in your CONFIG.SYS file. The device line looks something like this:

```
device=c:\dos\smartdrv.exe /double_buffer
```

This CONFIG.SYS entry is in addition to the SMARTDRV command you must place in your AUTOEXEC.BAT file. The SmartDrive DOUBLE_BUFFER parameter takes up about 2K of conventional memory.

Another, less common use of SmartDrive in the CONFIG.SYS file might occur if you have expanded memory on your system and prefer to use the older driver. SMARTDRV.SYS can use either extended or expanded memory to store the cached data. SMARTDRV.EXE uses only extended memory. You can tell SMARTDRV.SYS to use expanded memory by using the /A switch (expAnded). To use expanded memory for SmartDrive's cache, make sure you are using the SMARTDRV.SYS program from MS-DOS 5 (or earlier) and use the following in your CONFIG.SYS file:

```
device=c:\dos\smartdrv.sys 1024 /a
```

However, it's preferable whenever possible to run the cache in extended memory because reading extended memory takes less time than reading expanded memory does. Also, you should not use the /A switch with Microsoft Windows if your EMS memory is being created by EMM386.

For more questions and answers about SmartDrive, including how to tell if you need to use the double-buffering feature and how and why to run SMARTDRV from the DOS prompt, see Chapter 3, "SmartDrive." For a detailed description of the SmartDrive command, with all its switches and parameters, see the "SMARTDRV" entry in the *Command Reference*.

What's the difference between using BUFFERS and SMARTDRV?

If you're confused about the difference between the BUFFERS command and SmartDrive, you're not alone. Both commands share a common purpose: to speed up disk access.

The BUFFERS command establishes disk buffers. Each buffer holds data that is on its way to or from a disk. The more buffers, the more data that can be accumulated at one time, and the faster your system runs. However, the improvement resulting from adding more buffers is not dramatic.

SmartDrive creates a cache of recently used sectors, so programs that try to read one of these sectors again will be able to read it from memory rather than from the disk drive.

A disk cache, such as the one created by SmartDrive, has three advantages over internal buffers. First, disk caches tend to be faster than DOS, so you see more of a speed improvement than when using buffers. Second, disk caches allow you to use extended or expanded memory rather than conventional memory, and that means you have more free conventional memory for use by your programs. And third, data in a cache is preserved rather than thrown out when new data is read. Of course, when the cache is full, some data is thrown out to make room for newly requested data that is not already in the cache. But items that are called for frequently are likely to be retained.

On the other hand, you can also free up the conventional memory used by buffers if you load DOS into a high memory area (HMA). When you do that, DOS loads the buffers into HMA as well — if there's room. If there's not enough room, DOS puts them all into conventional memory, thus consuming up to 26K that could have gone to applications.

Don't allocate more than about 40 buffers if you want them all to reside in the HMA. (To find out where your BUFFERS are loaded, use the MEM /DEBUG command or look at the TSR Programs information using the MSD command.)

How many buffers should you allocate?

The number of buffers you allocate depends on two things: the size of your hard disk and whether you plan to use a disk-caching utility, such as SMARTDRV. Generally, if you're operating a cache, you don't need very many buffers.

Allocate 10 buffers for each 40 megabytes of hard disk space, to a maximum of 50 buffers (or 40 if you load DOS high). If you plan to use disk caching (a good way to use extended or expanded memory), you need to allocate only 10 buffers to handle floppy disk reads and writes.

If you don't have enough RAM (640K or less) to consider operating a disk cache, see Table 2-2 for guidelines regarding how many buffers you should allocate.

You don't get any advantage out of allocating more than 50 buffers. Above that number, DOS spends so much time looking through and managing buffers that you lose any time you might have saved in reading and writing disks.

Table 2-2: Suggested Buffer Settings

If your hard disk is	Use this buffer setting	Which takes up
Less than 40MB	Buffers=20	10K
40–79MB	Buffers=30	15K
80–119MB	Buffers=40	21K
More than 120MB	Buffers=50	26K

Some programs look for a specified minimum number of buffers, even if you are using a cache. In these cases, you have to increase the number of buffers to match the program's requirement.

What's the most effective way to organize the paths to your various programs?

A long path may require an increase in environment variable space. Windows users can get around this pretty easily, and DOS users can too, but they have to work a little harder at it.

Our favorite alternative in the DOS environment is to create a directory containing only batch files, where each batch file represents a program and runs the necessary command to launch the program. You can include the path to the program file as part of the actual launch command, or you can include a change directory command to move to the directory where the program resides. No matter how many programs you have on your system, and no matter how many batch files you choose to create, you only need to add the batch file directory name to the path (along with the path to your DOS directory).

Windows users can circumvent the need for long path statements in their AUTOEXEC.BAT files by including the path to a particular Windows program command as part of the command-line statement in the Program Item Properties dialog box. Access the dialog box by highlighting the icon in the Program Manager and selecting Properties from the File menu.

If you want to run a DOS program from inside Windows, you can use a PIF file and include the path along with the program filename in the Program Filename text box in the PIF Editor. Alternatively, you can launch a batch file from the same Program Filename text box, or specify the program's operating directory in the PIF Editor's Startup Directory text box.

You can also create and set environment variables in your AUTOEXEC.BAT file, using them later in Windows. For example, once you set the variable (see the *Command Reference* for a discussion of the SET command), you can use that variable — surrounded by percentage signs (%*variable*%) — in the Command Line text box in the Program Item Properties dialog box. Similarly, you can also use an environment variable when launching a DOS program from a PIF file by placing the variable in the Program Filename text box in the PIF Editor.

Part I: Problem Solver

What can you do if you get a startup message saying `Error: Unable to control A20 line`?

The A20 line controls whether the high memory area (HMA) is available or not. It is a hardware component of systems with 286 or higher processors that allows programs to access the first 64K of extended memory. If DOS cannot control the A20 line, then it is also unable to access the HMA. Sometimes HIMEM.SYS cannot determine how to control the A20 line, and you must help.

You need to identify your computer for the device driver by adding the /MACHINE switch to the HIMEM.SYS line in your CONFIG.SYS file. You can use either a number designation or an abbreviation to represent your system. For example, /MACHINE:1 and /MACHINE:AT both represent an IBM PC/AT. A chart is included with the HIMEM.SYS entry in the *Command Reference*.

Chapter 3
SmartDrive

SmartDrive is the MS-DOS disk-caching program, and it seems that many of the problems reported by users of MS-DOS 6.0 (not to mention the media) were caused not by DoubleSpace, but by SmartDrive. The new SmartDrive version introduced with DOS 6.0 had default settings that, in certain situations, resulted in file corruption, lost allocation units, and cross-linked chains. These problems occurred when a system was shut off before the write cache was flushed. In this section we show you how to prevent that from happening, whether you continue to use MS-DOS 6.0 or upgrade to 6.2. We also explain the basic concepts of caching and answer commonly asked questions about how SmartDrive works.

Disk Caching: Basic Concepts

Among the slowest parts of any computer — aside from dot-matrix printers — are the disk drives. That's because the disk drive is primarily mechanical rather than electronic. The drive has a platter that spins and a read/write head that slides back and forth. It takes time to find data on a disk using this approach. Disk caching is a way to speed up disk access.

You've heard a lot about the benefits of caching and the dangers of write caching? What do these terms mean?

The whole point of caching is to speed up communication between your relatively slow hard disk and the faster processing power of your system. Because there are two times when the system accesses the disk (to read and to write data), there are two kinds of disk caching. Caching during the read part of the access is a common and proven technology. Microsoft introduced write caching to SmartDrive with DOS 6.0 and, as with many new products, there were some problems.

Cache Read Only means that SmartDrive caches only the data being read from the disk. The recently used data is stored in the cache, and when it's needed again the system can get to it much faster because it's in RAM and not on a disk.

Cache Read and Write means that in addition to caching data read from the disk, SmartDrive also caches data being written to disk. Write caching is usually referred to as *write-behind caching* because an application thinks it's writing data to the disk, but in reality SmartDrive intercepts the data, holds it in the cache (in RAM), and writes it to disk a little later, "behind" the time the program thought the data was written (or, if your prefer, "behind" the application program's back).

Part I: Problem Solver

Holding on to data in the write cache can enhance system speed by making better use of system resources. Writing to disk immediately would slow down your next action. By waiting until the system is idle for a few seconds and writing to disk at that time, you are unlikely to experience a delay. The only danger is in losing your data if your system goes down before the writing takes place.

What does the phrase *flush the cache* mean, and is it important?

This term is used in conjunction with write-behind caching.

Flush the cache is another way of saying *empty the write-behind cache by writing the data to disk*. Once written to disk, the data is safe. It is on this concept that we base the prevention measures discussed in the next section.

Can you use Read Only caching on one drive and Read and Write on another?

If you are reading extremely critical data from one disk and never want to risk losing that data (no matter how small the risk), you might want to set the cache to Read Only. But meanwhile you're writing less critical information to another disk and would like to have the benefit of the Read and Write cache on that drive.

SmartDrive can run only one cache for any one drive, but it is capable of maintaining a different type of cache for each drive.

If you are a Windows user, you can set the type of caching for each drive independently by using the SmartMon Drive Controls. If you work in a DOS environment, you can control the cache for each drive by running the SMARTDRV command from the DOS prompt with the appropriate parameters and switches.

The *Command Reference* contains detailed descriptions of all the SMARTDRV parameters and switches.

Preventing File Corruption

First, we explain what was causing the problem, then we explain the difference between the MS-DOS 6.0 and 6.2 versions of SmartDrive, and finally we show you how to use the command switches to prevent it from happening to your system.

What is the problem with SmartDrive, and should you use it?

The problem is write-behind caching — not so much the concept (it does indeed improve performance), but the fact that it was incorporated into MS-DOS 6 as the default setting, and the fact that unsuspecting users were unaware that the return of a DOS prompt did not necessarily mean that the cache had been flushed.

If a system is turned off, rebooted, or reset (or downed by a power failure) before the write-cached data is written to disk, that data is lost and may cause cross-linked files and lost allocation units even in the absence of DoubleSpace.

However, there is no question that SmartDrive write-behind caching improves performance. So the ideal solution is to use SmartDrive caching but take steps to be sure that the cache is flushed prior to system shutdown.

Chapter 3: SmartDrive

What SmartDrive precautions can you take if you are using MS-DOS 6.0?

The version of SmartDrive included with MS-DOS 6.0 can be used in a safe and problem-free manner. The key is understanding fully how SmartDrive works. Once you understand its actions, you can use the SmartDrive switch settings to control its actions to suit your work needs.

First, you need to know that SmartDrive automatically flushes its cache if the system is idle for 5 seconds. So the easiest course of action is simply to wait several seconds before rebooting or shutting off your system. Of course, this is of no help if your system hangs or if you experience a power failure.

Next, you need to know that with MS-DOS 6.0 the return of the DOS prompt to your screen, which indicates the system's readiness for further action, does *not* mean that the cache has been flushed. Again, waiting for several seconds is an option. Just be sure to begin your waiting after the DOS prompt returns to your screen.

If you are uncertain or doubtful about whether the cache has been automatically flushed, you can always force it to complete its writing to disk by issuing a SMARTDRV command from the DOS prompt. Use the /C switch, like so:

```
C:\>smartdrv /c
```

This command tells SmartDrive to immediately write cached information to the disk that has not been written yet. If you really want to feel safe, run this command before you turn off your computer.

Yet another option is to set the cache to Read Only, or to disable the caching altogether. The Read Only option is accomplished by using the SmartDrive drive parameter without a plus (+) or minus (–) sign. To disable SmartDrive caching entirely, use the same drive parameter with a minus sign. (The plus sign specified Read and Write caching.)

The *Command Reference* contains a detailed description of the SmartDrive command with all its parameters and switches.

What's different about SmartDrive in MS-DOS 6.2, and how does it prevent file corruption?

In order to help users who may experience problems caused by turning off the machine with the write cache filled, Microsoft has a new SmartDrive version that is more conservative. They do not consider this to be a "bug fix," but the default settings are safer. The tradeoff is slightly slower disk-write performance, so if you prefer speed over vigilance, you can still use the switch settings to suit your own preferences.

SmartDrive has two new defaults. The first is Read Only, so if you want write caching, you will have to enable it yourself. If you enable write caching, the second new default takes effect: automatic cache flushing before returning to the DOS prompt. You can now be sure that the DOS prompt will not reappear until SmartDrive writes to disk all of the write-cached data.

Part I: Problem Solver

The new SmartDrive version has four new switches: /X, /F, /N, and /U. The /X switch is the default setting that disables write-behind caching for all drives. You can override this setting and enable write caching by using the drive parameter with a plus (+) sign. The /F switch is the default setting that forces the cache to write to disk before returning the DOS prompt. You can speed up performance some more by overriding that switch with the /N switch to have the cache write to disk when idle. The /U switch prevents CD-ROM caching.

The *Command Reference* contains a detailed description of the SmartDrive command with all its parameters and switches.

Commonly Asked SmartDrive Questions

In this section we address some of the most frequently asked questions about SmartDrive including how to evaluate the effectiveness of your cache settings, whether or not to use double buffering, altering your cache and/or element size, and caching DoubleSpace drives.

How can you see the current status of SmartDrive on your system?

If you want to know the size of your cache and what type of cache is running on each drive, you can run the SMARTDRV command from the DOS prompt.

When you enter

```
C:\>smartdrv
```

the SmartDrive program provides information similar to the following:

```
Cache size: 2,097,152 bytes
Cache size while running Windows: 2,097,152 bytes

            Disk Caching Status
   drive    read cache    write cache    buffering
   ---------------------------------------------------
   A:       yes           no             no
   B:       yes           no             no
   C:       yes           yes            no
```

The cache size is set when SmartDrive is loaded into memory from the AUTOEXEC.BAT file. If you do not specify a specific cache size, SmartDrive uses an appropriate default value.

If you look at the question/answer segment about the effectiveness of your cache later in this section, you notice that the cache size is equal to the number of elements multiplied by the number of bytes in each element.

The last column of the Disk Caching Status chart indicates whether or not you should use the SmartDrive double-buffering feature. It is most often needed when your system includes SCSI (small computer system interface) devices and is sometimes of benefit when running EMM386 or Windows 386 enhanced mode.

Chapter 3: SmartDrive

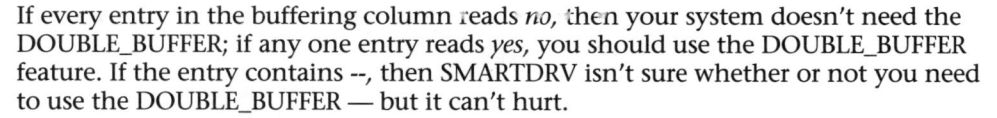

If every entry in the buffering column reads *no*, then your system doesn't need the DOUBLE_BUFFER; if any one entry reads *yes*, you should use the DOUBLE_BUFFER feature. If the entry contains --, then SMARTDRV isn't sure whether or not you need to use the DOUBLE_BUFFER — but it can't hurt.

For more information about using double buffering, see "Why would you run SMARTDRV from your CONFIG.SYS file?" in Chapter 2, "Startup Process," and the SMARTDRV entry in the *Command Reference*.

How can you determine whether you need to use SmartDrive's DOUBLE_BUFFER feature?

If you want some advice on whether or not you should use the DOUBLE_BUFFER feature, you can run the SMARTDRV command from the DOS prompt. The status chart displayed also indicates for each drive whether double buffering is advisable.

See previous question.

How can you tell if your cache is really effective?

In order to evaluate the effectiveness of your cache, you want to know the size of the data elements as well as how often the cache saves your system from having to read from the disk.

You can obtain this additional information by adding the /S switch to the SMARTDRV command run from the DOS prompt, like so:

```
C:\>smartdrv /s
```

In addition to the size and status information discussed earlier (in the question, "How can you see the current status of SmartDrive on your system?"), you also see something like the following:

```
Room for 256 elements of 8,192 bytes each
There have been 8,980 cache hits and 1,966 cache misses
```

The first line of information tells you how many elements (chunks of data) the SmartDrive cache can hold and the size of those elements. Element size is equal to the number of bytes that SmartDrive moves at one time. The calculation is based on the specified cache size and the element size. In this example, the specified cache size is 2,097,152. When divided by 8,192 (the default element size), the result is 256. Therefore, there are 256 elements, each containing 8,192 bytes.

The number of hits tells you how many times requested data was found in the cache. The number of misses indicates the number of times the requested data was not found in the cache, requiring hard disk access to retrieve the data.

Windows users may prefer to use the SmartMonitor program (SMARTMON) to get cache statistics and to control SmartDrive.

We discuss SmartMonitor later in this section as well as in the *Command Reference*.

If you want to alter the element size, see the "SMARTDRV" entry in the *Command Reference*.

Will changing the cache size, element size, or both increase SmartDrive's performance?

Computer users are forever in search of better and faster means for accomplishing their tasks. When used optimally, disk caching can achieve noticeable speed benefits.

In an earlier section on prevention, we talked about overriding some of the more conservative default settings for the version of SmartDrive in MS-DOS 6.2 and mentioned that some speed enhancement could be gained that way. Cache size (the maximum number of bytes that can be temporarily stored) and element size (the number of bytes that SmartDrive moves at one time) also affect SmartDrive's performance.

Generally, the larger the cache size, the more data is found in the cache, resulting in a higher amount of hits. This does not mean, however, that you should blithely increase your cache size. Allocating too much memory to a SmartDrive cache means less memory for other programs, potentially causing memory problems when running those programs.

Valid element sizes include 1,024, 2,048, 4,096, and 8,192 bytes. The larger the value, the more memory SmartDrive uses and the faster the SmartDrive performance. Because the default value is already 8,192, altering the element size would only slow the performance. (The only reason you might ever want to alter the element size is to reduce the amount of memory needed.)

Recommendations on cache size are discussed in the next question/answer segment, "What size should the cache be?" If you want to experiment with element size settings, see the "SMARTDRV" entry in the *Command Reference* for instructions on the use of the /E switch.

What size should the cache be?

Whereas disk caching can achieve noticeable speed benefits, determining the optimal cache size for your system configuration and work habits may be a matter of trial and error. But you can follow some general principles.

MS-DOS 6.0 (and later versions) uses fairly good default values for the cache size, based on the amount of extended memory supported by your system. The defaults are shown in Table 3-1.

Table 3-1: Default Cache Sizes

Extended memory available	*StartSize*	*WinSize*
0 to 1MB	All extended	0 (no cache)
1 to 2MB	1MB	256K
2 to 4MB	1MB	512K
4 to 6MB	2MB	1MB
6MB or more	2MB	2MB

With 2MB, 512K is probably a good size cache. 1MB is even better, but only if you can afford to spare that much memory. If you have more than 2MB of RAM, consider devoting about 1MB to the cache. We certainly recommend that size of cache if you have 4MB or more (and then 2MB might be even better). Again, it all depends on what your other memory needs might be.

What does the Windows SmartMonitor *hit rate* really measure, and can you alter it?

Hit rate *is the percentage of data that SmartDrive is able to deliver to a program without reading the disk again. The Cache Hit Rate area in the lower right-hand portion of the window displays a histogram showing the performance history of the SmartDrive cache. And here's how it works.*

The SmartDrive Monitor program for Windows (SMARTMON.EXE) allows you to monitor the hit rate. The histogram fluctuates with activity, and just under the histogram on the status bar you can see the Average Hit Rate percentage. (You can also enter **SMARTDRV** at the DOS prompt to obtain hit rate information.)

Without doing anything to alter SmartDrive's hit/miss ratio (such as changing the cache size), you can change the *sampling frequency,* which is a fancy term to describe how often the SmartDrive Monitor should check the hit rate of the cache. The Average Hit Rate fluctuates over time, so altering how often SmartDrive takes its measurements affects the average.

You can control the frequency by selecting the Options... button from the SmartDrive Monitor window. The default value is 500 milliseconds (every half second). The SmartDrive Monitor uses this sample information to create the histogram and calculate the Average Hit Rate.

Also see "How can you tell if your cache is really effective?" discussed earlier in this section.

Does sequence matter when you specify SMARTDRV parameters?

Generally, you can place command parameters and switches in any order you want. In the case of SmartDrive, however, the placement of the ElementSize switch (/E) has repercussions.

The only reason to use the ElementSize switch is if you are reducing the amount of data that SmartDrive moves at one time. (If this is not your intention, then you should not be using this switch.) The proper position for this switch is before you specify your initial and Windows cache sizes.

If you place the ElementSize switch after specifying these cache sizes, SmartDrive automatically reduces them by the same proportion that you have reduced the element size from its default. So, if you were to run SmartDrive with a misplaced ElementSize switch, as in

```
smartdrv 2048 1024 /e:4096
```

SmartDrive would cut the initial cache size to 1024 and the Windows cache size to 512 — each half of their originally specified size. Why? Because the default ElementSize is 8192, and you reduced it by half.

Part I: Problem Solver

Does SmartDrive really cache DoubleSpace drives?

DoubleSpace drives are really just files, and SmartDrive does not cache files. Nevertheless, when you run SMARTDRV from the DOS prompt, the Disk Caching Status chart shows YES under read cache for both your DoubleSpace and host drives. And if you've enabled write caching, it shows YES under write cache, too. How can that be?

SmartDrive doesn't directly supply a cache for compressed volume files, but it does cache the host drive. For example, if your drive C is a DoubleSpace drive, and DoubleSpace's hidden volume file is on drive H, SmartDrive caches all the reads and writes to drive H. The end result is that SmartDrive *does* provide caching for DoubleSpace drives.

If you want to enable, or prevent, some type of SmartDrive activity for a DoubleSpace drive, you must specify the host drive letter. So, continuing with our example, if you wanted to enable write caching for drive C, your compressed drive, you would enter the following:

```
C:\DOS\>smartdrv h+
```

If you were to enter

```
C:\DOS\>smartdrv c+
```

you'd get an error message saying `You must specify the host drive for a doublespace drive.`

Chapter 4
DoubleSpace

Uh-oh! DoubleSpace. You heard that DoubleSpace has problems. The media gave it a lot of attention. Should you use it? Is it safe? You desperately need more hard disk space, so it's either DoubleSpace, some other company's compression program, or buy a new hard drive. What to do?

Well, it turns out that the primary cause of the reported problems was not a malfunction of DoubleSpace. In fact, it was not a malfunction of any program. It turns out that the main cause of all those reported cross-linked chains and lost clusters was a function of the default settings for SmartDrive's write caching, default settings which have been changed in MS-DOS 6.2. (We talk more about that in Chapter 3, "SmartDrive.")

Now, that doesn't mean that there are not any DoubleSpace problems — there are a few, and we can help you work around them. First, we talk a little about how DoubleSpace works to save you space and then we explain some of the more confusing aspects (such as how DoubleSpace assigns drive letters). We also talk about converting from other compression programs to DoubleSpace as well as optimizing DoubleSpace, removing a compressed volume file, and what to do when you see those cryptic error messages. At the end of this chapter, we tell you about some of the programs, especially games, that are not compatible with DoubleSpace.

Understanding How DoubleSpace Works

DoubleSpace creates a disk-like structure in the form of a special file called a *compressed volume file* (CVF). This file masquerades as a real drive, complete with drive letter, while actually residing as a file on a host drive. Files stored on a compressed drive are actually compressed and stored inside the CVF by the DoubleSpace program.

What is disk compression?

Disk compression programs combine data compression algorithms with more effective disk-storage management techniques to make more effective use of your system's disk space.

Data Compression

On the simplest level, compression removes unneeded parts of a file for storage and replaces those parts when needed for use — sort of like removing air from dozens of balloons so that you can keep them in your kitchen drawer until the next party when you blow them up again. On a more sophisticated level, files are compressed using algorithms designed to replace repeated patterns of characters (such as the very common "er") with single symbols. When the file is decompressed, the character pattern is substituted for the symbol.

File compression programs, such as PKZIP, let you selectively compress one or more data files. You, the user, are the one who decompresses (PKUNZIPs) those same files before you can use them. Then there are programs, such as Stacker and DOS 6's DoubleSpace, which we generally refer to as disk compression programs because they create the illusion of a larger disk by automatically decompressing files as you need them and recompressing them when you are done. The process is transparent to the user and is called *on-the-fly compression*.

More effective storage management

An allocation unit is the smallest amount of disk space that DOS can use to store a file. Because each allocation unit generally contains 4 or 8 sectors (each sector is 512 bytes), the minimum byte size of an allocation unit is 2,048 bytes. Even a small file, one that contains only 640 bytes, still takes up a full allocation unit of space — all 2,048 bytes — when saved to disk. This means that 1,408 bytes of space are wasted, as shown in Figure 4-1. For the rest of our discussion, we use the word *slack* to refer to wasted space.

Uncompressed Disk

640 bytes — Contents of the file

Write to disk

One allocation unit with 4 sectors

Data uses only part of an allocation unit

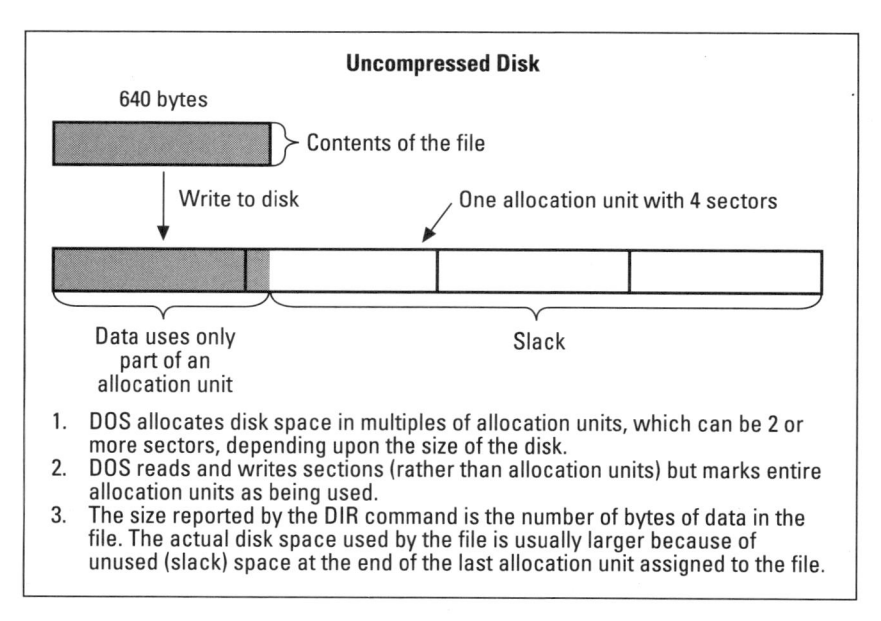

Slack

1. DOS allocates disk space in multiples of allocation units, which can be 2 or more sectors, depending upon the size of the disk.
2. DOS reads and writes sections (rather than allocation units) but marks entire allocation units as being used.
3. The size reported by the DIR command is the number of bytes of data in the file. The actual disk space used by the file is usually larger because of unused (slack) space at the end of the last allocation unit assigned to the file.

Figure 4-1: DOS writing a 640-byte file to an uncompressed disk.

The first big difference when using DoubleSpace is the size of allocation units. For all DoubleSpace volumes, allocation units are 8K, the equivalent of 16 sectors (or 8,192 bytes). You might think that larger allocation units would result in much more slack, but as you're about to see, it doesn't matter because DoubleSpace doesn't bother to store the slack.

The second big difference is, of course, the automatic file compression. Just as DOS is about to write to disk, DoubleSpace jumps in. Figure 4-2 shows what happens when DoubleSpace stores our 640-byte file.

Chapter 4: DoubleSpace

Uncompressed Disk

[Diagram: 640 bytes file — Contents of the file — Write to disk — One allocation unit with 4 sectors. Data uses only part of an allocation unit; remainder is Slack.]

Compressed Volumes

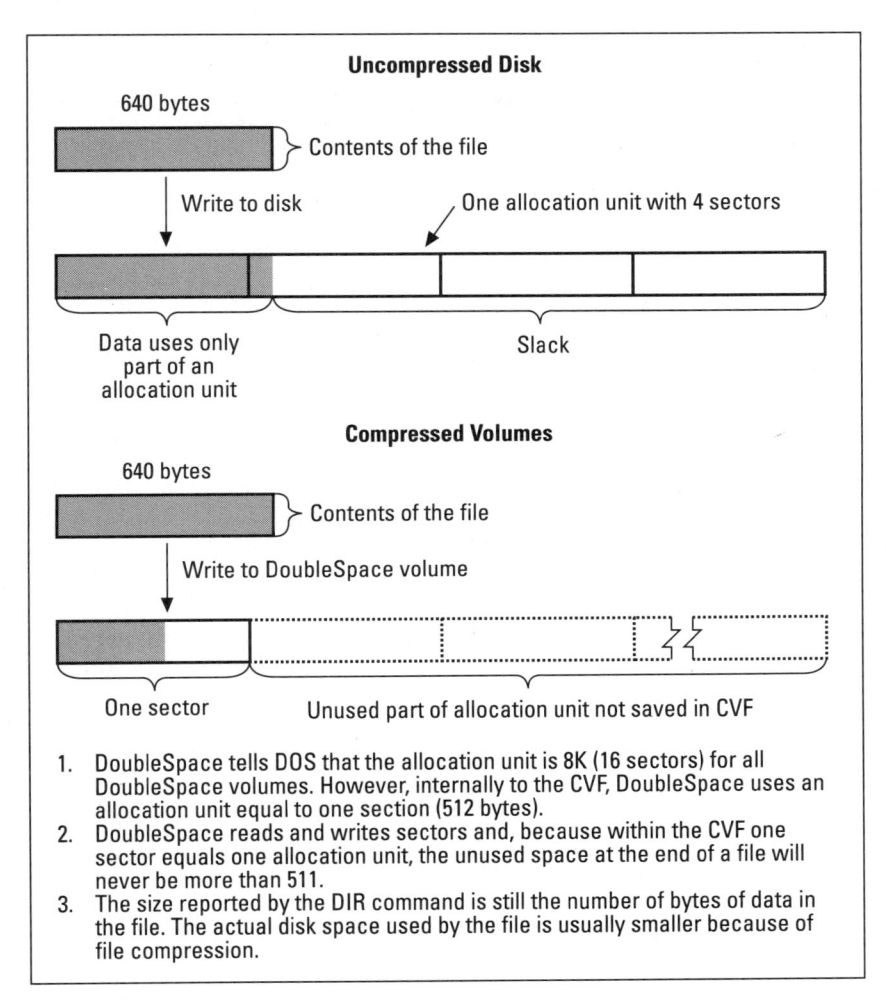

[Diagram: 640 bytes — Contents of the file — Write to DoubleSpace volume — One sector used; Unused part of allocation unit not saved in CVF.]

1. DoubleSpace tells DOS that the allocation unit is 8K (16 sectors) for all DoubleSpace volumes. However, internally to the CVF, DoubleSpace uses an allocation unit equal to one section (512 bytes).
2. DoubleSpace reads and writes sectors and, because within the CVF one sector equals one allocation unit, the unused space at the end of a file will never be more than 511.
3. The size reported by the DIR command is still the number of bytes of data in the file. The actual disk space used by the file is usually smaller because of file compression.

Figure 4-2: DoubleSpace writes a 640-byte file to a compressed volume.

First, DoubleSpace compresses the data so that it fills up fewer sectors (in our example, less than one sector). Then DoubleSpace stores only those sectors that contain compressed data inside the CVF. What happened to the other sectors? DOS thinks they've been used because it can't keep track of anything smaller than an allocation unit, but DoubleSpace simply ignores the slack.

DOS uses the *FAT (file allocation table)* to keep track of a file's disk address. Because the FAT can hold only approximately 65,000 addresses, DOS uses the concept of allocation units to control the number of addresses — the larger the disk, the larger the allocation unit, but always in multiples of 512 bytes (the size of a sector). DoubleSpace, however, is not faced with this restriction because it is placing the file inside another file, the CVF. Within the CVF, DoubleSpace has its own methods for keeping track of addresses, techniques that are based on individual sectors.

The same process, in reverse, applies when you ask DOS to retrieve a file. DOS looks at its FAT and figures out which allocation units contain the file. But when DOS tries to read from the disk, DoubleSpace intervenes again. This time DoubleSpace uses its own address list to find the location of your file inside the CVF, uncompresses the sectors, and hands the reconstructed data over to DOS. DOS is none the wiser.

How much can I really gain by using DoubleSpace?

Commercial compression programs talk about doubling your disk space, and even Microsoft calls the MS-DOS 6 program DoubleSpace. In reality, however, doubling is usually a figure of speech. The precise compression ratio varies from file to file. Some files have a lot of replaceable parts, making ratios of even 4:1 quite possible. Other files have very few, if any, extra parts, and the ratio can be as low as 1:1, meaning no space savings at all.

The compression ratio depends on the type of file and its contents. Text files can often achieve a ratio of 2:1. Compression programs can usually compress graphics files by a much larger ratio, sometimes 4:1 (or even better). This is possible because graphics files, which are composed of pixels instead of characters, generally have many more repetitive patterns. At the other end of the spectrum are executable files. These files contain programming code and don't usually leave much room for compression. Unfortunately, DoubleSpace can't calculate in advance exactly what the compression ratio will be for a given file, which can cause a slight problem. However, you can adjust the estimated compression ratio to reflect more accurate projections.

What's the difference between creating a CVF and compressing the current drive?

It is easy to become confused when Microsoft refers to creating a compressed volume file (CVF) as something different from compressing the current drive. After all, to compress a drive — any drive — DoubleSpace creates a CVF.

If you remember that there is really no such thing as compressing a drive, only compressing files, then it becomes clearer. What Microsoft is really talking about is the difference between compressing all of the currently existing files on the drive versus creating an empty compressed volume file.

Compressing the current drive

This means compressing all the files on the drive and placing them inside a CVF created from the free space on that drive. When you compress a drive, DoubleSpace reserves a little bit of uncompressed space on which to keep some essential files, gives that uncompressed space a drive letter all its own (making that the host drive), creates the CVF (taking over all the remaining space), and then moves your files to the compressed drive. All the files that were on your original drive C are still there, only now they've been compressed and are actually stored inside the CVF.

Creating an empty CVF

You want to create an empty CVF if you want to maintain your drive C uncompressed and use it as a host for a CVF, instead of the other way around. In this case, DoubleSpace creates the volume from the free space on whichever drive you select but does not touch any files that reside on the selected drive, so your existing files remain uncompressed. Your existing drive letter also remains unchanged. DoubleSpace asks you to select an unused drive letter and assigns it to your newly created compressed volume file. After DoubleSpace has created the compressed drive, only those files that you place on that drive are compressed.

You want to specify how much space you want left uncompressed when DoubleSpace compresses the current drive.

When you run DoubleSpace, the program gives you a choice between Express or Custom Setup. The Express option turns all control over to the Setup program and compresses your current drive.

If you want to control the amount of space left uncompressed on the host drive, you can use the Custom Setup option to compress the existing drive.

When you select Custom Setup, a screen appears giving you a choice between compressing an existing drive and creating a new, empty compressed drive. After you choose to compress your existing drive, another screen appears that allows you to specify how much space you want DoubleSpace to leave uncompressed on the host drive and what drive letter you want assigned to the host.

Use your arrow key to highlight the amount of space and press Enter. You can then type in the amount of free space you want and press Enter again to accept this. You can also highlight the drive letter, press Enter, and select the letter you want assigned to the host. When you're done making changes, highlight Continue and press Enter.

How does DoubleSpace assign drive letters?

The assignment of drive letters depends first on whether you are compressing the existing drive or creating a new empty compressed volume file. If you're compressing the existing drive, the drive letter assignment also depends on whether DoubleSpace detects Novell Netware in memory.

Compressing an existing drive means compressing all the files on the selected drive and placing them inside a CVF created from the free space on that drive. Your compressed drive maintains its original drive letter, and DoubleSpace assigns a new drive letter to the host drive. DoubleSpace looks for the last used drive letter, skips four more letters, and assigns the fifth letter to the host drive. If your hard disk is drive C, and D is a RAM drive, DoubleSpace skips letters E, F, G, and H and assigns the letter I to the host drive.

If, however, DoubleSpace detects Novell Netware, it looks for the LASTDRIVE setting and assigns the preceding letter. On a system with a LASTDRIVE set to T, for example, DoubleSpace assigns the letter S to the host drive. If for some reason S is unavailable (already in use), DoubleSpace tries the previous letter, R, and so on.

When you choose to create a new empty compressed drive, DoubleSpace creates a volume from the free space on the selected drive but does not touch any files that reside on the selected drive. In this case, the new CVF has its own drive letter, one selected by you (you can specify any drive letter that is not being used), and the host drive remains as is.

You want to change the drive letter that DoubleSpace has already assigned to the new host drive.

If you have devices, such as a RAM drive or CD-ROM, and you run DoubleSpace to compress the existing drive during a time when those devices are not loaded, you may find that you need to change the drive letter that was assigned by DoubleSpace.

You can do so by editing the DBLSPACE.INI file, but before you do, you must first disable your permanent swapfile (if you're running Windows) and then change the DBLSPACE.INI file attributes in order to edit the file.

Windows users have an extra step when changing the host's drive letter. A permanent Windows swapfile must reside on an uncompressed drive (the host). Because you are going to change the host's drive letter, you must delete the current swapfile and then re-create it on the "new" host drive. You do this from within Windows using the 386 Enhanced Control Panel. (Before you set swapfile to NONE, note its current size so that you can create a new one of the same size when you're done.)

Next, change drives to the current host drive (using drive I for the example) and use the ATTRIB command to make the file accessible. When DoubleSpace created its INI file, it created it as a system file that is hidden and read-only. Type the following ATTRIB command:

```
I:\>attrib dblspace.ini -s -h -r
```

Then use a text editor (such as the MS-DOS Editor) to change the first parameter in the ActiveDrive line to equal the drive letter you want used for the host drive. To continue our example, the current host drive letter is I, and the DoubleSpace entry looks like this:

```
ActiveDrive=I,xx
```

If you want the host drive letter to be changed from I to M, the new line should look like this:

```
ActiveDrive=M,xx
```

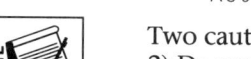

Two cautions: 1) Do not change the second parameter shown above as *xx*; and 2) Do not use a drive letter that represents a physical drive, such as A, that represents a floppy drive.

Save your DBLSPACE.INI file and then reset the file attributes, like so:

```
I:\>attrib dblspace.ini +s +h +r
```

Finally, reboot your system. And if you're running Windows, don't forget to re-create a permanent swapfile on the new host drive.

Can't find your compressed drive?

The importance of the Mount and Unmount commands in the Drive menu becomes clear when you remember that a compressed drive is not a real drive at all but a file masquerading as a drive. The Mount command creates the connection between a CVF and a drive letter; the Unmount command severs this connection.

Chapter 4: DoubleSpace

Thanks to the new AutoMount feature, introduced with MS-DOS 6.2, this should no longer be a problem. The *Command Reference* contains more information about this new feature.

To connect a CVF to its drive letter, select the Mount command from the Drive menu. DoubleSpace scans your system for any unmounted CVFs and displays a list from which you can choose CVFs. Highlight your choice in the scrollable window and select OK. DoubleSpace mounts the CVF and adds it to the list displayed on the main screen.

To sever the connection, select the CVF from the main screen listing and choose Unmount from the Drive menu. When you unmount a compressed drive, it is no longer listed on the main screen, and you are unable to access the files contained within that CVF. To regain access, you have to mount the CVF again.

Although CVFs residing on your hard disk automatically remain mounted, the Mount command is crucial for using compressed floppy disks with DOS 6.0 because DoubleSpace automatically unmounts the floppy whenever you remove it from the drive or reboot your system.

DoubleSpace treats compressed floppy disks and compressed hard drives pretty much the same, with one notable difference. Because floppy disks are removable, you have to mount a compressed floppy using the Mount command from the Drive menu in order for DoubleSpace to recognize the compressed volume. The floppy CVF remains mounted until you remove the disk from the drive, insert a new floppy into the drive, restart your computer, or select Unmount from the Drive menu.

You're running MS-DOS 6.0 and you want to use compressed floppy disks without running DoubleSpace Setup on your system.

When you run DoubleSpace Setup, the Setup program creates a DBLSPACE.INI file (among others) and places the DBLSPACE.BIN file in the root directory of the startup drive so that it loads automatically upon bootup. In order to use DoubleSpace compressed floppy disks, DoubleSpace must be loaded, and the INI file must be available, but you do not need to run Setup. Instead, you can create your own INI file and copy the BIN file to the root.

Thanks to the new AutoMount feature, introduced with MS-DOS 6.2, this should no longer be a problem. The *Command Reference* contains more information about this new feature.

To create the DBLSPACE.INI file, use the MS-DOS Editor (or any other ASCII text editor) to create a file containing the two lines

```
MaxRemovableDrives=2
LastDrive=driveletter
```

where *driveletter* is one letter after your last used drive letter. For example, if you already have a drive G, then the LastDrive letter should be H.

Save this file using DBLSPACE.INI as the filename and place it in your root directory. Then copy the DBLSPACE.BIN file from your DOS directory to the root directory of your startup drive and reboot. Now you should be able to mount the floppy disk using the Mount command. If the floppy disk drive is drive A, type

```
C:\>dblspace /mount a:
```

You haven't created any compressed volume files on your hard drive but you get a message saying `There are no more drive letters reserved for DoubleSpace to use...` **What should you do?**

This message appears whenever you try to mount a compressed floppy disk, and DoubleSpace cannot find the required DBLSPACE.BIN and DBLSPACE.INI files. If you have never run DoubleSpace to create a CVF on your hard drive, then these files do not exist yet. You have two choices.

If you are planning to compress your hard drive or create an empty CVF on your hard drive, do so first. Then try to mount your floppy disk. Everything should be fine.

If, on the other hand, you want to mount compressed floppy disks without ever running DoubleSpace Setup, you have to create your own DBLSPACE.INI file and then copy the DBLSPACE.BIN file to your root directory so that it will load on bootup. (Follow the directions in the preceeding question for using compressed floppy disks without running DoubleSpace Setup on your system.)

Optimizing DoubleSpace

When we talk about optimizing, we're talking about making the most efficient use of your resources — both RAM and hard disk space. First, you might want to adjust the estimated compression ratio to get a more accurate picture of how much space you actually have available. Then, depending on your systems needs and whether or not you're using Windows, you can reduce the size of the host drive to gain more compressed drive space. If it's uncompressed space you need, you can decrease the size of the compressed drive, but you need to defragment first. And then you can fine-tune DoubleSpace's use of RAM.

You want to adjust the estimated compression ratio to reflect more accurate projections of available free space.

DoubleSpace has two compression ratios: one for data already stored in your compressed volume file and the other for projecting free space. The first number is the average of all the compression ratios used when storing the files, and its value changes each time a file is added, modified, or deleted from the CVF. The second number is the ratio that DoubleSpace uses to estimate how much free space you have on a compressed volume. Initially, DoubleSpace uses 2:1 as the ratio for its estimated projection of available space, and this value remains constant unless you choose to alter it.

If you're going to be adding new files to your CVF, and you believe that the compression ratio will be different (perhaps you're adding a lot of graphic files to a CVF that so far contains only executable program files), you can change the estimated compression ratio to get a more accurate prediction of free space.

The Change Ratio option brings up a dialog box similar to that shown in Figure 4-3, indicating the estimated compression ratio that DoubleSpace anticipates using on future files, as well as the average ratio it uses for files currently in the CVF. (These ratios are the same as those shown in the Compressed Drive Information box.)

Chapter 4: DoubleSpace   51

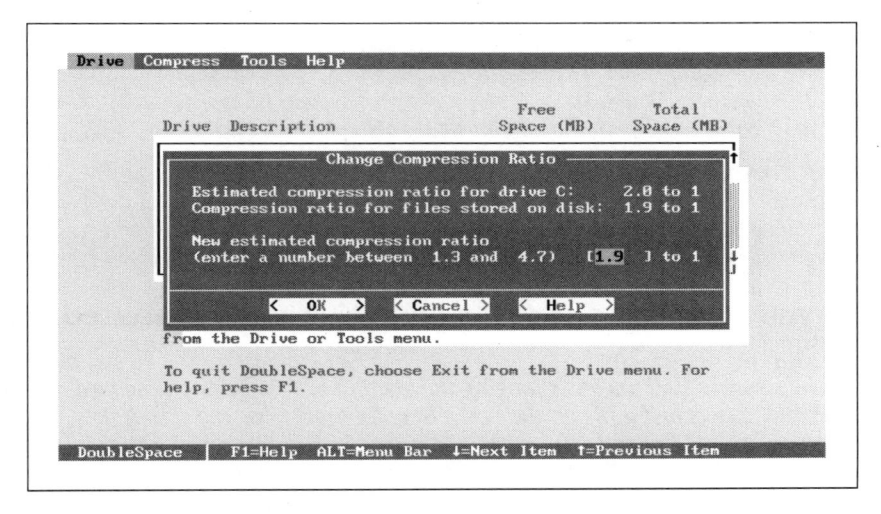

Figure 4-3: DoubleSpace Change Compression Ratio dialog box.

The screen instructions indicate a range of acceptable values (in Figure 4-3, between 1.3 and 4.7). If you're going to be adding a lot of graphic files, for example, you might want to change the ratio to 3:1, or even 4:1. On the other hand, if you're going to be adding a bunch of files that have already been compressed (ZIP files, for example), you might want to set the ratio at 1:1. Or you may prefer to match your estimated ratio with the average ratio used on the existing files.

After you type in the ratio number and select OK, DoubleSpace remounts the drive, applies the new ratio, and returns to the main screen displaying the newly calculated amount of free space.

Is there a way to automatically match the estimated free space ratio with the actual ratio used with existing files?

Yes. You can make the computer do all the work for you. After all, isn't that what the computer is for? You can bypass the menus and selection screens by using the Ratio switch with the DoubleSpace command.

From the DOS prompt of the compressed drive, type

```
C:\>dblspace /ratio
```

When you use the ratio switch, DoubleSpace calculates the average of compression ratios for existing files and adjusts the estimated free space ratio to match.

If you have more than one compressed drive and you want the estimated free space ratios to match the actual ratios for each compressed drive currently mounted, add the /ALL switch, like so:

```
C:\>dblspace /ratio /all
```

If you want to adjust the ratio each time you boot up, you can place this command line in your AUTOEXEC.BAT file.

Do you need all that uncompressed free space on the host drive?

When DoubleSpace compresses a drive, it leaves about 2MB of uncompressed space for the host drive. This is where DoubleSpace then places your system files. If you're a Windows user and have a permanent swapfile, DoubleSpace also places it on the host drive.

Chances are that unless you're a Windows user with a permanent swapfile you do not need most of the uncompressed space on the host drive. Take note of how much space is actually being used and then adjust the size of your host drive accordingly. The lowest value that DoubleSpace accepts for the size of the host drive is .54MB.

How do you adjust the size of the host drive and compressed volume file (CVF)?

Changing the size of a CVF means changing the amount of free space on the host drive. (Remember: the CVF is just a file on the host.) In order to increase the size of the CVF, you must use uncompressed free space from the host drive. Conversely, when you decrease the size of a CVF, you increase the amount of uncompressed free space available on the host drive. Space reappropriated from a compressed volume file must be contiguous, so you really should run the DoubleSpace defragment command first.

When you run DoubleSpace and select Defragment... from the Tools menu, a dialog box appears to inform you that *optimizing* (another word for *defragmenting* when applied to a disk) a compressed drive does not improve file access speed. It is, however, an excellent choice of action if you want to reduce the size of your compressed volume. By rearranging the files inside the CVF, placing them at the beginning of the file and all the empty space together at the end, you are able to reappropriate more of that space for the uncompressed or host drive.

When you select Change Size from the Drive menu, DoubleSpace examines your compressed drive and returns a dialog box (see Figure 4-4) with your cursor positioned next to the amount of free space on the uncompressed drive.

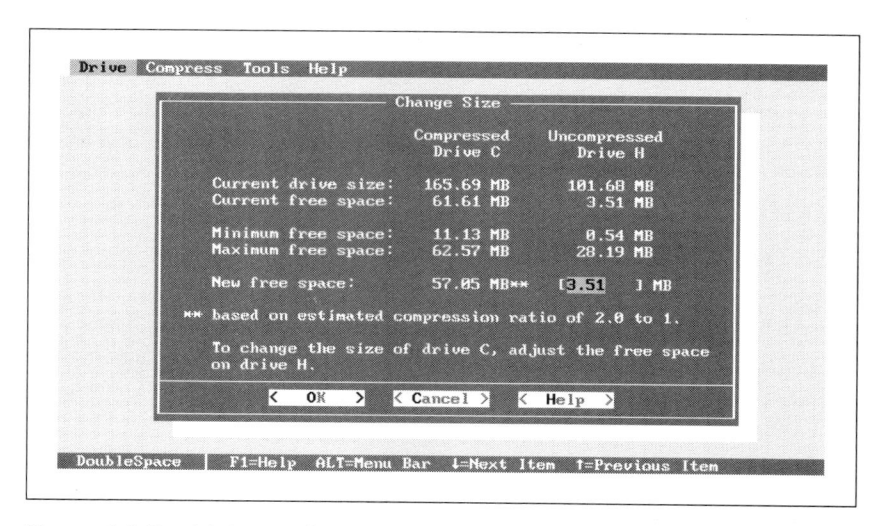

Figure 4-4: DoubleSpace Change Size dialog box.

When you type in a new amount, the program changes the size shown for the CVF. Then, when you select OK, DoubleSpace actually unmounts the CVF, adjusts the size, and remounts the compressed volume. If you have disks in your floppy drives, DoubleSpace prompts you to remove them, just in case there is a system failure and DoubleSpace has to reboot.

Should you use DEFRAG or DBLSPACE /DEF?

If you are confused by the abbreviated use of the word defragment *in two separate commands, you are not alone. Although the function of both the DEFRAG and the DBLSPACE /DEF commands is to use contiguous disk sectors, the goal of DEFRAG is to create contiguous sectors of related data on the disk, whereas the DBLSPACE /DEF command's goal is to create contiguous sectors of free space at the end of the compressed volume file.*

To add to the confusion, when you run DEFRAG from the DOS prompt on a DoubleSpace compressed drive, it first defragments the host drive and then automatically runs DBLSPACE /DEF. You can, however, run DBLSPACE /DEF (without running DEFRAG) when you want to reduce the size of your CVF.

When a disk has lots of scattered little pockets of free space, the *disk* is said to be fragmented. If there is no single pocket of free space large enough to store a file, DOS breaks up the file into pieces and stores each piece in different sectors scattered around the disk. When this happens, the *file* is said to be fragmented. So a fragmented file is one where the pieces of the file are scattered, and a fragmented disk is one where the free space is scattered.

DEFRAG

DEFRAG increases your data access speed by putting all of a file's pieces together in one location. That way the system does not have to go around to multiple locations to access a single file. All the pieces of one file are stored together in one location, followed by all the pieces of the next, and so on. As a by-product, all the free space ends up together after all the files, but the usefulness is the improved speed.

DBLSPACE /DEF

On the other hand, DBLSPACE /DEF works within the CVF and moves all the free sectors from wherever they are to the end of the file. Unlike the DEFRAG command, DBLSPACE /DEF does not put the file's pieces together when it rearranges them, so the files remain fragmented on the compressed drive. Speed is not gained with this command, but the free space is collected at the end of the file, and you can easily resize the CVF.

If desired, you can use the /Q switch to force DEFRAG to move all free sectors to the end of an uncompressed drive without rearranging the file pieces. You might want to do this to speed up the defragmentation process if your only goal is to create contiguous free space (perhaps for a permanent swapfile) rather than to increase processing speed.

Part I: Problem Solver

What can you do if you see this error message: `DoubleSpace cannot defragment because an unknown error occurred`?

If you see this message, chances are that you're running a screen saver program. The solution is easy.

All you have to do is temporarily disable the screen saver. Check your CONFIG.SYS or AUTOEXEC.BAT file and find the command that loads your screen saver program into memory. Disable the command by adding an REM command at the beginning of the line, save the file, and reboot. You should then be able to run your command. When done, you can edit your CONFIG.SYS or AUTOEXEC.BAT file to re-enable the screen saver program by removing the REM command and then reboot again.

How can you detect bad sectors in a DoubleSpace volume?

If you get a `data error reading drive X` *or* `sector not found reading drive X` *message, or if you cannot mount your host drive, you probably have a bad sector in your compressed volume file. (If you are running MS-DOS 6.2, see the 6.2 icon following this problem/answer segment.)*

The null test that we suggested in Chapter 1, "Installing MS-DOS 6," for testing your MS-DOS Setup Disks is also useful for diagnosing this problem. If you're able to copy the CVF to the null device, then your CVF doesn't have any bad sectors.

First, you need to copy the COMMAND.COM and DBLSPACE files from your compressed drive to your host drive. Assuming that C is your compressed drive and H is the host, enter the following:

```
C:\>copy command.com h
C:\>copy dblspace.inf h
C:\>copy dblspace.exe h
C:\>copy dblspace.bin h
C:\>copy dblspace.hlp h
```

Then clear the file attributes on the CVF file by moving to your host drive and typing

```
H:\>attrib -r -s -h dblspace.000
```

Then you need to unmount the CVF using the /U switch, as follows:

```
H:\>dblspace /u c:
```

Now you're ready to try to copy the CVF to the null device. Type

```
H:\>copy /b dblspace.000 nul
```

If you can't successfully copy the CVF to the null device, one of two things might be wrong. If you get a data error trying to read the file, then you probably do have a bad sector on the host drive. If you get a seek error or the sector not found error, it could be a CMOS problem. Check your CMOS settings for the host drive, and if they're correct, then you probably do have a bad sector on the host drive.

Chapter 4: DoubleSpace

If you have MS-DOS 6.2, you can use ScanDisk to detect and repair bad sectors. Enter **SCANDISK** from the DOS prompt of your DoubleSpace compressed drive and let ScanDisk do the rest. See the next question for a discussion of how ScanDisk is used to repair damaged volumes.

How can you repair bad sectors in a DoubleSpace volume?

The easiest way to repair bad sectors in a DoubleSpace volume is to upgrade to DOS 6.2 and use the ScanDisk utility. Or, if you already own a third-party surface scan utility such as Norton Disk Doctor (one of Symantec's Norton Utilities) or DiskFix from Central Point Software, you can use that. If you do not want to upgrade to MS-DOS 6.2 and you don't have any third-party utilities, you can use DOS 6 to reformat the disk.

Using ScanDisk

The first step is to determine whether DOS can mount the compressed volume. If, when you start your computer, you can list the directories stored on your compressed drive, then DOS was able to mount the drive. To fix any problems, simply run ScanDisk from the prompt for that drive.

If you've compressed your main disk drive, you could have a situation where DOS can't mount your compressed drive C because of damage to that volume, which means you won't have access to any of your DOS programs, including ScanDisk (because they're stored in the compressed volume file). In this case, you'll need to run ScanDisk from a floppy disk drive. Fortunately, ScanDisk is on the first DOS 6.2 installation disk in uncompressed form so you can run it from the floppy disk.

To repair your compressed C drive when DOS could not mount it, run the following command:

```
A:\>scandisk c:\dblspace.000
```

If you have the StepUp version of DOS 6.2 to upgrade from DOS 6.0, you won't be able to run ScanDisk off the floppy disk. Instead, you should make sure you put ScanDisk on a floppy disk before you have problems.

If the problem is that you have a second volume file that isn't currently mounted, you can run ScanDisk from your main volume (drive C). In this case drive C will use the volume file H:\DLBSPACE.000, so the second, unmounted, volume file will probably be called H:\DBLSPACE.001. The following command will check this volume file for errors:

```
C:\>scandisk h:\dblspace.001
```

As soon as you run this command, SCANDISK will switch to full-screen mode, where it uses dialog boxes to prompt you for responses.

For more detailed information about how ScanDisk works with compressed volume files, see the ScanDisk entry in the *Command Reference*.

Using a third-party surface scan utility

First, back up all your files on the compressed drive. Then copy the COMMAND.COM, DBLSPACE.INF, DBLSPACE.EXE, DBLSPACE.BIN, and DBLSPACE.HLP files to your host drive. (Remember: Your host drive is the one that is not compressed and that holds the compressed volume file.)

Next, you need to unmount the compressed volume file. Unmount it using the UNMOUNT command from the DOS prompt of your host drive. For example, if C is your compressed drive and H is your host drive, you would enter the following:

```
H:\>dblspace /unmount c:
```

Now you're ready to run the surface scan utility program to correct the bad sectors. After it's done, restart your computer. The compressed drive should mount automatically. (If it doesn't, you'll have to call Microsoft Technical Support.) We suggest you use the CHKDSK /F command to check for any file-allocation errors on your compressed drive. If you find any damaged files, you can then restore them from the backup that you made before you began this process. (You did do that, didn't you?)

Using MS-DOS 6 programs

First, you must back up all your files from the compressed drive. If you have any files on the host drive other than the system files and a Windows swapfile, you should back up those as well.

Now you can format your host drive. ***Note:*** *This will destroy all files on the drive!* Place your MS-DOS 6 Setup Disk 1 in your floppy drive. Then, from the DOS prompt of your floppy drive, type

```
A:\>format h: /s
```

where H is the host drive. (If you don't know which drive is the host, use the DBLSPACE /LIST command.)

Now, leaving the Setup Disk in your floppy drive, reboot your computer. Reinstall MS-DOS 6 and be sure to include the Backup program that you used to back up your files before you began this procedure. If you used the Windows version, you'll have to install Windows from your original disks. After MS-DOS 6 is reinstalled, run DBLSPACE to compress the drive. When that's done, you can use the Backup program (MSBACKUP or MWBACKUP) to restore your data.

You want to know how to handle Windows swapfiles when using DoubleSpace compression.

A permanent swapfile cannot reside on a compressed volume, but if you try to move it there, you do not get an error message. A temporary swapfile, on the other hand, is just a file and can reside anywhere. Nevertheless, it doesn't make much sense to place a temporary swapfile on a compressed drive because the purpose of a swapfile is to gain speed, and the DoubleSpace compression routines just slow it down.

Chapter 4: DoubleSpace

When you compress an existing drive, DoubleSpace creates a compressed volume and moves almost all of your files over to that volume, leaving some space uncompressed on a new drive that we refer to as the *host drive*. If your permanent swapfile exists before you run DoubleSpace, the compression program automatically places the swapfile on the host drive (the one that does not get compressed). In determining the size left over for the host, DoubleSpace doubles the size of the swapfile, leaving the remaining space free. However, you cannot increase the size of your swapfile afterwards! So set your size before running DoubleSpace or, if need be, you'll have to make your CVF smaller.

If you're going to have a permanent Windows swapfile, it's a good idea to set it up first, before running DoubleSpace. Swapfiles can't exist on compressed volumes, so be sure that you either leave enough uncompressed space for the swapfile or create and resize the swapfile first. If you want Windows to use temporary swapfiles, you still need to have enough uncompressed space.

Converting to DoubleSpace

If you are currently using a third-party compression program, such as Stacker, you may decide to convert your compressed drive to a DoubleSpace drive. In some cases conversion programs exist; in other cases you have to do it the hard way. As for why you may want to do this — well, it's a matter of convenience. Some people prefer DoubleSpace because the compressed drive is mounted first during the startup process. This means that unlike Stacker, for example, the program does not have to swap drive letters each time you boot up, and you do not have to make separate changes to different copies of your startup files (one for each drive) each time you want to modify your CONFIG.SYS or AUTOEXEC.BAT file.

You want to convert to DoubleSpace from third-party compression software.

Well, convert may be a misnomer here, unless you can find a conversion utility program for the third-party software in question (such as the Stacker conversion utility provided by Microsoft). However, there is a workaround.

You can back up all your data onto floppy disks or tape (or another hard drive — perhaps a laptop if you have one), reformat the hard drive that you compressed using other software, reload MS-DOS 6, run DoubleSpace to compress the drive, and then restore all your data from your backup disks.

Here are the steps, one by one. First, back up all the files on your compressed drive. If you have files on your host drive, other than the system files and Windows swapfile, back up those too.

If you have already installed MS-DOS 6, you can use the MSBACKUP or MWBACKUP commands. If you have an earlier version of DOS, use the BACKUP command. If you're using third-party backup software, be sure to reinstall that program when you are ready to restore the files. If you do not have a backup program, you can always use COPY to copy the files onto floppy disks or another drive. If you have a laptop, you might even use the MS-DOS 6 Interlink program to move the files from your host and compressed drives to the laptop drive.

Now you're going to format the hard drive that you compressed using third-party software. *Note: This will destroy all files on the drive!* Place your MS-DOS 6 Setup Disk 1 in your floppy drive. Then, from the DOS prompt of your floppy drive, type

    A:\>**format h: /s**

where H is the host drive. (If you don't know which drive is the host, try the DBLSPACE /LIST command.)

Now, leaving the Setup Disk in your floppy drive, reboot your computer. Reinstall MS-DOS 6 and be sure to include the Backup program that you used to back up your files before you began this procedure. If you used the Windows version, you'll have to install Windows from your original disks. (You should set the Windows swapfile size before proceeding.) After MS-DOS 6 is reinstalled, run DBLSPACE to compress the drive, and when that's done, you can use the Backup program (MSBACKUP or MWBACKUP or whatever method you used) to restore your data.

How to use the Stacker Conversion disk.

The Stacker Conversion program is quite straightforward. The only problem we've heard about is a syntax error message, which is presumed to relate to path problems. The solution is simple.

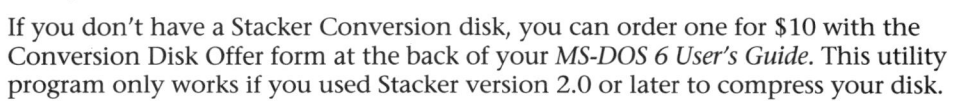

If you don't have a Stacker Conversion disk, you can order one for $10 with the Conversion Disk Offer form at the back of your *MS-DOS 6 User's Guide*. This utility program only works if you used Stacker version 2.0 or later to compress your disk.

To start the conversion, insert the Conversion disk in your floppy drive, make that your active drive, and enter the CONVERT command. For example, if A is your floppy drive, type

    A:\>**convert**

If you get a syntax error message, chances are that the Convert program can't find the DBLSPACE.EXE file. Check your path statement (in your AUTOEXEC.BAT file) to be sure that the directory where the file resides is part of the path (generally, C:\DOS). Or, even better, create a CONFIG.SYS file that contains only the Stacker drivers and an AUTOEXEC.BAT file that contains only a path statement pointing to the root, DOS, and STACKER directories. Then reboot and run the Stacker Conversion utility.

Removing DoubleSpace

DoubleSpace was introduced with MS-DOS 6, but Microsoft did not include a decompression utility until it released the MS-DOS 6.2 upgrade. In this section, we show you how to remove DoubleSpace compressed drives from your system if you are still running MS-DOS 6.0 and therefore do not have the new utility.

You can find information about the new decompress feature in the *Command Reference* portion of this book under DBLSPACE /DECOMPRESS.

Chapter 4: DoubleSpace

How can you remove DoubleSpace from your system?

The *Delete* command on the DoubleSpace *Drive* menu allows you to delete an entire CVF, files and all. However, just as with Format, DoubleSpace will not allow you to delete your setup drive. So, if you've compressed your startup drive — and most of us have — you need another option.

The simplest way around this restriction is to start by backing up all the files from your compressed drive and placing them on floppy disks or on some drive other than your startup drive. Of course, in the unlikely event that you have room on your host drive, you can put them all there.

Then use the ATTRIB command to reset the hidden, system, and read-only attributes of the DBLSPACE.000, DBLSPACE.BIN, DBLSPACE.INI, and DBLSPACE.OUT files, located in the root directory of your host drive. For example, using the ATTRIB command to reset the attributes of the DBLSPACE.000 file looks like this:

```
H:\>attrib +h +s +r dblspace.000
```

After you have reset the attributes for each of these files, delete (or erase) these same files and reboot your computer. All done. Now you just have to restore your files from the backup disk(s).

There's a slightly more cumbersome way that is useful if you don't have enough floppy disks for backup or another drive on which to place the files. This method involves making your compressed drive smaller to increase the amount of uncompressed free space and moving as many files as will fit onto the host drive. After you move some files from the compressed drive to the host, you can make the compressed drive smaller still and move some more files. You can continue to do this until you reach the minimum size allowable for a compressed drive (usually around .54MB). If you haven't copied over all the files by this time, you have to copy the last remaining files onto floppy disks or lose them.

After you've moved or copied all your files, use the ATTRIB command (as described earlier in this solution) to reset the attributes of the DoubleSpace files and then delete them.

DoubleSpace Incompatibilities

The biggest problems with DoubleSpace turned out not to be the cross-linked chains and lost allocation units that were actually caused by SmartDrive, but to be basic incompatibilities with other programs. Such incompatible programs include several games, as well as financial and spreadsheet programs among others. In general, the solution is to place these programs onto the uncompressed host drive. You may need to reduce the size of your CVF to free up enough space on the host.

Some of these problems may no longer exist with the introduction of the DoubleGuard feature in MS-DOS 6.2. Nevertheless, if a software manufacturer recommends running its software on uncompressed drives, we suggest that you follow its advice. You can find more information about DoubleGuard in the DoubleSpace entries of the *Command Reference*.

Part I: Problem Solver

You are a gamester and think DoubleSpace may be causing you problems.

Indeed, some games don't work well when run from a compressed drive. Here's what we know so far.

Tony LaRussa Baseball II simply does not work when run on a compressed drive, so don't try it. Furthermore, it doesn't work if you are using the RAM or NOEMS parameter with your EMM386 device command line in your CONFIG.SYS file.

Neither **Ultima** nor **Ultima Underworld** works properly when run on a compressed drive. This is true for DoubleSpace as well as third-party compression programs.

Because some of the game files get compressed and decompressed during play, it is not advisable to play **Links** or **Links 386** on a compressed drive. Your system may *hang*.

You use one or more financial and/or spreadsheet programs and think that DoubleSpace may be causing you problems.

Quite a few money-management and spreadsheet programs also seem to misbehave when run from a compressed drive. Here's what we know so far.

Argus Financial Software version 2.x must be run on an uncompressed drive. If you are planning to compress the drive on which Argus is already installed, you should move it to another drive beforehand. If you fail to do so, the copy-protection *key* is left on the host drive, and you have to uninstall the program to move the security back to the original diskettes before you can install it on the uncompressed hard drive. (Version 3 can run on compressed drives, but if you resize the CVF, you'll have trouble again, so it's still best to run it on an uncompressed drive.)

You can contact Argus Financial Software at 713-621-4343.

The **SuperLock protection in version 2.01 of Lotus 1-2-3** is not compatible with DoubleSpace. If you run the program after running DoubleSpace, you get the `1-2-3 has been uninstalled` error message. You can run Lotus 1-2-3 without the copy protection, but you need to run the 123.EXE file instead of the 123.COM. You can get this file with the Lotus Value Pack.

The telephone number for Lotus Development Customer Service is 800-343-5414. If you want to connect to their BBS, call 617-693-7000 at 2400 baud or 617-693-7001 at 9600 baud.

If you get a `divide overflow` error when running **Borland's Multimate 3.3 or 4.0** on a compressed drive, move the program to an uncompressed drive.

According to Intuit Technical Support, none of the versions of **Quicken for DOS** are likely to run properly on a compressed drive. If you need more information, call them at 415-858-6010.

What other programs have been identified as incompatible with DoubleSpace?

A few other programs have been reported as having difficulty when run from a compressed drive. Here's what we know so far.

Norton Utilities version 7 may not recognize the read-only, system, and hidden file attributes.

Complete PC Technical Support suggests that if you are using voice files, you should run **Complete Communicator** from an uncompressed drive.

Chapter 5
Memory Management

Second only to the processing power of your computer, no greater commodity exists in all of computing than memory. The CPU may do all the work, but everything that gets worked on has to be stored in memory. With more memory available, a computer can work on larger documents and can work with more of them at the same time. There's more room for TSR (terminate-and-stay-resident) programs and other helpful goodies. The system spends less time reading data from disk, so the overall system's speed increases. Life is good.

No matter how much memory your computer has, however, you never seem to have enough. So you have to make the best use of the available memory.

Understanding Memory Types

Before you can optimize your system through clever divvying up of your computer's memory, you need to understand the kinds and types of memory found in DOS computers. Knowing about memory — its potentials and limitations — helps you make decisions later on about how to apportion memory on your own computer.

What's the difference between RAM and ROM, EMS and XMA, HMA and UMB?

Computer terminology generates a lot of alphabet soup. Unfortunately, a lot of that alphabet soup is necessary for understanding the solutions to your problems. Here are some definitions.

Short-term memory is called *RAM*, for *random-access memory*. The densest RAM chips can hold 4 million bits of data (or about 125 pages of text). Each storage location in a RAM chip has an address. The CPU can read data starting at any address; hence, the random aspect of RAM. RAM requires a steady power supply, or data stored in it is lost forever.

Another type of electronic or chip memory is called *ROM*, for *read-only memory*. ROM cannot be written to, but the data stored in it is permanent and remains even when the power is turned off. On a PC, ROM is used to store vital operating system programs used to boot up your computer, so these programs have to be available when you turn your system on.

Because the original 8088 microprocessor used on the IBM PC could only address 1MB of memory, DOS was traditionally limited to 640K of RAM (*conventional memory*) and 384K of ROM. The first PC shipped with 16K of memory; at the time this seemed like a large number. Programs and data eventually grew beyond the 640K limits, however.

Lotus, Intel, and Microsoft (the LIM group) developed a new standard for *expanded memory*. This *LIM-EMS* memory (more commonly referred to as plain *EMS*) takes advantage of the fact that DOS does not use all the available ROM addresses. The EMS standard *maps* the available ROM addresses (called the EMS *page frame*) onto memory contained on a card that is inserted in one of the PC's slots. LIM-EMS memory offers a way for a PC that cannot address more than 1MB to have multiple megabytes of memory.

The new memory standard is called *extended memory*, or *XMS*. XMS memory requires an 80286 or later processor, one that can address more than 1MB of memory. XMS requires a device driver, as does EMS, and is available only to software that knows how to use it, also like EMS.

The first 64K of XMS memory is called the *High Memory Area* (*HMA*). DOS itself can be loaded into the HMA, saving conventional memory for applications.

Additional unused address space exists in the ROM address area, beyond that already taken by EMS. With an 80386 or later processor, these gaps can be filled with RAM remapped from extended memory. These *UMBs* (*Upper Memory Blocks*) can then be used for device drivers and TSRs.

On an 80386 or better processor, EMS can be simulated using extended memory and the proper software, which is included with MS-DOS versions 5 and later.

Use the MEM command to display the memory types and amounts that are available on your system, as well as to check whether MS-DOS is resident in the High Memory Area. The MEM command has switches with which you can obtain more detailed information.

You can find a detailed discussion of the MEM command and its switches in the *Command Reference* portion of this book.

You want to stop EMM386 from allocating expanded memory.

EMM386.EXE has two functions: It converts some of your extended memory into expanded memory and it can convert some extended memory into UMBs, which are useful for loading other device drivers and programs into upper memory. If you do not use any programs that need expanded memory, you can prevent EMM386 from using extended memory (XMS) to simulate expanded memory (EMS) and have more extended memory available for use by programs that need it (such as Windows).

You need to use the *NOEMS* parameter to tell EMM386 to create the UMBs but no expanded memory. If you are running MS-DOS 6, you should also use the *NOVCPI* parameter to tell EMM386 not to provide support for VCPI memory calls. The NOVCPI parameter must be used in conjunction with the NOEMS. Together, they restrict EMM386 to managing the UMB and providing no other services. The line in your CONFIG.SYS file should look something like this:

```
device=c:\dos\emm386.exe noems novcpi
```

If you neglect to use the NOVCPI parameter you may think that a page frame still exists and is allocating the minimum amount of EMS memory. In fact what you're seeing is the VCPI support, not EMS support. With just the NOEMS parameter, EMM386 still uses a portion of extended memory. It creates EMS memory to be mapped into the upper memory area. In addition, NOEMS enables VCPI and creates a 16K page frame. Add the NOVCPI parameter to disable this function.

Getting the Most out of Memory

The resources on your system may be ample or meager; but no matter what, they're still limited. You don't have an infinite amount of RAM. If your system is limited to 640K of RAM, you can't do much to optimize its use of memory; the memory you have is too limited. You can do a couple of things with buffers, but that's about it. On the other hand, if you have RAM beyond 1MB, you need the correct software before you can use this additional memory. In order to set up memory, you have to know what to put in the CONFIG.SYS file.

You use the CONFIG.SYS file to specify device drivers and other options that DOS installs at startup time. You can modify the CONFIG.SYS file with any text editor. DOS executes all statements in the file during bootup prior to running the AUTOEXEC.BAT file. In this section we suggest several commands that you can use to optimize your memory.

Throughout this chapter we refer to a number of powerful MS-DOS commands. Detailed descriptions of each of these commands can be found in the *Command Reference* section of this book.

You know you've got it (after all you paid for it) but you can't seem to access your expanded or extended memory.

In order to take advantage of expanded and/or extended memory, you must load the memory management drivers — HIMEM.SYS and EMM386.EXE.

The HIMEM.SYS driver sets up and manages extended memory. The driver EMM386.EXE manages expanded memory and provides upper memory on 80386 machines. If you're using expanded memory from a third party, be sure to install the third-party memory manager as well. Define memory-management devices early on in CONFIG.SYS with DEVICE commands.

You have extended memory available, but what you need is more conventional memory. Is there a way to move DOS to the extended region?

If you have determined that your programs need more conventional memory and you have extended memory to spare, you can load DOS into the High Memory Area (HMA).

With extended memory available, use the command

```
dos=high
```

in your CONFIG.SYS file to load DOS into the first 64K of extended memory, called the High Memory Area (HMA).

If you want DOS to manage the UMBs (Upper Memory Blocks), use the following command instead:

`dos=high, umb`

UMBs require an 80386 processor and a 386 memory manager (such as EMM386). Then you can use the DEVICEHIGH and LOADHIGH commands as well.

The DEVICEHIGH command loads device drivers into the Upper Memory Blocks, if available. This strategy moves device drivers out of conventional memory, freeing conventional RAM for applications.

The LOADHIGH command puts memory-resident programs (such as TSRs) into UMB memory. Use the LOADHIGH command from the command line or in a batch file such as AUTOEXEC.BAT.

You don't have any special memory but would like to get the most from what you have.

Without any expanded or extended memory, your best bet is to make use of the FILES and BUFFERS commands.

The FILES command establishes how many files can be open at one time. The BUFFERS command sets up areas of RAM in which data bound to or from disks is stored in preparation for reading and writing.

We talk more about FILES and BUFFERS in Chapter 2, "Startup Process." You can also find out more about the FILES and BUFFERS commands in the *Command Reference*.

Your system seems to run slowly, especially when accessing the disk or running certain programs.

If you're using a word processor, for example, and just typing away, chances are that you perceive your system as being fast, if you think about it at all. However, if you're using a database program, for example, and are doing a lot of searching to retrieve information, your system may seem to be moving rather slowly. This is because disk access, whether reading from or writing to disk, takes time. You may only be dealing with nanoseconds here, but there are ways to speed up this process.

Use SMARTDRV or other disk-caching software to create a disk cache in RAM, making frequently needed data available more quickly than if DOS had to read it off the disk each time. The minimum allowable cache size is 256K, but we recommend 512K if you have 2MB of RAM; 1MB if you have more than 2MB RAM. Using more than one disk-caching program at a time results in lost data.

A portion of RAM can simulate a disk, also called a *virtual disk* or *RAM disk*. Programs run from a RAM disk operate much faster than those stored on regular disks. RAM disks are also useful for storing TMP and swapfiles because they automatically disappear when you turn off your system (this does not apply to the Windows swapfile).

Chapter 5: Memory Management

? You receive an `Out of memory` **message, possibly when running one of the Microsoft utility programs.**

This message usually appears when a program cannot access enough conventional memory. However, if you are running a Windows-based program at the time, the program is more likely looking for extended memory. In either event, because memory is such an important part of your system, you should make sure you're getting the most from what you have.

Optimizing your system to free up more conventional memory means reducing the amount of conventional memory being used by MS-DOS, device drivers, and/or memory-resident programs (TSRs, terminate-and-stay-resident programs), and using upper memory and/or extended memory instead. If you have enough upper memory and/or extended memory, you can use the DEVICEHIGH and LOADHIGH commands to load the drivers and/or programs. MemMaker can accomplish this task for you automatically (we talk more about MemMaker later in this section). If you do not have enough free upper memory, you have to decide if some of the programs are not essential and refrain from loading them during startup.

The most effective way to free up extended memory is to disable EMM386.EXE. But before you take such a drastic step, you might try adding NOEMS to the EMM386 command line to prevent any of your extended memory from being configured for use as expanded memory. On the other hand, if you need to use some of your extended memory as expanded memory, add MIN=0 instead. If you are using RAMDRIVE and/or DOS=HIGH, you might also consider disabling them as well.

? What does `Error: Unknown command "/1:0;1"` **mean?**

This error occurs when LOADHIGH switches are not recognized by third-party shells (also known as command interpreters). With MS-DOS 6, the LOADHIGH command supports the use of the /L and /S switches to control the loading of programs into UMBs. MemMaker makes the most use of these switches in optimizing memory usage. Unfortunately, they are generally not compatible with third-party command interpreters such as 4DOS and NDOS.

Unless you can obtain an update for your third-party command interpreter that recognizes these switches, you have either to remove all occurrences of the /L and /S switches from your CONFIG.SYS and AUTOEXEC.BAT files or use COMMAND.COM as your command interpreter.

? You want to make more effective use of upper memory (UMBs) when loading drivers and TSRs, without using MemMaker. What can you do?

When the CONFIG.SYS file executes, the system reads through the file once and then on the second read loads all the device drivers in the same sequence as they appear in the file. You can do two things to optimize placement: either rearrange the sequence of command lines in your CONFIG.SYS file or indicate the specific upper memory region in which to load each driver.

The first solution is to rearrange the sequence of your command lines. For the most effective use of memory, you want your device drivers to be loaded by size, largest first. To find out the size requirements for each of your device drivers and TSRs, look at the Total column of the memory detail from the MEM /CLASSIFY output (see Figure 5-1).

```
Modules using memory below 1 MB:
  Name            Total  =  Conventional +    Upper Memory
  -----           -----     ------------      ------------
  MSDOS           60941    (60K)    60941   (60K)     0    (0K)
  SETVER            800     (1K)      800    (1K)     0    (0K)
  RAMDRIVE       369840   (361K)   369840  (361K)     0    (0K)
  COMMAND          4992     (5K)     4992    (5K)     0    (0K)
  DOSKEY           4144     (4K)     4144    (4K)     0    (0K)
  Free           211408   (206K)   211408  (206K)     0    (0K)
Memory Summary:
  Type of Memory   Total  =  Used   +  Free
  --------------   -----     ----      ----
  Conventional     652288  (637K)   440880  (431K)  211408 (206K)
  Upper                 0    (0K)        0    (0K)       0   (0K)
  Adapter RAM/ROM  396288  (387K)   396288  (387K)       0   (0K)
  Extended (XMS)  3145728 (3072K)  3145728 (3072K)       0   (0K)
  -------------   -------          -------          ------
  Total memory    4194304 (4096K)  3982896 (3890K) 211408 (206K)
  Total under 1 MB 652288  (637K)   440880  (431K) 211408 (206K)
  Largest executable program size  211312  (206K)
  Largest free upper memory block       0    (0K)
```

Figure 5-1: Output from the MEM /CLASSIFY command.

Unfortunately, this only shows the size requirements when loaded into memory. When launched, however, the program may need more memory. If you want to find the maximum size requirement, you can run the MemMaker program without accepting its suggested changes. The purpose of this is to allow MemMaker to create the MEMMAKER.STS file. You can then look at the MEMMAKER.STS file, find the SizeData section, and use the MaxSize entries as shown in Figure 5-2. Notice that the FinalSize entry is the one that matches the MEM /CLASSIFY output.

The second solution is for you to specify the upper memory region in which you want MS-DOS to load each driver. You can specify RAM regions in which to load a device driver by using the /L switch with the DEVICEHIGH or LOADHIGH commands in your CONFIG.SYS and AUTOEXEC.BAT files, respectively. First, however, you need to find the region in which available memory exists.

The MEM command has a switch for just this purpose — to hunt available memory. Typing

    C:\>**mem /free**

produces output similar to that shown in Figure 5-3. Notice that Region 1 has a total of 79K available. If you want to load the ANSI.SYS device driver into Region 1, use the line in your CONFIG.SYS file, as follows:

    devicehigh=/L:1 c:\dos\ansi.sys

```
[MemmakerData]
.
.
.
[SizeData]
Command=C:\DOS\SETVER.EXE
Line=8
FinalSize=720
MaxSize=12048
FinalUpperSizes=0
MaxUpperSizes=0
ProgramType=DEVICE

Command=C:\DOS\RAMDRIVE.SYS 360 /E
Line=13
FinalSize=1200
MaxSize=5888
FinalUpperSizes=0
MaxUpperSizes=0
ProgramType=DEVICE

Command=C:\DOS\ANSI.SYS
Line=15
FinalSize=4176
MaxSize=8960
FinalUpperSizes=0
MaxUpperSizes=0
ProgramType=DEVICE

Command=C:\DOS\SMARTDRV.EXE
Line=0
FinalSize=0
MaxSize=41824
FinalUpperSizes=28768
MaxUpperSizes=42384
ProgramType=PROGRAM

Command=C:\DOS\Mouse
Line=6
FinalSize=17088
MaxSize=56928
FinalUpperSizes=0
MaxUpperSizes=0
ProgramType=PROGRAM
```

Figure 5-2: Sample MEMMAKER.STS file.

```
Free Conventional Memory:
  Segment              Total
  -------       -----------------------
   0067D                   80           (0K)
   00693                   96           (0K)
   0271E                  192           (0K)
   0272A                88608          (87K)
   03CCC               403248         (394K)
 Total Free:           492224         (481K)
Free Upper Memory:
  Region      Largest Free         Total Free              Total Size
  ------      ------------         ----------              ----------
    1         126048 (123K)        126048 (123K)           126048 (123K)
```

Figure 5-3: MEM /FREE command output.

When you specify a region for a device driver, the driver is restricted to that region. However, if the device driver requires more memory than is available in one region, you can specify multiple regions by separating them with a semicolon, with syntax as follows:

```
devicehigh=/L:1;3 devicepathname
```

This command line enables the specified device driver to use memory in both regions 1 and 3. You can also specify a minimum available size in each region by following each region number with a comma and size using the LOADHIGH command. LOADHIGH has the following syntax:

```
loadhigh=/L:1,50;3,30 devicepathname
```

DOS loads the device driver into region 1 only when a minimum of 50K is available for use. If necessary, region 3 is also used, provided that a minimum of 30K is available.

? What can you do if you receive a message about Insufficient memory for UMBs or virtual HMA?

You see this message if, for example, you try to set up an HMA (High Memory Area) and a full UMA (Upper Memory Area) with only 1MB of RAM. You're 64K short.

Microsoft Technical Support on CompuServe has two suggestions for solving this problem. If you are loading DOS high, you can try to exclude an additional 64K from the UMA. To do this, use an /X switch to add an exclusion to the EMM386.EXE device line in your CONFIG.SYS file, excluding a specific range of address for UMB or EMS Page Frame use. The command should be as follows:

```
device=c:\dos\emm386.exe noems x=a000-cfff
```

Then use Custom Setup to run MemMaker, selecting Yes to the Keep current EMM386 inclusions and exclusions option. If you select No, MemMaker may remove or change the /X switch you just added.

Their second suggestion applies to systems with an AMI BIOS. Use the MSD command to review your system configuration. Select Computer from the main screen to obtain information about your system BIOS. If your system does have an AMI BIOS, disabling the Fast A20 Gating option may solve the problem.

You tried to free up XMS memory by loading everything in conventional memory but still find 1088K of XMS unaccounted for.

Chances are that you're loading SMARTDRV in your AUTOEXEC.BAT.

You can see how much memory SmartDrive is using by typing

    `C:\>`**`smartdrv`**

at the DOS prompt. Look at the line displaying Cache Size. If your cache is around 1024K, then you've found out what is using the majority of the XMS that was unaccounted for. HIMEM.SYS probably accounts for the remaining 64K.

You may choose to reduce the cache size, run without loading SmartDrive at all, or buy more memory.

Running MemMaker

MemMaker optimizes memory usage. In this context, *optimize* means that the program examines your CONFIG.SYS and AUTOEXEC.BAT files and loads the drivers and TSR programs in memory for maximum efficiency. MemMaker offers Express Setup, in which the program does everything while you sit back and watch, and Custom Setup, which prompts for answers to six key questions and then does everything for you.

Should you use MemMaker?

MemMaker optimizes memory usage. In this context, optimize means that the program examines your CONFIG.SYS and AUTOEXEC.BAT files and figures out where in memory to load the drivers and TSR programs for maximum efficiency. There are some restrictions in using MemMaker, and if you're a Windows user, other considerations come into play as well.

MemMaker only works on 80386 systems or better, and only with HIMEM.SYS and EMM386.EXE memory managers. Third-party utilities such as QEMM and 386MAX are not compatible with MemMaker, although they both have their own memory-optimization software.

MemMaker does not insert commands for you. The MemMaker program optimizes only what's already in your CONFIG.SYS and AUTOEXEC.BAT files. If it finds a more efficient position in memory in which to load a driver, for example, MemMaker alters your existing command (perhaps changing DEVICE to DEVICEHIGH or adding a parameter or switch). However, if you want a disk cache (SmartDrive) or a virtual drive (RamDrive), you have to place the appropriate commands in the CONFIG.SYS file. Then when you run MemMaker (which you can do more than once, by the way), MemMaker alters the CONFIG.SYS file as necessary for optimum effect.

Unless you have applications that require more than 512K of conventional memory, you should not try to free up conventional memory when running Windows. Making more conventional memory available means reducing the extended memory available to Windows, and the additional conventional memory most likely goes unused.

Can you use MemMaker to optimize memory usage on a diskless workstation?

MemMaker requires a hard disk drive and cannot be run on a diskless workstation.

Even though MemMaker does not run on a diskless workstation, you can optimize memory usage by using the DEVICEHIGH command in your CONFIG.SYS file and the LOADHIGH command in your AUTOEXEC.BAT file to load drivers into the UMA (Upper Memory Area).

When MemMaker's Custom Setup asks whether or not to `Optimize upper memory for use with Windows,` what should you reply?

Optimizing upper memory for use with Windows benefits DOS-based programs that are run from Windows.

Select Yes only if you are a Windows user and run DOS-based applications from inside Windows. If you are a Windows user and do not run DOS-based programs under Windows, then you don't need to optimize upper memory for use with Windows and should answer No. The command determines where portions of the Windows program are placed in memory.

How can you use MemMaker with multiple configurations?

The use of multiple configurations introduces some problems for MemMaker. MemMaker is designed to optimize a single configuration, providing the best integrated fit for the programs and device drivers loaded in your CONFIG.SYS and AUTOEXEC.BAT files. Basically, MemMaker works like an electronic puzzle solver, arranging the pieces to fill the available spaces in upper memory.

With multiple configurations, each configuration has a different set of pieces: From the CONFIG.SYS file you have the common commands plus those in the individual configuration block added to the commands from the AUTOEXEC.BAT file, which also may vary between configurations if you used labels and GOTO commands. Although each configuration shares many commands in common, the optimum placement of each program and device driver may vary when considered together with the commands specific to each configuration.

The solution is to break the multiple configurations down into individual configurations and run MemMaker for each. To do this you have to create one set of CONFIG.SYS and AUTOEXEC.BAT files for each configuration.

If you have already created your CONFIG.SYS and AUTOEXEC.BAT files using multiple configurations, you might want to start by renaming them with new extensions — perhaps CONFIG.ALL and AUTOEXEC.ALL. Then use a text editor to create individual files named CONFIG.1 and AUTOEXEC.1, CONFIG.2 and AUTOEXEC.2, and so on. (You can edit the ALL file and use the Save As option.) When you have all the files ready, you can use the RENAME command to change your CONFIG.1 and AUTOEXEC.1 files to SYS and BAT respectively and then run MemMaker. When MemMaker is done, rename the SYS and BAT files back to 1 and change the name of the MEMMAKER.STS to MEMMAKER.1. Next, repeat the process with your second set of files (the ones with the extension 2), and so on.

When you have finished running MemMaker on each of your configurations, it is up to you to evaluate the best way to reintegrate the files, creating your new CONFIG.SYS and AUTOEXEC.BAT files. Some commands that you had planned to put in the common block may have been optimized differently for each configuration, so when you reintegrate the files, you need to place these commands in the individual configuration blocks instead. The rule of thumb is to reserve the common block for only those commands that remain identical for each configuration after you run MemMaker.

What does it mean if your MemMaker memory adjustments do not match?

When MemMaker is finished, it displays a screen showing before and after figures for conventional memory and upper memory usage. Usually these differences match so that if you gain 50K in conventional memory, you lose 50K in upper memory. Occasionally, though, these figures do not match.

It is possible for a program to change size after loading into upper memory. One such program is SmartDrive. It is also possible that a program configured by MemMaker to run in upper memory failed to load there. A third possibility is that you are using a third-party memory manager. MemMaker uses EMM386 during optimization, but a third-party program may use upper memory in a different way. Each of these possibilities can account for reported differences.

What should you do if the MemMaker optimization process never finishes?

The last step in MemMaker's optimization process is to reboot your system using the updated CONFIG.SYS and AUTOEXEC.BAT files to ensure that everything works properly. If, right after the `Starting MS-DOS` *message, a screen appears saying that the computer was restarted before MemMaker had finished optimizing, chances are that you are executing a batch file from inside the AUTOEXEC.BAT file. A second possibility is that another program file (perhaps a TSR program) is in conflict with MemMaker and is causing it to freeze up before finishing.*

If you run a batch file from inside the AUTOEXEC.BAT file without using a CALL command, the batch file never returns control to the AUTOEXEC.BAT file and causes it to hang. Edit your AUTOEXEC.BAT file to use the CALL command. Use

CALL XYZ.BAT instead of simply XYZ.BAT. Then reboot and run MemMaker again. This time MemMaker should finish without a problem. But if you receive an `Invalid Session ID` message, you need to remove all MEMMAKER.STS files and MemMaker commands from your CONFIG.SYS and AUTOEXEC.BAT files as described in the next problem/solution.

If MemMaker still stalls, try remarking out all TSR programs loaded in the CONFIG.SYS file. Start with any virus-protection programs because some scanning software has been known to be incompatible with the SIZER program used by MemMaker. Use the REM command to remark out one command line at a time, until you find the conflicting command line. After you have successfully run MemMaker through to completion, you can reactivate the command lines that you deactivated using REM.

What if MemMaker fails to restart and then provides no choice to undo changes?

When MemMaker detects a restart before it has completed optimization, a screen appears listing possible reasons for the problem and providing instructions for continuing or aborting the process. You usually have the option of undoing any changes that MemMaker made. Even if MemMaker fails to give you this option, or if later after quitting MemMaker you decide that you want to undo MemMaker changes, you still can.

Make sure that you are not running any programs. Then at the DOS prompt type

    C:\>**memmaker /undo**

You are asked to confirm your intentions. Press Enter to restore your original files. When MemMaker is done, another screen appears notifying you that MemMaker has completed the undo task. Press Enter to reboot your computer with its original configuration.

> **NOTE:** Because MemMaker is restoring the original files, any changes that you made to your CONFIG.SYS, AUTOEXEC.BAT, or SYSTEM.INI files between the time that you first ran MemMaker and the time that you ran it with the Undo option will be lost. MemMaker warns you when this is the case and gives you the opportunity to stop the Undo process.

You want to undo changes made by MemMaker but you can't because you are running third-party compression software.

MemMaker is not able to restore the original CONFIG.SYS and AUTOEXEC.BAT files on systems using third-party compression software such as Stacker or SuperStor. When MemMaker fails, it still gives you the undo option but is unable to carry it out because the compressed drive is no longer mounted.

With third-party compression programs, the host drive and compressed drive letters are swapped after the compression software is loaded. So although MemMaker could restore the original files on the host drive, it cannot do so on the compressed volume. (This is not the case with DoubleSpace.)

To restore the files manually, quit MemMaker, and then copy the backup files (CONFIG.UMB and AUTOEXEC.UMB) from the host drive to the compressed drive, renaming them CONFIG.SYS and AUTOEXEC.BAT. If your host drive letter is E, and your compressed drive letter is C, then your copy commands would look like this when entered from the C prompt:

```
C:\>copy e:\config.umb config.sys
C:\>copy e:\autoexec.umb autoexec.bat
```

How can you remove all traces of an aborted MemMaker process?

When MemMaker does not finish properly, it leaves the MemMaker command in the AUTOEXEC.BAT file and the CHKSTATE.SYS line in the CONFIG.SYS file. The CHKSTATE.SYS device line in your CONFIG.SYS file is the telltale trace that alerts DOS to the fact that the optimization process is not finished. Also left behind are the MEMMAKER.STS files on your boot drive.

First, remove the CHKSTATE command line. It looks something like this:

```
device=c:\...\chkstate.sys ....
```

where the dots represent the path to the directory containing the CHKSTATE.SYS file.

Next, find the MemMaker command line with the /SESSION switch in your AUTOEXEC.BAT file and delete it. It looks something like this:

```
c:\dos\memmaker.exe /session:code
```

where the *code* represents a series of numbers. You also want to delete the MEMMAKER.EXE and/or SIZER.EXE command lines. Next, you need to delete the MemMaker log stored in MEMMAKER.STS. You can find the MEMMAKER.STS files by typing

```
C:\>dir c:\memmaker.sts /s
```

at the DOS prompt. Then reboot. Rerun MemMaker, and this time it should complete its process.

What can you do if MemMaker hangs with a SCSI hard drive?

SmartDrive has a double-buffering feature that is designed to assist devices, such as small computer system interface (SCSI) devices, that may have problems communicating with the memory provided when running EMM386 or Windows 386 enhanced mode. The MemMaker program can hang if a SCSI device driver loads into memory before SmartDrive's double-buffer driver.

Restart your computer and when MemMaker gives you the choice, select Cancel and Undo Changes. If you have already rebooted but did not choose to Undo changes made by MemMaker, you should do so now by typing

```
C:\>memmaker /undo
```

When the undo process is complete, edit your CONFIG.SYS file, adding the SmartDrive line to the beginning of the file. If your CONFIG.SYS file already has a SmartDrive line, move it to the beginning of the file. The device command line should look something like this:

```
device=c:\dos\smartdrv.exe /double_buffer
```

Save your CONFIG.SYS file, reboot your system, and run MemMaker again. It shouldn't hang this time.

What can you do if MemMaker conflicts with your ability to access CMOS setup?

This problem can occur when you use the aggressive scan option in MemMaker's Custom Setup. When MemMaker scans aggressively, it includes the area between F000 and F7FF (960K through 992K), which is usually reserved for ROM BIOS. Some computers, however, don't start properly when this area is used for UMBs.

If your system doesn't restart properly during the MemMaker process, choose Cancel and Undo Changes and then rerun MemMaker, this time saying No to the aggressive scan option. That prohibits MemMaker from searching for UMBs above the EFFF (959K) address.

Alternatively, you can add an exclusion parameter to your EMM386 line, protecting the BIOS area, before rerunning MemMaker. The command line should look something like this:

```
device=c:\dos\emm386.exe x=f000-f7ff
```

If you do this, you can still choose to scan aggressively, but don't forget to answer Yes to the option `Keep current EMM386 memory exclusions and inclusions`.

Why does MemMaker change the FCB line, and what's an FCB anyway?

The FCBs command is similar to the FILES command, except for older version programs. It looks something like this:

```
FCBS=16,8
```

where the first number is the number of files that FCBs can open at any one time, and the second number is the number of files opened that MS-DOS cannot automatically close.

For some reason the MemMaker program is hardcoded to add the FCBS number, even though the second number became invalid starting with MS-DOS 5. Microsoft Technical Support says that you can remove it without harming anything.

Chapter 6
The DOS 6 Utility Programs

Microsoft MS-DOS 6 comes with three optional utility programs to provide you with different ways of protecting your data. The Backup program provides you with automated functions for backing up your files. The Undelete program gives you three levels of protection, enabling you to restore erased or deleted files. And the Anti-Virus program protects your disks and files from computer viruses. Each of these programs comes in two versions: one for DOS and one for Windows. They are totally independent of one another, so you may install any of them in any combination that suits your purposes.

Installing and Running the MS-DOS 6 Utility Programs

Questions about the installation and running of the MS-DOS 6 utility programs usually involve the installation of one or more of the utilities after DOS 6 has already been installed on the hard drive. Other frequently asked questions in this area involve whether or not you can install both the DOS and Windows versions and whether or not you can run the DOS version from inside Windows.

Can you install the optional utility programs later, after DOS 6 is already installed?

The answer is yes. If you did not choose to install the Backup, Undelete, and Anti-Virus programs when you installed DOS 6, you can still do so quite easily.

Place your DOS disk in your floppy drive, change drives to make your floppy drive current, and type

```
A:\>setup /e
```

Using the /E switch moves you directly to the installation screens for the Windows and DOS optional programs, whereas entering the SETUP command alone launches the entire DOS installation procedure.

From the optional utility programs installation screen, you may select the program(s) you wish to install. (Figure 2-1 in Chapter 2, "Startup Process," shows a sample of this screen.)

Part I: Problem Solver

Can you install both the DOS and Windows versions of one or more of the MS-DOS 6 utility programs?

MS-DOS 6 includes three utility programs: Backup, Anti-Virus, and Undelete. And each program has two versions: one for DOS and another for Windows.

Whether you are running the Setup program for the first time or are running SETUP /E, when you select the programs you want to install from the utility programs installation screen, you must also indicate whether you want the DOS version, the Windows version, or both. You may choose DOS for one program, Windows for another, and both for the third, or any other combination that suits your purposes.

Can I run the DOS version of a utility program from Windows?

The answer to this question is both yes and no.

If by *from Windows* you mean shelling out to DOS or executing a command from the Windows File Menu in the Program Manager or File Manager, then the answer is no. You should not attempt to run the DOS version of a utility program from Windows, especially because a Windows version of each of the utilities exists. However, if absolutely necessary, you can safely run the DOS version from Windows by creating a PIF file and selecting the Exclusive and Full Screen options.

Questions about the Backup Utility Program

When you run Backup for the first time, you are prompted to run the configuration and compatibility test, and failing that test is the first problem we examine here. There are several possible causes for failing that test, which we discuss, as well as techniques for using compression with Backup and verification options to ensure backup data integrity.

Your computer failed the Backup compatibility test. What's wrong and what can you do now?

Reasons for test failure range from a lack of free disk space to incompatible hardware to software conflicts. In this section we list several possible causes and suggest a few ways to fix the most common problems.

There are four simple things that you should check first if you experience problems with Backup. If none of these fixes the problem, you may still be able to use the manual method.

The first step in attempting to identify the reason that your system cannot complete the compatibility test is to check the Three Little Things checklist:

1. Be sure that the diskette in your floppy drive (or tape in your tape drive, or cartridge in your SyQuest, and so on) is properly inserted.

2. Do not run the POWER command when using Backup.

3. Do not load APPEND.EXE because it causes the following error message:

    ```
    The file <filename> does not exist. The file cannot be compared.
    ```

Chapter 6: The DOS 6 Utility Programs

The second step is to check disk integrity and format compatibility. Be sure that the diskettes you use for backup are properly formatted and are not defective. Sometimes the compatibility test fails if you used third-party software utilities such as PC Tools or Norton Utilities for formatting or purchased preformatted diskettes at the store. To see whether this is the problem, reformat the diskettes using the MS-DOS FORMAT command and rerun the compatibility test.

If you are running Windows, you may be experiencing a problem with formatting from Windows. Try formatting a diskette using the Format Disk... option from the File Manager's Disk menu. It may turn out that Backup itself is not the problem.

The third step is to have available space on the disk. Backup needs to have enough free disk space in which to create temporary files.

The final step is a simple thing: check your FILES and BUFFERS settings. Before changing these settings in your CONFIG.SYS file, try running the compatibility test after a *clean start*. (A clean start means booting up without executing the CONFIG.SYS and AUTOEXEC.BAT files. To signal your system to bypass these files, boot up and press the F5 key as soon as you see the `Starting MS-DOS...` message on your screen.)

We talk more about interactive startups in Chapter 2, "Startup Process."

If the compatibility test still fails after a clean start, check the FILES and BUFFERS settings. If either setting is less than 30, edit the CONFIG.SYS file to increase both to 30, save the file, and reboot. This time when you reboot, press F8 during startup. This is called the *interactive boot*, and you are prompted to confirm each CONFIG.SYS command. Respond **N** to all commands except the FILES and BUFFERS commands.

You experience problems with the compatibility test when running Backup with Windows in 386 Enhanced Mode but not with Backup for DOS.

In addition to the simple problems and solutions described in the previous question, there is a much more complex issue associated with Microsoft Backup for Windows: third-party virtual device drivers. This problem can only occur when running Windows in 386 Enhanced Mode.

If the compatibility test fails when running Windows in 386 Enhanced Mode, exit Windows and restart running in Standard Mode (use the command WIN /S). Then try the compatibility test.

If the compatibility test works in Standard Mode, you need to get rid of any virtual device drivers (VxDs) that may conflict with VFINTD.386. Check the [386enh] section of your SYSTEM.INI file against the following list of VxD entries that can cause compatibility test failure:

```
device=myabu.386
device=fastback.386
device=vfd.386
device=cpbvxd.386
device=virwt.386
```

```
device=cmstape.386
device=cmstaped.386
device=cmsdtape.386
device=abackup.386
```

If you find an incompatible VxD, delete it from both your SYSTEM.INI and CONFIG.SYS files.

No matter what you try, your system continues to fail the compatibility test. What should you do now?

If the compatibility test continues to fail, you will not be able to select backup destinations, such as your floppy disk drive, from the Backup To dialog box. You should, however, be able to specify the desired destination manually by selecting MS-DOS Path from the dialog box and then entering the desired drive and path. This manual method was designed to provide the maximum possible compatibility with other systems.

If your system continues to fail the compatibility test, and you decide to try the manual method, we suggest that you test it first. Before you do, make sure the diskettes that you want to use for backup have already been formatted (the manual method requires that you format the diskettes ahead of time) using the FORMAT command.

To test the manual method, start the Backup program, click the Select Files button, and select about 2MB worth of files (enough to require more than one diskette for backup). When you have selected enough files, click OK. Then select MS-DOS Path from the Backup To dialog and type **A:** or **B:** (depending on which disk drive you'll be using). When ready, click Start Backup. If all goes well, Backup prompts you to change the disk in the floppy drive when necessary.

After the backup is complete, verify the integrity of the backup by running Compare. Click the Compare button (from the main screen if you're running the DOS version, MSBACKUP; or from the menu bar if you're running the Windows version, MWBACKUP), choose Select Files, selecting the same ones you backed up, and Start Compare. If the comparison is successful, then you can safely use the manual method with your system.

If this does not work, your problem might be caused by using a third-party memory manager such as QEMM with FL=0 and FEMS. Or your floppy drive controller card could be the culprit if it doesn't support direct memory access (DMA). In either case, you might want to call Microsoft Product Support Services. Their number is 206-646-5104, and their hours are 6 a.m. to 6 p.m. Pacific time.

Can I use DoubleSpace diskettes with Backup?

The answer to this question is no, but there is an alternative.

You cannot use DoubleSpace compressed floppy disks for your backup because DOS only sees the floppy's CVF as an ordinary file, and Backup would then prompt you to allow it to overwrite the file.

Chapter 6: The DOS 6 Utility Programs

If you want to get more mileage from your backup floppy disks, be sure to leave the Compress Backup Data option selected when setting your Disk Backup Options. This saves time and floppy disks by allowing the program to compress the files that are being backed up.

You get the `DMA Buffer Size Too Small` error message.

If the direct memory access (DMA) buffer used by EMM386.EXE is too small, the Backup compatibility test program issues this message.

If you start a backup or the compatibility test and get the message

```
DMA buffer size too small. You cannot back up,
compare, or restore files until you increase
the DMA buffer size
```

add a /D=32 switch to your EMM386 statement. Edit the line in your CONFIG.SYS file so that it reads

```
device=c:\...\emm386.exe /d=32
```

where . . . represents the appropriate path to your DOS system files.

If you are running Windows, you must also edit your SYSTEM.INI file to include a similar statement in the Enh386 section, as follows:

```
[Enh386]
DMABuffersize=32
```

Don't forget: Quit and restart Windows for the SYSTEM.INI change to take effect. (Of course, you have to reboot anyway for the change to EMM386 in your CONFIG.SYS file to take effect.)

How can you be sure that Backup creates reliable file copies?

The whole point of backing up the files on your hard drive is to protect your data. In case of hard drive failure, you should be able to reconstruct as much of your data as possible. This means that your backup disks must be reliable.

First, you should be sure that your system passed the compatibility test when you ran the Backup program for the first time. Then you can use the Verify Backup Data or Error Correction options when creating the backup disks. And finally, you can run the Compare program to ensure that your disks contain files identical to those you chose to back up.

Verify Backup Data option

Selecting the Verify Backup Data option instructs the Backup program to compare the backup files with the original files after backing up to ensure the integrity of the backup. Although this approach adds more time to the backup process, verifying backup data does provide great security; you can rest assured that your disks are readable and that the backup files are identical to the originals. If the program detects a bad sector on your floppy disk, it prompts you to replace the disk. To save time, you may prefer to choose the Error Correction option, or perhaps you'd prefer to run the Compare program separately when you have more time.

Use Error Correction on Diskettes option

When you select the Use Error Correction on Diskettes option, Backup uses about 10 percent of each backup floppy to store special information that enables you to restore files that were written to unreadable sectors. If you use the Verify Backup Data option, it may appear that you do not need to use this option. So what's the point? Verify takes more time; Error Correction uses up floppy disk space. Another thing to consider if you are planning on keeping you backups around for awhile is that while Verify is a bit more secure, this option only takes care of the files as they are copied onto the disk. If the disk gets damaged after the backup, you may end up with unreadable sectors. In this case, the Error Correction option would be your only salvation. We recommend you use Error Correction for all backup procedures.

You get the `Unable to open component file` **error message.**

If you choose to back up your files to a directory on your hard drive or to some drive other than a floppy drive, the Backup program creates a component file in a directory called FUL. (The component file has a 001 filename extension.) If this file is moved, you will be unable to restore your files.

In order to restore your backup files, you need to find the component file and place it back in the directory from which it originally came. (This might also mean rebuilding your original directory structure.) If you do not remember the name of the component file, rerun the compatibility test and take note of the error message when it appears; it tells you the name of the component file for which it is searching and includes the expected path.

Questions about the Anti-Virus Utility Program

The most important thing to remember about anti-virus programs is that they are always out of date because new viruses emerge every day. In this section we explain how virus-detection programs recognize a virus and how you can keep your MS-DOS 6 Anti-Virus program up-to-date.

Most viruses have a *signature* — a specific string of code embedded in a file or resident in a particular memory address. The Anti-Virus program maintains a table, with each entry containing a series of 37 two-character hexadecimal codes, that it uses to uniquely identify a signature. Usually, a virus alters the size of an infected file, although some viruses infect without changing the outer appearance of a file.

Searching for viral signatures is one of the methods anti-viral programs use to detect viruses. When an anti-virus program finds a suspicious series of characters that it suspects is a signature that it doesn't recognize, it usually tells you so with some sort of warning message, such as

```
unrecognized signature
```

Whenever this message appears on one of your computer systems, it serves as a good reminder that it's probably time to update your virus program with the latest vaccines.

Chapter 6: The DOS 6 Utility Programs

How can you update the viral signatures file, and where can you find the information?

Detection of a virus and curing a virus by cleaning it off your drive are two separate functions. You can update the viral signatures that MSAV or MWAV recognizes by adding new information to the signature file, and you can update the Anti-Virus program so that it can remove new viruses as well.

Signatures of new viruses can be downloaded from the Microsoft bulletin board, 24 hours a day, seven days a week. (You need a user identification code to use the BBS, but if you don't have one, you can obtain one by typing **NEW** when prompted for your code.) New signatures provide only the ability to *recognize* newly identified viruses. In order to remove or clean newly identified viruses from your system, you need to obtain the program updates by using the coupon found on the last page of your *MS-DOS 6 User's Guide*.

The modem number for the Microsoft Bulletin Board is 503-531-8100. The BBS handles speeds up to 9600 baud, and your modem communications settings should be 8 data bits, no parity, 1 stop bit.

When you upgrade your software, you get a lot of Anti-Virus warnings. What's the problem?

When you upgrade software, changes are often made to the program files. The Anti-Virus program may detect these changes and think they indicate virus activity. You can reduce the occurrence of these messages by taking the following steps.

First, protect your system by scanning the manufacturer's installation disks. When you determine that they are clean, write-protect them. Then install the upgrade. After you are done, update your Anti-Virus files by scanning the drive containing the new software.

If your Anti-Virus protection settings include the Verify Integrity and Prompt While Detect options, the Verify Error dialog box should appear indicating a change in an executable file. In this case you know that the change was intentionally caused by the software upgrade. Select Update to register the change.

You removed a virus and now the program won't run.

It is possible that when a virus is detected, the damage to the program file is irreparable. Usually the Anti-Virus program knows this and warns you with the `File was destroyed by the virus` *message. Sometimes, however, Anti-Virus may not detect the damage or might possibly cause the damage itself during the removal process.*

Once a program file doesn't run correctly, the only thing you can do is replace it. Delete the file from your system and replace it either by restoring from backup disks made before the infection took place, copying the file from a clean disk, or reinstalling the entire program from the manufacturer's disks (provided that they aren't the ones carrying the virus!).

Part I: Problem Solver

❓ You can't display the VSafe Warning Options screen using Alt-V.

Alt-V is the default key combination to bring up the Warning Options screen used with the DOS version of the Anti-Virus program. It only works with the DOS version and must be loaded into memory.

If you are running the DOS version of Anti-Virus and Alt-V fails to bring up the options box, check to see that VSafe was loaded into memory. You can load VSafe into memory by simply entering the VSAFE command from the DOS prompt, like so:

    C:\>**vsafe**

or by putting the command in your AUTOEXEC.BAT file. When you first load the program into memory, a message appears telling you that it was successfully installed and indicating the amount of memory used. If this message appears, it means that VSafe wasn't loaded previously.

If VSafe is loading correctly, the problem might be that the hot key setting has been changed from Alt-V to something else. When you load VSafe into memory, the installation message also indicates the hot key combination setting. Check to see if the setting has been changed. If VSafe is already in memory, you can unload it by pressing Alt-U and then load it again to see the hot key setting.

> **NOTE**
> You can change the hot key setting by using the /A switch, plus the letter you want to use, with the VSAFE command. For example, VSAFE /AZ changes the hot key setting to Alt-Z. If you want to use the Ctrl key instead of the Alt key, you can set the hot key using the /C switch with the VSAFE command. For example, VSAFE /CX changes the hot key setting to Ctrl-X.

If VSafe is in memory, and the hot key does not work to bring up the options screen, then it's likely that some other memory-resident program is in the way. Edit your CONFIG.SYS and AUTOEXEC.BAT files to remark out any memory-resident programs, reboot, and try again. If VSafe works, you can load the other memory-resident programs, one at a time, until you find the one that clashes. Edit your CONFIG.SYS and AUTOEXEC.BAT files accordingly.

Questions about the Undelete Utility Program

The Undelete utility program provides three possible levels of data protection, each of which is available for both the DOS and Windows versions. The most common questions about this utility can be answered by understanding the extent to which each level *protects* a data file.

❓ What's the difference between the various *conditions* of a deleted file?

The Undelete utility program uses five different conditions to indicate the likelihood of a successful restoration.

When DOS deletes a file, it doesn't actually touch the file's data. It simply modifies the file's bookkeeping entry. More to the point, it marks the space that the file occupies on the disk as *available*. If another file needs room in order to record more data,

DOS is then free to use the space and write over the existing data. Only then is that old data from the erased file gone for good. When it's gone for good, and the file can no longer be recovered, the condition is shown as *destroyed*.

Files in *poor* condition cannot be recovered by the Windows version of Undelete, but it is sometimes worth trying to recover that same file with the DOS version of Undelete.

Fragmented files are considered to be in *good* condition. A fragmented file is one in which the contents are stored in more than one location on the disk. When DOS finds the first part of the file, the allocation table tells DOS the address where the next part is stored. If address two does not contain the balance, it tells DOS where to look for part three, and so on until DOS locates the entire file. Sometimes it is not possible to follow all the forwarding addresses when undeleting a fragmented file, in which case some data from the file may not get retrieved.

The Tracker level of protection keeps track of file addresses. This greatly increases the chances of a successful undelete, so files deleted under Tracker protected files are said to be in *excellent* condition. However, even files in excellent condition can be overwritten if DOS reallocates any of the space used by the deleted file. When asked to undelete a file, Tracker uses its own address list to find the file and, as long as a new file does not cover it, restores the file.

Files deleted under Sentry protection are in *perfect* condition because Sentry hides copies of deleted files in a hidden directory. Space for the hidden directory is reserved, so there is no danger of DOS reallocating the space.

You are using Sentry protection but still can't undelete certain files.

Depending on the settings for Sentry protection, the file(s) that you want to undelete may not have been protected at all, their protection time may have expired, or they may have been overwritten by more recently deleted files.

There is nothing you can do to recover deleted files that were not protected or that were originally protected but are no longer. For the future, however, you can control the Sentry settings by editing the UNDELETE.INI file. Through these settings you can choose to protect more files, prolong the protection period, and allocate more space in which to store the deleted files under protection. The following is an excerpt from a sample UNDELETE.INI file:

```
[configuration]
archive=false
days=7
percentage=20
[sentry.drives]
c=
[mirror.drives]
[sentry.files]
s_files=*.* -*.tmp -*.vm? -*.swp
[defaults]
d.sentry=true
d.tracker=false
```

The [configuration] section determines three things: first, whether files with their archive bits turned on are protected (FALSE means no protection, TRUE saves the files); second, the number of days Sentry saves the protected files; and third, the percentage of disk space reserved for the deleted files.

The archive bit is one of four file attribute settings that may be turned ON or OFF. The archive bit is used to indicate whether or not a file has been modified since last backed up. The archive setting in the UNDELETE.INI file is used to determine whether files unchanged since the last backup are protected.

In our sample file, you can see that Sentry only saves the deleted file for 7 days, after which time you can no longer undelete it. You can also see that Sentry's reserved space allocation cannot exceed 20 percent of total disk space. To maintain the specified limit, Sentry removes the oldest hidden file(s) to make room for new ones as needed, and the file you're looking for may have been one of those removed to maintain space limitations.

The [sentry.drives] section of the file specifies which drive(s) are to be protected when Sentry is in force. In this sample, only files deleted from drive C are protected.

The [sentry.files] section of the INI file specifies which files (based on file extension) are protected and which are ignored. A hyphen preceding the extension indicates no protection (files with that extension are ignored). In our sample, all files are protected, except those with TMP, VM?, or SWP filename extensions.

In the [defaults] section of our sample, you can see that Sentry is set to TRUE, indicating that Sentry protection is in force, while Tracker protection is set to FALSE (not active).

You want to UNDELETE a directory.

Undelete protection in MS-DOS 6 is quite powerful, but not all of its features are available in both the DOS and Windows versions.

If you are using the DOS version of UNDELETE, you are not able to recover directories. End of story. However, if you are using the Windows version, you see that a deleted directory appears on the Files list with DIR shown in the size column. Of course, to see the directory entry you have to be displaying the files of the directory that is the parent directory to the directory you deleted.

If you're using the Tracking level of protection, you simply select the directory name and press Undelete. When the program has finished recovering the directory, you then use Change Drive/Dir to move into the recovered directory and see the list of deleted files in the newly recovered directory. You can now undelete the files that you want.

If you're using Sentry protection, undeleting a directory requires one little extra step. Undelete displays directories under Sentry protection with a question mark (?) as the first character of the directory name. So when you select the directory name and press Undelete, the program prompts you to enter a first character. The missing first character is due to the fact that Sentry does not actually protect directories — when you delete a directory, that directory's table of entries disappears, and DOS replaces the first character of the deleted directory name (in the parent directory's table of entries) with a special character. Undelete then uses a question mark instead of the special character. Once the directory is undeleted, you can Change Drive/Dir to the newly recovered directory and undelete the files you need.

Part II:

Command Reference

* and ? Wildcards   All DOS, Internal

Filename wildcard characters

The * and ? characters in filenames enable you to refer to a group of files instead of a single file. Use the ? and * wildcard characters by creating a pattern that tells DOS how to find filenames.

The ? wildcard

The ? wildcard character matches any single character that appears in a filename. Two rules determine how the ? behaves. When the ? character is in the middle of a filename, such as N?W, the ? indicates that there must be a character, which can be any character, in this position. So in this example, N?W matches any filename three characters long that starts with N and ends with W.

When the ? character is at the end of a filename or extension, on the other hand, the ? character matches either zero or one character. So the name NEW?? matches any name that starts with NEW and is between three and five characters long.

Note that these rules apply separately to the name and the extension.

The * wildcard

The * wildcard character matches zero or more characters at the end of a filename or extension. So, for example, the name NE* matches *any* filename that starts with NE, whether it be just these two characters, or an eight-character name that starts with NE.

When you put * in the middle of a filename, such as NE*T, DOS ignores any characters that appear after the * character. In other words, you *cannot* use * to find names that begin with one set of characters and end with another set of characters.

Note that these rules apply separately to the name and the extension, so you can have up to one * wildcard each for the filename and the extension.

Examples

Here is an example that uses the * and the ? wildcard characters together:

    n?m*.t*

This pattern matches any filename that starts with N, has any character in the second position, has an M in the third position, and can have anything else (or nothing at all) for the rest of the name. The extension must start with a T and can have anything else (or nothing at all) after the T.

One-character names

If you wanted to match only names that are one character long, you would type

    ?.*

Note that this only works for filenames, not for the extension. The pattern *.? matches all files that have either no extension or a single character in the extension. The reason for this difference is quite simple: each ? character is matching zero or one character, but a filename must have at least one character in it.

Part II: Command Reference

Matching names without extensions
If you ever want to work only with files that have no extension, here is the wildcard pattern to use:

```
*.
```

The period is very important, as some DOS commands interpret * without a trailing period as being the same as *.*.

One extension, any name
You can match all files that have a given extension, such as TXT, for example, by using an * wildcard in the filename's position:

```
*.txt
```

All files
There are two wildcard patterns that match all filenames. The first is the one you'll probably type when you want to refer to all filenames:

```
*.*
```

The other is the one that DOS uses internally when you specify *.*, and you'll see from time to time when DOS displays an error message:

```
????????.???
```

These are identical, but obviously *.* is easier to type.

@ — DOS 3.3 and later, Batch

Don't echo command

Put an @ sign in front of any line in a batch program to keep DOS from echoing this line to the screen.

When and why
Normally, when you run a batch program, DOS echoes each line to the screen before running the command. This can create a lot of screen output that you don't care much about. Use the @ command, along with the ECHO OFF command, to control when DOS echoes output to the screen. For most batch programs you'll want an @ECHO OFF line at the start to turn off echoing and some ECHO ... lines inside the batch program to display messages.

Syntax
@batch-command
Don't echo the *batch-command* to the screen before it's run by DOS.

Examples
Here is the most common use for the @ command, which is to turn the echo off when the batch file first starts:

```
@echo off
echo About to start copy...
copy *.* a:
```

This batch file starts by turning the echo off, but we've put an @ in front of the ECHO to keep this command from being echoed. The next ECHO command then displays just the text on the rest of the line (it doesn't display the echo). And finally, we copy some files to drive A.

See also

ECHO OFF   The ECHO OFF command allows you to turn off the echo for an entire batch file rather than just one line. This line itself, however, will be echoed unless you put an @ sign in front of it: @ECHO OFF.

ECHO *message*   Use this command to display any message you want on the screen.

?   DOS 6, CONFIG.SYS

Prompt for confirmation within CONFIG.SYS

Put a ? between a command and the = sign in a batch file whenever you want DOS to prompt you before it runs that command in the CONFIG.SYS file. This provides a very simple form of multiple configuration by allowing you to control which CONFIG.SYS commands are executed. DOS asks for confirmation for each command with the ? before the = sign.

When and why

You would use the ? only when you have commands in your CONFIG.SYS file that you don't want to run each time you start your computer. For example, if you sometimes have a CD-ROM drive attached to your computer, you might want to use a ? to load its device driver so you can control when it's loaded into memory. Another, less obvious use for the ? option is with the SET command; you can selectively set environment variables. If you have a few CONFIG.SYS commands that you want to exclude only rarely, you might find it easier to use the MENUITEM commands to set up a boot menu.

Syntax

command?=*setting*
Prompt for confirmation before executing the *command* while processing the CONFIG.SYS file.

Notes

How DOS processes CONFIG.SYS

DOS actually makes several passes through CONFIG.SYS, so DOS may ask you about a command near the end of your file before it asks you about a command near the start of your file. For example, DOS will always process DOS=HIGH before *any* DEVICE= commands, no matter where DOS=HIGH appears in your CONFIG.SYS file. To learn more about this, read the section in this reference on CONFIG.SYS.

Conflicting device drivers

You are responsible for monitoring which commands are executed. If you have two alternate drivers and must load one or the other, you should use the multiple configuration menus. Otherwise, it would be possible for you to mistakenly load neither driver or attempt to load both. For full implementation of the multiple configuration features, use the MENUITEM command.

Using the F8 key to bypass commands

You can press the F8 key whenever DOS starts to have it prompt you before running each line in your CONFIG.SYS file. When you see the message `Starting MS-DOS...`, you have 2 seconds to press the F8 key. Once DOS begins to prompt you for each command in CONFIG.SYS, you can press F5 to have DOS skip all the rest of the commands in CONFIG.SYS and to skip AUTOEXEC.BAT.

Using F5 to bypass CONFIG.SYS and AUTOEXEC.BAT

Pressing F5 after you see the message `Starting MS-DOS...` (you have about 2 seconds) will bypass both CONFIG.SYS and AUTOEXEC.BAT without running *any* of the commands in either file. This allows you to start a "clean" version of DOS (without any RAM-resident programs or device drivers loaded).

Comment lines in CONFIG.SYS

Another way to temporarily disable commands in your CONFIG.SYS file is to "comment out" lines. Whenever you put the word REM or a semicolon at the very start of a line, DOS will ignore everything else on the line.

Examples

Prompting for a device driver

If you occasionally do not install ANSI.SYS, you may use the statement

```
device?=ansi.sys
```

to prompt for confirmation during the startup process. This gives you the option of not loading the device driver.

Prompting for placing DOS in the HMA

Use this command to obtain some control over how memory is used during the configuration process. The statement

```
DOS?=high
```

prompts for confirmation before loading DOS into the HMA.

See also

MENUITEM	Provides support for multiple configurations based upon configuration blocks. Instead of being prompted to confirm each command, you are presented with a configuration menu.
REM, ;	Putting the word REM (followed by a space) or a semicolon at the start of any line in your CONFIG.SYS file tells DOS to ignore everything else on that line.
CONFIG.SYS	There are many secrets about how DOS processes the commands in your CONFIG.SYS file that you'll find documented under CONFIG.SYS.

;   DOS 6, CONFIG.SYS

Comment line

This character, when it is at the start of a line, allows you to add comments to a CONFIG.SYS file. DOS ignores all lines that start with a semicolon.

When and why

There are two things the semicolon command is useful for. First, you can use it to add comment lines to your CONFIG.SYS file to make it easier to read. And second, you can use it to comment out commands in CONFIG.SYS. Simply put a semicolon at the start of the line to comment it out.

Syntax

;[*comment*]

Puts a comment into the CONFIG.SYS file. The comment can be any text that you want, except that it must all be on one line.

Example

Disabling commands

Let's say you have a line in your CONFIG.SYS file that installs ANSI.SYS, but you'd like to turn this off for a while. Here is how you'd turn that line into a comment that DOS ignores:

```
; device=ansi.sys
```

Commenting CONFIG.SYS

When you add lines to your CONFIG.SYS file, you may not remember why you added them a year or so down the line. Adding comments can help you remember:

```
;
; Load SmartDrive with double buffering because I have a
; SCSI hard disk.
;
device=c:\dos\smartdrv.exe /double_buffer
```

See also

REM   This is another form of adding comments to CONFIG.SYS that works with DOS 5 and later, as well as in batch files.

| All DOS, Internal

Pipe output to another program

This character on a command line allows you to *pipe* the output from one command into another command.

When and why

Piping is most often used with programs called *filters*. These programs manipulate data in various ways, taking their input from the keyboard (via DOS) and outputting their results to the screen. The concept of filters never really caught on, so very few of them are available. DOS itself has three (MODE, FIND, and SORT) that you may find useful. You'll probably use piping mainly with these commands.

Syntax

program-1 | program-2
Pipe the output from *program-1* into the input of *program-2*.

Notes

Temporary files

DOS implements piping in a very simple manner. It runs the first program and redirects its output to a temporary file. Then it runs the second program by redirecting its input to this same temporary file. Finally, when both commands finish, DOS deletes the temporary files.

You can use the TEMP environment variable (DOS 5 and later) to determine where DOS creates such temporary files. It's a good idea to use either a RAM disk or a directory called C:\TEMP. Without this environment variable, DOS creates temporary files in the current directory.

Batch programs

You cannot use the | (pipe) character to pipe the output of batch programs, nor can you use the | character in a CALL command inside a batch program.

You can, however, use the | (pipe) in other commands inside a batch program.

Limitations on piping

Not all programs allow you to redirect their output. For example, many commercial programs write directly to the screen (Lotus 1-2-3, Microsoft Word, the Norton Commander), and such screen output can't be redirected because these programs aren't using DOS to display characters on the screen. Generally, you won't be able to redirect the output of any program that has a full-screen display.

Examples

It is common to use this command in conjunction with the MORE command to display screen output one page at a time. For example, you can use the TYPE command to view a file, but long files quickly scroll off the screen. The following command allows you to view the output of TYPE one page at a time by sending the output of the TYPE command to the MORE command:

```
C:\>type readme.txt | more
```

See also

<, >   These two characters provide input and output redirection, enabling you to read input from a file rather than the keyboard, and write output to a file rather than to the display.

MORE	Displays one page of output from a piped program at a time.
FIND	Allows you to display only lines that include a string you supply.
SORT	Sorts lines of text.

>, >>   All DOS, Internal

Redirect screen output

You can use either of these symbols inside a command to redirect the output of the command to a file. The > character will create a new file that contains the screen output from the command (or if the file exists, it will replace the contents of the file with the output of the command). The >> characters, on the other hand, tell DOS to append the screen output to the end of a file if it already exists or create a new file if it doesn't.

When and why
Output redirection is useful whenever you want to save, or even print, the output of DOS commands. You probably won't use it very often because most people don't need to save the output of DOS commands. If a file with the name *filespec* does not exist, DOS will create it.

Syntax

command >filespec
Write the output of *command* to a file rather than to the screen. If a file with the name *filespec* already exists, DOS will discard the previous contents.

command >>filespec
Write the output of *command* to the end of the *filespec*. If a file with the name *filespec* already exists, the information is appended to the end of the file.

Parameters

filespec
The name of the file or DOS device to write to. This can be any filename, or it can be one of the devices listed here:

Device	What the device is
NUL	Null device, ignores all output to it
CON	Console device (keyboard and screen)
AUX	Auxiliary device (normally the same as COM1)
COM*x*	Serial port (COM1, COM2, COM3, or COM4)
PRN	Printer (normally the same as LPT1)
LPT*x*	Printer port (LPT1, LPT2, or LPT3)

Notes

Spaces
Spaces between the > and >> characters and the *filespec* are ignored, so you can use spaces if you like, or use no spaces to separate these characters from the filename. It's your choice. We prefer not to use spaces as it makes it easier visually to connect the > and >> characters with the filename.

Batch programs
You cannot use the > or >> characters to redirect the output of batch programs, nor can you use redirection in a CALL command inside a batch program.

You can, however, use redirection in other commands *inside* a batch program.

Limitations on redirection
Not all programs allow you to redirect their output. For example, many commercial programs write directly to the screen (Lotus 1-2-3, Microsoft Word, the Norton Commander), and such screen output can't be redirected because these programs aren't using DOS to display characters on the screen. Generally, you won't be able to redirect the output of any program that has a full-screen display.

TSRs and redirection
Note: It's not a good idea to redirect the output of terminate-and-stay-resident (TSR) programs. Each time you redirect a TSR's output, you'll tie up one of the file handles available to other programs (see the description of the FILES= command).

Examples

Printing directories
Here is a good hint on how to keep track of what files are stored on floppy disks. You can print the output of the DIR command by redirecting screen output to the printer. Here is how you would print the directory for the disk in drive A:

```
C:\>dir a: >prn
```

If you have a special printer (such as a PostScript printer) that can't print text directly, you may need to save DIR's output to a file and then print that file:

```
C:\>dir a: >temp
C:\>lineprnt temp
C:\>del temp
```

Hiding output
There are times when you may want to hide the output of programs run by a batch file to keep the screen from filling with output. In such cases, you can redirect a program's output to the NUL device. NUL is a device that throws away anything you write to it (also known among programmers as a *bit bucket*). For example, if you copy files in your AUTOEXEC.BAT file, you can use the following command to keep COPY from displaying anything to the screen:

```
C:\>copy c:\nc\*.exe e: >nul
```

See also

| Use this character to redirect the output of a command to the input of another program.

<   Use this character to redirect the keyboard input of a command.

<   All DOS, Internal

Redirect keyboard input

You can use the < character inside a command to have the input for a command come from a file rather than the keyboard.

When and why

Redirection isn't difficult, and you'll probably start using output redirection (> and >>) fairly early on. Input redirection, using pipes (the | character) and the < character, is more advanced, and as a result isn't used very often.

Input redirection is generally used with filters (such as the MORE, FIND, and SORT commands), which read their input from the standard input. The standard input is usually connected to the console (also known as CON:). The console is an input/output device that uses the keyboard for input and the screen for output. You can, however, redirect the standard input so that it reads from a file rather than the keyboard. The SORT filter, for example, sorts lines that appear in the input, whether it be from the keyboard, from a pipe (see description of the | character), or redirected from a file.

Syntax

command <filespec
Read input for *command* from a file rather than from the keyboard.

Parameters

filespec
The name of the file or device to read keyboard input from. You'll find a list of DOS devices under the description of the > command (which appears just before this description).

Notes

Spaces

Spaces between the < character and the *filespec* are ignored, so you can use spaces if you like, or use no spaces to separate the < from the filename. It's your choice. We prefer not to uses spaces as it makes it easier visually to connect the < character with the filename.

Batch programs

You cannot use the < character inside a command that calls a batch program, nor can you use < in a CALL command.

You can, however, use the < input redirection in other commands that appear inside a batch program.

Limitations on redirection

Not all programs allow you to redirect their input. For example, many commercial programs don't use DOS to read characters from the keyboard (Lotus 1-2-3, Microsoft Word, the Norton Commander). Such programs won't be affected by input redirection. Generally, you won't be able to redirect the input of any program that has a full-screen display.

Examples
Filters

Input redirection is most frequently used with filters, such as the MORE, FIND, and SORT commands, which read their input from the standard input device (CON, which refers to the keyboard). You can tell MORE to read its input from a file with a command such as this:

```
C:\>more <readme.txt
```

DOS will send the contents of the file README.TXT to MORE's input.

Keyboard input

You can also use keyboard input redirection to provide canned input from a file to a program. The FORMAT command, for example, waits until you press Enter before it starts to format a floppy disk; then it asks you if you want to format another floppy disk. If you have a batch file that performs a number of operations and you want a floppy disk automatically formatted, you could provide a response file that contains three lines:

```
Line 1:
Line 2:     n
Line 3:
```

The first and third lines are blank, and the second contains a single *n*. Line 1 tells FORMAT to start formatting a floppy disk, while line 2 tells FORMAT that we don't want to format another disk (line 3 exists because we need an Enter at the end of line 2).

See also

|	Redirect the output of one command to the input of another.
>, >>	Redirect the output of a command to a file on the disk.

%n   All DOS, Batch files

Replaceable parameters in batch files

You'll need to use the % parameters whenever you want to use parameters in a batch file. There are ten parameters in all, numbered %0 through %9.

When and why

You'll need to use replaceable parameters whenever you create a batch file that uses parameters.

Syntax
%*n*

Replace these two characters with the parameter *n* when the batch file runs.

Notes

Meaning of the %n parameters
When you first start a batch file, %0 is the name of the batch file as you typed it on the command line (see examples below), and %1 will contain the first parameter you typed. You can use the SHIFT command to gain access to more parameters in a loop (see the SHIFT command for an example).

Using the % character
If you want to use the % character as an ordinary character, write it twice: %%. For example, the characters %1 refer to the first parameters, whereas %%1 is a percent sign followed by a 1 (see following examples).

Examples
Here is a short example batch file that you can use to see how the replaceable parameters work:

```
@echo off
echo %%0 = "%0"
echo %%1 = "%1"
echo %%2 = "%2"
```

Notice we've written %%0 on the left side of the equal sign. Using % twice like this tells DOS to insert a single % character instead of treating % as the start of a replaceable parameter. If you call this batch file TEST.BAT and run it, you'll see the following output:

```
C:\>test one
%0 = "test"
%1 = "one"
%2 = ""
```

See also

%*name*%	Use this form of parameters if you want to use environment variables within a batch file.
IF	You can use the IF command to test parameters and control the flow of your batch file's execution.
FOR	The FOR command has its own form of replaceable parameters, although you can also use the %*n* parameters in a FOR statement.
SHIFT	SHIFT allows you to work with a number of parameters (even more than ten if you like) within a batch file.

%*name*%   DOS 4.0 and later, Batch files

Use environment variable in batch file

This command allows you to use DOS environment variables (which you set using the SET command) as parameters to a batch file.

Syntax

%*name*%

Substitute the current value of the environment variable *name* for this parameter. If there is no environment variable called *name*, DOS substitutes an empty string (nothing at all) for this parameter.

Notes

No parameter of that name

If the name doesn't exist, DOS treats this parameter as being empty (which is the same thing it does with %*n* replaceable parameters that are empty).

Examples

The following batch file example displays the current setting of your path:

```
@echo off
echo Here is the current path:
echo %path%
```

See also

%*n*	Replaceable parameters for batch files. These allow you to use parameters you type on the command line.
COMMAND	You can use COMMAND to increase the size of the space reserved for environment variables.
SET	The SET command allows you to add, modify, and remove environment variables.

:*name*   All DOS, Batch files

A label in a batch file

Putting a colon as the first character on a line in a batch file defines that line as a label (DOS ignores any commands on the same line). You can use labels in the GOTO statement to control the execution of your batch file.

Syntax

:*name*

Defines *name* as a label in a batch file. You can use labels along with the GOTO statement to control the execution of batch files.

Notes

Repeated labels
DOS won't warn you when you've defined more than one label with the same name. Instead, the GOTO command will always branch to the first label in the file with the name you supply.

Valid labels
Labels can be up to eight characters long and can include any character except for the special and file separator characters:

% * - + = [ ] \ | : ; " < > , . and /

Example
This is an example that shows the use of a label and a GOTO statement within a batch file:

```
goto end
copy *.* c:
:end
```

The GOTO command here will skip the COPY command because it sends execution directly to the first command after the :END label. Notice that we don't use the colon in the GOTO statement; we use the colon only to mark lines that define labels.

See also
GOTO   The GOTO command jumps to the line with a given label.

ANSI.SYS   All DOS, Device driver

ANSI display device driver
This device driver provides support for a number of things. First, it allows the MODE command to change the number of lines on your screen. It also allows you to write batch programs that have full control over the screen, although this is a lot of work.

When and why
If you want to use the MODE command to change the number of lines on your screen (which you can do if you have an EGA or VGA card), you'll need to install ANSI.SYS.

The other uses of ANSI.SYS, namely all the escape sequences that allow you to control your screen, are beyond the scope of this book (and few people ever use them). Here we provide only the escape sequences that are useful for moving the cursor around the screen in a DOS prompt. You can find a complete list of all the escape sequences in your DOS manual.

Syntax
device=[*path*]**ansi.sys** [/x] [/k] [/r]
Load the ANSI.SYS console device driver into DOS.

Parameters

path
You'll want to provide a path to the ANSI.SYS device driver. This path will usually be C:\DOS.

Switches

/x
Use extended codes (DOS 4.0 and later). This switch tells ANSI.SYS to treat some of the new keys on extended keyboards as separate keys. For example, there are two Home keys, and this switch tells ANSI.SYS to use different codes for these two Home keys. This has no effect on most programs other than DOS. (Default is to generate the same codes for old and new keys.)

/k
Ignore extended keys (DOS 4.0 and later). This switch tells ANSI.SYS to treat the old and new keys on extended keyboards as the same key when they have the same label. This has no effect on most programs other than DOS.

/r
Adjust line scrolling (DOS 6). We're not quite sure what this switch does. The help says that /r "adjusts line scrolling to improve readability when ANSI.SYS is used with screen-reading programs (which make computers more accessible to people with disabilities)." Well, we couldn't see any difference with and without this switch.

ANSI escape codes

There are a number of escape sequences that you can use to send control messages to the ANSI.SYS device driver. In all the tables below, you should translate the Esc[sequence into an Escape character followed by a left bracket. Here's how you insert these two characters into Edit:

Esc[Ctrl-P Esc [

Edit requires that you press a Ctrl-P prior to pressing the Esc key to insert an Escape character. What you'll see on the screen is a left-pointing arrow (which is the Esc character) followed by a left bracket ([).

Cursor positioning

Action	Esc sequence	What it does
Cursor up	Esc[*nn*A	Moves the cursor up *nn* lines in the same column. Stops when the cursor reaches the top line. (1–50, default is 1.)
Cursor down	Esc[*nn*B	Moves the cursor down *nn* lines in the same column. Stops when the cursor reaches the bottom line. (1–50, default is 1.)
Cursor right	Esc[*nn*C	Moves the cursor right *nn* columns. Stops when cursor reaches the right side. (1–79, default is 1.)
Cursor left	Esc[*nn*D	Moves the cursor left *nn* columns. Stops when the cursor reaches the left side.

ANSI.SYS

Action	Esc sequence	What it does
Move cursor	Esc[*row;column*H	Moves the cursor to *row* and *column*. (row = 1–50, column = 1–79, default is 1;1.) You can omit the row or column, but you must include the semicolon.
	Esc[*row;column*f	Same as above.
Save Position	Esc[s	Saves the current position of the cursor. Use Restore Position to move it back here.
Restore Position	Esc[u	Moves the cursor back to the position saved by Save Position.

Erasing

Clear Screen	Esc[2J	Same as the CLS command.
Erase Line	Esc[K	Erases a line from the current cursor position to the end of the line (it doesn't erase any characters to the left of the cursor).

Text colors

You can also change the colors ANSI.SYS uses to display characters on the screen. Note also that the CLS command uses the current colors when ANSI.SYS is installed. Here is the escape sequence that allows you to change colors:

```
Esc[attr;...;attrm
```

The *attr* values can be one or more of the following:

Attr	Meaning	Attr	Foreground color	Attr	Background color
0	All attributes off	30	Black	40	Black
1	Bright	31	Red	41	Black
2	Normal intensity	32	Green	42	Green
		33	Yellow	43	Yellow
4	Underline*	34	Blue	44	Blue
5	Blink	35	Magenta	45	Magenta
		36	Cyan	46	Cyan
7	Reverse video	37	White	47	White
8	Invisible				

*Only available on monochrome display adapters.

Examples

Using ANSI.SYS in a prompt

This example shows how to use the ANSI.SYS to display a status line at the top of your screen showing the date and time in inverse video:

```
C:\>prompt $e[s$e[0;0H$e[7m$d $t$h$h$h$h$h$h $e[K$e[m$e[u$p$g
```

As you can see, there are a number of $E escape sequences, which we'll cover very briefly here. First, the $E[S saves the position of the cursor, which we restore at the very end with $E[U just before we display a regular path prompt PG. Next, we move the cursor to the top of the screen with $E[0;0H and set the color to inverse video, using $E[7M. We then display the date and time (removing the seconds). And finally, we clear the rest of this line with $E[K, set the color back to normal, $E[M, and move the cursor back to where it was.

APPEND — DOS 3.3 and later, External/Internal

Define search path for data

The APPEND command allows you to tell DOS where to look for data files if it can't find them in the current directory (similar to how the PATH command tells DOS where to look for programs). This command is called APPEND because it has the effect of appending the contents of other directories to the current directory. (Appended directories, however, won't be visible to the DIR command.)

Data files are any files with extensions other than COM, EXE, or BAT (which are extensions used by program files), although with DOS 4.0 or later you can also use this command to extend the search path for programs as well as data files.

When and why

You may never find a use for this command; it's provided mainly to help some older programs, which didn't know about subdirectories, work well with DOS 2.0 and later. DOS 1.x did not include subdirectories, so many programs that were written for DOS 1.x don't always know where to find their own files, such as overlay files (.OVL) and initialization files (.INI). Such programs require you to switch to their directory to run them; such cases are when the APPEND command is most useful. See the "Examples" section for more on this.

If you use APPEND with such old applications, you might want to use a batch file to start your programs. This batch file would first use APPEND to append the directory of the application, then call the application, and finally use "append ;" to turn off APPEND (so it won't confuse other applications). See the "Examples" section for more on this.

Note: You might also want to use the APPEND command to get access to some data files no matter what directory you're in. But be careful when you do this. APPEND lets you read files in appended directories, but if you modify these files, they won't always be saved back in the same directory. Some programs save changes you make by renaming the old copy (changing the extension to BAK) and saving the changes as a new file (with the old name). Such programs will save your changes in the current directory, rather than in the appended directory, because new files are always created in the current directory.

Syntax
There are several forms of the APPEND command:

To load APPEND
append [/x] [/e] (DOS 3.3)
append [/x[:on|:off]] [/e] (DOS 4.0 and later)
This form of the command is used to load the APPEND command into memory. The /E switch tells APPEND to use the APPEND environment variable rather than its own internal memory to save the search path. The advantage of using the /E switch is that you can also use the SET command to change the APPEND search path; the disadvantage is that it doesn't work with DOS shells.

append [/x] *path1;path2...* (DOS 3.3)
append [/x[:on|off]][/path:on|off] *path1;path2...* (DOS 4.0 and later)
This form of the command is used to load the APPEND command into memory and specify a search path for data at the same time.

After loaded
append *path1;path2...* (DOS 3.3)
append [/path:on|off] *path1;path2...* (DOS 4.0 and later)
This command allows you to change APPEND's search path for data. The search path you specify will replace the old search path (it won't add to it).

append ;
Clear APPEND's search path, which also has the effect of turning off the APPEND command until you issue another APPEND command with a path attached. APPEND will not, however, be removed from memory.

append
Display the current APPEND search path. If there isn't an APPEND path defined at the moment, this command reports "No Append."

Switches
/e
Use environment variable. This tells the APPEND command to use an environment variable, named APPEND, to save the APPEND path. The advantage of using the /E switch is that you can also use the SET command to change the APPEND search path; the disadvantage is that it doesn't work with DOS shells.

Note: You must use the /E switch before any other APPEND commands if you want to use the environment variable.

Note: You may get an `Out of environment space` message when you try to add a directory to the APPEND path. In such cases you can either use the COMMAND /E command to increase the size of your environment or not use the /E switch of the APPEND command.

/path:on|off
Path ignore (DOS 4.0 and later). This switch controls whether the APPEND command will affect searches when you put a path and/or drive letter in front of the filename. Setting this option to on will allow APPEND to use its search path even when you provide a path (such as \AUTOEXEC.BAT or C:\AUTOEXEC.BAT). (In DOS 3.3 this option is always turned on.) (Default: /PATH:ON.)

/x
Append programs. This switch allows you to run programs in appended directories by typing the program name at the DOS prompt. Normally, you'd use the PATH command to control the search path for programs, but you might want to use this command, with care, if your path becomes too long. If you do use APPEND, DOS will look for programs first in the current directory, then in appended directories, and finally in directories specified by the PATH command.

/x:on|off
Append programs (DOS 4.0 and later). This switch is the same as the /X switch except that you can use the on or off keyword; /X:ON is identical to /X, and /X:OFF is the same as no /X switch. (Default: /X:OFF.)

Notes
APPEND is an external command until you load it into memory, at which point it becomes an internal command until you restart your computer.

APPEND and shells
You won't be able to use the APPEND /E and SET commands if you're using a DOS Shell since these commands can't alter the environment of DOS Shells. In such cases, fortunately, the APPEND command will work if you don't use the /E option.

ASSIGN and APPEND
You must take care using both ASSIGN and APPEND. Any drive assignments you make after an APPEND command won't affect the command. For example, if you set the APPEND path to C:\TEST and then use ASSIGN to swap the A: and C: drives (see the "Examples" below), APPEND will report that its search path is C:\TEST and will continue to look on the original C: drive, even though you've used ASSIGN to swap the drive letters. Note also that initially you must load APPEND before ASSIGN (see the description of the "APPEND/ASSIGN conflict" message next).

Messages
```
APPEND/ASSIGN conflict
```
If you plan to use both the APPEND and the ASSIGN commands, you must install APPEND before you install the ASSIGN command. After you've installed both APPEND and ASSIGN, you can change the APPEND list and ASSIGN drive assignments in any order.

```
Incorrect DOS version
```
APPEND is matched to a specific version of DOS. You'll probably only see this message when you have files left behind from another version of DOS.

```
No APPEND
```
This message means that you don't have a search path defined for APPEND.

```
Out of environment space
```
This message means that the environment space DOS has provided isn't large enough to contain the information APPEND is trying to add. You have two options: (1) use the APPEND command without the /E option, which tells APPEND to use its own memory rather than the DOS environment, or (2) use the SHELL=COMMAND /E... in your CONFIG.SYS file.

Technical notes

The APPEND command is loaded into memory as a TSR program and occupies about 5K of memory (the actual amount depends on which version of DOS you're using). Note that this is true even when you use the /E switch to use an environment variable rather than APPEND's own internal memory.

For programmers, APPEND modifies the following DOS functions:

- Open File, FCB (0Fh)
- Open File, Handle (3Dh)
- Get File Size, FCB (23h)

When you use the /X or /X:ON switch, APPEND will also modify the following DOS functions:

- Find First File, FCB (11h)
- Find First File (4Eh)
- Execute Program, EXEC (4Bh)

Note that APPEND doesn't affect the Find Next Match calls, which means that you won't see a directory listing of appended directories. Also, DOS 4.0 and later modify many of the system commands such as DIR to ignore files in appended directories.

Examples

Older programs

The most common use for APPEND is to allow older programs, such as WordStar, to find their program files. If you find that you can run a program only when you're in its directory, you'll want to use the APPEND command. In such cases, however, it's a good idea to use a batch file to run the program so you can turn off APPEND when you're done. Here's a batch file called WS.BAT that uses APPEND with WS.COM (you use it by typing **WS** *filename*):

```
append /x              Make sure Append is loaded
append c:\progs\ws     Append WordStar's program directory
ws.com %1              Load file into WordStar
append ;               Turn off Append
```

You could also include the first line, APPEND /X, in your AUTOEXEC.BAT file rather than here. We've included it as a separate line so you can use the /X and /E options if you want.

In this case, we're using the /X option so you don't have to put your WordStar directory in your path. Instead, you can call this batch file WS.BAT and put it in any directory included in your path. Then when you type **WS** on the command line, DOS will execute WS.BAT (because it won't find WS.COM). WS.BAT then uses APPEND to append WordStar's directory to the current directory. Because we've specified the /X switch, we're allowing APPEND to search for program files in appended directories before searching the path; the WS %1 command will run WS.COM rather than WS.BAT — just what we want!

Part II: Command Reference

Note: We've been careful here to handle a special case. If you're in the directory that contains WS.BAT when you run it, DOS will look in this directory before the appended directory for programs. If our batch file contained the line WS %1 rather than WS.COM %1, DOS would look first in the current directory for a program file called WS, in which case it would find and run WS.BAT again, which isn't at all what we want. To make sure DOS doesn't do this, we've explicitly asked DOS to look for WS.COM (so it won't find WS.BAT).

See also
PATH — The PATH command allows you to define a search path for programs. Given the choice between using PATH and APPEND for programs, you should use PATH.

ASSIGN
PC-DOS 2.0, MS-DOS 3.0–5, External

Assign drive letter to disk drive

This command allows you to assign a different drive letter to an existing drive. It is mainly useful for older programs that look for files only on drive A: or B: (this is common for some older setup programs).

When and why

You may never find a use for this command. It is provided mainly to allow programs that insist on using drives A: or B: to work correctly with hard disks. Chances are you won't buy or use a program that has such problems, as it's been a long time since DOS learned about hard disks (DOS 2.0, which was the first version that knew about hard disks, was introduced in 1983).

This command is also useful for installation programs that expect to be run from the A: drive. For example, if your computer has a 5¼-inch floppy disk drive as drive A: and a 3½-inch floppy disk drive as drive B:, you may need to use ASSIGN if you're running an installation program from a 3½-inch disk in drive B:.

Note: In DOS 6, you must use the SUBST command instead of the ASSIGN command. In previous versions, we recommend using the SUBST instead of ASSIGN.

Syntax

assign *x=y* ...

Tells DOS to assign (or reassign if it's already in use) the drive letter *x* so that it actually refers to drive *y*. You can assign more than one drive letter at a time with this command. ASSIGN will clear any previous assignments before making the new assignments you've requested.

assign

Sets all drive letters back to their original meanings. Use this to clear an ASSIGN after you're done with it.

Switches

None.

Notes

ASSIGN is a TSR program that loads itself into memory the first time you use it, occupying about 1.5K of memory. It won't be removed from memory until you reboot your computer. ASSIGN does not become an internal command; it just loads code needed to redirect drive letters.

APPEND and ASSIGN

If you plan to use both the ASSIGN and APPEND commands, you'll need to install the APPEND command before you install the ASSIGN command (see the "Messages" section of the ASSIGN command).

Incompatibilities

Not all programs will work correctly with drive letter assignments made with ASSIGN. In particular, you should avoid using ASSIGN with the following DOS commands:

- ♦ BACKUP, RESTORE, JOIN, SUBST, and PRINT — these commands require drive information.

- ♦ COPY — ASSIGN can defeat the code in COPY that prevents a file from being copied over itself, which can destroy data.

- ♦ FORMAT, DISKCOPY, and DISKCOMP — these commands ignore drive reassignments.

Because drive letter assignments don't always behave the way you'd expect (in other words, they don't always work), you should only use ASSIGN for programs that absolutely need it. One way to do this is to create a batch file that turns ASSIGN on, calls your program, and then turns ASSIGN off again.

Messages

`Incorrect DOS version`
ASSIGN is matched to a specific version of DOS. You'll probably only see this message when you have files left behind from another version of DOS.

`Invalid parameter`
This message usually means that you've provided a drive on the right side of the equal sign that doesn't exist on your computer.

Technical notes

The ASSIGN command is loaded into memory as a TSR program, which occupies about 1.5K of memory (the actual amount depends on which version of DOS you're using).

Secret DOS: For programmers, ASSIGN modifies a number of DOS functions. Here is an overview of the INT 21h functions that ASSIGN modifies:

- ♦ FCB functions. ASSIGN modifies the drive number in the FCB for all the FCB functions: 0Fh..17h, 21h..24h, 27h, 28h.

- ♦ Filespec functions. A number of INT 21h functions expect DS:DX to point to a filespec that can have a drive letter at the beginning: 39h..3Dh, 41h, 43h, 4Eh, 5A, 5Bh. Also 6Ch, which expects DS:SI to point to a filespec.

- ♦ Drive number functions. Two calls expect a drive number in the DL register: 36h, 47h.

- Function 44h, IOCTL Functions: 4, 5, 8, and 9.
- Exec, Function 4Bh.
- Rename File, Function 56h, which expects two filespecs.
- Get Current Drive, Function 19h.
- Set Current Drive, Function 0Eh.

ASSIGN also traps two other DOS interrupts to make sure programs that work directly with the disk will have their drive letters reassigned as well:

- Absolute Disk Read, INT 25h.
- Absolute Disk Write, INT 26h.

Note that ASSIGN doesn't trap the ROM BIOS's disk calls, which means that some programs, such as disk caches and FORMAT, may not be affected by ASSIGN's drive letter assignments. Most programs, however, won't have any problems working correctly with ASSIGN.

Example

The most common use of ASSIGN is to allow a program to use A: or B: to refer to files on your hard disk:

```
C:\>assign a=c
```

This command tells DOS to reassign the drive letter A: so that it actually refers to your physical C: drive. So when you type **DIR A:**, you'll see the files on your hard disk (even if you have a floppy disk in drive A:).

Swapping drive letters

It is actually possible to swap two drive letters. For example, if you have a floppy disk drive A: and a hard disk drive C:, you can swap the drive letters with the following command:

```
C:\>assign a=c c=a
```

After this command, A: will refer to your hard disk drive and C: will refer to your floppy disk drive. Of course, if you use this command and your path points to files on drive C:, your path won't work correctly until you change it or use ASSIGN to restore the original drive letters. (*Note:* The external ASSIGN.COM command that you need to run is now on drive A: rather than drive C:, while your path probably tells DOS to look for external commands on drive C:. This means you'll have to change to the DOS directory on drive A:, which is really your hard disk, to run ASSIGN.COM.)

(Of course, the ASSIGN command will probably be in your path so you won't be able to run it to restore the drive letters without first switching to your DOS directory.)

See also

JOIN   Allows you to join two disk drives by making one disk drive a subdirectory of the other.

SUBST   Using this command instead of ASSIGN SUBST provides more flexibility and does a better job of making reassignments.

ATTRIB
DOS 3.0 and later, External

Displays and changes file attributes

Each file in the directory has certain information associated with it, such as the date and time that the file was last modified. The directory also contains other information, called attributes, that allows you a little more control over how DOS can deal with files. This command lets you display and change this attribute information for files and directories.

ATTRIB allows you to change various extra attributes that are connected with each file. The attribute information is part of the directory entry for each file. (The attributes are explained below in the "Attributes" section.)

When and why

The ATTRIB command gives you some added control over how DOS works with files on your hard disk. Historically, the most common use of this command is to use the +R and -R parameters to protect data in files that you don't need or want to change.

Later versions of DOS also allow you to control the archive attribute which, when used with commands like XCOPY and BACKUP, allow you more control over which files will be copied or backed up.

DOS 5 and later also allow you to control which files will be visible in directory listings. This can be useful for hiding details from other users of your computer, or as another mechanism along with the read-only attribute for protecting sensitive and valuable data. You can continue to use hidden files as long as you know their name and location (or you use a program such as the Norton Commander that allows you to see hidden files).

Syntax

attrib [*filename*] [/s]

This form of the ATTRIB command (without any of the ± parameters) displays the current attributes for a list of files in a directory (and its subdirectories if you use the /S switch) without changing the attributes. (The filename parameter is required for DOS versions before 5.)

attrib [±r] [±a] [±h] [±s] [*filename*] [/s]

This version of the ATTRIB command allows you to change the attributes on a single file or a group of files. The meanings of the various ± parameters are listed below. (The filename parameter is required for DOS versions before 5.)

Parameters

+r, -r
Read-only on and off. Using +R sets the read-only attribute, while -R turns off the read-only attribute, which is the default setting for new files.

+a, -a
Archive on and off (DOS 3.2 and later). Using +A sets the archive attribute, which is used to indicate that a file has been changed, and -A turns this attribute off. New files have their archive attribute turned on by default.

+h, -h
Hidden attribute on and off (DOS 5 and later). Turning this attribute on will hide a file so you don't see it in directory listings. Files are created with this attribute off by default.

+s, -s
System attribute on and off (DOS 5 and later). We're not sure why you're allowed to change this attribute, starting with DOS 5. It's normally used to indicate that special files are reserved for use by the system; DOS itself only uses this attribute on a few files.

Switches

/s
Subdirectories. Causes the ATTRIB command to search through subdirectories. Normally, ATTRIB will display or modify the attributes on the files only in the current directory (or the directory that you ask it to work in). Using this switch allows you to view or make changes to an entire branch of the tree, or an entire disk, with one command.

Attributes

Here is a description of each of the four attributes that ATTRIB can modify:

Read-only

The read-only attribute allows you to control write access to a file. When this attribute is set, you can read a file, but you won't be able to write over the file or delete it (you can rename or move the file).

Note: DOS Shell lets you know if a file is a read-only file and asks if you still want to delete it. Before DOS 6, the DOS Shell didn't warn you before deleting read-only files.

Archive

The archive attribute is generally set whenever you change a file or create a new file. This attribute is most useful to backup programs, as it identifies which files are new or changed since the last backup. Unfortunately, this doesn't always work. If you rename or move a file, the archive attribute won't be set, which means the file won't be backed up with its new name or location on your hard disk.

System

You'll probably never need to use this attribute. It is used mainly by some hidden system files that DOS uses for itself.

Hidden

You can hide files from most DOS commands by setting this file attribute. The DIR command won't show any hidden files. If you know they're there, however, you can use them. For example, the TYPE command will display the contents of hidden files. So this attribute hides files from view but allows you to use a hidden file if you know the name.

Notes

You can use ATTRIB to hide directories as well as files (DOS 5 and later).

ATTRIB before DOS 5 requires a filename; the DOS 5 and later ATTRIB command will assume *.* if you don't supply a filename.

Examples

Protecting files

You might want to protect all your program files from being altered or deleted by accident, which you can do by setting the read-only attribute on all your executable files. The following command will set the read-only attribute for all the EXE files on your hard disk:

```
C:\>attrib +r \*.exe /s
```

We've put a \ in front of *.EXE to tell ATTRIB to start in the root directory of the current drive. The /S switch then tells ATTRIB to apply the same operation on all the files in subdirectories as well.

You might also want to set the read-only attribute on all the files in your program directory. Be careful not to be overzealous: Some programs store configuration files in their directory that are often modified. If you set the read-only attribute, you might prevent the program from saving its configuration information.

Archive and backing up

ATTRIB is also a useful tool for controlling MSBACKUP (or, in versions prior to DOS 6, BACKUP). If you want to make sure a number of important files are backed up again, you can tell ATTRIB to turn on the archive attribute for all the files in a directory:

```
C:\>attrib +a *.*
```

Multiple attribute changes

You can turn off one attribute at the same time you turn on another. For example, to turn off the read-only attribute and turn on the archive attribute for all files in the DOS directory, you would type

```
C:\>attrib -r +a c:\dos\*.*
```

See also

There are several commands that can use the archive attribute to select which files they'll work on:

XCOPY   This command can copy entire subtrees (a directory and all of its subdirectories). You can also use its /A and /M switches to copy only files that have the archive attribute set.

BACKUP Allows you to back up files on your hard disk to floppy disks for safe storage. The /A and /M switches allow you to back up only those files that have been modified (indicated by having their archive attribute set).

RESTORE Allows you to restore files from a set of backup disks made by BACKUP. RESTORE's /M switch allows you to restore only those files that you've modified (indicated by the archive attribute) since you used BACKUP to create the backup disks.

BACKUP

DOS 2.0–5, External

Back up files to a set of floppy disks

This command allows you to back up an entire hard disk to a set of floppy disks, even when you have some files that are too large to fit on a single floppy disk. BACKUP automatically splits large files between multiple floppy disks. It can do this because it also saves information on the floppy disks that tells RESTORE, BACKUP's companion program, how to reconstruct files and where they should be restored to. DOS 6 users should see the MSBACKUP command, which in DOS 6 replaces the BACKUP command.

When and why

If you're running a version of DOS prior to DOS 6, this is a command you'll want to use frequently, unless you're using a commercial backup product such as FastBack or Norton Backup (the DOS 6 MSBACKUP and MWBACKUP are actually based on Norton Backup). Some people wonder if it's really worth all the effort to back up frequently; the answer is no, at least not until you lose some data. And you will lose data someday, and probably more than once.

We suggest that you use the SYS command to create a bootable floppy disk with DOS 5 on it and copy the RESTORE command to this floppy disk as well. This will allow you to boot your system and use the RESTORE command to rebuild your hard disk if you should lose all the data on your hard disk (hard disks do fail from time to time).

Syntax

backup *drive:[path\filespec] drive2:* [/s] [/m] [/a] [/f:size] [/d:date] [/t:time] [/l[:filespec]]
The BACKUP command allows you to specify which disk drive BACKUP should write to when it's creating a backup. This command is intended to write to a floppy disk drive. The parameter *d:path\filespec* is a filespec that describes what files you wish to back up. Note that this filespec *must* include a drive letter.

Parameters

drive:[path\filespec]
What to back up. This parameter tells BACKUP what files you want to back up. You must specify a drive letter. If you supply just a drive letter, BACKUP assumes you want to back up all files in the current directory (you still have to use the /S switch if you want to back up all files in subdirectories).

drive2:
Where to write to. This is the disk drive that you want backed-up files saved to. If you specify a floppy disk drive, BACKUP will erase all the files in the root directory, including read-only files, of floppy disks you provide (unless you use the /A switch to add files to an existing backup set); files in subdirectories won't be erased.

You can also back up files to another hard disk. When *x:* refers to a hard disk, BACKUP will create two files, BACKUP.001 and CONTROL.001 in a directory called \BACKUP, erasing any files already in this directory, including read-only files, before it starts the backup (unless you use the /A switch).

Switches

/s
Subdirectories. Backs up files in subdirectories as well as the current directory. You'll probably use this switch most of the time with BACKUP.

/m
Modified. Backs up only files that have been modified since the last BACKUP command. In reality, this switch tells BACKUP to back up files that have the archive attribute set. BACKUP will then clear the archive attribute on each file it backs up. This means you can use the ATTRIB command to control whether a file will be backed up, regardless of whether you've modified the file.

/a
Add. Adds files that are being backed up to an existing backup disk without erasing the files that are already on that disk. (*Note:* This switch is ignored if the backup disk was created with a DOS 3.2 or earlier BACKUP command.)

/f
Format (DOS 3.3 through DOS 5). Tells the BACKUP command to format the disk before starting the backup process for any disk that isn't already formatted. BACKUP actually passes control over to the FORMAT command, so you can format more than one disk. The backup process continues when you finish using the FORMAT command.

/f:*size*
Format (DOS 4.0 through DOS 5). Exactly like the /F switch, except that you can specify the size of the formatted disk. This is useful, for example, with a high-density 3½-inch disk drive that can format both 720K and 1.44MB disks when you want to format a normal density disk. Valid sizes are

5¼-inch disks: 160, 160K, 160KB, 180, 180K, 180KB, 320, 320K, 320KB, 360, 360K, 360KB, 1200, 1200K, 1200KB, 1.2, 1.2M, 1.2MB

3½-inch disks: 720, 720K, 720KB, 1440, 1440K, 1440KB, 1.44, 1.44M, 1.44MB, 2880, 2880K, 2880KB, 2.88, 2.88M, 2.88MB

The larger sizes (1.2, 1.44, and 2.88) require higher density floppy disk drives and are not always available.

/d:*date*
On or after. Backs up only those files that were changed (or created) on or after *date*. The normal format for dates (in the U.S.) is dd/mm/yy, where dd is the day of the month, mm is the month, and yy is the year (example: 3/21/91); although in the U.S. you can also use the format dd-mm-yy. The easiest way to determine your date format is to see what form the DIR command uses to display file dates. The date format is affected by the COUNTRY= setting in your CONFIG.SYS file. Valid formats are the same as for the DATE command.

/t:*time*
At or later. Backs up only those files that were changed (or created) on or after *time*. The U.S. time format is hh:mm:ss, where the seconds are optional. With DOS 5 and later, you can put an a or p after the time to denote a.m. and p.m. (for example, 3:45p). For DOS versions before 5 you have to use 24-hour format times to refer to

times after noon. For example, you would have to write 15:44 to refer to 3:44 p.m. The time format is affected by the COUNTRY= setting in your CONFIG.SYS file. Valid formats are the same as for the TIME command.

/l:*filename*
Log file (the letter L). This switch allows you to create a log file that lists all the files that were backed up. The log file begins with a line that gives the date and time of the backup, followed with one line for each file that was backed up; each line begins with a disk number, which is the number of the backup disk that contains the backed-up file, followed by the full pathname of the file that was backed up.

If you don't provide a filename, BACKUP will create a log file called BACKUP.LOG in the root directory of the drive you're backing up. If the log file already exists, BACKUP will add new entries at the end, creating a history of multiple backups.

Note: You shouldn't tell BACKUP to create a log file on a floppy disk since BACKUP may be trying to write to multiple floppy disks in the same disk drive.

Notes

ASSIGN, JOIN, and SUBST

You shouldn't use BACKUP while ASSIGN, JOIN, and SUBST are active, just as you shouldn't use RESTORE when these are active. This is because these commands can alter your directory structure between the time you back up and want to restore files. Since RESTORE can't restore files to a different location, you must have exactly the same directory structure as when BACKUP was active. This is one good reason to use a commercial backup program instead of BACKUP and RESTORE.

Previous versions

You cannot use RESTORE from DOS 3.3 or later to restore files created with BACKUP from DOS versions 3.2 and earlier. This is because the file format for backup files was changed with DOS 3.3 and later. For this reason it is a good idea to store a DOS bootable disk along with your backup disks that contains the same version of DOS and RESTORE you used to create the backup files.

Files created by BACKUP

BACKUP only creates two files on each floppy disk in the backup set (or in the \BACKUP directory on hard disks): BACKUP.XXX and CONTROL.XXX, where XXX is the number of the floppy disk within a backup set, starting with 001 for the first floppy disk. The file BACKUP.XXX contains the data from one or more files, while CONTROL.XXX contains information on what files are contained in BACKUP.XXX.

There are two advantages to this scheme of writing the files directly to the floppy disks. First, this allows BACKUP to back up files that are too large to fit on a single floppy disk by splitting the data between BACKUP.XXX files on more than one floppy disk. And second, BACKUP can pack the files more densely on the backup disks.

BACKUP also turns on the read-only attribute for these two files, providing some protection against accidental deletion of your backed-up data.

SYS files not backed up

BACKUP does not back up the system files IO.SYS, MSDOS.SYS, and COMMAND.COM. You must use the SYS command to copy these files to a floppy disk.

ERRORLEVEL returned

BACKUP returns information that batch files can test with the ERRORLEVEL command. Here are the exit codes that BACKUP returns:

0   The backup succeeded.

1   BACKUP didn't find any files that matched the conditions you asked for.

2   Some files could not be backed up because file-sharing didn't allow the files to be read.

3   You pressed Ctrl-C or Ctrl-Break to exit BACKUP before it finished.

4   There was an error of some type.

You can use this information in batch files to control the backup process.

Examples

Entire hard disk

The command you'll probably find yourself using at least once a week to back up your entire hard disk is

`C:\>`**`backup c:\*.* a: /s`**

This command will back up all files on your hard disk, including subdirectories, regardless of whether they've been modified since the last backup. This type of backup is called a full backup because you're backing up *all* the files on your hard disk.

Daily backups

For daily backups, you might want to do what's known as an incremental backup, where you back up only those files that have been created or modified since the last backup. Here is the command that will perform an incremental backup:

`C:\>`**`backup c:\*.* a: /s /m`**

The /M switch tells BACKUP to back up only files that have the archive attribute set.

You can also write just the files that have changed to the same backup set you used on the previous day, with this command:

`C:\>`**`backup c:\*.* a: /s /m /a`**

Formatting floppies during backup

Sometimes you may want to back up your hard disk to floppy disks that haven't been formatted first. This is useful when you don't know how many floppy disks you'll need for a backup set and you don't want to format a number of floppy disks beforehand. Imagine also that you're using a 1.44MB drive, but you've bought the less expensive 720K disks. In this case you'll need to tell BACKUP to format these disks, when necessary, as 720K disks rather than 1.44MB disks. The /F switch does this:

`C:\>`**`backup c:\*.* a: /f:720`**

Note that BACKUP won't reformat floppy disks that are already formatted.

See also

ATTRIB	BACKUP's /M switch allows you to back up only files that have been modified since the last backup, which really means those files with the archive attribute set. You can use the ATTRIB command to turn the archive attribute on or off for any files to give you more control over which files will be backed up.
COPY	This is the command to use when copying a small number of files to a floppy disk.
DATE	To use the /D switch effectively, you need to make sure your computer is using the current date. /D's date format is the same as that used by the DATE command.
DISKCOPY	This is the command you'll want to use if you need to back up a floppy disk because this command will create an exact copy of the original disk, which BACKUP doesn't do.
RESTORE	This is the companion command to BACKUP that allows you to restore backed-up files. You'll have to use this command since the backed-up files are not directly visible on the backup disks.
SYS	BACKUP doesn't back up the system files IO.SYS, MSDOS.SYS, and COMMAND.COM. Use this command to copy these files to a floppy disk, along with the RESTORE command, so you have a disk you can boot from and restore files to your hard disk in case your hard disk crashes.
TIME	To use the /T switch effectively, you need to make sure your computer is using the current time. /T's time format is the same as that used by the TIME command.
VERIFY	You should use the VERIFY command to turn on write verification before using BACKUP. This will give you a little extra error checking to ensure that your data is backed up correctly.
XCOPY	This command allows you to copy entire disks with all subdirectories. However, it can't write to multiple floppy disks, which puts a severe limit on how many files you can copy.

Break   DOS 2.0 and later, Internal

Controls Ctrl-C break checking

You can often use the Ctrl-C or Ctrl-Break key combinations to end (or, in computer jargon, terminate) a running program. This command lets you control, to a small degree, when DOS will check for these key combinations to allow you to terminate a program.

BREAK

When and why
In actual practice, the break flag mainly controls whether you can easily break out of a DOS command that makes frequent use of the disk without writing to the screen frequently, such as copying a very large file. (DOS doesn't write anything to the screen while it's copying a file.) On our computers, we generally keep the break flag turned on so we can stop long operations if we decide we don't really want to continue.

Syntax

break

Without any parameters, this command will tell you the current setting of the break flag. It will report "Break is on" or "Break is off."

break on

Turns on extended checking for Ctrl-C and Ctrl-Break. With extended checking on, DOS will check for a break signal whenever a program makes any DOS system call.

break off

Turns off extended checking for Ctrl-C and Ctrl-Break, which means that DOS checks for these break signals only when a program tries to read or write a character to a character device (for example, keyboard, screen, printer, or auxiliary port).

In CONFIG.SYS file

break=on
break=off

Use one of the two lines above in your CONFIG.SYS file to turn the break on or off when DOS first starts.

Notes

Mysterious changes

It is possible for applications to change the setting of this flag. Some applications turn this flag off while they're running and don't restore the previous setting. So if you find that BREAK is mysteriously turned off after running a program, you might want to create a batch file to launch that program so you can turn BREAK back on after the program finishes.

Ctrl-C and Ctrl-Break checking

If you press any key, such as the spacebar, before you press Ctrl-C, DOS may not recognize that you've pressed Ctrl-C. DOS will, however, recognize Ctrl-Break because these two key combinations are handled differently by the system. The ROM BIOS in your computer creates an interrupt signal whenever you press the Ctrl-Break key combination. DOS uses this signal to set a bit in memory (called a *flag*) that it uses to remember when you've pressed Ctrl-Break. Ctrl-C, on the other hand, is treated like any other character. The break detection code looks to see if the next character waiting to be read is a Ctrl-C. What this means is that if you press a key on the keyboard, such as the spacebar, before you press Ctrl-C, DOS won't see that a Ctrl-C is waiting because there's another character waiting to be read first.

Most commercial programs bypass DOS when reading from the keyboard, writing to the screen, and printing. In such cases the break flag will have no effect on keyboard input and screen and printer output.

Part II: Command Reference

Many commercial programs, such as the Norton Commander, also provide their own handling for Ctrl-C and Ctrl-Break, in which case this flag will have no effect at all while such a program is running.

Speed

In theory, turning BREAK on will slow down your system because DOS has to check if there was a break signal every time a program makes a call to DOS, but we've never noticed any difference in speed.

BUFFERS   All DOS, CONFIG.SYS

Set number of disk buffers

This command in your CONFIG.SYS file controls the number of buffers that DOS uses to speed up disk access.

When and why

This command allows you to fine-tune DOS so that you can get the best performance from your computer and disks. Here are some rules on how to use this command.

If your computer has no extended or expanded memory, you'll want to set the number of buffers according to the chart in the "Notes" section.

Otherwise, you'll want to use a cache, such as SMARTDRV.EXE, to provide the disk speed-up function. Disk caches have two advantages over DOS's internal buffers. First, disk caches allow you to use extended or expanded memory rather than conventional memory (which keeps more memory free for your programs). And second, disk caches tend to be faster than DOS, so you'll see more of a speed improvement if you use a cache rather than DOS's buffers.

Syntax

buffers=*nn*

(DOS 2 and 3.) Sets the number of buffers to *nn*, where *nn* is any number from 1–99. The default is 2 or 3, depending on your computer.

buffers=*nn* [,*mm*] [/x]

(DOS 4.0 and later.) Sets the number of buffers to *nn*, where *nn* is any number from 1–99. The default size depends on the amount of memory your computer has and varies from 2–15. The *mm* parameter allows you to set the size of the secondary buffer. The /x switch is not supported in DOS 5 or later.

Parameters

nn

Buffers. The number of buffers to use; can be any number from 1–99. See the table in the "Notes" section for recommended settings.

BUFFERS

mm
Read-ahead buffers (DOS 4.0 and later). Number of read-ahead buffers. Can be any number between 1 and 8, and specifies how many sectors of a file DOS should read at one time. Secondary buffers are used as a read-ahead buffer; when a program reads data from the disk, DOS will read extra sectors from the file to speed up future reads from that file (since DOS will already have the data in memory).

Switches

/x
Expanded memory (DOS 4.0 only). Tells DOS to use expanded memory rather than conventional memory for the disk buffers. If you have expanded memory, you'll probably want to use this switch because conventional memory is much more important than expanded memory for running most programs. Also, conventional memory is limited to 640K, while you can have megabytes of expanded memory.

DOS 5 and later automatically load buffers into the high memory area (HMA) when it loads itself into high memory, which is why this switch isn't supported in DOS 5 and later. The high memory area is the first 64K of extended memory and is managed by HIMEM.SYS. See the DOS=HIGH CONFIG.SYS command for more details on how to load DOS into the high memory area.

Notes

Buffers and SMARTDRV
If you're using a disk cache, such as SMARTDRV.EXE, you won't need to use DOS's buffers for hard disks because disk caches do a better job than DOS's buffers. In such cases you can set BUFFERS=10, which will provide a small number of buffers for when you read and write floppy disks.

Size of buffers
Each buffer uses about 531 bytes of memory, so you can calculate the amount of memory used for any number of buffers. Microsoft recommends that you choose the number of buffers based on the size of your hard disk. Here is a chart of recommended buffer sizes, including the amount of memory used by that number of buffers:

Hard disk size	Number of buffers	Buffer size, bytes
Less than 40MB	20	10,640
40 – 79MB	30	15,952
80 – 119MB	40	21,264
More than 120MB	50	26,576

If DOS is loaded into the high memory area, the file buffers will also be loaded into high memory — provided, however, that they are small enough to fit. The high memory area is 64K in size and is shared by DOS and the buffers. Our experience is that DOS can't fit more than about 40 buffers into high memory.

Note: If the buffers don't fit into high memory, all the buffers will be put in low memory, so you should be careful not to set the number of buffers too high when you load DOS into high memory.

Maximum buffer size

You won't want to set buffers to a number larger than about 50. Above 50, DOS actually takes more time looking for your data in its buffers than it would take to read the data from your hard disk.

Examples
Normal buffers

Our first example is an 8088-based laptop computer that has a 20MB hard disk drive but no extended or expanded memory. In this case, we'll set the number of buffers to 20 (as recommended in the "Notes" above).

```
buffers=20
```

Extended memory

This example shows how you would set the buffers for a computer that has extended memory and DOS loaded into the high memory area (the first 64K of extended memory). In this case, your CONFIG.SYS file will have something like the following in it:

```
buffers=40
device=c:\dos\himem.sys
dos=high
```

The first line sets the number of buffers to 40, which is about all we want when we use the high memory area (see note on "Size of buffers"). The next two lines tell DOS to load itself into high memory. DOS loads the buffers into high memory whenever it loads itself into high memory.

See also

DOS=HIGH	Tells DOS to load itself into the high memory area rather than low memory.
FASTOPEN	Keeps information on the locations of recently opened files. It will speed programs that open a large number of files, such as database programs and language compilers (used for writing programs). It uses conventional memory (the first 640K), however, so if you find FASTOPEN doesn't increase the speed of your computer, don't use it — keep the memory free for other uses.
FILES	Use the FILES command in your CONFIG.SYS file to control how many files can be open at the same time.
HIMEM.SYS	You'll need to have HIMEM.SYS installed in your CONFIG.SYS file if you want to load DOS, and the DOS buffers, into the high memory area. You'll also need a DOS=HIGH line in your CONFIG.SYS file.
SMARTDRV.EXE	A disk cache program that uses extended or expanded memory to speed up disk access. It does this by keeping recently used data in memory so later disk accesses will read from memory rather than disk. If you have lots of extended or expanded memory, this is a better way to speed up your computer than using buffers.

CALL   DOS 3.3 and later, Batch

Run second batch program
This command allows one batch program to run a second batch program. When the second batch program finishes, DOS will run the remaining commands in the first batch file. Without this command, DOS won't run the rest of the first batch file.

When and why
Whenever you want to run a batch command from within another batch file, you'll want to use the CALL command.

Normally, when you ask DOS to run a second batch command from within another batch file, DOS runs the second batch command without ever returning to the first batch file. The CALL command allows you to return to the original batch file and continue to run it. The only time you won't want to use CALL is when you write a batch file that works with a version of DOS before 3.3; in such cases, you'll need to use the COMMAND /C command to run the batch file.

Syntax
call *filespec* [*batch-parameters*]
Run another batch file and return to the current batch file when *filespec* finishes.

Parameters
filespec
Name of the batch file to call, which can be preceded by a drive letter and a path. You don't need to include the BAT extension in this filename, but the file itself must have a BAT extension.

batch-parameters
Any parameters that you want to send to the batch file.

Notes
Pipes and redirection
Don't use the > or | characters in a CALL command to redirect or pipe the output. DOS will never redirect the output. In the case of piping the output to another program, DOS will run the second program, but without any input. (The MORE command displays a `Divide overflow` error, or crashes, when it has no input from a pipe.)

CALL vs. the /C switch
You can also use the COMMAND /C command to run a second batch program and return to the first batch program when the second batch program finishes. There are two advantages to using CALL over COMMAND /C, however. First, the CALL command runs batch programs without creating a new copy of COMMAND (along with a new environment). What this means is that batch programs run with CALL can modify the current environment, whereas batch programs run with COMMAND /C modify a temporary copy of the environment (contained in the temporary copy of COMMAND), so any changes made will be lost when the second batch program finishes.

The second advantage is a little more subtle. Since COMMAND /C loads a new copy of the command-line interpreter, any TSR programs loaded into memory will be loaded into memory after this temporary copy. When the temporary copy of COMMAND exits, it leaves a small hole in memory, which reduces the amount of free memory available for programs to run.

Of course, the COMMAND /C method of running batch programs does have the advantage over CALL that it will work with versions of DOS before 3.3.

Examples

Your AUTOEXEC.BAT file is a good example of when you'd want to use the CALL command. When you have a lot installed on your computer, particularly when you're using a network such as Novell, you'll probably have a fairly large AUTOEXEC.BAT batch file. One thing you can do to make this batch file more manageable is to break it up into multiple batch files. For example, you might take the steps for initializing your network and put them into a batch file called STARTNET.BAT, which you'll then want to CALL from your AUTOEXEC.BAT file. Your AUTOEXEC.BAT file might then have some of the following lines in it:

```
path c:\dos;c:\prog\word;c:\prog\nc;c:\prog\nu
call startnet
nc
```

DOS will run the PATH command, then run the STARTNET batch command, and finally run NC (the Norton Commander).

See also

COMMAND /C   You'll need to use this command rather than CALL if you want a batch file to work in DOS versions before 3.3. See "Notes" on limitations using COMMAND /C.

CD

See CHDIR

CHCP   DOS 3.3 and later, Internal

Change or display code page (character set)

Code pages are provided as part of DOS's international support, so if you're using DOS in the U.S., you may never need this command.

The IBM PC defined a standard character set that contains 256 different characters, including a number of special symbols as well as foreign-language characters, such as ¿ and é. But there are also some foreign-language characters that aren't in this basic set. To support DOS in other languages, Microsoft had to create a number of different sets of 256 characters with special characters tuned to a particular language. Such character sets are called code pages.

CHCP

When and why
If you're using your computer in the U.S., chances are you'll never use any of the code page commands. If you're living in another country where you need characters that aren't available in the standard character set, however, you'll need to use all the code page functions described in the "Notes" section to use a different code page. Code page 850, in particular, is a universal code page that is designed to contain more language characters than the 437 code page that we use in the U.S. See the "Notes" section for a caveat on using code page 850.

Syntax
chcp
This command allows you to find out which code page is currently being used.

chcp [*nnn*]
This command allows you to change the code page to the code page numbered *nnn*.

Parameters
nnn
The number of the code page you want to switch to. It can be one of the following:

Code page	Country	Valid country codes
437	U.S.	001, 003, 031-034, 039, 041, 044, 046, 049, 055, 061, 358
850	Multilingual (Latin I)	All
852	Slavic (Latin II)	036, 038, 042, 048
860	Portuguese	351
863	Canadian-French	002
865	Nordic	045, 047

Note: There are only two code pages that will work with each COUNTRY= setting. Check the description of the COUNTRY= command for which code pages you can use.

Notes

CGA and monochrome displays
You cannot change code pages on CGA or monochrome displays. This is because these display adapters have character sets that are built into a ROM (read-only memory) chip and they can't be changed. More recent display adapters, including the EGA and VGA display adapters, allow you to change the character set.

Code pages and other programs
There are many programs that draw lines on the screen, double and single, using the line-drawing characters that are in the extended character set on the IBM PC (the upper 128 characters). Unfortunately, not all the line-drawing characters found in the U.S. (on code page 437) are available in other code pages. What you may see, then, are foreign-language characters on your screen where there should be line-drawing characters. If this bothers you, it's best to stick with code page 437 (which means not using any of the code page functions).

Part II: Command Reference

How to use code pages
There are a number of things you need to set up in order to use code pages. Here is a list of all the steps you must follow (and in this order):

- Put a COUNTRY= line in your CONFIG.SYS file to set the country code, which is used to set the country information (such as time and date formats). *(Optional.)*

- Add one DEVICE= statement to your CONFIG.SYS file for each device that you want to support code page switching (DISPLAY.SYS or PRINTER.SYS). This is required before you can use the MODE command to load a code page.

- Load NLSFUNC either using an INSTALL= line in your CONFIG.SYS or with a line in AUTOEXEC.BAT. You must supply the full pathname to the COUNTRY.SYS file if you didn't provide it in the COUNTRY= line. The NLSFUNC command is required before you can use CHCP to set a code page.

- One or more MODE *device* CP PREP commands to load (which DOS calls preparing) code pages. You need to load code pages before you can use CHCP to make one active.

- A keyboard (KEYB) command in your AUTOEXEC.BAT file to change the keyboard layout. You only need this if you're using a keyboard that doesn't have the U.S. keyboard layout. *(Optional.)*

- CHCP to set the active code page.

Messages
```
Code page nnn not prepared for all devices
```
You'll see this message, for example, when you have a printer that doesn't support code page switching (which is the case for most non-IBM printers). You can safely ignore this message.

```
Invalid code page
```
You'll see this message when you try to set the code page to a number that isn't supported by the current COUNTRY setting. See the table of code pages for which code pages are allowed for each country code.

Examples
CONFIG.SYS lines
Here are some typical lines that you'd put in your CONFIG.SYS file to use a code page other than 437 (the default):

```
country = 038,,c:\dos\country.sys
device = c:\dos\display.sys con=(ega)
install = c:\dos\nlsfunc
```

Here we've set the country code to 038 for Yugoslavia, and the display type as an EGA or VGA screen (DOS uses the same EGA.CPI file for both EGA and VGA screens).

AUTOEXEC.BAT lines
Here are the lines you would need in your AUTOEXEC.BAT file to load the code page 850, which works for all languages (but includes more international characters than the default code page 437):

```
mode con cp prep=((850)c:\dos\ega.cpi)
chcp 850
```

The first line loads the code page 850 into memory (in the DISPLAY.SYS driver), and the second line makes this code page active using the CHCP command.

See also

COUNTRY=	You need to use the COUNTRY= command in your CONFIG.SYS file to indicate where to find COUNTRY.SYS before you can switch code pages with CHCP. See the CONFIG.SYS section.
DISPLAY.SYS	Supports code-page switching for the display. You'll need this if you want to change the character set used on your screen.
KEYB	This command allows you to configure your keyboard for a language other than U.S. English.
MODE *device* CP PREP=	This command allows you to load code pages into memory, which you need to do before you can use CHCP to switch code pages.
MODE *device* CP SELECT=	This command allows you to switch to a different code page on a device (display, printer, or keyboard). It is better to use CHCP to switch code pages, as CHCP will change code pages for all the devices in your system, rather than just one.
NLSFUNC	You must install NLSFUNC (National Language Support Function) before you can use CHCP to switch code pages.
PRINTER.SYS	Supports code-page switching for some IBM printers. You'll need this if you want to change the character set on your printer.

CHDIR (CD) — DOS 2.0 and later, Internal

Change current directory

This command allows you to change between directories on any disk.

When and why
This command is an indispensable command for navigating around your hard disk; you'll probably use it often unless you use DOSSHELL or another program such as the Norton Commander, that allows a number of visual ways to change directories.

Syntax

chdir [*drive:*]
cd [*drive:*]
Displays the current directory on the drive you select or the current drive if you don't supply a drive letter.

chdir [*drive:*]*path*
cd [*drive:*]*path*
Change to a different directory. Without a drive, this command changes to another directory on the current disk. With a drive, this command changes the current directory on that drive. Note that changing the current directory on another drive doesn't make that drive the current drive. However, when you switch to that drive, the current directory will be what you've set with this command.

Parameters

drive
The drive on which you wish to change the current directory (the current drive is not changed by this command).

path
The path to the new current directory. This can be an absolute or a relative path.

Absolute path

name
Start at the root directory and then move down to the subdirectory called *name*. This is an absolute pathname.

Relative paths

..
Move up one level, changing to the parent of the current directory.

name
Without any \ moves down one level, changing to a subdirectory of the current directory.

..*name*
Go up one level and then change to the subdirectory called *name*. This allows you to move sideways to a sibling of the current directory.

The path can move down more than one level at a time. For example, you can type **\BIN\DOS** to move to a directory called DOS that is below a directory called BIN that is below the root directory. Or for a relative path, you can move to a nephew of the current directory by using a relative path such as ..\BROTHER\NEPHEW.

Switches

None.

Notes

You can use either form of this command, CD or CHDIR. Which you use really depends only on which you prefer to type.

Some programs change the directory during the course of running, which means that the current directory and drive could change after you run a program.

CHDIR (CD)

Typing a drive letter followed by a colon as a command allows you to switch to another drive (change the current drive).

Note: Pathnames are limited to 64 characters (this includes the \ at the start of the path but not a drive letter).

Messages
```
Invalid directory
```
This means that one of the directory names in the path you supplied doesn't exist.

```
Invalid drive specification
```
This means the disk drive letter that you specified doesn't exist.

Examples

Changing to the root
To change to the root directory on the current drive, type

```
C:\>cd \
```

Changing to the parent
To change to the parent directory of the current directory, type

```
C:\>cd ..
```

Change directories on other drives
There is one use of this command that may not be obvious: changing the current directory on a drive that isn't the current drive. Why would you want to do that? If you use a command, such as COPY A:*.* C: that contains two drive letters but no paths, the command will work with files in the current directory on each drive. It is often more convenient to type just the drive letters without having to specify the directory. In such cases you can use the CD command to change to the directories you want to work with and then use drive letters without a path. Here is an example that shows how you might move some files from one disk to another by first copying the files and then deleting them from the old location:

```
C:\>cd a:\original
C:\>cd new
C:\NEW>copy a:*.*
  ...
C:\NEW>del a:*.*
  ...
```

This command copies all of the files from the ORIGINAL directory on drive A to the NEW directory on drive C.

See also

MKDIR, MD	This command allows you to create a new subdirectory.
RMDIR, RD	This command allows you to delete a subdirectory when you're finished using it.
TREE	The TREE command will show you a visual tree of your directory structure.

CHKDSK
All DOS, External

Checks the disk structure for errors

This command checks, and optionally corrects, some errors in the directory and file structure of your disk. You can also use it to get some information on disk and memory usage. The section "About disk structures" contains a discussion of disk structures.

When and why

In DOS 6.2 or later, use ScanDisk instead of CHKDSK. ScanDisk can check for and fix far more problems than CHKDSK can find or fix.

Aside from CHKDSK's primary function checking the disk, you can also use this command to see how much free disk space and how much free memory you have. (The MEM command, however, is a faster way to check how much free memory you have since CHKDSK does all its checks before it reports anything.)

You'll want to check your disk for errors once a week or no less frequently than once a month because, like your own health, problems caught early are easier to fix. But we also suggest that you use a commercial disk utility product (Norton Utilities, Mace Utilities, or PC Tools) rather than CHKDSK because these products do a better job (see "Notes" section). If you do use CHKDSK, however, you might want to run it first without the /F switch to see what it reports. The /F switch will correct some errors without first asking you, which could actually make the problem worse.

Syntax

chkdsk [*drive*:][[*path*]*filespec*] [/**f**] [/**v**]

The CHKDSK command allows you to check the directory structure of a disk and to check files to see how fragmented they are (if you provide a filespec).

Parameters

drive
Tells CHKDSK which disk drive it should check.

[*path*]*filespec*
If you supply a filespec, CHKDSK will report on file fragmentation. In other words, it will report how many discontiguous pieces are in each file.

Switches

/f
Fix. Repair any errors found in the directory and FAT structures. Read the "Notes" section before you use this switch, as there are cases where it can cause data to be lost.

/v
Verbose. Lists each file on the disk as its directory entry is being checked. Allows you to see where the errors are as CHKDSK examines each file. For the most part, this switch isn't very useful as most people have hundreds, if not thousands, of files on their hard disks, and this option will list every file.

About disk structures

DOS has many pieces of information on any disk that it uses to locate and keep track of both files and free space. The two areas that CHKDSK checks are called the FAT (File Allocation Table) and the Disk Directory. We'll explain both of these after the next paragraph.

A concept closely connected with DOS's use of disks is the Allocation Unit. (Cluster is another name for allocation units.) DOS divides the disk into small chunks called allocation units; these are the smallest units of disk space that DOS works with. Allocation units are often around 2,048 bytes long. Each file, then, has a certain number of allocation units allocated to it. You can have a file of zero length, which would have no allocation units at all, but most files have at least one allocation unit.

The information about a file consists of three parts: a directory entry, a FAT entry, and the actual data stored in the file. The directory entry contains several pieces of information: the filename, the file attributes (see ATTRIB command), the time and date the file was last modified, the file size, and the first allocation unit in the file. The FAT is a map of allocation units that tells DOS which allocation units are free; for allocation units that are part of a file, it tells DOS how they're connected. So DOS uses the first allocation unit reported in the directory entry to find the start of a file, and it uses the FAT to find all the other allocation units used by that file. Finally, there is the actual data stored in the files.

There are several common errors that CHKDSK can report and fix in files. Probably the most common error you'll see is: "n *lost allocation units found in* i *chains. Convert lost chains to files (Y/N)?*" This message means that the FAT has *n* allocation units marked as being used by *i* files, but there are no directory entries that use these allocation units. In other words, the allocation units are marked as being used, but they're not actually being used by any file. In this case, the CHKDSK command (if you use the /F option) will create one or more files (*i* files, to be exact) named FILE*nnnn*.CHK (in the root directory) that contain the lost allocation units. You can look at these files to see if they contain any useful information, and if so, rename them. If these files don't contain useful information, you can delete them to free up the space. You probably won't see this error message often, but it is usually the result of the power to your computer being interrupted during a write or by a software bug that causes your computer to crash during a write. It can also be a sign of an impending disk problem, so you should use one of the commercial disk utilities to perform more extensive diagnostics when you see this message.

Another message you may see, which is less common, is "filename *is cross linked on allocation unit* n." This error message means that there are two chains of allocation units in the FAT that collide. In other words, two files are trying to share some of the same allocation units. This isn't allowed: Each file must have its own set of unique allocation units. When you see this error message, you'll want to copy both files to another disk and then run CHKDSK with the /F option to fix the cross-linking in the FAT. Next, you'll want to delete both files and then copy the files back onto your disk. At this point, you should look at the contents of the two files. Chances are that one file will have the correct information, whereas the other file may have some correct information at the start (this is because there may be allocation units that aren't shared at the start of the file) and the rest of the file will be information from the other file.

Notes

Using CHKDSK with DoubleSpace in DOS 6.0 only
The CHKDSK command will correctly scan and check a compressed volume, just as any other disk utility will. However, because CHKDSK can recognize compressed volumes, it also runs DBLSPACE /CHKDSK when it finishes. The reason for this is that there are two levels of disk structure when you're dealing with a compressed volume: There is the DOS FAT and directory structure, which CHKDSK checks, and there is an internal compressed volume file structure that only DoubleSpace knows about, and which DBLSPACE /CHKDSK checks for integrity.

DOS 6.2 and later have a new command, ScanDisk, that is much better than CHKDSK because ScanDisk checks for and corrects many more problems than CHKDSK could. ScanDisk also checks both physical drives and compressed volumes.

Alternatives to CHKDSK
In DOS 6.2 and later, use ScanDisk instead of CHKDSK. If you're using an earlier version of DOS, you're probably better off using a commercial disk utility rather than CHKDSK because such programs are written by companies who make their living learning how to do a better job than Microsoft at repairing problems with your disks. Such programs include the Norton Utilities (Symantec Corporation), the Mace Utilities (Fifth Generation Systems), and PC Tools (Central Point Software). All three programs provide much better checking and fixing of disk errors than CHKDSK and are well worth the money.

Networks
CHKDSK doesn't work across networks. You can only use it on hard and floppy disk drives that are inside your computer because most network software, such as Novell NetWare, uses its own proprietary operating system with a disk structure designed for speed and reliability rather than simplicity (as is the case for DOS). The result is that network servers often have disk structures that are internally quite different from DOS's. Programs that work directly with the disk, as opposed to letting DOS handle the disk, won't work across networks because of these differences. CHKDSK is such a program. In any event, network software usually has sophisticated error handling built into it, so CHKDSK isn't needed.

ASSIGN, JOIN, and SUBST
CHKDSK doesn't work on drives that have been ASSIGNed, JOINed, or SUBSTed. You must undo these assignments before you can use CHKDSK. Use ASSIGN (without any parameters) to cancel drive assignments, JOIN /D to disable directory joining, and SUBST *x*: /D to cancel the use of drive letter *x* for a directory.

Open files and windows
If you're running from within Microsoft Windows, or some other program is in memory that has a file open (such as a TSR program), CHKDSK will do one of two things. If you don't use the /F switch, CHKDSK may report some lost allocation units on the disk. This can happen when an open file has been changed, which would add allocation units to the file, but this information hasn't been recorded in

the directory yet (because the file hasn't been closed). If you do use the /F switch, CHKDSK will display an error warning that there are open files. It is best to avoid using CHKDSK in these cases.

Previous versions
Warning! Do not use this command with any version of DOS other than the version it was intended for. In particular, don't use the version of CHKDSK from DOS 2 with later versions of DOS, as it won't know, for example, about the support for larger disks that was added to later versions of DOS. Using an earlier version of CHKDSK can result in loss of data.

Redirecting output to save a report
Microsoft warns against redirecting the output of CHKDSK when you use the /F switch. We haven't been able to find a problem doing this, but there is a chance that CHKDSK could see the output file, which DOS opens before running CHKDSK, as lost clusters.

Messages
There are a number of error messages that CHKDSK can display, and most of them are fairly technical. Because of this, we'll list and describe most of the error messages.

```
filename Is cross-linked on allocation unit n.
```
This message means that two files are trying to share some of the same allocation units, which isn't allowed. Read the "About disk structures" section on how to deal with this message.

```
n lost allocation units found in i chains.
Convert lost chains to files (Y/N)?
```
There are some allocation units that aren't being used by any files but were probably used by some files in the past. Read the "About disk structures" section on how to deal with this message.

```
nnnnnn bytes disk space freed
```
or
```
nnnnnn bytes disk space would be freed.
```
Reports how much disk space was not allocated. If you use the /F switch, this space will be returned to the free disk space.

```
All specified file(s) are contiguous.
```
If you provide a filespec and none of the files are fragmented, CHKDSK displays this message (which isn't an error message).

```
Allocation error, size adjusted.
```
The file probably contains more allocation units than are needed for the size given in the directory entry. CHKDSK will free the extra allocation units at the end of the file (if you use the /F switch).

```
Cannot CHDIR to pathname,
tree past this point not processed.
```
There is serious damage to your directory structure that is preventing CHKDSK from being able to find its way to a given directory. One of the disk utilities mentioned in the "When and why" section might be able to fix the problem.

```
Cannot CHDIR to root.
Processing cannot continue.
```
There is serious damage to a directory that is preventing CHKDSK from finding its way back to the root directory. One of the disk utilities mentioned in the "When and why" section might be able to fix the problem.

```
Cannot CHKDSK a network drive.
```
or
```
Cannot CHKDSK a SUBSTed or ASSIGNed drive.
```
See "Notes" section.

```
Cannot recover .. entry, processing continued.
```
or
```
Cannot recover .. entry,
Entry has a bad attribute.
```
or
```
Cannot recover .. entry,
Entry has a bad link.
```
or
```
Cannot recover .. entry,
Entry has a bad size.
```
These messages all indicate a problem with the .. directory entry, which is created in each directory to allow DOS to find the parent of any directory. These are errors that CHKDSK should be able to fix when you use the /F switch.

```
CHDIR .. failed, trying alternate method.
```
CHKDSK couldn't use the .. directory entry to find the parent directory of one of the directories on your disk. It will try to find this directory by working down the tree so it can repair the .. directory entry to point to the correct parent directory.

```
Directory dir contains n non-contiguous blocks.
```
This is a report, not an error message. You'll see it when you ask CHKDSK to check for file fragmentation.

```
Directory is joined.
```
CHKDSK doesn't work when you have directories joined using the JOIN command. Use JOIN /D to turn JOIN off.

```
Directory is totally empty, no . or ..
```
Every directory must contain, at a minimum, a . and .. directory entry (the current and parent directory pointers). If you get this message, delete the empty directory and create it again.

```
Disk error reading FAT n.
```
or
```
Disk error writing FAT n.
```
Each disk has two FATs, so DOS can use the alternate FAT if it finds a bad sector in one of the FATs. When you see this message, you should copy all the files to another disk and dispose of the disk with the bad sectors in the FAT (lest a bad sector develop in the alternate FAT as well).

CHKDSK

```
Errors found, F parameter not specified.
Corrections will not be written to disk.
```
This message appears whenever CHKDSK finds some errors, but you haven't used the /F switch to ask that errors be corrected.

```
File allocation table bad, drive x:
```
Either the disk isn't an MS-DOS disk, or it is severely damaged. If the disk was readable before, you might be able to use UNFORMAT to repair the damage if you used MIRROR (in DOS 5 or on the DOS 6 Supplemental Disk) or UNDELETE /T (in DOS 6) to save the disk information.

```
First allocation unit is invalid, entry truncated.
```
The first allocation united reported by the directory entry for this file doesn't exist. CHKDSK will set the length of the file to 0 in this case (when you use /F).

```
Has invalid allocation unit, file truncated.
```
There was a pointer to an allocation unit that doesn't exist (in other words, it's off the end of the disk). CHKDSK will shorten the file (when you use /F) so that it includes only the allocation units up to, but not including, the one that doesn't exist.

```
Insufficient room in root directory
Move files from root directory and repeat CHKDSK.
```
The root directory can't have more than 512 files in it (can be more or less on floppy or RAM disks). If CHKDSK is trying to create files from lost chains, for example, and your root directory is full, it won't be able to create additional files. You shouldn't have many files in your root directory in the first place, so you should either delete some files or move most of the files into another directory and then try again.

```
Invalid current directory
Processing cannot continue.
```
There is a problem with the current directory that can't be fixed.

```
Invalid media type.
```
Each disk has a number stored on it that tells DOS what type of disk it is. If this number is not valid, DOS may not be able to read the disk correctly.

```
Invalid subdirectory entry.
```
The directory you supplied on the command line either doesn't exist or contains some characters that aren't allowed.

```
Probable non-DOS disk.
Continue (Y/N)?
```
Either the disk wasn't created by DOS (it could be a Macintosh or Unix disk), or it is so severely damaged that CHKDSK can't recognize it.

```
Unrecoverable error in directory.
Convert directory to file (Y/N)?
```
At this point, it's best to use one of the disk utilities mentioned in the "Notes" section to see if they can recover the directory. If you respond with Y, you'll lose all the files stored in the directory; you'll then want to delete the FILE*nnnn*.CHK file created by CHKDSK in the root directory since it won't contain any useful information.

Technical notes

Here are some of the directory errors CHKDSK looks for:

- Invalid pointers to the first allocation unit (as reported by a directory entry).
- Bad file attributes in directory entries.
- Damaged directory entries that make it impossible to navigate part of the directory structure.
- Damaged directories where none of the files can be accessed.

Here are some of the FAT (File Allocation Table) errors that CHKDSK looks for:

- Unreadable disk sectors in the FAT.
- Invalid next allocation unit pointers inside the FAT.
- Lost allocation units (that aren't assigned to any file).
- Cross-linking of files (when two files include some of the same allocation units).

Examples

If there is an error on the disk, such as lost allocation units, CHKDSK will report an error such as the following:

```
6 lost allocation units in 2 chains.
Convert lost chains to files (Y/N)?
```

If you use the /F switch, you can answer Y (and press Enter) to have CHKDSK convert these lost allocation units into files (two files in this example).

When we ran CHKDSK on our laptop computer, it reported the following:

```
C:\>chkdsk *.*

Volume DOS600 created 01-01-1990 12:06a
Volume Serial Number is 1682-857B

21,309,440  bytes total disk space
    73,728  bytes in 2 hidden files
   100,352  bytes in 45 directories
20,568,064  bytes in 840 user files
   567,296  bytes available on disk

     2,048  bytes in each allocation unit
    10,405  total allocation units on disk
       277  available allocation units on disk

   655,360  total bytes memory
   591,424  bytes free

C:\COMMAND.COM Contains 2 non-contiguous blocks
C:\TEST.BAK Contains 4 non-contiguous blocks
C:\MOUSE.SYS Contains 10 non-contiguous blocks
C:\MOUSE.COM Contains 2 non-contiguous blocks
```

CHKDSK

```
Instead of using CHKDSK, try using ScanDisk.  ScanDisk can
reliably detect and fix a much wider range of disk problems.
For more information, type HELP ScanDisk from the
command prompt.
```

As you can see, there is quite a bit of information that CHKDSK reports.

Volume label. The first line is only present if your disk has a volume label. You can also use the VOL command to view this label and the LABEL command to modify it.

Volume serial number. This is a unique number that DOS assigns to a disk whenever you format the disk. This number won't change until you format the disk again. Volume serial numbers are mainly for DOS's internal use since they allow DOS to tell which disk is in a disk drive. We have no idea why DOS displays this information. Disks formatted by DOS versions before 4.0 do not contain a volume serial number.

Total disk space. This is the total space on the disk.

Hidden files. DOS allows some files to be hidden so you won't see them in directory listings. Any disk that DOS boots from will have at least two hidden files (IO.SYS and MSDOS.SYS) that are part of DOS. Other programs might also create hidden files. For example, in DOS 5 (also on the DOS 6 Supplemental Disk), MIRROR creates a hidden file called MIRRORSAV.FIL in the root directory. And in DOS 6, UNDELETE /T (the tracker option) creates a file called PCTRACKR.DEL in the root directory.

Bad sectors. The example just given doesn't show this line, but your disk might have some sectors that are bad, which means that the disk drive can't read a sector for one reason or another. This line simply reports how many bytes are not available because there are bad sectors on your disk. It isn't unusual to have some bad sectors on your disk.

Allocation units. The next group of three lines (shown for DOS 4.0 and later only) displays information on the allocation units on your disk: the size of each allocation unit, the number of allocation units on a disk, and the number of unused allocation units that are available for use.

Memory. The final two lines show how much memory you have installed in your computer and how much is available for use by programs. (***Note:*** This display doesn't show how much extended or expanded memory you have in your computer — just the amount of memory in the first 640K.)

Noncontiguous blocks. For each file, if you've provided a filespec, CHKDSK will report the number of separate, noncontiguous pieces each file is divided into. This information isn't of much use except to give you an idea of how fragmented your disk has become. Disks that are heavily fragmented tend to run a little slower because DOS has to read from a number of different places to read a single file. If you want the maximum speed, there are a number of disk utilities that include a program to unfragment your hard disk. These include the Norton Utilities, the Mace Utilities, PC Tools, and Disk Optimizer.

See also

DIR   If you just want to know how much disk space is free, you can use the DIR command, which reports the amount of free disk space after it lists all the files.

LABEL	Allows you to change the disk's volume label. The LABEL command can create a volume label (if the disk doesn't have one), change a volume label, or delete the volume label.
MEM	If you're just interested in finding out how much memory is available, as opposed to disk space, you can use the MEM command, which will give you a report on memory much more quickly than CHKDSK (this is because CHKDSK scans the disk before it makes any report).
SCANDISK	Use this program instead of CHKDSK if you have DOS 6.2 or later. The ScanDisk command does a much better job of finding and fixing problems as well as checking more types of problems.
VOL	Reports the current volume label and serial number. This is faster than using CHKDSK for getting this information.

CHKSTATE.SYS — DOS 6 and later, Device driver

Used by MemMaker
MemMaker uses this file to monitor your system during the optimization process.

When and why
You will never want to use this device driver yourself: MemMaker uses CHKSTATE.SYS to help it optimize the use of your computer's memory. At the start of the optimization sequence, MemMaker inserts a line, DEVICE=CHKSTATE.SYS, at the beginning of your CONFIG.SYS file. When MemMaker terminates normally, the statement is removed from your CONFIG.SYS file. This file must be present for MemMaker to optimize your system. It is not needed at any other time.

Syntax
device=chkstate.sys
Loads MemMaker's device driver. You won't want to do this yourself.

See also
MemMaker	MemMaker is a new DOS 6 utility that modifies your configuration files to optimize your use of memory.

CHOICE — DOS 6 and later, External

Accepts single keystrokes from the keyboard
Displays a prompt and waits for you to type a character. You can supply the prompt and the list of allowed characters. You can then use the IF ERRORLEVEL command to choose which commands you want to run in a batch file.

CHOICE

When and why

You'll mainly want to use this command in batch files to add simple menus to your batch files. This command allows a batch file to obtain responses from you and simplifies the development of sophisticated menu systems with batch files. Use this command anytime you are designing a batch file that offers options.

For example, you could add a CHOICE command to your AUTOEXEC.BAT file to ask if you want to install certain programs (much like using the ? character or the MENUITEM command in CONFIG.SYS). You can provide a prompt, a set of allowed answers, and (this is the best part) you can provide a time-out value so DOS will continue running your batch file if you don't provide an answer within, say, 2 seconds. This allows your batch file to run without your input when you don't want to choose out-of-the-ordinary settings.

Syntax

choice [/c[:]*keys*] [/n] [/s] [/t[:]*choice,seconds*] [*text*]
Asks you a question and waits for a reply, returning the reply in the batch file ERRORLEVEL variable.

Parameters

text
Prompt. When you run CHOICE, it normally displays *text*, followed by a list of keys surrounded by brackets that CHOICE will accept, and finally a question mark. The *text* can contain any characters, except for the following: | / < and >. To include any of these characters, surround *text* with quotation marks, as follows: CHOICE "Run at 1/4th speed". You can also use the /n switch to suppress both the list of keys and the final question mark. If you don't supply *text*, CHOICE will not display a prompt.

Switches

/c[:]*keys*
Key list. The list of keys that CHOICE will accept. The positions of the characters in the list determine which value CHOICE will return to ERRORLEVEL when you press that key. The first character returns the value 1, the second returns 2, and so on. You can use any characters except for the following: | / < and >. CHOICE will beep whenever you press a key that isn't in this list of keys. The default key list is YN.

/n
Suppress key list. This switch tells CHOICE not to display the list of keys, which CHOICE normally displays in brackets after the prompt. When you use /n, the key list as well as the final question mark will not be shown, but CHOICE will still use the list to decide which keys to accept.

/s
Case Sensitive. This switch tells CHOICE to treat upper- and lowercase characters as distinct keys. By default, an uppercase letter, such as *A*, is treated the same as the lowercase letter, in this case, *a*. When you use this switch, be sure you specify both the upper- and lowercase characters in the key list when you want both to work, or else CHOICE will only accept the upper- or lowercase letter you supply, but not both. By default, CHOICE ignores the case of letters you type.

/t[:]*choice,seconds*
Default Key. When the time *seconds* and you haven't typed a valid letter, CHOICE will act as if you typed the letter *choice*. This is useful if you want your batch file to continue running after a delay, even if you haven't responded to CHOICE. The first parameter, *choice,* is any letter in the key list, and *seconds* is the number of full seconds you want CHOICE to wait for a response before continuing. Valid range is 0 to 99, where 0 means no pause. After the specified number of *seconds*, the value for *choice* is assigned to ERRORLEVEL and the processing continues.

Notes

Order of IF ERRORLEVEL statements

The IF ERRORLEVEL statements in your batch file must appear with the highest number first and the lowest number last because the IF ERRORLEVEL statement runs a command whenever the ERRORLEVEL is equal to *or higher* than the number you provide.

Using a colon in the key list

The colon can be specified as a character on the key list. To specify it as the first character, you must use the optional colon separator followed by the colon character.

Using CHOICE with DOS 4 and 5

Although CHOICE is new to DOS 6, it will run in DOS 4 and 5. We're not sure why Microsoft designed CHOICE so it won't work with versions of DOS before 4.0.

Return value for Ctrl-Break or Ctrl-C

If the you press Ctrl-C (or Ctrl-Break) to end the processing of the batch file while a CHOICE statement is waiting for input, CHOICE returns the value of 0 in ERRORLEVEL.

Error Conditions

If CHOICE encounters an error, such as an incorrect switch, it returns the value 255 in ERRORLEVEL.

Messages

```
Beep
```
CHOICE emits a beep whenever you press a key that isn't included in the key list.

```
CHOICE: invalid choice switch syntax. Expected form: /C[:]choices
```
This message appears if you specify an invalid key in the key list. The most common case is using / as one of the acceptable key values.

```
CHOICE: only one prompt string allowed. Expected Form:...
```
You'll probably see this error message when you use a / inside a prompt that looks like a switch. You can eliminate this error message by putting quote marks around your prompt, such as CHOICE "A /c switch in prompt".

```
CHOICE: Timeout default not in specified (or default) choices.
```
You'll see this error message whenever the *choice* your provided in the /t switch doesn't match one of the characters in the key list. You'll need to either change your key list to include the character after /t, or you'll need to use one of the characters in the key list after /t.

CHOICE

Technical notes

Testing ERRORLEVEL

You must use the IF ERRORLEVEL statement to test the value of the ERRORLEVEL variable. The ERRORLEVEL test is equivalent to a greater-than-or-equal comparison. As a result, you should first test for the highest possible value and use a GOTO statement to control the processing.

Examples

The default CHOICE statement

The CHOICE statement without any switches or parameters produces the following:

```
[Y,N]?
```

If you press *Y* or *y*, ERRORLEVEL is assigned the value 1. If you press *N* or *n*, ERRORLEVEL is assigned the value 2. CHOICE will beep if you press any other key. This statement is the equivalent of

```
choice /c:yn
```

Specifying a key list

To change the keystrokes that CHOICE recognizes, you must use the /c switch. The value of ERRORLEVEL is then assigned based on the order of the keys in the key list. The statement

```
choice /cba
```

would assign the value 1 to ERRORLEVEL when you press *B* or *b* and the value 2 to ERRORLEVEL when you press *A* or *a*. The only relationship between the keys in the key list (after /c) and the value assigned to ERRORLEVEL is the position of each key within the key list.

You should specify your keys in an order that makes sense when you see CHOICE's output. For example, you would probably want a quit option listed at the end of the list (such as, /cYNQ).

Specifying a prompt

The statement

```
choice Enter your response
```

produces the following:

```
Enter your response[Y,N]?
```

The value returned in ERRORLEVEL is based on the order of these letters (Y=1, N=2).

Specifying a prompt with the key list hidden

The statement

```
choice /n /c:yn Enter Y for Yes and N for No
```

produces the following:

```
Enter Y for Yes and N for No
```

Notice that the key list is not displayed. Even though CHOICE did not display the key list, it still uses the key list. The keys are interpreted in the same order as they appear in the key list (Y=1, N=2), which may or may not match the order in the prompt since CHOICE pays no attention to what's actually inside the prompt.

Specifying a default key

In many situations, you will want the processing of your batch file to continue after a set amount of time, even if you haven't pressed a key. To tell CHOICE to continue processing as though you pressed *Y* if you haven't pressed a key after 15 seconds, you would use the following statement:

```
choice /tY,15
```

The key you supply after /t must be in the key list. (In this case, we are using the default key list of *Y* and *N*.)

Forcing uppercase input

There may be times when you want to force the users to enter their response in uppercase letters, or where you want to distinguish between upper- and lowercases (for example, using *S* to indicate sort in increasing order and *s* to indicate sort in decreasing order). The /s switch makes CHOICE case sensitive. The statement

```
choice /s
```

forces you to enter either *Y* or *N*. Pressing *y* or *n* results in a beep.

Using CHOICE with GOTO

To provide three options, each of which performs a unique set of actions, you might structure your batch file as follows:

```
choice Please select by Size, by Name, by Date /cSND /tN,20
if errorlevel 3 goto ByDate
if errorlevel 2 goto ByName
if errorlevel 1 goto BySize
:ByDate
  actions to be performed for this condition
goto EndChoice
:ByName
  actions to be performed for this condition
goto EndChoice
:BySize
  actions to be performed for this condition
goto EndChoice
:EndChoice
  processing continues from here
```

Your segments do not have to be listed in the same order as they appear on the CHOICE statement, but it makes it easier to debug your batch file if you encounter problems. Because IF ERRORLEVEL checks whether the ERRORLEVEL is greater than or equal to the value specified, you must first test for the largest expected value. Otherwise, no matter what key the user presses, the action specified for the IF ERRORLEVEL 1 condition will be processed. Notice that in this example, the By Name option is selected after 15 seconds if the user does not respond.

See also

IF	Used to evaluate the value of ERRORLEVEL.
MENUITEM	Used to create your startup menu from within CONFIG.SYS.
?	Use this character in your CONFIG.SYS file when you want to be asked each time if you want to include a command in CONFIG.SYS.

CLS
All DOS, Internal

Clear the screen

Clears all the characters off your screen and moves the cursor to the top of the screen. The prompt will appear at the top of the screen.

When and why

There are two main uses for this command. First, and perhaps obviously, you can use it whenever the display becomes cluttered and you want to clean the slate.

And second, you can use CLS inside batch files to create menus and other displays that you want on a screen without any other lines.

Syntax

cls

Notes

Screen colors

There are some programs (such as the screen attributes command in the Norton Utilities) that allow you to set the screen colors, so you see DOS's output in colors other than black on white. When you use CLS to clear the screen, however, the screen colors may be set back to black and white. The way to preserve the screen colors you set is to install the ANSI.SYS driver, which will preserve screen colors (as long as the program that sets the colors sends an escape sequence to ANSI.SYS to tell it what colors to use).

EGA/VGA modes

On EGA and VGA monitors you can display more than 25 lines on the screen (43 on an EGA and 50 lines on a VGA) using the MODE command. In versions of DOS before 4.0, the CLS command may only clear the first 25 lines of your screen. There isn't a good solution for this, except to upgrade to DOS 6 (or DOS 5).

Escape sequences

If you have the ANSI.SYS display driver installed, CLS sends an escape sequence (Esc [2J) to ANSI.SYS telling it to clear the screen. You can capture this escape sequence using the following command:

```
C:\>cls > clear.txt
```

Part II: Command Reference

This redirects CLS's output to a text file (CLS will create the file even if you don't have ANSI.SYS installed). You can then use TYPE CLEAR.TXT at any time to clear the screen (provided you have ANSI.SYS installed).

See also
ANSI.SYS   Install ANSI.SYS to preserve screen colors when you clear the screen. You can also send escape sequences to the screen to change screen colors, the cursor position, etc.

MODE   Use the MODE CON: LINES= command to change the number of lines on the screen for EGA and VGA display adapters (between 25 and 43/50 lines).

COMMAND   All DOS, External

Start a new copy of the command line

This command starts a new copy of the command-line interpreter, which is the part of MS-DOS that handles anything you type on the command line. Type **EXIT** to leave the new copy of COMMAND and return to the previous copy.

When and why

This is a fairly advanced command that you may never use. (Except, of course, that you're using a copy of COMMAND whenever you see the DOS prompt. But you don't need to understand this command to use the DOS prompt.)

There are two cases when you'd want to use this command. The first, and most common, is to increase the size of the space DOS reserves for environment variables. You do this with the SHELL= line in your CONFIG.SYS file (see examples below).

Second, many commercial programs allow you to *shell out* to DOS to execute some DOS commands without exiting from your other program first. When you're done with DOS, you type **EXIT** to return to your other program. Such programs provide this feature by running another version of COMMAND, which is why you need to use the EXIT command to return to your program. *Note:* Don't use the /P switch in these cases because you can't use the EXIT command if you've used the /P switch.

Syntax

command [[*drive:*]*path*] [*device*] [/e:*nnnnn*] [/p] [/c *string*] [/k *program*] [/msg]
Start a new command processor or run a command.

command [[*drive:*]*path*] [*device*] [/e:*nnnnn*] [/p] [/y [/c *string*|/k *program*]] [/msg]
(DOS 6.2 and later.) Start a new command processor or run a command.

shell=[[*drive:*]*path*]**command.com** [[*drive*][*path*] [*device*] [/e:*nnnnn*] [/p] [/msg]
Use this form in your CONFIG.SYS file to modify setting for COMMAND.COM.

Parameters

[drive:]path
Reload path. Tells DOS where to look for COMMAND.COM when it needs to reload the command interpreter (after a program uses the memory that was occupied by it). See the "Notes" section for a discussion of reloading and the "Examples" section for why you'd want to use this parameter.

device
I/O device. Most people will never use this parameter. It allows you to change DOS's input/output device from the keyboard and screen to another character device, such as a terminal attached to one of your computer's serial ports. Note, however, that this only works for programs that get the input from DOS and use DOS to send their output to the screen. Most commercial programs bypass DOS for keyboard input and screen output, and therefore won't be affected by any changes in the input/output device. Legal devices include PRN, LPT1, LPT2, LPT3, CON, AUX, COM1, COM2, COM3, and COM4. The default is CON (the screen and keyboard).

Switches

/e:nnnnn
Environment size (DOS 3.2 and later). Allows you to set the minimum size of the environment in the new copy of COMMAND. You might want to do this if you're running a batch file that requires more space for environment variables than you currently have (you'll see `Out of environment space` messages if you don't have enough space reserved). The size is a number from 160 to 32768 (don't use commas) bytes and is rounded up to a multiple of 16. The default size is 256 (or 160 for DOS before Version 5).

/p
Make permanent. Only use this switch in your CONFIG.SYS file. This switch tells DOS to make this copy of COMMAND.COM the permanent copy. The effect is that you won't be able to use the EXIT command to exit the new copy of COMMAND. DOS also reruns the AUTOEXEC.BAT file in the root directory when you use this switch. It's best to use this switch only in the SHELL= line of your CONFIG.SYS file.

/y
Single step batch file (DOS 6.2 and later). This switch allows you to run a batch file one line at a time. DOS will ask `[Y/N]?` for each line in the batch file before it runs that line. Press Y followed by Enter to run that line or N followed by Enter to skip that line in the batch file. You might want to use this switch to help you debug a batch file you've written because you'll be able to see the individual steps more clearly. *Note:* You will need to place either the /C or /K switch on the command line after /Y for this switch to have any meaning.

/c string
Run command. Run the single command *string* and then exit the new copy of COMMAND. There are two main uses for this switch. First, in DOS versions before 3.3, this was the only way to run one batch file from within another (DOS 3.3 added the CALL command for this purpose). Second, most programs that allow you to run DOS commands, such as the Norton Commander, run the commands using a new copy of COMMAND with this switch. If you want to run a command and then have a new command prompt, use the /k switch. *Note:* You cannot use the /c and /k switches together — you can only use one at a time.

/k program
Run program and then show prompt (DOS 6 and later). This switch is like /c, in that it runs a batch file or program, but unlike /c, it does not exit the new copy of COMMAND after DOS finishes running *program*. This is most useful in Windows or the DOS Shell when you want to start a program but have DOS run a batch file first. The batch file you run first might set some environment variables or load some memory-resident programs (TSRs) into memory before your program starts. Type **EXIT** at the new command line to leave the new copy of COMMAND when you're finished. *Note:* You cannot use the /c and /k switches together—you can only use one at a time.

If you're using Windows, you can have DOS boxes automatically run a batch file before it shows you the DOS prompt (sort of like an AUTOEXEC.BAT for Windows). To do so, use the PIFEDIT program in Windows (press Alt-F-R and then type **PIFEDIT** from the Program Manager), and load in the file DOSPRMT.PIF from your Windows directory (press Alt-F-O to display the Open dialog box and then double-click on DOSPRMT.PIF). Finally, type **/k** *programname* in the Optional parameters section of PIFEDIT and save these changes (Alt-F-S). Now whenever you open a DOS box, DOS will run *programname* before it shows you the DOS prompt.

/msg
Messages in memory (DOS 5 and later). Keep all messages in memory rather than on disk. Must be used in conjunction with /P to keep the new copy, with messages, permanently in memory. You might use this switch when you're running DOS from a floppy disk rather than a hard disk. In this case, you'd want all the messages stored in memory so that you could remove the disk that contains DOS during some operations.

Notes

Reloading COMMAND

DOS has both a resident and a transient part. The transient part, which handles the command line, is loaded into high memory so that it can stay in memory without needing to be reloaded from disk after you run small programs. When you run large programs that use high memory, however, DOS will need to reload the command interpreter (the transient part) from disk after you exit from the large program. The path parameter allows you to tell DOS where to look for COMMAND.COM when it needs to reload its transient part.

Command and environment variables

Each copy of COMMAND that you start has its own area of memory set aside for storing environment variables. New copies of COMMAND receive a copy of the environment space from the previous COMMAND, so all the environment variables you've defined will still be there. But any changes you make to the environment will only be made to the current copy of COMMAND. In other words, when you use the EXIT command to exit the new version of COMMAND, you'll lose any changes you've made to environment variables.

Note: This means several things. First, if you're using a DOS shell, such as the Norton Commander or the DOS Shell, you won't be able to change environment variables without first quitting the shell. This is because shell programs start a new version of COMMAND to run DOS commands (they use the /C switch to run one

COMMAND

command), so these commands are actually modifying a temporary version of the environment rather than the shell's own environment. You can often get around this problem by using a batch file that changes the environment and then runs a command that needs the modified environment.

When environment size is a problem
Most of the time you don't need to be concerned with altering the size of the DOS environment because the environment size will expand as needed. However, if your AUTOEXEC.BAT file loads programs that stay in memory (TSR programs), these programs will fix the size of your environment so it can't expand. In such cases you may need to use the SHELL=COMMAND /E: line in your CONFIG.SYS file to set a larger size of your environment (see "Examples" for further details).

CALL vs. the /C switch
If you try to run one batch file from within another batch file, DOS will run the second batch file, but DOS won't return to the first batch file once the second finishes. There are two ways to run a second batch file such that DOS will continue running the first batch file after it finishes with the second one: You can use the CALL command (DOS 3.3 and later), or you can run the second batch file using COMMAND with the /C switch. In the latter case, however, any changes the second batch file makes to the environment (including the path) will be lost when that batch file finishes running. This happens because the second batch file modifies the environment of the new copy of COMMAND rather than the master copy. The CALL command does not have this limitation.

The /P switch
Warning! Be careful not to use the /P switch except with the SHELL command in your CONFIG.SYS file. If you use any type of shell program, such as the Norton Commander or the DOS Shell, you won't be able to return to your shell after running command /P because the new version of COMMAND will be the permanent version, which means you can't use EXIT to return to your shell. This also applies when shelling out to DOS from a word processor to run DOS commands. If you run COMMAND /P from this shell, you won't be able to return to your word processor.

You also shouldn't use this switch from within Microsoft Windows because you'll create a DOS window that you won't be able to close except by rebooting. (This happens because you can't exit from the new version of COMMAND when you use the /P switch.) In Windows 3.1, you can kill a DOS box without rebooting your computer by pressing Ctrl-Alt-Del when the DOS box is active.

Messages
Here are a few of the error messages that you might see. We've also put in some of the common command-line error messages that you'll see.

```
Bad command or file name
```
You'll see this message all the time. It usually means that DOS couldn't find a command that has the name you typed. There are a couple of reasons you'll run into this. One is that you've mistyped the command name. Another is that the command

exists, but DOS couldn't find it because the command is in a directory that isn't included in the PATH command. DOS looks for external commands only in directories that are listed in its search path.

`No free file handles`
DOS allows only a certain number of files to be open at one time. It is possible, though unlikely, that you can use up this limit. If you see this message, you'll want to increase the number in the FILES= line of your CONFIG.SYS file (default = 8 if there is no FILES= line).

`Parameter value not in allowed range.`
You'll see this message if the number you used with the /E switch is not between 160 and 32768.

`Required parameter missing`
You'll see this message if you use the /MSG switch without the /P switch.

Examples

Increasing environment size

By default, the minimum size of DOS's environment is 256 bytes, which may not be large enough for some programs, such as AutoCAD, that use a lot of environment variables. If you get the `Out of environment space` message, you can use a line like the following in your CONFIG.SYS file to increase the default size of DOS's environment:

```
shell=command.com /e:1024 /p
```

This increases the default size to 1,024 bytes. Note that the /P switch is required to make these changes permanent.

Emulating the CALL command

Let's say your AUTOEXEC.BAT file is rather large and you want to break it up into several smaller batch files, with a couple small ones to provide some services. For example, you might want a batch file that sets up your network without having all the lines to do the network initialization in your AUTOEXEC.BAT file. You'd then want a single line, DONET, to be in your AUTOEXEC.BAT file; DONET.BAT would then handle all the network initialization. The problem is that if you just put this line into your AUTOEXEC.BAT file, DOS will stop running AUTOEXEC.BAT when it runs DONET.BAT, so it won't run the rest of AUTOEXEC.BAT. The solution is to either use the CALL command to run the DONET.BAT file, or the /C switch of COMMAND:

```
command /c donet
```

This starts a new copy of COMMAND to run the second batch file so that when it finishes, our AUTOEXEC.BAT file will continue to run.

Note: It is best to use CALL rather than /C because batch files run with CALL can modify your environment (unlike batch files run with COMMAND /C). In this example, the DONET batch file needs to modify the path to include disk drives on the network, so COMMAND /C won't do exactly what you want. It would modify the path in the second shell, but those changes would be lost as soon as processing returned to the AUTOEXEC.BAT file.

Reloading COMMAND from a RAM disk

If you're a speed demon, you like everything to be as fast as possible. If you're running the Norton Commander, it has to load COMMAND every time you run a DOS command and then reload itself when that command finishes. Both of these take time, unless you have a RAM disk, in which case the reload takes almost no time. To load both the COMMANDER and COMMAND.COM from a RAM disk, you'll need to put the following lines at the end of your AUTOEXEC.BAT file (example assumes your RAM disk is drive E:):

```
copy command.com e:
copy nc*.exe e:
set comspec=e:\command.com
nc
```

Note that we didn't use the SHELL= line in your CONFIG.SYS file or the path parameter along with the /P switch of COMMAND. Why not? Because we need to copy COMMAND.COM to the RAM disk before we can load COMMAND.COM from it. But since a RAM disk loses its contents whenever you restart your computer, we can't copy COMMAND.COM to it until after DOS has finished going through your CONFIG.SYS file.

We could have used the path parameter in COMMAND, but we didn't do this because each copy of COMMAND that you make permanent in memory uses about 2.5K of memory. We can accomplish the same end by changing the COMSPEC environment variable, which tells DOS where to find COMMAND.COM whenever it needs to reload the transient part. If you wanted to use the path parameter of COMMAND, here is how you'd do it:

```
command e:\ /p
```

See also

CALL	This is a better way than COMMAND /C to call one batch file from within another if you're using DOS 3.3 or later.
CTTY	You can also use this command (rather than the *device* parameter of COMMAND) to change the input and output device for COMMAND.
EXIT	This command allows you to quit, or leave, the new copy of COMMAND you invoked. You'll use this to return to programs that allow you to shell out to DOS when you want to return from DOS.
PATH	The PATH command controls where DOS looks for external commands. You'll want to have a PATH command in your AUTOEXEC.BAT file to set up a search path when you first start your computer.
SHELL	The SHELL command in your CONFIG.SYS file can be used to increase the default size of your DOS environment.

Part II: Command Reference

COMP
DOS 1–5, External

Compares two files

The COMP command compares two files byte by byte to see if they are identical. COMP works mainly with files that have the same size (you can only compare files of different size if you use the /N switch) and reports characters that are different.

When and why

You'll want to use this command when you're cleaning up your hard disk and you find files in different directories that have the same name. You can use COMP to see if such files are identical so you can delete the extra copy without fear of losing anything.

You may also want to compare text or word processing files to see what lines are different between the two files. In such cases, you'll want to use the FC command rather than COMP. This is because the FC command knows a lot more about text and lines of text, and it will report which lines are different rather than just which characters are different. If you have a single new line inserted into one of the files, COMP will report a difference for each character in this new line rather than just that there is one line different.

Note: In DOS 6, the functions of the COMP command are now only available via the FC command. The COMP command is also available on the Supplemental Disk available from Microsoft.

Syntax

comp [[*drive1*:]*filespec1* [*drive2*:]*filespec2*]] [/d] [/a] [/l] [/n=*number*] [/c]

Compares two files and displays the differences between the two files.

Parameters

There are several combinations of file parameters that COMP can work with. Note that *filespec1* can include either of the DOS wildcard characters (* and ?), and DOS will then compare more than one file. Also, whenever you supply a drive letter without a filename, COMP will use the *.* filename, which will match the other filename that you supply (or it will compare all the files in the current directory of each drive if you supply two drive letters without filenames).

No parameters
COMP will ask you for both the "Name of first file to compare" and the "Name of second file to compare."

drive1 or *filespec1*
If you supply only one filename (or drive letter), COMP will ask you for the name of the second file to compare.

drive1 drive2
If you just supply two drive letters, COMP will compare all the files in the current directory on *drive1*: to all the files in the current directory on *drive2*:.

COMP

filespec1 drive2
Compare the file *filespec1* (with or without a drive letter) to a file of the same name on *drive2:* (in the current directory on that drive).

filespec1 filespec2
Compare the file(s) that match *filespec1* with the files that match *filespec2*. Either or both filespecs may include a drive letter.

Switches

/a
ASCII display (DOS 5 or later). Displays the bytes that are different as characters. Normally, COMP displays these bytes in hexadecimal notation.

/c
Ignore case (DOS 5 or later). Ignores case when doing the comparisons, so both a and A will be treated as the same letter.

/d
Decimal display (DOS 5 or later). Displays bytes that are different as decimal numbers. Normally, COMP displays these bytes in hexadecimal notation.

/l
Line numbers (DOS 5 or later). Displays the line number where each difference occurs. Normally, COMP displays an offset, in bytes, from the beginning of the file.

/n=*number*
Compare number lines (DOS 5 or later). Compares only the first *number* lines of each file. This is the only way to compare two files that are not of the same length (except by using the FC command).

Notes

Compare's prompts

When you don't supply any filenames (or just one filename) COMP will prompt you for the missing information, using the following prompts:

```
Name of first file to compare:
Name of second file to compare:
Option :
```

After each prompt, COMP waits for you to type a name (for the first two) or a switch (for OPTION). If you enter a switch after OPTION, COMP will ask you again for other options. Just press Enter when you see OPTION again to start the compare.

Wildcard characters

There are two ways that wildcard characters may not work the way you expect. First, COMP uses wildcard characters in the second filespec in the same way as the RENAME or COPY commands use wildcard characters — to create a second name based on the first name rather than to find files on the disk that match the second filespec. For example, if you ask COMP to compare CON*.SYS to MON??.SYS and there is a file called CONFIG.SYS, COMP will convert the second filespec into MONFI.SYS (the ?? characters substitute two characters from the first filename).

Secret DOS: The second has to do with the ? wildcard character in the second filespec. As it turns out, the DOS 5 COMP and FC commands introduced a slight bug in their support of the ? character. Any ? characters you use in the second filespec must match exactly one character in filenames produced by the first filespec. This means that CONFIG?.SYS won't match CONFIG.SYS because there is no character in position 7 (the position of the ?) of CONFIG.SYS for the ? to match. All other DOS commands allow ? characters at the end of filenames to match zero or one character rather than one and only one character as required by COMP and FC.

Hexadecimal numbers

The offset of mismatches inside a file is always reported as a hexadecimal number. Hexadecimal numbers are a little different from decimal numbers in that there are 16 digits rather than the usual 10; in other words, they're base-16 rather than base-10 numbers. Decimal numbers use the digits 0 through 9 (10 digits), while hexadecimal numbers use the digits 0 through 9, and A through F (for a total of 16 digits). In other words, we count up as follows: 1, 2, 3, . . ., 9, A, . . ., F, 10, ... The number 10 hexadecimal is really equal to 16 decimal. If you're wondering why COMP uses hexadecimal, so are we. Seriously though, programmers use hexadecimal numbers rather than decimal numbers, and COMP is a tool that is mainly used by programmers.

Offset in hexadecimal

When COMP finds a difference between two files, it displays a report such as the following:

```
Compare error at OFFSET 10
file1 = 54
file2 = 74
```

The numbers in this case are all in hexadecimal notation (see previous paragraph). You can also use the /D or /A switches to display the differences in decimal or ASCII (as characters). Here is what the same COMP would look like using the /D switch:

```
Compare error at OFFSET 10
file1 = 84
file2 = 116
```

Note that the OFFSET is still a hexadecimal number, even though the other two numbers (84 and 116) are now decimal numbers. COMP always displays the offset in hexadecimal.

Messages

```
10 mismatches - ending compare
```
COMP only displays information on the first ten characters (bytes) that differ between the two files. There really isn't a way to check for differences beyond the first ten mismatches.

```
Can't read file:
```
You'll probably see this error message on a network when someone else has opened and locked one of the files to keep other people from reading it while it's open. Wait for a while and try again. Or find out who has the file open and ask him or her to release it.

```
Compare more files (Y/N)?
```
You'll see this message after COMP finishes its work (or after it can't find some files). This allows you to enter another list of files to compare, if you want. Press Y to compare a new set of files or N to exit from COMP.

```
Could not expand second file name so as to match first
```
Secret DOS: This message did not appear in versions of COMP and FC before DOS 5 and is the result of an incorrect change made to how they handle the ? wildcard character. You'll see this message when you use the ? wildcard character in the second filename. COMP requires that each ? character in the second filespec match exactly one character in every filename generated by the first filespec. (See "Notes" on wildcard characters.)

```
Files are different sizes
```
COMP can only find differences between two files of the same size (unless you use the /N switch). Your best bet is to use the FC command, which knows about text and can compare files of different lengths.

```
Files compare OK
```
The two files are identical.

Examples

The following command compares the two batch files, TEST.BAT and TEST2.BAT, to see if they're the same:

```
C:\>comp test.bat test2.bat
```

Comparing disks

You can compare all the files on two disks with this command:

```
C:\>comp a: b:
```

When you don't supply a filename, COMP uses *.*, so we're asking COMP to compare A:*.* to B:*.* in this example.

Comparing directories

This example shows how you can compare all the Microsoft Word files in one directory to the same files in another directory (Word files use the DOC extension):

```
C:\>comp *.doc d:\writing\dos\backup
```

This compares all the *.DOC files in the current directory to the files with the same names in the \WRITING\DOS\BACKUP directory on drive D:.

See also

DISKCOMP   Compares two floppy disks to see if they're identical.

FC   This is the command you'll want to use most of the time to compare two files. FC is a lot more powerful. It can work with text files to find lines that are different, whereas COMP just reports what characters are different, which is useless once you start adding or removing lines.

CONFIG.SYS — All DOS, Configuration

System configuration file

This file contains configuration commands you can use to customize DOS when it first starts. It contains DOS options as well as commands to load device drivers into memory and to install memory-resident programs into memory. With DOS 6, you can also specify multiple configurations and develop a startup menu.

When and why

You probably won't need to learn about the CONFIG.SYS file and set options with it until you've become reasonably proficient with DOS. This file is automatically created when you use the Setup program to install DOS on your computer, and it contains fairly reasonable default settings. Even if your computer doesn't have a CONFIG.SYS file, DOS chooses reasonable settings for its options.

Every computer that's set up for DOS should have one CONFIG.SYS file. This file is located in the root directory of the disk that you're starting DOS from. So if you boot DOS from your hard disk (drive C:), this file will be located in the C:\ directory.

Syntax

The CONFIG.SYS file can contain any number of lines. Each line can be one of the following:

```
break         drivparm      rem
buffers       fcbs          set
country       files         shell
device        install       stacks
devicehigh    lastdrive     switches
dos           numlock
```

When specifying multiple configurations or a startup menu, the CONFIG.SYS file can also contain any of the following:

```
menuitem      submenu       menucolor
menudefault   include
```

These commands, as well as creating a multiple configuration CONFIG.SYS file, are explained under MENU in this command reference and are discussed under each topic individually.

Notes

No CONFIG.SYS file

If you don't have a CONFIG.SYS file, DOS uses the default values for all the lines that can be in your CONFIG.SYS file. You'll find these defaults in the descriptions of the individual commands.

Using Alt to show additional information

Some of DOS's device drivers display more information if you hold down the Alt key while they're loaded into memory: EMM386 and HIMEM.

Order of lines in CONFIG.SYS

Key Concept: If you've ever wondered which lines in CONFIG.SYS should be in what order, here's your answer. The following lines can be anywhere in your CONFIG.SYS file — the order isn't at all important or relevant (see, however, below about Stacker):

Lines that can be anywhere:

```
break        dos          lastdrive    shell
buffers      fcbs         numlock      stacks
country      files        set          switches
```

The order of the following lines, however, is important:

Lines whose order counts:

`device & devicehigh`	Device drivers are loaded in the same order as these lines appear in the file.
`drivparm`	This line must appear after the device driver that it affects. (You'll probably never use it, but it's nice to know where it should go in case you need it.)
`install`	The INSTALL= lines are processed after all the other lines in your CONFIG.SYS file. Memory-resident programs loaded with install are loaded in the same order as the INSTALL= lines appear in your CONFIG.SYS file.

How DOS processes CONFIG.SYS

Secret DOS: Not many people know that DOS actually makes several passes through your CONFIG.SYS file. This allows DOS to process items in the correct order. Here is the order in which DOS processes the lines in your CONFIG.SYS file:

1. On the first pass DOS looks at each line and remembers the type of information on each line. It doesn't actually process any of the lines, except to make some notes. For example, when DOS sees the DOS=HIGH line in your CONFIG.SYS file, it records that you've provided this line, but the actual work is done later.

2. On the second pass DOS loads all device drivers. These are the lines that start with DEVICE= or DEVICEHIGH=. DOS loads device drivers in the same order that they appear within the CONFIG.SYS file.

   During this second pass, DOS also checks all the BREAK, BUFFERS, STACKS, etc., lines to record the information present on these lines. At the end of this pass, DOS creates all the memory buffers for things like BUFFERS=, STACKS=, etc.

3. Next, DOS goes through the file again and loads all memory-resident programs that you've asked DOS to load using the INSTALL= lines in your CONFIG.SYS file. DOS 6 actually loads the resident part of COMMAND.COM before running any INSTALL= lines. By the way, it's at the end of this pass, after all the device drivers and all the memory-resident programs have been installed, that DOS tries to load itself into the high memory area.

4. At the end of the last pass, DOS starts the command shell, which will be COMMAND.COM unless you specify another name using the SHELL= line. The command shell runs AUTOEXEC.BAT as part of its startup process.

Stepping through CONFIG.SYS and AUTOEXEC.BAT

In DOS 6, you can press the F8 key during the startup process, and DOS will step through each line in your CONFIG.SYS file and, in DOS 6.2 and later, your AUTOEXEC.BAT file. You must press the F8 key while the message `Starting MS-DOS...` appears on your screen.

Skipping the CONFIG.SYS and AUTOEXEC.BAT processing

In DOS 6, you can skip the processing of CONFIG.SYS by pressing the F5 key while the message `Starting MS-DOS . . .` appears on-screen. We still recommend that you create an emergency system disk containing a minimum CONFIG.SYS and AUTOEXEC.BAT for starting your system.

DOS 6.2 also added Ctrl-F5 and Ctrl-F8 key combinations which, in addition to controlling CONFIG.SYS and AUTOEXEC.BAT, bypass the loading of DoubleSpace. Here is a summary of all these keys:

Key	Bypasses DoubleSpace	CONFIG.SYS and AUTOEXEC.BAT
F5	No	Bypasses
Ctrl-F5	Yes	Bypasses (DOS 6.2 and later)
F8	No	Steps through one entry at a time
Ctrl-F8	Yes	Steps through one entry at a time (DOS 6.2 and later)

Stacker and the order of lines

If you're using Stacker, the order of lines in CONFIG.SYS becomes more important because Stacker may swap drive letters on your computer while DOS is still processing CONFIG.SYS. In such cases, you should put the lines that load HIMEM.SYS and EMM386.EXE at the start of CONFIG.SYS with Stacker's DEVICE= lines immediately after:

```
device=c:\dos\himem.sys
device=c:\dos\emm386.exe
device=c:\prog\stacker\stacker.com c:\stackvol.dsk
device=c:\prog\stacker\sswap.com c:\stacvol.dsk /sync
    all other lines in CONFIG.SYS should appear here.
```

Organizing your CONFIG.SYS files this way will ensure that any other lines in CONFIG.SYS that look for files on drive C: will actually be looking on your compressed volume, which is probably where all your DOS files are (Stacker leaves just a few of DOS's files on the *host* drive).

Using INSTALL=

Some programs need to have a DOS environment (as in environment variables, which you set with the SET command) in order to load properly. You could not load such programs with INSTALL= in DOS 5. In DOS 6, however, DOS actually loads the resident portion of COMMAND.COM (using SHELL= if you have such a

CONFIG.SYS

line in CONFIG.SYS) *before* installing any memory-resident programs using INSTALL= lines. Because DOS 6 runs SET commands in CONFIG.SYS *before* installing memory-resident programs, these programs will have access to the environment (except for the COMSPEC environment variable which tells programs where to find COMMAND.COM). The SET command in CONFIG.SYS is also new to DOS 6.

Messages

`Bad or missing C:\DOS\RAMDRIVE`
You'll see a message like this one if you forgot to provide the extension (such as .SYS here) or you have the wrong path for a device driver. While DOS is processing your CONFIG.SYS file, it can't find files or programs unless you supply the correct path and the extension.

`Error in CONFIG.SYS line n`
You'll see this message during the boot process whenever DOS doesn't understand a line in your CONFIG.SYS file. Use the line number *n* to locate the line causing the problem.

Examples

Typical 8088 CONFIG.SYS file

This is an example of a typical CONFIG.SYS file that you'd find on an 8088-class computer.

```
device=c:\dos\ansi.sys
device=c:\dos\setver.exe

buffers=30
files=30
break on

shell=c:\dos\command.com c:\dos\ /p
```

Typical 80286 CONFIG.SYS file

```
device=c:\dos\himem.sys
device=c:\dos\ansi.sys
device=c:\dos\setver.exe
dos=high
buffers=10
files=30
break on

shell=c:\dos\command.com c:\dos\ /p
```

Typical 80386 CONFIG.SYS file

This example shows a typical CONFIG.SYS file on an 80386-class computer.

```
device=c:\dos\himem.sys
device=c:\dos\emm386.exe ram
```

Part II: Command Reference

```
devicehigh=c:\dos\ansi.sys
devicehigh=c:\dos\setver.exe
dos=high,umb
buffers=10
files=30
break on

shell=c:\dos\command.com c:\dos\ /p
```

See also

?   Requires confirmation before processing a line in the CONFIG.SYS file.

; and REM   Allow you to add comment lines to your CONFIG.SYS file.

MENUITEM   Used to develop multiple configuration menus.

SWITCHES   You can use the SWITCHES line in CONFIG.SYS to tell DOS not to pause for 2 seconds when it first starts. This will disable the F5 and F8 keys, unless you've created a CONFIG.SYS menu.

DBLSPACE /SWITCHES
    This command controls whether or not you can use the Ctrl-F5 and Ctrl-F8 keys to bypass loading DoubleSpace as well as either skipping or stepping through CONFIG.SYS and AUTOEXEC.BAT.

COPY

All DOS, Internal

Copy one or more files

This command allows you to make copies of files on your disks. You can copy files between disks and directories, and you can also create a copy that has a different name from the original file.

When and why

Some people never use the COPY command, particularly if they're using a DOS shell such as the Norton Commander or the DOS Shell program. You would use the COPY command if you want to keep around an unchanged copy of the file that you want to work on.

Starting in DOS 6.2, the COPY command is a little safer because it now asks you before it writes over files that already exist (however, this feature doesn't work if you use the COPY command from within any type of DOS shell program).

The combine feature of COPY (along with the /A and /B switches) is a fairly advanced feature that you may never find a use for. We almost never use it ourselves, but it's helpful to know it's there when you need it.

Syntax

copy [/y|-y] [/a|/b] *source* [/a|/b] [*destination* [/a|/b]] [/v]
Copies one file (or a group of files if you use DOS wildcard characters) from source to destination.

copy [/y|-y] [/a|/b] *source* [/a|/b] +*source* [/a|/b] [+...] [*destination* [/a|/b]] [/v]
Combines more than one source file into a single destination file. You can use DOS wildcard characters to combine groups of files.

Parameters

source
The file (or group of files) that you want to copy. If this name includes DOS wildcard characters, it will refer to a group of files. You can also include a drive letter and/or a path in front of the source name.

Note: If you're using + to combine files, and you're also using wildcard characters in some of the names, COPY will copy *all* the files matched by all the filespecs. So if you tell COPY to COPY *.TXT+*.BAK, all the TXT files will be at the start of the combined file, with all the BAK files at the end.

destination
Where to copy the file. This can be a drive or directory name, or it can be the name of a file.

Switches

Note: The meaning of the /A and /B switches depends on their location in the command and can be confusing. When the /A or /B switch appears before all the filenames, it applies to all the files on the command line, which is simple enough. The confusing part is when you place an /A or /B switch *after* a filename. In this case, the /A or /B switch applies to the file immediately before the switch *and* all files after the switch (until the next switch). See the "Examples" section for further details.

Source files

Here is the meaning of the /A and /B switches when applied to source files.

/a
ASCII copy. Use ASCII text copy mode, which copies all the characters in the file up to, but not including, the end-of-file character (Ctrl-Z). Default when combining files.

/b
Binary copy. Use binary copy mode, which copies all the characters in the file (it treats the end-of-file character as just another character to be copied). Default, except for combining files.

Destination file

Here is the meaning of the /A and /B switches when applied to the destination file.

/a
ASCII copy. Add an end-of-file character to the very end of the file.

/b
Binary copy. Don't add an end-of-file character. (Default.)

Option switches

/-y
Prompt before coping over files (DOS 6.2 and later). Tells COPY that it should ask before it overwrites a file that already exists. This is the default setting when you use COPY from the DOS command line. *Note:* You *will not* get an overwrite prompt if you run COPY from within a DOS shell, like the Norton Commander, or from within a batch file. In these two cases you will need to use the /-Y switch if you want to confirm overwriting existing files. You can change the default setting using the COPYCMD environment variable. Default: /-Y from DOS prompt, /Y from DOS shells or batch files.

/y
Overwrite without prompting (DOS 6.2 and later). Tells COPY to copy over existing files without first asking. This switch will override a /-Y switch in the COPYCMD environment variable. Default: /-Y from DOS prompt, /Y from DOS shells or batch files.

/v
Verify. Verify that files are written correctly. This switch tells DOS to read each block of a file as it's written to make sure the data can be read. *Note:* This doesn't check that the data read is, in fact, the same as the data you wrote. It does, however, slow down COPY a little (around 30 percent). See the VERIFY command for more details.

Notes

Date and time of new file

When you copy a file, DOS uses the same creation time and date on the copy as on the original file.

You can change the date of a file by putting "+,," after the filename. For example, COPY FILE1+,,. The commas mark the end of the source and destination parameter. Without these commas, COPY will report that it can't copy a file to itself.

Archive attribute

DOS sets the archive attribute on new files that it creates so a backup program will correctly back up new files.

End-of-file mark

DOS has two different ways to determine the length of a file. The one you're probably familiar with is the size of the file as indicated by the directory. But DOS sometimes uses another method — it looks for a character called the end-of-file character, which marks the end of the file. This character is a Ctrl-Z (decimal 26).

Combining files into one file

If you use DOS wildcard characters in the source that match more than one file, but the destination is the name of a single file (no wildcard characters), DOS will copy all the source files into a single file (which is the same as using the + character to combine files). For example, COPY *.TXT JKL will create a single file called JKL that contains the contents of all the TXT files in the current directory.

One thing you should be aware of, however, is that COPY may not copy all of each file in such cases. This is because COPY uses the /A switch by default when you're combining files because it assumes you'd only want to combine text files (the default copy mode when you're not combining files is /B).

Zero-length files
COPY doesn't copy files that have a length of zero. Use XCOPY to copy these files as well.

Messages

`Cannot do binary reads from a device`
You can't use the /B switch when the source is the name of a device, such as CON or AUX. Omit the /B switch and try again.

`Content of destination lost before copy`
You'll see this message whenever you're combining files and one of the files you're copying is also the destination file. For example, if you type **COPY FILE1+FILE2 FILE2**, COPY will copy FILE1 into FILE2 (overwriting its contents) before it tries to copy FILE2. When you see this message, you've already lost the original contents of the destination file, so be careful when combining files.

`File cannot be copied onto itself`
You've tried to copy a file onto itself. Make sure you provide a different name for the destination and try again.

`Invalid directory`
This can mean a couple of things. First of all, it can mean that you've typed a \ at the end of the pathname. DOS doesn't allow a pathname to be followed by a \ unless there is a filename after the path. You'll also see this if the pathname doesn't exist (which might mean that you mistyped the name).

Examples

Creating quick text files
Since COPY can copy from the keyboard (using the CON: device) to a file, you can create a file quickly by typing

```
C:\>copy con: file.txt
```

When you're done, press Ctrl-Z followed by Enter.

Printing files
An easy way to print a file (although without much control) is to copy a file to the printer device, which can be PRN, LPT1, LPT2, etc.:

```
C:\>copy file.txt prn
```

To other disks
If you want to copy a file to another disk, such as to a floppy disk, you can just provide the name of the disk drive as the destination:

```
C:\>copy file.txt a:
```

This copies the file FILE.TXT to the disk in drive A:.

To other directories
If you want to copy files to another directory, you can provide just the name of a path as the destination for the copy:

```
C:\>copy file.txt d:\writing\books
```

Notice that you don't write a \ at the end of the path.

Changing the name
You also have the option to change the name of a file as you copy it. For example, the following command will create a new copy of the file FILE.TXT called NEWFILE.TXT and store the new copy on a different drive and in a different directory:

```
C:\>copy file.txt d:\writing\books\newfile.txt
```

Confirming copying over existing files
Often, you may want COPY to ask before it copies files on top of existing files. To do this, you can use the /-Y switch:

```
C:\>copy file.txt d:\writing\books\newfile.txt
Overwrite d:\writing\books\newfile.txt (Yes/No/All)?
```

At this point you can press Y, N, or A followed by the Enter key. All means that COPY will copy any other files that match wildcard characters in a name without asking if you want to overwrite existing files.

Using the COPYCMD environment variable
You can set the COPYCMD environment variable so that COPY will always ask you before overwriting existing files (this environment variable also affects the MOVE and XCOPY commands). Here is the SET command you would place in your AUTOEXEC.BAT file to set up such an environment variable:

```
set copycmd=/-y
```

After you have this switch set, you can copy a file without COPY asking for confirmation by using the /Y switch:

```
C:\>copy /y file.txt d:\writing\books\newfile.txt
```

The /A and /B switches
Here is an example that shows you how COPY treats the /A and /B switches:

```
C:\>copy /b file1 + file2 /a + file3 newfile
```

The first /B switch tells COPY to copy all the following files in binary mode (copy all the characters in the file), which means that FILE1 will be copied to NEWFILE in its entirety. The /A switch after FILE2, however, tells COPY to switch to ASCII mode (copy only the characters up to the Ctrl-Z at the end of the file) for FILE2 and FILE3. Note that this /A doesn't apply to NEWFILE — you need to add an /A if you want COPY to add an end-of-file mark to the file.

See also

DISKCOPY	This command allows you to copy an entire floppy disk. This is the best way to create an exact copy of a floppy disk.
REPLACE	If you want to copy only files that exist in another directory and are more recent, this is a good command to use instead of COPY.
VERIFY	This command allows you to control whether or not DOS verifies that files being written can be read and provides functionality like the /V switch for other commands (not just COPY).
XCOPY	For copying all the files in a directory, as well as subdirectories, use XCOPY instead of COPY.

COUNTRY   DOS 3 and later, CONFIG.SYS

Set active country

DOS uses the current country setting to control its display of dates, times, numbers, currency, and in case conversions. Other programs also use this information.

When and why

If you're using a computer in the U.S., you won't need to use this command at all. This option allows DOS to support things such as time and date formats used in other countries. If, on the other hand, you're using DOS in another country, you might want to change the country code so the dates and times will be displayed using that country's formats.

Syntax

country=*nnn* [,[*code-page*] [,*filespec*]]   (DOS 3.3 and later)

Sets the country code for the date and time (etc.) formatting that DOS should support.

Parameters

nnn

The country code is a three-digit number that is usually the international long-distance telephone code for each country. See the table in the "Notes" section.

code-page

(DOS 3.3 and later.) The default code page (alternate character set) of the display adapter you're using. This tells DOS which code page to use for case conversions.

If you want to use a code page other than the default, you'll need to use CHCP or MODE to change the display's code page. In such cases, the case conversion tables will be changed by CHCP and MODE.

filespec

(DOS 3.3 and later.) DOS needs to know where to find the file that contains country-specific information, which is usually in a file called COUNTRY.SYS (if you don't specify a filespec, DOS looks for this file in the root directory). This file will usually be in your C:\DOS directory, in which case you'll want to provide C:\DOS\COUNTRY.SYS for this filespec.

The COUNTRY.SYS file is rather large because, among other information, it includes case-conversion tables for all the different languages. (For example, in Germany you need to be able to convert the lowercase ü to the uppercase Ü.)

Notes

What COUNTRY sets

Here is a list of what the country code affects:

- The date and time formats, both for display and for input. Input affects commands such as DATE, TIME, BACKUP, RESTORE, and XCOPY.
- The symbol used for currency and the location of this symbol (either before or after the number).
- The format for numbers: the character used to separate thousands (a comma in the U.S.) and the decimal character (a period in the U.S.).
- Case conversions: DOS provides a table to convert between lower- and uppercase letters based on the country code being used.
- (DOS 3.3 and later.) Sort order used to alphabetize filenames. This allows characters such as u and ü to be sorted together.

DOS commands affected

The country code specifies the time and date formats that are used by the following DOS commands: BACKUP, DATE, DIR, DOSSHELL, PROMPT, RESTORE, TIME, XCOPY.

Code pages

The subject of code pages is a little confusing, and you'll find a full discussion in the description of the CHCP command. In general, it's best to leave out the code page and let DOS figure out what it should be.

There is one aspect of the COUNTRY command and code pages that we will cover here, which is the issue of default code pages. The hardware itself has a default code page, which in most countries is 437. Here are the default hardware code pages for other countries: 860 for Portugal, 863 for French Canada, 865 for Norway/Denmark, and 852 for all the Slavic countries (Czech Republic, Slovakia, Hungary, Poland, and Serbia/Yugoslavia).

When DOS uses a default code page other than 437 (which is usually 850 except for the countries listed above), it doesn't actually load the code page into the display adapter if the code page is different from the hardware's code page — you still have to use the MODE CP PREP command to load the code page.

Countries and languages

Here is a table that shows all the country codes supported by MS-DOS, along with a list of code pages supported for each country (or language). The last column shows which versions of DOS support the country code; blanks in this column mean that all versions of DOS 2.1 and later support that country.

COUNTRY

Country	Country code	Default code page	Alternate code page	Date format	Time format	DOS version
Australia	061	437	850	dd-mm-yyyy	6:24:00p	
Belgium	032	850	437	dd/mm/yyyy	18:24:00	
Brazil	055	850	437	dd/mm/yyyy	18:24:00	5.0 +
French Canada	002	863	850	yyyy-mm-dd	18:24:00	3.3 +
Croatia	038	852	850	yyyy-mm-dd	18:24:00	6.0 +
Czech Republic	042	852	850	yyyy-mm-dd	18:24:00	5.0 +
Denmark	045	850	865	dd-mm-yyyy	18.24.00	
Finland	358	850	437	dd.mm.yyyy	18.24.00	
France	033	850	437	dd.mm.yyyy	18:24:00	
Germany	049	850	437	dd.mm.yyyy	18:24:00	
Hungary	036	852	850	yyyy-mm-dd	18:24:00	5.0 +
International English	061	437	850	dd/mm/yyyy	18:24:00	
Italy	039	850	437	dd/mm/yyyy	18.24.00	
Latin America	003	850	437	dd/mm/yyyy	6:24:00p	3.3 +
Netherlands	031	850	437	dd-mm-yyyy	18:24:00	
Norway	047	850	865	dd.mm.yyyy	18:24:00	
Poland	048	852	850	yyyy-mm-dd	18:24:00	5.0 +
Portugal	351	850	860	dd-mm-yyyy	18:24:00	3.3 +
Serbia/Yugoslavia	038	852	850	yyyy-mm-dd	18.24.00	6.0 +
Slovakia	042	852	850	yyyy-mm-dd	18:24:00	6.0 +
Slovenia	038	852	850	yyyy-mm-dd	18.24.00	6.0 +
Spain	034	850	437	dd/mm/yyyy	18.24.00	
Sweden	046	850	437	yyyy-mm-dd	18.24,00	
Switzerland	041	850	437	dd.mm.yyyy	18,24,00	
United Kingdom	044	437	850	dd/mm/yyyy	18.24.00	
U.S.	001	437	850	mm/dd/yyyy	6:24:00p	
Yugoslavia	038	852	850	yyyy-mm-dd	18.24.00	5.0 only

Note: There are special versions of DOS 5 and 6 that support Arabic, Hebrew, Japan, Korea, the People's Republic of China, and Taiwan.

Note: Because of changes in the borders of several countries, Microsoft has add and/or changed names for several countries: Czechoslovakia is now the Czech Republic and Slovakia; Yugoslavia is now Serbia/Yugoslavia, Slovenia, and Croatia. None of these new names have new country codes, just new entries in this table.

Examples

To convert the dates, times, and case conversion to German, put the following line in your CONFIG.SYS file:

`country=049,,c:\dos\country.sys`

This sets the country code to 049, uses DOS's default code page (437 for our U.S. version of MS-DOS), and looks for the country information in the C:\DOS\COUNTRY.SYS file.

See also

There are two groups of commands that you'll want to check out in addition to the COUNTRY command. First, if you're not interested in code pages (alternate character sets), there is only one other relevant command:

KEYB   Allows you to change the mapping of the keyboard for computers with country-specific keyboards. In Germany, for example, the Z and Y keys are swapped so the Z is between the T and U keys.

Part II: Command Reference

Code pages
The next group of commands are all related to code pages, which are alternate sets of characters that you may need to install. See the description of the CHCP command for details on how to use all these commands together.

CHCP Sets the active code page. You'll need to use this command if you use a code page different from your hardware's default.

DISPLAY.SYS Supports code-page switching for the display. You'll need this if you want to change the character set used on your screen.

MODE CP Allows you to load code pages into memory and change between code pages. It's better, though, to use CHCP to change code pages after you've used MODE to load the code page.

NLSFUNC Allows you to change the code page for more than one device (such as the keyboard and the display) at the same time. You'll need to install this before you use CHCP to set the active code page.

PRINTER.SYS Supports code-page switching for some IBM printers. You'll need this if you want to change the character set used on your printer.

CTTY All DOS, External

Change input/output device
This command allows you to change the console device from the normal keyboard and display to an external device, such as a computer terminal.

When and why
You'll probably never use this command. We know of only one common use for this command: File transfer programs, such as LapLink, use this command to control a second computer, which allows them to transfer a copy of themselves to another computer over a serial cable.

Syntax
ctty *device*

Parameters
device
The device that you want to use for console input and output. It can be any of the following devices:

PRN, LPT1, LPT2, LPT3, CON, AUX, COM1, COM2, COM3, COM4

Note: To change back to your computer's keyboard and screen, you'll have to issue the CTTY CON command from the new device (such as a terminal).

Notes

Full-screen programs
Most full-screen programs bypass DOS both to read from the keyboard and to write to the screen. As such, you won't be able to control or see the output of such programs from a remote device. This is one of the reasons the CTTY command isn't very useful.

Example
If you have a terminal attached to COM1 that is set up at a communications rate of 9600 baud, you would use these commands to control your computer from the serial port:

```
C:\>mode com1:9600,n,8,1,p
C:\>ctty com1
```

When you're done using the terminal, you'll have to issue this command from the terminal's keyboard to return control to your computer's keyboard:

```
C:\>ctty con
```

See also
COMMAND   You can also specify a device to use in place of CON when you start a second copy of the command-line processor.

MODE   MODE allows you to set up a serial port, which you'll want to do before you use the CTTY command.

DATE   All DOS, Internal

Report or set the date
This command displays the current date and allows you to change the date.

When and why
You'll want to make sure your computer's date and time are correct because DOS uses this date and time when it creates a new file (and programs such as BACKUP use this date and time information). If your computer doesn't seem to remember the date and time after you've turned it off, you'll need to read the following "Notes" section. You may also need to change your laptop's date if you travel across the international date line.

Syntax
date
Without any parameters, DATE displays the current date and prompts you to enter a new date. You can press Enter if you don't want to change the date.

date *mm-dd-yy*
Sets the current date.

Parameters

mm-dd-yy
The new date to use. The format that you use here actually depends on the country setting in your CONFIG.SYS file. If you're not sure what format to use, leave this parameter out and DATE will prompt you for the date and tell you what format it expects.

mm	Month	1 – 12
dd	Day	1 – 31
yy	Year	80 – 99 for the years 1980 – 1999 or 1980 – 2099 (allowed in DOS 3.0 and later)

You must separate the month, day, and year with periods (.), hyphens (-), or slash marks (/).

Notes

Number of days in a month
DOS knows the correct number of days in each month. So if you tell DOS to set the date to 6-31-91, it will display an error message because it knows that June only has 30 days.

Clock forgets date
If you leave your computer on when you leave on Friday, you may discover on Monday that DOS thinks it's still Saturday. As it turns out, DOS doesn't get the time from the clock built into your computer. Instead, it keeps tracks of system timer ticks since midnight. When the time passes midnight, a flag indicates that the day changed. This flag won't be checked until a program asks for the current time. So if more than one day has elapsed since a program asked for the time, DOS won't know that more than one day has passed.

Clock forgets date and time
If you have to reset your clock's date and time each time you start DOS, there are three things that could create this situation. First, your computer may not have a battery-backed clock that remembers the date and time with the power off (see the next note).

Second, the battery used to save the current date and time may have used up its charge. You'll need to get the battery replaced.

And finally, if you're using DOS 3.3 or earlier, the DATE and TIME commands don't actually change the time in the battery-backed clock — they only change DOS's date and time for the current session. In this case you'll need to run the Diagnostic program on the Utilities disk that came with your computer to change the internal clock's date and time.

Original IBM PC
The original IBM PC didn't have a built-in clock that would keep ticking with the power off, so you had to set the date and time each time you restarted your computer. If you're using such a computer, you'll need to run DATE and TIME in your AUTOEXEC.BAT file to set the clock each time you start DOS.

AUTOEXEC.BAT and DATE
If you don't have an AUTOEXEC.BAT file on your system, DOS will automatically run both DATE and TIME. Otherwise, DOS won't run either.

Messages
```
Invalid date
Enter new date (mm-dd-yy): _
```
You'll probably see this message when you've entered a day that doesn't exist in the month you've entered. For example, 6-31-91 isn't a valid date because June only has 30 days. You may also have entered the month and day in the wrong order (in some countries the day appears before the month in dates).

Examples
Setting a new date
Here is how you would set the current date to a different date:

```
C:\>date 6-17-91
```

This command sets the date to June 17, 1991 (for the U.S. version of DOS).

Letting DATE prompt you
If you type **DATE** without a parameter, the DATE command displays the current date and asks you to type in a new date:

```
C:\>date
Current date is Mon 06-17-1991
Enter new date (mm-dd-yy): _
```

At this point you can enter a new date or press Enter to keep the current date. Notice that DATE shows you what format to use when you enter a new date.

See also
COUNTRY   The date format is affected by the current setting of the COUNTRY= line in your CONFIG.SYS file.

TIME   The companion command for setting the current time.

DBLSPACE   DOS 6 and later, External

Access DoubleSpace program
This program allows you to compress existing disks and to create new compressed volumes. Once you have compressed volumes, DBLSPACE allows you to manage these compressed volumes and to create new compressed volumes. DBLSPACE has both a full-screen and a command-line interface for managing compressed volumes.

When and why
You'll want to run DLBSPACE whenever you want to create new compressed disks, whether they be hard or floppy disks, or manage existing compressed disks. Compressed disks, which are called *compressed volumes*, typically hold about twice as much data as an uncompressed disk, which is why this feature in DOS 6 is called DoubleSpace. Once you compress a disk, or use part of a disk to create a new compressed volume, these disks will behave just like any other disk drive. So in a sense, you're doubling your storage space almost for free. We say almost because disk reads and writes may be slightly slower (on 80286 computers). On the other hand, reads and writes may not be slower (on 80386 or later computers). Our own experience is that most people don't notice any change in their computer's speed either way after they compress their disks (DLBSPACE uses code that is much faster if you have an 80386 or later microprocessor).

The DBLSPACE program has two interfaces: the command-line interface and a full-screen interface. In this Command Reference we describe the command-line interface which provides a much easier way to use any of the command-line options, so we suggest you use the full-screen interface. In any case, you'll find that the descriptions of the command-line options will give you a good understanding of how to use the full-screen equivalents. Each DBLSPACE command has its own entry in this Command Reference, in alphabetical order.

Syntax
dblspace
Launches the full-screen interface to DoubleSpace, which is the easiest way to use DBLSPACE.

dlbspace /*command*
Runs a single DBLSPACE command. This is the command-line interface to DoubleSpace. You will find descriptions of all the commands in alphabetical order on the following pages.

Switches
Note: Each switch acts as a separate command, and you'll find descriptions of all these commands in individual entries in this Command Reference. They're listed in alphabetical order after the main command. Here is a list of all these commands, as well as a brief description:

/chkdsk	Looks for and fixes errors in a compressed volume. Replaced in DOS 6.2 by ScanDisk.
/compress	Compresses a disk, which creates a new compressed volume.
/create	Creates a new compressed drive, using free space on an uncompressed drive.
/defragment	Defragments a compressed volume, which you will need to do if you want to reduce the size of a compressed volume.
/delete	Removes a compressed volume. You will lose any files still in the compressed volume when you delete it.

/format	Formats a compressed volume. You probably won't want to use this command since it will erase everything contained in the compressed volume.
/info	Displays information about a compressed volume.
/list	Lists all of the drives on your computer (except for network drives) with a short description of the drive.
/mount	Allows you to "attach to" compressed volumes that are on removable disks, such as floppy disks and removable hard disks.
/ratio	Changes the estimated compression ratio for a compressed volume. This starts at 2:1, but you can change it to reflect the actual compression ratio for the files in the volume. You'll rarely need to use this because DoubleSpace adjusts the ratio each time you start your computer.
/size	Enlarges or reduces the size of a compressed volume.
/uncompress	(DOS 6.2 and later.) Uncompresses a drive that you compress with DoubleSpace. This will move all your files back to the uncompressed host volume and remove the compressed volume file.
/unmount	Disconnects a compressed volume so it will not be visible (until you mount it again). This is primarily useful with floppy disks and removable hard disks.

DBLSPACE.INI switches

The following switches all change settings in the DBLSPACE.INI file (a hidden/system/read-only file located in the root directory of the host drive), which controls how DoubleSpace works once it's loaded. These change are checked only when DOS first starts, so you'll need to restart your computer before any of these changes take affect.

Each switch acts as a separate command, and you'll find descriptions of all these commands in individual entries in this Command Reference. They're listed in alphabetical order after the main command. Here is a list of all these commands, as well as a brief description:

/automount	(DOS 6.2 and later.) Allows you to determine whether DOS will automatically mount floppy disks that have been compressed with DoubleSpace.
/doubleguard	(DOS 6.2 and later.) Turns the DoubleGuard feature on and off. DoubleGuard checks DoubleSpace's memory for damage created by other programs for additional safety.
/host	(DOS 6.2 and later.) Allows you to change the drive letter of the host (uncompressed) drive.
/lastdrive	(DOS 6.2 and later.) Similar to the LASTDRIVE command in CONFIG.SYS. Allows you to set the last drive letter that DoubleSpace will use.
/maxfilefragments	(DOS 6.2 and later.) Sets a limit on the maximum number of fragments allowed for a compressed volume file.

Part II: Command Reference

/maxremovabledrives	(DOS 6.2 and later) Sets the maximum number of DoubleSpace volumes that DoubleSpace can mount (in addition to the startup drive if that is a DoubleSpace drive).
/romserver	(DOS 6.2 and later.) Allows your computer to use disk compression services provided by your computer, if available, for faster DoubleSpace access.
/switches	(DOS 6.2 and later.) Determines whether or not you can use the Ctrl-F5 and Ctrl-F8 keys to bypass loading DoubleSpace.

Notes

Incompatibilities

You should not use programs like WipeInfo that wipe out the contents of a file since these programs can cause lost allocation units on a DoubleSpace volume.

Running DBLSPACE the first time

The first time you run DLBSPACE it asks you if you want to set up DoubleSpace, which will create a compressed volume and add a line to your CONFIG.SYS file that loads DBLSPACE.SYS (whose sole purpose is to control where DBLSPACE.BIN will end up in memory). You will be asked if you want to do an Express Setup or a Custom Setup. Custom Setup gives you the most control over DLBSPACE, and this is the option you want to choose if you want to create a new compressed volume using only space that is free on an existing disk, as opposed to compressing an existing disk, or if you want to compress a floppy disk. The Express Setup option will compress your boot disk, which is normally drive C.

Compressing an existing disk

When you compress an entire disk, DBLSPACE scans the disk looking for a Windows swapfile and to see how much disk space you have free. Since Windows swapfiles must be on uncompressed volumes, DBLSPACE reserves space for the existing swapfile plus a little extra (the default is 2MB) for other files on the uncompressed part of the disk. DLBSPACE uses all the space left over for your compressed volume. DoubleSpace then creates the compressed volume and begins copying files from the uncompressed portion of the disk into the compressed volume. As each file is copied into the compressed volume, it is deleted from the host. When DBLSPACE finishes compressing the disk, it assigns the original drive letter (such as C) to the compressed volume, and the physical hard disk (which contains the hidden DBLSPACE.*nnn* file) will be assigned a new drive letter, such as H.

The size of compressed volumes

The size of a compressed volume can actually change over time as you add and remove data. Here's what happens. DoubleSpace doesn't actually change the size of anything. Instead, it changes the number that it reports to DOS as the total size of the compressed volume. It changes the volume size so that DOS will see the amount of space that is currently being used, as well as the amount of space that is free. The free space, and therefore the total volume size, depends on how well DoubleSpace can compress the data stored in the compressed volume.

DBLSPACE

For example, let's say you used 5MB of real disk space to create a 10MB compressed volume (DoubleSpace initially assumes you'll get a 2 to 1 compression ratio). Then let's say you copy 6MB of data into this compressed volume and that it compressed at only 1.5 to 1. This means the 6MB of files will consume 6MB / 1.5 = 4MB of real disk space, leaving 1MB of real disk space free. If you assume that the compression ratio is 2 to 1 for any new data you write to this compressed volume, that would mean you would have 2MB of space still free. In other words, DoubleSpace will report to DOS that your compressed volume is now 8MB (calculated from 6MB used + 2MB free) rather than the original 10MB.

Compressing floppy disks

If you're using DOS 6.2 or later, DOS will automatically mount a compressed floppy disk when you try to use it, unless you've turned this feature off with DBLSPACE /AUTOMOUNT. In DOS 6.0, you must use the DBLSPACE /MOUNT command to mount a floppy disk manually.

You must use the DBLSPACE /COMPRESS command to compress a floppy disk. After compression, the disk will contain a file named READTHIS.TXT. This file contains a message indicating that the disk contains a DoubleSpace volume; it must be mounted using DLBSPACE /MOUNT in order to access files within the volume.

DoubleSpace volumes and Windows

You can access DoubleSpace volumes from within Windows, but you must mount the volume before starting Windows. (In DOS 6.2 and later, compressed removable volumes will be mounted automatically when you try to read from them, even in Windows.) None of the DoubleSpace commands are available from within the Windows environment. (*Note:* There is a special DoubleSpace Info command on the Tools menu with the Windows 3.1 File Manager.)

DoubleSpace and Windows swapfiles

The Windows swapfile must reside on an uncompressed volume. When you use DBLSPACE to compress an existing volume, it will automatically reserve enough room for the Windows swapfile.

Compressed volumes and host drives

Each DoubleSpace volume actually exists as a special file, which is called DBLSPACE.*nnn* and is marked as being hidden, system, and read-only to make sure you don't delete it by accident. The disk containing the actual DoubleSpace file is called the *host drive*. One host disk may contain several DoubleSpace volumes. Each volume would be an individual file on the disk.

DoubleSpace and LASTDRIVE

You don't actually have to use the LASTDRIVE= line in CONFIG.SYS because INTERLNK creates its own drive letters and completely ignores the LASTDRIVE= setting.

CVF

CVF stands for Compressed Volume File and is the term used to refer to the file which resides on the host drive. The CVF contains the information for the compressed volume. Normally, this file is hidden and protected by the read-only and system attributes.

Specifying a drive letter

If you specify a drive letter, DOS assumes that you want DoubleSpace information about that drive. Therefore, the command

```
C:\>dblspace a:
```

is the same as

```
C:\>dblspace /info a:
```

Compression ratios for small files

DoubleSpace will always report a compression ratio for very small files (512 bytes and less) of 16:1, and it will report an 8:1 compression ratio for slightly larger files. Is DoubleSpace really compressing small files more efficiently? No. Whenever DOS saves a file, it allocates a chunk of disk space to a file, which is called an *allocation unit*. Allocation units on hard disks are typically between 2,048 and 4,096 (although they can be smaller and larger than this). When you save a file with just a few bytes in it, most of this allocation unit will be unused. This unused space is called *slack*. DoubleSpace, on the other hand, allocates individual sectors (512 bytes) to files, so for small files, DoubleSpace makes much better use of your space than DOS can. This better use of space by DoubleSpace is exactly what leads to the high compression ratios for small files: DoubleSpace calculates compression ratios by comparing the size of allocation units on a CVF (8,192 bytes) to the number of sectors used by the file (one for small files), which gives a compression ratio of 16:1 for very small files. The bottom line is that DoubleSpace doesn't compress the data this much, but it does save disk space by having much less slack at the end of a file.

Technical notes

Booting from a compressed volume

If you boot from a disk containing a compressed volume, DBLSPACE automatically loads the DBLSPACE.BIN file into memory and then mounts the compressed volume. The configuration files used to start your system are then read from the compressed volume. The setup information is in a hidden, system, read-only file called DBLSPACE.INI.

Uncompressing a disk

DOS 6.2 now has a command to uncompress a volume, which is DBLSPACE /UNCOMPRESS. If you're using DOS 6.0, you can either upgrade to DOS 6.2 if you want to uncompress a volume, or you can use the following steps.

There are several steps you'll have to follow if you want to uncompress a volume. Because DBLSPACE doesn't provide an uncompress command, you'll want to begin by moving all the files inside your volume to another volume or disk drive. If you want to move the files to your host drive, you may not have enough room to move all the files. In this case, you can reduce the size of your compressed volume and free up space on your host drive using DBLSPACE /DEFRAGMENT followed by DBLSPACE /SIZE. Since this is a slow process, you'll only want to reduce your compressed volume when you run out of space on your host disk. Of course, if your host disk is smaller than the compressed volume, you'll need to either delete some of your files or move them to another disk. When you've removed all the files from your compressed volume, you can use DBLSPACE /DEL to remove the compressed volume.

Uncompressing your system disk

DOS 6.2 now has a command to uncompress a volume, including the startup disk, which is DBLSPACE /UNCOMPRESS. If you're using DOS 6.0, you can either upgrade to DOS 6.2 if you want to uncompress a volume, or you can use the following steps.

Because you can't delete a compressed volume that you booted from, you'll need to boot from a floppy disk if you want to remove a compressed volume that you were using as drive C:.

Compression ratios for small files

You'll sometimes see very high compression ratios such as 16:1 and 8:1 for very small files. As it turns out, these compression ratios aren't real compression ratios. For example, let's look at what happens when you compress a file with 512 bytes of data. In this case, DoubleSpace will compress this data so it takes less than 512 bytes to store, but since DoubleSpace stores data in segments (each 512 bytes), this file will never take up less than 512 bytes inside the CVF. When DoubleSpace calculates the compression ratio of a file, it looks at how much space the file actually uses inside the CVF (512 bytes) *vs* the size of the file user's allocation units (which are 8,129 bytes in the CVF). If you divide 8,192 by 512, you get a ratio of 16:1, which is exactly the compression ratio that DoubleSpace reports for any file of 512 bytes or less — always! The idea is that since you don't have to save the slack space at the end of the allocation unit, you have a net gain in disk usage: In other words, your file has been compressed. In reality, most hard disks have allocation unit size between 2,048 and 4,096 in size, rather than 8,192, so your real savings in disk space for very small files is more like 4:1 to 8:1.

Messages

```
You are running the MS-DOS Shell. To run DoubleSpace, you must
first quit the MS-DOS Shell.
```
DoubleSpace refuses to let you do anything while you have the DOS Shell running, which means you must exit from the DOS Shell to mount and unmount volumes or to do any type of volume management.

```
You are running Windows. To run DoubleSpace, you must first quit
Windows.
```
DoubleSpace refuses to let you do anything while you have Windows running. You'll have to quit Windows before you can mount or unmount any volumes.

See also

CHKDSK	Checks both the DOS level directory structure and DoubleSpace's internal structure. Since CHKDSK will call DBLSPACE /CHKDSK, it's best to use CHKDSK rather than DLBSPACE /CHKDSK alone.
DBLSPACE /CHKDSK	Checks a compressed volume for errors. We suggest you use CHKDSK instead in DOS 6.0. Use ScanDisk in DOS 6.2 and later.
DBLSPACE /COMPRESS	Compresses a disk and moves the files to the new DoubleSpace volume.

Part II: Command Reference

DBLSPACE /CREATE	Creates a new DoubleSpace volume on a disk.
DBLSPACE /DEFRAGMENT	Consolidates information on a DoubleSpace volume.
DBLSPACE /DELETE	Deletes a DoubleSpace volume.
DBLSPACE /FORMAT	Formats a DoubleSpace volume.
DBLSPACE /INFO	Displays information about a DoubleSpace volume.
DBLSPACE /LIST	Lists all available drives and volumes.
DBLSPACE /MOUNT	Permits access to a DoubleSpace volume.
DBLSPACE /RATIO	Changes the compression ratio used to estimate free space.
DBLSPACE /SIZE	Changes the size of an existing DoubleSpace volume.
DBLSPACE /UNCOMPRESS	Uncompresses a DoubleSpace volume, moving all files to the host volume and deleting the compressed volume file.
DBLSPACE /UNMOUNT	Releases a DoubleSpace volume.
DBLSPACE.SYS	Relocates DBLSPACE.BIN with this device driver.
DIR /C	You can find out the compression ratio for individual files using the /C switch on the DIR command.
LASTDRIVE	Controls which drive letters are available for use by DoubleSpace.

DBLSPACE /AUTOMOUNT   DOS 6.2 and later, External

Controls automatic mounting of compressed floppy disks

This command allows you to turn on or off the automatic mounting of DoubleSpace removable disks (such as floppy disks). After you change this setting, you'll need to restart your computer for it to take effect.

When and why

Probably the only reason you'd want to turn off this option is to save memory. The automatic mounting feature uses about 4K of memory.

The way this feature works is really quite simple. Whenever you insert a compressed floppy disk and try to read or write that floppy disk, DoubleSpace will automatically mount the floppy disk for you (even if you're running Windows). As long as this feature is turned on, you'll never need to manually mount or unmount a DoubleSpace volume.

Syntax

dblspace /automount=0|1|A..Z

Determines whether DoubleSpace will try to automatically mount removable disks (such as floppy disks) whenever you try to read from them. Default: 1.

Parameters

0
Automounting off. Turns off automatic mounting of any removable disk, which saves about 4K of memory.

1
Automounting on. Turns on automatic mounting of all removable disks, which uses about 4K of memory. Default: On.

A..Z
Automount some drives. Tells DoubleSpace to automatically mount disks only on the drive letters that you provide. This must be a list of drive letters with no space between the letters, such as AB to provide automounting only on drives A and B.

Notes
You must restart your computer before changes you make to AutoMount take effect.

See also
DBLSPACE   See this command for an overview of the DBLSPACE command options.

DBLSPACE /CHKDSK
DOS 6.0, External

Checks a compressed volume for errors

This command is the DoubleSpace equivalent of the CHKDSK command. Because the DoubleSpace volume is actually stored as a file on the host drive, DoubleSpace has its own list of checks it needs to perform on DoubleSpace volumes. When you run the standard CHKDSK command on a compressed volume, CHKDSK will do its checking of the FAT and directory structures, and then it will run DBLSPACE /CHKDSK to check the compressed volume's internal structures. You can use the standard CHKDSK command to check the integrity of the entire DoubleSpace volume.

DOS 6.2: This command has been replaced by the ScanDisk command in DOS 6.2 and later.

When and why
If you begin to experience trouble using the files on your DoubleSpace volume, or if you suspect that there might be a problem, run CHKDSK, which will also run DBLSPACE/CHKDSK. We recommend that you run CHKDSK without the /F switch first to see if errors exist. Then, if you want CHKDSK or DBLSPACE to attempt to correct the errors, run the command again with the /F option.

Full-screen access
Alt+T, C
When you run DLBSPACE without any parameters, this key combination will select Chkdsk... from the Tools menu. If you have more than one compressed volume, you'll need to use the arrow keys to select the volume you want to check before you select this command. You'll then see a dialog box that allows you to either Fix or Check a compressed volume.

Part II: Command Reference

Syntax
dblspace /chkdsk [/f] [*drive*:]
or
dblspace /chk [/f] [*drive*:]
Checks a compressed volume for any internal problems and allows you to correct them.

Switches
/f
Fix Errors. This switch tells DBLSPACE to attempt to correct any errors that it detects.

Parameters
drive
The drive letter that you want DBLSPACE to check (the trailing colon is optional). This must be a drive letter that refers to a compressed volume.

Notes
If you don't specify a drive, DBLSPACE checks the current volume.

Messages
```
Drive d is not a compressed drive.
```
You'll see this message when you provide a drive letter that refers to an uncompressed volume. The DBLSPACE /LIST command will tell you which drive letters refer to compressed drives and which drive letters refer to uncompressed drives.

See also
DBLSPACE	See this command for an overview of the DBLSPACE command options.
DLBSPACE /LIST	This command will tell you which drive letters refer to compressed volumes.
CHKDSK	Checks for errors in the DOS directory and FAT structures, which appear on all disks, including compressed disks. Use ScanDisk instead of CHKDSK if you have DOS 6.2 or later.
ScanDisk	This command replaces the DBLSPACE /CHKDSK command in DOS 6.2 and later, as well as the CHKDSK command.

DBLSPACE /COMPRESS — DOS 6 and later, External

Compress a disk
Generally, you use this command to compress a floppy disk to increase its storage capacity. You can also use it to compress a second hard disk on your computer when you have more than one hard disk. This command preserves all your files and gives you more free space.

DBLSPACE/COMPRESS

When and why
You'll want to use this command whenever you need more space on a hard or floppy disk. Compressing a disk drive will retain all your files and give you more space for new files. Usually, you'll end up with about twice as much total disk space as you started with (the actual number will vary with use) and perhaps as much free disk space as the previous size of your entire disk. In other words, compressing a disk is like getting a new disk drive for free.

If you just want to convert unused space on a disk drive to a compressed volume, you'll want to use the DBLSPACE /CREATE command instead of this one.

Full-screen access
Alt-C, E
When you run DLBSPACE without any parameters, this key combination pulls down the Compress menu and selects Existing drive..., which allows you to compress a disk drive, preserving all the files currently on the disk.

Syntax
dblspace /compress *drive*: [/**newdrive**=*host*] [/**reserve**=*size*] [/**f**]
or
dblspace /com *drive*: [/**new**=*host*] [/**res**=*size*] [/**f**]
Creates a new compressed volume by compressing all the files on an uncompressed hard or floppy disk.

Switches
/f
Eliminate final screen (DOS 6.2 and later). This switch tells DBLSPACE to bypass the final screen which displays information about the new compressed volume. Using this switch tells DBLSPACE /COMPRESS to exit back to DOS as soon as it finishes.

/newdrive=*host* or /new=*host*
Host drive letter. Tells DoubleSpace what drive letter you want to use to refer to your original disk drive. After you compress a disk, you'll have two drive letters: the original drive letter will refer to the compressed volume, and the *host* drive letter will refer to your original "uncompressed" drive that contains the DBLSPACE.*nnn* hidden file. You probably won't need to specify this drive letter most of the time. Default: next available drive letter.

/reserve=*size* or /res=*size*
Leave uncompressed. Tells DoubleSpace how much space, in megabytes, it should leave free on the host, which is the original uncompressed disk drive. You won't normally need to use this switch. If DoubleSpace sees a Windows swapfile, which must be on an uncompressed disk, it automatically reserves enough room for the swapfile and moves it to the host drive. Default: 2MB on hard disks and 0 on floppy disks.

Parameters
drive
The disk drive that you want to compress. After compression, this drive letter will be assigned to the compressed volume, and a new drive letter will be assigned to your

orginal disk drive. You cannot compress a drive that already has a compressed volume file on it, which would be the case if you use DBLSPACE /CREATE to create a compressed volume using free space on a disk.

Notes

Necessary free space
In order to compress an existing disk, DoubleSpace needs a minimum of 1.2MB free on a startup disk, .65MB for other hard and floppy disks. (DoubleSpace cannot compress 360K floppy disks.)

Accessing DoubleSpace volumes
A DoubleSpace volume must be mounted before you can use it. This is normally handled automatically for compressed hard disks and in DOS 6.2 and later for floppy disks. But if you're using compressed floppy disks or removable hard disks with DOS 6.0, you may have to mount the file using the DBLSPACE /MOUNT command. Before you mount a compressed volume, you'll see a single file called READTHIS.TXT, which tells you how to mount the volume. Of course, you can only mount a compressed volume if you have DOS 6 or later and already have DoubleSpace installed.

The DBLSPACE.000 hidden file
Whenever you use /COMPRESS to create a compressed volume, DoubleSpace creates a file called DBLSPACE.000, which is the file that actually contains all of the data in your compressed volume. When you use /CREATE rather than /COMPRESS, the hidden file will have the name DBLSPACE.*nnn*, where *nnn* is a three-digit number greater than 000 (such as 001, for example).

Installing DoubleSpace for use with floppy disk
If you only want to use DoubleSpace with floppy disks but you don't want to compress your hard disk, how do you install it? The first time you run DBLSPACE, it will ask you whether you want to do an Express Setup or Custom Setup. Make sure you have a floppy disk in the disk drive (you must do this first) and then select Custom Setup and tell DBLSPACE that you want to create a new compressed drive. DBLSPACE will then show you a list of floppy and hard disks in your computer (which is why you have to put the floppy disk into the drive first). You can now select the floppy disk and have DBLSPACE compress it. From now on, you will be able to mount and unmount compressed floppy disks, even if you don't have any compressed hard disks.

Examples
The command

```
C:\>dblspace /compress b: /newdrive=g: /reserve=.5
```

creates a compressed volume on the floppy disk in drive B, leaving 500K uncompressed. Assuming that the original disk was 1.4MB, the new compressed volume will have an estimated size of 1.8MB (based on a compression ratio of 2:1). This is in addition to the .5MB that you asked DBLSPACE to leave uncompressed and results in a total disk size of 2.3MB. If you compressed the entire floppy disk, you would have 2.8MB available. Any files that were on the disk prior to compression will be stored on the compressed volume. Note that you can still access these files on drive B:. Any files you put on drive G: will be placed on the uncompressed part of the floppy disk.

See also

DBLSPACE	See this command for an overview of the DBLSPACE command options.
DBLSPACE /AUTOMOUNT	(DOS 6.2 and later.) Controls whether DoubleSpace will automatically mount compressed floppy disks when you try to access them.
DBLSPACE /CREATE	Used to create a new DoubleSpace volume on a disk.
DBLSPACE /MOUNT	Used to access a DoubleSpace volume. You'll need to use this to gain access to compressed volumes on floppy disks.

DBLSPACE /CREATE   DOS 6 and later, External

Creates a new DoubleSpace volume

This command allows you to create new compressed volumes on hard disks (for floppy disks, use /COMPRESS instead). It uses free space on an uncompressed hard disk to create a new disk drive that uses space more efficiently. If you have existing files and want to make better use of the space on your disk, you'll probably want to use the DBLSPACE /COMPRESS command instead of /CREATE.

When and why

Most of the time you'll probably want to use DBLSPACE /COMPRESS rather than this command to enlarge the capacity of an existing hard or floppy disk. But there are times you might want to have both compressed and uncompressed space on a single hard disk drive. Why? The most common need, leaving room for the Windows swapfile, is handled automatically by the DLBSPACE /COMPRESS command, so this function is really a specialized command, designed more for power users who want complete control over their computers. You can also use this command, for example, to create more than one compressed volume. For example, if you had a 300MB hard disk, you might choose to convert it into a 100MB uncompressed drive, as well as two 200MB compressed volumes.

Full-screen access

Alt-C, C

When you run DLBSPACE without any parameters, this key combination pulls down the Compress menu and selects Create New Drive..., which allows you to convert free space on an uncompressed hard disk into a new compressed volume.

Syntax

dblspace /**create** *drive*: [/**newdrive**=*newdrive*] [/**size**=*UseSize* | /**reserve**=*ReserveSize*]

or

dblspace /**cr** *drive*: [/**n**=*newdrive*] [/**si**=*UseSize* | /**re**=*ReserveSize*]

Creates a new compressed volume using free space from an existing, uncompressed hard disk.

Switches

/newdrive=*newdrive*

or

/n=*newdrive*

New drive letter. This is the drive letter that the new compressed disk will have after you create it. Default: next available drive letter.

/size=*UseSize*

or

/si=*UseSize*

Size of space to convert. This is the amount of uncompressed space, in megabytes, that you want to hand over to DBLSPACE for the new compressed volume. With a compression ratio of 2 to 1, your compressed volume will be about twice as large as the amount of uncompressed space that you give to it. You cannot use both /SIZE and /RESERVE. Default: /RESERVE=1.

/reserve=*ReserveSize*

or

/re=*ReserveSize*

Reserve free space. Tells DBLSPACE how much free space you want left over on *drive* after it creates a new compressed volume. To obtain the largest possible compressed volume, use /RESERVE=0. You cannot use both /SIZE and /RESERVE. Default: /RESERVE=1, which leaves 1MB of space free on the uncompressed drive for DOS 6.0. Reserves 2MB for DOS 6.2 and later.

Parameters

drive

The disk drive that contains free space that you want to use to create a new compressed volume. This new volume will use a different drive letter.

Notes

If you don't use the /RESERVE or /SIZE switches, DBLSPACE will make sure you have at least 1MB of free space on *drive* after it creates the new compressed volume.

/CREATE and floppy disks

You cannot use the /CREATE command on floppy disks or removable hard disks. In these cases you'll need to use the /COMPRESS command.

The DBLSPACE.nnn hidden file

Whenever you use /CREATE to create a compressed volume, DoubleSpace creates a file called DBLSPACE.*nnn*, which is the file that actually contains all the data in your compressed volume. The extension, *nnn* is a three-digit number greater than 000 (such as 001). On the other hand, volumes that you create using /COMPRESS always create a volume file called DBLSPACE.000.

Installing DoubleSpace for use with floppy disks

If you only want to use DoubleSpace with floppy disks, how do you install it? The problem is that the DBLSPACE program insists on either compressing an existing *hard* disk or creating a new volume on a hard disk before you can do anything else with it. So here's what we suggest. First, select Custom Setup when you first start DBLSPACE. Then select Create a new empty compressed drive. Finally, let DBLSPACE create a new compressed drive using free space on your C: drive. Follow the directions on the screen and when DLBSPACE finishes all its work, you can use the DBLSPACE /DEL command to remove the compressed volume you just created. From then on you'll be able to use DBLSPACE with floppy disks.

Messages

`Drive A is removable, so you cannot create a compressed drive on it.` You can only use /CREATE to create compressed volumes on nonremovable hard disks. For floppy disks and removable hard disks, you'll need to use the /COMPRESS command to create a compressed volume.

Examples

To create a new compressed volume called drive G: using space on drive H:, you would type

```
C:\>dblspace /create h: /newdrive=g /reserve=2
```

Let's assume for this example that H: is a hard disk that has 15MB of space available. This command will then create a new compressed volume file using all this space except for 2MB (because the /RES=2 switch reserves 2MB), or 13MB. DBLSPACE will then create a new compressed volume called G: that is 26MB in size.

See also

DBLSPACE	See this command for an overview of the DBLSPACE command options.
DBLSPACE /COMPRESS	Use to compress a disk.

DBLSPACE /DEFRAGMENT DOS 6 and later, External

Defragments a DoubleSpace volume

This command moves all the files in a compressed volume to the start of the compressed volume file, leaving all the free space at the end of the file. Once you have all the free space at the end, you can use DBLSPACE /SIZE to reduce the size of the compressed volume file. Unlike using DEFRAG on an uncompressed drive, defragmenting a compressed volume will *not* speed up your system.

When and why

The only time you'll need to use this command is when you want to reduce the size of a compressed volume file. If you need more uncompressed space available on the original, host hard disk, you'll need to defragment the compressed volume first and then use the DBLSPACE /SIZE command to reduce the size of the compressed volume file.

Part II: Command Reference

> Defragmenting a compressed volume, either with DEFRAG or with DBLSPACE /DEFRAGMENT will *not* speed up your computer. So we don't recommend using either defragmenting program unless you need to reduce the size of your compressed volume file.

Full-screen access
Alt-T, D
When you run DLBSPACE without any parameters, this key combination selects the Defragment... option from the Tools menu. You should choose a compressed drive from the main screen before you choose this option.

Syntax
dblspace /defragment [/f] [*drive*:]
or
dblspace /def [/f] [*drive*:]
Defragments a compressed volume, which simply moves all the free space to the end of the compressed volume file.

Switches
/f
Full defragment (DOS 6.2 and later). Tells DBLSPACE /DEF to do a more complete job of defragmenting a DoubleSpace volume. Microsoft doesn't say exactly what this switch does.

Parameters
drive
The drive letter for the compressed volume that you want to defragment.

Notes
If you do not specify *drive*, DLBSPACE will defragment the current drive.

Stopping DBLSPACE /DEFRAGMENT
Since defragmenting a compressed volume can be a very time-consuming process, you can press the Escape key to stop the defragmenting. Press Escape, followed by Y (which means, Yes, you want to stop).

DEFRAG vs DLBSPACE /DEFRAGMENT
There are a number of major differences between what the DEFRAG command does and what DLBSPACE /DEFRAGMENT does. Both of these commands defragment a disk but for different reasons and using different approaches. The DEFRAG command consolidates all the pieces of each file so they're in one place, which speeds up access to your file. But the DBLSPACE /DEFRAGMENT command simply moves all the file information away from the end of the file so all the free space will be at the end of the file. It apparently doesn't do any type of reorganizing for speed.

Maximum defragmenting
Microsoft recommends using the following steps to reduce the size of a compressed drive as much as possible:

1. Use DEFRAG to defragment the host volume. *Note:* This step will *not* defragment the compressed volume file itself.
2. Run DBLSPACE /DEF /F to defragment the information inside the compressed volume file.
3. Run DBLSPACE /DEF without the /F switch. This second pass will create even more free space at the end of the compressed volume file.

Using DEFRAG on compressed volumes

DEFRAG will work on compressed volumes, but it probably won't give you an advantage. The reasons for this are rather technical, but it boils down to this: DoubleSpace has its own internal way that it stores all of its data, which is different from DOS's structure. Yet DOS and programs like DEFRAG aren't aware of this difference. So if you optimize the organization at the DOS level, you won't be optimizing the organization of the actual data inside the compressed volume. However, DEFRAG will take a long time to work, even though you won't gain anything from the process.

When you run DEFRAG on a compressed volume, DEFRAG will run DBLSPACE /DEFRAGMENT after it finishes defragmenting the DOS-level file system. We don't recommend, however, using DEFRAG on compressed volumes.

Defragmenting the hidden volume files

Neither DBLSPACE nor DEFRAG will defragment the hidden DBLSPACE.*nnn* files used by DoubleSpace. There is, however, a way you can get DEFRAG to defragment even these files. See the "Notes" section in the description of DEFRAG for a discussion of how to do this.

Messages

```
Cancel Defragment of drive H?
To continue, press N.
```
You'll see this message if you press the Escape key while DBLSPACE is defragmenting a compressed volume. Since defragmenting can be a long process, you may want to stop before it finishes. There is no risk in pressing Escape to stop DLBSPACE /DEFRAGMENT before it's done. Press Y if you want to stop and N to continue (confusing, huh?).

Examples

To defragment the current drive, use
`C:\>`**dblspace /defragment**

See also

DBLSPACE	See this command for an overview of the DBLSPACE command options.
DBLSPACE /SIZE	Changes the size of an existing DoubleSpace volume.
DEFRAG	Defragments an uncompressed volume to increase performance (although you can use it on compressed volumes, you won't gain speed, as explained in the notes above).

Part II: Command Reference

DBLSPACE /DELETE   DOS 6 and later, External

Deletes a DoubleSpace volume

This command deletes a compressed volume by removing the hidden compressed volume file from the host drive (the uncompressed drive that contains the CVF). If you just want to remove all the files from a compressed volume, leaving it empty, you can use the DBLSPACE /FORMAT command.

> ### When and why
> Use this command whenever you want to remove a compressed volume. **Warning:** When you delete a compressed volume, you will lose all the files contained inside that volume, and not even UNDELETE will be able to recover them, so be careful! This command will delete the hidden file, DBLSPACE.*nnn*, from the host (uncompressed) disk, freeing up space on your host drive. You can't use this command to delete the compressed volume from your boot disk (usually drive C:); you'll find some notes on how to uncompress your boot disk in the "Technical Notes" area in the description of the DBLSPACE command (without switches).

Full-screen access
Alt-D, D
When you run DLBSPACE without any parameters, this key combination selects the Delete... option from the Drive menu. You should choose a compressed drive from the main screen before you choose this option.

Syntax
dblspace /delete *drive*:
Deletes a compressed volume. This unmounts the compressed volume and then deletes the hidden volume file from the host disk.

Parameters
drive
The drive letter that refers to a compressed volume that you want to delete.

Notes

Accidentally deleting a compressed volume
If you accidentally delete the files used to contain the DoubleSpace volume, you can try using UNDELETE to recover them from the host drive. The file will be called DBLSPACE.*xxx* where *xxx* is a number, with 000 for the first compressed volume file on that host, 001 for the next CVF, and so on.

If you can't mount this volume with DBLSPACE /MOUNT, run ScanDisk (DOS 6.2 and later) to repair the volume file.

What this command does
This command does several things. First, it unmounts the volume *drive*, which makes the drive letter unused. Next, DBLSPACE deletes the hidden compressed volume file that contains all the data. And finally, DLBSPACE removes the reference

to this drive from the hidden DBLSPACE.INI file, which contains information on what volumes are mounted so DOS can automatically mount them the next time you start DOS.

Examples
To delete the DoubleSpace volume created as drive H, use

```
C:\>dblspace /del h:
```

See also

DBLSPACE	See this command for an overview of the DBLSPACE command options.
DBLSPACE /FORMAT	Used to format a DoubleSpace volume.
UNDELETE	Used to recover deleted files including the one containing the compressed DoubleSpace volume.
ScanDisk	Repairs compressed volume files that won't properly mount.

DBLSPACE /DOUBLEGUARD DOS 6.2 and later, External

Controls DoubleGuard safety checking

This command allows you to turn on or off the DoubleGuard feature of DoubleSpace. DoubleGuard constantly checks DoubleSpace's memory for damage done by other programs, which provides extra protection for the data on DoubleSpace volumes. After you change this setting, you'll need to restart your computer for it to take effect.

When and why
Probably the only reason you'd want to turn off this option is for speed. When DoubleGuard is turned off your computer might run slightly faster but at the risk of damaging the data in DoubleSpace volumes.

The DoubleGuard feature continually checks DBLSPACE.BIN in memory to make sure that no other program has accidentally damaged DBLSPACE.BIN. Such damage, if ignored, could cause a DoubleSpace volume to become damaged or for files in a DoubleSpace volume to be read or written incorrectly.

Whenever DoubleGuard detects damage, it halts your computer to "minimize" damage to your data. Of course, it means you'll lose any work you haven't saved, but at least you won't damage work you have saved.

Syntax
dblspace /doubleguard=0|1
Determines if DoubleSpace will continually test DBLSPACE.BIN in memory for damage. Default: On.

Parameters

0
 DoubleGuard off. Turns off testing of DBLSPACE.BIN's memory for damage. Turning this off may speed up your computer, but it will also decrease the protection of DoubleSpace from damage by other programs.

1
 DoubleGuard on. Turns on testing of DBLSPACE.BIN's memory. Default: On.

Notes
You must restart your computer before changes you make to DoubleGuard take effect.

See also
DBLSPACE   See this command for an overview of the DBLSPACE command options.

DBLSPACE /FORMAT — DOS 6 and later, External

Empties DoubleSpace volume

Formats a compressed DoubleSpace volume, which really does nothing more than delete all the files and directories on a compressed volume. You will not be able to use UNFORMAT to recover from using this command, so be careful.

When and why
You'll probably never want to use this command, and in fact it's a good idea to avoid it. You will lose **all** of your files and directories when you format a compressed volume, with no way to recover them; UNFORMAT will not work with a compressed volume. The only reason you would want to use this command is if you no longer have any reason to keep any of your files on a compressed volume, or you have backed up all of your files and wish to reconfigure your system.

Warning: This command will delete all your files and directories on a compressed volume, with no way to recover your files.

Full-screen access
Alt-D, F

When you run DLBSPACE without any parameters, this key combination selects the Format... option from the Drive menu. You should choose a compressed drive from the main screen before you choose this option.

Syntax
dblspace /format *drive*:
or
dblspace /f *drive*:

Warning: Erases all the files and directories from a compressed volume. You probably won't want to do this.

Parameters
drive
The compressed drive that you want to format. Everthing will be erased from this volume after you format it, so be careful!

Notes
You cannot use this command to delete the files on the boot volume.

The /FORMAT command will delete everything on a compressed volume, with no way to recover any of the files. Formatting a compressed volume is a very fast operation, so you won't have time to stop it once you've replied Y to its message asking if you really want to format the volume.

Messages
```
Formatting drive D will permanently erase all the files it
contains.
Are you sure you want to format drive D?
```
Be very careful when you see this message. If you really want to delete *everything* on a compressed volume, type **Y**. Otherwise type **N** to cancel your request to format a compressed volume.

Examples
To remove all of the files and directories on drive H (a compressed volume), leaving the volume empty, use

    `C:\>`**dblspace /format h:**

See also
DBLSPACE	See this command for an overview of all the DBLSPACE command options.
DBLSPACE /DELETE	Used to delete a DoubleSpace volume.

DBLSPACE /HOST   DOS 6.2 and later, External

Change host drive letter
This command allows you to change the drive letter that DoubleSpace assigns to the host (physical disk) of a compressed volume. For example, by default if you compress drive C, the original host drive (which contains DBLSPACE.000) will become drive H.

When and why

This is a somewhat advanced command that you may never have reason to use.

You'll want to use this command if the drive letter that DoubleSpace assigns to the original host drive of a compressed disk is a letter that you want to use for some other purpose. For example, DoubleSpace normally assigns drive letter H to the host drive of your compressed C disk. This command allows you to change the H to any other letter that isn't being used, as long as the drive letter is below the LastDrive setting in DBLSPACE.INI (see "Notes" later in this command entry for more information).

After you change the host drive letter, the change doesn't actually take effect until you restart your computer.

Syntax

dblspace *drive1*: **/host=***drive2*:
Changes the drive letter for the host (uncompressed) drive from *drive1* to *drive2*.

Parameters

drive1
Compressed/host drive letter. This is the drive letter of either the compressed drive (such as drive C) or the current host drive letter (such as drive H).

drive2
New host drive. This is the drive letter that you use to refer to the host (uncompressed) drive.

Notes

You must restart your computer before changes you make to HOST take effect.

How DoubleSpace chooses drive letters

When DoubleSpace assigns drive letters to compressed and host drives, it usually starts with the highest drive letter available to DoubleSpace, which means that the first drive you mount will use drive H (if DoubleSpace's LastDrive=H) and the next drive will use G.

In the case of mounting an entire disk that has been compressed, DoubleSpace *moves* the original, uncompressed disk drive to a new drive letter that it assigns (such as H). The old drive letter (such as C) is then given to the compressed volume.

However, if you're mounting a compressed volume that you created using only part of the space on a disk drive (using DBLSPACE /CREATE rather than DBLSPACE /COMPRESS), this drive receives a new drive letter (such as H) when it is mounted.

Limitations on host drive letters

The DBLSPACE.INI file has an entry called LastDrive that determines the highest drive letter that you can use as a host drive letter. You cannot use a drive letter higher than this value.

To determine the current setting, you need to look inside the DBLSPACE.INI file, which is located in the root directory of your startup host disk. For example, if your drive C is compressed and its host volume is H (you can find the host volume using

DBLSPACE /LIST, which tells you where the CVF is located), to see the current settings when the host drive is H, use EDIT to read the DBLSPACE.INI file (which is a read-only, hidden, system file):

```
C:\>edit h:\dblspace.ini
```

Messages

```
The drive letter D is not available for DoubleSpace's use.
```

You see this message when you try to use a drive letter after /HOST that is higher than the LastDrive setting in the DBLSPACE.INI file. See the "Notes" section for information about how to determine the current setting of this value. You can change the last drive letter available to DoubleSpace using the DBLSPACE /LASTDRIVE command.

Examples

Let's say that your drive C is compressed and drive C's host volume is H. The following command changes the drive letter from H to G:

```
C:\>dblspace c: /host=g:
```

The following command has exactly the same effect:

```
C:\>dblspace h: /host=g:
```

This shows that the first drive letter in this command can refer either to the compressed volume or to its host volume. You can use whichever approach works best for you.

See also

DBLSPACE	See this command for an overview of the DBLSPACE command options.
DBLSPACE /LASTDRIVE	This command allows you to control the last drive letter available to DoubleSpace.
DBLSPACE /LIST	Use this command to locate the host drive letters for all the mounted DoubleSpace volumes.

DBLSPACE /INFO — DOS 6 and later, External

Displays DoubleSpace drive information

This command provides information on compressed volumes: the location of the compressed volume file, the space used and free, the actual compression ratio for the used space, and the estimated compression ratio for free space.

When and why
This command is a handy command for finding out how well DBLSPACE is able to store your information in a compressed volume. It provides information on the amount of space free and used, plus information on compression ratios that is specific to compressed volumes. The higher the compression ratio, the better DBLSPACE is using your space. A compression ratio of about 2 to 1 is the average for most people's computers.

Full-screen access
Alt-D, I
When you run DLBSPACE without any parameters, this key combination selects the Info... option from the Drive menu. You should choose a compressed drive from the main screen before you choose this option.

Syntax
dblspace [/info] *drive*:
Displays information about a compressed volume called *drive*.

Switches
/info
Display volume info. This switch is optional. If you specify a DBLSPACE followed by a drive letter and no other switches, DBLSPACE provides the INFO listing. You can use DBLSPACE /INFO to obtain information about the current drive.

Notes
To find out the compression ratio for individual files, use the DIR /C command.

Examples
Entering the command on one of our systems

```
C:\>dblspace c:
```

provided the following listing:

```
DoubleSpace is examining drive C.
Compressed drive C is stored on uncompressed drive H in the file
H:\DBLSPACE.000.

         Space used:                96.30 MB
         Compression ratio:         1.9 to 1

         Space free:                71.79 MB
         Est. compression ratio:    2.0 to 1

         Total space:               168.09 MB
```

See also
DBLSPACE   See this command for an overview of the DBLSPACE command options.

DBLSPACE /LIST   Used to list all available drives and volumes.

DBLSPACE/LASTDRIVE

DBLSPACE /SIZE   This command will tell you even more about a compressed drive than /INFO, but be careful because it allows you to change the size of your compressed volume file.

DIR /C   You can find out the compression ratio for individual files using the /C switch on the DIR command.

DBLSPACE /LASTDRIVE   DOS 6.2 and later, External

Sets last drive letter available to DoubleSpace

This command allows you to set the last drive letter that is available to DoubleSpace.

When and why
Use this command if you want to be able to assign drive letters above H to DoubleSpace volumes or host volumes (the original uncompressed disk). Chances are you won't need to do this unless you have a large number of compressed drives.

Syntax
dblspace /lastdrive=*drive*:
Changes the setting of the LastDrive entry in DoubleSpace's DBLSPACE.INI file, which DoubleSpace reads only when it first starts.

Parameters
drive
Last available DoubleSpace letter. This is the highest drive letter that you permit DoubleSpace to use. Default: H.

Notes
You must restart your computer for changes you make to LASTDRIVE to take effect.

If any other devices use drive letters that DoubleSpace has set aside for itself, DoubleSpace uses one more drive letter past LastDrive for each drive letter that it lost to another device.

Examples
If you want to be able to use drive letters up to K with DoubleSpace, use the following command and then restart your computer:

    `C:\>dblspace /lastdrive=k`

See also
DBLSPACE   See this command for an overview of the DBLSPACE command options.

DBLSPACE /HOST   Allows you to change the drive letter assigned to a host drive.

DBLSPACE /LIST — DOS 6 and later, External

Lists information about drives

This command provides information about all of the local drives on your computer. It does not list any network drive letters.

> **When and why**
> You use this command to discover how the drive letters on your system are being used. With all the drive letters floating around, it's nice to be able to tell which drive letters refer to uncompressed drives, which to compressed drives, and so on. This is most important when you are trying to find out which drive letters are available for other uses.

Full-screen access

In Main Screen
The full-screen interface has no exact equivalent of the /LIST option. However, when you run DLBSPACE without any parameters, you will see a list of compressed drives (but you won't see uncompressed drives).

Syntax

dblspace /list
or
dblspace /li
Lists all compressed drives, floppy disks, and hard disks, and gives you information about each one.

Notes

DBLSPACE tends to be a bit greedy. Any unused drives are generally reported as Available for DoubleSpace. This does not mean that these drives are reserved for DoubleSpace, only that you can use them for new compressed volumes. You may also use them for other purposes.

Examples

Entering the command

```
C:\>dblspace /list
```

on one of our systems results in the following display:

```
Drive  Type                       Total Free   Total Size   CVF Filename
-----  ------------------------   ----------   ----------   ------------
  A    Removable-media drive      No disk in drive
  B    Removable-media drive      No disk in drive
  C    Compressed hard drive       71.79 MB     168.09 MB   H:\DBLSPACE.000
  D    Available for DoubleSpace
  E    Available for DoubleSpace
  F    Available for DoubleSpace
  G    Available for DoubleSpace
  H    Local hard drive             3.58 MB     101.68 MB
Double Guard safety checking is enabled.
Automounting is enabled for drive(s) AB.
```

See also

DBLSPACE	See this command for an overview of the DBLSPACE command options.
DBLSPACE /INFO	Used to get information about a specific DoubleSpace volume.
DBLSPACE /SIZE	This command will tell you even more about a compressed drive than /INFO, but be careful because it allows you to change the size of your compressed volume file.

DBLSPACE /MAXFILEFRAGMENTS DOS 6.2 and later, External

Sets the maximum fragmentation of DoubleSpace volumes files

This is a very advanced command that enables you to set the maximum number of fragments of a compressed volume file that DoubleSpace can handle on the host drive.

When and why

You'll probably never, ever want to change this setting, and you should be very careful if you ever do change it. Compressed volume files stored on the host drive can have gaps between the different parts of the file, which is known as *fragmentation;* each piece is called a *fragment.* In order to function properly, DoubleSpace needs to keep track of the location and size of each of these fragments. DoubleSpace reserves only enough memory to handle a certain number of fragments (the default is 113), using 6 bytes of memory to keep track of each fragment. Because the default number uses just 678 bytes of memory, you should not reduce this number in order to save memory. We strongly recommend that you keep this number at 113 or whatever the default setting is on your computer.

Syntax

dblspace /maxfilefragments=n

Sets the limit on the total number of fragments DoubleSpace can handle. These fragments are the separate pieces of the compressed volume file as stored on the host drive (and have nothing to do with fragmentation inside the DoubleSpace volume).

Parameters

n
   Maximum number of fragments. Sets the maximum number of file fragments for DoubleSpace volume files as stored on the host volume. Default: 113.

Notes

You must restart your computer for the changes you make to MaxFileFragments to take effect.

It is a good idea to run DEFRAG on any disk before you create a new compressed volume with DBLSPACE /CREATE. Doing so helps to minimize the number of fragments that will be in a new compressed volume file. Also, see the "Notes" section in DEFRAG for information on how to compress unmounted DoubleSpace volume files.

See also

DBLSPACE	See this command for an overview of the DBLSPACE command options.
DBLSPACE /CREATE	Allows you to create new compressed volumes using free space on an uncompressed disk drive.
DEFRAG	Allows you to defragment your disk, which you should do before creating new compressed volumes with DBLSPACE /CREATE.

DBLSPACE /MAXREMOVABLEDRIVES

DOS 6.2 and later, External

Sets the maximum number of removable drives

This command sets the number of removable drives and/or volumes (those created with DBLSPACE /CREATE) that can be mounted at one time. The default of 1 may be too low for your needs.

When and why

You should use this command whenever you need to have more than one removable volume mounted at the same time. Several types of volumes can be mounted and unmounted: compressed floppy disks, compressed cartridge hard disks (such as SyQuest drives), compressed magneto-optical drives, and volumes that you create from free disk space by using the DBLSPACE /CREATE command. All these volumes can be mounted on demand, and if you want to use more than one at a time, you need to use this command to increase the number of simultaneous removable volumes that DoubleSpace can mount at one time. We suggest setting this value to 3 or any other value higher than 1 or 2.

Syntax

dblspace /maxremovabledrives=n

Sets the maximum number of removable volumes that DoubleSpace can mount at the same time.

Parameters

n
  Maximum number of removable drives. Sets the maximum number of removable volumes that DoubleSpace can have mounted at the same time. Default: 1.

Notes

You must restart your computer for the change you make to MaxRemovableDrive to take effect.

DoubleSpace allocates 96 bytes of memory for each removable volume that it can mount. In other words, if you set MaxRemovableDrives to 3, DoubleSpace uses an additional 192 bytes (because the default is 1 removable volume).

Examples

The following command tells DoubleSpace to allocate enough memory so that it can have 3 removable volumes mounted at the same time:

    `C:\>dblspace /maxr=3`

Notice that you can abbreviate the name of the switch to the minimum number of letters that is unique (there is a /MAXFILEFRAGMENTS switch). You must restart your computer before these additional removable drives are available.

See also

DBLSPACE	See this command for an overview of the DBLSPACE command options.
DBLSPACE /CREATE	Allows you to create new compressed volumes using free space on an uncompressed disk drive.
DBLSPACE /MOUNT	Mounts removable volumes.

DBLSPACE /MOUNT   DOS 6 and later, External

Provides access to a DoubleSpace volume

This command connects a drive letter to a compressed volume file created by DoubleSpace. Compressed volume files are hidden until you mount them (normally, DOS will remount your volumes for you automatically). The command to unmount a volume (which removes the drive letter and hides the volume) is DBLSPACE /UNMOUNT.

When and why

If you're using DOS 6.2 or later, you'll probably never use this command since DOS automatically mounts and unmounts compressed floppy disks (unless you have AUTOMOUNT turned off).

If you're using DOS 6.0 or have AUTOMOUNT turned off, you'll probably use this command, along with /UNMOUNT, mainly with compressed floppy disks or removable hard disks. In these cases, you should unmount a volume before you remove the floppy disk. Then the next time you want to use the files on the floppy disk, you'll need to mount the compressed volume. Mounting a compressed volume basically connects a drive letter to a compressed volume file (which is a hidden file). If you see a file called READTHIS.TXT on a floppy disk (or a removable hard disk), it probably means you'll have to mount the disk before you can see its files.

You can also mount and unmount compressed volumes on nonremovable hard disks. Why would you want to do this? Most people probably won't, but if for some reason you decide to create several compressed volumes, you'll be able to keep them hidden (unmounted) until you need them.

Full-screen access
Alt-D, M
When you run DLBSPACE without any parameters, this key combination selects the Mount... option from the Drive menu. DBLSPACE will search for unmounted volumes and present you with a list, if it finds any. This is by far the easiest way to mount volumes since it will show you all the unmounted volumes, and you can choose which one to mount.

Syntax
dblspace /mount[=*nnn*] *host* [/**newdrive**=*drive*:]
or
dblspace /mo[=*nnn*] *host* [/**new**=*drive*:]
Mounts a compressed volume so that you can see all the files in the compressed volume.

Switches
/mount[=*nnn*] or /mo[=*nnn*]
Mount a DoubleSpace volume. Without a number (*nnn*), this switch tells DoubleSpace to mount a file called DBLSPACE.000. Any volume that you created by compressing a disk (/COMPRESS) will have a file with this name on it. On the other hand, compressed volumes that you create using the /CREATE command will have numbers higher than 000, such as 001. In such cases, you'll need to tell DBLSPACE which volume file to mount, and it's usually easier to use the full-screen interface to mount a volume (type **DBLSPACE** without any switches or parameters). Default: DBLSPACE.000.

/newdrive=*drive* or /new=*drive*
New drive. The way this switch works will be different depending on what type of volume you're mounting. If you mount a volume created with /COMPRESS, this drive letter will be the drive letter for the host disk, which is the original uncompressed disk. The original *host* drive letter will then refer to the compressed volume after it's mounted.

If, on the other hand, you used /CREATE to create a compressed volume that you want to mount, *drive* will be the drive letter of the compressed volume once it's loaded. Although this is a little confusing, you can use the DBLSPACE /LIST command to see what each drive letter refers to after you mount a volume. Default: next available drive letter.

Parameters
host
This is the letter of the disk drive that contains the compressed volume file. Compressed volume files are hidden files, so perhaps the only sign that you have a compressed volume is if you see only a single file called READTHIS.TXT and almost no free space. If you're not sure where your compressed volume files are located, you'll find it easier to use the full-screen interface to mount volumes (type **DBLSPACE** without any switches or parameters). The full-screen interface will show you a list of all unmounted volumes when you ask to mount a volume.

Notes

Volume labels and Mount
If you mount and unmount volumes, you should give each compressed volume a volume label, using the LABEL command. When you use the full-screen interface to mount a volume, DBLSPACE will show you all the volume labels for unmounted volumes, which makes it much easier to decide which volume you want to mount.

Mounting a second volume
There is one case of mounting a volume that may not be obvious. Let's say that you used /COMPRESS to create a compressed volume on a floppy disk in drive A, and that you use /RESERVE to reserve room for another compressed volume. After the /COMPRESS, your uncompressed floppy disk will have a new drive letter, such as H. If you have a second compressed volume on the floppy disk, you'll have to mount it from drive H:

```
C:\>dblspace /mount=001 h:
```

Messages

```
Cannot find the file D:\DBLSPACE.000.
```
You'll see this message whenever you try to mount a volume that you create with /CREATE rather than /COMPRESS.

```
DoubleSpace has used all the memory reserved by the settings in the
Options dialog box. To enable DoubleSpace to allocate more memory,
you should restart your computer now.
```
You see this message whenever you try to mount more removable volumes (such as compressed floppy disks and volumes that you create with DBLSPACE /CREATE) than DoubleSpace has allocated memory for. You can increase the number of mountable volumes DoubleSpace supports by using the DBLSPACE /MAXREMOVABLEDRIVES command in DOS 6.2 and later. Restarting doesn't actually increase the number of volumes —it simply unmounts any currently mounted removable drives.

```
Missing value - /new
```
You'll see this message whenever you forget to supply a value after /NEW or when you forget the equal sign after /NEW.

```
There are no more drive letters reserved for DoubleSpace to use. To
add more drive letters, choose the Options command from the Tools
menu.
```
If you tried to mount a floppy disk, this message may mean that you haven't installed DBLSPACE yet. If you have no other compressed volumes on your computer, you'll need to create at least one. (Use Custom Setup to create a new compressed volume; then use DBLSPACE /DEL followed by the drive letter of the new compressed volume to delete it; you will then be able to mount a floppy disk.)

Otherwise, you'll need to run DBLSPACE (without any switches) to change the number of removable volumes that you can mount.

Examples

The command

`C:\>dblspace /mount=001 d: /newdrive=j:`

searches for a file named DBLSPACE.001 on the disk on drive D. Once DOS locates the file, it mounts that file as a compressed volume and assigns it the drive letter J.

To mount a compressed floppy disk in drive A:, you would type the following:

`C:\>dblspace /mount a:`

Now A: will refer to your compressed floppy volume, and the original, uncompressed floppy disk will be renamed to a higher drive letter, such as H:.

See also

DBLSPACE	See this command for an overview of the DBLSPACE command options.
DBLSPACE /MAXREMOVABLEDRIVES	Lets you change how many removable drives and/or unmountable volumes DoubleSpace can support.
DBLSPACE /UNMOUNT	Releases a DoubleSpace volume and the drive letter assigned to it.
LABEL	Use this command to add volume labels to all your compressed volumes. These volume labels appear in DBLSPACE's full-screen interface when you ask to mount a volume.

DBLSPACE /RATIO   DOS 6 and later, External

Changes ratio used to predict free space

This command allows you to adjust how DoubleSpace calculates the amount of free space left on a compressed volume. Normally, DoubleSpace looks at how much real space it has free inside the compressed volume file and then multiplies it by 2 (because the default compression ratio DoubleSpace assumes is 2 to 1). If you know that your files compress at a different ratio, you can adjust the number that DoubleSpace uses to estimate free space. For example, you could use the DBLSPACE /INFO command to find how the actual compression ratio used for the files already in your compressed volume and then adjust the predicted compression ratio so it matches the actual number.

When and why

This is a fairly advanced command, and you'll need to really understand compression ratios and how DoubleSpace works before you use it. If you're still with us, the main reason you'd want to use this command is to adjust DoubleSpace's prediction of how much free disk space you have when you're about to copy some files that compress with a much higher compression ratio (like 4 to 1). For example, DoubleSpace may

DBLSPACE /RATIO

think you only have enough free space for 1MB of files, but you might be able to store 3MB of graphics files on the disk because you expect you can get a higher compression ratio. In this case you would set the estimated compression ratio for new files at 3 or 4 so DOS will think it has enough room to save the files to your compressed disk.

Another example is installing new software. In general, programs don't compress as well as text or graphics files. On the average, programs (EXE files) tend to compress at only about 1.5 to 1 rather than 2 to 1, which is the average for a typical mix of programs and files. Setting the ratio to 1.5 or an even smaller number will give you a more predictable idea of how much free disk space you have for a new program.

Full-screen access
Alt-D, R
When you run DLBSPACE without any parameters, this key combination selects the Change Ratio... option from the Drive menu. You should choose a compressed drive from the main screen before you choose this option.

Syntax
dblspace /ratio[=*r.r*] [*drive*: | **/all**]
or
dblspace /ra[=*r.r*] [*drive*: | **/all**]
Allows you to change the estimated compression ratio that DoubleSpace uses to calculate how much free space you have in a compressed volume.

Switches
/ratio[=*r.r*] or /ra[=*r.r*]
Compression ratio. Sets the ratio used to calculate the free space on a compressed volume to the current compression ratio. If you supply *r.r*, sets the ratio to *r.r* to 1. The allowed values for *r.r* are 1.0 to 16.0 (the maximum value may be less than 16).

/all
All drives. Sets the ratio for all the DoubleSpace volumes currently mounted. You cannot use this switch when you supply a drive.

Parameters
drive
The compressed drive for which you want to change the compression ratio.

Notes

Checking the compression ratio on files
The DIR /C command will display the compression ratio for individual files on your hard disk.

Changing the ratio on startup
Microsoft's on-line help states that DoubleSpace automatically sets the estimated ratio each time you start your computer so it matches the average ratio for data stored in the compressed volume. As we write this (using "final beta" software), DoubleSpace only changes the ratio from 2.0 to 1 when you run this command. It never changes the ratio during booting.

What happens when you change the ratio

Changing the compression ratio won't change the amount of space you have free. All it does is change DoubleSpace's estimate of how much free space you have. The larger the ratio, the more space DoubleSpace will say it has (DOS reports the numbers supplied to it by DoubleSpace). If you actually want to change how much you can put into a compressed volume file, you'll need to use the DBLSPACE /SIZE command to increase or decrease the size of your compressed volume file (assuming you have free space available on the uncompressed host disk).

Changing the estimated compression ratio has the effect of changing the apparent size of both the free space and the total space in a compressed volume. All this means is that DoubleSpace calculates the total size of a compressed volume by adding the estimated free space to the space already used by files.

Changing the compression ratio does *not* change how well DoubleSpace compresses data.

Examples

Synchronizing the estimated and actual ratios

Let's say that you want to change the estimated compression ratio so it matches the actual compression ratio for the files in your compressed volume. You could either do it the hard way, by using DBLSPACE /INFO to find out what the number is and then use DBLSPACE /RATIO to set it to this number. Fortunately, there is a much easier way. If you use the /RATIO switch without supplying a number, as follows:

```
C:\>dblspace /ratio
```

DoubleSpace will calculate the actual compression ratio and then set the estimated compression ratio so it matches.

Setting the compression ratio

To set the compression ratio on drive C to 1.2 to 1 (in preparation for installing a new application), you would use

```
C:\>dblspace /ra=1.2 c:
```

See also

DBLSPACE	See this command for an overview of the DBLSPACE command options.
DBLSPACE /SIZE	Use this command instead of /RATIO if you want to change the amount of space used for the compressed volume file.
DIR /C	You can find out the compression ratio for individual files using the /C switch on the DIR command.

DBLSPACE /ROMSERVER DOS 6.2 and later, External

Use ROM BIOS Compression
This is a fairly advanced option that controls whether DoubleSpace uses the ROM BIOS Microsoft Real-Time Compression Interface (MRCI) server.

When and why
Chances are you'll never want to change this setting unless you're directed to as a result of installing a special compression card in your computer. The purpose of this option is simple: Microsoft has defined a method for hardware manufacturers to build special add-in cards that provide compression for DoubleSpace via hardware. These hardware compression cards are much faster at compressing and uncompressing data than the software built into DoubleSpace. Installing special compression hardware gives you the fastest performance when using DoubleSpace.

Syntax
dblspace /romserver=0|1
Enables or disables checking for a ROM BIOS Microsoft Real-Time Compression Interface, which is usually provided by an add-in compression card. Default: 0.

Parameters
0
Disables MRCI checking. Tells DoubleSpace not to look for a ROM BIOS compression interface when it first loads. Default: 0.

1
Enables MRCI checking. Tells DoubleSpace to look for a ROM BIOS compression interface when it first loads. You should use this option only if you are sure you have a MRCI-compatible compression card installed in your computer. Default: 0.

Notes
You must restart your computer for the change you make to ROMSERVER to take effect.

Do not enable this feature unless you are sure that your computer contains a compression card which provides MRCI-compatible compression support.

See also
DBLSPACE   See this command for an overview of the DBLSPACE command options.

DBLSPACE /SIZE

DOS 6 and later, External

Changes size of a DoubleSpace volume

This command enlarges or reduces the size of a compressed volume file. It allows you to set the amount of free space available on the uncompressed host drive. Before you can reduce the size of a compressed volume file, you must make sure that the end of the volume file is empty. The DBLSPACE /DEFRAGMENT command moves all the free space to the end of the volume file.

When and why

By far the best way to use this command is in the full-screen interface of DBLSPACE (type **DBLSPACE** without any parameters or switches). You'll want to use this command whenever you want to change the amount of free space on the original, uncompressed volume (the host). For example, if you're adding or removing Microsoft Windows, the Windows swapfile must be on an uncompressed volume, so you might need to either increase or decrease the amount of uncompressed space on the host volume. This command allows you to do exactly that. You tell DBLSPACE how much free space, in megabytes, you want on the uncompressed host.

Before you reduce the size of a compressed volume file, you should run DBLSPACE /DEFRAGMENT, which will put all the free space at the end of the compressed volume file. When you reduce the size of a compressed volume, DBLSPACE can only reduce it by the amount of free space at the *end* of a compressed volume file.

Full-screen access

Alt-D, S

When you run DBLSPACE without any parameters, this key combination selects the Change Size... option from the Drive menu. You should choose a compressed drive from the main screen before you choose this option.

Syntax

dblspace /size[=*compressed*] | **/reserve**=*free*] *drive*:

or

dblspace /si[=*compressed*] | **/res**=*free*] *drive*:

Changes the size of a DoubleSpace volume file. If you don't use /RESERVE and you don't use a number after /SIZE, DBLSPACE will make the volume file as small as possible.

Switches

/size=*compressed* or /si=*compressed*

New volume size. Use this form to change the size of the volume file containing the compressed volume to *compressed*, which is a number in megabytes and can be a decimal number like 10.3. The size is measured in megabytes. You cannot combine this switch with the /RESERVED switch. Default, without /RESERVE, is to reduce the size of the compressed volume file as much as possible.

DBLSPACE /SIZE

/reserved=*uncompressed* or /res=*uncompressed*
Reserve uncompressed space. This switch tells DBLSPACE to change the size of the volume file so you will have *uncompressed* megabytes of free space on the uncompressed host disk. DBLSPACE will either increase or decrease the size of the volume file, depending on whether *uncompressed* is smaller or larger than the current free space. The number *uncompressed* is in megabytes and can be a decimal number, like 10.3.

Parameters

drive
The drive letter for the compressed volume that you want to resize. This command resizes the volume file located on the host disk, but you tell DBLSPACE which volume file you want to resize by supplying the drive letter for the compressed volume. This means that you must mount a volume before you can resize its volume file.

Notes

Limits on reducing the size

DoubleSpace will not reduce a volume beyond the minimum size needed to hold the files currently in the volume. To obtain the maximum reduction, always use the DBLSPACE /DEFRAGMENT command before you attempt to reduce the size of a volume file.

Using DBLSPACE /DEFRAGMENT first

Before you reduce the size of a volume file, you should always run DBLSPACE /DEFRAGMENT. If you don't run this command first, you may not be able to reduce the size of a volume very much. The /DEFRAGMENT option moves all the unused space to the end of the volume file, where /SIZE can simply eliminate it from the file. The /SIZE option can only eliminate free space when it's at the end.

Examples

Specifying the size of the volume file

Let's assume you have a 120MB hard disk, with a compressed volume file that currently uses 80MB of space on the host drive (called H). The following set of commands will reduce the volume file from 80MB to 70MB:

```
C:\>dblspace /size=70
```

Specifying the free space

You could also change the amount of unused space. For example, you can reserve 50MB of free space, which will reduce the volume file to 70MB, using the command

```
C:\>dblspace /size /reserve=50
```

Both of the commands above assume that the top 10MB of space in the volume file are free, but if your compressed volume is fragmented, this may not be true. You should always run DBLSPACE /DEFRAGMENT before you attempt to reduce the size of a DoubleSpace volume.

Part II: Command Reference

Reducing a volume to its minimum size

To reduce a compressed volume to the minimum possible size, use the following commands:

```
C:\>dblspace /defragment
C:\>dblspace /si
```

The first command moves all of the files to the bottom portion of the DoubleSpace volume. The second command converts all of the remaining free space back to uncompressed storage on the host disk.

See also

DBLSPACE — See this command for an overview of the DBLSPACE command options.

DBLSPACE /DEFRAGMENT — Use this command before you reduce the size of a compressed volume.

DBLSPACE /SWITCHES   DOS 6.2 and later, External

Allow or disable bypassing DoubleSpace

This command allows you to enable or disable the Ctrl-F5 and Ctrl-F8 keys, which will bypass loading of DoubleSpace when your computer first starts.

When and why

Two cases exist in which you might want to use this command. First, you can speed up DOS's loading a little by telling DOS to wait a shorter time before it loads DoubleSpace. Second, if you want to make sure that you can never bypass loading of DoubleSpace on someone's computer, you can turn off the Ctrl-F5 and Ctrl-F8 keys so that they can't bypass DoubleSpace.

Syntax

dblspace /switches=F|N

Either disable bypassing of DoubleSpace or shorten the length of time that DOS waits before it loads DoubleSpace.

Parameters

F
Faster loading. This option tells DOS to wait a shorter period of time between when it displays the `Starting MS-DOS...` message and when it loads DoubleSpace. This time period is the only time when you can press Ctrl-F5 or Ctrl-F8 to bypass loading of DoubleSpace. For instructions on how to turn this option off, see "Notes."

N
Never bypass. This option tells DOS to disable the Ctrl-F5 and Ctrl-F8 keys for bypassing the loading of DoubleSpace. For instructions on how to turn off this option, see "Notes."

DBLSPACE /SWITCHES

Notes

The difference between Ctrl-F5 and Ctrl-F8

The Ctrl-F5 and Ctrl-F8 keys work in exactly the same way that F5 and F8 do except that Ctrl-F5 and Ctrl-F8 also bypass the loading of DoubleSpace. When your computer first starts, you see the message `Starting MS-DOS...`. As soon as you see this message, you can press Ctrl-F5 or Ctrl-F8 to bypass DoubleSpace. Here is a summary of the key combinations that you can use:

Key	Bypasses DoubleSpace	CONFIG.SYS and AUTOEXEC.BAT
F5	No	Bypasses
Ctrl-F5	Yes	Bypasses
F8	No	Steps through one entry at a time
Ctrl-F8	Yes	Steps through one entry at a time

Turning off DBLSPACE /SWITCHES

The way this command works is a little strange. You can turn on either of these options, and you can switch between them (only one option can be on at one time). But you can't turn off both options using the DBLSPACE /SWITCHES command. In other words, you can't go back to the longer pause at the start while DOS waits for any of the F-key combinations.

Here's how you can turn off both options. Use an editor, like EDIT, to edit the hidden file DBLSPACE.INI, which is located in the root directory of the host startup disk drive. Find the line that reads SWITCHES with something after it. Delete this line and save DBLSPACE.INI. Then restart your computer.

Messages

```
You pressed CTRL+F5 or CTRL+F8 to bypass DBLSPACE.BIN. Therefore,
none of your compressed drives are available.
```
This is the message you see if you press Ctrl-F5 or Ctrl-F8 as soon as you see DOS display the message `Starting MS-DOS...`.

Examples

The following command turns on faster loading of DoubleSpace when your computer first starts:

    `C:\>`**`dblspace /switches=f`**

See also

DBLSPACE   See this command for an overview of the DBLSPACE command options.

SWITCHES   Use this command in your CONFIG.SYS file to control the F5 and F8 keys (without the Ctrl key).

Part II: Command Reference

DBLSPACE /UNCOMPRESS   DOS 6.2 and later, External

Uncompress a DoubleSpace volume

This command moves all the files in a compressed volume back onto the host volume. It also deletes the compressed volume file after it has moved all the files back to the host drive.

When and why

You might want to use this command for several reasons. First, you may decide that you really don't want to use DoubleSpace on your disk. This command allows you to go back to an uncompressed drive. Second, you may find that your hard disk is slightly slower after you compress it (it is also possible for it to be faster). Again, this command allows you to go back to an uncompressed volume. And finally, if you want to convert to another compression program, such as Stacker, you may want to uncompress your hard disk before you install the other disk compression program.

Full-screen access

Alt-T, U

When you run DBLSPACE without any parameters, this key combination selects the Uncompress option from the Tools menu. You should choose a compressed drive from the main screen before you choose this option.

Syntax

dblspace /uncompress [*drive*:]

or

dblspace /unc [*drive*:]

Uncompresses a disk drive by moving all the files from the compressed volume to the host disk drive. This command also deletes the empty compressed volume file after it has moved all the files to the host.

Parameters

drive

The drive letter for the volume that you want to uncompress. Default: current drive.

Notes

When you ask DoubleSpace to uncompress a volume, it runs ScanDisk first (to make sure there aren't any problems) before it uncompresses your DoubleSpace volume. This process of uncompressing a drive can take a long time — many minutes or even hours.

Examples

Uncompressing a floppy disk

Let's say that you have a floppy disk in drive A that is currently mounted, and that the uncompressed floppy disk is currently called G. This command uncompresses your floppy disk:

```
C:\>dblspace /uncompress a:
```

Now drive A will show your real, uncompressed floppy disk, and drive G won't exist anymore.

See also
DBLSPACE   See this command for an overview of the DBLSPACE command options.

DBLSPACE /CREATE   Use this command when you want to compress a disk.

DBLSPACE /UNMOUNT   DOS 6 and later, External

Releases a DoubleSpace volume
This command breaks the connection between a drive letter and a compressed volume file.

When and why
You'll want to use this command if you're using DOS 6.0 (this has been automated in DOS 6.2 and later) and you have compressed floppy or removable hard disks. In both cases, you should always unmount a volume before you remove the disk from your disk drive. To mount the volume again, use the DBLSPACE /MOUNT command. You might also use /UNMOUNT if you have some compressed volumes that you created with /CREATE on nonremovable hard disks. For more information on this, see the DBLSPACE /MOUNT command.

Full-screen access
Alt-D, U
When you run DLBSPACE without any parameters, this key combination selects the Unmount... option from the Drive menu. You should choose a compressed drive from the main screen before you choose this option.

Syntax
dblspace /unmount [*drive*:]
or
dblspace /unm [*drive*:]
Unmounts the compressed volume *drive* and hides the volume file. You'll need to use DBLSPACE /MOUNT before you can see the files in your compressed volume again.

Parameters
drive
The drive letter for the volume that you want to release. Default: current drive.

Switches
/unmount or /unm
Release volume. Instructs DoubleSpace to unmount a volume. What happens to the drive letter depends on how you created the compressed volume. After an unmount for volumes you create with /COMPRESS, the drive letter will refer to the uncompressed host drive. But for volumes you create with /CREATE, the drive letter won't be valid after you unmount the volume.

Notes

Use DBLSPACE /LIST to determine the relationships between mounted volumes and host drives.

Messages

```
Drive C is your startup disk drive and should not be unmounted.
```
DoubleSpace won't allow you to unmount the volume that you booted from, which is a good thing.

Examples

Unmounting a floppy disk

Let's say you have a floppy disk in drive A that is currently mounted, and the uncompressed floppy disk is currently called G. This command will unmount your floppy disk:

```
C:\>dblspace /unmount a:
```

Now drive A will show your real, uncompressed floppy disk, and drive G won't exist anymore.

To mount this floppy disk again so you can see the compressed volume, you would type

```
C:\>dblspace /mount a:
```

If you have DOS 6.2 and later, and the AUTOMOUNT option is turned on (the default), a floppy disk is mounted for you automatically as soon as you try to read from the floppy disk drive.

Unmounting a secondary volume

Let's say you used the DBLSPACE /CREATE command to create a new compressed volume using free space from your hard disk. When you mount such a volume, it will receive a new drive letter, such as H. To unmount such a volume, you would use this command:

```
C:\>dblspace /unmount h:
```

To remount this volume again, assuming the volume file is called C:\DBLSPACE.001, you would use this command:

```
C:\>dblspace /mount=001
```

Or, which is easier, type **DBLSPACE** without any switches or parameters to use the full-screen interface, which will show you a list of all unmounted volumes currently available.

See also

DBLSPACE	See this command for an overview of the DBLSPACE command options.
DBLSPACE AUTOMOUNT	Controls whether DOS 6.2 and later tries to automatically mount compressed disks.

DBLSPACE /DELETE   Use this command when you want to actually delete a volume rather than just hide it.

DBLSPACE /MOUNT   Permits access to a DoubleSpace volume.

DBLSPACE.SYS
DOS 6 and later, Device driver

Device driver for relocating DBLSPACE.BIN

Unlike other DEVICE statements in your CONFIG.SYS file, the DEVICE=DBLSPACE.SYS statement does not actually load a device driver. Instead, its sole purpose is to relocate the DBLSPACE.BIN driver. The control file for DBLSPACE (DBLSPACE.BIN) is loaded automatically when you boot your system from a drive that has been compressed with DoubleSpace. The DEVICE statement relocates the control file from the top of conventional memory to its final location, which can be lower or upper memory.

When and why

You should always use this command when you're using DoubleSpace. (DBLSPACE will automatically add this line to your CONFIG.SYS file when you first install DBLSPACE, so you probably won't need to add this line yourself.) This command simply moves the DBLSPACE.BIN driver into the correct part of memory, either lower or upper memory. Without this command, DBLSPACE.BIN will actually be at the end of lower memory (usually near the 640K limit), where it could get overwritten by an improperly written program. So it is always a good idea to move DBLSPACE.BIN.

Syntax

device=dblspace.sys /move [/nohma]
This line in CONFIG.SYS moves DBLSPACE.BIN to conventional memory (in the first 640K) along with other device drivers in lower memory.

devicehigh=dblspace.sys /move [/nohma]
This line in CONFIG.SYS moves DBLSPACE.BIN into upper memory. This line must appear after lines such as HIMEM.SYS and EMM386.SYS that create upper memory.

Switches

/nohma
Don't load into high memory area (DOS 6.2 and later). Without this switch, DOS tries to load part of DBLSPACE.BIN into the HMA (if there is enough room). This switch tells DOS not to use any of the HMA for DBLSPACE.BIN. Normally, if your CONFIG.SYS file contains a line DOS=HIGH, the compression server part of DBLSPACE.BIN is loaded into the HMA.

Notes

Device drivers and compressed drives

Some disk drives require device drivers in the CONFIG.SYS file in order to become visible to DOS. In such cases, you need to make sure that these device drivers are loaded in CONFIG.SYS *before* the line that loads DBLSPACE.SYS. If your device driver appears after the line that loads DBLSPACE.SYS, you won't be able automatically mount volumes located on those drives. The best advice we have is to load DBLSPACE.SYS as late in your CONFIG.SYS file as you can (we have ours at the very end of the CONFIG.SYS file). However, read the next "Note" for a warning.

Conflicts with DBLSPACE.SYS and other device drivers

A few device drivers can conflict with DBLSPACE.SYS if they're loaded in CONFIG.SYS before the line that loads DBLSPACE.SYS. Here's why.

When DOS first loads DBLSPACE.BIN, it loads it at the very top of conventional memory (usually at the end of the first 640K). DOS moves DBLSPACE.BIN to a lower location in memory (and possibly partly into the HMA) when it encounters the line in CONFIG.SYS that loads DBLSPACE.SYS. The problem is that some programs try to use memory at the top of conventional memory where DOS initially loads DBLSPACE.BIN. To prevent such a situation, the line that loads DBLSPACE.SYS *must* appear in CONFIG.SYS before lines that load any programs that use the top end of conventional memory. How do you know which programs have this problem?

The DoubleSpace setup program knows about most of these programs and automatically inserts a line that loads DBLSPACE.SYS before any such programs in your CONFIG.SYS file. You might also discover that your CONFIG.SYS has more than one line to load DBLSPACE.SYS. This is not a problem.

See also
DBLSPACE   The command that actually compresses and manages DoubleSpace volumes.

DEBUG — All DOS, External

Start the system debugger

This is a very advanced command that is almost always used by programmers (ordinary users usually use DEBUG only when they're told exactly what to type). As such, we won't cover DEBUG in this book. You'll find a full description in your DOS manual.

DEFRAG — DOS 6 and later, External

Rearranges files to eliminate fragmentation

DEFRAG moves the files on your disk so that every file is contiguous. *Contiguous* means that the file is arranged with its file segments in a continuous section of the disk with no wasted space between the file segments. This improves the speed of file access. To defragment a DoubleSpace volume, you must use DBLSPACE /DEFRAGMENT.

DEFRAG

When and why

Speed. Most of the time you'll probably use this command to speed up access to your files. When files become fragmented into a number of small pieces scattered across your disk, it takes DOS longer to find your files. This command will bring all the pieces back together so they're in one place.

You might also want to use this command before you create a large file, such as a DoubleSpace volume file, to make sure the file itself won't start life fragmented. Once you create a DoubleSpace volume file, DEFRAG won't let you unfragment it (for an advanced way to get around this limitation, see the "Notes" section below). You'll also find a more involved discussion of file fragmentation in the note "How DEFRAG works."

DEFRAG can either be run as a full-screen utility or from the command line. Each of the command options identified here is also available as a menu command or dialog box setting within the full-screen version. When started from the command line, DEFRAG creates a full-screen status screen and then automatically performs the requested tasks.

Syntax

defrag [/lcd | /bw] [/g0]
Starts the full-screen DEFRAG utility.

or

defrag [*drive*:] **/u** [/b] [/skiphigh] [/lcd | /bw] [/g0] [/h] [/q]
Relocates files so that each file is contiguous. Empty space may exist between files.

or

defrag [*drive*:] **/f** [/s[:]*order*] [/b] [/skiphigh] [/lcd | /bw] [/g0] [/h]
Arranges files so that each file is contiguous and no space exists between files.

or

defrag [*drive*:] **/q** [/b] [/skiphigh] [/lcd | /bw] [/g0] [/h]
Arranges empty space so there will be no gaps in the empty space.

Parameters

drive
Specifies the drive to be defragmented. If no drive is specified, the current drive is used.

Switches

/u
Unfragment files only. Moves the minimum amount to ensure that every file is contiguous. Empty space may exist between files. You cannot use /u with the /f, /q, or /s switches.

/f
Fully optimize. Places the files in contiguous segments with no space between the files. If you use the /s switch, the files will also be arranged in a specific order. Without the /s, DEFRAG will move the minimum number of files necessary to arrange them with no space between. You cannot use /f with the /u or /q switches.

/q
Unfragment free space (not documented by Microsoft). This option makes sure you have a single block of free space on your disk. This is useful if you want to create a larger file (such as a compressed volume) that will not be fragmented. DEFRAG will move the minimum number of files in order to put all the free space in one place. This option is faster than a full optimize but doesn't defragment the files. When you use this switch with a drive letter, DEFRAG will defragment your disk without asking for confirmation before it starts. The other two switches, /u and /f, always ask for confirmation first.

/s[:]*order*
Sorted defragmented files. Allows you to control the order in which files will be placed on the disk by DEFRAG. This option will move more files than any other option, which will make it the slowest. In some cases, files might even be moved more than once to put them into the correct order. Here is a list of additional sort parameters that you can supply after /S to control how DEFRAG orders files on your disk:

N	In alphabetic order by name
N-	In reverse alphabetic order by name (Z through A)
E	In alphabetic order by extension
E-	In reverse alphabetic order by extension (Z through A)
D	By date and time, earliest first
D-	By date and time, latest first
S	By size, smallest first
S-	By size, largest first

/b
Reboot. After defragmenting is complete, DEFRAG will reboot your computer.

/h
Hidden. Moves hidden files. Without this switch, DEFRAG will not move hidden files — it must work around them. This is important because some older programs expect, and require, that their hidden files never move on the disk. If you use this switch and you can't run an application, you may need to reinstall and re-create the hidden files. In any event, files marked with the system attribute will never be moved (DoubleSpace's volume files are marked with the system attribute).

/skiphigh
Load in conventional. Without this switch, DEFRAG uses upper memory if it is available. This switch tells DEFRAG to use conventional memory only.

/lcd
LCD display. Configures DEFRAG for display on LCD systems, such as laptops. Without this switch, you may not be able to read everything on your laptop screen. You cannot use this switch with the /BW switch.

/bw
Black and white. Configures DEFRAG to display in black and white. You cannot use this switch with the /LCD switch.

/g0
No graphics. Disables the graphic mouse and graphic character display on EGA or VGA screens. This switch should permit running the DEFRAG utility on any monitor. You can also combine this switch with either the /LCD or the /BW switch.

Notes

DOS 6.2 improvements
The version of DEFRAG introduced in DOS 6.2 makes much better use of extended memory, which allows it to defragment much larger hard disks. DEFRAG can also handle many more files and directories than the version in DOS 6.0.

DEFRAG and Windows
You cannot run DEFRAG from within Microsoft Windows. Because of the way Windows handles writing file segments to disk, you would risk losing data during the defragmentation process, so DEFRAG refuses to run while Windows is running. You should only run DEFRAG from the DOS prompt with no other programs running.

DEFRAG and the DOS Task Swapper
You cannot run DEFRAG from within the DOS Task Swapper. Because other programs may have files open, and because moving open files confuses DOS, DEFRAG refuses to run whenever the DOS Task Swapper is active. You'll need to quit from the DOS Shell before you run DEFRAG.

DEFRAG and SmartDrive
DEFRAG is compatible with the read and write buffering features of SmartDrive. You do not need to turn off the SmartDrive caching to run DEFRAG.

Defragmenting DoubleSpace's hidden volume files
Even though DEFRAG has the /H switch to allow it to move hidden files, it will never defragment DoubleSpace's hidden files because they're also marked with the system attribute. However, if you're feeling really brave, you can defragment DoubleSpace's volume files.

Here's how you do it. First, and this is very important, you must unmount all the volumes that have DBLSPACE.*nnn* files on the volume you want to defragment (you cannot use this method if your C drive is a compressed volume). Next, you'll need to clear the system attribute from the hidden DBLSPACE.*nnn* files on the host disk (you can use DBLSPACE to find all unmounted volumes and DBLSPACE /LIST to find the host files for mounted volumes). Then use DEFRAG /H to defragment the host volume and move hidden files. Once DEFRAG finishes, turn on the system attribute for all the DBLSPACE.*nnn* files you defragmented. And finally, mount any of these volumes again.

How DEFRAG works
A file is fragmented when the parts of the file are not located in a continuous section on the disk. Fragmentation occurs as a result of modifying the files on the disk. Creating new files, deleting old files, or simply changing the contents of a file may create fragmentation. The greater the fragmentation of files on a disk, the slower the access time. DEFRAG is a utility designed to eliminate file fragmentation. It reorganizes the files on the disk so that every file occupies a continuous section on the disk.

Part II: Command Reference

The easiest way to understand fragmentation is to imagine that you have a series of files tightly packed together. You decided to modify one of the files in the middle and add several pages. Rather than move all of the other files, DOS inserts a pointer at the end of the file you are modifying and locates the new portion somewhere else on the disk. If a disk becomes too fragmented, DOS wastes time tracking down all the pointers (and the little fragments of the file they reference) and your system slows down.

In its simplest, and fastest, form, DEFRAG takes each file and makes sure it is written in a continuous section on the disk. In its most elaborate form, DEFRAG rewrites all of the files in a specific order (perhaps alphabetically by filename), closely packed and with no empty space between files. This results in all of the empty space being grouped together at the end of the disk.

ERRORLEVEL returned

DEFRAG returns information that batch files can test with the IF ERRORLEVEL command. Here are the exit codes DEFRAG returns:

0   DEFRAG finished without errors.
1   There was some type of internal error.
2   The disk didn't have any free clusters. DEFRAG needs at least 1 cluster free.
3   You pressed Ctrl-C or Ctrl-Break to exit DEFRAG before it finished.
4   There was an error of some other type.
5   DEFRAG had a problem reading a cluster (usually from a bad sector).
6   DEFRAG had a problem writing a cluster (usually from a bad sector).
7   There was a problem with the FAT. You need to use CHKDSK /F to fix the problem.
8   DEFRAG had a problem with memory.
9   Not enough memory to DEFRAG the disk.

You can use this information in batch files to take an action if DEFRAG failed.

Examples

Defragment drive C and place files in alphabetical order

In order to fully defragment drive C and arrange the files in alphabetical order (from A to Z), you would use the following command:

```
C:\>defrag c: /f /h /sn
```

This example would also move the hidden files on drive C and place them in the appropriate alphabetical order.

See also

DBLSPACE /DEFRAGMENT   Used to consolidate the files on a DoubleSpace volume.

DEL (ERASE)   All DOS, Internal

Delete (erase) a file from a disk
This command removes one or more files from your disk.

When and why
This is a command you should become familiar with unless you're using a shell program such as the Norton Commander or the DOS Shell. Deleting files from your disk is the only way to free space on your disk for new files. If you don't delete files, you'll eventually run out of space on your hard disk, which will probably happen much sooner than you expect.

From time to time you might want to do a little hard disk maintenance, which involves deleting files you don't need anymore and reorganizing your directory structure and files so you can find things more easily.

Syntax
del *filespec* [**/p**]
or
erase *filespec* [**/p**]
Deletes one or more files from a disk.

Parameters
filespec
The name of the file that you want to delete. This can include a drive letter, pathname, and filename. You can delete groups of files by using the DOS * and ? wildcard characters.

Note: If you provide just a path for *filespec*, DEL assumes that you want to delete all the files in that directory. In this case DEL will ask you for confirmation before it deletes any files (DEL normally doesn't ask before it deletes files). There is a single confirmation message for all of the files in the directory.

Switches
/p
Prompt (DOS 4.0 and later). Ask for permission before deleting each file. This makes it easy to selectively delete some of the files in a group.

Notes
What DEL and ERASE do
This command deletes a file from the disk by erasing the directory entry for that file. The actual contents of the file remain on the disk, but the space they used is marked as being available for use by new files. This is what allows the UNDELETE command to bring back files that you deleted accidentally (it also means that DEL is very fast because it doesn't have to write over the contents of the file). If you have confidential data that you need to wipe off your disk, you'll find programs in

commercial utility products (such as the Norton Utilities, PC Tools, and the Mace Utilities) that actually write over the contents of the files so that even UNDELETE won't be able to recover the files.

DEL vs. ERASE
You're probably wondering whether you should use DEL or ERASE to delete files. Most people use DEL rather than ERASE because it involves less typing. But consider also that DEL and DIR are a lot alike, so you might accidentally type **DEL** when you meant to type **DIR**. For this reason you might consider using ERASE rather than DEL.

Using the /P switch
The /P switch is a good way to selectively delete files from a directory. When you use the /P switch, DOS will ask for confirmation before deleting each file:

```
filename,    Delete (Y/N)?
```

Type **Y** and then Enter to delete this file or **N** followed by Enter to keep the file.

Wildcard characters
You can use both of the DOS wildcard characters (? and *) to delete groups of files. If you tell DOS to delete all the files in a directory, using *.*, DOS will ask you to confirm this request before it continues:

```
All files in directory will be deleted!
Are you sure (Y/N)?_
```

which allows you to press **N** followed by Enter to back out of deleting all the files.

If, however, you use any wildcard specification other than *.*, DOS won't confirm your request, it will just delete all the files that match the specification you provided. So be careful when using wildcard characters!

Using DIR to check wildcards
If you want to use wildcard characters to delete a group of files, you can use the DIR command to see what group of files you'll delete before you use the DEL command.

Note: There is one case where DIR and DEL treat wildcard characters differently: when you provide no extension or period after the filename. If, for example, you type **DIR *** (without a trailing period), DIR takes this to mean *.*. On the other hand, DEL * will only delete files that have no extension (in other words, DEL takes * to mean *. rather than *.*).

Messages
```
Access denied
```
The file is probably marked as a read-only file. Use the ATTRIB command to turn off the read-only attribute and then try again. *Note:* The DOS Shell allows you to delete read-only files directly.

```
File not found
```
DEL couldn't find any files that matched the name (or wildcard pattern) that you provided. You can use DIR to see what files are there and then try DEL again once you've found the files you want to delete.

```
Path not found
```
One of the directory names in the path you provided doesn't exist. Check your path and try again.

Examples
To delete all the BAK files (which are usually old copies of other files) in the current directory, you can type

```
C:\>del *.bak
```

You can also delete all the files in a directory by providing the name of a directory (without a filename or wildcard pattern). For example, to delete all the files in the \TEMP directory, type

```
C:\>del \temp
```

Here's a shortcut for deleting all the files in the current directory (which is usually DEL *.*):

```
C:\>del .
```

The period refers to the current directory, so DEL will delete all the files in the current directory.

See also

MIRROR   (DOS 5 only.) You can use the MIRROR /T command to load a TSR program that will track files that you delete. This makes the UNDELETE command more reliable when recovering files. In DOS 6, the functions of MIRROR have been incorporated into the UNDELETE command.

RMDIR   Deletes a directory from your disk. Note that you must remove all the files in a directory using DEL before you can use RMDIR to remove a directory.

UNDELETE   This command serves two purposes. First, it allows you to recover files that you deleted accidentally. Note that it can't always recover deleted files. You can also use UNDELETE with either the /T or the /S switch to load a TSR program that will track files that you delete. This makes it much easier for UNDELETE to recover files.

DELOLDOS   DOS 5 and later, External

Delete previous version of DOS

This command allows you to remove the previous version of DOS from your hard disk. The DOS 5 and 6 install programs save your old version of DOS to a directory called OLD_DOS.*n*, where *n* will be 1 unless you already have a directory with this name.

Part II: Command Reference

When and why
The INSTALL command, which you probably used to install DOS 5 and later, saves the previous version of DOS that was installed on your computer. This allows you to go back to your old version if you have problems with DOS 5 and later. You'll want to run this command once you're satisfied that the new DOS is working properly since the old version takes up space on your disk.

Syntax
deloldos [/b]
Remove the previous version of DOS saved by INSTALL from your hard disk. This is a full-screen program that will prompt you.

Switches
/b
Black and white. Displays in black-and-white mode, which is useful on laptop computers, or black-and-white displays connected to color cards. DELOLDOS is a full-screen program that will display in color unless you specify this option.

Note
This command also deletes itself from your DOS directory when it finishes. Also, DELOLDOS deletes all former DOS directories, even if you have more than one (such as if you upgraded to DOS 5 and then DOS 6).

DELTREE   DOS 6 and later, External

Delete an entire directory (and subdirectories)
DELTREE provides a single command for pruning entire branches from your directory tree. DELTREE will remove directories that contain files, subdirectories, or both files and subdirectories. It is most useful for removing applications.

When and why
Use this command when you want to delete an entire directory without having to empty it first. The RMDIR command will only delete directories that contain no files or subdirectories, which meant that in DOS 5 and earlier, it took a lot of work to remove a directory if it had a lot of subdirectories.

The most common use for DELTREE is to remove an application's directories. Many applications install a series of subdirectories for organizing their support files. DELTREE provides a single command for removing the application's entire directory branch. You should always check first, though, to ensure that there are no documents that you want to keep inside the directory or subdirectories.

Syntax
deltree *path* [/y]
Deletes all of the files and subdirectories contained within *path* and then deletes the directory *path* itself.

Switches

/y
Yes, delete entire tree. This switch is probably one of the most dangerous in DOS. It confirms the delete operation and suppresses the standard confirmation prompt. We don't recommend using this switch!

Notes

Deleting files and directories

The DELTREE command actually deletes both files and directories that match *path*. For example, if you type

```
C:\SOME_DIR>deltree c*.*
```

the DELTREE command will delete all files and directories that start with the letter *C* in the directory SOME_DIR. DELTREE will, however, ask you before it deletes each file and subdirectory.

DELTREE and attibutes

DELTREE ignores any attributes on files within directories, so marking files as read-only will not protect them from DELTREE. Be careful that the directory that you are deleting does not contain any hidden files that may contain important information.

Wildcard characters

Be very, very careful when using wildcard characters with DELTREE. Wildcard characters allow you to delete a number of directories. Fortunately, DELTREE will ask you before it deletes each directory.

DELTREE and relative paths

Although DELTREE fully supports relative paths, it does not expand them to the absolute path when displaying the confirmation message. The confirmation prompt displays the path as you entered it. If you use relative paths, be extremely careful to check your specification.

Deleting the current directory

DELTREE will not permit you to delete the current directory. You may move to the parent directory or any other directory.

Examples

Delete the branch \PROGS\GAMES

To remove the GAMES subdirectory and all of its contents, you enter the command

```
C:\>deltree \progs\games
```

DOS prompts for confirmation with the message

```
Delete directory "\progs\games" and all its subdirectories?
[yn]
```

If you press **Y** and then Enter, the directory and its contents will be deleted. To cancel the operation, press **N** and then Enter.

Part II: Command Reference

Using wildcard characters

Let's say you have three subdirectories in the current directory, called

```
FIRST
FOURTH
SIXTH
```

You can delete the two directories that start with F using the following command:

```
C:\SOME_DIR>deltree f*
Delete directory "first" and all its subdirectories? [yn] y
Deleting first...
Delete directory "fourth" and all its subdirectories? [yn] y
Deleting fourth...
C:\>
```

As you can see, DELTREE asks you before it deletes each directory that matches the wildcard name you supplied.

See also

RMDIR   Removes an empty directory.

DEL   Removes a file or group of files.

DEVICE — All DOS, CONFIG.SYS

Install device driver

This command is used in your CONFIG.SYS file and allows you to load device drivers into DOS. Device drivers are small programs that add extra features to DOS during the startup process.

When and why

You may or may not work with this command directly. Most installation programs, including the DOS 6 INSTALL, automatically insert DEVICE= lines into your CONFIG.SYS file with the correct settings. You'll want to work directly with a DEVICE= line when you want to modify settings made by install programs or when you want to install a device driver yourself.

A device driver, by the way, is a program that controls a physical device, such as a display screen, a keyboard, or a mouse. Device drivers can also create logical devices, which are not real devices but appear as devices to the system. For example, the EMM386.EXE device driver creates a logical device by making some of your extended memory look like expanded memory on an expanded memory card (a physical device).

Syntax

device=_filespec_ [_device-command-line_]
Installs the device driver _filespec_ into DOS.

DEVICE

device?=*filespec* [*device-command-line*]   (DOS 6 and later)
DOS asks you if you want to install the device driver *filespec* into DOS.

Parameters

filespec
The name and location of the device driver you want to install. You must include the extension on the filename (DEVICE does not assume the name has the SYS extension). You'll also have to include a pathname unless the device driver is in the root directory.

device-command-line
Many device drivers allow you to provide extra parameters after the driver's name.

Notes

Device driver extensions
Most device drivers have the SYS extension to tell you that they're device drivers rather than executable files (which end in EXE or COM). There are two files with the SYS extension, however, that are not device drivers: COUNTRY.SYS and KEYBOARD.SYS. See the COUNTRY and KEYB commands on how to use these two files. Do not load COUNTRY.SYS or KEYBOARD.SYS as a device driver!

DISPLAY.SYS and console drivers
If you're using a console driver such as ANSI.SYS as well as the DISPLAY.SYS device driver (used for international support), make sure you load ANSI.SYS *before* you load DISPLAY.SYS.

DOS device drivers
Here is a list of the standard device drivers that come with DOS:

Name	DOS version	Description
ANSI.SYS	2.0 +	Provides some extra functionality for the display and the keyboard.
CHKSTATE.SYS	6.0 +	This device driver is used by MemMaker and should not be installed into your CONFIG.SYS file.
DBLSPACE.SYS	6.0 +	Provides support for disk compression and controls where DBLSPACE.BIN is loaded in memory.
DISPLAY.SYS	3.3 +	Provides code-page switching on EGA and VGA screens (and the IBM PC Convertible's LCD display) for international character sets.
DRIVER.SYS	3.2 +	Provides support for floppy disk drives that DOS supports but which your computer's ROM BIOS doesn't know about.
EGA.SYS	5.0 +	Allows the task switcher in the DOS Shell to save and restore graphics screens on EGA displays.

(continued)

Name	DOS version	Description
EMM386.EXE	5.0 +	This is both a device driver and a command. The device driver makes extended memory look like expanded memory on 80386 or better processors. (Prior to DOS 5, the file was EMM386.SYS and shipped with Windows 3.0.)
HIMEM.SYS	5.0 +	Provides a memory manager for extended memory (XMS).
INTERLNK.EXE	6.0 +	Provides a way to connect two computers using a parallel or serial cable.
POWER.EXE	6.0 +	Power-management functions for laptops.
PRINTER.SYS	3.3 – 5.0	Provides code-page switching for some IBM printers to support international character sets.
RAMDRIVE.SYS	3.2 +	Uses RAM to create a very fast disk drive.
SETVER.EXE	5.0 +	This is both a command and a device driver. The device driver keeps a table in memory of programs that need to think they're running on a different version of DOS.
SMARTDRV.SYS	5.0	Provides disk caching. (Replaced by SMARTDRV.EXE in DOS 6.)
SMARTDRV.EXE	6.0 +	Provides disk caching. (Prior to DOS 6, the file was SMARTDRV.SYS.)
VDISK.SYS	IBM 3.0 +	Uses RAM to create a fast disk drive. The MS-DOS version is RAMDRIVE.SYS.

Messages

The error messages displayed by DOS usually appear early in the boot process, and you have to keep a sharp eye out for them (you can use the Pause key to stop the display). When DOS does display an error message, it tells you what line in your CONFIG.SYS file is creating a problem. With DOS 6, you can use the new interactive startup (described under the CONFIG.SYS entry) to step through your CONFIG.SYS file. You can also put a ? after DEVICE to have DOS 6 ask you before it loads each device driver.

```
Bad or missing filespec
Error in CONFIG.SYS line nn
```

You'll usually see this message when DOS can't find the device driver you asked it to load.

```
Unrecognized command in CONFIG.SYS
Error in CONFIG.SYS line nn
```
You'll see this message if you mistyped DEVICE=. Check your CONFIG.SYS file to make sure all the lines are correct.

Examples
To load the ANSI.SYS display device driver from your DOS directory, you would enter this line into your CONFIG.SYS file:

```
device=c:\dos\ansi.sys
```

You'll find more examples of using DEVICE= under the descriptions of the standard device drivers that come with DOS.

See also
CONFIG.SYS   You'll find more information on how to use and set up your CONFIG.SYS file in the description of CONFIG.SYS in this reference section. You will also find a discussion of the new interactive startup option.

DEVICEHIGH   If your computer has an 80386 or better microprocessor, you can use the DEVICEHIGH= line (rather than DEVICE=) with EMM386.EXE to load a device driver into the upper memory block (UMB).

REM   You can comment-out lines in your CONFIG.SYS file by putting REM in front of the DEVICE= line.

DEVICEHIGH — DOS 5 and later, CONFIG.SYS

Load device driver into upper memory
This command in a CONFIG.SYS file is identical to the DEVICE= command except that it loads the device driver into the upper memory blocks (UMBs) rather than in conventional memory.

When and why
Loading device drivers into the UMBs is a good way to keep conventional memory free for applications programs or other programs that don't use the UMBs.

To use this command, you must have a program installed (as a device driver) that provides UMBs, such as EMM386.EXE. Most of the UMB programs run only on 80386 or faster microprocessors.

Don't use this command, however, if you have a commercial memory manager (such as 386MAX, BLUEMAX, CEMM, or QEMM). These programs provide their own versions of DEVICEHIGH and LOADHIGH that are more flexible, more reliable, and work better with programs that try to load themselves into upper memory.

Syntax

devicehigh=*filespec* [*device-command-line*]
Installs the device driver *filespec* into the UMBs. The syntax is identical to the syntax for DEVICE=, except that the command is called DEVICEHIGH instead of DEVICE.

devicehigh [[/l:*block1*[,*size1*][;*block2*[,*size2*] [/s]]=*filespec* [*device-command-line*]
(DOS 6 syntax)

devicehigh size=*hex-size filespec* [*device-command-line*] (DOS 5 syntax)
Loads a device into a block of memory at least *hex-size* bytes large.

devicehigh? [[/l:*block1*[,*size1*][;*block2*[,*size2*] [/s]]=*filespec* [*device-command-line*]
(DOS 6 and later)
When you add a question mark after the DEVICEHIGH statement, DOS will ask before it loads a device when this line appears in CONFIG.SYS.

Parameters

filespec
The name and location of the device driver you want to install. You must include the extension on the filename (DEVICE does not assume the name has the SYS extension). You'll also have to include a pathname unless the device driver is in the root directory.

device-command-line
Many device drivers allow you to provide extra parameters after the driver's name.

hex-size
Specifies the minimum size of the memory block into which DOS can load a device driver. This is required for some device drivers that allocate extra memory when they're loaded and crash if there isn't enough memory available. This size must be a hexadecimal number, which you can obtain from the MEM command (see the "Notes" section).

Switches

/l: *block1*
or
/l: *block1;block2*,
Location (DOS 6 and later). Loads the device driver into a specific Upper Memory Block (UMB). The *block1* and *block2* parameters specify the block number where the device is to be placed. Only some devices can be split between blocks. Use MEM /M to determine how a specific device driver uses memory. Use MEM /F to identify free blocks of memory.

/l: *block1, size1; block2, size2*
(DOS 6 and later.) The *size1* parameter specifies the minimum size for *block1*. If *block1* is smaller than *size1*, no attempt is made to load the device driver into that UMB. You must use this format if you are specifying the /S switch.

/s
Shrink block (DOS 6 and later). This switch can only be used in conjunction with the /L switch and when a minimum block size has been specified. The /s switch causes the memory block to be reduced to the size specified, and any remaining memory is redefined as a new UMB.

DEVICEHIGH

Notes

Warning! Before you install any device drivers into upper memory, create a bootable floppy disk with DOS on it. This will allow you to start your computer from a floppy disk in case changes you make to your CONFIG.SYS file (on your hard disk) create problems that keep DOS from starting off your hard disk. Starting with DOS 6 you can also use the F5 key to bypass the CONFIG.SYS and AUTOEXEC.BAT files, or the F8 key to select which lines in CONFIG.SYS you want to include. You'll have about 2 seconds after DOS displays `Starting MS-DOS...` (unless you've eliminated this delay using the SWITCHES=/F or /N lines in your CONFIG.SYS file).

UMB memory

The upper memory blocks are areas of memory located between the 640K limit for DOS programs and the end of conventional memory (1MB). This area of memory is normally reserved for ROMs (read-only memory) that provide support for various hardware items in your computer (such as your display adapter). There are usually gaps between these ROMs which contain no memory.

If your computer has at least an 80386 microprocessor, you can use a 386 control program, such as EMM386.EXE, 386MAX, CEMM, or QEMM, to fill in these gaps with memory called UMBs.

DOS=UMB

To use the DEVICEHIGH command, you need to tell DOS to manage the UMBs. You do this by providing a DOS=UMB line in your CONFIG.SYS file (this can be anywhere in the file). You also need to install HIMEM.SYS and EMM386.EXE (or a commercial equivalent that replaces both) in your CONFIG.SYS file.

MemMaker

DOS 6 introduces a memory configuration utility, MemMaker. To obtain the optimum memory usage with Microsoft drivers, you can have MemMaker try to find an optimal usage of UMB for you. See the MemMaker entry in this Command Reference for details.

Other memory managers

If you're using another memory manager, such as 386MAX, BLUEMAX, QEMM, or CEMM, you should use their versions of DEVICEHIGH and LOADHIGH rather than DOS's version (and don't use DOS=UMB). This is because DOS's versions aren't as flexible or reliable as the commercial program's versions.

Using the size parameter

There are some device drivers that need to be able to enlarge their use of memory as they're being installed. For these device drivers you'll need to provide a size parameter that tells DEVICEHIGH how much memory the device driver must have in order to install correctly. The easiest way to get a value for this parameter is to first load the device into low memory (using the DEVICE= command). Then you can use the MEM /C command to see how much memory the device driver actually uses:

```
mem /c /p
```

MEM will list all the programs that are installed in memory, with the size (in hexadecimal notation) after each device driver name. Just use the number you see in MEM's display for the number in DEVICEHIGH's size parameter. (In versions prior to DOS 6, you need to pipe MEM's output through MORE so that you can see the information one page at a time.)

Note: Any changes you make in a device driver's parameters may change the memory needed. When you change parameters, repeat the process described here for determining a new size parameter.

SmartDrive and UMB

Some disk drive adapters may have problems if you load SMARTDRV.EXE into UMB. In such cases, you'll need to use the double-buffer solution provided in DOS 6 (or simply load SMARTDRV.SYS into low memory for DOS before 6). The reasons for this aren't at all simple and have to do with disk drive hardware. Some disk drive controllers won't know how to write to the UMBs because these areas of memory are actually mapped in from extended memory. When the disk drive controller tries to write to those addresses, it sees that the memory isn't really there (the 80386 processor fools all programs, but not all hardware, into thinking there is memory there).

Messages

Same as messages for the DEVICE command in CONFIG.SYS.

Examples

Basic steps

There are a series of steps you must follow in order to use the DEVICEHIGH command. First, you need to install the HIMEM.SYS and EMM386.EXE device drivers (unless you're using a program like 386MAX, QEMM, or CEMM which provides both functions in one program). You'll also need a DOS=UMB line:

```
device=c:\dos\himem.sys
device=c:\dos\emm386.exe ram
dos=umb
devicehigh=c:\dos\mouse.sys
```

The RAM parameter after EMM386 tells it to support the UMBs. You can also use the NOEMS parameter, which supports upper memory, but doesn't support expanded memory. Using NOEMS will give you a little more upper memory for loading your programs.

Device drivers you can load high

Here is a list of device drivers that you might want to load into the UMBs:

ANSI.SYS, DBLSPACE.SYS, DISPLAY.SYS, DRIVER.SYS, EGA.SYS, INTERLNK.EXE, RAMDRIVE.SYS, and SETVER.EXE

See also

DEVICE   This is the original version of the command that loads a device driver into conventional memory (the first 640K).

DIR

DOS=UMB	You'll need this command in your CONFIG.SYS file before you can load device drivers into high memory.
EMM386.EXE	This device driver can supply UMB memory required for loading device drivers into high memory.
HIMEM.SYS	You'll need to install HIMEM.SYS before you can install EMM386.EXE. And you'll need both (or a commercial equivalent) to load device drivers into upper memory.
LOADHIGH	This is the command to use if you want to load TSR programs into the UMBs.
MEM	You can use the MEM /CLASSIFY command to see how much memory is used by a device driver in conventional memory before you load it into high memory (so you can provide a size limit for the program).
MEMMAKER	This program will help you optimize the use of upper memory. It will automatically set up DEVICEHIGH lines for you in CONFIG.SYS.

DIR   All DOS, Internal

Display list of files in directory

This command displays information about files on your disks.

When and why
Almost everyone uses the DIR command at some point. The only people who don't use the DIR command are those who use a DOS shell program.

Syntax
dir *filespec* [**/p**] [**/w**]   (DOS before 5.0)
dir *filespec* [**/p**] [**/w**] [**/s**] [**/b**] [**/l**] [**/a**[**:**][*attributes*]] [**/o**[**:**][*sort-order*]]
                                                                        (DOS before 6.0)
dir *filespec* [**/p**] [**/w**] [**/s**] [**/b**] [**/l**] [**/c** | **ch**] [**/a**[**:**][*attributes*]] [**/o**[**:**][*sort-order*]]
Displays directory information on the files defined by *filespec*.

Parameters
filespec
The files you want to see directory information for. This filespec can include a drive letter, a directory, and/or a filename (which can include the ? and * wildcard characters). (Default is *.*.)

Switches
/p
Page output. Pauses after each screenful of directory information. This switch allows you to view one screenful of files at a time. Press any key to see the next screen (there is no way to back up).

/w
Wide display. Rather than size, date, and time information, displays five columns of filenames. This is a good way to view as many filenames as possible.

/s
Subdirectories (DOS 5 and later). Lists all the files in subdirectories as well as the current directory that match *filespec*. This is a good way to find a file if you know its name, but you forgot where you put it.

/b
Brief display (DOS 5 and later). Displays only file and directory names (in other words, doesn't display the volume label, serial number, current directory, or directory information for any of the files). This switch is useful when you're redirecting the output of DIR to a file or another program. The /B switch overrides the /W switch. Using the /S switch with this switch causes each filename to be preceded by a drive letter and path.

/l
Lowercase (DOS 5 and later). The /L switch displays names in lowercase letters; normally DIR uses uppercase letters for all names.

/c
Compression ratio (DOS 6 and later). Displays the compression ratio for files on a DoubleSpace volume based upon an 8K cluster size. This switch is not compatible with the /B or /W switches.

/ch
Compression on host ratio (DOS 6 and later). Displays the compression ratio for files on a DoubleSpace volume based upon the cluster size used by the host drive. This switch is not compatible with the /B or /W switches. This switch is a variant of, and cannot be used with, the /C switch.

/a[[:]*attribute*[...]]
Attribute display (DOS 5 and later). Displays only the names of files that have the file attribute *attribute* set. By default, DIR displays all files except for hidden and system files. The /A switch without an attribute displays *all* files (including hidden and system). You can supply more than one attribute (don't separate them) which displays only the files with those attributes:

h	Show hidden files.
-h	Don't show hidden files.
s	Show system files.
-s	Don't show system files.
d	Show directories as well as files.
-d	Don't show directories — show only files.
a	Show only files with the archive bit set (need to be backed up).
-a	Show files that haven't changed since the last backup.
r	Show read-only files.
-r	Don't show files that are marked as read-only.

The colon between the /A switch and the attribute is optional.

DIR

/o[[:*sort-order***[...]]**
Sort order (DOS 5 and later). Sorts the filenames according to *sort-order*. By default, DIR displays the files unsorted. This switch without a sort order is equivalent to /OGN (alphabetical, with directories listed first). You can combine more than one sort order (don't use spaces to separate them), in which case DIR sorts by the first order first and then by the second, etc. For example, /OEN sorts first by extension and then by name for files with the same extension. Here is the list of sort orders:

n	Sort in alphabetical order by name.
-n	Sort in reverse alphabetical order by name (Z through A).
e	Sort in alphabetical order by extension.
-e	Sort in reverse alphabetical order by extension.
d	Sort by date and time, with the oldest first.
-d	Sort by date and time, with the newest first.
s	Sort by file size, with the smallest first.
-s	Sort by file size, with the largest first.
c	(DOS 6 and later.) Sort by compression ratio, with the smallest first.
-c	(DOS 6 and later.) Sort by compression ratio, with the largest first.
g	List the directories before all the files.
-g	List the directories after all the files.

The colon between the /O switch and sort specification is optional.

Notes

Directories

Starting with DOS 5, the DIR command surrounds directories in a wide listing with square brackets (such as [SUB-DIR]). This allows you to determine which names in a wide directory listing refer to directories rather than files.

Directory size

(DOS 5 and later.) After directory listing, the total number of files and the total size for all files combined is displayed. If you use the /S switch to display a series of subdirectories, the totals for each subdirectory are displayed and a grand total is displayed at the end of the listing.

Date and time formats

The format for the date and time you see in the directory listing is determined by the country setting (see the description of the COUNTRY command).

Setting default DIR options

(DOS 5 and later.) You can set default switches for the DIR command using the DIRCMD environment variable. Simply set this environment variable to the list of switches that you want DIR to use by default. For example, to set the sort order to name, display directories first, and display names in lowercase only, you would use this command:

```
C:\>set dircmd=/ong /l
```

You can override switches set in the DIRCMD environment variable by using a minus sign after the /. For example, to turn off use of lowercase letters, you would type

`C:\>`**`dir /-L`**

Examples

Using sort order

We like to see the files in our directories in alphabetical order, with the directories listed first so they're easy to find. The following command sets both sort orders and displays names in lowercase letters:

`C:\>`**`dir /ong /l`**

Using the DIRCMD environment variable

We set our DIRCMD environment variable so DIR will display filenames sorted alphabetically, with the directories shown first. We also like the filenames in lowercase letters since we find them easier to read. Here is the SET command placed in our AUTOEXEC.BAT file used to set up such an environment variable:

`set dircmd=/ong /l`

To override the /L switch, for example, you would type

`C:\>`**`dir /-l`**

Finding a file

If you've forgotten where you put a file, you can use the DIR command to find it. For example, to find the file NC.EXE on your C: drive, type

`C:\>`**`dir \nc.exe /s`**

See also

COUNTRY   This CONFIG.SYS command determines the time and date format used by DIR when it displays information on files.

SET   Use the SET command to set the DIRCMD environment variable.

DISKCOMP   All DOS, External

Compare two floppy disks

This command compares two floppy disks of the same size to see if they're identical. It does a track-by-track comparison, so if you have the same files on both disks but they're not in the same order, DISKCOMP will report that the disks are not identical. Use the COMP command when you just want to check that the files are the same.

DISKCOMP

When and why
Most people only use this command to make sure DISKCOPY worked properly. DISKCOMP can only compare two floppy disks that are the same logical size (by size we mean the number of bytes the disk holds, like 360K vs. 1.2MB). If two disks aren't formatted to exactly the same capacity, or they weren't created with the DISKCOPY command, DISKCOMP won't be able to compare them. For this reason, you'll probably use the COMP command most of the time instead of DISKCOMP.

Warning! Be careful not to type **DISKCOPY** by accident because this will write over any contents currently on the second disk.

Syntax
diskcomp [*drive1*: [*drive2*:]] [/1] [/8]
Compare two disks to see if they're the same.

Parameters
drive1
The floppy disk drive that contains one of the disks. (Default is current drive.) You can omit this parameter only if the current drive is the drive you want to use for both disks.

drive2
The floppy disk drive that contains the other disk. This can be the same as the first drive letter if you want to use the same disk drive (see "Examples" below). (Default is current drive.)

Switches
/1
One side compare (the number one). Compares only the first sides of the disk. You'll probably never use this switch; it's mainly useful for comparing two single-sided floppy disks (chances are you'll never see one).

Notes
Incompatibilities
DISKCOMP works only with floppy disk drives. It does not work on any drive letters created by ASSIGN, or by disk drives that are connected to another drive via the JOIN command.

ERRORLEVEL returned
DISKCOMP returns information that batch files can test with the IF ERRORLEVEL command. Here are the exit codes DISKCOMP returns:

0   The two floppy disks are identical.
1   The two floppy disks are not identical.
2   You pressed Ctrl-C or Ctrl-Break to exit DISKCOMP before it finished.
3   DISKCOMP encountered a disk error reading one of the floppy disks.
4   DISKCOMP had an internal problem.

You can use this information in batch files to take an action if DISKCOMP fails.

Messages

```
Compare error on
side 1, track 3
```
This is the kind of message you'll see when the two disks are not the same. Side can be 0 or 1, and track can be from 0 to 79 (or one less than the number of tracks on the disk). As you can see, this message doesn't give you any information on what's different, except that one of the tracks differs.

```
Drive types or diskette types
not compatible
```
You'll see this message when you try to compare two disks that aren't formatted for the same size (for example, when you try to compare a 360K disk to a 1.2MB disk). Or when you try to compare a 3 ½-inch to a 5¼-inch floppy disk. DISKCOMP can only compare two floppy disks of the same logical size. You can use the COMP command, however, to compare all the files on these two disks.

```
Invalid drive specification
Specified drive does not exist
or is non-removable
```
You can use DISKCOMP only on floppy disk drives. Make sure the drive letter you supplied (or the current drive if you supplied one or no drive letters) is a floppy disk drive. You'll also see this message when you use DISKCOMP with a drive letter created by ASSIGN or that is visible on another drive via JOIN.

Examples

Using one disk drive

If you only have one floppy disk drive, you can compare two floppy disks by swapping disks when DISKCOMP tells you to. To use a single floppy disk drive, use the same drive letter for both drive1 and drive2. For example:

```
C:\>diskcomp a: a:
```

See also

COMP   (DOS 5 and earlier.) Use this command when you're only interested in whether or not the files are the same on two disks.

FC   Since the COMP command doesn't exist in DOS 6, you'll have to use this command to compare files rather than entire disks.

DISKCOPY Use this command to make an identical copy of a floppy disk.

DISKCOPY — All DOS, External

Copy a floppy disk

This command makes an exact copy of a floppy disk. The second floppy disk doesn't have to be formatted — DISKCOPY can format a disk as it writes to it.

DISKCOPY

When and why
You should use this command whenever you purchase a program, to make backup copies of all your disks. Save the original disks in a safe place and use the backup copies to actually install the software on your disk.

Starting in DOS 6.2, you can copy an entire disk (even a 1.44MB floppy disk) without swapping disks a number of times, which you had to with previous versions of the DISKCOPY command. The DISKCOPY command in DOS 6.2 and later use hard disk space to store a copy of the entire floppy disk.

Syntax
diskcopy [*drive1*: [*drive2*:]] [/1] [/8] [/v] [/m]

Makes an exact copy of the disk in *drive1* on the floppy disk in *drive2*. If you have only one floppy disk drive, you can supply the same drive letter for *drive1* and *drive2*, and DISKCOPY will tell you when to swap floppy disks.

Parameters
drive1
The floppy disk drive that contains one of the disks. You may omit this parameter if you want to use the current drive to perform the diskcopy. (Default is the current drive.)

drive2
The floppy disk drive that contains the other disk. This can be the same as the first drive letter if you want to use the same disk drive (see "Examples" below). (Default is the current drive.)

Switches
/1
One side compare (the number one). Copies only the first side of the disk. You'll probably never use this switch; it's mainly useful for copying single-sided floppy disks (chances are you'll never see one).

/8
Eight sectors only (DOS 1–5). Copies only the first eight sectors on each track. This is another switch you'll probably never use. It's useful only when you're copying 160K or 320K disks (which were the type created by DOS 1.0).

/v
Verify (DOS 6 or later). Checks that the copy is accurate. This switch slows the copying process.

/m
Use conventional memory (DOS 6.2 or later). Use conventional memory instead of hard disk space for storage. Starting in DOS 6.2, DISKCOPY copies the contents of a floppy disk to your hard disk so that you don't have to swap floppy disks more than once. This switch tells DISKCOPY that you want it to use memory rather than hard disk space, which means that you probably need to swap floppy disks several times. We're not sure why this flag exists because DISKCOPY automatically switches to using conventional memory if there isn't enough hard disk space free on the boot disk (drive C).

Notes

Incompatibilities
DISKCOPY only works with floppy disk drives. It does not work on any drive letters created by the ASSIGN command or by disk drives connected to another drive via the JOIN command. Also, you can't use DISKCOPY to copy between 3½-inch and 5¼-inch disks (you must use the COPY command for this).

Drive compatibility problems
You may have some problems with normal-density disks (such as 360K) that you create on high-capacity disk drives (such as 1.2MB drives). This usually happens when you originally format the disk in a normal-density disk drive and then use DISKCOPY to make a copy on a 1.2MB drive of a 360K disk. The problem comes when you try to read this new disk on a 360K disk drive; the wider read head on the 360K disk drive will see both the new information on the thin track and some leftover information from the old, thick track. The result is that a 360K disk drive may not be able to read a disk created by DISKCOPY in a 1.2MB disk drive. The best solution is to use an unformatted floppy disk when you're creating a copy of a 360K disk in a 1.2MB disk drive.

Volume serial numbers
If the source disk contains a volume serial number (DOS 4.0 and later), DOS will create a new volume serial number on the new disk. This ensures that you won't have two disks with the same volume serial number.

ErrorLevel returned
DISKCOPY returns information that batch files can test with the IF ERRORLEVEL command. Here are the exit codes DISKCOPY returns:

0   DISKCOPY finished without any errors.
1   There was a read/write error during the copy.
2   You pressed Ctrl-C or Ctrl-Break to exit DISKCOPY before it finished.
3   There was a hardware error.
4   DISKCOPY had an internal problem.

You can use this information in batch files to take an action if DISKCOPY fails.

Messages

```
Drive types or diskette types
not compatible
```
You'll see this message when you try to copy two disks that aren't the same size (for example, when you try to copy a 3½-inch to a 5¼-inch floppy disk). Or when you try to copy a 720K disk to a high-density disk (1.44MB). DISKCOPY can only copy two floppy disks of the same physical size. You can use the COPY command, however, to copy all the files to another disk.

```
Invalid drive specification
Specified drive does not exist
or is non-removable
```
You can use DISKCOPY only on floppy disk drives. Make sure the drive letter you supplied (or the current drive if you supplied one or no drive letters) is a floppy disk drive. You'll also see this message when you use DISKCOMP with a drive letter created by ASSIGN or that is visible on another drive via JOIN.

```
Target diskette may be unusable
```
or
```
Target diskette unusable
```
There are probably some bad sectors on the floppy disk that you're trying to copy to. Try another floppy disk.

```
Write protect error
Press CTRL+C to abort,
or correct this problem and press any other key to continue_
```
You'll see this when the floppy disk you're trying to copy to has the write-protect tab set.

Examples

Using one disk drive

If you only have one floppy disk drive, you can copy two floppy disks by swapping disks when DISKCOPY tells you to. To use a single floppy disk drive, use the same drive letter for both drive1 and drive2. For example:

```
C:\>diskcopy a: a:
```

See also

COPY   If you just want to copy the files on a disk, the COPY or XCOPY commands are more flexible because they'll work between different types of disks.

DISKCOMP   You can use this command after DISKCOPY to ensure the disk was copied correctly.

DISPLAY.SYS   DOS 3.3 and later, Device driver

Display code page device driver

This device driver provides support for code-page switching, which allows you to use alternate character sets on the screen to support languages other than U.S. English.

When and why

You'll need to use this device driver whenever you want to use language characters that aren't in the standard U.S. character set (code page 437).

Syntax

device=[*path*]**display.sys con**[:]=(*type* [,*hw-cp*] [,*n*])
device=[*path*]**display.sys con**[:]=(*type* [,*hw-cp*] [,(*n*,*m*)])

This line in your CONFIG.SYS file loads the display device driver.

Parameters

path
You'll want to provide a path to the DISPLAY.SYS device driver. This path will usually be C:\DOS.

type
Type of display. It can be one of the following:

Abbreviation	Type of display
CGA	Color/Graphics Adapter. Doesn't support code-page switching.
MONO	Monochrome display adapter. Doesn't support code-page switching.
EGA	Supports code-page switching on both EGA and VGA displays.
LCD	IBM PC Convertible LCD display.

hw-cp
Hardware code page. This tells the display driver what the default hardware code page is. It can be one of the following (when in doubt, leave out this parameter):

437	U.S.
850	Multilingual (Latin I)
852	Slavic (Latin II)
860	Portuguese
863	Canadian-French
865	Nordic

n
Pages supported. Number of code pages the device can support in addition to the primary code page. Valid numbers are 0 to 6 (for LCD, the maximum is 1; it is 0 for CGA and MONO).

m
Subfonts supported. Number of subfonts the hardware supports for each code page. The default value is 2 for EGA, 1 for LCD, and 0 for the CGA and MONO.

Notes

DISPLAY.SYS is a device driver that is loaded into memory when DOS starts. See the description of the CHCP command for a discussion of code pages and how to use them.

Memory usage

DISPLAY.SYS needs to reserve memory for both itself and for the code pages you'll want to load with MODE CP PREP. DISPLAY.SYS without any room for code pages consumes about 5K of memory. The first code page requires about 13K of memory; additional code pages require approximately 10K. For example, DISPLAY.SYS uses about 28K of memory when you want it to hold two code pages.

CGA and monochrome displays

Using DISPLAY.SYS with a CGA or monochrome display adapter has no effect because these two display adapters don't allow their character sets to be modified.

ANSI.SYS

If you plan to use ANSI.SYS or another console device driver, you'll need to install ANSI.SYS *before* DISPLAY.SYS (in other words, ANSI.SYS's DEVICE= line in the CONFIG.SYS file should appear before DISPLAY.SYS's DEVICE= line).

Examples

This is the command that you'll probably use for code-page switching:

```
device=c:\dos\driver.sys con=(ega)
```

Installs the display driver for EGA and VGA displays using the default settings.

If you're using a display adapter in a country that doesn't support the 437 default code page (see description of CHCP for more details), you'll have to provide the default code page for your display adapter. For example, a display adapter made for Portugal would need a line like this:

```
device=c:\dos\driver.sys con=(ega,860)
```

See also

For a full description on how to use code pages, see the description of the CHCP command.

CHCP	Read this command first — it contains a discussion on code pages and how to use them. Sets the active code page. You'll need to use this command if you use a code page different from your hardware's default.
DEVICEHIGH	Loads a device driver into the upper memory area. You can use this if you have an 80386 or better processor in your computer and you're using a program such as EMM386.EXE to provide an upper memory area.
KEYB	Allows you to change the mapping of the keyboard for computers with country-specific keyboards. In Germany, for example, the Z and Y keys are swapped so the Z is between the T and U keys.
MODE CP	Allows you to load code pages into memory and change between code pages. It's better, though, to use CHCP to change code pages after you've used MODE to load the code page.
NLSFUNC	Allows you to change the code page for more than one device (such as the keyboard and the display) at the same time. You'll want to install this before you use CHCP to set the active code page.
PRINTER.SYS	Supports code-page switching for some IBM printers. You'll need this if you want to change the character set used on your printer.

DOS

DOS 5 or later, CONFIG.SYS

Controls DOS's use of high memory

This command has two options, each of which controls a different aspect of high memory usage.

The DOS=HIGH option tells DOS to load itself into the High Memory Area (HMA), which is the first 64K of extended memory.

The DOS=UMB option tells DOS to manage the Upper Memory Blocks (UMBs), which are chunks of memory between 640K and 1MB that memory managers can provide for loading programs and device drivers into UMB.

When and why

If your computer has at least an 80286 microprocessor and at least 64K of extended memory, you'll want to use the DOS=HIGH command to load part of DOS into the HMA. This should free up about 45K to 55K of extra memory for your applications, which can make a real difference.

Syntax

dos=[high | low] [,umb | noumb]

Tells DOS whether to load itself into high memory, and whether it should control upper memory for loading device drivers and TSR programs.

Note: These two parameters can be in either order (HIGH,UMB or UMB,HIGH), or you can supply just one. There is really no reason to ever specify the LOW or NOUMB options.

Parameters

high|low
High loading of DOS. Tells DOS whether or not DOS should try to load itself into the HMA. HIGH tells DOS to load itself into HMA, and LOW tells DOS to load itself into low memory (the first 640K). (Default is LOW.)

umb|noumb
Control of upper memory. Tells DOS whether it should manage the UMBs. You'll need to tell DOS to manage upper memory if you're going to use DOS's DEVICEHIGH and LOADHIGH commands. (Default is NOUMB.)

Notes

HMA
The HMA is the first 64K of extended memory (which starts at 1MB). Intel 80286 or better microprocessors allow the first 64K of extended memory to be addressed directly by DOS, which is what allows DOS to load itself into the HMA.

HIMEM.SYS or XMS provider
There are two things you'll need in order to use the DOS=HIGH option. First, you'll need some extended memory (at least 64K) for DOS to load itself into high memory. And second, you'll need HIMEM.SYS or another extended memory manager (XMS) installed. Commercial 386 memory managers provide this function in addition to providing expanded memory management.

UMB provider
You'll need a UMB provider to load programs into the upper memory blocks. The upper memory blocks are gaps in the memory area between 640K and 1MB that are filled in by mapping extended memory into these areas. You'll need at least an 80386 microprocessor to allow this kind of mapping and a memory manager to do the actual mapping of extended memory into the UMBs. You'll also need enough extended memory installed to fill in these gaps.

When DOS loads into the HMA
As it turns out, DOS tries to load itself into the HMA after it has loaded all the device drivers in your CONFIG.SYS file and before it starts to load any of the INSTALL= programs. If DOS doesn't find an XMS provider at this point, it loads the rest of itself into low memory, above all the device drivers.

HMA conflicts with other programs

There are some device drivers that use the HMA, which will prevent DOS from loading itself there. Two such programs are DesqView and the XMS version of the NetWare driver. If you're using either of these, you will not see an increase in the amount of memory available for DOS programs because DOS won't load itself into high memory.

UMB conflicts

There are some programs (primarily programs written before DOS 5), both device drivers and memory-resident programs, that load themselves into upper memory. If you use the DOS=UMB option, however, these programs may not be able to load themselves into upper memory because DOS takes control of upper memory as soon as it sees any.

In the case of memory-resident programs, DOS 5 provided a new way for programs to ask for upper memory. Programs updated to support DOS 5 should be able to use upper memory with DOS=UMB.

DOS, however, still does not provide a way for device drivers to ask for upper memory whenever you use DOS=UMB. The best solution is to buy a third-party memory manager and set DOS=NOUMB.

Message

```
HMA not available : loading DOS low
```
You'll see this message when DOS can't use the HMA. You must have an XMS memory manager, such as HIMEM.SYS, loaded before you can load DOS into high memory.

Examples

Loading DOS into HMA

If you want to load DOS into the HMA, you'll need these two lines in your CONFIG.SYS file:

```
device=c:\dos\himem.sys
dos=high
```

If you're using a commercial memory manager, which provides the functionality of *both* HIMEM and EMM386, you can substitute the DEVICE= line to load your memory manager instead of HIMEM.SYS.

Using HMA and UMB

If you want DOS to load itself into high memory and manage the UMBs (which requires an 80386 or 80486 microprocessor), use the following lines in your CONFIG.SYS file (the DOS= line can be anywhere in the file):

```
dos=high,umb
device=c:\dos\himem.sys
device=c:\dos\emm386.exe ram
```

You can replace the last two lines with a DEVICE= command to load a commercial memory manager since they provide the functions of both device drivers in a single file.

See also

DEVICEHIGH   This command in your CONFIG.SYS file allows you to load device drivers into the UMBs.

EMM386.EXE   This is a device driver that can supply the UMB memory required for loading device drivers into upper memory.

Part II: Command Reference

HIMEM.SYS	You'll need to install HIMEM.SYS before you can install EMM386.EXE. And you'll need both (or a commercial equivalent) to load devices into upper memory.
LOADHIGH	Use this command if you want to load TSR programs into the UMBs.
MEM	You'll find a discussion of the different types of memory in the description of the MEM command.
MEMMAKER	The new DOS 6 utility for optimizing your memory usage.

DOSKEY   DOS 5 and later, External

Memory-resident command-line extender

This program extends the functionality of the DOS command line, adding an editable command line, a memory of recent commands, and macros.

When and why
If you use the DOS command line a lot and you're not using a DOS shell, DOSKEY provides some nice improvements to the command line. The command-line editing and history are the easiest to learn and use, and they're nice to have. If, on the other hand, you're using a DOS shell, DOSKEY won't be very useful.

Syntax
doskey [**/reinstall**] [**/bufsize=***size*] [**/macros**] [**/history**] [**/insert|overstrike**] [*macroname*=[*text*]...]

or

doskey [**/reinstall**] [**/bufsize=***size*] [**/m**] [**/h**] [**/insert|overstrike**] [*macroname*=[*text*]...]

Loads the DOSKEY program into memory and/or defines macros.

Parameters
macroname=[*text*]
Define macro. This parameter allows you to define macros to carry out one or more commands. Macros are like batch files, but they're stored in memory, and you can use them to replace internal DOS commands (which you can't do with batch files). Macro names can contain any characters except for the following: = | > and <.

You remove macros from DOSKEY by leaving the *text* part of the definition blank.

Switches
/reinstall
Install new copy. Installs a fresh copy of DOSKEY into memory, even if another copy is already installed. Because you can't remove DOSKEY from memory, you'll need to use this switch when you want to increase the size of DOSKEY's buffer (or you can restart your computer and load a fresh copy of DOSKEY with the /BUFSIZE switch).

/bufsize=*size*
Set buffer size. Sets the size (in bytes) of DOSKEY's internal buffer, which is used both to remember commands and to store macros you've created. Minimum size is 256. (Default is 512 bytes.)

DOSKEY

/macros *or* /m
Display macros. Displays all the macros that are currently defined. Each macro will be displayed the way you typed it (except the macro name will be in uppercase letters).

/history *or* /h
Display history. Lists the most recent commands you've run. The number of commands DOSKEY can remember depends on the size of its internal buffer and the amount of memory used to remember macros. If you remove some macros, for example, DOSKEY will have more memory for remembering commands.

/insert
/overstrike
Set overstrike mode. Tells DOSKEY whether you want keys typed in the middle of a line to be inserted or to write over characters. This switch determines the mode to use for each new DOS command. Within a single DOS command you can use the Ins key to toggle between insert and overwrite modes. (Default is /overstrike.)

Notes

Multiple commands

DOSKEY allows you to type more than one command at a time. You separate each command with a Ctrl-T, which appears on the screen as ¶. For example, to run the VER command followed by CD, type **VER**, then press Ctrl-T, and then **CD**:

```
C:\>ver¶cd
```

Memory usage

DOSKEY uses about 4K of memory by default (with a 512-byte buffer). If you set a buffer size using the /BUFSIZE switch, DOSKEY uses about 3.5K of memory for the program, plus the size of your buffer.

DOS shells and DOSKEY

DOSKEY isn't active at the command line in programs such as the Norton Commander. This is because such programs create their own command line so they can provide their own command-line editing and history.

When you can't use macros

You can't use macros from within batch files or other macros — you can only use macros from the command line.

Recalling commands

There are a number of keys you can use to recall recent commands you've run since installing DOSKEY:

Up arrow	Previous command: shows the command you ran before the one that's being displayed.
Down arrow	Next command: shows the command you ran after the one that's being displayed.
PgUp	Shows the oldest command that's still in DOSKEY's buffer.
PgDn	Shows the most recent command you ran.

Part II: Command Reference

Command-line editing

Here are the keys that you can use to edit the DOS command line when DOSKEY is installed:

Ctrl-T	Command separator. When you want to write more than one command on the command line, type a Ctrl-T between the commands. DOSKEY will display this as a ¶ on the command line.
Esc	Clears the command line.
Home	Moves the cursor to the start of the line.
End	Moves the cursor to the end of the line.
Left arrow	Moves the cursor left one character.
Right arrow	Moves the cursor right one character. If you're at the end of the line, DOSKEY starts to recall characters from the previous command you ran. This is a little confusing and is best understood through experimentation.
Ctrl-Left arrow	Moves the cursor left one word.
Ctrl-Right arrow	Moves right one word. Or, at the end of a line, recalls one word from the previous command.
Ins	Switches between Insert and Overwrite modes. The cursor will change shape when you switch to the other mode (whichever mode isn't the default).
F1 – F6	Same meaning as the DOS command line.
F7	Displays the previous commands remembered by DOSKEY in its history queue. You can use the numbers with the F9 key to recall a command. This is a lot faster than typing (DOSKEY /H).
Alt-F7	Clears the command history queue.
F8	Finds the previous command. Type the first few characters of a recent command; then press F8 to recall the most recent command that starts with what you've typed. Press F8 again to find the next most recent command that matches the characters you typed.
F9	Recalls a command by number. Press F7 to display command numbers. When you press this key, DOSKEY will prompt you to type a number. Press Enter to show the command.
Alt-F10	Deletes all macros from DOSKEY's buffer.

Creating macros

The right side of a macro definition (after the =) can be any DOS command. In addition, you can use any of the following special macro parameters inside a macro (letters can be either upper- or lowercase):

$g	Same as > to redirect output to a file. You must use $G in a macro definition rather than > because DOS doesn't pass the > onto DOSKEY. The G stands for greater-than.
gg	Same as >> to append output to a file. You must use GG in a macro definition rather than >> because DOS doesn't pass the >> on to DOSKEY.

DOSKEY

$l   (The letter L.) Same as < to redirect keyboard input so it will read from a file. You must use $L in a macro definition rather than < because DOS doesn't pass the < on to DOSKEY. The L stands for less-than.

$b   Same as | to pipe the output to another command. You must use $B in a macro definition rather than | because DOS doesn't pass the | on to DOSKEY. The B stands for bar (which is one name used for the | character).

$t   Separates commands when you want more than one command in a macro. (On the command line, as opposed to in a macro definition, use Ctrl-T instead.)

$$ Inserts a dollar-sign character ($).

$1 – $9   The same as %1 through %9 batch-file parameters but for DOSKEY macros. These parameters refer to the first nine parameters on the command line when you run the macro.

$*   Includes everything you type on the command line after the macro name (when you run the macro).

See the following "Examples" for how to use the parameters in a DOSKEY macro.

Replacing internal commands

Macros you create can have any name, including the names of internal DOS commands, in which case DOSKEY runs the macro rather than the internal DOS command. As it turns out, you can still get to the internal DOS command by typing a space before the command name because DOSKEY only recognizes commands that don't start with a space, whereas DOS ignores spaces in front of commands.

Messages

```
Cannot change BUFSIZE.
```
You can't change the size of DOSKEY's buffer once it's been loaded into memory. You have two options: Restart your computer and load DOSKEY again with the /bufsize switch. Or load another copy of DOSKEY using both the /REINSTALL and /BUFSIZE switches.

```
Insufficient memory to store macro. Use the DOSKEY command with the
/BUFSIZE switch to increase available memory.
```
You'll see this message when you've run out of memory in DOSKEY's internal buffer. You'll need to either restart your computer and load DOSKEY using the /BUFSIZE switch, or load another copy of DOSKEY using both the /REINSTALL and /BUFSIZE switches.

```
Invalid macro definition
```
You'll see this message whenever you mistype a switch or leave out an equal sign in a macro definition. By the way, if you mistype a switch that's followed by an equal sign, DOSKEY will enter what you type as a macro rather than display this error message.

Examples

A simple macro

Some people like short commands, such as CP instead of COPY. Here is a macro that would create such a command:

```
C:\>doskey cp=copy $1 $2
```

This allows you to type **CP FILE.TXT NEW.TXT** to copy a file called FILE.TXT. You'll notice, however, that this command doesn't allow you to use any of COPY's switches. In cases such as this it's better to pass on the entire command line, which you can do using $*:

```
C:\>doskey cp=copy $*
```

Multiple commands

Here is a simple macro called MOVE that allows you to move a file from one directory to another by first copying and then deleting the original:

```
C:\>doskey move=copy $1 $2 $t erase $1
```

The $T separates the COPY and the ERASE commands. This isn't actually the best way to move a file if you're using DOS wildcard characters because you'll end up copying all of the files before you move any of them. (And, in DOS 6, there's a new MOVE command.)

Reloading macros

You may have noticed that DOSKEY doesn't provide a way to save macro definitions to a file or to load them back into memory. There is, however, a way you can do this, although it takes a bit of work. First, define all the macros you want to use. You can then redirect DOSKEY's output to a file to create a list of macros:

```
C:\>doskey /m > macros.bat
```

Then edit this file to put the word "doskey" in front of each definition. You can then run this batch file from within your AUTOEXEC.BAT file, which might have these two lines in it:

```
doskey /insert
call macros
```

Deleting macros

You can delete macros by giving a macro's name (followed by an equal sign) without any macro text. For example, if you have a macro called DO, you can remove it with the following command:

```
C:\>doskey do=
```

DOSSHELL   DOS 4.0 and later, External

Start the DOS Shell

This command starts the DOS Shell program, which you can use to manage your files and directories. It provides a more visual interface to DOS than the DOS command line.

> **When and why**
>
> The DOS Shell program is a lot easier to work with when you're doing directory and file maintenance than the DOS commands for the same types of operations. You'll want to use this program from time to time to clear out old files or reorganize your hard disk (spring cleaning).

DOSSHELL

> The DOSSHELL program is included with MS-DOS 6.0 and available on the MS-DOS 6.2 supplemental disk.

Syntax
dosshell (DOS 4.0 only)
dosshell [/t|g[:*res*]] [/b] (DOS 5 and later)
Starts the DOS Shell program. If you don't use any switches, DOS uses the display mode you last used with the Shell (whether set by the command line or within the Shell).

Parameters
res
Screen resolution. Sets the screen resolution to use. The following table shows the values you can use for *res*, along with the number of lines you'll see on the three types of screens supported.

Switch	Res	Monochrome/CGA	EGA	VGA
/T:	L	25	25	25
	M, M1, H, H1	-	43	43
	M2, H2	-	43	50
/G:	L	25	25	25
	M, M1	-	43	30
	M2	-	43	34
	H, H1	-	43	43
	H2	-	43	60

Switches
/t
Text mode. Starts the DOS Shell program in text mode.

/g
Graphics mode. Starts the DOS Shell program in graphics mode.

/b
Black and white. Starts the DOS Shell program using a black-and-white color set. This is useful for laptop computers that don't show shades of gray.

Notes

Display mode
If you start DOSSHELL without specifying a screen resolution, it will use the last screen resolution you used. You can also change the screen resolution from within the DOS Shell using the Display item in the Options menu.

DOS 4.0 Shell
The DOS Shell program was rewritten extensively between version 4 and 5 of DOS. In DOS 4.0, DOSSHELL is a batch file that sets a number of switches for the SHELLC program. We won't describe any of the details of the DOS 4.0 Shell in this book.

DRIVER.SYS DOS 3.2 and later, Device driver

Define disk drive characteristics

This is an advanced device driver that has two uses. First, if you install a floppy disk drive that your computer doesn't recognize, you can use this device driver to assign a drive letter to your floppy disk. Second, you can create a new drive letter for an existing floppy disk that uses different drive characteristics.

> **When and why**
>
> This device driver has two main uses.
>
> First, it's useful when you install a floppy disk drive in a computer that doesn't know how to handle it. For example, we used to have an old IBM PC/AT that didn't know about 3½-inch floppy disk drives, but we wanted to install one. We had to use the DRIVER.SYS device driver to tell DOS how to access this disk drive.
>
> As it turns out, you can also use this device driver to create new drive letters for existing floppy disk drives. For example, if you have a 1.2MB floppy disk drive, but most of the time you want to work with 360K disks, you can create a new drive letter (which will probably be D:) that treats this disk drive as a 360K floppy disk drive. Then you won't have to remember to use the correct format switches whenever you format a disk in your drive.

Syntax

device=[*path*]**driver.sys** **/d:***number* [**/c**] [**/f:***type*] [**/h:***heads*] [**/s:***sectors*] [**/t:***tracks*]
Load the DRIVER.SYS device driver into DOS.

Switches

/d:*number*
Drive number. This is the physical number of the disk drive. A drive's number is determined when you install it by its physical location and by switch settings on the hardware. Valid range is 0 to 127 (drive 0 = drive A:, 1 = B:, and so on).

/c
Change line. This switch indicates that the disk drive can sense when the drive door is open. Check your drive's documentation to determine if your drive supports change-line error detection. (Most 1.2MB and 3½-inch disk drives support change lines, but most 360K disk drives don't.)

/f:*type*
Drive type. Defines the maximum storage capacity of the disk drive. (Default is 2.)

Type	Description
0	Standard 5¼-inch floppy disk (160K to 360K)
1	High-density 5¼-inch (1.2MB)
2	720K 5¼-inch disk drive
7	1.44MB 3½-inch disk drive
9	2.88MB 3½-inch disk drive (DOS 5 and later)

DRIVER.SYS

Note: You usually don't need to use the /H, /S, or /T switches if you use the /F switch.

/h:*heads*
Sides per disk. The number of read/write heads (sides) on the drive. Valid range is 1 – 99. (Default is 2.)

/s:*sectors*
Sectors per track. The number of sectors per track on this device. Valid range is 1 – 99. (Default is 9.)

/t:*tracks*
Tracks per side. The number of tracks on each side of the drive. Valid range is 1 – 999. (Default is 80, except for type 0, which is 40.)

Notes

How DOS assigns drive letters

When DOS loads your device driver, it's already located all the disk drives it knows about, so if you have a hard disk, DOS has probably assigned A:, B:, and C:. The next available drive letter will be assigned to a drive created by DRIVER.SYS (in the example here, it would be D:). You'll see a message when DRIVER.SYS is loaded saying what drive letter was assigned to your drive.

The change line

Some floppy disk drives support what's known as a change line. This is a switch that DOS can check to see if the drive door is open or closed. Drives that support such a change line (such as 1.2MB 5¼-inch floppy disk drives) can report much more quickly as to whether or not a disk is in the drive (since you can only close the door when a disk is in the drive). We suggest you use the /C switch when you can (check your hardware's manual).

Common settings

Here is a table that shows common settings for the /H, /S, and /T switches on different size disk drives:

Drive	/f	/h	/s	/t
5¼-inch disk	0	1 or 2	8 or 9	40
1.2MB, 5¼-inch	1	2	15	80
720K, 3½-inch	2	2	9	80
1.44MB, 3½-inch	7	2	18	80
2.88MB, 3½-inch	9	2	36	80

Examples

Installing foreign drive

Let's say you have a 1.44MB 3½-inch disk drive installed on a computer that doesn't recognize 3½-inch disk drives, and that this disk drive is set to hardware drive number 2. Here is how you would make DOS aware of this disk drive:

```
device=c:\dos\driver.sys /d:2 /f:7
```

A new drive letter

We have a laptop computer that has a single 1.44MB 3½-inch floppy disk and a hard disk. The 3½-inch floppy disk drive gets the A: and B: drive letters assigned to it, and the hard disk gets the C: drive letter. Just for fun, we created a new drive letter that treats the single floppy disk drive as a 720K disk drive. The first floppy disk is hardware drive number 0, and drive type 2 is a 720K 3½-inch disk:

```
device=c:\dos\driver.sys /d:0 /f:2
```

When you create a new drive letter for an existing drive, DOS allows only one drive letter to be active at one time. In this example, our floppy disk can be A:, B:, or D:. The first time you try to access the D: drive letter, you'll see a message like this:

```
Insert diskette for drive D: and press any key when ready
```

You can then type a command like

```
C:\>copy a:*.* d:*.*
```

to copy files between two disks using one floppy disk drive; DOS will display a message so you can insert the correct disk for each drive.

See also
DRIVPARM — This CONFIG.SYS command allows you to modify the device characteristics for an existing disk device.

DRIVPARM — DOS 3.2 and later, CONFIG.SYS

Define disk drive characteristics

This is an advanced command that allows you to redefine the physical characteristics of an existing disk drive. Only use this if you know what you're doing or your hardware manual tells you to use this command.

Syntax
drivparm=/d:number [/c] [/f:*type*] [/h:*heads*] [/i] [/n] [/s:*sectors*] [/t:*tracks*]
Changes the drive characters for a drive. This line should appear in your CONFIG.SYS file after the line that loads the affected device drive (if any).

Switches
/d:*number*
Drive number. The physical drive number. Valid range is 0 – 255 (drive 0 = drive A:, 1 = B:, etc.)

/c
Change line. This drive can detect whether the drive door is open or closed (for example, 1.2MB drives can tell whether the drive door is closed, but most 360K drives can't).

/f:type
Drive type. Set the type of drive, which can be one of the following (default is 2 if DRIVPARM is used and this switch is omitted):

Type	Description
0	Standard 5¼-inch floppy disk (160K to 360K)
1	High-density 5¼-inch disk (1.2MB)
2	720K 3½-inch disk drive
3	8-inch single-density floppy disk
4	8-inch double-density floppy disk
5	Hard disk
6	Tape drive
7	1.44MB 3½-inch disk drive
8	Read/write optical drive
9	2.88MB 3½-inch disk drive (DOS 5 and later)

/h:heads
Sides per disk. The number of read/write heads on the drive. Valid range is 1 – 99. The default value depends on the drive type.

/i
Standard 3 ½-inch disk drive (DOS 4.0 and later). Use this switch when your ROM BIOS doesn't support 3½-inch disks to tell DOS how to work with the drive.

/n
Nonremovable. The drive has a nonremovable media (such as a sealed hard disk).

/s:sectors
Sectors per track. The number of sectors per track on this device. Valid range is 1 – 99. The default depends on the drive type.

/t:tracks
Tracks per side. The number of tracks on each side of the drive. Valid range is 1 – 999.

Notes

The change line
Some floppy disk drives support what's known as a change line. This is a switch that DOS can check to see if the drive door is open or closed. Drives that support such a change line (such as 1.2MB 5¼-inch floppy disk drives) can report much more quickly as to whether a disk is in the drive (since you can only close the door when a disk is in the drive). We suggest you use the /C switch when you can (check your hardware's manual).

See also
DRIVER.SYS — This device driver allows you to create a drive letter to support disk drives that your computer doesn't know how to support.

ECHO
All DOS, Internal batch

Echo line to the screen

This command turns command echoing in batch files on and off. When echoing is on (the normal case), DOS echoes each line of a batch file to the screen just before it executes the line.

When and why

Most people like their batch files to be fairly quiet when they're running, which means they don't want DOS to echo each command it executes. The ECHO OFF command as the first line in a batch file turns off echoing for the entire batch file. You'll probably want to use either ECHO OFF or @ECHO OFF (with DOS 3.3 and later) as the first line in every batch file you write.

Note: You might want to leave ECHO on until you have your batch file working properly so that you can see what your batch file is actually doing.

Syntax

echo
Without any parameters, reports whether ECHO is currently on or off within. This is rarely used, and we're not sure why you'd want to know since ECHO is turned on whenever a batch file starts.

echo.
This form of the command allows you to echo a blank line to the screen.

echo on|off
Turns echoing of commands on or off. With DOS 3.3 and later you can use @ECHO OFF to turn ECHO off without displaying the current line. When you use this command at the DOS prompt, ECHO controls whether you see the DOS prompt.

echo *message*
Echoes the rest of the command line (*message*) to the screen. This is the most commonly used form of the command, aside from ECHO OFF.

Notes

DOS prompt

When you use the ECHO command at the DOS prompt rather than in a batch file, ECHO OFF turns off display of the DOS prompt. You can display the prompt again using ECHO ON.

Keeping ECHO OFF from echoing

You can precede the ECHO command with an @ sign to keep the ECHO OFF command itself from echoing (DOS 3.3 and later).

ECHO and batch file output

There are two batch file commands (other than ECHO) that are often used to produce output — PAUSE and CHOICE. The PAUSE command produces the message as follows:

```
Press any key to continue . . .
```

Many people place an optional prompt message on the PAUSE command line. Because this line is not really output, if ECHO is OFF, you cannot see the message. On the other hand, the CHOICE command produces a prompt line in several different formats which appear even if ECHO is OFF. These commands are discussed in detail in their own Command Reference entries.

Disallowed characters

You cannot display the following characters with an ECHO command: <, |, and >. These characters are intercepted by DOS and used to support input/output redirection.

ECHO state

Each time you run a batch file, echoing is turned on if the DOS prompt is visible (ECHO ON). Very few people ever use ECHO to turn off their DOS prompt, so it's safe to assume that ECHO will be on when your batch file starts. The only exception is when one batch file runs another. In this case the first batch file controls the state of echoing when it starts the second batch file.

Examples

Here's a simple example of the ECHO command in a batch file. We'll show both the batch file and its output. Here is the batch file:

```
@echo off
echo This is a simple batch file.
echo.
echo We just had a blank line.
```

If we call this batch file TEST.BAT, this is what its output looks like:

```
C:\>test
This is a simple batch file.

We just had a blank line.
C:\>_
```

See also

@   Putting an @ at the start of any line in a batch file keeps that line from being echoed.

PAUSE   The PAUSE command allows you to pause a batch file's output.

Part II: Command Reference

EDIT
DOS 5 and later, External

Edit a text file
This command provides a full-screen text editor that you can use to edit text files.

When and why
This program is a nice editor for writing batch files and modifying your CONFIG.SYS and AUTOEXEC.BAT files. The program is very easy to use and has on-line help. Press F1 at any time to get help on using the editor.

Syntax
edit *filespec* [**/b**] [**/h**] [**/nohi**] [**/g**]
Starts the editor and loads the text file *filespec* into the editor.

Parameters
filespec
The name of the file (with optional drive letter and path) that you want to edit.

Switches
/b
Black and white. Uses black and white rather than colors. This option is useful on laptop computers with EGA screens that display colors as shades of gray (which can be hard to read).

/h
High resolution. Uses as many lines as possible: 43 lines on an EGA display and 50 lines on a VGA display adapter.

/nohi
Eight colors. Only uses 8 colors on the screen, rather than 16. This is useful for displays that don't support 16 colors (most do). You'll need to use this switch if you don't see the menu and item shortcut keys highlighted.

/g
Fast CGA display. For a CGA display adapter, uses fast screen writing. Older computers that used a CGA card based on IBM's design display "snow" when you write quickly to the screen, so most programs slow down on CGA screens. You can try this switch to see if it improves screen output speed.

Notes
Needs Basic
The EDIT command uses the QBasic program's editor (or for PC-DOS 5, the Basic editor in ROM on IBM computers), so EDIT won't work properly if this file isn't either in the current directory or in your search path. In fact, the EDIT.COM is a very short file whose sole function is to start QBasic with the /EDITOR switch.

See also
QBASIC   The editor is actually provided by the QBasic program.

EDLIN DOS 1–5, External

Line-oriented text editor
This command allows you to edit text files using a set of line-oriented commands.

When and why
You'll almost certainly not want to use this program because it's rather difficult to work with. EDLIN first appeared in DOS 1.0 and hasn't been modified substantially since. Back then Microsoft wrote DOS so it could run on any computer with an 8088 microprocessor, including computers that used teletypes (a combination of a keyboard and a printer) rather than an attached keyboard and screen. For this they needed a text editor that could work much like DOS: You issue commands and look at output.

If you really want to use EDLIN, you can find a complete description in your DOS manual.

See also
EDIT   The EDIT command is a full-screen editor that's much easier to use than EDLIN.

EGA.SYS DOS 5 and later, Device driver

EGA display driver
This command allows you to use the DOS Shell Task Swapper with EGA displays.

When and why
If you're going to use the DOS Shell Task Swapper in the DOS Shell on an EGA display adapter, you'll need to install this device driver. (You don't need this device driver for VGA display adapters.) This device driver helps the task switcher keep track of the screen mode used for each program running so it can correctly set the screen mode for each program.

Syntax
device=[*path*]**ega.sys**
Load the EGA.SYS device driver into DOS.

Parameters
path
You'll want to provide a path to the EGA.SYS device driver. This path will usually be C:\DOS.

Notes
Mouse and EGA.SYS
If you're using a Microsoft mouse, you can save some memory by installing the EGA.SYS device driver before you install the mouse device driver. You do this by making sure the DEVICE= line for EGA.SYS appears before the DEVICE= line for MOUSE.SYS.

```
device=c:\dos\ega.sys
device=mouse.sys
```

Part II: Command Reference

EMM386.EXE DOS 5 and later, Device driver

386 expanded memory manager

This file is both a device driver and a program. The device driver works with computers that have at least an 80386 (or 80486) microprocessor, and provides two functions. First, it converts some of your extended memory into expanded memory. And second, it can convert some extended memory into the UMBs, which are useful for loading other device drivers and programs into upper memory.

As a program, EMM386 displays the status of the EMM386 drive and the UMBs. It also allows you to turn expanded memory on and off.

When and why

If your computer has an 80386 (or 80486) microprocessor, you'll probably want to use this, or another 386 memory manager, to provide the UMBs so you can load device drivers and memory-resident programs in upper memory (outside the first 640K of memory). Make sure you use the RAM or NOEMS parameter if you want upper memory available. You'll also need to use the DOS= command.

This device driver can also make some of your extended memory look like expanded memory, which is quite useful.

In DOS 6, you can use MemMaker to configure all of your memory managers (including EMM386) automatically to obtain the optimal memory usage with Microsoft drivers.

Syntax

device=[*path*]emm386.exe [*memory*] [**min**=*minsize*] [**ram**=mmmm-nnnn][**noems**] [**L**=*minXMS*] [**w**=on|off] [**mx**|**frame**=*address*|/*paddress*] [**pn**=*address*] [**x**=*mmmm-nnnn*] [**i**=*mmmm-nnnn*] [**b**=*address*] [**a**=*altregs*] [**h**=*handles*] [**d**=*nnn*] [**novcpi**] [**highscan**] [**verbose**] [**win**=*mmmm-nnnn*] [**nohi**] [**rom**=*mmmm-nnnn*] [**nomoveexbda**] [**altboot**]
Loads the device driver.

emm386 [on|off|auto] [w=on|off]
This command allows you to control the EMM386 device driver after it's been installed. Without any parameters, reports information on expanded and upper memory.

Parameters

memory
EMS memory. The maximum amount of EMS memory (in kilobytes) to create out of extended memory. EMM386 actually uses a little more extended memory (96K extra) than the amount of expanded memory you ask for. Valid range is 16 through 32,768 and is rounded down to the nearest multiple of 16. The minimum EMS size created is 64K. (Default is 256.)

Note: If you're letting EMM386 create the UMBs, it uses an additional amount of extended memory.

EMM386.EXE

min=*minsize*
Minimum EMS memory (DOS 6 and later). This is the minimum amount of memory dedicated to EMS memory. Depending upon the demands of the programs running, EMM386 may adjust the EMS pool down to *minsize*. Only if extended memory is available will EMM386 increase the amount of EMS memory (up to the amount specified by *memory*).

on|off|auto
EMM386 enable. This parameter of the EMM386 command allows you to turn the EMM386 EMS and UMB functions on and off. The AUTO setting tells EMM386 to turn these functions off until they're needed by a program. The AUTO option allows you to keep your memory available as extended memory until some program needs expanded memory. *Note:* You can't turn EMM386 off if a program is using EMS memory or if you have programs loaded into upper memory.

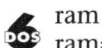

ram   (DOS 5 and later)
ram=*mmmm-nnnn*   (DOS 6 and later)
EMS and upper memory. Tells EMM386 to create both expanded memory and the UMBs. (Default is expanded memory, without upper memory blocks.)

In DOS 6, you can specify the range to use for creating the UMBs.

noems
Upper memory only. Tells EMM386 to create the UMBs but no expanded memory. (Default is expanded memory, without upper memory blocks.)

novcpi
Disable VCPI support (DOS 6 and later). Tells EMM386 to provide no support for VCPI memory calls. This parameter must be used in conjunction with the NOEMS. Together, they restrict EMM386 to managing the UBM and providing no other services.

L=*minXMS*
Leave some XMS free. Tells EMM386 to leave at least minXMS kilobytes of extended memory free. Use this parameter if you want to set memory to a large number so you can have as much expanded memory as possible, but you still need some extended memory available for other programs. (Default is 0.)

w=on | w=off
Enables or disables support for the Weitek floating-point processor. Most people don't have a Weitek processor, but if you do, it may interfere with the operation of some old DOS programs. Use this parameter to turn support on and off as needed. (Default is off.)

verbose
or
v
Display messages (DOS 6 and later). Instructs EMM386 to display status messages during the load process. You may also activate the status messages by holding down the Alt key as EMM386 is loading.

Part II: Command Reference

highscan
Second memory scan (DOS 6 and later). Instructs EMM386 to scan upper memory a second time for additional memory blocks. On some systems, this may cause EMM386 to identify blocks that are not really available. Be extremely cautious when using this option.

rom
Shadow RAM (DOS 6 and later). Specifies a segment of memory for use as shadow RAM. This may improve performance on your system if it does not have its own shadow RAM system.

altboot
Alternate boot control (DOS 6 and later). Use this switch only if you experience trouble restarting your system using Ctrl-Alt-Del.

nomovexbda
Extended BIOS location (DOS 6 and later). This parameter instructs EMM386 to leave extended BIOS data in conventional memory.

EMS page options

The following options allow you to control where EMM386 puts its expanded memory pages in the first 1MB of memory. These are very advanced options that you won't want to use unless instructed to by your hardware or software manuals. MemMaker may install some of these options if you use it to optimize your memory. This provides you with the best performance possible using Microsoft drivers.

mx
Advanced option. Sets the address where EMM386 will put the EMS page frame. You'll need a 64K block of memory for the page frame. Here is a table of the values you can use for x, along with the address of the page frame for each value (in hexadecimal notation):

x	Address	x	Address	x	Address
1	C000h	6	D400h	11	8400h
2	C400h	7	D800h	12	8800h
3	C800h	8	DC00h	13	8C00h
4	CC00h	9	E000h	14	9000h
5	D000h	10	8000h		

Warning! Don't use the values between 10 and 14 unless your computer has only 512K of memory.

Default: EMM386 normally chooses the highest address that allows a 64K page frame without overlapping any ROM or RAM locations.

frame=*address*
/p*address*
Advanced option. Sets the address where EMM386 will put the EMS page frame (like the Mx parameter, but allows you to specify the address directly). The *address* is the segment number (same as the addresses in the table above) in hexadecimal notation. Valid values are from 8000h to 9000h and C000h to E000h in 400h increments (the h means these are hexadecimal numbers).

EMM386.EXE

Default: EMM386 normally chooses the highest address that allows a 64K page frame without overlapping any ROM or RAM locations.

/p*n*=*address*
Advanced option. Sets the segment address for a single EMS page rather than for the entire page frame. *N* is the number of the page, between 0 and 255. And *address* is the segment address, which is the same address used in the FRAME= parameter above.

This option is usually used to add extra EMS pages (the first four pages 0 to 3 must all be together). It's best to control the address of these first four pages using either the /P*address* or the FRAME=*address* parameter.

x=*mmmm-nnnn*
Advanced option. Prevents EMM386 from using this range of memory for EMS pages. You may want to use this if EMM386 doesn't recognize some memory being used by an add-on card, such as a network adapter. The numbers *mmmm* and *nnnn* are segment addresses and must be between A000h and FFFFh. They're automatically rounded down to the nearest multiple of 100h. The X parameter overrules any I parameters.

i=*mmmm-nnnn*
Advanced option. Allows EMM386 to use this range of memory for EMS pages, even if EMM386 finds option ROM or RAM at these addresses. Be very careful using this option, and don't use it unless you know what you're doing. These numbers have the same restrictions as the numbers in the X parameter above.

win=*mmmm-nnnn*
Advanced option (DOS 6 and later). Reserves the specified memory addresses for use by Windows rather than EMM386. These numbers have the same restrictions as those specified for the x parameter.

b=*address*
Advanced option. Sets the lowest address for EMS bank switching, which is a form of memory swapping allowed by EMS 4.0. This is used by programs such as DesqView to swap DOS programs in and out of memory. Only change this if your software manual tells you what it needs. Valid range is 1000h through 4000h. (Default is 4000h.)

Other advanced options

Here are some other fairly advanced options. If you don't understand these options, only change them if you're instructed to do so by a software manual or a knowledgeable person.

a=*altregs*
Advanced option. Tells EMM386 how many alternate fast register sets to allocate. This feature is used by multitasking programs such as DesqView to speed up switching between DOS programs. *Note:* Each register set adds 200 bytes to the size of EMM386 in memory. Valid range is 0 – 255. (Default is 7.)

h=*handles*
Advanced option. Sets the number of handles that will be available from EMM386. Valid range is 2 – 255. (Default is 64.)

d=*nnn*
Advanced option. Sets the number of kilobytes that EMM386 will reserve for buffered DMA. This value should be as large as the largest DMA transfer that can occur. Valid range is 16 to 256. (Default is 16.)

Notes

Types of memory

Here is a quick chart that shows you what types of memory you'll get when using no parameter, or the RAM or NOEMS parameters:

Parameter	Expanded memory	Upper memory
none	yes	no
ram	yes	yes
noems	no	yes

Changing advanced options

Warning! Be very careful changing any of the advanced options. You should create a boot floppy before changing these options because some may cause EMM386 to crash.

Windows and EMM386

Caution: When running windows, do not use a disk cache, like SMARTDRV.EXE, that uses EMS memory, or your system may crash.

Windows Tip: If you're running Windows in 386 enhanced mode, Windows provides expanded memory support to DOS applications. You might, however, still want to load device drivers and memory-resident programs into upper memory: install EMM386 with the NOEMS parameter to create the UMBs without creating expanded memory.

Messages

```
EMM386 not installed - insufficient memory
```
You'll see this message if you don't have enough extended memory installed on your computer or if EMM386 doesn't see your extended memory for some reason.

```
EMM386 not installed - protected mode software already running.
```
You have another device driver loaded before EMM386 that uses the protected mode of the processor (which EMM386 needs to use to map extended memory into expanded memory and UMBs). Try making EMM386 the second device driver you load (HIMEM.SYS must be loaded before you load EMM386).

```
EMM386 not installed - XMS manager not present.
```
You need to install HIMEM.SYS before you can install EMM386. Make sure you have a DEVICE= line in your CONFIG.SYS file before the line that loads EMM386.

```
Unable to deactivate EMM386 as UMBs are being provided
and/or EMS is being used.
```
You'll see this message when you use the EMM386 OFF command. This message tells you that at least one program is using EMS memory, or the UMBs. You can use MEM /C to see what programs are loaded in upper memory and MEM /D to see what programs are using EMS memory.

```
WARNING: Option ROM or RAM detected within page frame.
```
If you specify the address of the page frame, you may have provided a 64K area that overlaps the location of ROM or RAM that's reserved for use by an add-on card, such as your VGA display adapter. EMM386 will install itself, but it's a good idea not to run

any programs that use expanded memory until you change the address of the page frame to remove this conflict. Or better yet, let EMM386 choose an address of the page frame.

Examples

Typical CONFIG.SYS file

Your typical CONFIG.SYS file might contain the following lines to load EMM386:

```
device=c:\dos\himem.sys
device=c:\dos\emm386.exe ram

dos=high,umb
```

The first two lines load the HIMEM and EMM386 device drivers. The RAM parameter tells EMM386 to provide both expanded and upper memory. The next line makes use of the UMBs (DOS=UMB).

See also

DOS	You'll need to use the DOS= command in your CONFIG.SYS file if you want to use the UMBs created by EMM386.
HIMEM.SYS	You need to load HIMEM.SYS before you can load EMM386.
MEM	The MEM command contains a discussion of the different types of memory. You'll also find it useful for determining how memory is being used.
MEMMAKER	The new DOS 6 utility for configuring your memory management.

ERASE   All DOS, Internal

Erase file from the disk (see DEL)

The ERASE command is exactly the same command as DEL. DOS provides both names, and you can use whichever you're most comfortable with. Some people prefer DEL over ERASE because it's less typing. On the other hand, since DEL and DIR are somewhat similar, some people who use DEL (rather than ERASE) sometimes type **DEL** accidentally when they meant to type **DIR**. The choice is yours.

See the DEL command for a full description.

EXE2BIN   DOS 1–5, External

Convert EXE file to BIN file

This command was provided in earlier DOS versions for use by software developers, not for ordinary users. As such, we won't discuss it at all in this book. If you need to know more about EXE2BIN, read your *DOS Technical Reference* manual.

Part II: Command Reference

EXIT
All DOS, Internal

Exit COMMAND.COM
This command allows you to exit a copy of COMMAND.COM.

When and why
There are two cases where you'll need to use the EXIT command. First, many programs allow you to shell out to DOS, which gives you access to the DOS command line without having to quit your program. Such programs do this by starting another copy of DOS's command interpreter. You'll need to type **EXIT** at the DOS prompt to return to your program.

You might also load a second copy of COMMAND.COM yourself. EXIT will allow you to leave the second copy, returning to the first.

Syntax
    exit
    Exits the temporary copy of COMMAND.COM (if there is one).

Notes
COMMAND's /P switch
    If you run COMMAND.COM with the /P switch, the new copy of COMMAND.COM will become permanent, which means EXIT won't leave this copy.

See also
    COMMAND.COM   This is the command you use to load another copy of DOS's command-line interpreter.

EXPAND
DOS 5 and later, External

Expand compressed DOS files
This command allows you to "copy" individual files from your original DOS disks to your hard disk.

When and why
Most of the files on your original DOS disks are compressed so they'll take up less space. The INSTALL program normally does all the work of expanding these files, but if you accidentally delete a file, you'll need to use this command to copy files from your original DOS disks.

Syntax
    expand *filespec1* [*filespec2* ...] *destination*   (DOS 5 and later)
    Expands one or more files from one of your DOS floppy disks to the destination.

EXPAND

expand [*filespec1*] (DOS 6 and later)
Prompts you for information on which file you want to expand and where you want to put the expanded file.

Parameters

filespec1
Compressed name. The name of a file you want to expand. This filename cannot include wildcard characters — it must be the name of a single file on a floppy disk.

destination
Expanded name. The name and location on your hard disk (or floppy disk) where you want the expanded file stored. If you supply a path without a filename, you'll need to rename the file or files so they have the correct extensions (see "Notes" for a table).

Notes

EXPAND and hard disks
The DOS 5 EXPAND can only read compressed files from floppy disks. If you try to read a file from a hard disk, EXPAND will report an error. The DOS 6 version of expand *can* expand files that you copied to your hard disk.

Finding files
There is a file called PACKING.LST on Disk 1 (Disk 2 for DOS 5) that lists which disk each file is stored on. You can view this file rather than searching through all the disks to find out which disk you need.

Extensions
The extensions of all the compressed files have their last character replaced by an underscore character (_). You'll need to tell EXPAND the new name for each file you expand. Here is a chart that shows what extension to use for the expanded files for most extensions:

Compressed	Expanded
38_	386
ba_	bas
co_	com
cp_	cpi
dl_	dll
ex_	exe
hl_	hlp
ov_	ovl
pr_	pro
sy_	sys

The files that end with the extensions in the following table supply display-specific information to the DOSSHELL program. You'll need to choose a file based on the type of adapter you have (such as EGA) and use the full names here:

Part II: Command Reference

Compressed	Expanded
*.in_	dosshell.ini
*.gr_	dosshell.grb
*.vi_	dosshell.vid

Finally, any of the extensions listed below are used by network-specific files. See the *Getting Started* manual that comes with DOS for more information on how to install these files:

bi_   ob_   do_   1x_   2x_   ov_

Messages

```
Destination directory does not exist: name
```
(DOS 5 only.) You'll see this message when you've only supplied one filespec on the command line. EXPAND always assumes the last parameter on the command line (even if it's the only one) refers to the destination directory. Try again with an explicit destination directory, which can just be a single period to refer to the current directory.

```
Sector not found reading drive C
Abort, Retry, Ignore, Fail?_
```
(DOS 5 only.) You'll see this message when you've copied a compressed file to your hard disk and then tried to run EXPAND on this file. EXPAND can only read files from floppy disks.

Example

Let's say you deleted the file EMM386 by accident and you want to get it back. Here's what you'd do: First, you'll need to look through your original DOS disks for a file called EMM386.EX_. Once this disk is in your A: drive, type the following command to expand this file into your DOS directory:

```
C:\>expand a:emm386.ex_ c:\dos\emm386.exe
```

FASTHELP   DOS 6 and later, External

Displays syntax for DOS commands

This command is a fast way to get simple help on DOS commands. When you enter FASTHELP by itself, it displays a listing of all of the DOS commands in alphabetical order with a brief one-line description for each command. You can get additional information (about a screen full) for each command by supplying the command name after FASTHELP (or by running a command with the /? switch).

When and why

You'll want to use this command whenever you can't remember the name of a command, or when you want to see the list of switches and parameters you can use with a command. This command is invaluable for those times when the name of a command is on the tip of your tongue, but you simply can't remember the proper name — or when you can't remember what switches a particular command supports. FASTHELP provides a very brief description of each DOS command. When you

> supply a command name (or use the /? switch), FASTHELP provides a slightly longer description with a detailed syntax (including every parameter and switch). The HELP utility provides the most comprehensive on-line help, with notes and examples. This Command Reference you're reading provides the most comprehensive help available.

Syntax
fasthelp [*command*]
Provides a brief description of DOS commands.

Parameters
command
Whenever you provide the name of a command after FASTHELP, it displays more detailed information about the command. You can also get this same information by running the command with the /? switch.

Notes
Undocumented commands
FASTHELP only contains information about those commands that you can execute from the DOS prompt. It does not contain information about DOS commands that are normally placed in your CONFIG.SYS file or information about device drivers.

Examples
To display the command list
To see a list of all DOS commands, enter

   `C:\>`**`fasthelp`**

To display information about a specific command
If you specify the command name, FASTHELP displays a one-page listing of information related to that command. For example, if you enter

   `C:\>`**`fasthelp xcopy`**

FASTHELP displays information about using the XCOPY command. This command is exactly the same as typing

   `C:\>`**`xcopy /?`**

See also
HELP   Provides a cross-referenced on-line help system. The information in this book is more detailed than the on-line reference, however.

FASTOPEN   DOS 3.3 and later, External

Cache directory information
This command keeps directory information on recently used files in memory so that DOS can open the files quickly, without having to read the directory information from the disk. FASTOPEN does this by keeping the file's name and location in memory for up to n of the most recently opened files.

When and why

If you have enough expanded or extended memory for a disk cache such as SMARTDRV, you'll want to use it rather than FASTOPEN. This is because modern disk caches are typically better at speeding up *all* disk accesses, not just opening files. In theory, FASTOPEN should be faster at speeding up opening files than disk caches, but in practice it doesn't really provide a noticeable speed improvement, and a disk cache speeds up almost all types of disk access.

Warning! Even if you don't have enough memory for a disk cache, you may not want to use FASTOPEN. We've heard of a number of problems with FASTOPEN and other programs, and it's not clear you get much speed improvement. Your best solution when you can't use a disk cache is to use BUFFERS.

If you're using software that works with a number of files, such as a database program or a programming language compiler, FASTOPEN should provide a noticeable improvement in speed. FASTOPEN speeds up any program that opens files frequently because it keeps a list in memory of recently opened files, along with information on the location of those files. Whenever DOS tries to open a file, FASTOPEN first checks to see if that file is listed in this list, and if so provides DOS with the location of the file (without this memory list, DOS has to read several sectors from the disk to locate a file).

Syntax

fastopen *drive*:[=n] ... [/x]

Allows you to cache directory information on one or more drives and to store this cache in expanded memory rather than conventional memory.

Parameters

drive:

Drive to monitor. The disk drive for which you want FASTOPEN to remember directory information. You can tell FASTOPEN to work with more than one drive (see "Examples").

=n

Number of files. The number of files that you want FASTOPEN to keep directory information on. Can be any number between 10 and 999. The default value is 48 (34 for versions of DOS before 5). *Note:* The equal sign (=) is optional.

Switches

/x

Expanded memory (DOS 4.0 and later). Uses expanded memory rather than conventional memory to store the directory information on recently used files. You must have a memory manager that conforms to the Lotus/Intel/Microsoft Expanded Memory Specification (LIM EMS) to use this switch.

Notes

Networks

FASTOPEN doesn't work with network drives, only on hard disks attached directly to your computer. Most network software, such as Novell NetWare, uses its own proprietary operating system with a disk structure designed for speed and reliability rather than simplicity (as is the case for DOS). The result is that the network servers often have disk structures that are internally quite different from DOS's. As a result, FASTOPEN has no way to save relevant location information for network drives since this is all handled internally by the network software (DOS just sends the server a request to open the file; it doesn't know where the file's stored).

Memory used
FASTOPEN reserves about 48 bytes of memory for each file that it tracks (the sum of all the n's for all the disk drives you ask it to track). So, for example, for the default of 48 files on one hard disk, FASTOPEN will reserve 2,304 bytes of memory. Of course, if you use the /X switch, this memory will be in expanded memory rather than conventional memory, which will leave more room for your programs.

DOS Shell and Windows
Don't install the FASTOPEN command from the command line in the DOS Shell or from a DOS task inside Microsoft Windows. Instead, install FASTOPEN in your CONFIG.SYS or AUTOEXEC.BAT file so it will be loaded before the DOS Shell or Microsoft Windows starts.

Disk optimization programs
Warning! Don't run disk optimization programs (also known as disk defragmenting programs) when you have FASTOPEN installed. These programs move files around on your hard disk to remove fragmentation from the files (fragmentation is when a file has several pieces scattered across the disk). The information FASTOPEN keeps on the location of files on the disk may not be correct after the disk optimization program finishes.

Messages
```
Cannot use FASTOPEN for drive x:
```
FASTOPEN only works on local hard disks. It doesn't work with network drives, floppy disks, or drives that are affected by the SUBST, JOIN, or ASSIGN commands.

```
FASTOPEN already installed
```
Once FASTOPEN has been installed, you can only change the settings by restarting DOS. This message indicates that FASTOPEN has been installed already and the tracking hasn't changed.

```
FASTOPEN EMS entry count exceeded. Use fewer entries
```
You need to reduce the number of entries you want FASTOPEN to track. Expanded memory is divided into blocks called pages, with each page holding about 16K of data. The total entry count needs to be small enough so all the entries will fit into one page, which in our experience is about 300 (the sum for all the n's for the disk drives tracked by FASTOPEN).

```
Too many drive entries
```
FASTOPEN can't track more than 24 hard disks at one time (this number was smaller for versions of DOS before 5). Reduce the number of disk drives that you want FASTOPEN to track.

```
Too many file/directory entries
```
FASTOPEN is limited to tracking 999 file and directory entries for all disk drives. What this means is that the sum of all the n's must be 999 or less.

Part II: Command Reference

Examples

Using from the command line

You can type **FASTOPEN** directly at the command line or put it in your AUTOEXEC.BAT file. The following line tells FASTOPEN to track files on drive C:, using the default number of files:

```
C:\>fastopen c:
```

Installing in CONFIG.SYS

To install FASTOPEN in your CONFIG.SYS file, use the following line (FASTOPEN remembers directory information for 50 files on drive C:), assuming FASTOPEN.EXE is in the \DOS directory on drive C:

```
install=c:\dos\fastopen.exe c:=50 /x
```

We've also added the /X switch, which tells FASTOPEN to use expanded memory rather than conventional memory to save the information.

Multiple drives

You can have FASTOPEN remember directory information for more than one drive. This example tells FASTOPEN to remember directory information for 50 files on drive C: and for 70 files on drive D:.

```
C:\>fastopen c:=50 d:=70
```

See also

BUFFERS	DOS maintains some internal data buffers that you can also use to speed up disk accesses. Using a disk cache such as SMARTDRV is a better method.
EMM386.EXE	If your computer has an 80386 or better microprocessor, you can use this device driver to turn extended memory (which FASTOPEN can't use) into expanded memory (which it can use).
MEM	You can use the MEM command to see if you have any expanded memory on your computer, which you'll need if you want to use the /X switch on FASTOPEN.
SMARTDRV.EXE	You might want to use SMARTDRV instead of FASTOPEN to speed up disk accesses. SMARTDRV is a disk cache that will speed up all disk operations, whereas FASTOPEN only speeds up opening files.

FC   MS-DOS 2 and later, External

Compare two files

FC stands for File Compare, and it compares two files to see what the differences are. The FC command can do a byte-by-byte comparison to see if two files are identical; or for text files, FC can report which lines are different between two files.

When and why
This command is useful for comparing two text files to see what lines are different. You'll probably want to use it when you're trying to figure out which version of a file you want to keep.

Syntax
fc *filespec1 filespec2* [**/a**] [**/c**] [**/l**] [**/lb***n*] [**/n**] [**/t**] [**/w**] [**/***nnn*]
Compares the two text files and reports the differences.

fc *filespec1 filespec2* **/b**
Does a byte-by-byte (or binary) comparison of the two files to see if there are any differences. This is similar to the COMP command.

Parameters
filespec
Files to compare. The name of one of the two files to compare. Each of the two filespecs must refer to a filename (they can't be directory names), but you can use the DOS * and ? wildcard characters to compare several pairs of files. If only one filespec contains wildcard characters, FC will compare all the files that match the filespec to the other (single) file.

Switches
/a
Abbreviate. Abbreviates the report on what lines are different. Normally, when FC finds a group of lines that differ, it displays all the lines in that group. This switch tells FC to display only the first and last line of each group. FC then displays . . . on a line by itself to indicate that there are more lines in the group.

/c
Ignore case. Ignores the case of letters when doing the comparison.

/l
Text compare (the letter L). Forces FC to compare two files in text mode rather than binary mode. You'll need this switch whenever you want to do a text comparison on files with the following extensions: EXE, COM, SYS, OBJ, LIB, or BIN.

/lb*n*
Size of line buffer. Sets the size (in lines) of FC's internal buffer which it uses to store lines that differ. You may need to increase this number if the files you're comparing have a large number of lines that are different in any one area of the file. (Default is 100.)

/n
Line numbers. Displays the line numbers for lines that are different. This is a very useful switch when you're trying to find the differences in the file itself.

/t
No tab expansion. Doesn't expand tabs into spaces during the comparison. Normally, FC expands tabs into enough spaces to move to the next tab stop; tab stops are every eight spaces from the start of the line.

/w
Compress white space. Compresses white space (tabs and spaces) into a single space during comparison. Also, tells FC to ignore white space at the start and end of a line.

/nnn
Resynchronize line count. Sets the number of consecutive lines that must match before FC considers itself to be resynchronized. (Default is 2.)

/b
Binary compare. Compare the files in binary mode (byte-by-byte). This mode reports the offset into the file of any differences. This option is most useful for checking whether or not two files are identical. This is the default option for files with the following extensions: EXE, COM, SYS, OBJ, LIB, or BIN.

Notes

Hexadecimal numbers

When you use the /B switch, all the numbers displayed are hexadecimal numbers. Hexadecimal numbers are a little different from decimal numbers in that there are 16 digits rather than the usual 10; in other words, they're base-16 rather than base-10 numbers. Decimal numbers use the digits 0 through 9 (10 digits), while hexadecimal numbers use the digits 0 through 9, and A through F (for a total of 16 digits). In other words, we count up as follows: 1, 2, 3, . . ., 9, A, . . ., F, 10, ... The number 10 hexadecimal is really equal to 16 decimal.

Binary differences in hexadecimal

When FC using the /B switch finds a difference between two files, it displays a report such as the following:

```
00000021: 2E A6
```

The numbers in this case are all in hexadecimal notation (see "Notes" on "Hexadecimal numbers"). The first number is the offset from the start of the file to the difference reported (the first byte in the file is at offset 0). The next two numbers report the value of the byte at that location from the first and second file, respectively.

Wildcard characters

Wildcard characters may work in two unexpected ways. First, FC uses wildcard characters in the second filespec in the same way as the RENAME or COPY commands use wildcard characters — to create a second name based on the first name rather than to find files on the disk that match the second filespec. For example, if you ask FC to compare CON*.SYS to MON??.SYS and there is a file called CONFIG.SYS, FC will convert the second filespec into MONFI.SYS (the ?? characters substitute two characters from the first filename).

The second has to do with the ? wildcard character in the second filespec. As it turns out, the DOS 5 COMP and FC commands introduced a slight bug in their support of the ? character. Any ? characters you use in the second filespec must match exactly filenames produced by the first filespec. This means that CONFIG?.SYS won't match CONFIG.SYS because there is no character in position 7 for the ? to match. All other DOS commands allow ? characters at the end of filenames to match zero or one character rather than one and only one character as required by COMP and FC.

Messages

```
Could not expand second filename so as to match first
```
This message did not appear in versions of COMP and FC before DOS 5 and is the result of an incorrect change made to how COMP and FC handle the ? wildcard character. You'll see this message when you use the ? wildcard character in the second filename. FC requires that each ? character in the second filespec match exactly one character in every filename generated by the first filespec. (See "Notes" on wildcard characters.)

```
Incompatible switches
```
Secret DOS: You'll see this message when you try to use one of the text-comparison switches and either you've used the /B switch (for binary comparison), or you're trying to compare files that FC considers to be binary files. Either remove the /B switch or use the /L switch to force FC to do text comparisons.

```
Resync failed. Files are too different
```
You'll see this message when the files you're comparing are very different. There are two ways you can eliminate this message. First, you can increase the size of FC's line buffer to handle more lines at a time. And second, you can set the */nnn* switch to a smaller number (the default of 2 works fairly well) for the number of lines that must match before FC can resynchronize.

Examples

This example shows you what FC's output looks like for a simple set of files. We'll show you the two files first and then the output of the FC command. Here are the two files:

```
first.bat                       second.bat
```
```
@echo off                       @echo off
echo This is a test.            echo This is a test.
Here is new line 1              echo.
Here is new line 2              echo Just had a blank line
Here is new line 3
echo.
echo Just had a blank line
```

As you can see, these files are the same except for three lines added to the middle of FIRST.BAT. Here is the output of the FC command:

```
C:\>fc first.bat second.bat /n
Comparing files FIRST.BAT and SECOND.BAT
***** FIRST.BAT
    2:  echo This is a test.
    3:  echo.
***** SECOND.BAT
    2:  echo This is a test.
    3:  Here is new line 1
    4:  Here is new line 2
    5:  Here is new line 3
    6:  echo.
*****
```

See also

CONTENT_COMP — The COMP command is available in all IBM versions of DOS (FC isn't), but it's not as useful as FC.

DISKCOMP — This command allows you to compare two floppy disks of the same size to see if they're identical.

FCBs *DOS 3 and later, CONFIG.SYS*

Set maximum number of open files

This command is similar to the FILES= commands, except that it affects how many files old-style programs can open. It sets the number of File Control Blocks (FCBs) available in the system.

When and why

The FILES= command sets the number of file handles available in the system, but file handles didn't appear in DOS until DOS 2.0. As a result, there are a few programs that still use the DOS 1.0 method of opening files, using FCBs. So unless you have such a program, you may never need to use this CONFIG.SYS option.

Syntax

fcbs=*n*

Sets the number of FCBs available in the system for old-style programs.

Parameters

n

Sets the number of FCBs available. Valid range is 1 – 255. (Default is 4.)

Notes

You'll probably never need to use this command. Only use it when you're instructed to do so by your program's documentation.

Memory used by FCBs=

Each FCB that you want to be available adds approximately 60 bytes to the size of DOS in low memory.

See also

CONFIG.SYS — This entry explains more about how to use the CONFIG.SYS file and where it's located.

FILES= — This command affects how many files can be opened for programs written for DOS 2.0 and later.

FDISK
IBM 2.0 and later, DOS 3.2 and later, External

Configure hard (fixed) disk
This command allows you to set up a new hard disk or to change the number and size of logical drives you create when you partition your hard disk into more than one partition.

When and why
Since most computers come with DOS already set up on the hard disk, you'll probably never need this command.

This is a dangerous command, so you should be aware of what it does and what it can damage before you use it. You'll want to use FDISK whenever you install a new hard disk or first set up your computer. FDISK creates a partition table, which is a table at the start of your hard disk that tells DOS how it's organized. In other words, whether it's set up as one large hard disk or partitioned into several smaller logical drives.

Warning! When you create, remove, or resize hard disk partitions, you'll lose all the information on your hard disk. So if you have information on your hard disk, you'll need to back it up before you change your partition table. You'll also want to make sure you create a DOS floppy disk that you can boot from which contains the FDISK and FORMAT commands, as well as the program you need to restore the contents of your hard disk.

Syntax
fdisk [/status]
Starts the FDISK program, which is a full-screen program. In other words, there are no parameters or switches because FDISK displays prompts and asks for answers to questions.

Switches
/status
Displays the partition information for the drive without starting the FDISK utility.

See also
FORMAT After you've created a partition on your hard disk, you'll need to format it using the FORMAT command.

FILES
All DOS, CONFIG.SYS

Set maximum number of open files
This command in your CONFIG.SYS file allows you to set the maximum number of files that can be open at one time. DOS keeps track of open files using file handles, which are just numbers. The FILES command sets the number of file handles that are available in the system.

When and why
Many commercial programs need to work with a number of files simultaneously. This command allows you to make sure the programs have enough file handles. Most programs that open a number of files at the same time have their own installation program that modifies your CONFIG.SYS file to make sure the FILES= limit is high enough. The best thing to keep in mind, however, is that if a program does increase this number in your CONFIG.SYS file, you shouldn't reduce it. A good number for most programs is 20. Or 30 if you're using Microsoft Windows.

Syntax
files=*n*
Sets the maximum number of open files to *n*.

Parameters
n
The maximum number of files that can be open at one time. Valid range is 8 – 255. (Default is 8.)

Notes

Memory used by FILES=
Each file handle adds approximately 60 bytes to the size of DOS in low memory. Setting FILES=20, for example, increases DOS's size by about 720 bytes (since the default is FILES=8).

Files too small
Note: Be careful not to set FILES at too small a number. Some programs, such as Microsoft Windows, won't run if FILES is set too low, and they may not tell why they're not running. A good minimum is 20.

Memory-resident programs
If you're loading memory-resident (also known as TSR) programs, don't redirect their output to the NUL device (for example, TSR >NUL). Each such redirection will tie up one file handle until that program is no longer in memory. Memory-resident programs may also have several files open when other programs are running, so if you're using a memory-resident program that uses files, you might need to increase the FILES= number slightly.

Microsoft Windows
Windows Tip: Microsoft Windows needs a large number of file handles so it can support several programs running at the same time. By default, the Windows Setup program modifies CONFIG.SYS to include FILES=30, but this number may not be enough for all applications. If a program reports that it doesn't have enough file handles, increase this number.

Example
The following line in your CONFIG.SYS file sets maximum number of open files to 20:

```
files=20
```

See also

CONFIG.SYS — This entry explains more about how to use the CONFIG.SYS file and where it's located.

FCBs — Old-style programs (and there aren't many left) didn't use file handles. Instead, they used File Control Blocks (FCBs). This CONFIG.SYS line allows you to set the number of FCBs that are available.

FIND
All DOS, External

Search for text inside files

This command allows you to find a specific string inside files.

When and why
This command is useful for finding text within a file. You might also want to search for files that contain a given string. The FIND command by itself can't do this, but you can use the FOR command to search more than one file at a time (see "Examples").

Syntax
find *"string"* [*filespec*] [/c] [/n] [/v] [/i]
Searches for *string* inside a single file (you cannot use wildcard characters).

Parameters

"string"
Search string. The string that you're searching for. This can be any set of characters, as long as you enclose them between quotation marks. You can include quotation marks inside a string by repeating it twice ("quote mark"" is in the middle").

filespec
Search files. The name of the single file you want to search for the string (this filespec cannot include wildcard characters). If you don't supply the name of a file, FIND searches the text that appears from the standard input device. This allows you to use FIND as a filter (using the | PIPE command).

Switches

/c
Count matches. Displays only a count of the number of lines that contain the string. In other words, doesn't display any of the actual lines that contain the string.

/n
Line numbers. Displays the line number in front of each line that includes the string. This line number is displayed in brackets (for example, [1] for line 1).

/v
Nonmatching lines. Displays all the lines that do not contain the string. This is an inverse search.

/i
>**Ignore case** (DOS 5 and later). Ignores the case of letters during the search. This is a very useful switch. By default FIND only finds strings that use the same case for all the letters in the string you supplied.

Notes

Multiple word strings

When you use FIND to look for a string with more than one word (such as "two words"), it may not find the string even though it actually does appear in the file. This happens because some programs wrap paragraphs by putting a carriage-return character between words. If the two words you're looking for appear on two lines (one at the end of the first line and the other at the beginning of the next line), FIND may not locate the string.

Messages

```
File not found - name
```
You'll see this message either when FIND couldn't find the filenames or when you use the DOS * and ? wildcard characters in the filename; FIND doesn't allow wildcard characters (see "Examples" for a solution to this problem).

Examples

Searching multiple files

There are a couple of approaches you can take if you want to search more than one file at a time and they both use the FOR command. First, we'll show you how to use the FOR command on the command line to search all the *.TXT files:

```
C:\>for %n in (*.txt) do find "string" %n
```

This is a lot to type, so you might want to create a batch file, called SEARCH.BAT, that does the work for you:

```
rem Wildcard Find
@echo off
if "%1" == "" goto help
if "%1" == "/?" goto help
for %%n in (%2) do find %1 %%n %3 %4 %5 %6 %7 %8 %9
goto end
:help
echo Syntax: search "string" file [switches...]
:end
```

This batch file uses almost the same syntax as FIND. The parameters %3 through %9 at the end of the FOR command allow you to supply switches to the FIND command. As a result, SEARCH.BAT requires that you list switches at the end of the command, whereas the FIND command allows switches to be in any order. Now, to search all the *.TXT files, you can type

```
C:\>search "string" *.txt
```

FIND and DIR

(DOS 5 and later.) The FIND and DIR commands together are useful for finding files on your hard disk. For example, if you don't remember the name of a file, but you know that it contains "may", you can use the following command to find this file:

```
C:\>dir \*.* /s /b | find "may" /i
```

You can also use the DIR and FIND commands together to find files that were created (or last modified) on a certain date. This is useful if you know exactly when you last changed a file, but you don't remember its name or where you saved it to. For example, to find a file you created on 3-17-93, you would use the following command:

```
C:\>dir \*.* /s | find "03-17-93"
```

This won't tell you what directories the files are in, just their names. You can then use the DIR /B/S command to locate the directory where the file's stored.

FOR
All DOS, Batch command

Run command on a list

This command allows you to repeatedly run a single command on a list of strings or on a group of files. This is much more powerful and general than using the DOS wildcard characters.

When and why

This command is useful for adding wildcard processing to commands that don't support DOS wildcard characters (see the "Examples" that follow).

You can also use this command when you want to work on a group of files that can't be described by a single DOS wildcard pattern. For example, you may want to work with all *.DOC and *.BAK files. FOR is a powerful command. It's not the sort of command that you'll always remember how to use, but it allows you to build powerful batch files.

Syntax

for %%v in (set) do *command* [*parameters*]
Batch files. Runs one command for each item in *set*. This is the form of FOR that you need to use in batch files.

for %v in (set) do *command* [*parameters*]
Command line. Command-line version of FOR. Use this version of the command outside of batch files.

Parameters

%%*v* (in batch files)
%*v* (at the command line)
Replaceable parameter. Refers to one of the items in *set*. You can use this parameter in *command* to refer to a value from *set*. The *v* can be any character except 0 through 9 and / | < or >.

set
Parameter list. The list of items that you want to use in *command*. This set can be a list of names separated by spaces. Filenames in the set can also include the DOS * and ? wildcard characters, in which case FOR expands the wildcard name into a list of filenames. You refer to the items in the set using the %*v* or %%*v* parameters.

Notes

Running batch files with FOR
The command that appears after the DO command must be either an internal command or an external EXE or COM program. It can't be a batch file. You can run a batch file, however, by using CALL (or COMMAND /C) followed by the name of the batch file.

Lists
The *set* part of the FOR command can be a list of strings or filenames separated by spaces. When you're using filenames, you can also include DOS * and ? wildcard characters. FOR expands wildcard patterns into a list of filenames that match the pattern. This makes it easy to write a command that can work with DOS wildcard patterns. Here are some valid sets:

```
(*.txt)
(first.txt second.txt *.bat)
(john clint peter devra)
(*.txt %1 %2 %path%)
```

Examples
This is a simple example of using the FOR command (at the command line) to echo three names in a list:

```
C:\>for %n in (john clint peter) do echo %n
```

To perform a similar command from within a batch file, you would use

```
C:\>for %%n in (john devra peter) do echo %%n
```

Note that in the batch file, the variable must have a double percent sign.

Searching multiple files
This example shows how you can create a batch file, called SEARCH.BAT, that allows you to search a set of files for a specific string. This batch file uses the FIND command, which doesn't work with DOS wildcard characters.

```
rem Wildcard Find
@echo off
if "%1" == "" goto help
if "%1" == "/?" goto help
for %%n in (%2) do find %1 %%n %3 %4 %5 %6 %7 %8 %9
goto end
:help
echo Syntax: search "string" file [switches...]
:end
```

This batch file uses the same syntax as FIND. The parameters %3 through %9 at the end of the FOR command allow you to supply switches to the FIND command. To search all the *.TXT files, you can type

```
C:\>search "string" *.txt
```

See also
CALL	Use this command to run a batch file from within the FOR statement.
COMMAND	If you're using DOS versions before 3.3, you'll have to use COMMAND /C rather than CALL.

FORMAT   All DOS, External

Format a disk
This command allows you to format blank floppy disks, which you'll need to do before you can use them.

When and why
You'll want to use this command whenever you format a new floppy disk. The FORMAT command creates tracks and sectors on a floppy disk, which is known as *formatting*. It also writes several areas to the disk, including the root directory and the file allocation table (which describes which parts of the disk are used or free). FORMAT also checks for and marks bad sectors so they won't be used by DOS.

When you ask FORMAT to create a system disk, it also creates a boot sector, which enables you to load your DOS off the disk.

Syntax
format *drive*: [/**v**[:*label*]] [/**q**] [/**u**] [/**f**:*size*] [/**b**|/**s**] [/**t**:*tracks*] [/**n**:*sectors*] [/1] [/4] [/8][/c]

Parameters
drive:
The letter of the disk drive that contains the disk you want to format.

Switches
/**v**   (DOS 4.0 and later)
/**v**[:label]   (DOS 5.0 and later)
Volume label. Writes a volume label to the disk. If you don't supply a label here, DOS will prompt you for the label. Volume labels can be up to 11 characters long and can include any character (including spaces) except for ^ & * ( ) + = [ ] \ | : ; " / , . < > and ?. You cannot use this switch with the /8 switch.

/**q**
Quick format (DOS 5 and later). Builds a new file allocation table and root directory, without scanning the disk for bad sectors. This is very fast and is useful for reformatting disks that are in good condition. Saves information for UNFORMAT.

/**u**
Unconditional format (DOS 5 and later). Does a complete format of the disk. This switch prevents FORMAT from writing the UNFORMAT information to the disk. On a floppy disk, it also tells FORMAT to actually format each track, which will destroy all your data so UNFORMAT won't be able to recover it.

You'll want to use this switch to reformat a floppy disk that is reporting read or write errors, or when FORMAT has problems formatting a blank floppy disk.

/**f**:*size*
Set format size (DOS 4.0 and later). Tells FORMAT what size to use when it formats a floppy disk. This is useful when you want to format a low-capacity disk in a high-capacity drive. Use this switch rather than the /T and /N switches when you can. The size can be any of the following:

Part II: Command Reference

    5¼-inch disks: 160, 160K, 160KB, 180, 180K, 180KB, 320, 320K, 320KB, 360, 360K, 360KB, 1200, 1200K, 1200KB, 1.2, 1.2M, 1.2MB

    3½-inch disks: 720, 720K, 720KB, 1440, 1440K, 1440KB, 1.44, 1.44M, 1.44MB, 2880, 2880K, 2880KB, 2.88, 2.88M, 2.88MB

The larger sizes (1.2, 1.44, and 2.88) require higher density floppy disk drives and are not always available.

/b
Reserve room for DOS. Reserves space on the disk for installing DOS (the files installed by the SYS command). This command isn't needed for DOS 4.0 and later since the SYS command doesn't need space reserved beforehand for the system files.

/s
Transfer system. Copies the system files to the floppy disk after it's been formatted. The files copied are IO.SYS and MSDOS.SYS (for MS-DOS) or IBMIO.COM and IBMDOS.COM (for IBM and some other versions of DOS). DOS 5 and later also copy the COMMAND.COM file (you'll need to copy this file yourself if you're using an earlier version of DOS).

DOS 6 also copies the DBLSPACE.BIN file onto the new system disk. This file is necessary to access drives compressed with DoubleSpace.

/t:*tracks*
Tracks per side. The number of tracks to format on the disk. You should use the /F: switch rather than this switch if you're using DOS 4.0 or later. For earlier versions of DOS, you'll use this switch in conjunction with the /N switch. (See table for values to use with the /N switch).

/n:*sectors*
Sectors per track. The number of sectors per track. You should use the /F: switch rather than this switch if you're using DOS 4.0 or later. For earlier versions of DOS, here is a table of values you should use with /T and /N:

Drive	Formatted Size	/t:*tracks*	/n:*sectors*
5¼-inch	360K	9	40
	1.2MB	15	80
3½-inch	720K	9	80
	1.44MB	18	80
	2.88MB	36	80

/1
Single-sided disk (the number one). Formats a single-sided floppy disk. This is for compatibility with single-sided disk drives, which haven't been built into IBM PCs since 1982. You'll probably never need this switch.

/4
360K disk. Formats a 5¼-inch, 360K disk in a 1.2MB floppy disk drive.

/8
320K disk. Formats a 5¼-inch, 320K disk. This allows you to format a disk that can be read by DOS 1.1. You'll probably never use this switch.

/c
Test for bad clusters (DOS 6.2 and later). Tells FORMAT to retest bad clusters to see if they're still bad. The DOS 6.2 and later FORMAT command normally doesn't bother to

FORMAT

test clusters that are already marked as being bad. You can use this command, however, to force FORMAT to retest these bad clusters. In versions of DOS before 6.2, FORMAT always tested all clusters, even if they were already marked as bad.

Notes

The /U switch
Contrary to what the DOS manual states, FORMAT does not erase the contents of a hard disk when you use the /U switch: it only erases the contents of floppy disks. It also prevents FORMAT from creating the UNFORMAT information, which could make it difficult to recover the data on your disk.

Bad sectors
Some disks may have some errors that prevent parts of the disk from being used. FORMAT will mark these areas as being bad in the file allocation table so they won't be used to store files or data. The process of marking bad sectors is done whenever you format a disk unless you use the /Q option. In MS-DOS 6.2, you must use the /C switch to force FORMAT to check for bad sectors when reformatting a disk.

Incompatibilities
You should not use FORMAT to format a drive letter created by ASSIGN or SUBST, or one currently attached to another disk via the JOIN command.

Drive compatibility problems
You may have some problems with disks that you format in 1.2MB disk drives when they were previously formatted in a 360K floppy disk drive. This happens because the 360K floppy disk drive writes wider sectors than a 1.2MB disk drive (the 1.2MB drive writes 80 tracks in the same space that the 360K disk drive writes 40). When you try to read this floppy disk again in a 360K disk drive, that drive's wider read head will read both the new format tracks created by the 1.2MB disk drive and the part of the wider tracks created by the 360K drive that weren't covered by the 1.2MB disk drive's tracks. The best solution is to use an unformatted floppy disk when you're creating a 360K disk in a 1.2MB disk drive. This will ensure there are no wide tracks left behind. Fortunately, most modern 1.2MB disk drives don't have this problem.

ERRORLEVEL returned
Format returns information that batch files can test with the IF ERRORLEVEL command. Here are the exit codes FORMAT returns:

    0 FORMAT finished without errors.
    3 You pressed Ctrl-C or Ctrl-Break to exit FORMAT before it finished.
    4 There was an error.
    5 You pressed N to exit FORMAT before it actually formatted your disk.

You can use this information in batch files to take an action if FORMAT failed.

Messages
The FORMAT command has a number of error messages, so we can only show a few of the more common messages here.

```
Cannot format an ASSIGNed or SUBSTed drive.
```
Disable the ASSIGN or SUBST setting that affects the disk you're trying to format and then try again.

`Disk unsuitable for system disk.`
You'll see this error message when there are bad sectors in the area where DOS writes DOS system files. You'll need to try another disk (you can still use this disk for storing data files).

`Invalid media or track 0 bad - disk unusable`
There is a bad sector in the first track of the disk, where DOS needs write information to make a disk usable. You'll need to use another disk (the disk with this error won't be useful).

`Invalid Volume ID.`
You'll see this message when the volume label you typed has some characters that aren't allowed in volume labels. You can use any character (including spaces) except for ^ & * ( ) + = [ ] \ | : ; " / , . < > and ?.

`Parameters not supported by drive.`
You'll usually see this message when you've asked FORMAT to use a size (or track and sector switches) that isn't available on the disk drive. For example, if you ask FORMAT to create a 360K disk in a 3½-inch disk drive.

`Unable to write BOOT.`
You'll see this message when there is a bad sector in the boot area of the disk. Try another disk.

`Write protect error`
`Format terminated.`
This means that the disk you're trying to format is currently write-protected. Remove the write-protect tab (5¼-inch disks) or slide the tab so it covers the hole (3½-inch disks) to make the disk writeable; then try again.

`You must use "DBLSPACE /FORMAT d:" to format that drive`
You'll see this message when you try to format a DoubleSpace volume. The Format command only works with uncompressed disks.

Examples

To create a survival disk, you could type

`C:\>`**`format a: /s /v:survival`**

Formatting a lower capacity disk

This example shows the command used to format a 720K disk in a 1.44MB 3½-inch disk drive:

`C:\>`**`format a: /f:720`**

Reformatting

When you're reformatting a floppy disk, there are two commands you might want to use. First, if the floppy disk had read or write errors, you'll want to do a full format to ensure FORMAT creates new tracks and marks bad sectors. Here is the command to do this:

`C:\>`**`format a: /u`**

If, on the other hand, you want to remove all the files on the floppy disk so you have a blank disk, you can type

`C:\>`**`format a: /q`**

This will do a quick format, which is very fast.

See also

DBLSPACE /FORMAT	You'll need to use this command to format compressed DoubleSpace volumes.
LABEL	You can change (or create) a disk's volume label at any time using the LABEL command.
SYS	The SYS command transfers the current version of DOS to another disk so that you can boot DOS from that disk.
UNFORMAT	This command allows you to recover the contents of a disk after you format it by accident.
VOL	Displays the current volume label for a disk.

GOTO   All DOS, Batch files

Branch to another line in batch file

This command allows you to control the order in which DOS executes lines in a batch file. When DOS sees a GOTO command, it looks for the first label in the batch file that matches the name you supply.

When and why
The GOTO command is useful, along with the IF command, for building intelligent batch files. You'll want to use this command when you're programming batch files.

Syntax
goto *name*
Starts executing commands with the first line after the label name. In the examples below, notice that we use a colon to define the label, but we don't use the colon in the GOTO statement.

Notes

GOTO ignores case
The GOTO command ignores case, so the name you provide will match any combination of upper- and lowercase letters in labels.

Valid labels
Labels can be up to eight characters long. You can use any character except for the special and file separator characters: % * - + = [ ] \ | : ; " < > , . and /. GOTO ignores any characters after the first eight.

Messages
```
Label not found
```
You'll see this message when there is no label with the name in a GOTO command.

Examples

Here is a simple example that shows the use of a label and a GOTO statement:

```
goto end
copy *.* c:
:end
```

The GOTO command here skips the COPY command and sends execution directly to the line after the label :END.

Using GOTO and multiple configurations

Starting with DOS 6, you can have multiple configurations in your CONFIG.SYS file (see the entry on MENUITEM for details). When you have multiple configurations, DOS defines an environment variable called CONFIG and assigns it the name of the menu you choose. In your AUTOEXEC.BAT file (or any other batch file) you can refer to an environment variable using the form %*name*%. If you have a menu called Windows and one called DOS, you could then use code like this to either launch Windows or run the Norton Commander (our favorite DOS shell) based on which CONFIG.SYS configuration you choose:

```
goto %config%
:windows
    win
    goto done
:dos
    nc
:done
```

You can also use the IF command to run single commands.

Replaceable parameters in GOTO

You can use a replaceable parameter, such as %1, in a GOTO statement to run a set of commands based on the parameter you supply. For example, some people like to create a menu batch file that contains a set of commands they often run. Such a batch file, called DO.BAT, might look something like this:

```
if "%1" == "" goto syntax
if %1 = word goto StartWord
    .
    .
    .
:StartWord
    .
    .
    .
goto exit
:syntax
echo Syntax: DO word ...
:exit
```

See also
:name   Lines that start with a colon define labels.

IF   This command allows you to run one command if a condition is true. This one command is often the GOTO command.

GRAFTABL
DOS 3.0–5, External

Support code pages on CGA
This command has limited use and, as a result, was dropped with DOS 6. It supports the display of international characters and code-page switching (used for national language support) on the Color Graphics Adapter (CGA) in graphics mode.

When and why
Unless you have a CGA display and plan to use code-page switching, you won't need this command. EGA and VGA display adapters have this function built into the hardware. We're not even sure why you'd want to use this function on a CGA display since it can only change the character set when you're in graphics mode, and most programs run in text rather than graphics mode.

All display adapters have a total of 256 characters they can show. CGA display adapters, however, can only display the first 128 characters when in graphics mode. This is because the ROMs on original IBM PCs only had enough room to store the first 128 characters. So if you plan to use extended characters (the upper 128 characters) on a CGA display adapter in graphics mode, you'll need to use this command to load the upper 128 characters.

This command isn't needed on EGA or VGA cards because they can display and change their entire character set (all 256 characters) in both text and graphics mode.

Note: This command was dropped with the release of DOS 6.

Syntax
graftabl [*nnn*] [**/status**]

Parameters
nnn
Code page (DOS 3.3 and later). The number of the code page to load into GRAFTABL. This can be any of the following:

437	U.S.
850	Multilingual (Latin I)
852	Slavic (Latin II) (DOS 5 and later)
860	Portuguese
863	Canadian-French
865	Nordic

Part II: Command Reference

Switches
/status
/sta
Displays the current code page loaded into GRAFTABL.

Notes
Display adapters
The GRAFTABL command only works on CGA screens. You don't need GRAFTABL for EGA and VGA screens since this function is built directly into the hardware on those display adapters.

Text mode
The GRAFTABL command doesn't change any of the characters in text mode. It only affects characters you see on the screen while the display is in graphics mode. Note that the CHCP command *does* change the text-mode character sets on EGA and VGA screens.

See also
CHCP   If you're using an EGA or VGA display, you can use the CHCP command to change character sets.

GRAPHICS   All DOS, External

Enable graphics print screen
This command allows you to use the Print Screen key on your keyboard to print graphics screens.

When and why
This command allows you to use the Shift-PrtScr key combination to print the screen to your printer when you're in graphics mode. If you need to print graphics screens, and you have one of the supported printers, you can use this command.

Syntax
graphics [*type*] [*filespec*] [/r] [/b] [/lcd] [/printbox:std|lcd]   (DOS 4 and later)
graphics [*type*] [/r] [/b] [/lcd] [/c] [/f] [/p*n*]   (Prior to DOS 4)
Loads the memory-resident program that supports graphics-mode screen dumps (using the Print Screen key to print a graphics screen).

Parameters
type
Printer type. The type of printer that you want to print to. It can be one of the following (grouped by the printer manufacturer):

deskjet   (DOS 5 and later.) Hewlett-Packard DeskJet printer.
hpdefault   (DOS 5 and later.) Hewlett-Packard LaserJet printer.

GRAPHICS

laserjet	(DOS 5 and later.) Hewlett-Packard LaserJet printer.
laserjetii	(DOS 5 and later.) Hewlett-Packard LaserJet II printer.
paintjet	(DOS 5 and later.) Hewlett-Packard PaintJet printer.
quietjet	(DOS 5 and later.) Hewlett-Packard QuietJet printer.
quietjetplus	(DOS 5 and later.) Hewlett-Packard QuietJet Plus printer.
ruggedwriter	(DOS 5 and later.) Hewlett-Packard RuggedWriter printer.
ruggedwriterwide	(DOS 5 and later.) Hewlett-Packard RuggedWriterwide printer.
thinkjet	(DOS 5 and later.) Hewlett-Packard ThinkJet printer.
color1	IBM Personal Computer Color Printer with black ribbon.
color4	IBM Personal Computer Color Printer with an RGB (red, green, blue) ribbon. Can produce four colors.
color8	IBM Personal Computer Color Printer with a CMYK (cyan, magenta, yellow, and black) ribbon. Can produce eight colors.
graphics	IBM Personal Graphics Printer, IBM Proprinter, or IBM Quietwriter. Also many Epson printers.
graphicswide	(DOS 4.0 and later.) IBM Personal Graphics Printer with an 11-inch wide carriage.
thermal	IBM PC-Convertible Thermal Printer.

filespec
Printer information file (DOS 4.0 and later). The name and location of the file that contains the information on all the printers supported. By default, DOS looks for a file called GRAPHICS.PRO both in the current directory and in the directory that contains the GRAPHICS.COM program.

Switches

/r
Reverses the image. Normally, GRAPHICS prints white areas as black and black areas as white (since the background is often black). This switch tells GRAPHICS to print black as black and white as white.

/b
Prints the background in color. This is only supported on color printers (COLOR4 and COLOR8).

/lcd
Prints IBM PC Convertible screen. The Convertible used an LCD screen which required this switch. Same as the /PRINTBOX:LCD switch.

/c
Center image (MS-DOS 3.2 and 3.3 only). Centers an image on the page printed with the /F option. This works for image resolutions of 640 × 200 or 320 × 200.

/f
Flip page (MS-DOS 3.2 and 3.3 only). Flips the printed image so it's printed sideways on the page (rotated 90 degrees). Supports images with resolutions of 640 × 200 or 320 × 200.

/p*n*
Printer port (DOS before 4.0 only). Selects the printer port to use. The number *n* can be 1, 2, or 3 for LPT1, LPT2, or LPT3.

/printbox:std
/printbox:lcd
Aspect ratio (DOS 4.0 and later). Chooses which aspect ratio to use: STD uses the aspect ratio of a standard screen; LCD uses the aspect ratio of IBM's PC Convertible's LCD screen.

Notes

Memory used
The GRAPHICS command uses about 6K of memory when it's loaded; the actual size will depend on which printer you're using. You can load it into upper memory using the LOADHIGH command.

Changing the printer
You can change the printer that you want GRAPHICS to work with as long as that printer's description is small enough to fit into GRAPHICS's buffer. The size of this buffer was set when you first loaded GRAPHICS. If you need to reload a larger printer description, you'll have to restart your computer.

HELP   DOS 5 and later, External

Display DOS help

This command activates the hypertext Help program in DOS 6. In DOS 5, it displays a single screen of help information for any DOS command, just as the FASTHELP command does in DOS 6. For information on using HELP in DOS 5 or FASTHELP in DOS 6, see the entry for FASTHELP.

When and why
This command is a quick way of getting information on DOS commands without having to pick up a book. If you know the name of the command, the /? switch is probably your fastest way of getting information. When you don't know the name of the command, just type **HELP**, and you'll see a list of commands.

Syntax

    help [/b] [/g] [/h] [/**nohi**] [*command*]   (DOS 6)
    help [*command*]   (DOS 5)
Starts the full-screen help program (DOS 6 and later). The following are the common syntaxes.

    help
Starts the DOS 6 hypertext Help utility.   (DOS 6)
Displays an alphabetical list of DOS commands with one-line descriptions.   (DOS 5)

help *command*
Starts the DOS 6 Help program with the syntax page for *command* displayed. (DOS 6)
Displays help information for *command*. (DOS 5)

command /? (DOS 5 and later)
Displays brief (less than one page) syntax information for a DOS command.

Parameters
command
The DOS command for which you want help.

Note: Most of the material from here on applies to the DOS 6 version of HELP. For information on how to use HELP in DOS 5, see the description of the DOS 6 FASTHELP command (which was called HELP in DOS 5).

Switches
/b
Black and white. Uses black and white rather than colors on systems that have a color graphics card. This option is useful on laptop computers with EGA or VGA screens that display colors as shades of gray (which can be hard to read). On systems with monochrome cards, the display is automatically set to black and white.

/h
High resolution. Uses as many lines as possible: 43 lines on an EGA display and 50 lines on a VGA display adapter.

/nohi
Eight colors. Uses only 8 colors on the screen rather than 16. This is useful for the few displays that don't support 16 colors. You'll need to use this switch if you don't see the menu and item shortcut keys highlighted.

/g
Fast CGA display. For a CGA display adapter: uses fast screen writing. Older computers that use a CGA card based on IBM's design display "snow" when you write quickly to the screen, so most programs slow down on CGA screens. You can try this switch to see whether it improves screen output speed.

Notes
Moving through the Help utility
Although it is easiest to use Help with a mouse, you can also use the keyboard. For all commands, you may either click on a command or menu item or use the keyboard equivalent. Press the Alt key to activate the menu bar and then the first letter of the menu you want to pull down (**F**ile or **S**earch). Here are keystrokes that you can use to move through HELP:

Alt-C   Table of Contents. Shows a list of all DOS commands, in alphabetical order.

Alt-N   Next Page. Moves to next page in the help file. You can use this command, for example, to move from the Syntax section, to the "Notes" section, and finally to the Example section.

Part II: Command Reference

Alt-B	**Back.** Moves back to previous page. Previous page means the last page you were looking at rather than the previous page in the help file. This command is *not* the opposite of Next Page.
PgDn	**Page Down.** Move down one screen. Each "page" in the file can be more than one screen long. This key allows you to scroll down in one page.
PgUp	**Page Up.** Move up one screen. This allows you to browse backwards (and with PgDn, forwards) through a single page in the help file.
Tab	**Next Jump item.** Move to next jump topic mark. These are keywords in the text, or at the top of the screen, that allow you to jump to related topics.
Enter	**Jump.** Move to selected topic. Allows you to jump to a related topic. Alt-B will bring you back after you jump.

Organization of the Help file

The pages of the Help file are organized alphabetically by command. Within each command, the Syntax page is followed by the Notes page (if included) and then the Examples page (if included). All commands have a Syntax page. Some commands, such as DBLSPACE, have a number of extra pages for all the switches.

Searching the Help file

You can use the Find command from the Search menu to search the Help file for a particular word or phrase. Use the F3 key to move to the next occurrence of the word.

Examples

You can also get help on any command by using the /? switch after the command. For example, to get help on the XCOPY command (we always have to), you might start with the following:

```
C:\>xcopy /?
```

This provides you with a short listing of the syntax of the XCOPY command, such as:

```
Copies files (except hidden and system files) and directory trees.

XCOPY source [destination] [/A | /M] [/D:date] [/P] [/S [/E]] [/V] [/W]

  source       Specifies the file(s) to copy.
  destination  Specifies the location and/or name of new files.
  /A           Copies files with the archive attribute set; doesn't change
               the attribute.
  /M           Copies files with the archive attribute set; turns off the
               archive attribute.
  /D:date      Copies files changed on or after the specified date.
  /P           Prompts you before creating each destination file.
  /S           Copies directories and subdirectories except empty ones.
  /E           Copies any subdirectories, even if empty.
  /V           Verifies each new file.
  /W           Prompts you to press a key before copying.
```

If this command doesn't provide you with enough information, you can use the DOS 6 Help command by entering

```
C:\>help xcopy
```

HELP opens to the Syntax page for XCOPY. The explanations for each switch are much more detailed. For example, the syntax description for the /M switch is

```
/M Copies source files that have their archive file attributes
   set. Unlike the /A switch, the /M switch turns off archive
   file attributes in the files specified in source. For
   informtion about how to set the archive file attribute,
   see the <ATTRIB> command.
```

Whenever you see a word with angle brackets around it, such as <ATTRIB>, you can jump directly to an explanation of that command or concept: Either click on this word, or move the cursor so it's on this word and press Enter. On a color screen, the angle brackets will be in green, while the rest of the text will be white. You can also use the Tab key to move between these *jump* words.

HIMEM.SYS   DOS 4.0 and later, Device driver

Extended memory manager

This device driver manages extended memory, using the eXtended Memory Specification (XMS). It also manages the High Memory Area (HMA) that DOS uses to load itself into high memory.

When and why

If you're using a computer with extended memory (any computer with at least an 80286 microprocessor and more than 1MB of memory), you'll want to use this device driver. The only exception is when you're using another memory manager that provides the same function.

HIMEM manages extended memory using the XMS, which many programs use to work with extended memory. For example, DOS gets the memory it needs to load itself into high memory by requesting the HMA from HIMEM.SYS (or any other XMS device driver).

Syntax
device=[*path*]**himem.sys** [**/machine:***code*] [**/cpuclock:on|off**] [**/int15=***xxxx*] [**/shadowram:on|off**] [**/hmamin=***mm*] [**/numhandles=***hh*] [**/a20control:on|off**] [**eisa**] [**/testmem:on|off**] [**/verbose**]
Loads the HIMEM device driver into memory.

Switches
/machine:*code*
If you have problems loading DOS into high memory, or you see a report that there is a problem with the A20 handler (which allows access to the HMA), you may need to tell HIMEM what machine you're using. This is the message you'll probably see:

```
Unable to control A20
```

Use one of the machine abbreviations or numbers listed in this table for the code or check the README.TXT file in your DOS directory for additional information (and codes). (Default is 1, which is the IBM PC/AT.)

Computer	Number	Abbreviation
Acer 1100	6	acer1100
AT&T 6300 Plus	5	att6300plus
Bull Micral 60	16	bullmicral (Abbrev. in DOS 6 and later)
CompuAdd 386 systems	1, 8	
CSS Labs	12	css
Datamedia 386/486	2	
Dell XBIOS	17	dell
Hitachi HL500C	8	
HP Vectra	14	fasthp
HP Vectra (A and A+)	4	hpvectra
IBM 7552 Industrial Computer	15	ibm7552 (DOS 6 and later)
IBM PC/AT	1, 11	at, at1
IBM PC/AT (alternative delay)	12, 13	at2, at3
IBM PS/2	2	ps2
Intel 301z or 302	8	
JDR 386/33	1	
Philips	13	philips
Phoenix Cascade BIOS	3	ptlcascade
Phoenix BIOS	1, 8	
Toshiba 1600, 1200XE, 5100	7	toshiba
Tulip SX	9	tulip
UNISYS PowerPort	2	
Wyse 12.5 MHz 286	8	wyse
Zenith ZBIOS	10	zenith

/cpuclock:on|off
Slow clock disable. If your computer slows down when you install HIMEM.SYS, you may need to provide the /CPUCLOCK:ON switch to keep HIMEM.SYS from slowing your computer down. (Default is OFF.)

/int15=*nnn*
Old-style extended. You'll probably never need to use this option. Sets the amount of extended memory (in kilobytes) that will be available for old-style programs that don't use the XMS to access extended memory (but instead use INT 15h). This memory won't be available to programs that use XMS. If you use this switch, set *nnn* so you request 64K more memory than you'll need; this is because DOS uses the first 64K of old-style extended memory for the HMA. Valid range is 64 to 65535 (64K to 64MB). (Default is 0.)

HIMEM.SYS

/shadowram:on|off
Shadow RAM enable. Tells HIMEM.SYS if it should turn shadow RAM on or off. Shadow RAM is RAM that's used to hold a copy of a ROM for faster access to the ROM. If your computer has shadow RAM (many computers don't), this option will free up the extended RAM used for shadowing the ROM. (Default is /SHADOWRAM:OFF if your computer has less than 2MB of RAM.)

/verbose or /v
Display status during loading. This switch causes HIMEM.SYS to display status messages during the boot process. It is useful for tracking down problems in memory management. You can also have these messages display by holding down the Alt key while HIMEM loads (you have to press it and hold it down *before* HIMEM starts to load).

/testmem:on|off
Test extended memory (DOS 6.2 and later). Controls whether HIMEM will test your extended memory before it loads. Before DOS 6.2, HIMEM never tested extended memory, relying instead on the memory test (if any) done when your computer first starts. HIMEM's new memory test, however, does a better job of finding bad memory chips than the test done by most computers when you first turn them on. For safety's sake it's a good idea to let HIMEM test your memory (because a bad memory chip can cause you to lose your work). The only reason you'd want to turn off memory testing is for speed: HIMEM's memory test can take several seconds on some computers. Default: /TESTMEM:ON.

Advanced switches

The following switches are fairly advanced. You probably won't want to use any of these unless instructed to do so by a software manual or a knowledgeable person.

/hmamin=*mm*
High memory threshold. Sets a lower limit on the amount of high memory that a program can use. High memory is the first 64K of extended memory and is allocated as an entire chunk to one and only one program. This switch keeps programs from using the HMA unless they're going to use at least *mm* kilobytes of the HMA. You might use this switch to keep some program that uses only a small amount of the HMA from stealing it from DOS, which uses most of the HMA when given the chance. Valid range is 0 – 63. (Default is 0, which allows any program to request the HMA.)

/numhandles=*hh*
Set number of handles. Sets the maximum number of extended memory blocks that can be in use. Programs use handles to refer to these blocks, so the number of handles available determines how many blocks can be used at one time. *Note:* HIMEM's size in memory will increase by 6 bytes for each handle. Valid range for hh is 1 – 128. (Default is 32.)

/a20:control:on|off
A20 control. This is a rather technical option. The A20 line controls whether the HMA is available or not. This switch tells HIMEM.SYS whether it should take control of this line. ON tells HIMEM.SYS to take control, while OFF tells HIMEM to take control of the A20 line only if it was off when HIMEM.SYS was loaded. (Default is /A20CONTROL:ON.)

eisa
Allocate all memory. Necessary only on EISA computers with over 16MB of memory. This switch tells HIMEM to grab all available extended memory, which it normally does on most computers. If you have an EISA computer with more than 16MB of memory, you may need to use this switch to make all of extended memory available to your programs.

Notes

Loading DOS high

You must have this device driver or another device driver that supports XMS in order to load DOS into the HMA. Then you'll need to use DOS=HIGH in your CONFIG.SYS file.

DOS can't load into high memory

If you discover that DOS refuses to load into high memory, even when you have DOS=HIGH in your CONFIG.SYS file and you have a line that loads HIMEM.SYS, you may have some device driver that is stealing the HMA from DOS. If you think this is happening, you might try using the /HMAIN switch to keep programs that don't use much of the HMA from using any of it. Only one program can use the HMA, and it's on a first come, first served basis.

Messages

```
ERROR: An extended memory manager is already installed.
```
You have another device driver you're loading before HIMEM.SYS that provides extended memory management. If you're using a third-party 80386 memory manager, it provides the functionality of both HIMEM.SYS and EMM386.EXE in a single device driver, so you don't need HIMEM.SYS. Otherwise, check your manuals to see which device driver you should use.

```
ERROR: HIMEM.SYS requires an 80x86-base machine.
```
You can't use HIMEM.SYS on 8088- or 8086-based computers because these microprocessors don't support extended memory.

```
ERROR: VDISK memory allocator already installed.
       XMS driver not installed.
```
You'll see this message when a device driver loaded before HIMEM.SYS allocates some extended memory using the old-style INT15 interface. Make sure HIMEM.SYS is the first device driver loaded (by putting it first in the CONFIG.SYS file) and then use the /INT15 switch to set aside some old-style extended memory for the other device driver.

```
Unable to control A20
```
You'll need to set the machine type, using the /MACHINE switch, so HIMEM.SYS will know how to handle the A20 line (which allows access to the HMA).

```
WARNING: The A20 line was already enabled.
```
You'll see this when you install a device driver before HIMEM.SYS that controls the A20 line. Make sure you really want both device drivers. If you do, you can use the /A20CONTROL:OFF switch.

Examples

Most of the time you'll use HIMEM.SYS without any switches. In such cases, HIMEM.SYS should be the first device driver loaded by your CONFIG.SYS file. The following should be the first line in your file:

```
device=c:\dos\himem.sys
```

If, on the other hand, you're using a computer listed in the machine-type table (see "Switches"), you may need to use the /MACHINE switch, which can be abbreviated /M. For an IBM PS/2 computer, for example, you would type

```
device=c:\dos\himem.sys /m:2
```

See also

DOS=	This command in your CONFIG.SYS file tells DOS to load itself into high memory.
EMM386	You'll need to load this device driver after HIMEM.SYS if you want to use expanded memory or the upper memory blocks on an 80386 (or 80486) computer.
MEM	The MEMORY command will give you information on the types of memory in your computer, as well as where programs and device drivers are loaded.
MEMMAKER	In DOS 6, you can use this utility to automatically optimize the use of your memory.

IF   All DOS, Batch command

Test condition in batch file

This command allows you to program batch files which allows you to create intelligent commands.

When and why

If you're writing batch files, you'll almost certainly want to use this command. IF allows you to actually program your batch files, rather than just write a set of commands that DOS will execute in sequence.

Most of the time you'll probably use the GOTO command as the IF command runs. These two commands together make it possible for you to write loops that have an end. You can also run different sets of commands based on the results of IF tests.

Syntax

if [**not**] *string1* == *string2 command*

Tests to see if *string1* is the same as *string2* and runs *command* if they're the same. The NOT keyword tells IF to run *command* if the two strings are not the same.

if [not] exist *filespec command*
Checks to see if *filespec* exists, and if so runs *command*. The NOT keyword tells IF to run *command* if the file does not exist.

if errorlevel *number command*
This form of IF allows you to test the error level returned by the previous external command (if it returns an error level). IF runs *command* if the error level returned by the previous command is greater than or equal to *number*. Used with the new DOS 6 CHOICE command to provide a method for obtaining user responses during the processing of a batch file.

Parameters

command
The command to run if the condition is true (or not true if you use the NOT parameter). This can be any DOS command. If you want to run another batch file, you should use either CALL or COMMAND /C to run the batch file.

not
Tells IF to run the command if the condition is not true.

string1 == string2
"string1"=="string2"
This expression will be true only if the two strings are the same. A string can be a set of characters, a filename, a batch-file parameter (%0 through %9), or a combination. It's usually a good idea to put quotation marks (") around both strings so you can include all characters inside the string. The only characters you can't include are = and a single % (you must write it twice: %%). IF is case-sensitive.

exist filespec
True only if the file given by *filespec* exists on your disk. The filespec can include the DOS * and ? wildcard characters, in which case IF checks to see if at least one file exists that matches *filespec*.

errorlevel number
True if the error level returned by the previous command is greater than or equal to (>= in programming notation) *number*. You can use this to test the output of some DOS commands, as well as other programs that return an error level. (Many programs don't.) You can test for a specific value by testing ERROR LEVEL and then NOT ERRORLEVEL (we show you how in the "Notes" section).

Examples

Testing for an empty string

The easiest way to test for an empty string is to put quote marks (or any character that you won't find in either string) around both parts of the test. For example, if you wanted to test %1 to see if it's empty, the following line works:

```
if "%1" == "" goto empty
```

Batch file loops

This short batch file, which we'll call DELETE.BAT, shows you how you might write a loop that processes all the parameters you type on the command line. It allows you to list more than one file to delete (without using wildcards or multiple DEL statements):

```
@echo off
:loop
if "%1" == "" goto end
del %1
shift
goto loop
:end
```

Friendly batch files

It's a good idea to write batch files that can display help information when you use the /? switch (just like DOS's commands) or when you don't supply the right number of parameters. The IF command makes this very simple. Here is a short batch file that displays help information:

```
@echo off
if "%1" == "" goto help
if "%1" == "/?" goto help
  .
  .
  .
:help
echo Syntax: delete filespec1 [filespec2 ...]
```

Using multiple configurations

Starting with DOS 6, you can have multiple configurations in your CONFIG.SYS file (see the entry on MENUITEM for details). When you have multiple configurations, DOS defines an environment variable called CONFIG and assigns it the name of the menu you choose. In your AUTOEXEC.BAT file (or any other batch file), you can refer to an environment variable using the form %*name*%. If you have a menu called Windows and one called DOS, you could then use code like this to either launch Windows or run the Norton Commander (our favorite DOS shell) based on which CONFIG.SYS configuration you choose:

```
if %config% == windows win
if %config% == dos nc
```

You can also use the GOTO %config% command if you want to run more than a single command.

Using ERRORLEVEL to test for no errors

You might want to create a batch file that builds some floppy disks. This batch file should check the FORMAT command to make sure it worked before continuing. If it didn't work, the batch file should allow you to insert another blank floppy disk and try again. Here is how you check to see if FORMAT worked properly:

```
format a:/s /v:label
if errorlevel 1 goto error
  ...
:error
Handle the error here.
```

The IF ERRORLEVEL command branches to the label ERROR if the error level number returned by FORMAT is greater than or equal to one (zero means that FORMAT finished without errors).

Using ERRORLEVEL to test for specific values

The DOS 6 CHOICE statement places a value into ERRORLEVEL to indicate how you answered a question. When working with the CHOICE statement (and in more complex batch files testing for exit conditions from other commands), you have two options for identifying specific ERRORLEVEL values.

The first (and easiest) is to test for the largest possible value first. The default CHOICE statement returns the value 1 for yes and 2 for no. To perform different actions for each possible response, you can structure your batch file as follows:

```
@echo off
choice
if errorlevel 2 goto NoAction
if errorlevel 1 goto YesAction
:NoAction
echo The answer was No
goto end
:YesAction
echo The answer was Yes
goto end
:end
```

But there is a cleaner way that will test for specific values, or even for a range of values, using *nested IF* statements. A nested IF has a second IF statement as the action for the first IF statement. For example, if you want to see if ERRORLEVEL is between *start* and *stop*, you can use this form:

```
if errorlevel start if not errorlevel stop+1 command
```

Here is an example to bring this back to reality. The following batch file uses CHOICE to give you three choices: **Y**, **M** (for maybe), and **N**:

```
@echo off
choice /c:ymn "Yes, Maybe, No: "
if errorlevel 1 if not errorlevel 3 echo Maybe, Yes...same thing.
if errorlevel 3 if not errorlevel 4 echo OK, OK.
```

Notice that, unlike the previous batch file, here the tests are in increasing numerical order (rather than decreasing). You'll also notice that you get the same message for both Y and M (ERRORLEVELs 1 and 2). This approach is a really powerful and clean approach when you use the GOTO command to run different pieces of code — particularly since you can place these nested IF statements in any order.

See also

CALL	Use this command to run a batch file from within the IF statement.
CHOICE	This is a good way to ask questions in batch files, and you can use the IF command to respond to these answers.

COMMAND   If you're using DOS versions before 3.3, you'll have to use COMMAND /C rather than CALL.

GOTO   You'll probably use the GOTO command with IF more often than any other command. GOTO allows you to branch to another location in your batch file when a condition is true.

INCLUDE   DOS 6 and later, CONFIG.SYS

Include one menu block within another

This command allows you to include the CONFIG.SYS lines from one menu block in another. You can use it with multiple configurations (see MENUITEM) to simplify your CONFIG.SYS file when you have lines that you share between several menu blocks. A menu block is a series of CONFIG.SYS lines that DOS will use when you select a startup configuration from a menu.

When and why

This command is useful only if you're using a CONFIG.SYS menu, also known as multiple configurations. (See the MENUITEM command for more details.) In such cases, you can use INCLUDE to include the commands from other menu blocks, which means you won't have to repeat commands that are common in more than one menu block. Without INCLUDE, you would have to repeat the commands for each menu item.

Syntax

include=*menublock*
Include the CONFIG.SYS lines from another menu block, named *menublock*.

Parameters

menublock
Identifies the name of the block to be included. A menu block is identified with a header that consists of the block name enclosed in square brackets (for example, [network]). Menu blocks do not have to be connected with a MENUITEM.

Notes

To use a configuration menu, your CONFIG.SYS file must contain a menu section, consisting of the header [menu], followed by a series of MENUITEM commands. Each MENUITEM tells DOS which menu block it should "run" when you select that menu. You can add an INCLUDE line inside any of these menu blocks to include all of the lines from another menu block. For example, you might have some commands that are common to some menu items, but not others. In this case, you can create a menu block that isn't connected to a menu to hold the shared lines; then you can use INCLUDE to include these shared lines in other menu blocks. You'll find more information on creating menus and menu blocks under the MENUITEM entry in this reference.

Shared common blocks

You can create common blocks that aren't connected to a MENUITEM, which is very useful if you want to create blocks that you can include with INCLUDE.

Examples

Including common devices

The following lines in CONFIG.SYS define three menu blocks: Windows, DOS, and Shared. Only the first two are actually attached to menus, so the [shared] block is used only by the INCLUDE lines in the other two blocks. The INCLUDE lines cause all the lines in the [shared] block to be run as if they appeared where DOS sees INCLUDE=shared.

```
device=c:\dos\himem.sys

[menu]
menuitem=Windows
menuitem=DOS

[dos]
device=c:\dos\emm386 ram
device=c:\dos\ramdrive 2048 /e
include=shared

[windows]
device=c:\dos\emm386 noems
include=shared

[shared]
device=ansi.sys
install=c:\dos\share.exe

[common]
```

This format avoids having to repeat the lines in the [shared] block and instead references them using the INCLUDE statement.

See also

MENUITEM Used to create a menu item on a configuration menu. You'll also find a discussion here of the [common] blocks, which are a special type of menu block.

CONFIG.SYS Discusses the typical CONFIG.SYS commands.

INSTALL=

DOS 4.0 and later, CONFIG.SYS

Load memory-resident program

This command in your CONFIG.SYS file allows you to load memory-resident programs. These programs will be loaded after all the device drivers have been loaded but before DOS runs AUTOEXEC.BAT.

When and why

Memory-resident programs are programs that stay in memory until you restart your computer. They're also called terminate-and-stay-resident (TSR) programs. DOS has a number of memory-resident programs. You can use this command to install the following programs in your CONFIG.SYS file: FASTOPEN, KEYB, NLSFUNC, and SHARE. But you're certainly not limited to these four programs.

You have two options when installing memory-resident programs. You can install them with this command, or you can install them by running them from your AUTOEXEC.BAT file. It is a matter of personal preference, except when you want to load memory-resident programs into upper memory, in which case you can't use the INSTALL= command (see "Notes").

Syntax

install=*filespec* [*parameters*]
Runs the program *filespec* so it can install itself into memory.

Parameters

filespec
Program to install is the name of the file you want to install. *Note:* You must include the program's path and extension since the command interpreter (which searches for programs) isn't loaded yet when INSTALL= tries to run your program.

parameters
Program parameters. This is the same command line that you would normally supply to the program you're installing.

Notes

Loading into upper memory

If you want to load a program into the upper memory area, you'll have to use the LOADHIGH command in your AUTOEXEC.BAT file because INSTALL= doesn't allow you to run the LOADHIGH command.

If you're using a third-party memory manager (such as 386MAX, BLUEMAX, CEMM, or QEMM), you can use their versions of LOADHIGH in the INSTALL= line to load programs into upper memory.

When INSTALL= lines run

DOS makes several passes through your CONFIG.SYS file, and it processes the INSTALL= lines last. This means that DOS will load all device drivers using DEVICE=

Part II: Command Reference

or DEVICEHIGH= lines before it loads any programs with INSTALL=. DOS loads the command-line interpreter (COMMAND.COM) after it finishes installing all the INSTALL= programs.

Installing programs that use environment variables

(DOS 5 only.) The INSTALL= command loads programs into memory without creating an environment for the program, which might cause problems. Don't use INSTALL= to load programs that use either environment variables or COMMAND.COM to handle disk errors.

(DOS 6 and later.) In DOS 6 Microsoft allows you, for the first time, to use the SET command to set environment variables from within the CONFIG.SYS file. This means that DOS actually creates an environment before running any programs that use INSTALL= (contrary to Microsoft's manual). In fact, you could run the Commander using an INSTALL= line. You wouldn't want to do this, but just for fun, here are the lines you would need in your CONFIG.SYS file (we actually tried this):

```
set comspec=c:\dos\command.com
set path=c:\dos;c:\prog\nc;
install=c:\prog\nc\nc.exe
```

The two SET commands define environment variables that the Commander needs to function properly: the current PATH and COMSPEC, which tells the Commander where to find COMMAND.COM. However, and this is also interesting, DOS doesn't load itself into high memory until after it finishes running all commands in CONFIG.SYS. So if you run the MEM command when the Commander starts, you'll see a large chunk of memory being used by MS-DOS. When you quit the Commander, which causes DOS to finish running CONFIG.SYS and then run AUTOEXEC.BAT, you'll notice that the message "MS-DOS is resident in the high memory area" appears after you exit from the Commander that was run by the INSTALL= line.

Messages

```
Bad or missing filespec
Error in CONFIG.SYS line n
```
You'll see this message when DOS can't locate the file you asked it to load. Check the pathname and filename to make sure they're correct. *Note:* You must include the program's extension since the command interpreter (which searches for programs) isn't loaded yet when INSTALL= tries to run your program.

Example

Windows Tip: Put this line in your CONFIG.SYS file to load the Share program (which you should load if you're running Microsoft Windows or the DOS Shell's Task Swapper):

```
install=c:\dos\share.exe /l:40
```

See also

DEVICE=   The equivalent command for loading device drivers is the DEVICE= command in CONFIG.SYS.

LOADHIGH   If you want to load your program into upper memory, you'll need to use the LOADHIGH command in your AUTOEXEC.BAT file instead of the INSTALL= command.

INTERLNK   DOS 6 and later, External

Control client's connection on Interlnk network

Interlnk is a DOS 6 feature that allows you to connect two computers together using a special serial or parallel cable. Using this command, and INTERSVR, you can have the disk drives and/or printers on one computer appear on the other computer. In a sense, this is a very simple network between two computers. This command serves three primary functions. First, it displays the status of the Interlnk connections with a host system (server). Second, it establishes connections between a client and a host system. Finally, it releases connections established between a client and a host system.

When and why

Use this program whenever you want an easy way to connect two computers together in a mini network. This program, along with INTERSVR, allows you to have the disk drives and printers on one of your computers appear as if they were attached to your other computer. Before you can use this command, you'll need the proper cables. Many computer stores should be able to sell you these cables that work with Interlnk (you might have to ask for LapLink cables).

When two computers are connected together with Interlnk, one computer will act as a *client*, and the other computer will act as a *server*. The server is the computer providing services to the other computer, such as disk drives or printers, while the client is the computer making use of these services.

On the server, you must run the program INTERSVR before your client computer will be able to use any of the server's disks or printers. INTERSVR will completely take over your server computer until you exit from INTERSVR, which will also disconnect your two computers.

On the client side, you'll need to do a couple of things to set up the link. First, you'll need to install the INTERLNK.EXE program as a device driver in CONFIG.SYS. See the INTERLNK.EXE description in the next section for details. Once you have this device driver installed, you can control the connection using the INTERLNK program (it acts both as a device driver and a program).

Syntax

interlnk
Displays the status of the Interlnk connections. If no connection exists, establishes the default connections controlled by the INTERLNK.EXE line in your CONFIG.SYS file.

interlnk *client*[:]=*server*[:]
Establishes an Interlnk drive connection. If no other connection exists, it also establishes the default connections controlled by the INTERLNK.EXE line in your CONFIG.SYS file.

interlnk *client*[:]=
Releases an Interlnk connection, which also frees up the drive letter *client*.

Parameters

client
A drive letter on the client computer. This is either a letter that is connected to an Interlnk drive or an unused drive letter. You can assign unused drive letters to disk drives on the server as well as disconnect drive letters from the server.

server
The drive letter for a disk drive on your server computer that you want to connect to an unused drive letter on your client computer. This drive letter should be the letter of the actual disk drive on your server computer. You cannot connect to network drives or CD-ROM drives attached to your server.

Notes

Using INTERLNK with a non-DOS 6 computer

One of your computers must be running DOS 6 for you to use the Interlnk feature. (This isn't true in theory, but it is true if you want to satisfy the license agreement for using DOS 6.) If the other computer isn't running DOS 6, you can copy the INTERLNK.EXE and INTERSVR.EXE files to your other computer, via floppy disk. If, however, you can't or don't want to use a floppy disk, INTERSVR has a nice remote copy feature that allows you to copy both files to another computer connected only by a serial cable. You'll find details on how to do this in the discussion of INTERSVR.

What drives are available

By default, all the floppy and hard disk drives on your server will be available, but you can also use the /X switch when you run INTERSVR to exclude some of your disk drives so they won't be available. See the description of INTERSVR for more details. Also, you can set INTERLNK so it doesn't reserve any drive letters if you only want to use a printer attached to the server. See the description of INTERLNK.EXE in the next section.

Using volume labels

If you use volume labels to label your disks, these volume labels will appear in INTERLNK's list of drive letters when you type **INTERLNK** at the command line without any parameters or switches. This makes it much easier to identify which drive is which if you have more than one disk drive.

Number of Interlnk drives

The maximum number of drive letters that you can work with is determined by the line in CONFIG.SYS that loads the INTERLNK device driver. By default, INTERLNK reserves enough memory so you can work with up to three drives, but you can change this using the /DRIVES switch with INTERLNK (see the description of INTERLNK.EXE in the next command entry).

Interlnk and LASTDRIVE

The manual says that you must have LASTDRIVE set so you'll have enough available drive letters, but this isn't true. Device drivers, including INTERLNK

INTERLNK

allocate their own drive letters and have nothing to do with the LASTDRIVE line in your CONFIG.SYS file. The LASTDRIVE line is important only for commands that allow you to add and remove drive letters from the DOS prompt, such as the SUBST command and the NET command in Workgroup Connection. The INTERLNK command always reserves a fixed number of drive letters for itself, based on the /DRIVES switch on INTERLNK.EXE in your CONFIG.SYS file.

INTERLNK serial cables

The serial cable used by INTERLNK is different from the ordinary serial cable and is commonly known as a *null-modem* cable. You can find such cables at many computer stores. Another name people often use to refer to these cables is *LapLink cables*, after the name of the most successful product that connects two computers together via a serial or parallel cable. If you're handy with a soldering iron and want to try to build the cable yourself, you'll find detailed information in the INTERLNK "Notes" section of the HELP command.

INTERLNK parallel cables

The parallel cable used by INTERLNK is different from the ordinary printer cable and is often called a *LapLink cable*, after the name of the most successful product that connects two computers together via a serial or parallel cable. You should be able to purchace such a cable from many computer stores. If you're handy with a soldering iron and want to try to build the cable yourself, you'll find detailed information in the INTERLNK "Notes" section of the HELP command.

Messages

```
Drive assignment syntax error
```
This is a really frustrating error message. You'll see it whenever you try to use a drive letter that INTERLNK didn't create. When you load INTERLNK.EXE in your CONFIG.SYS file, it creates some special drive letters for its own use. You can only use these drive letters with INTERLNK. How do you know which drive letters INTERLNK created for your use? When DOS first loads INTERLNK.EXE into memory (from your CONFIG.SYS file), INTERLNK displays a list of drive letters that it has commandeered. You'll simply have to remember which drive letters belong to INTERLNK.

```
Invalid unit reading drive F
Abort, Retry, Fail
```
You'll see this message whenever you try to use one of INTERLNK's drive letters when it's not connected to a disk drive on the server. Use the INTERLNK *client=server* to connect a drive letter on the client with a drive letter on the server. Use the /DRIVES switch with the INTERLNK line in your CONFIG.SYS file to change the number of drive letters INTERLNK reserves for its use.

```
Not ready reading drive F
Abort, Retry, Fail
```
You'll see this message when you try to use one of INTERLNK's drive letters before you've connected to the server. You'll need to run INTERSVR on the server and then run INTERLNK, without any parameters, to connect the two machines. You can now connect any of INTERLNK's drive letters to a drive on the server. Use the /DRIVES switch with the INTERLNK line in your CONFIG.SYS file to change the number of drive letters INTERLNK reserves for its use.

Part II: Command Reference

```
Too many block devices
```
If you see this message while DOS is loading INTERLNK from your CONFIG.SYS file, it probably means you have the /DRIVES set to more drive letters than you have available. In this case you may not be able to access your INTERLNK drives at all. You'll need to reduce the number of drives you ask for and reboot.

Examples

To display the status of Interlnk

To check on the available Interlnk services, enter **INTERLNK** without any parameters. The message that appears is similar to the following:

```
C:\>interlnk
    Port=LPT1

    This Computer            Other Computer
      (Client)                  (Server)
    ---------------          --------------
        E:           equals       A:
        F:           equals       B:
        G:           equals       C: (169Mb) HOST_SYS

C:\>_
```

In this example, three drivers have already been mapped between the two systems.

To release a drive

To release drives F and G, you would enter

```
C:\>interlnk F= G=
```

This removes the connection between the client drive letters F and G and disk drives on the server. After you run this command, the drive letters F and G will still exist, but you'll get an error if you try to read from them.

To connect a drive

To attach the drive letter G on your client to the floppy disk drive A on your server, you would enter

```
C:\>interlnk G=A
```

See also

INTERLNK.EXE   This device driver must be loaded to use the Interlnk connections.

INTERSVR   You must run this command on the server computer to make resources available to your client.

INTERLNK.EXE — DOS 6 and later, Device driver

INTERLNK device driver

This device driver must be installed on the client computer before you can use Interlnk to connect two computers together (you'll also need the right type of cable, as explained under "Notes" in the previous section).

INTERLNK.EXE

When and why
You must install this device driver any time you want to use INTERLNK to connect as a client to another computer via a parallel or serial cable. Place the INTERLNK.EXE line in your CONFIG.SYS file.

Syntax
device=[*path*]**interlnk.exe** [**/drives:***n*] [**/noprinter**] [**/com**[:][*n|address*]] [**/lpt**[:][*n|address*]] [**/auto**] [**/noscan**] [**/low**] [**/baud:***rate*] [**/v**]

Loads the INTERLNK device driver into memory and creates drive letters that you can use to access disks on the server. You'll need this program before you can use disks and printers made available by another computer running INTERSVR.

Parameters
path
The location of the INTERLNK.EXE file, which is usually in your DOS directory.

Switches
/drives:*n*
Maximum drive connections. This switch determines how many drive letters you can redirect. INTERLNK creates *n* drive letters when it loads into memory. The only way you can increase this number is to change the number *n* and reboot. Valid range is 0 to 26. The value 0 tells INTERLNK to redirect only printers. (Default is 3).

/lpt[:][*n|address*]
Search parallel ports (LPT). This switch tells INTERLNK to look for a connection with the server on a parallel port. If you don't supply either *n* or *address*, INTERLNK uses the first parallel port that it finds connected to the server. Supplying a number tells INTERLNK which specific port you want to use. Supply *n* when you know the LPT number, such as LPT1, or supply *address* if you know the I/O port for that parallel port (the *address* is an advanced feature). You can have INTERLNK search only parallel ports by using the /LPT switch without the /COM switch. The default is to search all parallel and serial ports, which is equivalent to /COM /LPT.

/com[:][*n|address*]
Search serial ports (COM). This switch tells INTERLNK to look for a connection with the server on a serial port. If you don't supply either *n* or *address*, INTERLNK uses the first serial port that it finds connected to the server. Supplying a number tells INTERLNK to look for a connection on a specific port. Supply *n* when you know the COM number, such as COM1, or supply *address* if you know the I/O port for that serial port (the *address* is an advanced feature). You can have INTERLNK search only serial ports by using the /COM switch without the /LPT switch. You might also want to limit the search to a single serial port, like /COM2, if you have a serial mouse installed on COM1. This will keep INTERLNK from intefering with your mouse. The default is to search all parallel and serial ports, which is equivalent to /COM /LPT.

/baud=*n*
Serial baud rate. This switch sets the maximum speed for serial transfers (the actual speed can vary during the connection but will never be higher than this number). The acceptable values for *n* are 9600, 19200, 38400, 57600, and 115200. The default is 115200.

/v
Correct timing. If you have problems with INTERLNK only when one of your computers uses a disk drive or printer, you can try using this switch to see if it fixes the problem. These problems can be caused by conflicts with one of your computer's system timers, which tick 18.2 times every second.

/noprinters
Load normally but do not establish printer connections. This switch tells INTERLNK not to load the code to handle printer connections. If you know you're not going to use a printer on the server, you can use this switch to reduce the amount of memory used by INTERLNK. (Default is to allow printer redirection.)

/auto
Load only if connection is available. With this switch, the INTERLNK device driver loads only if it can immediately establish a connection with a server. If no server is available, INTERLNK won't load into memory. If you later want to establish a link, you'll need to start the server on the other computer and then reboot the client. By default, INTERLNK loads into memory even if it finds no server. We recommend using this switch unless you use INTERLNK a lot and don't want to reboot the client to start INTERLNK.

/noscan
Load without establishing a connection. This switch tells INTERLNK to load into memory without looking for a server. You'll need to run INTERLNK from the command line to actually establish a link. By default, INTERLNK tries to connect to a server when it's first loaded into memory.

/low
Use low memory. Loads INTERLNK into low memory, rather than into upper memory. By default, INTERLNK loads itself into upper memory when it's available.

Notes

Loading INTERLNK into upper memory
INTERLNK automatically loads itself into upper memory (unless you use the /LOW switch), so there is no reason to use the DEVICEHIGH command to load INTERLNK.

Using printer redirection with Windows
If you ask INTERLNK to redirect LPT1 or LPT2 to a printer attached to the server, you'll need to select LPT1.DOS or LPT2.DOS from the Printer Control Panel in Windows before you can print to the server's printer. Using these printer port names tells Windows not to bypass the normal printer code in your computer; Windows normally writes directly to the hardware for maximum speed, but INTERLNK cannot redirect LPT*n* when Windows writes directly to the hardware.

How INTERLNK uses drive letters
When DOS loads the INTERLNK.EXE device driver, INTERLNK creates as many drive letters as you ask it to. These drive letters will not be available to any other device drivers, nor will they be available for use with commands like SUBST that use drive letters. In other words, these drive letters are for INTERLNK's use only. As such, you should be careful not to ask for too many drive letters. Since INTERLNK

INTERLNK.EXE

grabs drive letters when it loads, the drive letters might change for other device drivers, such as RAMDRIVE, that also create drive letters. For this reason, you might want to load INTERLNK after you load other device drivers.

INTERLNK and LASTDRIVE

You don't actually have to use the LASTDRIVE= line in CONFIG.SYS because INTERLNK creates its own drive letters and completely ignores the LASTDRIVE= setting.

DoubleSpace, Interlnk, and RAMDrive

Device drivers, such as DBLSPACE, INTERLNK, and RAMDRIVE, create their own drive letters. They ignore the setting of LASTDRIVE, so you don't need to set LASTDRIVE in order to use any of these commands or any other device driver that creates drive letters. The LASTDRIVE command sets aside memory for programs, such as SUBST and networks, that allow you to create and destroy drive letters from the DOS prompt. Device drivers, on the other hand, reserve drive letters when they're loaded from within CONFIG.SYS.

Let's say you have a DoubleSpace drive C, which means that the uncompressed physical disk will normally be drive H. If you have INTERLNK.EXE /DRIVES:6 in your CONFIG.SYS file followed by RAMDRIVE.SYS, you'll have the following drive letters when you finish booting:

- C   Your compressed hard disk
- D–I   The six drive letters grabbed by INTERLNK
- J   The RAM disk
- O   Your uncompressed hard disk

DoubleSpace always tries to leave a gap between its drive letter and the other drive letters, which is usually four unused drive letters if you have only one compressed drive. DoubleSpace allocates new drive letters working down from its first drive letter. In this example we also have LASTDRIVE set to D, so you can see that the device drivers ignore the setting of LASTDRIVE.

Incompatibilities

You cannot use any of the following commands on drive letters created by INTERLNK:

chkdsk	diskcopy	mirror	unformat
defrag	fdisk	sys	
diskcomp	format	undelete	

Examples

To request LPT1 and 2 drives

The following statement in the CONFIG.SYS file loads INTERLNK whether or not a server is available:

```
device=c:\dos\interlnk.exe /drives:2 /lpt1
```

Part II: Command Reference

If a server is available, it establishes a connection via a cable attached to LPT1, and it uses the first two available drive letters. If INTERLNK doesn't find a server, it still grabs the drive letters and loads into memory, but you'll need to run the INTERLNK command to establish the connection.

An example of a specific connection

This statement establishes a connection for remote printing (no drives will be available for the connection), and INTERLNK won't be loaded if it couldn't find a server. The format is as follows:

```
device=c:\dos\interlnk.exe /drives:0 /com /auto
```

If the server is not available at startup, INTERLNK will not load. This means that if the server later becomes available, you must reboot the client before you can take advantage of the server's printer. The advantage of this strategy is that no memory is wasted on a device driver that you're not using.

We recommend using the /AUTO switch unless you use Interlnk a lot. This will keep INTERLNK from loading itself unless you have a server running when you boot your computer. Not only will this save memory, but you'll also have the extra drive letters only when you're actually using INTERLNK.

See also

INTERLNK   The actual client software.

INTERSVR   The host system (server) software.

INTERSVR   DOS 6 and later, External

Starts the server portion of the Interlnk system

This command is half the Interlnk system, which allows you to connect two computers together with a serial or parallel cable in order to share disks and/or printers. The other half is INTERLNK. This program provides resources to the other computer.

When and why

You'll want to use this command in connection with the INTERLNK command. These two commands together allow you to connect two computers together via a serial or parallel cable. When you run this command on one computer, it takes over the computer and makes disk drives or printers available to a second computer. See the INTERLNK command for more details.

This command also allows you to copy the INTERLNK software to another computer attached only by a serial cable (called a null-modem cable). You don't even need a floppy disk on the second computer.

Syntax

intersvr [*drive1*[*drive2*...]] [/**x**=*drive1*[*drive2*...]] [/**lpt:**[*n*|*address*]] [/**com:**[*n*|*address*]] [/**baud:***rate*] [/**b**] [/**v**]

Makes Interlnk resources available.

INTERSVR

intersvr /rcopy
Copies the Interlnk files to a remote system connected with a null-modem cable.

Parameters

drive1 drive2
Available drive. This is a list of drive letters for all the drive letters you want to make available to the client. Any drives that are not in this list will not be available to the client. You can use the /X switch to exclude a specific drive. By default, all drives are made available.

Switches

/x=drive1 drive2
Exclude drive. A drive letter, or a list of drive letters, that you want hidden from the client. By default, all drives are made available.

/lpt[:][n|address]
Search parallel ports (LPT). This switch tells INTERSVR to look for a connection with the client on a parallel port. If you don't supply either *n* or *address*, INTERSVR uses the first parallel port that it finds connected to the client. Supplying a number tells INTERSVR which specific port you want to use. Supply *n* when you know the LPT number, such as LPT1 or supply *address* if you know the I/O port for that parallel port (the *address* is an advanced feature). You can have INTERSVR search only parallel ports by using the /LPT switch without the /COM switch. The default is to search all parallel and serial ports, which is equivalent to /COM /LPT.

/com[:][n|address]
Search serial ports (COM). This switch tells INTERSVR to look for a connection with the client on a serial port. If you don't supply either *n* or *address*, INTERSVR uses the first serial port that it finds connected to the client. Supplying a number tells INTERSVR to look for a connection on a specific port only. The number *n* refers to a specific serial port, such as COM1, while *address* is the I/O address for the serial port (an advanced feature). You can have INTERSVR search only serial ports by using the /COM switch without the /LPT switch. The default is to search all parallel and serial ports, which is equivalent to /COM /LPT.

/baud=*n*
Serial baud rate. This switch sets the maximum speed for serial transfers (the actual speed can vary during the connection but will never be higher than this number). The acceptable values for *n* are 9600, 19200, 38400, 57600, and 115200. The default is 115200.

/v
Correct timing. If you have problems with INTERLNK only when one of your computers uses a disk drive or printer, you can try using this switch to see if it fixes the problem. These problems can be caused by conflicts with one of your computer's system timers, which tick 18.2 times every second.

/b
Black and white. Tells INTERSVR not to use color to display its status screen. You'll probably want to use this switch if you're planning to run INTERSVR on a laptop screen that shows colors as shades of gray.

/rcopy
Remote copy. This command copies the INTERSVR.EXE and INTERLNK.EXE files to another computer connected by a serial cable. To use this command, the two computers must be connected with a 7-pin, null-modem serial cable. When you run INTERSVR /RCOPY, it will provide instructions on what you need to type on the other computer to start the transfer.

Notes

To use Interlnk, you need to have either a parallel or serial (null-modem) cable to connect the two systems. You can either purchase one or create one following the directions in the on-line Help utility under the Notes for the Interlnk command. If you already have a cable, you may be able to purchase an adapter to convert it for use as an Interlnk cable.

Using INTERSVR with Windows or the DOS Task Swapper

You can run INTERSVR from within either Windows or the DOS Shell's Task Swapper. But when you do, INTERSVR will take over your computer, disabling all other programs, until you exit from INTERSVR. You can exit at any time by pressing Alt-F4.

Examples

To make only drive A available

This command allows the client to access information on drive A only:

```
C:\>intersvr a:
```

All other drives will be hidden from the client.

To establish a 9600 baud connection

If you want to establish a relatively slow serial connection, you can use

```
C:\>intersvr /lpt1 /baud:9600
```

In general, direct serial connections can support much higher speeds, and Interlnk automatically adjusts the serial speed if necessary.

To copy the Interlnk files to another computer

You must first physically connect the two computers with a null-modem cable. Next, confirm that the computer that is to receive the files has the MODE command installed. Finally, enter the following command on the computer that has the Interlnk files:

```
C:\>intersvr /rcopy
```

Follow the directions that INTERSVR displays on the screen, and it will copy the Interlnk files to the other computer. You will then need to configure the Interlnk files on the other computer before you can establish a full Interlnk connection.

To exclude several drives

Here is how you would have all drives, except for A and B, available to the client:

```
C:\>intersvr /x=ab
```

JOIN

You can also write this same command as

```
C:\>intersvr /x=a: b:
```

Both forms are equivalent.

See also

INTERLNK   The client portion of the Interlnk software.

INTERLNK.EXE   The device driver used for the client. You must load this on one of your computers before you can use Interlnk.

MODE   Used by the RCOPY switch of INTERSVR to help copy the Interlnk files to another computer.

STTY   INTERSVR also uses this command when you use the /RCOPY switch.

JOIN   DOS 3.0–5, External

Attach drive as a subdirectory

This command allows you to attach an entire disk drive as a subdirectory on another disk. In this way you can make more than one disk appear as a single, large disk.

When and why

Many of the uses for this command are historical. DOS versions before 3.31 didn't support hard disks larger than 32MB. To install a larger hard disk you had to partition it into virtual drives no larger than 32MB. If you really wanted one larger hard disk, you could use the JOIN command to join all these partitions together so your hard disk would look like one large hard disk.

With DOS 3.31 and later, however, you can create a single partition the size of your hard disk. JOIN can still be useful when you have more than one hard disk, but this isn't very common. You should also be aware that there are a number of DOS commands that you shouldn't use when JOIN is active (see "Notes").

Note: For these reasons, JOIN was dropped as a command in DOS 6.

Syntax

join
Displays the list of JOIN assignments that are currently in effect.

join *drive*: [*path*]
Joins the disk *drive:* to the directory *path* on another disk.

join *drive*: /d
Deletes the JOIN of *drive:* so it's no longer attached to another disk. *Drive* is the drive letter for this disk that now appears as a subdirectory on another disk. In other words, this is the same drive letter you used in the initial JOIN command.

Parameters

drive
Drive to join. The drive letter for the disk drive that you want to appear as a subdirectory on another drive.

path
Where to join. The directory you want the other drive attached to. This path will refer to the root directory of the drive you're joining; all the drive's subdirectories will appear as subdirectories of this directory. The directory *path* must be empty if it exists; JOIN will create the directory if it doesn't exist. In versions of DOS before 4.0, this directory had to be directly off the root directory (such as C:\TEMP). DOS 4.0 and later allow you to attach a disk drive to any directory below the root.

Switches

/d
Delete JOIN assignment. Deletes a JOIN assignment. This cancels the effect of the JOIN on a drive.

Notes

Joined drives
When you join two disk drives, the drive letter from the first drive won't be available until you cancel the JOIN. When you try to switch to the old drive, you'll get the message `Invalid drive specification`.

Networks
JOIN doesn't allow you to attach network drives to other drives. In other words, you can use the JOIN command only with disk drives attached to your computer.

Incompatibilities
You should not use any of the following commands on drives that are affected by JOIN:

```
assign     diskcomp    format    recover
backup     diskcopy    label     restore
chkdsk     fdisk       mirror    sys
```

Because of these restrictions, you should be very careful when using the JOIN command.

Messages

`Cannot JOIN a network drive`
The JOIN command doesn't allow you to attach network drives to other drives.

`Directory not empty`
The directory that you want to join to another disk drive must first be empty. Either remove all the files from the directory (and all its subdirectories) or use another directory name.

`Invalid parameter`
You'll see this message when you've provided a directory that JOIN can't use. In DOS 3.x, JOIN displays this message whenever the directory you provide isn't directly off the root; you need to make sure your path is just below the root (for example, C:\DISK).

Examples

Simple join

One of our computers has two hard disks: the original 110MB disk and a new 210MB hard disk. We can use JOIN to make these two disks appear as though they're a single disk drive. Here is how you'd use JOIN to attach the D: drive so it appears as the subdirectory C:\DATA:

```
C:\>join d: c:\data
```

If you're using DOS 4.0 or later, you can attach a drive farther down in your directory structure, like this:

```
C:\>join d: c:\data\writing
```

Joining a drive to the current directory

When you want to join an entire disk drive to the current directory, there is an easier way than typing the entire pathname of the current directory: You can use a period to indicate the current directory:

```
C:\>join d: .
```

Canceling JOIN

When you want a drive letter to be available again, you need to cancel its JOIN assignment. For example, if we joined D: to the C:\DATA directory, we can cancel the assignment with this command:

```
C:\>join d: /d
```

See also

ASSIGN	ASSIGN allows you to assign different drive letters to existing drives.
SUBST	This command allows you to assign a drive letter to a directory. In a way it's the opposite of the JOIN command.

KEYB DOS 3.3 and later, External

Set keyboard layout

This command supports keyboards that have keys in different locations than the U.S. keyboard. It loads itself into memory and remaps the keyboard.

When and why

If you're using a non-U.S. keyboard (usually the case if you bought your computer outside the U.S.), you'll need this command. The KEYB command remaps the keys on the keyboard to support the layout for any non-U.S. keyboards. You'll want to load KEYB either in your AUTOEXEC.BAT file or in your CONFIG.SYS file using the INSTALL command.

Syntax

keyb
Without any parameters it reports the current keyboard code and code page being used by the keyboard.

keyb *keybd* [,*code-page*] [,*filespec*] [/e] [/id:*nnn*]
Loads the keyboard remapping program into memory.

Parameters

keybd
The keyboard code for the keyboard layout you want to use. See table in the "Notes" section.

code-page
The code page to use with this keyboard. This is used to translate keys that need to generate extended codes (language characters such as Ü) into the correct screen character. This code page must be installed before you run KEYB.

filespec
The location of the keyboard information file (which is usually KEYBOARD.SYS). In DOS 5, you'll need to provide this filespec unless you place KEYBOARD.SYS in the root directory. In DOS 6 and later, KEYB can find KEYBOARD.SYS as long as it is in the same directory as KEYB.COM.

Switches

/e
Enhanced keyboard. Tells KEYB that you're using an enhanced keyboard. You'll need to provide this only if you're using an enhanced keyboard on an 8086 computer (all other computers can sense the type of keyboard you have installed).

/id:*nnn*
Keyboard ID. Specifies which keyboard is being used when there is more than one type of keyboard for a given country.

Notes

KEYB is loaded into memory after you run it, consuming about 10K of memory. You may be able to use the LOADHIGH command to load KEYB into the upper memory area.

Location of KEYBOARD.SYS and KEYB.COM files

These two files *must* be in the same directory. The DOS 6 manual states that KEYB can find KEYBOARD.SYS as long as it is in the search path. Not! KEYB will find KEYBOARD.SYS as long as they are both in the same directory, which is usually the C:\DOS directory. If for some reason you want these files in different directories, however, you can supply a full filespec to KEYB, telling it where to find the KEYBOARD.SYS file.

Switching keyboard layouts

You can switch back to the default keyboard layout by pressing Ctrl-Alt-F1. Return to the layout you set with KEYB using Ctrl-Alt-F2.

Dead keys

In some languages (French, German, and Spanish) there are characters that you type on the keyboard by typing two-key sequences. The first key of this sequence is called a *dead key* since it doesn't actually generate a character — it modifies the character created by the second key press. Here is a table of dead keys:

Keyboard	Dead key	U.S. key	Modified characters produced
French (fr)	^	[	â, ê, î, ô, û
	Shift + ^	{	ä, è, ï, ö, ü, Ä, Ë, Ï, Ö, Ü
German (gr)	'	+	á, é, í, ó, ú, É
	`	=	à, è, ì, ò, ù
Spanish (sp)	'	[	á, é, í, ó, ú, É
	`	]	à, è, ì, ò, ù
	Shift + '	{	ä, è, ï, ö, ü, Ä, Ë, Ï, Ö, Ü
	Shift + `	}	â, ê, î, ô, û

Note: The dead keys shown here are the keys you push on keyboards made in these countries. The column labeled "U.S. key" shows the dead key to press on a U.S. keyboard to get the same dead keys (once you have the keyboard layout for these languages loaded).

Possible keyboard codes

Here is a table of all the possible keyboard codes, along with a list of code pages that are valid for each keyboard.

Country	Keyboard code	Default code page	Alternate code page	Keyboard ID values
Belgium	be	850	437	
Brazil	br	850	437	
French Canada	cf	863	850	
Czechoslovakia (Czech)	cz	852	850	
Czechoslovakia (Slovak)	sl	852	850	
Denmark	dk	850	865	
Finland	su	850	437	
France	fr	850	437	120, 189
Germany	gr	850	437	
Hungary	hu	852	850	
Italy	it	850	437	141, 142
Latin America	la	850	437	
Netherlands	nl	850	437	
Norway	no	850	865	
Poland	pl	852	850	
Portugal	po	850	860	
Spain	sp	850	437	
Sweden	sv	850	437	
Switzerland (French)	sf	850	437	
Switzerland (German)	sg	850	437	
United Kingdom	uk	437	850	166, 168
U.S.	us	437	850	
Yugoslavia	yu	852	850	

ERRORLEVEL returned

KEYB returns information that batch files can test with the IF ERRORLEVEL command. Here are the exit codes that KEYB returns:

- 0 The keyboard definition file (KEYBOARD.SYS) was loaded.
- 1 The keyboard code, code page, or syntax of the command line wasn't valid.
- 2 The keyboard definition file (KEYBOARD.SYS) has a problem, or KEYB couldn't find it.
- 4 KEYB couldn't communicate with the CON (console) device.
- 5 The code page you supplied in KEYB has been prepared for the system.

Messages

```
Active code page not available from CON device
```
KEYB gets the active code-page information from the DISPLAY.SYS device driver, which means DISPLAY.SYS has to be loaded into memory. You also must have NLSFUNC loaded and run CHCP *code-page* once to set the current code page.

```
Bad or missing keyboard definition file
```
Either KEYB couldn't locate the KEYBOARD.SYS file, or the filename you provided doesn't refer to a valid keyboard definition file. Make sure you have a KEYBOARD.SYS file and that you've provided a correct, full pathname (such as C:\DOS\KEYBOARD.SYS), or that you've put the KEYBOARD.SYS file in the root directory that DOS starts from (usually drive C: if you have a hard disk). If neither of these solutions work, erase the KEYBOARD.SYS file and copy it over again from your original DOS disks.

```
Code page requested (nnn) is not valid for given keyboard code
```
Each keyboard code has two code pages that you can use with that keyboard (see table in "Notes" section). Make sure the code page you provide to KEYB is one of the two code pages that work with the keyboard code.

```
Code page specified has not been prepared
```
If you want to provide a code page to KEYB, you'll need to load (prepare) a code page into the DISPLAY.SYS driver using the MODE CON CP PREP before you load KEYB.

```
Code page specified is inconsistent with the selected code page
```
You'll see this message when you've set up an active code page using CHCP that is different from the code page you specified in KEYB. Make sure these two numbers are the same (you can use CHCP without any parameters to get the current code page for the display).

```
Device error during prepare
```
You may see this message if you didn't provide the name and location of the font file (which has a CPI extension).

```
Invalid keyboard code specified
```
or
```
Invalid keyboard ID specified
```
or
```
Invalid code page specified
```

The table in the "Notes" section lists all the valid combinations of keyboard codes, keyboard IDs, and code pages. All options that you provide must be from the same line in this table.

```
KEYB has not been installed
```
You need to install KEYB before you can type KEYB without any parameters to report the current settings.

```
One or more device code pages invalid for given keyboard code
```
If you have more than one code page loaded, this message tells you that some of the code pages aren't allowed with the new keyboard layout. See previous table for the code pages that are allowed for each keyboard code.

```
Unable to create KEYB table in resident memory
```
You may see this message when you try to change the keyboard layout after KEYB has already been installed. In such cases you'll need to restart DOS and load KEYB again with the new keyboard layout.

Examples

Use Italian keyboard layout
Here is the command you'll have to use for the Italian keyboard layout (this will even work on a U.S. keyboard, although not all the key legends will be correct):

```
C:\>keyb it,,c:\dos\keyboard.sys
```

Display current settings
You can also display the current settings any time:

```
C:\>keyb
Current keyboard code: IT code page: 437
Current CON code page: 437
```

Changing the layout
If you've already installed KEYB , you can change the keyboard layout without providing the location of the KEYBOARD.SYS file:

```
C:\>keyb us
```

This switches back to the U.S. keyboard layout. *Note:* If you're experimenting with different keyboard layouts, you might discover that you can't type KEYB because some of these keys have moved. In such cases you can press Ctrl-Alt-F1 to switch back to your U.S. keyboard layout.

See also

For a full description on how to use code pages, see the description of the CHCP command.

CHCP	Read this command first — it contains a discussion on code pages and how to use them. Sets the active code page. You'll need to use this command if you use a code page different from your hardware's default.

Part II: Command Reference

DISPLAY.SYS	Supports code-page switching for the display. You'll need this if you want to change the character set used on your display.	
LOADHIGH	Loads a memory-resident program into the upper memory area. You can use this if you have an 80386 or better processor in your computer, and you're using a program such as EMM386.EXE to provide an upper memory area.	
MODE CP	Allows you to load code pages into memory and change between code pages. It's better, though, to use CHCP to change code pages after you've used MODE to load the code page.	
NLSFUNC	Allows you to change the code page for more than one device (such as the keyboard and the display) at the same time. You'll want to install this before you use CHCP to set the active code page.	
PRINTER.SYS	Supports code-page switching for some IBM printers. You'll need this if you want to change the character set used on your printer.	

LABEL   DOS 3.1 and later, External

Change disk volume label

This command allows you to create, change, or delete disk volume labels.

When and why

This command is easy to learn and use. You'll probably want to use it to assign volume labels to your disk (you can also enter volume labels using FORMAT as you format a disk).

Any disk can contain a volume label, which is a single 11-character name that you can use to identify a disk. Volume labels are mainly useful for floppy disks because you can have hundreds of floppy disks, whereas you'll probably have only one or two hard disks. But volume labels are also useful on hard disks because many backup programs use the volume label to help identify the backup disks.

Syntax
label [*drive*:][*label*]

Parameters
drive:
The drive letter for the disk that you want to label. (Default is current drive.)

label
The volume label you want to put on this disk drive. If you leave this blank, LABEL will prompt you to type in a label. You can use any character (including spaces) in the volume label, except for the following: ^ & * ( ) + = [ ] \ | : ; " / , . < > and ?. Lowercase letters will be converted to uppercase.

Notes

Networks
LABEL doesn't work on network drives.

Incompatibilities
The LABEL command doesn't work with drive letters affected by the JOIN, SUBST, or ASSIGN commands. Nor does it work with Interlnk drives.

Messages

```
Cannot label a JOINed, SUBSTed or ASSIGNed drive
```
You can't use the LABEL command to label any drive that's affected by the JOIN, SUBST, or ASSIGN commands.

```
Cannot label a network drive
```
You can't create or change volume labels on network drives using the LABEL command.

```
Cannot make directory entry
```
You'll see this message when your root directory is full. The volume label is stored as a directory entry in your root directory, so you'll need to delete at least one file before you can create a volume label. Root directories are limited to 512 files.

```
Invalid characters in volume label
```
You'll see this message when the volume label you typed has some characters that aren't allowed in volume labels. You can use any character (including spaces) except for ^ & * ( ) + = [ ] \ | : ; " / , . < > and ?.

```
Too many characters in volume label
```
Volume labels cannot be longer than 11 characters. Choose a shorter volume label.

Examples

Setting a volume label
The following command sets the volume label on drive C: to 386 LAPTOP:

```
C:\>label c:386 laptop
```

Valid label characters
You can use any character in a volume label except for the following:

^ & * ( ) + = [ ] \ | : ; " / , . < > and ?

A volume label can contain as many as 11 characters and can include spaces (but not tabs). Consecutive spaces may be interpreted as a single space.

Deleting a volume label
Let's say you have a volume label on drive C: that you'd like to delete. Here is the way you delete it:

```
C:\>label c:
Volume in drive C is 386 LAPTOP
Volume Serial Number is 16E3-8DA9
Volume label (11 characters, ENTER for none)?_
```

Press Enter to tell LABEL that you don't want a volume label. LABEL will then display

```
Delete current volume label (Y/N)?_
```

Answer Y and press Enter to delete the volume label.

See also
FORMAT   FORMAT allows you to add a volume label to the disk when it finishes formatting the disk.

VOL   Displays the current volume label and serial number on a disk.

LASTDRIVE   DOS 3.0 and later, CONFIG.SYS

Set highest drive letter

Sets the highest letter that you can use as a drive letter with either the SUBST command or for a network drive letter.

When and why

You'll want to use this command either when you're using a network or when you're using the SUBST command to define new drive letters. The LASTDRIVE command sets the maximum number of drive letters that DOS can define (hardware drive letters aren't constrained by this limit). If you're not using a network or the SUBST command, you won't need to set LASTDRIVE.

By default, DOS allows drive letters A through E. If you're using a network, it's not uncommon to have drive letters such as K or even Z that are defined by your network logon script. So if you're using a network, you'll probably want to set LASTDRIVE=Z to allow up to 26 drive letters.

Syntax
lastdrive=*drive*
Set the last drive letter that can be assigned.

Parameters
drive
Last letter. The last drive letter that you want to be able to use with either SUBST or a network drive. This is a single letter, with no colon. Valid range is the letters A through Z. (Default is E.)

Notes

Memory used
DOS increases in size by about 40 bytes for each drive letter beyond E. In other words, when you set LASTDRIVE=Z, DOS is about 840 bytes larger than without a LASTDRIVE= line in your CONFIG.SYS file.

Hardware drives

Setting LASTDRIVE to a drive letter lower than your highest disk drive won't remove any drive letters. It will simply set LASTDRIVE to the drive letter of your highest hard disk. After you've done this, you won't be able to create any new drive letters for network drives or with the SUBST command.

LASTDRIVE and Netware

If you're using Novell Netware, you might want to set LASTDRIVE=Y to leave room for drive Z since, we understand, Netware needs one drive letter that it allocates *after* the last drive available. If you set LASTDRIVE=Z, you won't have such a drive letter after the last available drive letter.

DoubleSpace, Interlnk, and RAMDrive

Device drivers, such as DBLSPACE, INTERLNK, and RAMDRIVE, create their own drive letters. They ignore the setting of LASTDRIVE, so you don't need to set LASTDRIVE in order to use any of these commands or any other device driver that creates drive letters. The LASTDRIVE command sets aside memory for programs, such as SUBST and networks, that allow you to create and destroy drive letters from the DOS prompt. Device drivers, on the other hand, reserve drive letters when they're loaded from within CONFIG.SYS.

Let's say you have a DoubleSpace drive C, which means that the uncompressed physical disk will normally be drive H. If you have INTERLNK.EXE /DRIVES:6 in your CONFIG.SYS file followed by RAMDRIVE.SYS, you'll have the following drive letters when you finish booting:

C   Your compressed hard disk
D–I   The six drive letters grabbed by INTERLNK
J   The RAM disk
O   Your uncompressed hard disk

DoubleSpace always tries to leave a gap between its drive letter and the other drive letters, which is usually four unused drive letters if you have only one compressed drive. DoubleSpace allocates new drive letters working down from its first drive letter. In this example we also have LASTDRIVE set to D, so you can see that the device drivers ignore the setting of LASTDRIVE.

Messages

```
Bad command or parameters
Error in CONFIG.SYS line n
```
You'll see this message when the drive letter you supplied isn't a valid drive letter. Make sure it's a single letter between A and Z.

Examples

If you're using a network, you may want to set LASTDRIVE to Z so you can define any drive letter. To do so, put this line in your CONFIG.SYS file:

```
lastdrive=z
```

See also
SUBST   This command allows you to create new drive letters that refer to directories on your disk. SUBST uses drive letters made available with the LASTDRIVE command.

LOADFIX
DOS 5 and later, External

Load program after first 64K of memory
This program loads another program into memory, ensuring that it doesn't start in the first 64K of memory.

When and why
The only time you would want to use this command is if you get the message `Packed file corrupt` when you try to run a program. Some older programs have problems when they're loaded too low into memory. Before DOS 5 this was never a problem because DOS always used more than the first 64K of memory. But starting with DOS 5, you can actually have DOS use less than 64K of memory.

Some programs have their own code compressed, and they uncompress themselves when they're loaded into memory. But some of these programs have a bug that keeps them from running if they start too low in memory. You can either use this command to run your program that has this problem, or you can upgrade your program to a newer version that doesn't have this problem.

Syntax
loadfix *program* [*parameters*]
Run the program and make sure it doesn't start in the first 64K of memory.

Parameters
program
Program to load. The name (along with an optional drive letter and path) of the program that you want to load into upper memory beyond the first 64K of memory.

parameters
Program parameters. The parameters that you normally pass to the program you want to run it.

Notes
What LOADFIX does
LOADFIX is actually a very simple program (it is only 1,131 bytes long). It looks to see how much memory is being used after it loads, and if it's less than 64K, LOADFIX allocates enough so 64K will be in use, and then it runs your program. When your program finishes running, LOADFIX will exit and release the memory it used.

Examples

Let's say you have a program called BOGUS that displays the message `Packed file corrupt` when you run it:

```
C:\>bogus stuff
Packed file corrupt
C:\>_
```

You would use the following command line to run this program:

```
C:\>loadfix bogus stuff
```

LH   DOS 5 and later, Internal

See LOADHIGH

LOADHIGH (LH)   DOS 5 and later, Internal

Load program into upper memory

This internal command allows you to load terminate-and-stay-resident (TSR) programs into the upper memory blocks. You'll need a memory manager (such as EMM386) that supports UMBs before you can use this command.

When and why

If you have at least an 80386 microprocessor in your computer, you'll probably want to use this command (or the equivalent command available in commercial memory manager packages). It allows you to keep more conventional memory free by moving some resident programs into the upper memory blocks (UMBs), which are free areas between 640K and 1MB.

In order to use this command, you must have a program installed (as a device driver) that provides UMBs, such as EMM386.EXE. Most of the UMB programs run only on 80386 or better microprocessors.

Don't use this command, however, if you have a commercial memory manager (such as 386MAX, BLUEMAX, CEMM, or QEMM). These programs provide their own versions of DEVICEHIGH and LOADHIGH that are more flexible, more reliable, and work better with programs that try to load themselves into upper memory.

Syntax

loadhigh *program* [*parameters*]
lh *program* [*parameters*]
Loads a program into upper memory. The syntax is identical to installing a program in low memory, except that you put a LOADHIGH in front of the command.

loadhigh [/l:*region1*[,*minsize1*]][;*region2*[,*minsize2*]...] [/s]] *program* [*parameters*]
(DOS 6 and later.) Loads a program into upper memory. This syntax gives you more control over how your programs will be loaded into upper memory.

Switches

/l: *block1*
or
/l: *block1;block2*,
Location (DOS 6 and later). Loads the program into a specific Upper Memory Block (UMB). The *block1* and *block2* parameters specify the block number where the device is to be placed. Only some programs can be split between blocks. Use MEM /M to determine how a specific program uses memory. Use MEM /F to identify free blocks of memory.

/l: *block1, size1; block2, size2*
(DOS 6 and later.)The *size1* parameter specifies the minimum size for *block1*. If *block1* is smaller than *size1*, no attempt is made to load the program into that UMB. You must use this format if you are specifying the /S switch.

/s
Shrink block (DOS 6 and later). This switch can only be used in conjunction with the /L switch and when a minimum block size has been specified. The /s switch causes the memory block to be reduced to the size specified, and any remaining memory is redefined as a new UMB.

Parameters

program
Program to load. The name (along with an optional drive letter and path) of the program that you want to load into upper memory.

parameters
Program parameters. The parameters that you normally pass to the program you want to load into upper memory.

Notes

DOS programs you can load high

Here is a list of DOS TSR (terminate-and-stay-resident) programs that you might want to load into the UMBs:

APPEND, DOSKEY, GRAPHICS, KEYB, MODE, NLSFUNC, PRINT, and SHARE

Programs that won't load high

Both VSAFE and UNDELETE won't load into upper memory even if you run them using LOADHIGH. These two programs will always reside in lower memory. We're not sure why this limitation exists, and we certainly hope they fix this in the next version of DOS.

LOADHIGH (LH)

Not enough UMBs
When there isn't enough memory to load a program into a UMB, DOS automatically loads it into low memory. DOS won't tell you when it has done this. Some of the commercial memory manager programs are a lot easier to set up since they provide more advice on what you can and can't load into the UMBs.

UMB memory
The UMBs are areas of memory located between the 640K limit for DOS programs and the end of conventional memory (1MB). This area of memory is normally reserved for ROMs (read-only memory) that provide support for various hardware items (such as your display adapter). There are usually gaps between these ROMs that contain no memory.

If your computer has at least an 80386 microprocessor, you can use a 386 control program, such as EMM386.EXE, 386MAX, CEMM, or QEMM, to fill in these gaps with UMBs.

To use the LOADHIGH command, you need to tell DOS to manage the UMBs. You do this by providing a DOS=UMB line in your CONFIG.SYS file (anywhere in the file). You also need to install HIMEM.SYS and EMM386.EXE (or a commercial equivalent that replaces both) in your CONFIG.SYS file.

Other memory managers
If you're using another memory manager, you should use their versions of LOADHIGH and DEVICEHIGH rather than DOS's version (and don't use DOS=UMB).

INSTALL and LOADHIGH
You can't use LOADHIGH in an INSTALL= line in your CONFIG.SYS file to load a memory-resident program into upper memory. Commercial memory managers, on the other hand, allow you to load programs into upper memory in the INSTALL= line.

Incompatibilities
There are a number of programs that install themselves automatically into upper memory. Unfortunately, if you specify DOS=UMB, such programs will no longer be able to load themselves into upper memory because DOS takes over all of upper memory when you specify DOS=UMB; you can then use only the DOS DEVICEHIGH and LOADHIGH commands to load programs into upper memory. Programs that have been updated for DOS 5 (or DOS 6) shouldn't have this problem.

You may want to use a commercial memory manager (such as 386MAX, CEMM, or QEMM) rather than EMM386, which will allow you to set DOS=NOUMB. These programs provide their own versions of DEVICEHIGH and LOADHIGH that are compatible with other programs and don't require DOS=UMB. They're also more flexible and reliable than the DOS 5 LOADHIGH (the DOS 6 version is quite powerful).

Examples
Basics of loading high
To load programs into the UMBs, you need to have the following lines in your CONFIG.SYS file:

```
device=c:\dos\himem.sys
device=c:\dos\emm386.exe ram
dos=umb
```

Then you can load any resident program into the UMBs. For example, to load SHARE into upper memory, type

```
loadhigh share
```

See also

DEVICEHIGH	This is the command to use in your CONFIG.SYS file to load device drivers into upper memory.
DOS=UMB	You'll need this command in your CONFIG.SYS file before you can load device drivers into high memory.
EMM386.EXE	This is a device driver that can supply UMB memory needed for loading device drivers into high memory.
HIMEM.SYS	You'll need to install HIMEM.SYS before you can install EMM386.EXE. And you'll need both (or a commercial equivalent) to load devices into upper memory.
MEMMAKER	This command will automatically determine the best location for programs in the upper memory blocks, and it will use the new DOS 6 switches to control which memory blocks programs will be loaded into.

MD

See MKDIR

MEM   DOS 4.0 and later, External

Display information on memory

This command displays information on what memory is available and how it's being used. It covers conventional, expanded, extended, and upper memory areas.

When and why
MEM is a quick way to find out how much memory you have and how it's being used. Many people who learned how to use DOS before version 4.0 are accustomed to using CHKDSK. But CHKDSK takes a lot longer, and it doesn't provide as much information.

MEM

The MEM command by itself will tell you how much memory of each type is installed and available. (You'll find a discussion on the types of memory in the "Notes" section.) You can also use the MEM /CLASSIFY option to learn what programs are using memory. This is useful when you're tracking down memory-resident programs and how much memory they're using.

If you are not using DOS 6, you may want to pipe MEM's output through MORE since MEM generates a lot of information (MEM /C | MORE).

Syntax

    mem [/classify | /program | /debug]   (DOS 4.0 and 5)
    mem [/c | /p | /d]   (DOS 5)
    mem [/classify | /debug | /free | /module *program***] [/page]**   (DOS 6 and later)
    mem [/c | /d | /f | /m *program***] [/p]**   (DOS 6 and later)
    Displays information on memory.

Switches

    /classify   (DOS 4 and later)
    /c   (DOS 5 and later)
    Group programs by memory location. This option is easiest to read. It shows you all programs (as well as device drivers) that are in memory, and it groups them according to whether they're in conventional memory or the upper memory area. This switch also reports how much upper memory is available.

    /module *program*
    /m *program*
    Module information (DOS 6 and later). Displays information about how a specific program is using memory. This switch is similar to the /PROGRAM switch in earlier versions of DOS, except it displays information on a single program.

    /free
    /f
    Show free memory (DOS 6 and later). This switch tells MEM to display all the areas of memory that are free. In particular, it will show you which areas of upper memory are free and how much space is free in each region. This is very useful if you're trying to optimize your use of memory by loading programs in specific areas of upper memory.

    /debug   (DOS 4 and later)
    /d   (DOS 5 and later)
    Group programs and devices by memory location. The debug option provides all the information shown by /PROGRAM, along with additional information on device drivers and EMS memory usage.

    /page
    /p
    Page output (DOS 6 and later). Use this option to display the information one screen at a time. Before DOS 6, you had to pipe the output from MEM into MORE to keep MEM's output from scrolling by too fast.

Part II: Command Reference

/program   (DOS 4 and 5)
/p   (DOS 5)

Group by program. Use this option if you want more technical details on the programs installed in memory. The program option displays the absolute address for every program and device driver installed in your system, along with the name, size, and type of program. All the numbers are in hexadecimal notation. Replaced with the /M switch in DOS 6.

Notes

Types of memory

There are a several types of memory you may have on your computer: conventional, upper memory, expanded memory, extended memory, and extended memory managed by an extended memory manager.

Conventional memory

All MS-DOS computers have conventional memory. This is the memory where DOS runs your programs, and most computers made today have 640K of conventional memory. Some of this memory is used by DOS and memory-resident programs, leaving a smaller number (such as 590K) available for running programs.

Extended memory

Extended memory is any memory above the 1MB mark on a PC with at least an 80286 microprocessor. Computers that use the original 8088 or 8086 microprocessor cannot have extended memory.

Expanded memory

Expanded memory is a type of memory that was developed by Lotus, Intel, and Microsoft and can be installed on any kind of computer. Computers that have an 8088 or a 80286 microprocessor usually need special hardware to provide expanded memory (many laptop computers have this hardware built in). On computers with 80386 microprocessors or better, you can use the EMM386 device driver to convert portions of extended memory into expanded memory.

Expanded memory is memory that, in a sense, is tacked onto the side of your computer. You can have several megabytes of expanded memory, but programs generally have access to only 64K at a time. Expanded memory is provided either by an add-on board plus an expanded memory manager or by an 80386 memory manager that can remap memory to make some of extended memory behave like expanded memory.

Expanded vs. extended memory

The easiest way to keep these two types of memory clear is to think of extended memory as extending beyond the first megabyte of memory. The 80286 and above microprocessors were designed to access more than 1MB of memory, so they can access this memory directly.

Expanded memory, on the other hand, is generally tacked onto the side of regular memory. Expanded memory is accessed indirectly through several pages that appear in the first megabyte of your computer's memory.

EMS, XMS, UMB, HMA

You'll encounter these four acronyms often in connection with memory. EMS stands for Expanded Memory Specification and is the name of a specification that describes how programs interact with expanded memory managers.

XMS stands for eXtended Memory Specification and describes how programs interact with extended memory. There are two, incompatible interfaces that programs use to allocate extended memory: XMS and the old Vdisk method. Most programs use the XMS specification, but a few programs still use Vdisk. If you have such a program, you'll want to use the /INT15 switch on HIMEM.SYS.

UMB stands for Upper Memory Block and refers to the areas of free memory between the 640K address mark and the 1MB mark. Some computers, and any 80386 or better computer using EMM386 (or another 386 memory manager), have upper memory that DOS can use for loading device drivers and memory-resident programs.

HMA stands for High Memory Area and is the first 64K of extended memory. DOS can load about 45K of itself into this memory area.

SYSTEM program

If your computer has UMBs, you may notice a program called SYSTEM that can be quite large (160K on our computer). Yet it doesn't seem to reduce the amount of memory you have available. What's going on? It turns out that the program called SYSTEM really isn't a program at all. Instead, it represents the memory reserved for your video display adapter and BIOS extensions.

LIM 4.0 EMS

The MEM command requires that your expanded memory manager conform to at least version 4.0 of the Lotus/Intel/Microsoft (LIM) expanded memory specification (EMS).

Messages

```
Too much of memory fragmentation; MEM /C cannot be done
```
You'll rarely see this message. It usually appears only when some program has allocated many small chunks that divide memory into many small pieces. This message will probably disappear if you reboot and run MEM /C again.

Examples

Memory

Here is what the output of MEM looks like on one of our computers:

```
Memory Type          Total   =   Used   +   Free
-----------          -----       ----       ----
Conventional          637K        27K       610K
Upper                 187K        79K       108K
Reserved              131K       131K         0K
Extended (XMS)      5,189K     2,269K     2,920K
-----------         ------     ------     ------
Total memory        6,144K     2,506K     3,638K
```

```
Total under 1 MB        824K        106K        718K

Largest executable program size         610K (624,240 bytes)
Largest free upper memory block          51K  (52,144 bytes)
MS-DOS is resident in the high memory area.

    655360  bytes total conventional memory
    652288  bytes available to MS-DOS
    621024  largest executable program size
    655360  bytes total EMS memory
    262144  bytes free EMS memory
   1310720  bytes total contiguous extended memory
         0  bytes available contiguous extended memory
    327680  bytes available XMS memory
            MS-DOS resident in High Memory Area
```

You'll notice that there is no extended memory available. This is because we've used the extended memory for three other types of memory: some upper memory blocks, some expanded memory, and the rest is allocated as XMS memory, which is extended memory that's being managed by HIMEM.SYS or another memory manager.

See also

DEVICEHIGH	The CONFIG.SYS command that allows you to load device drivers into the UMBs.
DOS=	This command allows you to control DOS's use of high memory and UMBs. If you're running EMM386, you'll need to use this before you can load device drivers or memory-resident programs into upper memory.
EMM386	On an 80386 (or 486) computer, can convert extended memory into UMBs and/or expanded memory.
HIMEM.SYS	This device driver manages extended memory. You'll need to load it before you can load DOS into high memory or use the EMM386 device driver. If you're using a third-party memory manager, however, the function of HIMEM is probably provided by the third-party memory manager.
LOADHIGH, LH	The command to load memory-resident programs into upper memory.
MEMMAKER	You can use this program to optimize the use of your memory, automatically.
CHKDSK	CHKDSK also displays information on memory, but not as much. It also takes longer than MEM because CHKDSK has to check your disk for problems first. If you're using DOS versions before 4.0, you'll have to use CHKDSK.

MEMMAKER DOS 6 and later, External

Optimize memory usage
MemMaker is Microsoft's memory optimizer. It configures the statements in your CONFIG.SYS and AUTOEXEC.BAT to maximize the amount of available conventional memory.

When and why
MemMaker is a program that can rearrange your programs in memory to make more memory available for your applications programs. Unless you are using a memory manager not provided by Microsoft, such as 386MAX or QEMM, you should run MemMaker after installing DOS 6. You should also run MemMaker after making any changes to the device drivers in your CONFIG.SYS file or adding memory-resident programs to your AUTOEXEC.BAT file. If you are using a third-party memory manager, use the memory optimizer provided with that program.

MemMaker will run your computer through a number of tests; then it will rewrite your CONFIG.SYS and AUTOEXEC.BAT (and possibly SYSTEM.INI if you're using Windows) using DEVICEHIGH and LOADHIGH commands to control which and where programs will be loaded into upper memory. You will need some upper memory, created by EMM386 or some other memory manager, before you can use MemMaker. These programs require an 80386 or better microprocessor.

Syntax
memmaker [/b] [/batch] [/undo] [/swap:*drive*] [/t] [/w:*winbuf1*, *winbuf2*] [/session]

Switches
/b
Black and white. Use this switch to run MemMaker with a monochrome monitor. You might want to use this option if you're using MemMaker on a laptop computer to make its screen more readable.

/batch
Run unattended. This switch causes MemMaker to automatically accept the default value at all prompts. Unless you want to exercise greater control over the optimization process, this is the easiest way to run MemMaker. If MemMaker encounters a problem, it will restore your original system.

/undo
Undo changes. When you use MemMaker to optimize your memory, it stores your previous configuration before it makes any changes. Use this switch to restore your configuration files to the way they were before the last time you ran MemMaker. You might use this option if your computer has problems running properly after you run MemMaker or if you're not happy with the changes MemMaker made for you.

/swap:*drive*
Starting drive. Use this switch if your drive configuration changes during system startup, which might happen if you're using a disk compression program like Stacker that swaps drive letters as a result of a command in your CONFIG.SYS file. Here *drive* is

the letter that contains the CONFIG.SYS and AUTOEXEC.BAT files when DOS first starts your CONFIG.SYS file. If the drive letter has changed, MemMaker may not be able to find your configuration files. You only need this switch if you are using a compression program that MemMaker does not recognize. (You do not need this switch if you're using DoubleSpace, Stacker 2.0 or later, or SuperStor.)

/t
Ignore Token-Ring. Use this switch only if you experience problems running MemMaker on a system connected to a Token-Ring network.

/w: *winbuf1*, *winbuf2*
Window buffers. Reserves space for Windows translation buffers in upper memory. You may need to use this switch if you run MemMaker and then experience a loss of performance within Windows.

/session
Used by MemMaker during the optimization process. Don't use this switch yourself!

Notes

MemMaker and multiple configurations

Unfortunately, MemMaker does not recognize menus in your CONFIG.SYS file, which are also known as multiple configurations. If you're using multiple configurations (see the MENUITEM command for details), you'll need to break your CONFIG.SYS file into separate pieces, with the commands for each menu item in a separate CONFIG file. You'll then need to run MemMaker once for each of these files (you'll need to rename each file to CONFIG.SYS, run MemMaker, and then rename the file to another name). After you optimize each configuration, you can recombine all the pieces into a single CONFIG.SYS file.

Fine-tuning device driver placement

MemMaker loads any device drivers into memory in the same order as they appear in your CONFIG.SYS file. You may be able to fine-tune the memory management by changing the order of the DEVICE statements in your CONFIG.SYS file.

Fine-tuning MemMaker

There are a couple of choices you can make that can help MemMaker load even more programs into upper memory (assuming you have more programs that you can load into upper memory). If you choose Custom Setup rather than Express Setup, MemMaker will ask you a number of questions. Here are two of the more useful, and safe, options:

EMS usage	If you don't use any programs that use EMS memory, MemMaker can make an additional 64K of upper memory, but you won't have any expanded memory at all when MemMaker finishes.
Use monochrome region	If you have an EGA or a standard VGA card, you can make an extra 32K of memory available. Do not use this option if you have a Super VGA card or you also have a monochrome display card.

Examples

Running MemMaker unattended
To run MemMaker and automatically accept all of the default settings, use

    `C:\>`**`memmaker /batch`**

If MemMaker encounters a problem, it will return your configuration to its previous settings. After MemMaker finishes, you should try all of the programs on your computer to make sure that everything works with the new configuration.

Reversing MemMaker's changes
If you run into a problem after running MemMaker, you may need to undo any changes it made during the optimization process. Fortunately, there is a simple command to do that:

    `C:\>`**`memmaker /undo`**

This reverses the last set of changes made by MemMaker. You should always test a configuration after MemMaker completes its optimization.

See also

CONFIG.SYS	See this entry for more information on how DOS loads device drivers.
DEVICE	For information about loading device drivers into conventional memory.
DEVICEHIGH	For information about loading device drivers into upper memory.
EMM386.EXE	You will need this device driver installed, as well as HIMEM.SYS or some other memory manager, before you can load programs into upper memory.
HIMEM.SYS	You will need this device driver installed, as well as EMM386 or some other memory manager, before you can load programs into upper memory.
INSTALL	For information about loading TSRs into memory.
MEM	For information about current memory usage and free memory. You'll also find a discussion of the various types of memory in the "Notes" section of the MEM command.

MENUCOLOR   DOS 6 and later, CONFIG.SYS

Set startup menu colors
This sets the colors for a CONFIG.SYS startup menu.

When and why
This command allows you to control the colors used for menus you create in your CONFIG.SYS file, which are also known as multiple configurations. If you're not using multiple configurations, you won't need to use this command. For more details on using multiple configurations, see the description of the MENUITEM command.

Syntax

menucolor=*textcolor*[, *background*]
Set the menu color, as well as the color of the background (optional).

Parameters

textcolor
Text color. This is a number (see the chart in the "Notes" section) that tells DOS what color to use for the text in the menus. Valid range is 0 to 15. (Default is 7.)

background
Backround color. This is a number (see the chart in the "Notes" section) that tells DOS what color to use for the background. Valid range is 0 to 15. (Default is 0.)

Notes

Where you can use MENUCOLOR commands

You can only use the MENUCOLOR command inside a menu block. A menu block is a set of MENUITEM, SUBMENU, MENUDEFAULT, and MENUCOLOR commands that appears on lines after the following line:

```
[menu]
```

The MENUCOLOR command can appear either before or after MENUITEM and SUBMENU lines in your CONFIG.SYS file.

Side effect of menu colors

There is one interesting side effect of changing the color of CONFIG.SYS menus. All your DOS output will have the same exact colors as the menu color you set with this command until some program (or the CLS command) clears the screen.

Color table

The following table lists the colors that you can use for the startup menus. Background color numbers of 8 and above will cause the text to blink.

0	Black	8	Gray
1	Blue	9	Bright blue
2	Green	10	Bright green
3	Cyan	11	Bright cyan
4	Red	12	Bright red
5	Magenta	13	Bright magenta
6	Brown	14	Yellow
7	White	15	Bright white

Examples

Out favorite colors are bright white against a blue background. Here is the command to set the CONFIG.SYS menus to these colors:

```
[menu]
menucolor=15,1
....
```

Green text on a yellow background
It's not easy on the eyes, but it certainly is eye-catching.

```
menucolor=2, 14
```

See also
MENUITEM   This entry details the use of multiple configurations.

MENUDEFAULT   DOS 6 and later, External

Default startup menu item
This command allows you to select which item from your startup menu will be highlighted initially. You can also tell DOS to select this item automatically if you don't touch your keyboard for *N* seconds.

When and why
This command is useful only if you've set up your CONFIG.SYS file to support a startup menu, which is also known as multiple configurations (see the description of the MENUITEM command for more details). If you are using multiple configurations, you may want a configuration that DOS will use if you start your computer and walk away. You can use this command to pick one of the menu items and to indicate how long the menu should be displayed before DOS will use your default selection:

Syntax
menudefault=*blockname*[, *time*]
Defines the default menu item as well as an optional timeout value.

Switches
blockname
Default menu block. This is the name of a menu block, which identifies which menu item you want DOS to highlight when it displays the CONFIG.SYS menu. Each MENUITEM and SUBMENU has a menu block associated with it, and this is the name you must supply in this command.

time
Wait time. The amount of time, in seconds, that DOS should wait before you press a key. If you don't press a key within *time* seconds, DOS will start running your CONFIG.SYS file as if you selected the menu for *blockname*. If you do type a key before *time* seconds expire, DOS stops counting down and will wait until you press the Enter key. While DOS counts down, it displays a countdown timer on the screen, showing you how many seconds you have left before DOS uses the default *blockname*. If you don't supply this value, DOS will wait until you press the Enter key. Valid range is 0 to 90 (0 means use *blockname* without waiting). (Default is wait for Enter.)

Notes
Where you can use MENUDEFAULT commands
You can only use the MENUDEFAULT command inside a menu block. A menu block is a set of MENUITEM, SUBMENU, MENUDEFAULT, and MENUCOLOR commands that appear on lines after the following line:

```
[menu]
```

The MENUDEFAULT command can appear either before or after MENUITEM and SUBMENU lines in your CONFIG.SYS file. You can have DOS select an item other than the first item when it displays the menu. But in general, it's best to have the default menu item be the first one in the menu.

Examples
Activate the Windows block
Here is a simple example that will use the menu block for the Windows item if you don't press any key within 15 seconds after DOS displays your CONFIG.SYS menu:

```
[menu]
menuitem=windows
menudefault=windows, 15
```

See also
MENUCOLOR   This command allows you to set the color DOS will use for a menu.

MENUITEM   Read this entry for more details about how to build and use CONFIG.SYS menus.

MENUITEM — DOS 6 and later, CONFIG.SYS

Create Startup menu item

This command inside your CONFIG.SYS file defines a single menu item and must be part of a larger menu block. You use this command to create a CONFIG.SYS multiple that allows you to choose between multiple configurations. Read this command to learn all about CONFIG.SYS menus.

When and why
You'll want to use this command if you ever have a need for multiple CONFIG.SYS files. For example, if you sometimes use Windows and you sometimes use a network, you might want to have DOS load different device drivers or use different settings for these different ways that you use your computer. The multiple configurations commands added to DOS 6 allow you to set up a menu when DOS first starts and then use this menu to control which commands DOS will process inside your CONFIG.SYS file. Of the six multiple configuration commands, this is the only one that is required to create a startup menu. You must have a MENUITEM line for each option in your startup menu.

MENUITEM

Syntax
menuitem=*blockname* [, *description*]
Creates a menu item on the startup menu.

Parameters
blockname
Name of menu block. This is the name of a section in your CONFIG.SYS file that you want DOS to process if you select the menu created by this MENUITEM line. The *blockname* must appear elsewhere within your CONFIG.SYS file on a line by itself surrounded by square brackets, which marks the start of a block of commands (see "Examples" section). The name can have up to 70 characters in it, but you cannot use any of the following characters in a name: space \ / , ; = [and].

description
Menu title. This is the text that DOS displays as the menu entry. If you don't supply *description*, DOS uses *blockname* as the name of this menu item on the screen. The title can be up to 70 characters long and can contain any character. (Default is *blockname*.)

Notes

Defining configuration blocks
A configuration block consists of a series of configuration commands grouped under a block name. The block name is a name enclosed in square brackets on a line by itself in your CONFIG.SYS file. There are two special block names. The [Menu] block defines the entries for the main startup menu. [Common] blocks include configuration commands that you want DOS to run always. DOS only runs other blocks as a result of your referring to blocks using MENUITEM, SUBMENU, and INCLUDE lines.

When you have [common] blocks and a [menu] block, DOS processes the commands in the [common] blocks in the same order as these blocks appear in your CONFIG.SYS file. So if you have a [common] block before you have a [menu] block, DOS will run these common commands before it processes any of the commands in the menu blocks. Also, if you have a [common] block after all the menu blocks, DOS will run these commands after processing all the menu commands. Any commands that you have in your CONFIG.SYS file before a [menu] block are treated as a common block, even if you don't have a [common] line in front of them. The examples below show how all this works.

Note: You should always have a [common] block at the very end of your CONFIG.SYS file so that DOS will run the commands that SETUP programs add to the end of your CONFIG.SYS file.

Empty configuration blocks
In certain situations, you may want to create empty configuration blocks. An empty configuration block executes only those commands found within the [common] blocks. What makes this useful is that DOS assigns the block name to the CONFIG environmental variable, which you can use in your AUTOEXEC.BAT file to select between different commands. This is particularly useful if you want the same configuration with different paths. Of course, with DOS 6 you can also use the SET command in CONFIG.SYS to set your path.

Optimizing multiple configurations

To use MemMaker to optimize the CONFIG.SYS file with multiple configurations, you must create a CONFIG.SYS and an AUTOEXEC.BAT file that contain only the command for a single configuration. You can then run MemMaker and then merge these commands back into a CONFIG.SYS file with multiple configurations.

Making individual commands optional

If you use ?= on any CONFIG.SYS command that normally contains an equal sign (=), DOS will prompt for confirmation before executing the command. You can also combine this feature with startup menus.

Designing multiple configurations

There are two ways to design multiple configurations: methodically or on the fly. In this section we'll describe a method you can use (if you're the "on the fly" type of person, you can skip this section).

Before you start, you may want to think about what configurations you're going to want. Do you want a single Windows menu and a DOS menu, or do you want to set up different configurations for different people using a computer? Do you want to use submenus or just a single main menu?

Once you decide on a menu structure, you can then decide what commands you want to run for each menu item. For each configuration, write down the commands you want to run for that configuration. No matter what you design, you try to keep your menu structure as simple as possible. When you design your menus, you may also want to have a default menu that DOS will use if you don't press a key within, say, 10 seconds after the menu appears. Of course, if you're setting up a computer that several people will use, you might not want to use this timeout default.

You are now ready to create your [Menu] block. The [Menu] block contains the items that appear on the opening startup menu. Each item is represented by either a MENUITEM or SUBMENU command. You must decide in what order you want items to appear on the menu and then place the MENUITEM and SUBMENU commands in that order in the [Menu] block. The actual blocks containing the commands for each menu item can appear in any order within the file. Enter the header [Main] on a line by itself followed by one line for each MENUITEM or SUBMENU entry.

At this point, you should enter the MENUDEFAULT statement. The format for the MENUDEFAULT statement is MENUDEFAULT=*blockname, time* where *blockname* is the name of the block that you want DOS to run after *time* seconds if you haven't pressed any keys. You can also specify the color for the menu using the MENUCOLOR command.

If you are using submenus, the blocks for each submenu should come next. This lets you see the statements for your menu structure separate from the commands. For each submenu, create a header with the submenu's blockname in square brackets on a line by itself (for example, [DOS]). Within each submenu block, insert a MENUITEM (or SUBMENU) line for the menu choices. You may also use a different menu color for each submenu.

MENUITEM

You are now ready to create the block of commands for each configuration. Each configuration block must start with the block name on a line by itself, and it must be enclosed in square brackets. This block name should be the same as a name in a MENUITEM command. Also, your CONFIG.SYS file will be easier to read if you leave a line blank before each block header.

Communicating choices to AUTOEXEC.BAT

DOS uses a special environment variable, called CONFIG, to keep track of which menu you finally chose. This variable will contain the block name for the block of commands that DOS ran once you selected a menu. You can use the IF or GOTO commands in your AUTOEXEC.BAT to control which commands you run in your AUTOEXEC.BAT file based on which menu item you chose in your CONFIG.SYS file.

You can refer to the CONFIG environment variable in the IF or GOTO commands using the form %CONFIG%. For example, you might have a line of this form in your AUTOEXEC.BAT file:

```
if %config%=blockname goto label
```

where *blockname* is the name of a configuration block that DOS ran in your CONFIG.SYS file and *label* is a name of a line in your AUTOEXEC.BAT file. If you use IF, you must have one IF statement for each configuration block.

Alternatively, you can use a command like this one:

```
goto %config%
```

This command will jump directly to a line in your CONFIG.SYS file that has the same name as a configuration block.

The lines that you can jump to in your AUTOEXEC.BAT file must be labels, which are lines that start with a colon:

```
:blockname
```

After this line you can include any AUTOEXEC.BAT commands. The last line in this list of commands should be a command like the following:

```
goto common
```

And the last line in your AUTOEXEC.BAT file should be the label COMMON:

```
:common
```

Examples

A simple example

Here we'll show you a very simple menu with two choices and two blocks of commands you might run.

```
[menu]
menuitem=dos, Pure DOS
submenu=windows, Windows and DOS

[dos]
Device=ansi.sys
device=mouse.com
```

```
[windows]
device=c:\dos\himem.sys
```

Obviously, this sample CONFIG.SYS file doesn't have as many commands in it as a real CONFIG.SYS file. When you start DOS, you'll see a menu that looks like this:

```
MS-DOS 6 Startup Menu
=====================

    1. Pure DOS
    2. Windows and DOS

Enter a choice: 1
```

A more realistic multiple configuration

In this example we'll show you a more realistic CONFIG.SYS file. Whether you're running DOS or Windows, there are some commands you'll probably always want to run. You might want to run some of these commands before the menu commands, and you might want to run some of these commands after you run the menu commands. Fortunately, DOS makes this very easy using [common] blocks. These are blocks of commands that DOS will run for *all* menus, and DOS runs them in the same order as the appear inside the file. Also, if you place commands before the [menu] line, DOS will run these lines before it runs any of the commands in the menu blocks.

Here is an example that shows using [common] blocks:

```
dos=high,umb
buffers=10
device=c:\dos\himem.sys

[menu]
menuitem=windows, Windows environment
menuitem=dos, DOS programs only

[windows]
device=c:\dos\emm386.exe noems

[dos]
device=c:\dos\emm386.exe ram

[common]
devicehigh=c:\dos\setver.exe
. . .
```

The only difference between the DOS and Windows configuration is the EMM386 line. We've set this up so EMM386 will create expanded memory for the DOS configuration but not for the Windows configuration. DOS will run the first three lines in this file for all menus. Then it will run the commands in the menu blocks. And finally, DOS processes the commands in the [common] block at the end.

Using shared blocks of commands

There are times when you might have a whole set of commands that are common between two configurations but that you don't use in a third. In these cases, you can use the INCLUDE line to include a set of commands:

```
[menu]
menuitem=windows, Windows environment
menuitem=dos, DOS programs only

[windows]
device=c:\dos\emm386.exe noems
include=shared

[dos]
device=c:\dos\emm386.exe ram
include=shared

[shared]
dos=high,umb
buffers=10
device=c:\dos\himem.sys

[common]
devicehigh=c:\dos\setver.exe
. . .
```

You'll notice that this example is nearly identical to our previous example. The only difference is that we're using an included block rather than a common block at the start. You can use any name you like for include blocks (we used SHARED), as long as the name is different from all the other block names.

Multiple configurations in AUTOEXEC.BAT

In this last example, we show you how to continue the process of selecting multiple configurations in the processing of your AUTOEXEC.BAT file. Using the previous example with two menus, you might have some code in your AUTOEXEC.BAT file that looks like this:

```
goto %config%

:windows
path c:\dos;c:\win;
goto common

:dos
path c:\dos;c:\prog\nc;
goto common

:common
```

In this example, the menu that you select in your startup menu will control how you set the path. In a real example, you might want to do much more than we've shown you here, but we're just trying to give you ideas.

See also

CONFIG.SYS	Describes the standard format for the CONFIG.SYS file.
IF	This command will help you react to startup menu choices when DOS runs your AUTOEXEC.BAT file.
INCLUDE	Allows you to use the contents of one menu block within another.
GOTO	Use this command along with %CONFIG% to add multiple configuration support to your AUTOEXEC.BAT file.
MENUCOLOR	Sets the text and background color for the startup menu.
MENUDEFAULT	Specifies the menu block to be used if none is selected within a timeout period.
NUMLOCK	Sets the state of the Num Lock key at startup.
SUBMENU	Allows second-level menus.

MIRROR · DOS 5, External

Save disk information

This command saves information about your disks that can be used by UNDELETE and UNFORMAT to recover information from your disk.

DOS 6 Note: Part of MIRROR is now in UNDELETE, but other equally important parts are not in DOS 6 at all. If you upgraded from DOS 5, you will still be able to use MIRROR. An updated version of MIRROR is also available from Microsoft on a supplemental disk.

When and why

This is a command you'll definitely want to use if you have DOS 5 and even if you have DOS 6 or later! There are two parts you can utilize: saving the disk information and deletion-tracking. Saving the disk information will help you recover your hard disk should something happen that wipes it out. You may be able to recover most of your hard disk if you've taken the time to use the MIRROR command.

The deletion-tracking feature is also useful. MIRROR will keep track of the most recent files you've deleted (you can tell it how many deleted files to remember) so that you can recover any of these files using UNDELETE.

Your AUTOEXEC.BAT file should contain a line that both saves the disk information and loads the deletion-tracking program into memory. You should also run MIRROR at the end of each day. You'll want to create a floppy disk you can boot from that has the MIRROR command on it.

MIRROR

> You'll also want to save your partition table information to a floppy disk. Most people never change their partition table after they set up their hard disk. Saving this information using the MIRROR /PARTN command will allow you to use UNFORMAT to restore your partition table if there is ever a problem.
>
> *Note:* Back up your disk frequently. Don't rely on MIRROR and UNFORMAT to protect your data.

Syntax

mirror [*drive*:[...]] [/**1**] [/**t***drive*[-*entries*]]
Saves information about one or more disks for use by UNFORMAT and UNDELETE.

mirror /partn
Saves the partition table information on the current hard disk to a floppy disk. MIRROR will prompt you to insert a formatted disk and ask which floppy disk drive you want to save partition information to.

mirror /u
Removes the deletion-tracking part of MIRROR from memory. Deletion-tracking is loaded using the /T switch. You may not be able to unload MIRROR if you've loaded other memory-resident programs after it.

Parameters

drive:
This is the hard disk from which you want MIRROR to record information. If you don't provide a drive letter, MIRROR uses the current drive.

Switches

/1
One copy (the number one). Deletes the previous copy of the disk information. Normally, MIRROR keeps two copies of the disk information: the current copy and the next most recent copy. This switch tells MIRROR to save only the current copy (it also deletes any old copies that are around).

/t*drive*: [-*entries*]
Deletion tracking. Loads the deletion-tracking module of MIRROR into memory. This program will record information on each file you delete (the name and location of the file) so UNDELETE can do a better job of recovering deleted files. This switch takes one or two parameters: *drive:* is the disk drive for which you want MIRROR to record information, and *entries* is the number of deleted files that you want MIRROR to keep track of. You'll find a table in the "Notes" section that shows the default values for entries, along with file sizes for different values of *entries*. Valid range is 1–999.

Notes

Size in memory

When you enable deletion-tracking, MIRROR loads part of itself into memory so it can record which files you've deleted and where they're stored on the disk. MIRROR uses about 6.5K of memory. If you have enough free upper memory (see the MEM command) MIRROR automatically loads itself into upper memory. As a result, you don't need to use LOADHIGH (or LH) to load MIRROR into upper memory.

Part II: Command Reference

What's restored
If you use UNFORMAT to restore a damaged hard disk, it restores your file allocation table (the information on which parts of the disk are being used by files) and root directory to the state it was in when you saved the disk information with the MIRROR command. As a result, it's a good idea to save this information frequently.

Partition information
The partition table is at the beginning of your hard disk and describes how it's set up (including whether it's all one hard disk or divided into several logical drives). It's a good idea to save this information once to a floppy disk so you can restore it later if something happens to your hard disk's partition table. You need to save it to a floppy disk because MIRROR won't be able to access your hard disk if its partition table isn't valid.

Files created
MIRROR creates up to four files in the root directory of your hard disk; you need to be careful not to erase these files (they're marked as read-only to make them more difficult to delete) unless you decide to stop using the MIRROR command.

MIRROR.FIL	Saves a copy of the File Allocation Table (FAT) and the root directory.
MIRROR.BAK	The previous copy of the MIRROR.FIL file. MIRROR renames the previous file whenever you save the disk information (unless you use the /L switch).
MIRORSAV.FIL	This is a short, hidden file that MIRROR uses to keep track of the MIRROR.FIL file. This is important when you're unformatting a disk. Because none of these files will be in the directory, MIRROR searches the disk for a pattern in this file and then uses the information to locate MIRROR.FIL.
PCTRACKR.DEL	This file contains the deletion-tracking information created by the memory-resident part of MIRROR (when you use the /T switch). It contains information on the names and locations of deleted files. The size of this file depends on the number of files you want to track. Here is a table that shows the default values for different disk sizes:

Disk size	Default entries	Tracking file size
360K	25	5K
720K	50	9K
1.2MB	75	14K
20MB	101	18K
32MB	202	36K
> 32MB	303	55K

Networks
MIRROR doesn't support network drives. This is because MIRROR records very low-level information on where the files are located that isn't available from networks (since they have their own operating system and disk structure that's different from DOS).

160K and 360K disks
The MIRROR command doesn't support 160K or 320K disks that were formatted with versions of DOS before DOS 5.

Messages
```
Cannot unload resident deletion-tracking software.
Vectors or memory have been altered.
```
When you see this message, it means you've installed another memory-resident program after MIRROR, and MIRROR can't unload itself from memory as a result. You'll need to restart your computer to remove MIRROR from memory.

```
Invalid parameter(s) specified
```
If you're using the /PARTN or the /U switches, you can't specify any other parameters on the command line. You'll need to run MIRROR twice if you want to use these options plus save the disk information.

Examples

Running in AUTOEXEC.BAT
This example shows the line that you should have in your AUTOEXEC.BAT file:

```
C:\>mirror c: /ta /tc
```

This command saves the information for drive C: and loads the deletion-tracking program so it will track all files you delete on the A: and C: drives.

Controlling deletion tracking
Here is how you would increase the number of deleted files that MIRROR keeps track of:

```
C:\>mirror /tc-600
```

This command does several things. First, it saves the disk information for the current drive (the FAT and the root directory). And second, it installs the deletion-tracking software in memory and sets to 600 the number of deleted files that MIRROR will track.

Partition table information
You'll want to save the partition table information for your hard disk at least once. This information tells the computer how your hard disk is set up: whether it's being used as one large hard disk or several logical drives. Saving this information to a floppy disk will allow you to restore the partition table if something should ever happen to it. You need to save it to a floppy disk rather than your hard disk because DOS can't access a hard disk until it has a valid partition table on it.

To save the partition table for the current disk drive, type the following:

```
C:\>mirror /partn
```

Part II: Command Reference

MIRROR will then prompt you to insert a floppy disk and press Enter (you can also change the drive letter):

```
Disk Partition Table saver.
The partition information from your hard drive(s) has been read.
Next, the file PARTNSAV.FIL will be written to a floppy disk. Please
insert a formatted diskette and type the name of the diskette drive.
What drive? A
```

Type in a new drive letter if you don't want to use the A: drive and then press Enter (make sure you write to a floppy disk and save the floppy disk in a safe place).

See also
FORMAT	The FORMAT command usually saves the same information as MIRROR when you format a disk.
UNDELETE	Recovers files accidentally deleted from your disk. You should try to undelete these files as soon as you can so the files won't be overwritten by new files.
UNFORMAT	This command allows you to recover the files on a disk that you formatted by accident.

MKDIR, MD   All DOS, Internal

Create a directory
This command allows you to create a new directory on your hard or floppy disk.

When and why
You'll almost certainly use this command. The only people who won't need MKDIR are people using a DOS shell program, such as the Norton Commander or the DOS Shell. Directories allow you to organize your files into separate groups. And this is the command that you use to create directories.

Syntax
mkdir [*drive:*]*path*
md [*drive:*]*path*
Creates a new directory.

Parameters
drive
The disk drive on which you want to create the new directory. (Default is the current drive.)

path
The name of the new directory. If this is a simple name (no backslashes), the directory will be created inside the current directory (in other words, as a subdirectory). Otherwise, the directory will be created in the path you provide. Pathnames can't include any of the following characters: * + = [ ] | ; : " < > , / or ?.

Notes

Multipart paths
When you provide a long pathname, all the parts of the path must exist except for the final name. For example, if you tell MD to create a directory called \WRITING\BOOKS\DOS, both WRITING and BOOKS must exist before you can create the DOS directory.

Long paths
The entire directory path, from the initial \ to the last character, can be no longer than 64 characters.

Messages
```
Unable to create directory
```
or
```
Invalid keyword
```
or
```
Parameter format not correct
```
There are two things that might cause these messages. First, some of the characters in the name you typed aren't allowed in pathnames. Or you may be creating a directory whose full pathname (all the way back to the root) is longer than the 64-character limit.

Examples

Creating a subdirectory
Our first example shows how you would create a subdirectory in the current directory. Let's say you're in the directory called C:\WRITING, and you want to create a directory called BOOKS. Here is the command to do this:

```
C:\WRITING>md books
```

(Note that you can type either MD or MKDIR to create a directory.) This command creates the directory C:\WRITING\BOOKS.

Absolute name
You can also create directories on disks other than the current disk. Let's say we're currently on the C: drive. You can create a directory on the A: disk in the root directory with this command:

```
C:\>mkdir a:\data
```

See also

CHDIR	This command allows you to change the current directory. You'll use this command (or a DOS shell program) to navigate around your disk.
DELTREE	This command allows you to delete directories from your disk, even if they have files and subdirectories inside them.
RMDIR	This command allows you to delete empty directories from your disk.
TREE	The TREE command will show you a visual tree of your directory structure.
XCOPY	XCOPY allows you to copy entire branches of your directory structure. If you want to copy all the files in a directory and all the files in that directory's subdirectories, this is the command you'll want to use.

MODE COM — DOS 3.2, IBM 1.1 and later, External

Set serial port parameters
Sets the various parameters for the serial communications port (also known as RS-232 port).

When and why
If you're going to attach a serial printer to your serial port, you'll probably have to use this command to set up the port before you can print. You'll also want to use the MODE LPT command to redirect printer output to the serial port.

You don't need to use this command, however, if you're going to use communications programs since they set the serial port themselves.

Syntax
mode com$n$[:] [*baud*] [,*parity* [,*data* [,*stop* ,*retry*]]]
Sets the parameters on a serial port.

mode com$n$[:] [**baud**=*baud*] [**parity**=*parity*] [**data**=*data*] [**stop**=*stop*] [**retry**=*retry*]
(DOS 4.0 and later.) Sets the parameters on a serial port.

Parameters
com*n*
The serial port that you want to change the settings for. Can be COM1 or COM2 (all DOS versions) or COM3 or COM4 (DOS 3.3 and later).

baud
The data transmission speed (in bits per second, which is also known as baud) that you want to use for this serial port. Here are the values you can use (you only need to write the first two digits):

110	600	4800
150	1200	9600
300	2400	19200*

*The speed 19200 isn't supported on all computers.

parity
The parity bit is an extra bit sent along with each character that can be used for detecting transmission errors. Here are the values you can use for this parameter:

parity	Meaning
n	None, don't check the parity bit.
e	Even parity checking.
o	Odd parity checking.
m	(DOS 4.0 and later.) Mark.
s	(DOS 4.0 and later.) Space.

Not all computers support Mark or Space checking. (Default is E.)

MODE COM

data
The number of data bits used for each character. Most of the time you'll want to set this to 8 or 7. Valid options are 7 or 8 (or 5 through 8 in DOS 4.0 and later), although not all computers support 5 and 6. (Default is 7.)

stop
The number of stop bits at the end of each character. Valid options are 1, 1.5, or 2 (1.5 is available in DOS 4.0 and later). Not all computers support 1.5. (Default is 2 at 110 baud; otherwise, 1.)

retry
This option is useful when you're redirecting a parallel printer's output to a serial printer (using the MODE LPT command). It tells DOS how to handle time-out errors that occur when the printer doesn't respond quickly enough. Here are the options:

retry	**Meaning**
e	Return an error when the port is busy.
b	Return "busy" when the port is busy.
p	Keep trying until the printer accepts the characters.
n, none	Take no action.
r	(DOS 5 and later.) Return "ready" if the port is busy.

(Default is E [DOS 4.0 and earlier] or N [DOS 5 and later].)

Notes

Continuous retry
If you use the P retry option and your printer isn't responding, your computer may appear to freeze. You can break out of this retry loop by pressing Ctrl-Break.

Messages

```
Illegal device name
```
You'll see this message when the name you provide isn't COM1, COM2, COM3, or COM4. Or when you don't have a serial port with that name. Most computers, for example, come with a single serial port installed, which is COM1. You'll see this message if you try to set COM2 since it doesn't exist.

```
Invalid parameter
```
You'll see this message when one of your parameters is incorrect. Check your parameters to make sure they're legal values and try again.

Examples
We have an Apple LaserWriter (a PostScript laser printer) attached to COM1, so we use the following command to set up COM1 before we print:

```
C:\>mode com1:9600,N,8,1,P
```

With DOS 4.0 and later, you can write this:

```
C:\>mode com1 baud=9600 parity=n data=8 stop=1 retry=p
```

You can also change just one parameter, such as the retry setting, using this command:

```
C:\>mode com1 retry=b
```

Part II: Command Reference

If you're using the other form of the MODE command, you need to make sure you have enough commas so MODE will know which parameter you're changing. For example, to change the retry:

```
C:\>mode ,,,,b
```

See also
MODE LPT   You can use this command to redirect printer output from the LPT ports to a serial port.

MODE CON   DOS 4.0 and later, External

Set keyboard repeat rate and delay

This command allows you to control the keyboard's repeat rate and the delay before keys repeat. This repeat action is also known as the typematic rate.

When and why
This is a useful command if you find the keyboard repeat rate too fast or slow or if the delay before keys start to repeat is too fast or slow. We tend to speed up our keyboards because we like to move around quickly using the cursor keys.

Syntax
mode con rate=*r* **delay=***d*
Sets the keyboard repeat rate and the delay before automatic repeating.

Parameters
rate=r
How quickly to repeat characters, in characters per second. Valid range is 1 – 32, which represents keyboard repeat rates of between 2 and 30 characters per second. (Default is 20 for most keyboards and 21 for IBM PS/2 keyboards.)

delay=d
The delay before typematic action begins. Valid range is 1 – 4, which represent delays of ¼, ½, ¾, and 1 second. (Default is 2 [½ second].)

Value	Delay
1	0.25 second
2	0.5 second
3	0.75 second
4	1 second

Notes
Nonrepeating keys
There are a few keys that don't automatically repeat: Ins, and the state keys Caps Lock, Num Lock, and Scroll Lock. The Ins key doesn't repeat because IBM viewed this key as a state key that toggles between INSERT and OVERWRITE modes.

Unsupported keyboards

Not all keyboards allow you to change the repeat rate. Such keyboards are mostly limited to computers with 8088 microprocessors, such as the original IBM PC.

Messages

```
Invalid parameter -
```
This is the message you'll see if the rate or delay is a number that isn't allowed. Make sure the delay is between 1 and 4, and the rate is between 1 and 32.

```
Rate and delay must be specified together
```
This command requires that you provide both the delay and the repeat rate. Run the command again providing both numbers.

Examples

Here is an example that sets the keyboard repeat rate to its maximum with the delay kept at the default of ½ second:

```
C:\>mode con rate=32 delay=2
```

If the normal repeat rate and initial delay is too fast for you, here is a rate and delay that might be more pleasing:

```
C:\>mode con rate=15 delay=3
```

MODE *device* CP   DOS 3.3 and later, External

Code page functions

The MODE command has four subfunctions that deal with code pages, which are alternate character sets that your printer and display can use. See the description of the CHCP command for more information on code pages.

Syntax

The MODE command allows several abbreviations. We've shown the syntax below using CP, which is an abbreviation of code page. You can also abbreviate PREPARE to PREP, REFRESH to REF, and SELECT to SEL. In DOS 6 and later, you can also use the full word CODEPAGE in place of CP.

mode device **cp prepare**=((*page* [...]) *filespec*)
PREPARE loads a code page into the DISPLAY.SYS or PRINTER.SYS device driver. You must use the CHCP command or the SELECT option to load the code page into the hardware.

mode *device* **cp refresh**
Reloads the current code page into the hardware. You may need to do this if there is a hardware problem (such as losing power on a printer) that causes the current code page to be lost.

mode *device* **cp select=***page*
Changes the current code page to *page*. You must first prepare a code page with the PREPARE option. It's better to use CHCP, which will change the code page for all devices rather than just one.

mode *device* **cp** [**/status**]
Displays information on the device. See "Notes" section for details.

Parameters
device
The device that you want to work with. Valid names are CON, PRN, LPT1, LPT2, and LPT3.

page
The code page to prepare or select. Valid code pages are

Code page	Country
437	United States
850	Multilingual (Latin I)
852	Slavic (Latin II)
860	Portugal
863	French Canada
865	Nordic

filespec
The location and name of the file that contains the code-page information. This can be one of the following:

File	Supports
EGA.CPI	Both EGA and VGA display adapters
LCD.CPI	The IBM PC Convertible computer's display
4201.CPI	IBM Proprinters II and III Model 4201
	IBM Proprinters II and III XL Model 4202
4208.CPI	IBM Proprinter X24E Model 4207
	IBM Proprinter XL24E Model 4208
5202.CPI	IBM Quietwriter III printer

Notes

Using code pages
There are a number of steps you need to follow to use code pages correctly. You'll find a full discussion of code pages and how to use them in the description of the CHCP command.

Status information
When you ask for a device's current status, MODE reports information on the current code page, the hardware code page, and what code pages are prepared for the device. For example, if you've set up DISPLAY.SYS to support two code pages in memory and you've prepared code page 850, you may see a display such as this:

MODE *device* CP

```
C:\>mode con cp
Active code page for device CON is 437
Hardware code pages:
  code page 437
Prepared code pages:
  code page 850
  code page not prepared
```

CHCP vs. MODE select
In general it's a better idea to use the CHCP command rather than the MODE CP SELECT command. There are two reasons for this. First, CHCP will change the code page on all devices rather than just one device. And second, CHCP makes sure the code page that you're selecting is compatible with the currently selected country code.

Messages

```
Code page not prepared
```
You need to prepare a code page with the PREPARE option before you can select it.

```
Code page operation not supported on this device
```
You need to load either the DISPLAY.SYS or the PRINTER.SYS device driver before you can use the MODE command to load a code page. See the description of the CHCP command for a discussion of how to use code pages.

```
Current keyboard does not support this code page
```
Each keyboard code supports only two code pages (see KEYB for a list of supported code pages).

```
Device or code page missing from font file
```
The code page you're asking for may not be in the font file you've provided. You'll see this mainly when working with printers, so you should check your printer documentation to make sure it supports the code page you're requesting.

```
Device error during refresh
```
The code page needed to refresh the device may not be in memory. You may have to prepare the code page again. You may also see this error message when your printer isn't connected or turned on (if you're using code pages with the printer).

```
Device error during select
```
You'll see this message when you try to select a code page for a device when you haven't loaded the DISPLAY.SYS or PRINTER.SYS device driver. Make sure you load the device driver in your CONFIG.SYS file. You'll also see this error message when you try to select a code page for a printer that isn't connected to your computer or that is turned off.

```
Error during read of font file
```
There was an error reading the CPI file that you provided. Make sure you typed the name correctly. If you've provided the correct name, delete the file and copy it over again from your original DOS disks.

```
Failure to access code page font file
```
This means that MODE couldn't find a file of the name you provided. Make sure you typed the name correctly.

```
Font file contents invalid
```
You may have provided the wrong name for the font file (it's usually KEYBOARD.SYS in your DOS directory). If you have provided the correct name, your font file may have been damaged. Delete it and make a new copy from your original DOS disks.

```
Invalid number of parameters
```
You may have left out one of the words (such as CP) from the MODE command. Check to make sure you've provided all the words and information needed. A common error is to forget the right parenthesis at end of the command line.

```
Unable to perform refresh operation
```
This may mean that there is a hardware failure or that the code-page information is no longer in the DISPLAY.SYS or PRINTER.SYS device driver. You can use the MODE *device* CP command to see what code pages are currently loaded into the device driver. If the code page is there, you might want to turn your computer or printer off and then on again to reset the hardware.

Example

Preparing CON code pages

Here is an example of how to prepare and use the 850 code page (which is supported for all countries):

```
C:\>mode con cp prep=((850)c:\dos\ega.cpi)
C:\>chcp 850
```

For more details on code pages and how to use them, see the description of the CHCP command.

See also

For a full description on how to use code pages, see the description of the CHCP command.

CHCP	Read this command first — it contains a discussion on code pages and how to use them. Sets the active code page. You'll need this command if you use a code page different from your hardware's default.
DEVICEHIGH	Loads a device driver into the upper memory area.
DISPLAY.SYS	Supports code-page switching for the display. You'll need this if you want to change your display's character set.
KEYB	Allows you to change the mapping of the keyboard for computers with country-specific keyboards. In Germany, for example, the Z and Y keys are swapped so the Z is between the T and U keys.
NLSFUNC	Allows you to change the code page for more than one device (such as the keyboard and the display) at the same time. You'll want to install this before you use CHCP to set the active code page.
PRINTER.SYS	Supports code-page switching for some IBM printers. You'll need this if you want to change your printer's character set.

MODE *display* — DOS 3.2, IBM 2.0 and later, External

Change display characteristics
This command allows you to make changes to the display. There are several versions of this command, depending on which display adapter you have.

When and why
There are two main uses for this command. First, if you're using a laptop computer with an LCD (Liquid Crystal Display) screen which only shows shades of gray, you may want to use the MODE BW80 command to disable color. Many, but not all, programs check to see if the display is set for color or black and white and then use the appropriate colors.

The other use is to change the number of lines visible on the screen. You can only use this option if you have an EGA or VGA display adapter installed since other displays don't allow you to change the number of lines. This feature is implemented in the ANSI.SYS display device driver, so you'll need to install this using a DEVICE= line in your CONFIG.SYS file before you can change the number of lines on your screen.

Syntax
mode con[:] [cols=*c***] [lines=***n***]**
(DOS 4.0 and later.) Sets the number of lines on the screen and the width of the screen (in characters).

mode [*display***] [,***n***]**
(DOS 4.0 and later.) Allows you to change the number of lines on the screen (like the previous form) and change the display mode (like the following form).

mode [*display***] [,l|r [,t]]**
Allows you to switch display modes or between displays. On CGA display adapters you can shift the screen left and right (this was designed with the idea of using a TV for display — we're talking ancient history here). This form of the MODE command is designed for CGA and monochrome displays. Most people never use this form.

Parameters
cols=*c*
(DOS 4.0 and later.) The number of columns you want on the screen. The only valid values are 40 and 80.

lines=*n*
(DOS 4.0 and later.) The number of lines on the screen. You must have an EGA or VGA display adapter to use this feature, and you also have to install ANSI.SYS. The number can be 25, 43, or 50 (VGA only for 50 lines).

display
This parameter has two uses. First, if you have two display adapters installed (one must be a monochrome display and the other color), you can use this to select which is the active monitor. And second, on color displays you can use it to turn off color (which most, but not all, programs honor). Here are the valid values for this parameter:

Part II: Command Reference

    40 or 80   Sets the number of characters per line (this is the same as the COLS= parameter).

    bw40 or bw80 Sets the number of characters per line to 40 or 80 and disables color (this is an internal flag that isn't honored by all programs).

    co40 or co80 Sets the number of characters per line to 40 or 80 and enables color.

    mono   Switches to the monochrome display adapter, if installed. If you have a VGA card, this switches to the monochrome display adapter mode, which allows only black and white.

l|r
CGA displays only. This command allows you to shift the screen left or right. It is rarely useful these days since there are few CGA display adapters in use.

t
CGA displays only. Shows a test pattern so you can see whether the entire display is visible on the screen. This is used with the left and right shift parameter. Again, it's ancient history and rarely used.

Notes
You'll need to install ANSI.SYS before you can change the number of lines on the screen of an EGA or VGA display.

Messages
`ANSI.SYS must be installed to perform requested function`
MODE uses the ANSI.SYS device driver to change the number of lines on the screen. Install ANSI.SYS in your CONFIG.SYS file and reboot before you try again.

Examples

More lines on-screen
If you're using an EGA or VGA display adapter, you can change the number of lines on your screen from the normal 25 to 43 (EGA and VGA) or 50 (VGA). Here is how you would switch to 43-line mode:

    `C:\>`**`mode con lines=43`**

Laptop control of color
If you're using a laptop computer, you might want to put the following line into your AUTOEXEC.BAT file:

    `C:\>`**`mode bw80`**

This will turn off the color bit (which doesn't change the screen). Many programs look at this bit to see if they should display in color or black and white. If you have a program that ignores this setting, you'll probably have to change the colors either from within the program or by using that program's installation program.

See also
    ANSI.SYS   You'll need to install this device driver before you can change the number of lines on the screen.

MODE LPT · All IBM, DOS 3.2 and later, External

Control printer output

There are several forms of this command that provide various types of control over your printers.

When and why

The most common use of this command is to redirect printer output to a serial port, but you may never have to do this. Most programs allow you to print directly to any parallel (LPTn) or serial (COMn) port without having to use redirection. Using a program's built-in code is better than using printer redirection. But if you have a serial printer and your software can't print to a serial printer, you'll have to use printer redirection.

The other options are even less commonly used. The retry options are something you should avoid using unless your software manual suggests that you use them.

As to changing the printer settings, you need an IBM- or Epson-compatible printer that accepts the control codes used to change printer settings. Very few people use this option. But if you have a compatible printer, you might find it useful.

Syntax

mode lpt*n*[:] [*cols*] [,[*lines*] [,*retry*]]

or

mode lpt*n*[:][**cols**=*cols*][**lines**=*lines*][**retry**=*retry*]

(DOS 4.0 and later.) Sets the number of columns and lines per page on the printer and determines how DOS will handle printer errors. The second form of this command is easier to work with and was introduced in DOS 4.0. Under DOS versions before 4.0, the only retry option available is P.

mode lpt*n*[:] = **com***m*[:]

Redirects printer output. This command allows you to reroute the printer LPT*n* so anything sent to it will actually be sent to a printer attached to a serial port. LPT*n* can be LPT1, LPT2, or LPT3, while COM*m* can be COM1, COM2, COM3, or COM4. You'll want to set up the COM port with the MODE COM command before you print to the printer. *Note:* DOS versions before 3.3 don't support COM3 or COM4.

Parameters

lptn
The printer that you want to control. Can be LPT1, LPT2, or LPT3.

cols
IBM- and Epson-compatible printers only. The number of characters per line (columns) on the printer. Valid values are 80 and 132. (Default is 80.)

lines
IBM- and Epson-compatible printers only. Sets the number of lines per inch. Valid values are 6 and 8. (Default is 6.)

retry
Tells MODE how to handle printer delays that cause time-out errors (which can happen if you forget to set the printer on-line). When you choose one of these options, MODE loads a small program into memory to handle these time-out errors:

- e   Returns an error when the printer is busy after a time-out. (Default before DOS 5.)
- b   Returns "busy" when the printer is busy after a time-out.
- p   Keeps retrying until the printer accepts the output.
- r   Returns "ready" when the printer is busy after a time-out.
- n   Takes no action when the printer is busy after a time-out. (DOS 5 Default.)

Notes

Canceling printer redirection

You can cancel printer redirection by using the MODE LPT*n* command without any other parameters. For example, to cancel printer redirection on LPT1, use the following command:

```
C:\>mode lpt1
```

Setting COLS or LINES or redirected printer

You can't use the MODE commands to change the printer LINES or COLS if you're using printer redirection (because MODE LPT*n* turns off redirection). The best solution is to create some text files that contain the control codes needed to switch printer modes. Then copy one of these text files to your printer whenever you want to change modes. You can find the necessary control codes in your printer's documentation.

Network printers

Don't use any of the retry options with network printers — only use these options for printers that are attached directly to your computer.

The P retry option

If you're using the P retry option, which keeps trying to send output to the printer until it accepts the output, you can press Ctrl-Break to cancel continuous retries.

Messages

```
LPTn: not redirected
```
This message means that printer redirection to a serial port is currently turned off. If you use any of the MODE LPT*n* commands (even if you just want to change the number of lines per inch) MODE turns off printer redirection.

```
Printer error
```
You'll see this message if your printer isn't connected, turned on, and on-line when you try to change the LINES or COLS setting of your printer. This is because MODE needs to send control codes to your printer, which it can't do if your printer isn't ready.

```
Resident portion of MODE loaded
```
You'll see this message whenever you set a retry option or use printer redirection. MODE loads a small piece of code into memory (about 500 bytes) to provide the retry and redirection services.

Examples

This example shows how to change the number of lines per inch from the default 6 to a tighter 8 lines per inch:

```
C:\>mode lpt1 lines=8
```

You can also use the short form (the only form for DOS versions before 4.0) of this command, which is

```
C:\>mode lpt1, 8
```

Note that you must use the comma to tell MODE what you're setting.

See also

MODE COM   If you're redirecting printer output, you'll want to use this command to set up the serial port before you print to the serial printer.

MODE CP   Use this command if you need to change your printer's character sets for international support (not supported by all printers).

MODE *device* STATUS   DOS 4.0 and later, External

Display information about a device

This command displays information about several types of devices installed in your computer.

When and why

You probably won't get much useful information from this command. MODE mainly displays information about some of the options it can set. But if you're using printer redirection or code pages, you might find this command useful.

Syntax

mode [*device*] [**/status**]

Displays the information about one device (or all the devices if you don't give a device name).

Parameters

device

The name of the device for which you want information. Device can be any of the following:

COM1 – COM4	The serial communications ports
CON	The console (keyboard and display) device
LPT1 – LPT4	The printer ports
PRN	The default printer port (usually LPT1)

If you don't give a device name, MODE displays the current status for all the devices installed in your computer.

Switch

/status
Displays status information on a device. This switch is purely optional.

Example

This is the kind of output you'll see when you run MODE to display information on the CON (console) device:

```
C:\>mode con

Status for device CON:

Columns=80
Lines=25

Code page operation not supported on this device
```

MORE — All DOS, External

Display output one screen at a time

This command displays the output of another program (or the contents of a file) one screenful at a time.

When and why

This command is useful for viewing the output of other commands that are longer than one screen. Some commands provide a switch (usually /P) to display only one screenful of text at a time. But many commands don't provide such a switch. This is where you'll want to use the MORE command. You can pipe (using the | character) the output of any such program into MORE.

MORE is a type of program called a filter because it reads characters from the standard input (which can be redirected using the < or | redirection characters) and it writes to the standard output.

Syntax

command | **more**
Shows the output of a command one page at a time.

more < *filespec*
Displays a file one page at a time.

Notes

Next page
After MORE displays a page, it prints - - More - - at the bottom of the screen. Press any key to see the next screen.

Stopping MORE
You can stop MORE at any time by pressing Ctrl-Break (or Ctrl-C).

Long lines
Your computer screen can display 80 characters across, so MORE can't display lines longer than 80 characters without breaking the line into smaller lines. This is called wrapping. MORE wraps long lines without any regard to words, so when it hits the 80th character, it will move to the next line on the screen (even if it breaks the line in the middle of a word).

Examples
The MEM command is an example of a command that can generate more than one screenful of information (starting with DOS 6, MEM supports the /P pause switch). Here is how you would use MORE to display MEM's output one page at a time:

    C:\>mem /classify | more

MORE also works well for viewing text files (although you can't page backwards, as you can with the Norton Commander's or the DOS Shell's file viewers):

    C:\>more < readme.txt

See also
| The pipe command allows you to send the output of one program into the input of another.

<   The less-than sign allows you to redirect a command's input (the MORE command in this case) to a data file.

MOUSE   DOS 6 and later, External

The Microsoft mouse driver
If you use a Microsoft mouse (or compatible pointing device), this command updates the mouse driver for full compatibility with DOS 6.

When and why
You'll need to install a mouse driver, like this one, if you want to use a mouse with your DOS software (Windows doesn't require this driver). If your mouse is a Microsoft mouse or it's compatible with a Microsoft mouse, you can use this device driver. If, however, your mouse is not compatible with the Microsoft mouse, you won't want to use this mouse driver. Of course, if your mouse is Microsoft compatible, your mouse driver may have already been updated when you installed DOS 6.

Syntax
mouse [**on**|**off**] [/**c***n* | /**z**] [/**l***language*] [/**r***rate*] [/**h***horz*] [/**v***vert*] [/**s***both*] [/**p***accel*] [/**y**]
This line in your AUTOEXEC.BAT loads the mouse driver into memory.

mouse [/**c***n* | /**z**] [/**l***language*] [/**r***rate*] [/**h***horz*] [/**v***vert*] [/**s***both*] [/**p***accel*] [/**y**]
Allows you to change the settings of the mouse driver.

mouse [on|off]
Enables and disables the mouse driver. When you turn the mouse driver off, it will remove itself from memory if it can. The message you see will tell you whether MOUSE was able to remove itself from memory or not.

Switches

/cn
Serial mouse. This switch tells MOUSE to use a specific serial port for the connection instead of automatically searching for the correct port. Telling MOUSE which port to use can speed up loading MOUSE. You can also use this switch to choose which mouse to use if you have more than one mouse installed on your computer. Valid numbers are 1 and 2 (COM1 and COM2).

/z
PS/2 mouse. This switch tells MOUSE to look for the mouse on a PS/2 mouse port instead of searching for the correct port. Your mouse is using a PS/2 mouse port if the connector is a small round connector that plugs into the back of your computer. Using this switch can speed up the loading of MOUSE. You can also use this switch to choose which mouse to use if you have more than one mouse installed on your computer.

*/l*language*
Language for messages. You can change the language that MOUSE will use to display all its messages using this switch. Here are all the possible /L switches:

/L	English	/LNL	Dutch
/LD	German	/LP	Portuguese
/LE	Spanish	/LS	Swedish
/LF	French	/LSF	Finnish
/LI	Italian		

(Default is English.)

*/r*rate*
Interrupt rate. This switch controls how often a PS/2 mouse will relay position information to MOUSE. You probably won't need to change this setting. Valid numbers: 0, 1, 2, 3, and 4. (Default is 1.)

*/h*horz*
Horizontal sensitivity. This switch controls just the horizontal sensitivity. For a description of sensitivity, see the /S switch below. You'll probably want to use the /S switch instead of this switch. Valid range is 5 to 100. (Default is 50.)

*/v*vert*
Vertical sensitivity. This switch controls just the vertical sensitivity. For a description of sensitivity, see the /S switch below. Valid range is 5 to 100. You'll probably want to use the /S switch instead of this switch. (Default is 50.)

*/s*both*
Vertical and horizontal sensitivity. This switch controls both the horizontal and the vertical sensitivity of your mouse. The higher this number, the faster the on-screen cursor will move when you move your mouse. When you set this number to 5, for example, the on-screen mouse will seem very sluggish. Whereas using a value of 100 produces a very *fast* cursor. Valid range is 5 to 100. (Default is 50.)

MOUSE

/p*accel*
Acceleration profile. This setting controls the feel of your mouse. Acceleration causes your mouse sensitivity to increase as you move your mouse faster. Since this setting is really a matter of feel, you'll probably want to try different settings. Valid numbers: 1, 2, 3, 4. (Default is 2.)

1 Slow
2 Medium
3 Fast
4 No acceleration

/y
Disable hardware cursor. Normally, MOUSE draws the cursor itself, but some display cards (such as VIDEO7 cards) have a hardware cursor. What this means is that you can see an arrow cursor that moves smoothly even in text-mode programs like the Norton Commander. This switch turns off support for this feature. To turn support on again, you'll have to restart your computer and load MOUSE without this switch. (Default is to use hardware cursor if available.)

Notes

MOUSE.SYS vs. MOUSE.COM
Originally, you could load the mouse driver either from your CONFIG.SYS file (as MOUSE.SYS) or as a command (MOUSE.COM). Microsoft now only supports MOUSE.COM. You can load the mouse driver automatically at startup by inserting a command in your AUTOEXEC.BAT file.

Using the most recent version
Microsoft is constantly updating the mouse driver, so you should make sure you're using the most recent version of MOUSE.COM. The version shipped with DOS 6 is version 8.2. If you have more than one mouse driver, there are two ways you can tell which is most recent. First, you can run MOUSE.COM, and it will tell its version number. Second, you could look at the dates on the two programs and use the most recent version. This latter method isn't as reliable because you can change the dates on files, but MOUSE will always report its version number when you run it.

There are several ways you might obtain a new mouse driver. Whenever you upgrade to a new version of DOS (starting with DOS 6), you'll get a new mouse driver. You'll also get the latest mouse driver when you buy a Microsoft Mouse. And finally, you can contact Microsoft to upgrade to the latest and greatest mouse driver.

Using your mouse with Windows
If you are using Windows, you do not need to load any mouse driver from DOS. Windows has its own set of internal mouse drivers, which you select using the Setup command within Windows. However, if you plan to run DOS software that uses a mouse from within Windows, you will need to load a DOS-based mouse driver such as MOUSE.COM.

The MOUSE.INI file
The mouse device driver in DOS 6 actually has a lot of new features that are supported by settings in a MOUSE.INI file. In order to use this file, you'll need to do two things. First, before you load MOUSE into memory, you'll need to set an

environment variable that tells MOUSE which directory contains the MOUSE.INI file. For example, if you put MOUSE.INI into your DOS directory, you'll need the following lines in your AUTOEXEC.BAT file:

set mouse=c:\dos
c:\dos\mouse

Next, you'll need to add some lines to your MOUSE.INI file. This file can have a section (which your file may already have) called [DOSPointer] which controls how the mouse cursor behaves for DOS programs. (For Windows you would make changes to a section called [WindowsPointer], which has the same set of options.) Here is what a typical MOUSE.INI file might look like:

```
[DOSPointer]
PointerSize=Medium
PointerColor=Normal
Growth=On
Threshold=20
Delay=3
```

The main purpose of these lines is to control the size of your mouse cursor, and these options are especially helpful on a laptop computer where the cursor can sometimes be hard to find. As in the example above, you can have MOUSE increase the size of your mouse cursor whenever you move the mouse. Here are descriptions for each of these lines:

PointerSize   Controls the size of the mouse cursor. If you have GROWTH=ON, this setting changes the size of the cursor only when you move the mouse. The size can be any of three values, and they're shown below. Valid values: NORMAL, MEDIUM, and LARGE. (Default is Normal.)

Normal ■   Medium ■▟■   Large ■▙■

PointerColor   This option has three settings, but it doesn't seem to have much effect on non-graphics programs. Valid values: NORMAL, REVERSE, and TRANSPARENT. (Default is Normal.)

Growth   When you turn this option on, the cursor will keep its normal size until you move the mouse, at which point it will switch to the size you've set using the PointerSize setting. Valid values: ON and OFF. (Default is Off.)

Threshold   This setting controls how much you have to move the mouse before the mouse cursor will grow (MOUSE ignores this setting when GROWTH=OFF). The values correspond roughly to pixels. In text mode each character is treated as about 8 pixels wide. Valid range is 1 – 100.

Delay   How long MOUSE shown waits before restoring the mouse cursor to its normal size after you stop moving the mouse (MOUSE ignores this setting when GROWTH=OFF). This number is a relative value, where 100 is about 10 seconds. Valid range is 1 – 100.

Examples

Activating mouse support
To start using your mouse if the mouse driver wasn't loaded during system startup, use

    C:\>**mouse**

Setting mouse acceleration
If you want to make your mouse more sensitive, you might try this command:

    C:\>**mouse /s100**

This command will change both the horizontal and vertical sensitivity to the maximum value.

If, on the other hand, you thought the default setting of 50 was too much, you could decrease the sensitivity using this command:

    C:\>**mouse /s20**

Changing the language for messages
At any time you can tell MOUSE to display its messages in a different language. For example, if you have MOUSE loaded, you can change its messages to German by typing

    C:\>**mouse /ld**

```
Microsoft (R) Mouse Treiber-Version 8.20
Copyright (C) 1983-1992 Microsoft Corp.   Alle Rechte vorbehalten.
Optionswerte an vorhandenen Maustreiber weitergeleitet

C:>_
```

MOVE   DOS 6 and later, External

Move files or rename a directory
This command has two uses. First, as its name suggests, it can move a file or group of files from one directory to another. You can even move files from one disk to another. The second function is less obvious; you can rename directories.

When and why
If you want to move files between directories, or you want to rename directories, this is the command for you. This command is very handy when you're reorganizing your files and directories since you'll probably want to move files between directories and change the names of some directories.

But if you're doing a lot of work, you'll probably find it easier to use either the Commander or the DOS Shell.

> Starting in DOS 6.2, the MOVE command is a little safer because it now asks you before it writes over files that already exist (however, this feature doesn't work if you use the MOVE command from within any type of DOS shell program).
>
> *Note:* Use RENAME to change the names of a group of files.

Syntax

move [/y|/-y] [*drive:*][*path*]*filename*[,[*drive:*][*path*]*filename*[...]] *destination*
Moves one or more files to a new directory, *destination*.

move [/y|/-y] [*drive:*][*path*]*directory* [*drive:*][*path*]*newname*
Changes the name of a directory to *newname*.

Parameter

[*drive:*][*path*][*filename*]
File(s) to move. You can use a single filename, a group of filenames (separated by commas), or a file specification that includes the * and ? wildcard characters. If you're moving only a single file, you can also rename the file (see "Notes" below).

destination
New location for files. When moving more than one file, this must be a directory name. This directory name may be a relative path or an absolute path, and may include a drive letter if you want to move the files to another disk.

[*drive:*][*path*]*directory*
Directory to rename. This is the name of a directory that you want to rename. If the name isn't a directory, MOVE will treat it as a file and try to move it.

newname
New directory name. The new name that you want to use for a directory. Note that if the directory you're renaming isn't a subdirectory of the current directory, you'll have to use the same *drive* and *path* that you supplied before the *directory* name. You have to supply the path in this case so MOVE doesn't think you're asking to move a directory, which you can't do.

Switches

/-y
Prompt before copying over files (DOS 6.2 and later). Tells MOVE that it should ask before it overwrites a file that already exists. This is the default setting when you use MOVE from the DOS command line. *Note:* You *will not* get an overwrite prompt if you run MOVE from within a DOS shell, such as the Norton Commander, or from within a batch file. In these two cases, you need to use the /-Y switch if you want to confirm overwriting existing files. You can change the default setting using the COPYCMD environment variable. Default: /-Y from DOS prompt, /Y from DOS shells or batch files.

/y
Overwrite without prompting (DOS 6.2 and later). Tells MOVE to write over existing files without asking first. This switch overrides a /-Y switch in the COPYCMD environment variable. Default: /-Y from DOS prompt, /Y from DOS shells or batch files.

Notes

How MOVE moves files

When you move a file to a new directory on the same disk, MOVE is very fast because it doesn't actually move the contents of your file. Instead, it simply moves the information about the file (the name, attributes, date, etc.) from one directory table to another directory table.

When you move a file between disks, however, DOS actually copies the file to the second disk and then deletes the file from the first disk once it finishes copying the file. This is much slower since MOVE has to move the entire file rather than just the directory data.

Changing a file's name and location

If you're moving a single file, you can both move it to a new directory and give it a new name. See the "Examples" section for an example of doing just this.

Working with relative paths

Because the MOVE command works with both files and directories, it is less flexible in the way that it processes relative paths than commands like COPY that only work with files. For example, you can use the command

    C:\>**copy . b:**

to copy all of the files from the current directory to a floppy disk in drive B. On the other hand, the command

    C:\>**move . b:**

produces an error message because MOVE can't determine whether you want to MOVE the files in the current directory or rename the current directory.

Furthermore, if you use a relative path to rename a directory, and the directory is *not* a subdirectory of the current directory, you'll need to use the same relative path for the new name as well:

    C:\>**move temp\oldname temp\newname**

Messages

    Cannot move test1 - No such file or directory

There are a couple of cases when you'll see this message. First, if you mistyped a file name, this message simply means that MOVE couldn't find a file with the name that you typed. You'll also see this message when you use a relative path and MOVE doesn't know whether you're asking to rename a directory or move all the files in that directory.

    [Unable to open source]

You'll see this message if you ask to rename a directory and you used a relative path for the first name but not for the second name. You'll need to include the same relative path in front of the new directory name. We're not sure why MOVE uses this error message for this error. MOVE might also use this same error message if it has some other problem reading the file.

```
[Unable to write destination]
```
You may see this message when you try to move a file to a floppy disk that doesn't have enough room for the file or files.

ERRORLEVEL returned

MOVE returns information that batch files can test with the ERRORLEVEL command. Here are the exit codes that MOVE returns:

0   MOVE was able to move all your files

1   MOVE wasn't able to move one or more of your files.

Examples

Moving files to a floppy disk

To move all of the files from the current directory to a floppy disk, use

```
C:\>move *.* b:
```

The MOVE command will show you the status of each file that it moves (the [ok] doesn't appear until MOVE finishes moving that file):

```
c:\john.doc  => b:\john.doc  [ok]

c:\devra.doc => b:\devra.doc [ok]

c:\clint.doc => b:\clint.doc [ok]
```

Changing a directory name

To change the name of a directory, use

```
C:\>move \dos-book\working \dos-book\done
```

Notice that you have to specify the entire path for the new directory name when you used a path for the old name. The path up to the final directory name must be the same for both the old and the new name.

Moving a file and changing its name

Let's say you have a file called SOMEFILE.TXT and you have a directory called \DOS-BOOK. The following command will move the file SOMEFILE.TXT to this directory and change its name to NEWFILE.TXT:

```
C:\>move somefile.txt \dos-book\newfile.txt
```

Confirming moving over existing files

Often, you may want MOVE to ask before it moves files on top of existing files. To make MOVE ask first, use the /-Y switch (which works even from within batch files):

```
C:\>move file.txt d:\writing\books\newfile.txt
```
```
Overwrite d:\writing\books\newfile.txt (Yes/No/All)?
```

At this point you can press Y, N, or A, followed by Enter. All means that MOVE moves any other files that match wildcard characters in a name without first asking whether you want to overwrite existing files.

Using the COPYCMD environment variable

You can set the COPYCMD environment variable so that MOVE always asks you before overwriting existing files (this environment variable also affects the COPY and XCOPY commands). Here is the SET command you can place in your AUTOEXEC.BAT file to set up such an environment variable:

```
set copycmd=/-y
```

After you have this switch set, you can have MOVE copy a file without asking for confirmation by using the /Y switch:

```
C:\>move /y file.txt d:\writing\books\newfile.txt
```

See also

COPY   Used to make duplicates of files.

RENAME Used to rename groups of files.

XCOPY   Used to copy directory structures.

MSAV   DOS 6 and later, External

Microsoft Anti-Virus for DOS

This is a DOS program (as apposed to the Windows MWAV) that will scan your memory and disks for viruses. It can also remove viruses that it finds.

When and why

Whenever you get a new disk or program from a perhaps dubious source (many bulletin boards, for example), you should use this program or the Windows equivalent (MWAV) to make sure the disk and/or programs don't contain a virus. You'll want to do this before you use the disk or programs. You might also want to load VSAFE into memory to protect against viruses in case you forget to run MSAV on new programs before you run them.

Computer viruses are like human viruses — they can make your computer sick, which could mean losing some of your files and data. This program will scan for and remove viruses from your computer, even if they're dormant.

Syntax

msav [/*video-switch*]
Starts the full-screen anti-virus program.

msav [*drive*: ...] [/s | /c] [/r] [/a | /l] [/*video-switch*]
Starts the full-screen anti-virus program and starts running the task you asked for with a switch.

msav [*drive*: ...] /p [/s | /c] [/r] [/a | /l] [/f] [/*video-switch*]
Starts the command-line interface for the anti-virus utility and performs any requested task.

msav [*drive*: ...] /n [/s | /c] [/r] [/a | /l] [/f]
Performs the requested task without an interface.

msav /video
Displays the available video switches.

Parameters
drive:
Which drive or drives you want MSAV to scan and/or clean. If you don't supply any drive letters, MSAV will scan the current drive (unless you used the /A or /L switch).
Note: If you supply more than one drive letter, MSAV will process them in alphabetical order rather than the order you supplied. (Default is current drive.)

Switches
/s
Scan only. Tells MSAV to look for viruses but not to remove them. Using this switch tells MSAV to start scanning without waiting for you to start the process, which you have to do if you don't use the /N or /P switches.

/c
Clean. Tells MSAV to remove any viruses if it finds any. MSAV will try to remove the virus from the file without destroying the file. Using this switch tells MSAV to start scanning without waiting for you to start the process, which you have to do if you don't use the /N or /P switches.

/r
Report. Creates a report of what MSAV checked and found, and saves this report in MSAV.RPT in the root directory of each drive it scans. This report contains information about the number of files scanned, the number of viruses found, and the number of viruses removed.

/a
All drives (except A: and B:). This switch tells MSAV to scan all disks except for your floppy disks A and B. MSAV will also scan network drives and CD-ROM drives, which you may not want it to do.

/l
All local drives (including A: and B:). This switch tells MSAV to scan only drives attached to your computer. It will scan floppy disks (drives A and B) as well as any local hard disks. But it will not scan network drives.

/p
Prompt interface. Use this switch if you don't want to use MSAV's full-screen interface *and* if you want MSAV to quit automatically when it finishes. If you don't use this switch (or /N), you'll have to select Exit from the full-screen program to return to DOS. This switch is useful if you want to run MSAV from a batch file.

/n
No interface. We're not exactly sure why you'd want this option. It tells MSAV not to display any messages at all while it works. Instead, MSAV will display a text file called MSAV.TXT if it exists and then start scanning. This file must be in the same directory as the MSAV.EXE program.

/f
Do not display filenames. You can use this with /P or /N to turn off the automatic display of filenames as they are scanned.

MSAV

/video
Display video options. This switch lists all the valid video switches that you can use with MSAV.

/video-switch
Video mode. You can use this option to control how MSAV works with your screen. Here is a list of all the possible values:

/25   Sets screen display to 25 lines. This is the default setting.

/28   Sets screen display to 28 lines. Use this switch with VGA display adapters only.

/43   Sets screen display to 43 lines. Use this switch with EGA and VGA display adapters.

/50   Sets screen display to 50 lines. Use this switch with VGA display adapters only.

/60   Sets screen display to 60 lines. Use this switch with Video 7 display adapters only.

/IN   Runs MSAV using a color scheme, even if MSAV doesn't detect a color display adapter. You'll probably never have need for this switch.

/BW   Runs MSAV using a black-and-white color scheme, which is really shades of gray. Use the /MONO switch if you want to actually use just two colors.

/MONO Runs MSAV using a monochromatic color scheme.

/LCD   Runs MSAV using an LCD color scheme. Our experience is that this scheme isn't always easy to read on a laptop. You might prefer to use the /MONO switch.

/FF   Uses the fastest screen updating on computers with CGA display adapters. Using this switch may decrease video quality but only if you have a CGA display adapter.

/BF   Uses the computer's BIOS to display video. (We couldn't get this to work.)

/NF   Disables the use of alternate fonts. Use this switch if you don't want MSAV to use graphical characters on an EGA or VGA screen. Use /NGM to tell MSAV to use a non-graphical mouse cursor as well.

/BT   Allows use of a graphics mouse in Windows. (We couldn't get this to work.)

Mouse switches

/NGM   Runs MSAV using the default mouse character instead of the graphics character. Normally, MSAV displays an arrow mouse that moves very smoothly. Use this switch if you want to use an inverse character for the mouse cursor. Use /NF if you also want to turn off other special graphics.

/LE   Exchanges left and right mouse buttons.

/PS2   Resets the mouse if the mouse cursor disappears or locks up.

Notes

What files MSAV checks

Unless you've asked MSAV to check all your files, it normally checks only program files, which it defines as any file with the following extensions: EXE, COM, OVL, OVR, SYS, BIN, APP, or CMD. The Windows version, MWAV, also adds a number of other extensions.

Note: If you have Windows installed on your computer, you should use MWAV instead because it scans Windows-specific files (such as DLLs) for viruses, whereas MSAV does not.

Checklist files

Normally, MSAV saves a special file called CHKLIST.MS in each directory that it scans. This file contains a list of checksum values for each program (COM, EXE, SYS, etc.) stored in that directory. It contains information about each file's size, attributes, date, time, and a checklist. This file helps MSAV determine when a new type of virus that MSAV doesn't know about infects one of your files.

MSAV creates the checklist files only if you have that option set. By default, MSAV creates checklist files on hard disks but not on floppy disks.

Deleting checklist files

You can delete all the checklist files on a disk using the full-screen interface. First, start MSAV with a list of drive letters that you want to delete checklist files from. Then press the F7 Delete key and press Enter when the dialog box appears. This will delete all the CHKLIST.MS files.

Using Windows and DOS

If you use both the Windows and the DOS programs (MWAV and MSAV), you should be aware that they each have their own settings files (MWAV.INI and MSAV.INI). So any options that you change in one program will not appear in the other program.

Using the MSAV.INI file

If you use the MSAV.INI file to save settings, there are two places where you can store this file. First, you can put it into the same directory as MSAV.EXE. If you're working on a network, however, and MSAV.EXE is on a network drive, you might prefer to have your own private copy of MSAV.INI instead. In this case you will want to set the MSDOSDATA environment variable so it tells MSAV where to find your MSAV.INI file. For example, to tell MSAV to use your own DOS directory (let's say MSAV.EXE is on drive G), you would use this line in your AUTOEXEC.BAT file:

```
set msdosdata=c:\dos
```

ERRORLEVEL returned

When you run MSAV with the /N switch, it sets the ERRORLEVEL variable to let your batch file know that MSAV found an error. Here are the error codes returned by MSAV:

- 0   MSAV did not detect any viruses.
- 86   MSAV found a virus.

You can use the IF ERRORLEVEL command to test for this error condition in a batch file.

Examples

Scan the disk in drive B for viruses

It's a good idea to either install VSafe as on-going protection or to use the Anti-Virus utility to scan floppies before using them (we prefer the latter). To detect (but not clean) viruses on a disk placed in drive B, use

```
C:\>msav b: /s
```

If the MSAV detects a virus, you can either choose not to use that floppy in your machine or attempt to remove the virus by using the /C switch.

After you install DOS 6, you might want to run MSAV to check your system for any existing viruses. To do this from the command line, use

```
C:\>msav /l /c
```

This searches for and attempts to remove viruses on all your local drives.

See also

VSAFE   A TSR that provides on-going virus protection.

MWAV   The Windows version of the Anti-Virus program.

MSBACKUP   DOS 6 and later, External

Microsoft Backup for DOS

This command allows you to back up an entire hard disk to a set of floppy disks, even when you have some files that are too large to fit on a single floppy disk. MSBACKUP automatically splits large files between multiple floppy disks. It can do this because it also saves information on the floppy disks that tells MSBACKUP how to reconstruct files and where they should be restored to.

When and why

If you do any real work on your computer, you should be using this program or a commercial backup program to back up your work regularly. And you should keep backup copies of your work at a different location, in case everything is destroyed by a fire or other disaster. If you don't back up your computer and something goes wrong, you might not be able to recover your work. So back up your data!

Microsoft Backup is a very powerful, full-screen program that gives you a lot of control over what files you back up.

Syntax

msbackup [*setup_file*] [/**bw** | /**lcd** | /**mda**]

Starts the Microsoft Backup utility. This is a full-screen program.

Parameters

setup_file
Setup file to load. The name of the setup file you want to load into MWBACKUP (it won't start to back up until you press the Start Backup button). A setup file includes information about the files to be included in the backup, the type of backup to perform, and the settings of all the backup options. This simplifies, but does not completely automate, the backup process. You create such setup files using MSBACKUP, and all backup sets have the extension SET.

Switches

/bw
Black and white. Tells MSBACKUP to use black and white (not shades of gray) to display its screen. This option should make it easier to read MSBACKUP's screen on a laptop computer. (*Note:* The /BW, /LCD, and /MDA switches all seem to have the same effect.)

/lcd
LCD displays. Use this switch if you're running MSBACKUP on a laptop computer with an LCD screen. This option should make it easier to read MSBACKUP's screen on a laptop computer. (*Note:* The /BW, /LCD, and /MDA switches all seem to have the same effect.)

/mda
Monochrome display adaptor. Use only if your system requires this switch to display MSBACKUP properly. This option should make it easier to read MSBACKUP's screen on a laptop computer. (*Note:* The /BW, /LCD, and /MDA switches all seem to have the same effect.)

Notes

Using Backup in Windows

If you're using Windows, you should use MWBACKUP instead of MSBACKUP. The MSBACKUP program may not work properly while Windows is running, but MWBACKUP will.

Setup files

Microsoft Backup's design is centered around setup files, which contain information on all the files you want to back up, the type of backup (full, incremental, or differential), and other options. To create new setup files, choose the files and options you want; then select Save Setup As... from the File menu. You can also type in a long description of the setup file, which will help you identify setup files if you have several of them.

Types of backup

MSBACKUP offers three different types of backup: Full, Incremental, and Differential. In this note we explain what these terms mean.

Full backup. This type of backup will back up all the files in your backup set, even if they haven't changed since the last backup. You should perform a full backup of your data periodically. For daily backups, you'll probably want to do an incremental backup. Full backups turn off the archive attribute for all files you back up.

Incremental backup. An incremental backup backs up only those files in your backup set that have changed or are new since the last time you did either a full or incremental backup. This is probably the best type of backup to perform between full backups. MSBACKUP uses the archive attribute to tell which files have been modified since the last time you did a backup. Incremental backups turn off the archive attribute for all files you back up.

Differential backup. Different backups back up all files that you've changed since the last time you did a *full* backup. This option does not turn off the archive attribute.

Using the MSBACKUP.INI file

If you use the MSBACKUP.INI file to save settings, there are two places where you can store this file. First, you can put it into the same directory as MSBACKUP.EXE. If you're working on a network, however, and MSBACKUP.EXE is on a network drive, you might prefer to have your own private copy of MSBACKUP.INI instead. In this case you will want to set the MSDOSDATA environment variable so it tells MSBACKUP where to find your MSBACKUP.INI file. For example, to tell MSBACKUP to use your own DOS directory (let's say MSBACKUP.EXE is on drive G), you would use this line in your AUTOEXEC.BAT file:

```
set msdosdata=c:\dos
```

The MSBACKUP.INI file is an encoded file, so you can't make changes directly to this file, as you can for other INI files. The only way to change settings is from inside MSBACKUP.

Backup catalogs

Whenever you back up files on your computer, MSBACKUP creates a catalog that lists all the files MSBACKUP backed up for you. The sole purpose of catalog files is to make it easier for you and MSBACKUP to restore a file at some time in the future. When you ask to restore a file, MSBACKUP will display a restore dialog box, with the catalog for your last backup selected. You can select a different catalog or retrieve a catalog from your backup floppy disks. In any event, once you select a backup set, MSBACKUP will allow you to select which files you want to restore. You'll see the full directory of your hard disks as it existed when you backed up your computers. But the only files that will be visible are the ones you backed up. Catalogs make this all possible.

There are also two types of catalogs: master catalogs and backup-set catalogs. The master catalog contains information from the last full backup, plus all incremental and differential backups, whereas the backup-set catalogs contain information on what files were backed up during a single backup session. What this means is that you can select a master catalog when you want to restore files, and MSBACKUP will tell you which backup set of disks you'll have to insert. As long as you're consistent about which backup set you use, then you won't need to remember the name of the last catalog MSBACKUP created.

Note: Make sure you label all the disks in your backup sets with the name of the catalog since this is how MSBACKUP will ask for backup disks when you restore files. You'll find the catalog name in the Backup Set Information of the backup screen.

How MSBACKUP names catalog files

One sticky point about catalogs is that the names may appear to be somewhat cryptic. That's because MSBACKUP actually encodes quite a bit of information into the name, and you can use this information to figure out which catalog you want to use. For example, you can tell a lot from the following name:

```
CD30323A.FUL
```

This says that you backed up drives C through D on March 23, 1993, and it was a full backup. Here is a table that shows you how to decode catalog names:

Characters	Example	Meaning
1	C	First drive letter you backed up in this catalog. C: in this example.
1	D	Last drive letter that you backed up in this catalog. This will be the same as the first character if you only backed up one drive letter. D: in this example.
1	3	The last digit of the year, which is 1993 in this example.
2	03	The month that you backed up these files. March in this example.
2	23	The day of the month that you created this backup set. The 23rd in this example.
1	A	The sequence letter. This will have a value other than A only if you backed up more than once on the same day, and it keeps track of which backup you did first.
Extension	FUL	The type of backup. This can be FUL (full backup), INC (incremental backup), or DIF (differential backup).

Examples

Let's say you created a backup set called FRIDAY.SET which you run every Friday afternoon to do a complete backup of all your data files (you probably won't back up your programs). To use this backup file, you would type the following:

```
C:\>msbackup friday
```

This will load the backup set FRIDAY into MSBACKUP, but you'll have to select the Backup option before MSBACKUP will actually start backing up your files.

See also

ATTRIB	You can use this command to turn on (or off) the archive bit for files.
COPY	Copies a file or set of files. This command can be used to copy a few files to a floppy disk for safe-keeping.

REPLACE   You can use this command to copy more recent files to another disk, which you could use for a simple backup system.

XCOPY   This command allows you to copy files in directories and subdirectories. You could use it to copy files to a floppy disk for a simple backup system. XCOPY can also alter a file's archive flag.

MSCDEX   DOS 6 and later, External

Assigns drive letter to CD-ROM

This program allows you to use CD-ROM drives with DOS. Once the device driver for your particular CD-ROM drive has been installed, this command allows you to assign a drive letter to your CD-ROM drive.

When and why

You'll need this command if you have a CD-ROM drive that you want to use. If you used a setup program to install the software for your CD-ROM drive, chances are this command will already be in your AUTOEXEC.BAT file. Using this command will allow you to view and work with the files on your CD-ROM drive, except that you won't be able to write to this drive.

CD-ROMs give you access to large amounts of information. Accessing that information requires a special device for reading CD-ROMs (often called a CD-ROM drive or player). The first step in using such information is to install the appropriate device driver for your particular CD-ROM drive. Once this device driver is installed, you can access CD-ROMs only from programs that recognize this device driver. However, if the CD-ROM contains programs or files that are meant for use from DOS, you must assign a drive letter to the CD-ROM player. The MSCDEX program does just that.

Most programs today that use CD-ROMs use drive letters created by MSCDEX to read from the CD-ROM, so if you use any CD-ROMs, the chances are fairly good that you'll need to use MSCDEX.

Syntax
    mscdex **/d:***driver* [**/d:***driver2*...] [**/e**] [**/k**] [**/s**] [**/v**] [**/l:***letter*] [**/m:***number*]
    Associates a drive letter with a CD-ROM drive.

Parameters
    driver, driver2
    Name of the device. When you load a CD-ROM's device driver (with DEVICE or DEVICEHIGH in your CONFIG.SYS file), you'll need to use /D followed by a name to give your device driver a name. You'll need to use this same exact name in the MSCDEX command /D switch. See the examples for how this works with a real CD-ROM drive.

Switches

/e
Expanded memory. This switch tells MSCDEX to load its sector buffers (see /M) into expanded memory, if available. Normally, the sector buffers are loaded into conventional memory.

/k
Kanji. This switch tells MSCDEX to recognize CD-ROMs encoded in Kanji, which is an alphabet used in Japan. By default, MSCDEX will not recognize such disks.

/s
Share disk. Enables sharing of CD-ROM drives on MS-NET or Windows for Workgroups servers. You must supply this switch if you want others to be able to read a CD-ROM drive attached to a computer acting as a server.

/v
Verbose. Directs MSCDEX to display memory statistics when it starts.

/l:*letter*
First drive letter. This is the drive letter that you want MSCDEX to assign to the first CD-ROM drive. Additional drives will receive drive letters after this letter. Drive letters are assigned in the same order as the /D switches. (Default is first available drive letter.)

/m:*number*
Memory buffers. Specifies the number of sector buffers. More sector buffers can increase the performance of your CD-ROM drive, but they also consume more memory.

Notes

Using the most recent version

You should use whatever version of MSCDEX that you have. The way you can tell which version is most recent is to look at the date and time on the MSCDEX.EXE file. Then in your AUTOEXEC.BAT file, you can add the path in front of MSCDEX so it points to the location with the most recent version.

Availability of drive letters

You'll need to make sure you have LASTDRIVE set high enough so you have a drive letter free for use by MSCDEX.

Many other devices and utilities (such as DoubleSpace) also require drive letters. In addition, most networks require assigning drive letters for accessing information on remote volumes. You may need to carefully plan the use of your drive letters and, in extreme cases, may need to use the multiple configurations in your CONFIG.SYS file to control which devices are active.

SmartDrive and CD-ROM drives

If you're using DOS 6.2 or later, SmartDrive (version 5.0 or later of SMARTDRV.EXE) *does* provide caching for CD-ROM drives, which in general is better to use than MSCDEX's /M cache because SmartDrive's cache can be in extended memory.

If you want SmartDrive to be able to cache CD-ROM drives, you must make sure that you load SMARTDRV after you load MSCDEX. For example, you might have the following lines in your AUTOEXEC.BAT file:

```
mscdex /d:sony_000
smartdrv.exe
```

Before DOS 6.2 (SMARTDRV versions before 5.0), SMARTDRV did *not* provide a cache for CD-ROM drives, so if you're using an older version of SMARTDRV you'll have to rely on the cache provided by MSCDEX's /M switch. Unfortunately, you can't place these sector buffers into extended memory — they can only be in conventional or expanded memory.

Examples

Using a CD-ROM device

The first step in accessing a CD-ROM is to load the device driver in the CONFIG.SYS file using a statement such as:

```
devicehigh=\cdrom\cdrdrv.sys /d:romsys
```

The /D switch on the device driver provides the device name that must be used on the MSCDEX command line. To assign this drive as drive K, use the command

```
C:\>mscdex /d:romsys /l:k
```

You can either place this command into your AUTOEXEC.BAT file or execute it from the command line. You should not attempt to associate a drive once Windows has been started on your system.

Using an NEC CDR-74

This is a real example, taken from one of our computers that has an NEC CDR-74 CD-ROM drive attached to it. The following line appears in the CONFIG.SYS file to load NEC's device driver into memory, with the device name NECCD:

```
device=c:\prog\nec\neccdr.sys /d:neccd
lastdrive=k
```

The LASTDRIVE line ensures that you have enough drive letters so MSCDEX will have one available to it (and a few left over in this example). Here is the line that loads MSCDEX and assigns drive G to the CD-ROM drive:

```
mscdex.exe /s /d:neccd /l:g /m:10
```

You'll notice that the name after the /D switch is identical in both lines, as it must be. The /S switch allows other people in the office to share this CD-ROM drive, courtesy of Windows for Workgroups. And the /M switch adds some extra buffers to speed up access to the CD-ROM drive (they're usually pretty slow).

See also

LASTDRIVE   You may need to use this command to allocate some additional drive letters for MSCDEX.

MENUITEM   Describes the creation of multiple configuration menus.

MSD
DOS 6 and later, External

Miscrosoft System Diagnostics
Records the configuration of your system for use in tracking down and troubleshooting problems.

When and why
This is a program you probably won't need, but it can be very useful. At its simplest level, it provides information on your computer, such as the type of microprocessor in your computer, how much memory you have, and so on. But it can also be a very useful, although somewhat technical, troubleshooting tool. For example, if you call Microsoft for help with DOS, they may ask you to run this program and report what you see on the screen.

MSD also performs some simple consistency checks on your computer. For example, if you have your TEMP environment variable set to a drive or directory that doesn't exist, MSD will display a dialog box warning you of this problem.

Syntax
msd [/b] [/i]
Runs this full-screen version of MSD.

msd [/i] /f*filename* | /p*filename* | /s[*filename*]
Generate an MSD report.

Parameters
filename
Report file. This is the name of the file you want MSD to use when it saves a report on how your computer is set up.

Switches
/i
Turn off hardware detection. Use this switch only if you are having problems starting MSD. This turns off MSD's automatic hardware detection. When you start the full-screen program, you can then select the options one at a time (by typing the highlighted letter in one of the buttons) to see where the problem is.

/b
Black and white. Tells MSD to use a black-and-white display rather than color. You might need to use this on some computers, such as laptops, to make the screen readable.

/f*filename*
Full report. Tells MSD to write a full report to *filename*. This report includes information used to identify your computer, and you'll generally use it to send a report to a technical support line. MSD will prompt you for some extra information including your name, company name, address, and phone number.

MSD

/p*filename*
Partial report. Includes all of the detailed system information, but none of the identifying information, from a full report.

/s[*filename*]
Summary report. Provides a quick listing of your system configuration. You may direct this report to the screen by omitting a filename.

Notes

Quitting MSD
To exit from MSD's full-screen display, simply press F3 (or select Exit from the File menu).

MSD's menus
MSD has three menus in a menu bar at the top of the screen. You pull down these menus either by clicking on a menu with the mouse, or by pressing the Alt key and then using the cursor keys and Enter.

The File menu, in particular, will show you information on a number of files that control your computer. For example, if you're using DoubleSpace to compress your hard disk, MSD will allow you to view the hidden DBLSPACE.INI file. The Utilities menu provides two options for looking into memory, which can be quite interesting.

MSD's buttons
Here is a brief discussion of what additional information you can find out by selecting each of MSD's buttons. You'll see these buttons when you run MSD as a full-screen program, and you can select any of these buttons by typing the letter that's highlighted in red on a color display, or in black with the /B switch.

Computer. . . (Press **p**). Displays a dialog box showing detailed information about your computer.

Memory. . . (Press **m**). Displays a dialog box with lots and lots of information on your memory. It shows a map of the upper memory area, between 640K and 1MB, as well as a table with lots of information on your memory.

Video. . . (Press **v**). Displays a dialog box with information about your display adapter. If you're wondering if your VGA card is a SuperVGA card that follows the VESA standard (which most graphics programs know how to work with), this dialog box will tell you.

Network. . . (Press **n**). Displays information about your network, if you're computer is connected to a network.

OS Version. . . (Press **o**). This dialog box will tell you which version of DOS and Windows you have on your computer, and it also shows you the settings of all your environment variables (see the SET command for a discussion of environment variables).

Mouse. . . (Press **u**). Use this dialog box to see the settings currently in use for your mouse. The MOUSE program can change these settings, but it doesn't display them. See the description of the MOUSE command for more details on mouse settings.

Other Adapters... (Press **a**). Displays information on other adapters, such as a Game Adapter, that you might have installed in your computer.

Disk Drives... (Press **d**). Displays detailed technical information on your disk drives, including the bytes per sector and the number of sectors per track. It will also tell you the current setting of LASTDRIVE, and whether or not you have SHARE installed (you should if you're using Windows or the DOS Task Swapper).

LPT Ports... (Press **l**). Displays information about your parallel printer ports, including the I/O ports.

COM Ports... (Press **c**). Displays the current settings for your COM ports, as well as the I/O address.

IRQ Status... (Press **q**). This is the information you might need if you're about to install a new card into your computer. It will tell you which hardware interrupts are being used and what they're being used by. You can usually use this display to identify hardware interrupts that are available for use by an add-in board, such as a network card.

TSR Programs... (Press **t**). Tells you what programs are memory-resident, how large they are, where they're stored, and what command line they received.

Device Drivers... (Press **r**). Shows you what device drivers you have loaded into memory. This display contains a lot of technical information that only a programmer would understand.

Examples

Generating a summary report

The command to generate a summary report to the screen is

```
C:\>msd /s
```

The output for one of our systems was

```
      Computer: American Megatrend, 486DX
        Memory: 640K, 4096K Ext, 1024K XMS
         Video: VGA, Quadtel
       Network: No Network
    OS Version: MS-DOS Version 6.00, Windows 3.10
         Mouse: Serial Mouse 8.20
Other Adapters: Game Adapter
   Disk Drives: A: B: C: H:
     LPT Ports: 1
     COM Ports: 2
```

This information can be extremely useful when talking to a technical support person about your system configuration. The information provided by the /P switch on the same system produced a 19-page report.

See also
MEM   This command provides information about the memory usage of your system.

MSHERC   DOS 5 only, External

Support for Hercules graphics card
This command installs support for the Hercules graphics card when running QBasic programs.

When and why
You only need to use this command if your video card is a Hercules graphics card and if you are running QBasic programs. The Hercules cards were a very early standard and are no longer sold. Most modern computers have a VGA or SVGA card.

Syntax
msherc [/half]
Installs support for the Hercules card.

Switches
/half
Shared support. Use this switch if you are also using a color graphics adapter (such as a VGA) on your computer.

MWAV   DOS 6 and later, External

Anti-Virus for Windows
This is a Windows program (as opposed to the DOS MSAV) that will scan your memory and disks for viruses. It can also remove viruses that it finds.

When and why
Whenever you get a new disk or program from a perhaps dubious source (many bulletin boards, for example), you should use this program or the DOS equivalent (MSAV) to make sure the disk and/or programs don't contain a virus. You'll want to do this before you use the disk or programs. You might also want to load VSAFE into memory to protect against viruses in case you forget to run MWAV on new programs before you run them.

Computer viruses are like human viruses — they can make your computer sick, which could mean losing some of your files and data. This program will scan for and remove viruses from your computer, even if they're dormant.

If you are a Windows user, this is one of three new DOS 6 utilities that SETUP may have installed in the Microsoft Tools group in the Program Manager. If you didn't install these programs, you can run SETUP /E to install them at any time.

Syntax
You can either double-click on the Anti-Virus icon in the Microsoft Tools group in the Program manager, or you can click on the File menu and select **Run...** to display the Run dialog box and then enter **MWAV**.

Notes
The Tools menu
The SETUP program will add a Tools menu to the File Manager in Windows 3.1 and later. You can directly launch the Windows Backup and Anti-Virus programs from this window.

What files MWAV checks
Unless you've asked MWAV to check all your files, it normally checks only program files, which it defines as any file with the following extensions: EXE, COM, OV*, SYS, BIN, APP, CMD, PGM, PRG, DRV, DLL, 386, FON, ICO, or PIF. The DOS version, MSAV, has a much shorter list of extensions that it scans.

Note: If you have Windows installed on your computer, you should use MWAV instead because it scans Windows-specific files (such as DLLs) for viruses, whereas MSAV does not.

Checklist files
Normally, MWAV saves a special file called CHKLIST.MS in each directory that it scans. This file contains a list of checksum values for each program (COM, EXE, SYS, etc.) stored in that directory. It contains information about each file's size, attributes, date, time, and a checklist. This file helps MWAV determine when a new type of virus that MWAV doesn't know about infects one of your files.

MWAV creates the checklist files only if you have that option set. By default, MWAV creates checklist files on hard disks but not on floppy disks.

Deleting checklist files
To delete all the checklist files on a disk, first select the disk and then select the Delete CHKLIST files command from the **S**can menu.

Using Windows and DOS
If you use both the Windows and the DOS programs (MWAV and MSAV), you should be aware that they each have their own settings files (MWAV.INI and MSAV.INI). So any options that you change in one program will not appear in the other program.

See also
MSAV	The DOS anti-virus program.
VSafe	The memory-resident program (TSR) used to scan for new viruses and virus activity.

MWAVTSR DOS 6 and later, External

VSafe Manager

This Windows 3.1 program allows the VSAFE virus-detection program to display warning messages when you're running Windows. You must install VSAFE in DOS before you start Windows.

When and why
If you're using VSAFE and Windows 3.1, you'll want to run this program whenever you start Windows. MWAVTSR allows VSAFE to display its error messages while Windows is running. If you don't use this program (which you can't with Windows 3.0), VSAFE won't be able to display warning messages as long as you're running Windows programs.

You can also use this program to change the current settings used by VSAFE. These changes will remain in effect until either you restart your computer or you unload VSAFE from DOS.

See also
- MSAV — The DOS anti-virus program that scans all your files looking for dormant viruses.
- MWAV — The Windows anti-virus program that scans all your files looking for dormant viruses.
- VSafe — The memory-resident program (TSR) used to scan for new viruses and virus activity as you run your programs.

MWBACKUP DOS 6 and later, External

Microsoft Backup for Windows

This command allows you to back up an entire hard disk to a set of floppy disks, even when you have some files that are too large to fit on a single floppy disk. MWBACKUP automatically splits large files between multiple floppy disks. It can do this because it also saves information on the floppy disks that tells MWBACKUP how to reconstruct files and where they should be restored to.

When and why
Microsoft Backup is a very powerful, full-screen program that gives you a lot of control over what files you back up. If you do any real work on your computer, you should be using this program or a commercial backup program to back up your work regularly. And you should keep backup copies of your work at a different location, in case everything is destroyed by a fire or other disaster. If you don't back up your computer and something goes wrong, you might not be able to recover your work. So back up your data!

Syntax
msbackup [/m] [*setup-file*]

Parameters
setup-file
Setup file to load. The name of the setup file you want to load into MWBACKUP (it won't start to back up until you press the Start Backup button). A setup file includes information about the files to be included in the backup, the type of backup to perform, and the settings of all the backup options. This simplifies, but does not completely automate, the backup process. You create such setup files using MWBACKUP (use the Save, and all backup sets have the extension SET).

Switches
/m
Minimize. This switch tells MWBACKUP to run as a minimized program, which we don't think is a good idea since it will take over your computer for a while as it scans your hard disk.

Notes

The File Manager Tools menu
The SETUP program will add a Tools menu to the File Manager in Windows 3.1 and later. You can directly launch the Windows Backup and Anti-Virus programs from this menu.

Setup files
Microsoft Backup's design is centered around setup files, which contain information on all the files you want to back up, the type of backup (full, incremental, or differential), and other options. To create new setup files, choose the files and options you want and then select Save Setup As... from the File menu. You can also type in a long description of the setup file, which will help you identify setup files if you have several of them.

Types of backup
MWBACKUP offers three different types of backup: full, incremental, and differential. In this note we explain what these terms mean.

Full backup. This type of backup will back up all the files in your backup set, even if they haven't changed since the last backup. You should perform a full backup of your data periodically. For daily backups, you'll probably want to do an incremental backup. Full backups turn off the archive attribute for all files you back up.

Incremental backup. An incremental backup backs up only those files in your backup set that have changed or are new since the last time you did either a full or incremental backup. This is probably the best type of backup to perform between full backups. MWBACKUP uses the archive attribute to tell which files have been modified since the last time you did a backup. Incremental backups turn off the archive attribute for all files you back up.

Differential backup. Different backups back up all files that you've changed since the last time you did a *full* backup. This option does not turn off the archive attribute.

Using the MWBACKUP.INI file

If you use the MWBACKUP.INI file to save settings, there are two places where you can store this file. First, you can put it into the same directory as MWBACKUP.EXE. If you're working on a network, however, and MWBACKUP.EXE is on a network drive, you might prefer to have your own private copy of MWBACKUP.INI instead. In this case you will want to set the MSDOSDATA environment variable so it tells MSAV where to find your MWBACKUP.INI file. For example, to tell MWBACKUP to use your own DOS directory (let's say MWBACKUP.EXE is on drive G), you would use this line in your AUTOEXEC.BAT file:

```
set msdosdata=c:\dos
```

Backup catalogs

Whenever you back up files on your computer, MWBACKUP creates a catalog that lists all the files MWBACKUP backed up for you. The sole purpose of catalog files is to make it easier for you and MWBACKUP to restore a file at some time in the future. When you ask to restore a file, MWBACKUP will display a restore dialog box, with the catalog for your last backup selected. You can select a different catalog or retrieve a catalog from your backup floppy disks. In any event, once you select a backup set, MWBACKUP will allow you to select which files you want to restore. You'll see the full directory of your hard disks as it existed when you backed up your computers. But the only files that will be visible are the ones you backed up. Catalogs make this all possible.

There are also two types of catalogs: Master catalogs and backup-set catalogs. The master catalog contains information from the last full backup, plus all incremental and differential backups, whereas the backup-set catalogs contain information on what files were backed up during a single backup session. What this means is that you can select a master catalog when you want to restore files, and MWBACKUP will tell you which backup set of disks you'll have to insert. As long as you're consistent about which backup set you use, then you won't need to remember the name of the last catalog MWBACKUP created.

Note: Make sure you label all the disks in your backup sets with the name of the catalog, since this is how MWBACKUP will ask for backup disks when you restore files. You'll find the catalog name in the Backup Set Information of the backup screen.

How MWBACKUP names catalog files

One sticky point about catalogs is that the names may appear to be somewhat cryptic. That's because MWBACKUP actually encodes quite a bit of information into the name, and you can use this information to figure out which catalog you want to use. For example, you can tell a lot from the following name:

```
CD30323A.FUL
```

Part II: Command Reference

This says that you backed up drives C through D on March 23, 1993, and it was a full backup. Here is a table that shows you how to decode catalog names:

Characters	Example	Meaning
1	C	First drive letter you backed up in this catalog. C: in this example.
1	D	Last drive letter that you backed up in this catalog. This will be the same as the first character if you only backed up one drive letter. D: in this example.
1	3	The last digit of the year, which is 1993 in this example.
2	03	The month that you backed up these files. March in this example.
2	23	The day of the month that you created this backup set. The 23rd in this example.
1	A	The sequence letter. This will have a value other than A only if you backed up more than once on the same day, and it keeps track of which backup you did first.
Extension	FUL	The type of backup. This can be FUL (full backup), INC (incremental backup), or DIF (differential backup).

See also

ATTRIB	You can use this command to turn on (or off) the archive bit for files.
COPY	Copies a file or set of files. This command can be used to copy a few files to a floppy disk for safe-keeping.
MSBACKUP	This is the DOS version of Backup.
REPLACE	You can use this command to copy more recent files to another disk, which you could use for a simple backup system.
XCOPY	This command allows you to copy files in directories and subdirectories. You could use it to copy files to a floppy disk for a simple backup system. XCOPY can also alter a file's archive flag.

MWUNDEL   DOS 6 and later, External

Undelete for Windows

This program allows you to recover files that you deleted by accident and provides features similar, although easier to use, than the DOS UNDELETE program. Use this program, rather than UNDELETE, to recover files while you're running Windows. *Note:* Do not use the DOS UNDELETE command from a DOS window.

MWUNDEL

When and why

If you delete a file by accident while you're running Windows, you should run this program immediately. This program will allow you to recover a file, or group of files, that you deleted by accident. However, if you don't run this program right away, other files may use the space freed when you delete the file or files.

If you use Windows, this is the way to recover a file that you deleted by accident. It provides a graphical interface that allows you to select which file you want to delete. If you're using Windows 3.1, SETUP probably added the Undelete command to the File menu in the File Manager. You'll also find an Undelete icon in the Microsoft Tools program group in the Program Manager.

Notes

The Windows Undelete program can be rather complicated to use, especially with the interactions with the memory-resident part of UNDELETE when you're using Delete Sentry or Delete Tracker.

Using MWUNDEL with the File Manager

The SETUP program will add an Undelete... item to the File menu in the File Manager in Windows 3.1 and later. You can directly launch the Windows Undelete program from this menu.

Order of Sentry files

If you're using the Delete Sentry option of UNDELETE, you'll notice that any of these files that you delete appear at the end of MWUNDEL's list of deleted files. So before you despair that DOS has forgotten about the files you just deleted, scroll through the list of deleted files to see if your files are perhaps at the end of the list.

Setting type of delete protection

You can set the type of delete protection offered by UNDELETE by selecting Configure Delete Protection... from the Options menu. Any changes you make will apply in both DOS and Windows. The actual delete protection is provided by running UNDELETE /LOAD from your AUTOEXEC.BAT file, and the options are controlled by the UNDELETE.INI file. You can also use switches when you load the UNDELETE command, and these changes will be reflected in the UNDELETE.INI file.

Removing Delete Sentry files

When you're using the Delete Sentry feature of UNDELETE, you won't need to worry about removing files that it keeps around. UNDELETE will automatically purge files as you need more space. But if you turn off the Delete Sentry feature, UNDELETE won't purge these files automatically. In this case you may need to remove them yourself. The easiest way to remove these files is to use the /PURGE switch of UNDELETE. For example, to purge the files on drive C, you would type

```
C:\>undelete /purgec
```

The last letter is the drive letter on which you want UNDELETE to remove all your sentry files. You can only purge the files from one drive at a time.

When you run this command, UNDELETE will also delete the hidden \SENTRY directory.

Undeleting directories

If you accidentally delete a directory, using DELTREE for example, retrieving your files may not be as simple as you would hope. First of all, you must use the MWUNDEL program — the DOS UNDELETE program cannot undelete directories. There are some strange quirks about how MWUNDEL works when you undelete a directory, which we've tried to explain as best as we can. How MWUNDEL undeletes a directory, and how well it does, actually depends on whether or not you've installed any type of tracking using the memory-resident part of UNDELETE.

There are three types of delete tracking, and we'll explain how to use MWUNDEL to recover deleted directories for each type of tracking.

Standard, no delete tracking. The standard form of delete tracking gains no help from UNDELETE and relies solely on DOS's method for deleting files, which sets the first character in the directory name to a special character and releases the allocation units that were being used by the directory. MWUNDEL usually allows you to recover directories that you deleted by accident, although you'll need to supply the missing first letter. However, you may or may not be able to recover the files inside that directory. We had a lot of problems doing so.

Delete Tracker (UNDELETE /T). When you have UNDELETE loaded with the Delete tracking option turned on, UNDELETE remembers the directory information whenever you delete any file or directory. This means that you can undelete a directory without having to supply the missing first letter of the name. However, you may or may not be able to recover the files inside that directory. We had a lot of problems doing so.

Delete Sentry (UNDELETE /S). This is the highest level of protection. When you use the Sentry option, UNDELETE moves the files to a special directory instead of actually deleting them, so you'll almost certainly be able to recover your files. However, UNDELETE does not save information on directories you delete, so if you delete a directory, you'll see a ? in front of its name in the MWUNDEL window, and you may not be able to undelete this directory. Fortunately, there is a simple workaround. If you can't undelete the directory, you can create a new directory with the same name as the directory you deleted. Then when you run MWUNDEL again, you'll be able to recover the files that were in the old directory with the same name.

Messages

```
There is no more deleted directory data on this disk.
```
You'll see this message when you try to undelete a directory and MWUNDEL is being uncooperative. We got this message fairly often. If you deleted your files while Delete Sentry was active on your drive, you can try to make a new directory that has the same name as the directory you deleted and then MWUNDEL to recover the files that were in this directory. For files deleted with Delete Sentry active, MWUNDEL doesn't care whether the directory is the original directory or a new directory with the same name —it can recover your files in either case.

See also

UNDELETE You can improve the chances of being able to recover a deleted file if you load the memory-resident part of UNDELETE to track files that you delete.

UNFORMAT This command is used to recover information from disks that have been formatted by mistake.

NLSFUNC   DOS 3.3 and later, External

National Language Support Function

This is a command that you run once to load it into memory. It provides support for the code-page switching functions in the CHCP and MORE CP commands.

When and why
If you're going to use code pages (see the description of CHCP for details on code pages), you'll need to install NLSFUNC. It's that simple.

Syntax
nlsfunc [*filespec*]
Loads the National Language Support Function into memory.

Parameters
filespec
Location and name of the COUNTRY.SYS file. You don't need to provide this if you've already provided the file's location in the COUNTRY= line of your CONFIG.SYS file.

Notes
NLSFUNC is loaded into memory the first time you run it. It consumes about 3K of memory.

Messages
```
NLSFUNC already installed
```
You'll see this message if you run NLSFUNC after it's already been installed.

Examples

Install in CONFIG.SYS
If you're using DOS 4.0 or later, you can install NLSFUNC from within your CONFIG.SYS file rather than running it in your AUTOEXEC.BAT file:

```
install=c:\dos\nlsfunc
```

Loading in high memory
With DOS 5 and later you can load NLSFUNC into the Upper Memory Blocks (UMBs), leaving more room in the first 640K for other programs. Type this line in your AUTOEXEC.BAT file:

```
loadhigh nlsfunc
```

See also

CHCP	Read this command first — it contains a discussion on what code pages are and how to use them. This is the command you should use to change code pages.
COUNTRY=	You need to use the COUNTRY= command in your CONFIG.SYS file to indicate where to find COUNTRY.SYS before you can switch code pages with CHCP.
DISPLAY.SYS	Supports code-page switching for the display. You'll need this if you want to change your screen's character set.
KEYB	This command allows you to configure your keyboard for a language other than U.S. English.
LOADHIGH	Loads a memory-resident program into the upper memory area. You can use this if you have an 80386 or better processor in your computer and you're using a program such as EMM386.EXE to provide an upper memory area.
MODE CP	Allows you to load code pages into memory and change between code pages. It's better, though, to use CHCP to change code pages after you've used MODE to load the code pages.
PRINTER.SYS	Supports code-page switching for some IBM printers. You'll need this if you want to change the character set on your printer.

NUMLOCK   DOS 6 and later, CONFIG.SYS

Set NumLock at startup

This command controls whether the Num Lock state is turned on or off (normally you have to press the Num Lock key to change this state).

When and why

You'll want to use this command if you don't like the state of the Num Lock light on your keyboard when DOS first starts. For example, if your computer always starts with Num Lock on, you can use this command in your CONFIG.SYS file to turn it off.

The Num Lock light and key control how the numeric keypad on your keyboard behaves. With Num Lock turned on, the keypad keys will act as number keys. When you turn Num Lock off, these keys will act as cursor control keys. Most enhanced keyboards (which have both a numeric keypad and separate cursor control keys) initially have Num Lock turned on. While older, AT-style keyboards that do not have separate numeric and cursor groups usually start with Num Lock turned off.

Syntax

numlock=on

Turns Num Lock on, which means the numbers on your numeric keypad will be active on startup.

numlock=off
Turns Num Lock off, which means the cursor keys on your numeric keypad will be active on startup.

PATH   All DOS, Internal

Define search path for programs
This command defines a list of directories DOS searches for external commands.

When and why
You'll need a PATH command in your AUTOEXEC.BAT file to tell DOS where to find commands. At a bare minimum, this command should tell DOS where to find its own external commands (usually C:\DOS).

This search path is a list of directories DOS will search when you ask it to run a command that either isn't an internal command or isn't stored in the current directory. Commands are programs with the COM or EXE extensions or batch files with the BAT extension.

Syntax
path
Displays the current search path.

path ;
Clears the search path so DOS will search for external commands only in the current directory.

path [*drive*:]*dir*;[...;]
Sets a list of directories DOS should search for commands. You can provide more than one directory; separate directories by putting a semicolon between them.

Parameters
drive:
You should include a drive letter in front of each directory in your path statement so DOS will know what drive that directory is on.

dir
A directory that DOS should search for commands.

Notes
Drive letters
Make sure your paths are absolute paths and that they include drive letters. If you don't include a drive letter, you'll discover you won't have access to your commands when you switch to another disk.

Search order
DOS has three different places it looks for commands. First, DOS looks for internal commands that match the name you typed. If it doesn't find a match there, it looks

for a command in the current directory. Failing that, DOS searches the path list, starting with the first directory in the list. It searches one directory after the other in the path list until it finds the command (or displays

```
Bad command or file name
```

if it fails to find the command anywhere).

In each directory, DOS searches first for a command with the COM extension, then for a command with the EXE extension, and finally for a command with the BAT extension. DOS looks for a command with one of these three extensions and only moves on to the next directory after its search fails. DOS will run the first program it finds during this search (even if you have another program with the same name later in the path).

Note: Prior to DOS 5, DOS ignored any file extension you typed after a command on the command line. So if you had both a batch file and a program named DOIT.BAT and DOIT.EXE, DOS would run DOIT.EXE when you typed DOIT.BAT at the command line. In current versions of DOS, you can use the extension to select between files. If you use batch files to start your applications, you should place the directory containing your batch files at the start of the path (after C:\DOS) so DOS will find your batch files before searching the rest of the path (this is for speed).

Maximum length of PATH

The PATH command cannot be longer than 127 characters. If your PATH statement is longer than this, DOS simply truncates the path. One solution if you find yourself running out of room is to use shorter names for some of your directories. For example, instead of using PROG for your programs subdirectory, use P, as in

path c:\dos;c:\p\word;...

Another, perhaps better, solution is to create batch files that launch your programs using the full pathname of your program. Most modern programs allow you to run them by supplying the full path:

C:\>**c:\prog\nc\nc**

If you create batch files, you can put all your batch files into the same directory, BELFRY (since bats live in belfries), and put this directory in your path statement. Your batch files should look something like this:

```
drive:path\program %1 %2 %3 %4 %5 %6 %7 %8 %9
```

This will launch *program* and pass it the same parameters as on the command line you supplied when you ran the batch file. Your batch file should have the same name as the program.

Examples

Minimum PATH command

At a bare minimum, your AUTOEXEC.BAT file should contain a PATH command that tells DOS where to find its external commands:

path c:\dos

More complex PATH
Here is an example that allows you to find external DOS commands, Microsoft Windows, and the Norton Commander, regardless of what directory you're currently in:

```
path c:\dos;c:\windows;c:\prog\nc
```

See also
APPEND   The APPEND command lets you build a search path for your data files, although we don't recommend you use it.

SET   The SET command also allows you to change the search path by changing the PATH environment variable.

PAUSE   All DOS, Batch file

Pause a batch file
This command pauses the running of a batch file until you press any key.

When and why
You may find this command useful when writing batch files. If you've just displayed a page of text, you can use this command to pause the output. You can also use PAUSE while you do something, such as put a floppy disk into drive A:.

When DOS encounters a PAUSE command, it displays

```
Press any key to continue . . .
```

Syntax
pause
Pauses the output of the batch file and waits for you to press any key.

Notes
Stopping a batch file
You can press Ctrl-Break or Ctrl-C to stop a batch file. DOS will then display the message

```
Terminate batch job (Y/N)?_
```

to allow you to continue running the batch file.

Note: Ctrl-Break or Ctrl-C will stop a batch file immediately (without displaying this message) if you run a batch file from within a DOS shell program (such as the Norton Commander or the DOS Shell program).

Examples

Here is a short batch file that shows how you might use the PAUSE command:

```
@echo off
echo Insert a blank disk in drive A: and
pause
format a:
```

This batch file actually displays the following output (before you press a key to continue):

```
Insert a blank disk in drive A: and
Press any key to continue . . .
```

Using a different message

If you want to use your own message, rather than the `Press any...` message, you can use the ECHO command to display a message and redirect PAUSE's output to the NUL device (which discards everything you write to it):

```
@echo off
echo Press Enter to continue...
pause >nul
```

This batch file will display the following output:

```
Press Enter to continue...
```

See also

ECHO   You can use the ECHO command to display a message just before PAUSE.

POWER   DOS 6 and later, External

Conserve power on laptop systems

To use this command, you must load the POWER.EXE device driver. The POWER command allows you to change the power management settings on a laptop computer from the command line.

When and why

You'll want to use this command, along with the POWER.EXE device driver, to conserve battery power on your laptop, which should allow your laptop to run longer between charges. Depending on what you are doing, you may want to adjust the level of power management.

Syntax

power [adv[:max|reg|min]|std|off]

Reports or sets power management levels. You must install the POWER.EXE device driver before you can use this command.

Parameters

off
: **Turns off power management.** This switch disables the power management features but leaves the POWER.EXE driver installed in memory. Some programs might run slower when you have power management turned on.

std
: **Sets standard power management.** If your computer has support for the Advanced Power Management specification (APM), this setting uses your laptop's built-in power management. If your system does not support APM, this setting is the same as off (which disables power management).

adv:max
: **Maximum power management.** Try this setting to obtain the longest battery life. Your power savings can be up to 25 percent for computers that support the Advanced Power Management specification (APM), and 5 percent for computers that don't support APM. If you experience performance problems, try the default setting (REG) or the minimum setting (MIN).

adv
adv: reg
: **Regular power management.** This setting tries to strike a balance between conserving your battery's power and reducing the performance of your computer. You can use this option if the MAX setting slows your computer down too much, or try the MIN setting if even this setting is too slow. (Default is MIN.)

adv: min
: **Minimum power management.** This setting will conserve less of your battery power, but it will speed up some programs on your computer. Use this option only if your computer (or some program) was not fast enough with the REG setting.

Notes

You must install the POWER.EXE device driver in your CONFIG.SYS file to use this feature. If your system does not support the Advanced Power Management (APM) specification, and the performance loss with adv:min is too great, you should not install the device driver. You should probably use the power management software that came with your laptop computer (almost all laptop computers have power management software). You can also buy commercial products like BatterWatch, which supports most of the popular laptop computers and provides more features than POWER.

Messages

`Power Manager (POWER.EXE) not installed.`
You'll need to install the POWER.EXE device driver in your CONFIG.SYS file before you can use POWER to change power management settings.

Examples

Using maximum power conservation

Assuming that it is not already at its maximum, you can increase the level of power management by entering

```
C:\>power adv:max
```

Part II: Command Reference

This setting stays in effect until you reboot your computer or you change it by entering the POWER command using another level of power management.

Temporarily suspending power management
To suspend power management but leave the driver installed in memory, enter

```
C:\>power off
```

This setting disables all power management features provided by POWER. You can reactivate power management by entering the POWER command with any other level of activity.

See also
POWER.EXE   The power management device driver.

POWER.EXE   DOS 6 and later, Device driver

Power management device driver
This device driver provides power management facilities for laptop computers. Power management will help your computer run longer on a single battery charge than without power management.

When and why
If you don't have a laptop, you won't need this device driver. This device driver is designed to lengthen the amount of time that you can run a laptop computer before recharging its battery. (Many laptop computers already have their own power management software, which may be better than POWER.)

If your computer does not support the Advanced Power Management (APM) specification, you'll probably get better results using the power management software that came with your laptop computer.

Syntax
device=*path***power.exe** [**adv**[**:max** | **reg** | **min**]|**std** | **off**] [**/low**]
Installs the power management device driver.

Parameters
off
Turns off power management. This switch installs the device driver with the power management features disabled. Because the driver is loaded into memory, you can use the POWER command to activate power management later.

std
Sets standard power management. If your system conforms to the Advanced Power Management specification (APM), this setting uses your laptop's built-in power management. If your system does not support APM, this setting is the same as off (power management will be disabled on installation).

POWER.EXE

adv:max
: **Maximum power management.** Try this setting to obtain the longest battery life. If you experience performance problems, try the default setting (REG).

adv
adv: reg
: **Regular power management.** This is the default setting and if your system does not support the MAX option, you should use this setting unless you experience performance problems.

adv: min
: **Minimum power management.** If you suffer performance loss with the default option, the MIN setting may allow you to obtain some power management features.

Switches

/low
: **Loads into low memory.** By default, POWER.EXE is loaded into upper memory. This switch tells POWER.EXE to load itself into lower memory.

Notes

The POWER.EXE device driver does all the power management, so you must install it in CONFIG.SYS before you can gain any benefit. Running POWER from the command line simply reconfigures how the POWER.EXE device driver controls power management. You can expect to see up to a 25 percent savings in battery power if your computer supports the Advanced Power Management (APM) specification. Otherwise, you'll only see about a 5 percent savings. Most laptop computers come with software that can do better than 5 percent in savings, so if your computer doesn't support APM, you should use your laptop's power management software rather than POWER.

Examples

To install the maximum level of power management

The following line in your CONFIG.SYS file will turn on the maximum level of power management:

    device=c:\dos\power.exe adv:max

You can change the level of power management later by using the POWER command.

Install the power management features for later use

To install the driver but not activate the power management features, you would use

    device=c:\dos\power.exe off

Upon startup, POWER will load into memory, but it won't activate any of the power management features. You can then use the POWER command to turn on power management later.

See also

POWER
: You can use the POWER command at any time to control the POWER.EXE device driver's power management.

PRINT

All DOS, External

Print files to the printer

This command allows you to print files on your printer in the background (while you run other programs).

When and why

This command allows you to print files in the background; in other words, you can run other programs while PRINT continues to send files to your printer. It does this by loading itself into memory.

The problem with PRINT is that it doesn't know anything about the different types of printers, so your printer has to be able to print text files (PostScript printers can't without a program). As a result, you may not find this command useful if you need to print other kinds of files.

Syntax

print [/**d**:*device*] [/**b**:*size*] [/**s**:*timeslice*] [/**m**:*maxticks*] [/**u**:*busyticks*] [/**q**:*qsize*] [*filespec* ...]
This is the form of the PRINT command you'll use when you first load PRINT into memory. You can't use any of these switches to change the way PRINT is set up when it is already loaded.

print [/**t**] [/**c**] [/**p**] [*filespec* ...]
Adds or removes files from the print queue. This is the form of the PRINT command you'll use after you initially load PRINT into memory.

Parameters

filespec
File to print. The name of the file(s) that you want to print. If you use the /C switch after a filename, it removes this file from the print queue. You can use the DOS * and ? wildcard characters to print a group of files.

Switches

/t
Clear queue. Removes all files from the print queue.

Note on /C and /P: The meaning of the /C and /P switches depends on their location in the command. Each /C or /P switch applies to the file immediately before the switch (if there is one) and to all files after the switch (unless they're affected by another /C or /P switch).

/c
Remove file. Removes the file(s) from the print queue. See note above for how to use the /C switch.

/p
Add file. Adds a file(s) to the print queue. See note above for how to use the /P switch.

/d:*device*
Printer (DOS 3.0 and later). The printer you want PRINT to use. This can be LPT1, LPT2, LPT3, COM1, or COM2, and for DOS 3.3 and later, COM3 or COM4. The /D switch must precede any filenames on the command line. (Default is PRN, which refers to LPT1.)

/q:*qsize*
Queue size. Sets the number of files that can be in the print queue at any one time. Valid range is 4 – 32. Default is 10.

/b:*size*
Buffer size (DOS 3.0 and later). Sets the size (in bytes) of the internal buffer PRINT uses to store data before it sends it to the printer. You'll only want to set this value if you have a very fast printer and you want PRINT to be faster. Valid range is 512 – 16,384. (Default is 512.)

/s:*timeslice*
Time slices per second (DOS 3.0 and later). Sets the number of times per second that PRINT can receive a time slice. Increasing this number speeds up PRINT but slows down other programs running in the foreground. Valid range is 1 – 255. (Default is 8.)

/m:*maxticks*
Length of time slice (DOS 3.0 and later). Sets the maximum length of time PRINT keeps control during each time slice it gets. It's a good idea to keep this number relatively low. Valid range is 1 – 255. (Default is 2.)

/u:*busyticks*
Busy time-out delay (DOS 3.0 and later). Sets the time-out delay (in clock ticks) for PRINT to wait for the printer to be available before giving up its time slice (PRINT will try again later). You'll generally want to keep this number low. Valid range is 1 – 255. (Default is 1.)

Notes

There are a few things the PRINT command does that can affect how it works. First, since it assumes you're printing text files, it expands tabs into spaces (PRINT assumes tab stops are every eight characters, which is what the TYPE command also assumes). Second, PRINT looks for end-of-file characters (ASCII code 26) and stops printing as soon as it sees one. If you use PRINT to send a nontext file to your printer, it won't print the entire file if there is an end-of-file character.

Memory used

With the default settings, PRINT uses about 5.5K of memory.

Warning! You should not rename, move, delete, or change a file in any way between the time you place it in the queue and it finishes printing. This is because PRINT works directly with the contents of the file on your disk — it doesn't save a copy.

Clock ticks

The system clock (this is not the same as your CPU's clock speed) inside your computer ticks 18.2 times every second, so a clock tick is about 0.05 seconds.

Time slices

PRINT works in the background by using time slices. These are periods of time during which PRINT takes control from the foreground application (whatever other program you're running). The three switches /M, /U, and /S control how PRINT uses time slices.

There is a small piece of code inside PRINT called a scheduler, which DOS calls at least 18.2 times every second (it can be more often at the DOS prompt or within cooperative programs). This scheduler determines when, and for how long, it should turn control over to the part of PRINT that actually sends characters to the printer.

The /S switch tells PRINT how many times per second it can take control, which it needs to do before it can send any characters to the printer. Each time PRINT takes control (to try to send characters to the printer), one of two things can happen. The printer can be ready to accept characters, in which case PRINT sends characters to the printer until it's used up its maximum time for a time slice (set by the /M switch). And finally, if the printer is busy and can't accept characters, the /U switch determines how long PRINT waits before it gives up its time slice and returns control to the foreground program.

Messages

```
Errors on list device indicate that it
may be off-line. Please check it.
```
You'll see this error message when you don't have a printer attached, the printer isn't turned on, or your printer is not set on-line (which allows it to accept output from your computer).

```
Pathname too long
```
You'll see this message when the full pathname on a file (including the drive letter and \ at the front and the filename at the end) is longer than 63 characters.

```
PRINT queue is empty
```
You'll see this message when there are no files waiting to be printed.

Examples

If you use PRINT often, you might want to load it during your boot process, which you can do by running PRINT from your AUTOEXEC.BAT file. The following command loads PRINT into memory and tells it to print to a serial printer on COM1:

> **print /d:com1**

You can then add a file to the print queue with a command such as this:

> C:\>**print readme.txt**

See also

MODE COM   You can use this command to set up a serial port, which you'll need to do before you print to a printer attached to your serial port.

PRINTER.SYS   DOS 3.3–5, Device driver

Printer code-page device driver
This device driver provides support for code-page switching, which allows you to use alternate character sets on some IBM printers to support languages other than U.S. English.

When and why
Unless you have an IBM printer listed in the "Parameters" section, you won't find a use for this command.

Note: This command was dropped in DOS 6.

Syntax
device=[*path*]**printer.sys lpt***x*=(*type* [,*hw-cp*] [,*n*])
This line in your CONFIG.SYS file loads the printer device driver.

Parameters
path
Path to driver. You'll want to provide a path to the PRINTER.SYS device driver. This path will usually be C:\DOS.

lpt*x*
Printer Port. Which printer port the printer is attached to. *X* can be between 1 and 3.

type
Printer type. The type of printer for which you want to support code-page switching. It can be one of the following:

Type	Printer
4201	IBM Proprinters II and III Model 4201
	IBM Proprinters II and III XL Model 4202
4208	IBM Proprinter X24E Model 4207
	IBM Proprinter XL24E Model 4208
5202	IBM Quietwriter III Model 5202

hw-cp
Hardware code page. This tells the display driver what the default hardware code page is. It can be one of the following (when in doubt, leave out this parameter):

- 437   United States
- 850   Multilingual (Latin I)
- 852   Slavic (Latin II)
- 860   Portuguese
- 863   Canadian-French
- 865   Nordic

n
Pages supported. Number of code pages the device can support in addition to the primary code page. Valid range is 0 – 6 (although for LCD the maximum is 1, and it is 0 for CGA and monochrome).

Notes

PRINTER.SYS is a device driver that is loaded into memory when DOS starts. See the description of the CHCP command for a discussion of code pages and how to use them.

Memory usage

PRINTER.SYS uses about 11K of memory when it's installed.

Examples

This is the command that you'll probably use for code-page switching on a Model 4208 Proprinter:

```
device=c:\dos\printer.sys lpt1=(4208,850,2)
```

See also

CHCP	Read this command first — it contains a discussion on code pages and how to use them. Sets the active code page. You'll need to use this command if you use a code page different from your hardware's default.
DEVICEHIGH	Loads a device driver into the upper memory area. You can use this if you have an 80386 or better processor in your computer and you're using a program such as EMM386.EXE to provide an upper memory area.
DISPLAY.SYS	Supports code-page switching for the display. You'll need this if you want to change the character set used on your display.
KEYB	Allows you to change the mapping of the keyboard for computers with country-specific keyboards. In Germany, for example, the Z and Y keys are swapped so the Z is between the T and U keys.
MODE CP	Allows you to load code pages into memory and change between code pages. It's better, though, to use CHCP to change code pages after you've used MODE to load the code page.
NLSFUNC	Allows you to change the code page for more than one device (such as the keyboard and the display) at the same time. You'll want to install this before you use CHCP to set the active code page.

PROMPT
All DOS, Internal

Set the command-line prompt

This command allows you to customize the command line's prompt.

When and why

Most people like to set their prompt to PG, which displays the current directory followed by a > sign. Putting the PROMPT PG command in your AUTOEXEC.BAT file will do this for you.

Syntax

prompt
Sets the command-line prompt back to the default, which is the drive letter followed by a greater-than sign (for example, C>).

prompt *text*
Sets the command-line prompt to *text*.

Parameters

text
Prompt text. The command-line prompt that you want to use. This can be any text, and it can also include some special characters (see "Notes" section for a table).

Notes

Special $ parameters

There are a number of $ parameters that you can include in a prompt to insert special characters or text. The following table shows what you can insert:

Characters	Example	Description
$q	=	Equal sign.
$$	$	Dollar sign.
$t	12:14:08.92	Displays the current DOS time. (*Note:* The time is not updated as the time changes.)
$d	Tue 07-09-1991	Displays the current DOS date.
$p	C:\DOS	The current directory.
$v	MS-DOS Version 6.00	Shows DOS version number.
$n	C	Displays current drive letter.
$g	>	Greater-than sign.
$l	<	Less-than sign.
$b	|	Vertical bar (pipe) character.

Characters	Description
$_	Advances to start of the next line (allowing multiline prompts).
$e	Esc character — generates escape sequences for the ANSI.SYS functions.
$h	Backspace — moves the cursor left, erasing one character in the process.

Date and time

When you insert the date and time into a prompt, they won't be updated after they've been displayed. In other words, you'll have to press Enter to display a new prompt when you want to see the current date and time.

Path prompt and empty floppy drives

DOS reads the disk before it displays a path ($P), which will slow down the display of the prompt on floppy disks. If there is no floppy disk in the drive, you'll see the following message:

```
Not ready reading drive A
Abort, Retry, Fail?_
```

You'll need to choose the FAIL option (type **F**) to get rid of this error message and display the DOS prompt, which will change to

```
Current drive is no longer valid>_
```

Prompt in Windows 3.1

If you're using Windows 3.1, you can have a different prompt appear whenever you run a DOS prompt from inside Windows (you'll need to set this up before you start Windows). To set the prompt for DOS boxes in Windows 3.1, you use the WINPMT environment variable. For example, you can put the following line in your AUTOEXEC.BAT file:

set winpmt=Win: pg

Then when you start a DOS box from inside Windows 3.1, you'll see this prompt:

```
Win: C:\>_
```

Using a special prompt like this will tell you when you're actually inside Windows rather than running DOS by itself. You'll want to know this before you turn off your computer, in case you have any Windows programs running with files that you haven't saved yet.

Examples

Standard path prompt

Most people like to display both the current drive letter and the current path. Here is the PROMPT command that sets up such a prompt:

```
C:\>prompt $p$g
C:\TEST>_
```

This examples assumes that you are in a subdirectory called TEST when you change your prompt.

Using backspace

Here is an example that shows how you'd use the $H backspace character. The time display shows both the seconds and the hundredths of a second. Since this time display isn't updated after it's displayed, you might want to display just the hour and minutes. The $H command allows you to erase the seconds part. Here is such a prompt, along with a sample of its output:

```
C:\>prompt $t$h$h$h$h$h$h  $p$g
7:15 C:\TEST>_
```

Using ANSI.SYS

This example shows how to use the ANSI.SYS to display a status line at the top of your screen showing the date and time in inverse video:

prompt $e[s$e[0;0H$e[7m$d thhhhh$h $e[K$e[m$e[u$p$g

As you can see, there are a number of $e escape sequences, which we'll cover very briefly here. (They are covered in more detail in the ANSI.SYS entry.) First, the $e[s saves the position of the cursor, which we restore at the very end with $e[u just before we display a regular path prompt. Next, we move the cursor to the top of the screen with $e[0;0H and set the color to inverse video, using $e[7m. We then display the date and time (removing the seconds). And finally, we clear the rest of this line with $e[K, set the color back to normal, $e[m, and move the cursor back to where it was.

See also
ANSI.SYS   This device driver provides a number of escape sequences that you can use to control your display.

SET   You can also set the PROMPT environment variable using the SET command. And you can set the WINPMT environment variable to control the DOS prompt when Windows is running.

QBASIC DOS 5 and later, External
Quick Basic programming system

This command starts the Quick Basic editor and interpreter. Since you can fill an entire book describing Quick Basic, we're only going to describe the syntax of the QBASIC command. You'll need to check your DOS manual, or another book, for full details on the Quick Basic language and system. Press F1 inside QBASIC to obtain on-line help.

When and why
QBASIC is a programming language and development system that comes free with DOS. It is based on the Quick Basic programming language and system sold by Microsoft. Earlier versions of DOS contained either BASICA or GW-BASIC, which are much less capable than QBASIC.

If you want to learn how to use QBASIC, we suggest you buy a book about QBASIC programming.

Syntax
qbasic [**/b**] [**/editor** [*filespec*]] [**/g**] [**/h**] [**/mbf**] [**/run** *filespec*] [**/nohi**]
Starts Quick Basic.

Parameters
filespec
File to load. The name of the BAS (basic's extension) file you want to load or run. (If you use the /EDITOR switch, this file can be any text file.)

Switches
/b
Black and white. Uses black and white rather than colors. This option is useful on laptop computers with EGA screens that display colors as shades of gray (which can be hard to read).

/editor [*filespec*]
Editor only. Launches the editor part of QBASIC. This is equivalent to running the EDIT command. You cannot use this switch with the /RUN switch.

Part II: Command Reference

/g
Fast CGA display. For a CGA display adapter, uses fast screen writing. Older computers that used a CGA card based on IBM's design display "snow" when you write quickly to the screen, so most programs slow down on CGA screens. You can try this switch to see if it improves screen output speed.

/h
High resolution. Uses as many lines as possible: 43 lines on an EGA display and 50 lines on a VGA display adapter.

/mbf
Converts the built-in Basic functions MKS$, MKD$, CVS, and CVD to MKSMBF$, MKDMBF$, CVSMBF, and CVDMBF, respectively.

/nohi
Eight colors. Only uses 8 colors on the screen rather than 16. This is useful for displays that don't support 16 colors (most do). You'll need to use this switch if you don't see the menu and item shortcut keys highlighted.

/run *filespec*
Run program. Runs the Basic program *filespec* immediately after loading QBASIC. A filename is required after the /RUN switch. You may not use this command with the /EDITOR switch.

RAMDRIVE.SYS   DOS 3.2 and later, Device driver

RAM disk device driver

This program allows you to turn some of your memory (conventional, extended, or expanded) into a virtual disk drive, which is called a RAM disk. In earlier versions of DOS, this program was called VDISK.SYS.

When and why

A RAM disk is an area of memory that's made to look like a disk drive. Since it's located in memory and has no moving parts, a RAM disk is extremely fast. On the other hand, anything you write to a RAM disk will be erased whenever you restart your computer or turn it off. As such, you shouldn't put valuable data into a RAM disk.

A RAM disk can be very useful if you have some expanded or extended memory to spare, and you have some files you want quick access to that rarely change. For example, we like to put the Norton Commander into a RAM disk so it reloads almost instantaneously whenever DOS finishes running a command. If, on the other hand, you want to speed up access to all files, you're better off using a disk cache such as SMARTDRV.EXE.

Syntax

device=[*path*]**ramdrive.sys** [*size* [*sector* [*entries*]]] [/**e** | /**a**]
Loads the device driver that creates a RAM disk.

Parameters

path
Path to driver. You'll want to provide a path to the RAMDRIVE.SYS device driver. This path will usually be C:\DOS.

size
RAM drive size. The size (in kilobytes) of the RAM drive you want to create. Valid range is 16 – 4,096. (VDISK range is 1 to all of memory.) (Default is 64.)

sector
Sector size. The size you want to use for sectors in your RAM disk. We suggest you don't change this value from the default of 512 unless you have a very good reason. Valid values are 128, 256, and 512. (Default is 512 [128 for VDISK].)

entries
Root directory entries. The number of directory entries (files and directories) that can be in the root directory of your RAM disk. Rounds the number of entries up to the nearest multiple of entries that fit into a sector. You might need to increase this value if you have a large RAM disk and you plan to store more than 64 files in the root directory. (A better solution is to create a subdirectory, which doesn't have a limit on the number of entries.) Valid range is 2 – 1,024 (maximum of 512 for VDISK). (Default is 64.)

Switches

/e
Extended memory. Uses extended memory to create the RAM disk.

/a
Expanded memory. Uses expanded memory to create the RAM disk. (Not available with VDISK.)

Notes

Drive letter
DOS assigns the next available drive letter to your RAM disk. So if your computer has an A: and C: drive, the RAM disk will be created as drive D:.

Using extended memory
You'll need an extended memory manager (such as HIMEM.SYS, 386MAX, CEMM, or QEMM) that provides XMS (eXtended Memory Specification) memory before you can use RAMDRIVE.SYS with extended memory. Make sure the extended memory manager is loaded by CONFIG.SYS before RAMDRIVE.SYS.

Using expanded memory
You'll need an expanded memory manager (such as 386MAX, CEMM, or QEMM) that provides Lotus/Intel/Microsoft Expanded Memory Specification (LIM EMS 4.0) support before you can use RAMDRIVE.SYS with expanded memory. Make sure the expanded memory manager is loaded by CONFIG.SYS before RAMDRIVE.SYS.

Messages

`Expanded memory manager not present`
You need an expanded memory manager installed before you can use RAMDRIVE.SYS with extended memory. Make sure your CONFIG.SYS file installs an extended memory manager before it installs RAMDRIVE.SYS.

`Extended memory manager not present`
You need an extended memory manager installed that provides XMS memory management before you can use RAMDRIVE.SYS with extended memory. Make sure your CONFIG.SYS file installs an expanded memory manager before it installs RAMDRIVE.SYS.

`Insufficient memory`
You'll probably see this message when you're trying to create a large RAM disk in extended or expanded memory, but you forgot the /E or /A switch. Make sure you include such a switch in the DEVICE=RAMDRIVE.SYS line in your CONFIG.SYS file.

`No extended memory available`
You'll probably see this message when you've used the /E switch and your computer doesn't have any extended memory installed.

Examples

Installing in upper memory

If you're using a 386 memory manager that provides upper memory blocks (UMBs), you can install RAMDRIVE.SYS into upper memory. This command in your CONFIG.SYS file loads RAMDRIVE.SYS into upper memory and creates a 1MB RAM disk using extended memory:

`devicehigh=c:\dos\ramdrive.sys 1024 /e`

More directory entries

This example shows how you would create a 512K RAM disk in expanded memory that allows 512 files in the root directory:

`device=c:\dos\ramdrive.sys 512 512 512 /a`

See also

DEVICE=	You'll need to use either DEVICE= or DEVICEHIGH= to load the RAMDRIVE.SYS device driver.
DEVICEHIGH=	This command allows you to load RAMDRIVE.SYS into the UMB, if you have upper memory (which isn't the same as extended or expanded memory).
EMM386.EXE	This device driver provides expanded memory support on computers with at least an 80386 microprocessor.
HIMEM.SYS	You should install HIMEM.SYS before you install RAMDRIVE.SYS. This is because HIMEM.SYS manages extended memory.
MEM	You'll find a good discussion of the different types of memory in the description of the MEM command.

SMARTDRV.EXE If you're interested in speeding up access to all your files, not just a few select files, you'll probably want to use SMARTDRV.EXE rather than RAMDRIVE.SYS.

RD

See RMDIR

RECOVER

DOS 1–5, External

"Recover" files from a damaged disk

This command recovers files that are unreadable because they contain bad sectors. Unfortunately, this command doesn't actually recover all the data in your files.

Warning! You can easily destroy the data and directory structure on a disk if you're not careful when using this command.

When and why

You don't want to use this command. It is designed to recover files that have bad sectors inside the file. Unfortunately, all it does is remove the bad sectors from inside the file, leaving a file that, although readable, won't contain any of the information that was in the bad sectors. You're better off using similar programs in commercial utilities products, which tend to be much safer and do a better job. In fact, most utilities packages have programs designed to undo the damage done by the DOS RECOVER command.

Asking RECOVER to recover an entire disk is even worse. It will change your directory structure, moving all your files to the root directory and renaming them to computer-generated names that have no meaning. If all your files won't fit in the root directory, RECOVER adds injury to insult by losing track of these files entirely.

Because of the problems with this command, you might want to delete the RECOVER program from your DOS directory. If you want to keep it around, move it to a subdirectory that isn't in your path.

Note: In DOS 6, this command has finally been removed.

Syntax

recover *filespec*
Recovers a single file.

recover *drive*:
Warning! Don't use this form! This tells RECOVER to recover all the files on a disk. Unfortunately, you'll lose all your directories, and RECOVER will change all the filenames to computer-generated names of the form FILEnnnn.REC. RECOVER will do its dirty work even if there are absolutely no bad areas on your disk!

Parameters

filespec
File to recover. The name of the file you want to recover. If there are no bad areas (sectors) in the file, RECOVER will report that it recovered all the file. Otherwise, it will modify the file by cutting out any bad sectors. You can't use wildcard characters in the name.

drive:
Disk to recover. The disk you want to recover. Don't use this!

Notes

Limitations
RECOVER doesn't work on network drives, which is just as well considering how dangerous it can be. RECOVER also doesn't work with drive letters created by SUBST or drives affected by JOIN or ASSIGN.

What RECOVER does
Disks are divided into sectors, which are usually 512 bytes long; a file is made out of one or more sectors. The RECOVER command checks each sector used by a file to make sure it's readable. If the sector isn't readable, RECOVER marks it as bad and removes the bad sector from the file. This means files recovered by this command will have areas that are completely missing. Most programs (such as spreadsheets, word processors, and graphics programs) won't be able to read the partial files created by RECOVER. In other words, RECOVER doesn't make your data useful again.

Messages
```
The entire drive will be reconstructed,
directory structures will be destroyed.
Are you sure (Y/N)?_
```
Warning! Answer N to stop RECOVER! When you see this message, you don't want to continue because you will lose data, even if there are no bad sectors on your entire disk.

REM   All DOS, Batch file/ DOS 4.0 and later, CONFIG.SYS

Remark line
This command in a CONFIG.SYS file (DOS 4.0 and later) or a batch file allows you to add comments that will be ignored by DOS.

When and why
There are two things the REM command is useful for. First, you can use it to add comment lines to your batch and CONFIG.SYS files to make them easier to read them. And second, you can use it to comment-out commands in your CONFIG.SYS or AUTOEXEC.BAT file. Simply put a REM in front of the command to comment it out.

Syntax
rem [*remark*]
Puts a remark into a batch or CONFIG.SYS file. The remark can be any text that you want, except that it must all be on one line.

Note
The DOS manual states that you can't include the < > and | characters in a remark inside a batch file. Not true! You can include all these characters and any others in the remark after the REM statement.

Example
Disabling commands

Let's say you have a line in your CONFIG.SYS file that installs EMM386, but you'd like to turn this off for awhile. Here is how you'd turn that line into a remark that DOS ignores:

```
rem device=c:\dos\emm386.sys ram
```

See also
;   Starting with DOS 6, you can also comment out lines in CONFIG.SYS by putting a semicolon at the start of the line.

REN
See RENAME

RENAME (REN)   All DOS, Internal

Rename a file
This command changes the name of a single file or a group of files (when you use the * and ? wildcard characters).

When and why
You may never use the RENAME command, particularly if you're using a DOS shell such as the Norton Commander or the DOS Shell program. You'll usually use RENAME when you're cleaning up or rearranging your directory structure, and you need to rename some files so they're easier to find.

Syntax
rename [*path*]*oldname newname*
or
ren [*path*]*oldname newname*
Renames a file (or a group of files if you use the DOS * and ? wildcard characters).

Parameters
path
The directory that contains the file(s) you want to rename. This is optional. Note that you can only supply a path before the old name, which means you can't use this command to move files between directories (see "Notes" section).

oldname
The current name of the file(s) you want to rename. You can use the DOS * and ? wildcard characters to specify a group of files you want to rename.

newname
The new name you want to use for the file(s). This name can't have a directory or drive letter in front of it since you can't rename (move) files to other directories.

Notes

Renaming directories
The RENAME command doesn't allow you to rename directories. You'll have to use the Norton Commander, the DOS Shell program, or another third-party program to rename directories. Most DOS shells allow you to rename directories using the same command you'd use to rename files. In DOS 6 and later, you can also use the MOVE command to rename directories.

Moving files
You can use any DOS shell to moves files between directories on the same disk without having to copy and delete them. DOS 6 now has a MOVE command that allows you to move files.

Replacing existing files
The RENAME command doesn't allow you to rename a file if it would overwrite an existing file.

Messages

```
Duplicate file name or file not found
```
There are several things that can cause this message. First, you'll see this message when a file already exists with *newname*. When you use wildcard characters, RENAME will rename as many files as it can without overwriting existing files; it displays this message only once even if there are several files with name conflicts. You can get into this same situation unintentionally if you use wildcard characters in *oldname* but not in *newname*. You'll also see this message when there are no files that match *oldname*.

```
Required parameter missing
```
This message means you haven't supplied both *oldname* and *newname*.

Examples

Suppose you have a file you're working on that you called CHAP19.DOC, but you decide to move this chapter in your book so it will be Chapter 20. This command changes the name of that file:

```
C:\>rename chap19.doc chap20.doc
```

Continuing with this example, let's say we started by naming our chapters C1.DOC, C2.DOC, etc., to refer to Chapter 1, Chapter 2, etc. These names are easy to type, but they won't be easy to read in a few months after we've finished the book. This command will rename all these files to names such as CHAP1.DOC, which are much easier to read:

```
C:\>rename c*.doc chap*.doc
```

See also

COPY	The COPY command allows you to create a copy of an existing file (or group of files) that has a new name.
DEL	Deletes a file (or group of files).
LABEL	The LABEL command allows you to "rename" disks by changing their volume label.
MOVE	This command allows you to move files between directories.
XCOPY	XCOPY allows you to copy entire directories (including all the subdirectories).

REPLACE

DOS 3.2 and later, External

Update or add files to a directory

This command allows you to keep two disks or directories up to date. You can either copy files that don't exist in the other directory or copy only those files that are more recent.

When and why

If you're using two computers or a network, this is a great way to make sure two directories always have the same information. Let's say, for example, you sometimes take work home on a floppy disk, and you have the same work directory on both your home and office computers. You want to make sure these two directories contain the same set of files, and they're both up to date. The REPLACE command is ideal for this task (see "Examples").

Syntax

replace *filespec* [*path*] [/a] [/p] [/r] [/s] [/w] [/u]

Replaces the files on *path* with files defined by *filespec* (and according to the options set by the switches).

Parameters

filespec
Source files. The set of files that you want to consider copying. Which files are actually copied depends on the switches that you use. Without any switches, REPLACE copies all the files, and only the files, that already exist in *path*. In other words, it replaces the files that already exist with the versions defined by *filespec*.

path
Destination. Where you want to copy the files to. This can be a drive letter and/or a pathname, but it cannot include a filename. (Default is the current directory.)

Switches

No switches
Copy common files. Without any switches, REPLACE copies all the files, and only the files, that already exist in *path*. In other words, it replaces the files that already exist with the versions defined by *filespec*. Any files defined by *filespec* that don't exist in *path* won't be copied.

/u
Update (DOS 4.0 and later). This switch tells REPLACE to copy only the files from the source that are newer than files in the destination, which is what you'll usually want. Normally, REPLACE copies both files that are newer and files with the same date and time. You can't use the /U and /A switches together.

/a
Add files. This option only copies files that don't exist in the other directory (*path*). You can't use the /A with the /S or /U switches.

/p
Prompt. Prompts for confirmation. REPLACE will ask for confirmation for each file it wants to copy.

/r
Read only. Replaces read-only files. Normally, REPLACE displays an error message and stops when it tries to replace a file that is marked as read-only. This switch tells REPLACE that it can replace those files.

/s
Subdirectories. This switch doesn't work quite the way you might expect. It searches all the subdirectories of *path* (the destination disk) for any files that match files in the single-source directory (REPLACE doesn't search source subdirectories). You can't use the /S and /A switches together.

/w
Wait for new disk. This switch displays the message `Press any key to continue . . .` so you can insert another floppy disk before REPLACE starts.

Notes

Hidden and system files

You can't use REPLACE to update hidden or system files. If you need to use REPLACE with such files, you'll have to use the ATTRIB command to turn off the hidden or system attributes on the files you want to update.

ERRORLEVEL returned

REPLACE returns information that batch files can test with the IF ERRORLEVEL command. Here are the exit codes that REPLACE returns:

0	Successfully replaced or added files.
1	(DOS 3.3 and earlier.) Syntax error in the command line.
2	Couldn't find any files to match the source.
3	Couldn't find the source or destination path.
5	Could not replace files, perhaps because a file is marked read-only.
8	Not enough memory to run REPLACE.
11	(DOS 4.0 and later.) Syntax error in the command line.
15	The command line includes an invalid drive letter.

You might find this information useful to write a batch file that moves information between two computers. For example, if you get ERRORLEVEL 3, you might want to create a directory where you'll save the files.

Messages

```
Access denied
```
This is the message you'll see if one of the files in the destination path is marked as read-only. Use ATTRIB to turn off read-only and try again.

```
File cannot be copied onto itself
```
You'll see this message when the source and destination refer to the same disk and directory. You may have left off the destination drive or directory.

```
No files found
```
REPLACE couldn't find any files that match the source *filespec* you provided.

```
No files replaced
```
REPLACE didn't copy any files. This might happen because the file you want to update doesn't exist on the destination (assuming you didn't use the /A switch) or the files are already up to date (if you used the /U switch).

```
Source path required
```
You'll probably see this message when you didn't provide any parameters. You must supply at least the source *filespec*.

Examples

Two computers

In this example we're going to look at how you can create a directory on your home computer that you want to keep up to date with a directory on your office computer. Let's call this directory WORK, and we'll show you the steps you need to take.

- *Office setup.* First, you'll want to create a floppy disk that contains all the files from your office computer. You can either use the COPY or the REPLACE command. We'll use the REPLACE command to copy all the files from your office hard disk to the floppy disk you'll take between home and work:

  `C:\OFFICE>` **`replace c:\work\*.* a: /a`**

- *Home setup.* Next, you'll want to create this directory on your home computer and copy all the files over from the floppy disk you brought home:

  `C:\HOME>`**`mkdir c:\work`**
  `C:\HOME>`**`replace a:*.* c:\work /a`**

- *Home to office.* After doing some work at home, you'll need to run this command to copy all the new files back to your floppy disk which you'll take back to the office:

  `C:\HOME>`**`replace c:\work\*.* a: /u`**

  Once you get to your office, you'll run this command to copy all the new files to your hard disk:

  `C:\OFFICE>`**`replace a:*.* c:\work /u`**

- *Office to home.* At the end of the day, when it's time to take your work home again, you'd run this command on your office computer:

  `C:\OFFICE>`**`replace c:\work\*.* a: /u`**

  And then this command when you get home:

  `C:\HOME>`**`replace a:*.* c:\work /u`**

See also

ATTRIB   The ATTRIB command allows you to change the read-only attribute on files.

COPY   You can also use the COPY command to copy files between disks and directories.

XCOPY   This command allows you to copy an entire directory structure rather than just the files in one directory.

RESTORE

All DOS, External

Restore files backed up with BACKUP

This command allows you to restore files from backup floppy disks you created with the BACKUP command.

When and why

If you've backed up your hard disk using the BACKUP command, this command is the only way you have to restore files from your backup disks.

Note: This command is included in DOS 6 for compatibility with disks you created using BACKUP in earlier versions of DOS (2 through 5). If you are using DOS 6, you should use MSBACKUP or the Windows Backup program to back up your computer.

Syntax

restore *drive*: *path*\[*filespec*] [/**s**] [/**m**] [/**n**] [/**d**] [/**p**] [/**d**:*date*] [/**a**:*date*] [/**b**:*date*][/**e**:*time*] [/**l**:*time*]

Parameters

drive:
Backup disks. The disk drive that contains the backup disks you want to restore files from.

path\filespec
Files to restore. The name and location of the file(s) you want to restore. The *filespec* can include the DOS * and ? wildcard characters. You can specify a drive as part of the *path*.

Note: The path must be the same as you supplied when you backed up these files.

Switches

/s
Subdirectories. Restores all files in subdirectories that match *filespec*.

/m
Modified files. Restores only the files that have been modified since the last backup. This has the effect of undoing any work you did on those files.

/n
Nonexistent files. Restores only files that have been deleted since the last backup. This is an easy way to recover files you deleted by accident if UNERASE doesn't bring back your files successfully.

/d
Display files (DOS 5 and later). Lists all the files on the backup disk that match the name and location you provided. This switch doesn't restore any of these files, it just lists them. It's a good idea to use this switch to see what you'll restore before you actually restore any files.

/p
Prompt for read-only or archive. RESTORE will ask for permission before it restores each file that is marked as read-only or has been modified since the last backup (based on having its attribute bit set).

/a:*date*
Modified after. Restores only those files that have been modified on or after a certain date. You can use this option to "revert" to the previous versions of files you're working on if you decide you made a mistake. You can run DATE to see what format to use for the date.

/b:*date*
Modified before. Restores only files that were modified on or before a certain date. You can run DATE to see what format to use for the date.

/e:*time*
Modified earlier than. Restores only files that were modified at or earlier than a given time of day. You can run TIME to see what format to use for the time.

/l:*time*
Modified later than. Restores only files that were modified at or later than a given time of day. You can run TIME to see what format to use for the time.

Notes

ASSIGN, JOIN, and SUBST

You shouldn't use RESTORE while ASSIGN, JOIN, and SUBST are active, just as you shouldn't use BACKUP when these are active. This is because these commands can alter your directory structure between the time you back up and restore files. Since RESTORE can't restore files to a different location, you must have exactly the same directory structure. This is just one good reason to use a commercial backup program instead of BACKUP and RESTORE.

System files
You can't use RESTORE to restore the system files (IO.SYS and MSDOS.SYS on MS-DOS, and IBMBIO.COM and IBMDOS.COM on PC DOS). You can, however, use the SYS command to restore these files, provided you have a system floppy disk (which it's a good idea to keep around).

Previous versions
You cannot use RESTORE from DOS 3.3 or later to restore files created with BACKUP from DOS versions 3.2 and earlier. This is because the file format for backup files was changed with DOS 3.3 and later. For this reason it is a good idea to store a DOS bootable disk with your backup disks that contains the same version of DOS and RESTORE you used to create the backup files.

ERRORLEVEL returned
RESTORE returns information that batch files can test with the IF ERRORLEVEL command. Here are the exit codes that RESTORE returns:

- 0   Restored the file(s).
- 1   Could not find any files to restore.
- 3   You pressed Ctrl-C or Ctrl-Break to exit RESTORE before it finished.
- 4   There was an error of some type.

You can use this information in batch files to control the restore process.

Examples
To restore a single file, such as CHAP13.DOC, you would use a command such as this:

```
C:\>restore a: c:\books\dos\chap13.doc
```

To restore all the files in a directory, type

```
C:\>restore a: c:\books\dos\*.*
```

See also

BACKUP	(DOS 5 and earlier.) Creates the disks RESTORE reads. You'll need to use BACKUP before you can use RESTORE.
COUNTRY	Controls the current format you'll need to use for time and date input. You can run the DATE and TIME commands to see how it's currently set.
DATE	You can use the DATE command to show you the format for dates.
MSBACKUP	The DOS 6 Backup utility for DOS.
MWBACKUP	The DOS 6 Backup utility for Windows.
SYS	Use the SYS command to restore DOS's two system files.
TIME	You can use the TIME command to show you the format for times.

RMDIR (RD) All DOS, External

Remove a directory
This command allows you to remove (delete) empty directories from your disk, whether it be a hard or floppy disk. In DOS 6, you can use the DELTREE command to remove directories, whether or not they contain files or subdirectories.

When and why
This is a command you'll probably use at some point when you're doing spring cleaning. The only people who won't need RMDIR are people using a DOS shell program, such as the Norton Commander or the DOS Shell.

Syntax
rmdir [*drive*:]*path*
rd [*drive*:]*path*
Removes a directory. The directory must be empty (no files or subdirectories) before you can remove it.

Parameters
drive:
Drive contain directory. The disk drive from which you want to remove a directory. (Default is the current drive.)

path
Directory to delete. The name of the directory you want to remove. This can be a full pathname (starting at the root directory: \) or a relative pathname. If you provide a name without any backslashes, this refers to a subdirectory in the current directory.

Notes
Deleting directories
The directory you want to delete must be empty. That is, it can't have any files or subdirectories. You'll have to use ERASE and RMDIR to remove all the files and subdirectories first. (In DOS 6, you can use the DELTREE command to remove directories that are not empty.)

Multipart paths
When you provide a long pathname, DOS only removes the directory whose name appears at the end of the path. For example, the command

```
C:\>RMDIR \WRITING\BOOKS\NEW
```

just removes the NEW directory.

Messages
```
Invalid path, not directory,
or directory not empty
```
This is a catch-all message that covers all types of errors. Here are some of the things that can cause RMDIR to display this message.

Part II: Command Reference

- The directory isn't empty. You need to delete all files and subdirectories before you can delete this directory.
- The name you provided is the name of a file, not a directory. Make sure you've typed the correct name.
- The directory name you provided doesn't exist. Check the name (using the DIR command) and try again.

Examples
For this example, let's say we have a directory called C:\WRITING\BOOKS that we want to remove. We'll show you two ways you can remove this directory. First, if the current directory is C:\WRITING, you can use this command:

```
C:\WRITING>rmdir books
```

You can also type the full pathname:

```
C:\>rmdir \writing\books
```

See also
DELTREE   This DOS 6 command allows you to remove directories that are not empty.

ERASE   You'll need to erase all the files in a directory before you can remove that directory.

MKDIR   This command allows you to create directories.

SCANDISK   DOS 6.2 and later, External

Scan disk for defects
This command can check and correct many types of disk errors, including directory and file structure errors. ScanDisk provides far more functionality than the CHKDSK command did in previous versions of DOS. Many of the ScanDisk commands have a full-screen interface.

> **When and why**
> You should check your disk for errors, including performing a surface scan, once a week — at the very least once a month — because, as is the case with a doctor's routine checkup, problems caught early on are easier to fix. ScanDisk detects and corrects errors in physical disks and in DoubleSpace volumes.

Syntax
scandisk
Checks the current disk drive for errors. If the current disk drive is a DoubleSpace volume, ScanDisk asks you whether you want to check the host drive (the actual physical disk drive) before checking the DoubleSpace drive.

SCANDISK

scandisk [*drive*: [*drive*: ...] | **/all**] [**/checkonly** | **/autofix** [**/nofix**] | **/custom**] [**/surface**] [**/mono**] [**/nosummary**]
Scans one or more disks for errors and enables you to control exactly what ScanDisk scans for and repairs.

scandisk *volume* [**/checkonly** | **/autofix** [**/nosave**] | **/custom**] [**/mono**] [**/nosummary**]
This form of SCANDISK enables you to check a DoubleSpace volume that isn't currently mounted.

scandisk /fragment [*drive*:][*path*]*filespec*
Checks one or more files for fragmentation.

scandisk /undo [*undo-drive*:] [**/mono**]
Warning! *Do not* use this command if you've made changes to your disk since you ran ScanDisk. Running SCANDISK /UNDO after you've made any changes to your disk, such as changing files or making changes to directories, can damage your disk.

This command undoes the fixes that ScanDisk made. You can *only* use this command if ScanDisk created an undo disk before it made changes to your disk. You should undo changes only if you haven't made subsequent changes to the files on your disk.

Switches

/all
Scan all disks. Checks and fixes problems on all floppy and hard disks connected directly to your computer. This does not check network drives.

/autofix
Fix without asking. This switch tells ScanDisk to correct any errors it finds without first asking for permission. Normally, ScanDisk asks you whether you want it to fix errors before it fixes them.

/checkonly
Check but don't fix. Use this switch when you want to see whether any problems exist but you don't want ScanDisk to try to fix them. You cannot use this switch with the /AUTOFIX or /CUSTOM switches.

/custom
Use settings in SCANDISK.INI. This switch tells ScanDisk to take its commands and settings from an area of the SCANDISK.INI file, which you can edit with any text editor (including the DOS EDIT command). You may want to use this switch if you set up ScanDisk to run from a batch file. The SCANDISK.INI file itself has numerous comments on the various settings that you can change.

/mono
Use black and white. Tells ScanDisk not to use colors on the screen. This is useful if you're running ScanDisk on a laptop computer that doesn't have a color screen. You can also change the Display line in the SCANDISK.INI file so that it reads Display=mono instead of having to use this switch every time you start ScanDisk.

/nosave
Don't save lost clusters. Normally, when ScanDisk (or CHKDSK) finds any lost clusters, it saves them as files in the root directory on your disk. This switch tells ScanDisk to free the clusters without saving them to files. You can only use this switch along with the /AUTOFIX switch.

/nosummary
Don't display report. This switch tells ScanDisk to skip the summary report after it tests a disk drive, which also means that ScanDisk automatically moves on to the next drive or quits, as long as there are no errors. Normally, ScanDisk asks whether you want to review a more detailed report before it exits or moves on to the next disk drive. You probably want to use this switch when you run ScanDisk from within a batch file.

When you use this switch, ScanDisk also skips the surface scan unless you use the /SURFACE switch.

/surface
Automatic surface scan. Tells ScanDisk to perform a surface scan after all other tests without first asking whether you want it to perform a surface scan. A surface scan checks your disk for bad sectors, marking them as bad and moving the data to undamaged sectors. ScanDisk normally asks you whether you want it to perform a surface scan. If you're using the /NOSUMMARY switch, ScanDisk performs a surface scan only if you also provide the /SURFACE switch. Default: ask first; skip if you use the /NOSUMMARY switch.

Parameters

drive:
Disk drive to scan. A drive letter of the disk drive that you want to scan. The drive letter must refer either to a physical disk attached to your computer (hard or floppy disk) or to the drive letter assigned to a DoubleSpace volume that is currently mounted.

[*drive*:][*path*]*filespec*
File to test for fragmentation. The name of a file that you want to test for fragmentation. The *filespec* can contain DOS wildcard characters, which allows you to test multiple files with one call to ScanDisk.

undo-drive:
Drive that contains undo disk. When ScanDisk finds errors on a disk drive, it gives you the option of creating an *undo disk* that you can later use to undo the fixes that ScanDisk made to your disk. The files on the undo disk contain information about which drive the undo information applies to as well as information about all the changes ScanDisk made to that drive.

volume
DoubleSpace volume file. The name, with drive letter (if it's on a different drive), of a DoubleSpace volume that isn't currently mounted (meaning it doesn't have a drive letter assigned to it). DoubleSpace volume files have names such as [*drive*:\]DBLSPACE.*nnn*, where the extension is a different number for each volume file. To find out the names of unmounted DoubleSpace volumes, run DBLSPACE and select Mount from the Drive menu — this shows a list of unmounted DoubleSpace volume files.

Notes

Warning about SCANDISK/UNDO

If you have made *any change at all* to your disk (including deleting files, writing files, renaming files, and so on) since you ran ScanDisk, *do not run SCANDISK /UNDO*. Undoing ScanDisk's fixes after you've made changes to your disk will almost certainly damage some of your data. If you want to undo ScanDisk, do so immediately after you run it.

Repairing a compressed drive C
If you've compressed your main hard disk (drive C) with DoubleSpace, and this volume becomes damaged, DOS may not be able to mount the DoubleSpace volume file. In this case, you need to run ScanDisk from a floppy disk. If you have the full DOS 6.2 installation, ScanDisk is available uncompressed on the first disk, so you can run ScanDisk directly from your DOS floppy disks.

However, if you have the StepUp version that upgrades from DOS 6.0 to DOS 6.2, ScanDisk is stored compressed on the upgrade floppy disk. If you upgraded to DOS 6.2 using this StepUp disk, make sure that you copy SCANDISK.EXE and SCANDISK.INI to a floppy disk that you keep near your computer in case you have problems with your startup disk.

To repair the compressed volume that couldn't be mounted as drive C, enter the following command:

```
A:\>scandisk c:\dblspace.000
```

Searching for marginal sectors
Sometimes hard disks develop *soft* errors, which are errors that don't appear every time you read a sector from the disk. ScanDisk can find weak sectors and mark them as bad. To find weak sectors, you need to change a line in the SCANDISK.INI file, which should be located in your DOS directory. Open this file in a text editor, such as EDIT, and change the NumPasses line so that it reads NumPasses = 10. This tells ScanDisk to read each sector ten times instead of just once. Reading a sector ten times instead of once gives you a better chance of finding a marginal sector.

ScanDisk vs. CHKDSK
The ScanDisk command is far more extensive than CHKDSK in terms of the kinds of problems it can detect and repair. Here is a short list of some of the cases in which ScanDisk can solve problems that CHKDSK can't:

Test/Repair	ScanDisk	CHKDSK
Cross-linked clusters	Yes	No
Lost clusters	Yes	Yes[*]
Surface scan for bad sectors	Yes	No
Repair damaged DoubleSpace volumes	Yes	No
Undo repairs	Yes	No

[*]CHKDSK cannot check or repair problems inside DoubleSpace compressed volumes.

ScanDisk: networks, CD ROMs, and so on
There are a number of types of drives that ScanDisk cannot scan or repair. Here is a list of drives that ScanDisk doesn't work on:

- CD-ROM drives

- Network drives
- Drive letters created by ASSIGN, JOIN, or SUBST
- Drive letters created using INTERLNK
- Compressed drives created by Stacker

ScanDisk and DOS Task Swapper

You cannot run ScanDisk while the DOS Task Swapper is active unless you use the /CHECKONLY switch, which looks for but doesn't correct problems on your disk. Exit the DOS Shell and run ScanDisk again to repair any problems.

ScanDisk and Windows

Although you can run ScanDisk from within Windows or other multitasking environments, problems can arise from doing so. First, if any other programs are in the process of writing a file, ScanDisk may see a difference between the directory structure and the FAT because DOS doesn't always update these structures immediately. Such "errors" are not really errors, and you certainly don't want ScanDisk to correct them. For this reason, ScanDisk sets the /CHECKONLY switch for you when you run ScanDisk from within Windows. For best results, especially if you're going to make any repairs, you should always exit Windows before running ScanDisk.

ScanDisk and Stacker

If you're using Stacker to compress your hard disk, ScanDisk displays a message saying that it cannot correct disk problems while Stacker is running. If you encounter this problem, you need to reboot your computer without Stacker — which probably means that you need to put ScanDisk on a floppy disk because you won't have access to the files on your compressed disk without Stacker. Run ScanDisk without Stacker running and then reboot your computer again after you finish running ScanDisk.

Technical notes

What ScanDisk checks

ScanDisk checks two different types of disk drives: physical drives and DoubleSpace volumes. Because a DoubleSpace volume is actually stored inside a file on a physical volume, testing these two types of drives involves checking a number of different types of information. The following two notes give an overview of what ScanDisk checks for in each type of drive.

Tests on physical disk drives

Here is a list of what ScanDisk checks on physical disk drives:

Media descriptor	ScanDisk checks to see if the disk type, as stored on the disk drive, is a correct disk type.
File allocation tables	DOS uses the File allocation table (FAT) as a road map to the information contained in all the files on a disk. Most disk drives (except for RAM disks) contain two copies of the FAT, in case one should become damaged. ScanDisk tries to determine which copy is damaged and uses the other copy to repair the damaged copy.

SCANDISK

ScanDisk also ensures that no two files overlap on the disk. Overlaps, known as *cross-linked clusters,* are one of the more common types of damage to the FAT. ScanDisk ensures that only one file uses any location on your disk.

Another type of damage occurs when you delete a file and DOS crashes before it completely records the fact that you deleted the file. This type of error is known as *lost clusters*.

Directory structure	ScanDisk checks every directory on your computer to make sure they're free of errors. Sometimes invalid directory entries prevent other programs, such as CHKDSK, from recognizing lost clusters or from running at all.
File system	After ScanDisk ensures that the FAT and directory structures are both valid, it looks for other problems such as lost clusters and cross-linked files. (See the section "About disk structures" under CHKDSK for more information on these two topics.)
Surface scan	(Optional) When ScanDisk does a surface scan, it tries to read every sector on your disk to see if that sector can be read without errors. If it finds any bad sectors (sectors that it cannot read), ScanDisk marks these sectors as *bad* so that DOS doesn't try to use these sectors in a file. In the case of sectors that are marginally readable, ScanDisk moves the data to an undamaged sector so that you don't lose any data.

Tests on DoubleSpace volumes

Here is a list of what ScanDisk checks inside DoubleSpace volumes:

DoubleSpace file header	This is an area at the beginning of the compressed volume file that contains information about the compressed volume, such as size of drive, size of root directory, and a number of pointers to other structures that DoubleSpace uses to find, compress, and uncompress information.
Directory structure	ScanDisk checks every directory on your computer to make sure they contain no errors. Sometimes invalid directory entries prevent other programs, such as CHKDSK, from recognizing lost clusters or from running at all.
File system	This checks the DOS directory structure and FAT for lost or cross-linked clusters and repairs both of these problems. Note that DoubleSpace volumes actually have *two* levels of FATs and can contain lost or cross-linked files at either level. The MDFAT (described next) allows DoubleSpace to use disk space more efficiently than DOS does because it allows DoubleSpace to save partial clusters (DOS only works with whole clusters).

DoubleSpace file allocation table	Also known as the MDFAT, it contains information on exactly where to find each piece of compressed data that is part of any file. If errors occur in this structure, you may get incorrect data when you try to read a file. ScanDisk makes sure the MDFAT has no errors.
Compression structure	This check makes sure that one — and only one — file refers to each chunk of compressed data. If no file actually refers to a cluster that is marked as being used, ScanDisk frees the cluster so that it is available again.
Volume signatures	The volume signatures (there are two of them) help DoubleSpace to ensure that the compressed volume file is a valid DoubleSpace volume. ScanDisk ensures that these signatures are correct and sets them if they're invalid.
Boot sector	In order to make the DoubleSpace volume look like a real disk, DoubleSpace stores a copy of the startup disk's boot sector. ScanDisk makes sure that the boot sector in the DoubleSpace volume matches the startup disk's boot sector.
Surface scan	(Optional) The surface scan for a DoubleSpace volume reads each compressed cluster to make sure it can be read without any errors.

ERRORLEVEL returned

ScanDisk returns information that batch files can test with the ERRORLEVEL command. Here are the exit codes that ScanDisk returns:

Code	What It Means
0	There are no problems with the drive or drives.
1	There was an error with the command line, such as an invalid switch.
2	ScanDisk ran out of memory while it was running.
3	You exited scan disk before it finished all the checks.
4	You stopped a surface scan before it completed, but there were no errors with other tests. ScanDisk doesn't return this value if you chose to bypass the surface scan.
254	ScanDisk found and corrected at least one problem.
255	ScanDisk found one or more errors and couldn't fix at least one of these errors.

Note: You can use this information in batch files to control testing of your disks.

SCANDISK

Messages

```
All specified file(s) are contiguous.
```
You see this when you use the /fragment switch to test files for fragmentation and none of the files are fragmented.

filespec contains *n* noncontiguous blocks.
This is the message that you see when you use the /fragment switch and the file is fragmented.

filespec is not a valid name for a DoubleSpace volume file.
There are two cases when you see this message. If you meant to check a file for fragmentation, this message means that you didn't supply the /fragment switch to ScanDisk. But if you meant to check an unmounted DoubleSpace volume, you may get this message if you didn't put the correct drive letter in front of the volume name or if you didn't type a correct volume name. To see the list of valid volume names (with drive letters), run DBLSPACE and select Mount from the Drive menu.

Examples

Repairing a DoubleSpace C drive

If you've compressed your main disk drive, a situation could arise in which DOS can't mount your compressed drive C because of damage to that volume, which means you don't have access to any of your DOS programs, including ScanDisk (because they're stored in the compressed volume file).

In this case, you need to run ScanDisk from a floppy disk drive. Fortunately, ScanDisk is on the first DOS 6.2 Installation Disk in uncompressed form, so you can run it from that floppy disk. (*Note:* If you have the StepUp version of DOS 6.2, which upgrades from DOS 6.0, you won't be able to run ScanDisk from the floppy disk. Instead, you should make sure that you put ScanDisk on a floppy disk *before* you have problems.

To repair your compressed C drive when DOS cannot mount it, run the following command:

```
A:\>scandisk c:\dblspace.000
```

Checking an unmounted DoubleSpace volume

Suppose you have a compressed drive C as well as a second volume file that isn't currently mounted. In this case, drive C uses the volume file H:\DBLSPACE.000, so the second, unmounted volume file is probably called H:\DBLSPACE.001. The following command checks this volume file for errors:

```
C:\>scandisk h:\dblspace.001
```

As soon as you run this command, ScanDisk switches to full-screen mode, in which it uses dialog boxes to prompt you for responses.

See also

CHKDSK   ScanDisk supersedes CHKDSK. However, the description of CHKDSK in this book explains more about disk structures, which you may find helpful in understanding what the ScanDisk command does.

SET

All DOS, Internal

Set environment variables

This command allows you to create, modify, and remove string variables from your environment space. Starting with DOS 6, you can also use this command in the CONFIG.SYS file.

When and why

DOS sets aside an area of memory, called the *environment*, that it uses to save some pairs of names and strings. These names are called *variables*. DOS itself uses several environment variables that it automatically sets up.

Most people never use the SET command, but you might want to use it to set the DIRCMD environment variable, which controls how the DIR command displays its output.

Syntax

set
Displays all the environment variables that are currently set.

set *variable=*
Erases *variable* from the environment space.

set *variable=string*
Sets the environment variable *variable* to *string*. If there is already a variable with this name, changes its value to *string*.

Parameters

variable
Variable name. The name of the environment variable that you want to define or change. This name can be anything you want, except that you can't use the following characters in a name unless you surround the name with quotation marks ("): < > | =. Note that *variable* can include spaces, and it can be longer than eight characters.

string
New value. String can also be anything you want, with the same restrictions as the *variable* name.

Notes

DOS's environment variables

DOS defines several environment variables that it uses for itself (but other programs can read this information if they want):

COMSPEC — This variable defines the location of the COMMAND.COM file. It's usually C:\COMMAND.COM, unless you have a SHELL= line in your CONFIG.SYS file.

PROMPT — If you've changed the DOS prompt, this environment variable contains the current prompt setting.

SET

PATH   This environment variable contains the path you set using the PATH command.

WINPMT   (Windows 3.1 and later.) This is just like the PATH environment variables, but if it's defined, it controls the appearance of the DOS prompt while Windows is running (see the PROMPT command for details).

DIRCMD   (DOS 5 and later.) This environment variable allows you to define a set of switches and parameters that the DIR command will use by default (see the DIR command for details).

Using environment variables in batch files

You can get the value of any environment variable in a batch file using the %*name*% parameter. This substitutes the string for the variable called *name* into the batch file.

Using SET within DOS shells

The SET command changes the current environment, which in the case of a DOS shell program is a temporary copy of the environment that is active only for executing one command. In other words, you can't change the master environment variables from within DOS shells, such as the Norton Commander or the DOS Shell.

Messages

`Out of environment space`

You'll see this message when DOS has no more room for environment variables. Normally, you'll see this message when you've loaded a memory-resident program, which prevents DOS from expanding its environment space. You can use COMMAND to set a larger minimum size for the environment space.

Examples

Some programs use environment variables to identify directories that they might want to use. A common environment variable, called TEMP, tells programs where they should create temporary files. You'll usually want this to be a very fast disk (or even a RAM disk). Here is how you would set TEMP to a RAM disk called F:

    set temp=f:

Setting the DIRCMD variable

The DIR command has an environment variable called DIRCMD you can use to customize the way DIR works. For example, if you want DIR to always alphabetize filenames and display them in lowercase, you can use the following command in your AUTOEXEC.BAT file:

    set dircmd=/on /l

See also

%*name*%   Allows you to use environment variables as parameters inside batch files.

COMMAND   You may need to adjust the minimum size of the environment variable if you encounter the `Out of environment space` message. You can use this command or the SHELL command.

Part II: Command Reference

DIR	The DIR command has an environment variable called DIRCMD that can set frequently used switches.
PATH	The usual way to set the PATH environment variable.
PROMPT	The usual way to set the PROMPT environment variable.
SHELL	You can use this command, with COMMAND, in your CONFIG.SYS file to set a minimum size for your environment space.

SETUP
DOS 5 and later, External

DOS Installation program
This program installs DOS and, in DOS 6, the Microsoft utilities.

When and why
There are actually several cases when you might want to use this command. Certainly the first time you install DOS 6 you'll need to use the SETUP program (unless your computer came with DOS 6 already installed).

Starting with DOS 6 you can also use SETUP to install some optional programs at a later time. These programs include the DOS and Windows versions of Undelete, Backup, and the Anti-Virus software. If you didn't install these programs when you first installed DOS, or if you just installed Windows and want to install the Windows versions of these DOS programs, run SETUP /E.

Syntax
setup [/b] [/e] [/f | /m | /q] [/i | /h | /g] [/u]

Installs DOS and, in DOS 6, the Microsoft utilities. The SETUP program is on the floppy disk labeled Microsoft DOS *N.N*, Disk 1.

Switches
/b
Black and white. Use this swich if you have a monochrome monitor. This switch tells SETUP not to show its display in full color. You might also need this switch if you're installing DOS on a non-color laptop computer.

/e
Add utilities (DOS 6 and later). Use this switch after you have installed DOS 6 to install any of the new DOS or Windows Utilities (Undelete, Backup and Anti-Virus).

/f
Floppy installation. Installs a minimum configuration of DOS onto a floppy disk. The only time you want to do this, rather than using the SYS command, is when you don't want to install DOS on your hard disk or if you don't have a hard disk.

/m
Minimal installation (DOS 6 and later). Installs a minimum configuration of DOS 6 onto a hard disk. You would use this switch when you don't have a lot of room on your hard disk. With DOS 6 you can use DoubleSpace to increase your disk space after you've installed DOS.

/q
Copy files (DOS 6 and later). Use this switch for manual installs. This switch tells SETUP to copy the DOS files to your hard disk, but it doesn't actually install DOS 6. You'll need to use the SYS C: command to copy the system files over to your hard disk (you will need to boot from a DOS 6 floppy disk first). Then you should be able to boot your computer with DOS 6.

/i
Disable hardware detection (DOS 6 and later). If Setup freezes prior to beginning the actual installation, you may want to try using this switch. The /I switch disables the automatic hardware detection. You must then select your hardware configuration from the lists provided.

/h
Use Setup defaults (DOS 6 and later). You should use this command only when you are sure that the default installation is what you want.

/g
No Uninstall (DOS 6 and later). This option provides a faster install and uses less space on your hard disk (because SETUP doesn't have to save your old DOS files), but you will not be able to uninstall the new version of DOS. You should use this option only if you have tested DOS 6 on a similar machine and are sure you will experience no compatibility problems.

/u
Unconditional (DOS 6 and later). This installation option ignores any partitions that DOS 6 recognizes as incompatible. You should use this switch only as a last resort for installing DOS 6 or when you intend to delete the incompatible partitions after installation.

Notes
You must run SETUP from your original DOS floppy disks.

When you don't have enough free space
Here's how you can install all of DOS 6 on your computer when you don't have enough free disk space on your hard disk.

- Install the minimum DOS 6 configuration on your hard disk so you can get DOS 6 up and running. Run the following command:

    `C:\>`**`a:setup /m`**

    If your DOS floppy disk is in drive B, you'll need to substitute B: for the A: above.

- Reboot your computer using DOS 6. Then run the DoubleSpace program to compress your hard disk, following the directions that appear on your screen:

    `C:\>`**`dblspace`**

- Run SETUP again to install the full DOS 6 onto your hard disk.

Uninstalling DOS

The SETUP programs in DOS 5 and later keep your old version of DOS around on your hard disk, in a directory called OLD_DOS.*nnn*, where *nnn* is a number such as 000, in case you've upgraded your version of DOS more than once (such as from DOS 3.3 to 5.0 and finally to 6.0). It also writes some uninstall information to a floppy disk, such as your old AUTOEXEC.BAT and CONFIG.SYS files. You can return to a previous version of DOS in one of two ways:

1. Put your uninstall floppy disk into drive A and reboot your computer.

2. Log onto your uninstall floppy disk and run the UNINSTALL program.

Any time you decide you don't want to go back to your previous version of DOS, you can run the DELOLDOS program to remove all the files from your previous version of DOS.

Note: If you installed DOS 6 on a computer with a hard disk compressed by Stacker or another compression program, DOS won't create an uninstall disk or save your old DOS files. In other words, you won't be able to uninstall DOS 6 on computers that already have some type of disk compression.

See also

DBLSPACE	Allows you to make room available on your hard disk.
DELOLDOS	Deletes the old copies of DOS that the SETUP program puts into directories called OLD_DOS.*nnn* so you can uninstall DOS.
EXPAND	You can use this command to retrieve individual files from your original DOS floppy disks.
SYS	Allows you to create a bootable DOS floppy disk.

SETVER — DOS 5 and later, External and Device driver

Set DOS version number

This command is both a device driver and a DOS command. As a device driver, it fools some programs into thinking they're running under previous versions of DOS. And as a program, you can add or remove programs from the version table.

When and why

You'll need to use this program only if you have programs that don't run under your version of DOS. Don't add a program to this version table unless you have to!

This program allows you to fool certain programs into thinking they're running an earlier version of DOS. You may need to do this for programs that haven't been updated for the current version of DOS. Programs that don't run under DOS 5 or 6 usually contain code that makes sure the program only runs under versions of DOS that the programmer knew about. SETVER, then, allows you to fool such programs into thinking they're running under a previous version of DOS.

SETVER

> To use SETVER, enter the name of the program (with extension) that you want to run, along with the version number of the DOS you were running before you upgraded. You'll then need to restart your computer to make this new version table active.

Syntax

device=[*path*]**setver.exe**
This line in your CONFIG.SYS file tells DOS to load the SETVER device driver into memory (which uses about 400 bytes). The Setup program that you used to install DOS 5 or later usually adds this line to your CONFIG.SYS file.

setver *program n.nn*
Adds a program to the version table. The program name must include an extension (COM or EXE) and no path. You can also use this to change the version number for programs already in the version table. You'll need to restart DOS to use the new version table.

setver *program* **/delete** [**/quiet**]
Removes a program from the version table. The program name must include an extension. You'll need to restart DOS to use the new version table.

setver
Without any parameters, lists the programs and DOS version numbers currently in the table.

Parameters

path
Path to driver. You'll want to provide a path to the SETVER.EXE device driver. This path will usually be C:\DOS.

program
Program to add or remove. The name of the program you want to add to or remove from the version table. You must include the program's extension (COM or EXE), but don't include a drive letter or path. You also can't use the * and ? wildcard characters.

n.nn
Version. The version of DOS you want this program to think it's running under. Valid range is 2.11 – 9.99.

Switches

/delete
/d
Deletes a program from the version table.

/quiet
Tells SETVER not to display the message it normally displays when you delete a program from the version table. This message is only two lines long, so we're not sure why you'd want to keep it from being displayed.

Notes

Memory used

The SETVER device driver uses about 400 bytes of memory. You can use the DEVICEHIGH= line instead of DEVICE= to load SETVER into upper memory if your computer has upper memory blocks.

Location of version table

SETVER.EXE reserves an area inside itself for saving the version table. Whenever you add or remove a program, SETVER modifies this table, but it doesn't modify the version stored in memory. As a result, you have to restart DOS before the new version table will take effect.

You also have to make sure you have a DEVICE= (or DEVICEHIGH=) line in your CONFIG.SYS file that loads the SETVER.EXE device driver into DOS. The DOS 5 and later Setup program usually creates this line for you when you install DOS.

ERRORLEVEL returned

SETVER returns information that batch files can test with the IF ERRORLEVEL command. This is probably only of interest to software developers who write setup programs. Here are the exit codes SETVER returns:

0 SETVER finished without errors.
1 You used a switch that SETVER doesn't understand.
2 The filename isn't valid or doesn't exist.
3 There isn't enough memory to run SETVER properly.
4 The version number isn't correctly formatted.
5 SETVER couldn't find the name in the version table.
6 SETVER couldn't find the SETVER.EXE file.
7 You supplied an invalid drive letter.
8 Too many command-line parameters.
9 One of the command-line parameters is missing.
10 SETVER had problems while reading SETVER.EXE.
11 The SETVER.EXE file is corrupt.
12 The SETVER.EXE program you ran doesn't support a version table.
13 Not enough room left in the version table for a new entry.
14 SETVER had problems writing to the SETVER.EXE file.

As you can see, the information returned by SETVER is very detailed—the kind of thing that programmers love and need.

Messages

```
Specified entry was not found in the version table.
```
You'll see this message when you try to delete entries from the version table. You can run SETVER without any parameters to see if the program you're trying to delete is, in fact, in the table. If it is, make sure you type the program name and the extension exactly as you see it in this list.

```
There is no more space in the version table new entries
```
SETVER has a fixed-sized table. You'll have to delete some entries from the table before you can add other entries.

```
Version table is corrupt.
```
You'll need to delete the SETVER.EXE file and get a fresh copy off your original DOS disks (using the EXPAND command).

Examples

The easiest way to see what programs are listed in the version table is with this command:

    C:\>**setver | more**

Adding programs

Let's say you have a program called MYPROG.EXE that reports it can't run under DOS 6. You can try to fool it into thinking it's running under DOS 3.31. First, use SETVER to set a table entry and then restart your computer:

    C:\>**setver myprog.exe 3.31**

Removing programs

The LapLink (LL3.EXE) program is listed in the default table as needing to run under DOS 4.01. If you purchase a new version of LapLink that knows about DOS 5 or 6, you can remove this entry from the table:

    C:\>**setver ll3.exe /d**

See also

DEVICE=   This command allows you to load device drivers into DOS.

DEVICEHIGH= Same as DEVICE=, except that it allows you to load device drivers into upper memory.

SHARE   DOS 3.0 and later, External

Provides safe file sharing

This command loads itself into memory when you run it to provide file sharing and locking facilities.

When and why

You'll want to use this command with task-switching programs, such as the DOS Shell Task Swapper, DesqView, or Microsoft Windows. Without SHARE , it's possible for several programs to try to write to the same file at the same time, which can lead to unpredictable results, including losing your data.

You may also need to load SHARE if you're using a network. Contact your network manager to find out.

SHARE ensures that two programs don't try to write to a file at the same time. Instead of your data being altered quietly, one of the programs will probably display an error message about permission not available (or something about SHARE) and give you a chance to try again. You can then switch to the program that's currently using the file and make it available to the other program.

Syntax

share [/**f**:*bufsize*] [/**l**:*files*]

Loads SHARE into memory. You can also use an INSTALL= line in your CONFIG.SYS file to load SHARE, in which case you'll also have to supply the path and extension.

Switches

/f:*bufsize*
Size of file lock buffer. This switch allows you to set the size (in bytes) of SHARE's buffer (in memory) where it keeps track of what files (or parts of files) are currently locked. (Default is 2048.)

/l:*files*
Number of locked files. Sets the maximum number of files that can be locked at any one time. (Default is 20.)

Notes

DOS 4.0 and SHARE

This is a strange one. According to the DOS 4.0 manuals, you need to load SHARE if you have a hard disk partition larger than 32MB. But we know a number of people who run DOS 4.0 on large hard disks without using SHARE and have no problems. And if you think about it, DOS has to be able to access your hard disk before it can load SHARE, so why does it need SHARE? We don't know. We've even heard a story that the IBM programmers who wrote DOS 4.0 say you don't need to load SHARE.

Our guess is that IBM wanted to require SHARE for safety reasons but knew that existing users would complain if they had to load it. However, since support for hard disk partitions larger than 32MB was new to DOS 4.0, IBM may have felt they could require SHARE for such large partitions without users complaining (since they couldn't have large partitions before). But this is just a guess by one programmer about other programmers' intentions.

Memory used

SHARE uses about 6K in memory with the default settings. If you have a 386 memory manager, you may be able to load SHARE into upper memory using the LOADHIGH command.

Examples

Installing in CONFIG.SYS

It's often convenient to load SHARE from within your CONFIG.SYS file. Here is an example of how you'd do that:

```
install=c:\dos\share.exe
```

Installing in AUTOEXEC.BAT

If, however, you want to load SHARE into upper memory, you'll have to install it from your AUTOEXEC.BAT file:

```
loadhigh share
```

See also

INSTALL=   You can use this command in your CONFIG.SYS file to load SHARE there rather than in your AUTOEXEC.BAT file.

LOADHIGH   You can use this command to load SHARE into upper memory.

SHELL   All DOS, CONFIG.SYS

Load command-line interpreter

This command in your CONFIG.SYS file allows you to load a command-line processor other than COMMAND.COM or to set options on COMMAND.COM.

When and why

You may never create or modify this line in your CONFIG.SYS file. The DOS Setup program automatically adds such a line to your CONFIG.SYS file when it installs DOS. But your computer will run just fine without it.

There are two cases when you'll want to create or make changes to this line. First, you might want to use some of COMMAND's switches to change its default settings. For example, you might want to set the minimum size of DOS's environment. The examples that follow show how to do this. And second, you might want to use a third-party replacement for COMMAND.COM.

Syntax

shell=*filespec* [*parameters*]

Loads a command-line interpreter of your choice, which is usually COMMAND.COM.

Parameters

filespec

Program. The name of the program (with its extensions and path if it's not in the root directory) you want to use as the command-line interpreter. The only time you'll want to use a program other than COMMAND.COM is if you have a COMMAND.COM replacement. (See the description for COMMAND on what parameters and switches to use.) If there is no SHELL= line in your CONFIG.SYS file, DOS uses \COMMAND.COM as the command-line interpreter.

Notes

Warning! Be careful when you use this command with a filename other than COMMAND.COM. If DOS can't find the program you name in SHELL=, it won't be able to boot, and you'll have to boot from a floppy disk (in DOS 6 and later you can press F5 to bypass CONFIG.SYS when DOS first starts). So it's a good idea to make sure you have a DOS floppy disk around.

The DOS Shell

Don't confuse the SHELL= command in CONFIG.SYS with the DOS Shell program — they're not related. The SHELL= line loads COMMAND.COM (or an alternate

Part II: Command Reference

command-line processor), whereas you start the DOS Shell program (which is a graphical interface) by typing **DOSSHELL**.

Messages
`Bad or missing command interpreter`
You'll see this message when DOS can't find the program you specified in the SHELL= line of your CONFIG.SYS file. At this point DOS will stop trying to boot; you'll have to insert a floppy disk that contains DOS and restart your computer. Then modify the CONFIG.SYS file so SHELL= contains the correct name.

Examples

Increasing environment size
By default, the minimum size of DOS's environment is 256 bytes, which may not be large enough for some programs, such as AutoCAD, that use a lot of environment variables. If you get the `Out of environment space` message, you can use a line such as the following in your CONFIG.SYS file to increase the default size of DOS's environment:

```
shell=command.com /e:1024 /p
```

This increases the default size to 1,024 bytes. Note that the /P switch is required to make these changes permanent.

A replacement program
You might also have a third-party program that is designed as a replacement for COMMAND.COM. There aren't many such programs, and their documentation will always tell you how to install them with SHELL=. For example, here is the line for one such program (called NDOS):

```
shell=c:\ndos.com /p
```

This, of course, assumes you've copied NDOS.COM to the root directory of your hard disk. It's better, however, to keep it in its own directory and supply its full pathname in the SHELL= line.

See also
COMMAND	The description of COMMAND will tell you what switches and parameters you can use.
CONFIG.SYS	The description of CONFIG.SYS in this reference section tells you more about how DOS uses this file.
DOSSHELL	This is the command you want to use (and not SHELL=) if you want to start the DOS Shell program.

SHIFT All DOS, Batch file

Shift batch file parameters left
This command provides access to more than nine parameters on the command line. It's also useful for processing parameters within a loop.

SHIFT

When and why
You'll only use this command if you're writing batch files. SHIFT is very useful when you want a batch file to work with a set of parameters. You normally are limited to working with nine parameters, %0 through %9, (plus the name of the program). SHIFT allows you to supply more than nine parameters to a batch file. It also allows you to write batch files that work with any number of parameters.

Syntax
shift

There are no parameters or switches for the SHIFT command.

Notes

What SHIFT does
Each time you execute SHIFT in a batch file, all the parameters will be shifted left one place. In other words, %0 takes on the contents of %1, %1 in turn takes on the contents of %2, and so on, and %9 takes on the value of any unused parameters. The chart below shows how parameters will change after each shift (this is for the batch command "test one two three", where TEST is the name of the batch file):

	%0	%1	%2	%3	%4
At start:	test	one	two	three	
after SHIFT	one	two	three		
after SHIFT	two	three			
after SHIFT	three				
after SHIFT					

You can see that the parameters become empty after enough shifts.

Examples
This short example, which we'll call DELETE.BAT, shows how you can create a version of the DEL command that accepts more than one file parameter:

```
@echo off
:loop
if "%1" == "" goto end
del %1
shift
goto loop
:end
```

You can apply the same logic to extend any DOS command so that it accepts more than one parameter. For example, to create a batch file called VIEW.BAT that allows you to view several text files, one after the other, you could replace the line in the batch file above

```
del %1
```

with

```
type %1 | more
```

Part II: Command Reference

This creates a TYPE command that lets you view several files as if they were one large file.

See also
%n   These are the replaceable parameters that are affected by the SHIFT command.

FOR   The FOR command is another method you can use for working with lists of files (as opposed to multiple parameters).

SIZER   DOS 6 and later, External

Used by MemMaker to optimize memory usage

This file is used by MemMaker during the memory optimization process. You should not run it yourself.

When and why
You don't want to use this program directly. MemMaker uses SIZER to help it optimize your use of memory. This program helps MemMaker determine how much space each device driver and memory-resident program uses.

SMARTDRV   DOS 4.0 and later, Device driver

Creates a disk cache

SMARTDRV creates a cache of recently used sectors from the disk in expanded or extended memory.

A disk cache can dramatically increase the speed of disk access. It does this by caching recently used disk sectors so programs that try to read one of these sectors again will be able to read it from memory rather than the disk drive. (*Note:* Prior to DOS 6 and Windows for Workgroups, the driver was SMARTDRV.SYS.)

When and why
As long as you've got some extended or expanded memory to spare, you'll probably want to use SMARTDRV or a commercial disk cache program. Most of the commercial disk utility packages (such as the Norton Utilities, PC Tools, and the Mace Utilities) include disk caches that are at least as good as SMARTDRV, if not better. Any disk cache will speed up disk access.

Here's a brief discussion of why a cache increases your computer's speed. Disk drives have a performance figure, called the average access time, that is a measure of how long it takes to read a single piece of information from your disk drive. For hard disks, this figure is typically in the 10 – 65ms (1/1000 seconds) range, while floppy disks are in the 200ms range (unless the motor is off, in which case it can be even longer). Reading the same data from memory, on the other hand, takes less than 1ms, which is very fast.

SMARTDRV

> Caches use a large area of memory to keep copies of sectors that have been read or written recently. When a program needs to read one of these sectors again, the cache can return the data in less than 1ms (if it's in the cache), which can speed up a program. Once the cache fills up, the cache program will throw out the oldest sectors to make room for new ones.
>
> *Note:* SmartDrive was extensively revised for the release of DOS 6. The most obvious change is the conversion from a device driver to a command.

Syntax

device=[*path*]**smartdrv.sys** [*startsize* [*winsize*]] [**/a**]   (DOS 4 – 5)
Use this line in your CONFIG.SYS file to create a disk cache.

device=[*path*]**smartdrv.exe /double_buffer**   (DOS 6 and later)
Use this line in your CONFIG.SYS file to load the device driver for double buffering (see "Notes" later for details). You must start SmartDrive from your AUTOEXEC.BAT file.

smartdrv [[*drive*[+|-]]...] [**/x**] [**/e:***elementsize*] [*startsize*][*winsize*]] [**/b:***buffersize*] [**/u**] [**/c**|**/r**] [**/f**|**/n**] [**/l**] [**/v**|**/q**|**/s**] [**/v**]
This command loads SMARTDRV into memory and creates a disk cache. Normally, you'll put this line into your AUTOEXEC.BAT file. Once SMARTDRV is loaded, you can use the following form to control which drives will be cached.

smartdrv [[*drive*[+|-]]...]] [**/c**] [**/r**]
smartdrv [**/x**] [[*drive*[+|-]]...]] [**/c**|**/r**] [**/f**|**/n**] [**/q**|**/s**]   (DOS 6.2 and later)
Use this command to manage the disk cache and control which drives SMARTDRV will cache.

smartdrv [**/s**]
Displays information about the SmartDrive cache.

Parameters

path
Path to driver. The location of the SMARTDRV.EXE device driver, which will usually be in the same directory as all your DOS commands (often the C:\DOS directory).

drive[+|-]
The drive to cache. The drive or drives that you want SmartDrive to cache or to stop caching. You have three choices: when you supply a drive without a + or - after it, SmartDrive will cache reads. Add a plus (+) and SmartDrive will cache both reads and writes. If you put a minus sign (-) after the drive, SmartDrive will disable caching for that drive.

By default (if you don't list any drive letters), SmartDrive caches reads for floppy disk drives and InterLnk drives, while SmartDrive caches both reads and writes for hard disks. SmartDrive provides no cache for CD-ROM drives, network drives, and Microsoft Flash memory cards. (SmartDrive caches the host drive for DoubleSpace volumes.)

startsize
Initial cache size. The initial size, in kilobytes, of the cache, which uses extended memory. Can be any number between 128 and 8,192. (Default is 256 for DOS 4 and 5. For DOS 6 it depends on how much extended memory you have — see "Notes.")

winsize
Windows cache size (Windows 3.0 or later). If you're running under Microsoft Windows, programs can change and reduce the size of the memory cache. You can set the minimum cache size so that programs won't reduce it below this number. Can be any number between 128 and 8,192. (Default is 0. In DOS 6 or later, see "Notes" for default.)

Note: This parameter has no effect if you're not running Microsoft Windows.

Switches

/e:*elementsize*
Bytes moved by SmartDrive (DOS 6 and later). This switch controls how much data SmartDrive moves at a time. Since SmartDrive uses extended memory and DOS uses conventional memory, SmartDrive needs to move data back and forth between conventional and extended memory. The only reason you would want to change this number is to reduce the amount of memory SmartDrive uses in either upper or lower memory. SmartDrive uses more memory with larger values, but it is also faster. Valid values: 1024, 2048, 4096, and 8192 (all measured in bytes). (Default is 8192).

/b:*buffersize*
Buffer size (DOS 6 and later). The size of the read-ahead buffer in kilobytes (K). The read ahead buffer controls how much data SmartDrive will read from the disk at a time. Without SmartDrive, DOS often reads single sectors at a time (512 bytes). In order to speed up programs that read several sectors in a row (which is very common), SmartDrive pre-reads a chunk much larger than a single sector. That way the next sector will already be waiting in memory for DOS when it asks to read the next sector. This size must be a multiple of the *ElementSize* used in the /E switch divided by 1024. Using larger buffer sizes increases the amount of lower or upper memory used by SmartDrive, so you won't want this number to be too high. (Default is 16.)

/c
Write cache (DOS 6 and later). This command tells SMARTDRV to immediately write cached information to the disk if it hasn't been written yet. This switch only has an effect on drives with both read and write caching enabled. You'll want to run SMARTDRV /C before you turn your computer off.

/x
Disable delayed write cache (DOS 6.2 and later). This switch prevents SmartDrive from using a write-behind cache, which buffers writes in memory so that the data isn't actually written to the disk until later (usually within a few seconds). Using this switch keeps your data safer but at the expense of speed. This switch turns off write caching for *all* drives. Use a drive letter without a plus sign to turn off write caching for a single drive.

/r
Restart (DOS 6 and later). This switch clears the contents of the disk cache (writing cached writes first) and restarts the cache, using any new settings. We're not sure why you would want to use this switch.

/f
Write cache before prompt (DOS 6.2 and later). This switch tells SmartDrive to write the cache before showing the DOS prompt again. We suggest using this option because most people are taught that they can turn their computer off as soon as they see the

SMARTDRV

DOS prompt. *Note:* if you're using a DOS shell, such as the Norton Commander, that shows a DOS prompt, SmartDrive may not write the cache before you see this prompt because it isn't really DOS's prompt. To be absolutely safe, exit any DOS shell if you're using this switch before you shut off your computer. Default setting.

/n
Write cache when idle (DOS 6.2 and later). Tells SmartDrive to write data in the write cache only when your computer is idle, which could be several seconds or more after a program thinks it has written data to your disk drive. Use this setting with caution: it is possible to lose data with this setting if you shut off your computer before SmartDrive writes the write cache to the disk drive. You can manually write all data to the disk drive using the /C switch.

/l
Load low (DOS 6 and later). SMARTDRV automatically loads itself into upper memory if it is available. This switch forces SmartDrive to load into lower memory even if UMBs are available. You might need to use this switch if you're using the Double Buffering feature and SmartDrive seems to be too slow. (Default is load into upper memory.)

/q
Quiet (DOS 6 and later). Suppresses the display of status messages. This switch isn't useful in your AUTOEXEC.BAT since SMARTDRV doesn't display the status information when you first load it (unless you use the /V switch). However, you can use it whenever you run the SMARTDRV command to *change* which or how drives are cached. In this case SMARTDRV normally displays status information, but you can use the /Q switch to suppress this information. (Default: /Q when you install SMARTDRV into memory, /V thereafter.)

/v
Verbose (DOS 6 and later). Display status messages during the startup process. This switch cannot be used with the /Q switch. (Default: /Q when you install SMARTDRV into memory, /V thereafter.)

/s
Status (DOS 6 and later). Provides additional information about cache size and usage. This switch displays information about how well the cache is doing, such as how many blocks can fit into the cache, how many times SMARTDRV found data already in memory, and how many times it had to read from the disk. If you're using Windows, you can get even more information by running the SMARTMON program.

/u
Don't load CD-ROM support (DOS 6.2 and later). Tells SmartDrive not to load code that provides caching for CD-ROM drives. Normally, SmartDrive can cache reads from a CD-ROM drive, which can dramatically speed up CD-ROM drives. However, if you either have no CD-ROM drives or you don't want to use this support, you can save some memory by disabling this feature. After you disable this feature, you won't be able to cache individual CD-ROM drives until you restart your computer and load SMARTDRV without this switch. See "Notes" section about using SmartDrive with CD-ROM drives.

/double_buffer
Double Buffering (DOS 6 and later). Loads the double-buffering device driver. To use this switch, you must install SmartDrive as a device in your CONFIG.SYS file. Loading SMARTDRV as a device driver doesn't actually create the cache; it just creates a small 2K buffer in low memory. You'll need to use this option with some types of disk drive controllers. Some disk controllers, particularly SCSI (Small Computer System Interface) disk controllers, may write to the wrong area of memory when you have SMARTDRV loaded into upper memory (the default). You may also need to use double buffering with ESDI (Enhanced System Device Interface) or MCA (MicroChannel Architecture) devices.

/a   (Only available with SMARTDRV.SYS)
Expanded memory (DOS 4 and 5). Uses expanded memory rather than extended memory. (Default is extended memory.)

Windows Note: Do not use the /A switch with Microsoft Windows if your EMS memory is being creatd by EMM386 or another 386 memory manager.

Notes

SmartDrive and CD-ROM drives
If you want SmartDrive to be able to cache CD-ROM drives, you must make sure that you load SMARTDRV after you load MSCDEX. For example, you might have the following lines in your AUTOEXEC.BAT file:

```
mscdex /d:sony_000
```
```
smartdrv.exe
```

SmartDrive and data loss in DOS 6
There have been a number of reports of data loss when using SmartDrive in DOS 6.0 that all seem to stem from a design decision made by Microsoft when it built DOS 6.0. Starting with DOS 6, SmartDrive supports a feature known as write-behind caching, which saves data in memory that needs to be written to the disk. This data isn't actually transferred to the disk drive right away. Instead, many different writes to a disk can be buffered into memory, and they're only written to the disk drive during idle time or when the write cache becomes full.

The problem with write-behind caching is that it is possible for you to turn off your computer before SmartDrive has written all the new data to the disk. Many people have been taught that they can safely turn off their computer as soon as they see the DOS prompt. But with the SmartDrive in DOS 6.0 this wasn't true. To solve this problem, Microsoft made another change to SmartDrive in DOS 6.2 — they made the new /F the default setting, which causes the write cache to be written to the disk before DOS displays the prompt.

However, if you're using a DOS shell, such as the Norton Commander, that provides a simulation of the DOS prompt, SmartDrive may still not have written its cache when you see the prompt inside such programs.

You have several options to protect yourself. First, run SMARTDRV /C before you turn off your computer. This always writes changes to your disks. Second, turn off write-behind caching using the /X switch. This always works, but it also means that

SMARTDRV

disk writes slow down because SmartDrive no longer buffers writes. Finally, keep the /F switch on and make sure that you exit all programs, including DOS shells or menuing programs, before you turn off your computer.

Write-behind caching and Windows
Whenever you exit Windows, Windows automatically tells SmartDrive to write all changes to the disk, even if you have write-behind caching enabled.

SmartDrive and Windows
Microsoft Windows comes with its own version of SmartDrive, which you should use only if it is more recent than your DOS version of SMARTDRV. All versions of Windows up to and including Windows 3.1 shipped with a version of SMARTDRV.SYS. Windows for Workgroups 3.1, however, is the first version of Windows to ship with SMARTDRV.EXE. That version is version 4.0, while the version shipped with DOS 6 is version 4.1 (version 5.0 in DOS 6.2). You can find out the version of SMARTDRV.EXE by simply typing **smartdrv** at the command line. SMARTDRV will display a message like this, as well as much status information:

```
C:\>smartdrv
Microsoft SMARTDrive Disk Cache version 5.0
Copyright 1991,1993 Microsoft Corp.
    . . .
```

You should always use whichever version of SMARTDRV has the highest version number.

SmartDrive and DoubleSpace
SmartDrive doesn't directly supply a cache for compressed volumes. But it does cache the host disk drive. For example, if your drive C is a DoubleSpace drive, and DoubleSpace's hidden volume file is on drive H, SmartDrive will cache all reads and writes to drive H. The end result is that SmartDrive does provide caching for DoubleSpace drives. For example, here is the default settings on one of our laptop computers:

drive	read cache	write cache	buffering
A:	yes	no	no
B:	yes	no	no
C:*	yes	yes	no
H:	yes	yes	no

* DoubleSpace drive cached via host drive.

Default cache sizes
In DOS 6 and later, SmartDrive uses fairly good default values for the size of the cache, depending on how much extended memory you have.

Extended memory available	StartSize	WinSize
0 to 1 MB	All extended	0 (no cache)
1 to 2 MB	1MB	256K
2 to 4 MB	1MB	512K
4 to 6 MB	2MB	1MB
6 MB or more	2MB	2MB

SMARTDRV and DEVICEHIGH

Warning! If you are using a version earlier than DOS 6, don't load SMARTDRV.SYS into the upper memory area using the DEVICEHIGH command! Some disk drive controllers, particularly SCSI disk controllers, may write to the wrong area of memory when you have SMARTDRV.SYS loaded in the upper memory area. And don't use EMS memory with a disk cache when running Windows if the EMS memory has been created from extended memory. In DOS 6, you can use double buffering to address this problem.

What SMARTDRV caches

(DOS 6 and later.) SMARTDRV.EXE in DOS 6 and later is much improved over previous versions. SMARTDRV reads large chunks of your disk at one time (the chunk size is controlled by the /B switch and is normally 8,192 bytes) whenever DOS wants to read a sector (512 bytes) from the disk. By reading larger chunks at a time, the data your program needs is very likely to be in memory. And since reading from memory is a lot faster than reading from disk, this helps speed up disk access. SMARTDRV can also keep around a large number of these chunks, which increases the chance even more that the data your programs need will already be in memory.

(DOS 4 and 5.) SMARTDRV.SYS reads entire disk tracks, which typically hold 17 sectors each (high-capacity disks can have 25, 33, or more sectors per track). When DOS loads SMARTDRV, you'll see a message that reports how many sectors are contained in each track, as well as how many tracks SMARTDRV can cache:

```
Microsoft SMARTDrive Disk Cache version 3.13
    Cache size: 512K in Extended Memory
    Room for 60 tracks of 17 sectors each
    Minimum cache size will be OK
```

Size of the cache in DOS 4 and 5

(DOS 4 and 5 only.) SMARTDRV rounds the actual size down to a multiple of the largest track size for all the hard disks in your system. If there isn't enough memory for this size cache, SMARTDRV will create a smaller cache using as much memory as it can.

Writing the cache to disk

Turning off your computer may cause you to lose any information currently in the cache that hasn't been written to disk yet. There are several approaches you can take to avoid this. First, any time you restart your computer using Ctrl-Alt-Del, SMARTDRV automatically writes any unwritten data to the disk. You can also use SMARTDRV /C to tell SMARTDRV to immediately write cached data back to the disk (the Windows SMARTMON program has a button that does the same thing). The final option is that you can disable write caching on all drives since the problem we've described here only applies to write caching.

Types of memory

If you're not familiar with extended vs. expanded memory, you'll find a good description of the different types of memory in the description of the MEM command.

SMARTDRV

You'll probably get the best results by using extended rather than expanded memory (extended memory is your only option in DOS 6 and later). This is because access to extended memory is generally faster than access to expanded memory.

Using extended memory

You'll need to install HIMEM.SYS or another XMS (eXtended Memory Specification) memory manager to use extended memory with SMARTDRV. If you're using DOS 4 or 5, this HIMEM.SYS line must appear in your CONFIG.SYS file before the line that installs SMARTDRV.SYS (otherwise, the XMS memory manager won't be running when SMARTDRV asks for extended memory).

Networks

SMARTDRV does no caching on network drives or in DOS 4 and 5 to floppy disks. It only works with hard disks attached to your computer (SMARTDRV does, however, provide read caching for InterLnk drives).

Determining when you need double buffering

If you're using an 80286 computer, you won't need double buffering. You may need double buffering only if you have at least an 80386 computer, and you're using Windows, EMM386, or some other program that creates Upper Memory Blocks out of extended memory. And in these cases, you'll only need to use double buffering if you have a disk controller that isn't compatible with these schemes, such as SCSI, or sometimes ESDI and MCA devices. If you're not sure, here's how you can test to see if you need double buffering:

♦ First, you'll need to add the following line to your CONFIG.SYS file to turn on double buffering. In case you do need it, this will keep your computer from having problems:

```
device=c:\dos\smartdrv.exe /double_buffer
```

♦ Next, you'll want to add the following line to your AUTOEXEC.BAT (unless it's already there) to actually create a disk cache:

```
c:\dos\smartdrv
```

You should put this line at the very start of your AUTOEXEC.BAT file (or right after an @ECHO OFF line) so it will speed up processing of your AUTOEXEC.BAT file itself. We've put a path in front of this command in case you have this line before the PATH statement.

♦ Next, you'll want to make sure you've set up your computer so you have enough Upper Memory Blocks so SMARTDRV can load itself into upper memory. You can use the MEM /C/P command to determine whether SMARTDRV is loading itself into upper memory. If it's not, you might want to run MemMaker to optimize your use of memory.

♦ Finally, run SMARTDRV by itself to see if it's using buffering for any of the disk drives. You will see a listing that looks something like this:

drive	read cache	write cache	buffering
A:	yes	no	no
B:	yes	no	no
C:	yes	yes	yes
D:	yes	yes	-

If you see a yes anywhere in the buffering column (such as the example above), you definitely need to use double buffering. A hyphen in the buffering column, such as for drive D, means that SMARTDRV couldn't determine whether it needed double buffering. This could be the case if SMARTDRV isn't actually being loaded into upper memory. Use the MEM /C/P command to ensure that SMARTDRV is not being loaded into upper memory. If the buffering column contains a no in every line, you can remove the SMARTDRV.EXE line from your CONFIG.SYS file.

Messages

Here are some of the more mysterious messages you'll encounter with the DOS 4 and 5 versions of SMARTDRV.SYS:

```
Incompatible disk partition detected.
```
or
```
WARNING: SMARTDrive will not check for incompatible disk partitions.
         Data corruption may result.
```
(DOS 4 and 5 only.) SMARTDRV works at a very low level, so it needs to know about the disks it's working with. There are some disk partitioning programs that don't follow the normal specifications for partitioning hard disks. In these cases SMARTDRV won't be able to read tracks from the disk. You can either find a commercial cache program that works with your hard disk or use a disk partitioning program that is compatible with SMARTDRV.

```
No hard drives on system
```
(DOS 4 and 5 only.) SMARTDRV only works on local hard disks (it doesn't work on floppy disks or networks), so you need at least one local hard disk for SMARTDRV to work.

```
Too many bytes per track on hard drive
```
(DOS 4 and 5 only.) You probably have a hard disk with very large tracks. You might want to use a commercial disk cache program that can handle your hard disk.

Here's a message that you see with SMARTDRV.EXE in DOS 6 and later:

```
    You must specify the host drive for a DoubleSpace drive.
```

To turn on write caching for a DoubleSpace volume, you need to give the drive letter for the host drive rather than the DoubleSpace volume's drive letter.

Examples

Controlling caching options

Let's say that you have floppy disk drive A, a hard disk C, and a CD-ROM drive D. In this case, the following command turns on read caching for drive A, read/write caching for drive C, and no caching for drive D:

```
C:\>smartdrv a c+ d-
```

A drive letter without a plus sign tells SmartDrive to provide read caching only. A plus sign says to use both read and write caching. And a minus sign tells SmartDrive to provide no caching at all.

The normal installation

Normally, you'll install SMARTDRV without any switches or parameters since the defaults are quite good. In DOS 6 or later you should install SMARTDRV in your AUTOEXEC.BAT file, using a line like this:

smartdrv

In DOS 4 and 5, you'll need to install SMARTDRV using a line in your CONFIG.SYS file, like the following:

device=c:\dos\smartdrv.sys 1024

In any event, you'll need to make sure you have an extended memory manager such as HIMEM.SYS loaded so SMARTDRV can use extended memory.

Using double buffering

If you have a computer that has problems using SMARTDRV.EXE in upper memory (such as a SCSI disk drive), you might need to use double buffering. To do this, you'll need two lines to load SMARTDRV: one in your CONFIG.SYS file and the other in your AUTOEXEC.BAT file. Here is the line you would want in your CONFIG.SYS file:

device=c:\dos\smartdrv.exe /double_buffer

This line creates a small buffer in low memory, but it doesn't actually load the disk cache. To load the disk cache, add this line to your AUTOEXEC.BAT file:

c:\dos\smartdrv.exe

This command will create your disk cache and use the buffer in low memory that SMARTDRV created as a result of the line in your CONFIG.SYS file.

Using expanded memory

(DOS 4 and 5 only.) If you're using expanded memory, you'll need to install an expanded memory manager before you install SMARTDRV. If your computer uses an 80386 or better microprocessor, you can use the EMM386 device driver for this purpose. Otherwise, you'll have to use the device driver supplied with your computer (in the case of laptop computers that have expanded memory hardware built in) or with your expanded memory board. Here is how you'd use a cache in expanded memory:

device=c:\dos\smartdrv.sys 1024 /a

This allocates 1MB of expanded memory for use as a disk cache.

Microsoft Windows

Use the version of SMARTDRV that comes with Windows if it has a more recent date than the SMARTDRV that is in your DOS directory. If the file is SMARTDRV.SYS (as it is for Windows 3.1), it's definitely older than any version named SMARTDRV.EXE. (Windows for Workgroups 3.1 ships with version 4.0 of SMARTDRV.EXE, while DOS 6.0 ships with version 4.1 of SMARTDRV.EXE.) You may also want to provide a minimum size for the cache since Windows programs can change the cache size:

C:\>**c:\dos\smartdrv.exe 1024 256**

This will set the cache size to 1MB, with a minimum size (under Windows) of 256K.

Here is how Microsoft Windows changes your cache size. If your cache is in extended memory and you start Windows in standard mode or 386 enhanced mode, Windows immediately reduces the size of the cache to the minimum value. This minimum value is 0 for SMARTDRV.SYS if you don't specify a minimum value. For SMARTDRV.EXE, the minimum value depends on the amount of free extended memory you have (see "Notes" section above). This allows Windows to manage this memory and work with SMARTDRV to provide both disk caching and memory management for Windows programs. As soon as you exit Windows, the cache will return to its normal size.

If your cache is in expanded memory (SMARTDRV.SYS only), Windows will only reduce the size of the cache when you run Windows in real mode (which uses expanded memory because real mode can't use extended memory). It will reduce the size of the cache only as Windows needs more expanded memory (rather than reducing the cache size as soon as it starts).

See also

BUFFERS	DOS maintains some internal data buffers that you can use to speed up disk access. Using a disk cache such as SMARTDRV is better than using DOS's buffers, if you have the memory for SMARTDRV.
EMM386.EXE	If your computer has an 80386 or better microprocessor, you can use this device driver to turn extended memory into expanded memory.
FASTOPEN	FASTOPEN speeds up opening files. While in theory this can complement SMARTDRV, in practice you won't need to use FASTOPEN if you're using SMARTDRV.
HIMEM.SYS	You'll need to install this device driver before you install SMARTDRV if you want SMARTDRV to store its cache in extended memory.
MEM	You can use the MEM command to see if you have any expanded or extended memory on your computer. You'll need one or the other to use SMARTDRV.
RAMDRIVE.SYS	If you're working with a small number of files that don't change, you might want to create a RAM disk instead of, or in addition to, a disk cache.
SMARTMON	This is a Windows program that allows you to control SMARTDRV's cache. It also displays performance data.

SMARTMON   DOS 6 and later, External

Windows controller for SmartDrive

SMARTMON is a Windows program that lets you control and monitor your SmartDrive disk cache.

When and why

If you're running Windows, you'll want to use this program, rather than SMARTDRV, to make changes to SMARTDRV after you've loaded it into memory. You still have to install SMARTDRV *before* you start Windows.

This program allows you to turn caching on and off for individual disk drives, and it also has a number of monitoring features that the DOS SMARTDRV program doesn't have. Any changes you can make with SMARTDRV you can also make with SMARTMON.

Notes

To run SMARTMON, you can either install a new icon in Program Manager (as shown above) or use the Run command from the File menu and enter **SMARTMON** as the command name.

The SmartDrive Monitor displays a bar graph showing the performance history of the SmartDrive cache. SMARTMON uses buttons and drop-down lists (combo boxes, in Windows jargon) to provide the same configuration options as the switches on the SMARTDRV command. You can even append the SMARTDRV configuration to the batch file of your choice (including AUTOEXEC.BAT).

Note: You can press the Help button to read SmartDrive Monitor's own on-line help. When you click on the Help button, you may discover that SmartDrive Monitor's window stays in front of the Help window. If this happens, click on the system menu (the gray box in the upper-left corner of the SmartDrive Monitor window) and select Always on Top to remove the check mark next to this item. Finally, click on the Help button again.

See also

SMARTDRV   This is the actual disk-caching program.

SORT   All DOS, External

Filter for sorting lines

This command allows you to sort lines in alphabetic (or numeric) order. Because it is a filter, you must use either input redirection (the < character) or piping (the | character) as the source for lines.

When and why

This is a useful program if you have some lines to sort. We haven't used it much ourselves since our word processor has a SORT command built into it.

Syntax

sort [/**r**] [/+*column*] <*filespec1* [>*filespec2*]
Sorts the lines in a file.

command | **sort** [/**r**] [/+*column*] [>*filespec2*]
Sorts the lines from the output of another command.

Parameters

<filespec1>
File to sort. The file that contains lines you want to sort. Note that you must use the < input redirection character to provide input to the SORT command.

Switches

/r
Reverse order. Sorts lines in reverse order, from Z to A, and 9 to 0. The normal sort order is 0 to 9, followed by A to Z.

/+column
Sort column. Starts the sort in column *n* instead of at the start of each line (which is column 1). (Default is 1.)

Notes

Maximum size
SORT cannot sort lines in files larger than 64K.

Upper- vs. lowercase
SORT doesn't distinguish case, so the words *Sort* and *sort* will be grouped together.

Collating sequence
DOS 3.3 and later contain sort tables for each language that describe how to sort characters. This allows characters such as ü, Ü, u, and U to be grouped together. The SORT command uses the table inside DOS.

Messages

```
SORT: Too many parameters
```
You'll see this error message whenever you forget the < or the > before a filename. SORT doesn't allow you to directly type in a filename, so you must use one of these characters to redirect the input or the output of SORT. *Note:* The DOS 6 manual states incorrectly that the < for the input file is optional — it is required.

Examples

Sorting a list
If you have a phone list, called PHONE.TXT, that you want to sort, you can use the following commands:

```
C:\>sort <phone.txt >phone.new
C:\>del phone.txt
C:\>ren phone.new phone.txt
```

Whenever you sort a file, you should always use a different name for the output file. If you use the same name, you might lose all your data.

SORT and MORE
You can use the pipe redirector (|) to pass the output from SORT through MORE so that the information is displayed one screen at a time. Before the update of the DIR

command in DOS 5, which has switches to sort DIR's output, people often used SORT to sort their directory listings:

`C:\>dir | sort | more`

This series of commands was necessary to produce an alphabetical listing of the contents of a directory. Of course, today you can use the DIR /ON/P command to get the same results, but when we were young . . .

See also

| Use this character to redirect the output of a command to the input of another program.

<, >   These two characters provide input and output redirection, which allows you to read input from a file rather than the keyboard and write output to a file rather than to the display.

STACKS   DOS 3.2 and later, CONFIG.SYS

Reserve stack space for programs

This command reserves extra space for hardware interrupt handlers.

When and why

You'll probably want to avoid this command until you're ready to fine-tune your computer for optimum memory use. (In DOS 6, this command is often inserted by MemMaker.) The only other time you'll want to use STACKS is when you see the error messages listed in the "Messages" section; in that case, you may need to add a STACKS= line to your CONFIG.SYS file that increases the number of stacks from the default. For more information on stacks, see the "Notes" section.

Syntax

stacks=n**,**s

This line in your CONFIG.SYS file sets the number of independent stacks that are available for hardware interrupts.

Parameters

n

Number of stacks. Sets the number of independent stacks that DOS reserves for hardware interrupts. Valid range is 0 and 8 – 64. (Default size is 0 on IBM 8088-based computers and 9 on all other computers.)

s

Stack size. Sets the size (in bytes) for each of the independent stacks. Valid range is 0 and 32 – 512. (Default is 0 on IBM 8088-based computers and 128 on all others.)

Notes

What stacks are

The STACKS command is very technical, but we'll try to explain it in simple terms. Your computer has a number of pieces of hardware that work at the same time, such as your keyboard, display, and disk drives. These devices often need to get the attention of the microprocessor. For example, when you press a key on your keyboard, its hardware sends a signal to the microprocessor asking for attention. These signals are called *interrupts*. Each interrupt signal is handled by a small program called an *interrupt handler*.

The interrupt handlers need a small amount of memory, called a *stack*, to run. Without the stacks, interrupt handlers use memory from the program that's currently running. But if your computer receives several interrupts in quick succession, the interrupt handlers might use too much of the current program's memory. The STACKS command avoids this problem by reserving a separate stack for each interrupt handler.

Memory usage

Increasing the number of stacks, or the size of each stack, increases the size of DOS in memory, so you should not set STACKS= to too large a number and size. Some people also like to set STACKS=0,0. We don't suggest this, but you can certainly try it to see how it works.

MemMaker and STACKS

When you run MemMaker, it will often place the following line into your CONFIG.SYS file:

```
stacks=9,256
```

This is considered these days to be the standard setting for the STACKS command.

Zenith computers and GRAPHICS

If you're using the GRAPHICS command on Zenith computers, you'll need the following line in your CONFIG.SYS file:

```
stacks=9,256
```

Messages

```
Exception error 12
```
or
```
Internal stack overflow
```
If you see either of these messages, you should increase the number of stacks in the STACKS= command. The most common setting is STACKS=9,256.

```
Invalid STACK parameters
```
Make sure the STACKS= line in your CONFIG.SYS file is correct.

Example

This example shows how you might increase the number of stacks available for interrupts from the default of 9 to 10:

```
stacks=10,128
```

SUBMENU   DOS 6 and later, CONFIG.SYS

Create a submenu for a configuration menu

This command allows you to display a second level of menu choices in a CONFIG.SYS menu, also known as multiple configurations (see MENUITEM for details). You create first-level menus using the MENUITEM command in your CONFIG.SYS files.

When and why
If you're not using menus in your CONFIG.SYS file, you won't need this command. (See the MENUITEM command for more details.) This command allows a menu item in your startup menu to bring up another menu. Startup menus are menus that appear when DOS starts to process your CONFIG.SYS file and allow you to control which commands DOS will use from this file.

Syntax
    submenu=*menublock* [,*description*]
    Defines a menu item that will cause a secondary menu to appear when you select it.

Parameters
menublock
Name of menu block. The name of the block that has a submenu. This block elsewhere in your CONFIG.SYS file must start with a name in square brackets (such as [network]) followed by menu lines. Menu lines can include MENUITEM and SUBMENU, as well as a MENUCOLOR and MENUDEFAULT line. The name can have up to 70 characters in it, but you cannot use any of the following characters in a name: space \ / , ; = [and].

description
Menu title. This is the text that DOS displays as the menu entry. If you don't supply *description*, DOS uses *menublock* as the name of this menu item on the screen. The title can be up to 70 characters long and can contain any character. (Default is *menublock*.)

Notes
In order to use SUBMENU in your CONFIG.SYS file, you must first have a main menu, which is a section that starts with the line [menu]. This line must be followed by one or more MENUITEM and/or SUBMENU lines, which define items in the main menu. MENUITEM lines are connected to blocks that have a sequence of CONFIG.SYS commands, while SUBMENU items are connected to another menu block. In both cases, these blocks start with the *menublock* name in square brackets, such as [network]. This name must match the *menublock* name in the MENUITEM or the SUBMENU line. You'll find more details on how to use all these commands in the MENUITEM entry of this Command Reference.

Examples
Define a submenu
    This example shows a main menu with three items. Two of these menus will bring up submenus. The Windows submenu allows you to select between Workgroup and

Stand-alone. The net menu also has a submenu for selecting network options, but we haven't shown you this option.

The main menu block must exist for DOS to create a configuration menu. This is the first menu displayed by DOS. The main menu block is identified with the [menu] header. Each of these entries generates a menu entry. The actions for each menu entry is specified in an independent menu block.

```
[menu]
menuitem=Standard DOS
submenu=Windows
submenu=net, Network Options

[Standard DOS]
Device=ansi.sys
device=mouse.com

[Windows]
menuitem=Workgroup
menuitem=Stand-alone

[Workgroup]
. . .
[[Stand-alone]
. . .
[net]
menuitem. . .
```

The main menu will look something like this:

```
MS-DOS 6 Startup Menu


   1. Standard DOS
   2. Windows
   3. Network Options

Enter a choice: 1
```

When you select option 2, you'll see a menu that looks like the following:

```
MS-DOS 6 Startup Menu


   1. Workgroup
   2. Stand-alone

Enter a choice: 1
```

See also
CONFIG.SYS   Discusses the typical CONFIG.SYS commands and processing.

MENUCOLOR   Allows you to control the color of a menu or submenu.

MENUDEFAULT This command allows you to have a menu choice that will be used by default if you don't choose a menu item within *N* seconds.

MENUITEM This is the main command for designing configuration menus.

SUBST DOS 3.1 and later, External

Assign drive letter to directory

This command allows you to create a new drive letter that you can use to refer to a directory. It is mainly useful for older programs that don't allow you to type pathnames.

When and why

You may never find a use for this command. It allows you to use different directories with programs that didn't know about directories but could work with different drive letters. Chances are you won't buy or use such a program. (DOS 2.0, which was the first version of DOS with subdirectories, was introduced in 1983.)

The SUBST command allows you to treat a subdirectory as if it were another disk drive. For example, you might want the directory C:\WRITING to appear as the disk drive D:. All of its files and subdirectories will then appear in the root directory of the new D: drive. This disk drive isn't a real disk drive, of course, but most programs won't care.

Syntax

subst *drive*: *path*
Creates a drive letter that refers to a directory.

subst *drive*: **/d**
Deletes a drive letter created by SUBST.

subst
Without any parameters, displays all of the SUBST drive letters currently defined.

Parameters

drive:
New drive letter. The new drive letter you want to create.

path
Directory for new disk. The name of the directory that you want to appear as a new disk drive. The path can include a drive letter.

Switches

/d
Delete drive letter. This switch deletes a drive letter that you created with the SUBST command.

Notes
Relative paths
If the pathname you provide is a relative path (doesn't include a \ at the start), SUBST automatically converts it into a full path.

Incompatibilities
Not all programs will work correctly with drive letters created by SUBST. In particular, you should avoid using SUBST drive letters with the following DOS commands:

BACKUP, RESTORE, CHKDSK, DEFRAG, DISKCOMP, DISKCOPY, FDISK, FORMAT, LABEL, MIRROR, RECOVER, SYS, AND UNDELETE — all these commands need to work with real disk drives.

SUBST is fairly safe because all these commands refuse to work on drive letters created by SUBST.

Messages
```
Cannot SUBST a network drive
```
You can't use a path from a network drive in the SUBST command. In other words, you can't create a new drive letter that refers to a directory on a network drive.

```
Drive already SUBSTed
```
You've already created the drive letter with the SUBST command. If you want to change which directory the drive letter refers to, you'll have to delete it first.

```
Invalid parameter
```
When this message appears with a drive letter, it probably means you're off the end of the list of drive letters you can use. You might need to modify the LASTDRIVE= line in your CONFIG.SYS to allow more drive letters.

The other case where you might see this message is when you're trying to create a new drive letter using a directory on another drive created by SUBST. The path in the SUBST command must refer to a real disk drive.

Examples
Creating
To create the drive D: that contains all the contents of the C:\WRITING directory, type

```
C:\>subst d: c:\writing
```

Listing
You can then list the SUBST drive letters that are currently defined:

```
C:\>subst
D: => C:\WRITING
```

Deleting
And finally, to delete the drive letter:

```
C:\>subst d: /d
```

See also
ASSIGN	You can use the ASSIGN command to reassign drive letters between disk drives.

LASTDRIVE	To create drive letters with SUBST, you must make sure the LASTDRIVE= line in your CONFIG.SYS file is set to a high enough drive letter.

SWITCHES   PC-DOS 4.0, MS-DOS 5 and later, CONFIG.SYS

Controls various startup options

This command provides special command switches for the startup process. Among the features that it controls are making an enhanced keyboard perform like a standard keyboard, relocating the WINA20.386 file for Windows 3.0, and controlling the DOS 6 interactive startup process.

When and why

You'll probably never use this command for its original purpose. It was provided for programs written before IBM introduced its enhanced keyboard, which had a number of new keys. Some older programs didn't behave well when they saw these new keys, so IBM added this command to tell DOS not to generate the new keys on enhanced keyboards.

When DOS 5 was released, a second switch was added (/W). This switch was used to allow you to relocate the WINA20.386 file to a directory other than the root of the startup disk. This switch is necessary only if you are running Windows 3.0.

In DOS 6, two very important switches were added. These two switches, /F and /N, provide a way to disable the interactive startup process, a very important consideration in environments where you want to protect your system configuration.

Syntax

switches=[/k] [/w] [/n] [/f]

This command in your CONFIG.SYS file controls the startup process. Each switch controls a different function.

Switches

/k
Configure enhanced keyboard. You'll need this only for very old programs that don't recognize the enhanced keyboard. You'll probably never, ever, need to use this switch.

/w
WINA20 relocation. Do not use this switch with Windows 3.1 and later. You'll need this switch only if you're using Windows 3.0 and you want to move the WINA20.386 out of your root directory. If you do this, you must change a line in your SYSTEM.INI file. You will need a DEVICE= line in the [386enh] section that gives the full path and name of WINA20.386. You do not need this switch with Windows 3.1 or later.

/n
No interactive startup (DOS 6 and later). This switch disables the F5 and F8 key interactive startup features, which allows you to skip all or parts of your CONFIG.SYS file. For more information on these features, see the CONFIG.SYS entry in this command reference.

/f
Fast Start (DOS 6 and later). By default, DOS pauses two seconds after displaying the `Starting MS-DOS . . .` message upon startup. This switch eliminates that pause. If you specify the /N switch, you will probably want to use the /F switch as well since the only reason to pause is to allow you to press the F5 and F8 keys.

Notes

The /K switch and ANSI.SYS

If you're using the ANSI.SYS console device driver, you should place the /K switch at the end of its command line rather than using the SWITCHES= line in CONFIG.SYS.

What the /K switch affects

Note: This command only affects programs that read their keyboard input through DOS. Most programs bypass DOS and read keys directly from the ROM BIOS, which is the internal set of programs that work with the hardware such as the keyboard.

Examples

Disabling interactive startup

To completely disable interactive startup, your CONFIG.SYS file should contain

```
switches /n /f
```

This command is particularly useful if you want to configure a computer for someone who will be using a menu that doesn't give him or her access to DOS. This command in CONFIG.SYS will prevent such users from changing the way their computer starts. *Note:* Even with this switch, you can still press Ctrl-Break when DOS starts running your AUTOEXEC.BAT file to stop running that file, so it is still possible for someone to get inside CONFIG.SYS and make changes.

If you use these switches, be sure to have an emergency boot disk available. You will not be able to skip over the commands contained in your CONFIG.SYS file should there be a problem during startup.

See also

ANSI.SYS   If you're using the ANSI.SYS device driver, you should use its /K switch rather than this command to force a program to recognize the enhanced keyboard.

CONFIG.SYS   You'll find more information on using the F5 and F8 keys during DOS startup in the discussion on CONFIG.SYS.

SYS   All DOS, External

Transfer DOS (system) files

This command allows you to create a disk that you can boot DOS from or to update a boot disk created with an older version of DOS.

When and why

You'll probably use this command at some point. It allows you to create disks you can use to start DOS from. It is most commonly used when creating a survival floppy disk which you should keep near your computer in case you can't start DOS from your hard disk.

The SYS command copies four files (three in DOS 5 and two in versions before 5) to another disk: the two hidden files from your root directory, IO.SYS and MSDOS.SYS for MS-DOS, or IBMBIO.COM and IBMDOS.COM for some other versions of DOS (not just IBM), and the COMMAND.COM command-line interpreter (in DOS 5 and later). DOS 6 also copies the hidden DoubleSpace file DBLSPACE.BIN so DOS will be able to recognize a compressed hard disk when you start your computer from DOS on a floppy disk.

You can also use this command to update existing DOS floppy disks to DOS 6, which you'll definitely want to do if you've used DoubleSpace to compress your hard disk. Unlesss you boot with a DOS 6 hard disk, you won't be able to see any of your DoubleSpace disks.

Syntax

sys *drive2*:
sys [*drive1*:][*path*] *drive2*:   (DOS 4.0 and later)
Transfers the system files to another disk.

Parameters

[*drive1*:][*path*]
Source drive (DOS 4.0 and later). This drive and path, if present, tell the SYS command where to find the system files that you want it to copy to another disk.

drive2:
Destination drive. This is the drive

Notes

DOS 3.3 and earlier

In the old days, DOS 3.3 and earlier, you sometimes had to reformat your floppy disk before you could run SYS on it. This happened because DOS required that the two hidden system files had to be at the very start of the disk. This is no longer a problem. As long as you have enough free disk space, you can run SYS to copy all the files to the floppy disk.

Part II: Command Reference

DOS 4.0 and earlier
If you're not using DOS 5 or later, you'll have to copy the COMMAND.COM file after you run SYS (or use the /S switch on FORMAT).

ASSIGN, JOIN, and SUBST
You can't use SYS with drive letters created by ASSIGN or SUBST or drives affected by JOIN. Nor can you use SYS on network drives — you can only use it on disk drives connected directly to your computer.

Examples
Here is the command that will put MS-DOS on a disk in drive A:

```
C:\>sys a:
```

If you're not running DOS 5 or later, you'll also have to type

```
C:\>copy c:\command.com a:                              (DOS 4 and earlier)
```

See also
FORMAT   You can also use the /S switch to have FORMAT transfer the system files when it finishes. *Note:* If you're running DOS 4.0 or earlier, you'll have to copy COMMAND.COM.

TIME   All DOS, Internal

Report or set the time
This command displays the current time and allows you to change it.

When and why
You'll want to make sure your computer's date and time are correct since DOS uses them whenever it creates a new file (programs such as BACKUP use this date and time information). If your computer doesn't seem to remember the date and time after you've turned it off, read the "Notes" section. You'll also need to use this command to correct the time when you switch between Daylight Savings and Standard Times (or when traveling between time zones with a laptop computer).

Syntax
time
Without any parameters, TIME displays the current time and prompts you to enter a new time. You can press Enter if you don't want to make a change.

time *hours* [:*minutes* [:*seconds* [.*hundredths*]]][a|p]
Sets the current time.

Parameters
hours
The hours. Valid range is 0 – 23 (many countries use 0:01 rather than 12:01 a.m.). If you want to use the 12-hour format, you'll need to add a P at the end of times in the afternoon. (You have to use the 24-hour format for DOS versions before 4.0.)

minutes
The minutes. Valid range is 0 – 59.

seconds
The seconds. Valid range is 0 – 59.

hundredths
Hundredths of a second. Valid range is 0 – 99.

a|p
12-hour clock (DOS 4.0 and later). Refers to a.m. or p.m. for 12-hour format. Default is a.m. You can also provide the time in 24-hour format. *Note:* The A and P must immediately follow the time (without any space).

Notes

Clock forgets date and time

There are three things that could cause you to have to reset your clock's date and time each time you start DOS. First, your computer may not have a battery-backed clock that remembers the date and time with the power off (see the next note).

Second, the battery used to save the current date and time may need replacing.

And finally, if you're using DOS 3.3 or earlier, the DATE and TIME commands don't change the time in a battery-backed clock — they only change DOS's date and time for the current session. In this case you'll need to run the Diagnostic program on the Utilities disk that came with your computer.

Original IBM PC

The original IBM PC didn't have a built-in clock that would keep ticking with the power off, so you had to set the date and time each time you restarted your computer. If you're using such a computer, you'll need to run DATE and TIME in your AUTOEXEC.BAT file to set the clock each time you start DOS.

AUTOEXEC.BAT and time

If you don't have an AUTOEXEC.BAT file on your system, DOS will automatically run DATE and TIME. Otherwise, it won't run either.

Messages

```
Invalid time
Enter new time: _
```

You'll see this message when you enter a time that isn't valid. If you've supplied an A or P after the time, you'll see this message if there is a space between the time and the A or P. Simply retype the command without any space.

Examples

Setting a new time

The following command sets the time to 11:43 a.m.:

```
C:\>time 11:43
```

Both of the next two examples set the time to 12:03 a.m.:

```
C:\>time 12:03a
C:\>time 0:03
```

Note that we need to put an A after 12:03 to let TIME know that we want 12:03 a.m. The last example shows two ways to set the current time to 2:00 p.m.:

```
C:\>time 2:00p
C:\>time 14:00
```

Letting TIME prompt you

If you type **TIME** without a parameter, it displays the current time and asks you to type in a new time:

```
C:\>time
Current time is 11:20:01.51a
Enter new time: _
```

At this point you can enter a new time or press Enter to keep the current one.

See also

COUNTRY   The TIME format is affected by the current setting of the COUNTRY= line in your CONFIG.SYS file.

DATE   The companion command for setting the current date.

TREE   IBM 2.0, DOS 3.2 and later, External

Display directory structure

This command displays a visual tree of the directory structure on your disk (also known as the directory tree).

When and why

Most people never use this command, except to print a picture of the directory structure on their hard disk, because you can't browse through this display. It's better to use the directory tree in the DOS Shell or a third-party program such as the Norton Commander. Both programs provide a live directory tree that allows you to move between directories.

Syntax

tree [*path*] [/f] [/a]
Displays a visual directory tree.

Parameters

path
Top of tree. The drive and/or path of the directory where you want TREE to start (it doesn't automatically list all the files starting at the root directory). (Default is the current directory.)

Switches

/f
List files. Lists all the files in each directory. This is useful if you want to print a listing of all the files in your directories (you probably won't want to view it on the screen).

/a
Text lines (DOS 4.0 and later). This switch tells TREE to use text characters (|, +, and -) rather than the line-drawing characters in your computer. This allows you to print the tree on a printer that doesn't support the line-drawing characters.

Messages

```
Invalid path
```
Make sure the directory you supplied to TREE is correct and exists.

```
No subdirectories exist
```
You'll see this message if you run TREE from a directory that doesn't have any subdirectories. If you wanted to see the directory structure on your entire disk, run TREE again and supply \ as the path.

Examples

If you use TREE without any parameters, it will display the structure of the directory tree beginning with the current directory. This means you won't see any directories above the current directory. For example, if you're in a directory that doesn't have any subdirectories, you'll see something like this:

```
C:\VERY\DEEP\PATH>tree
Directory PATH listing for Volume 386 LAPTOP
Volume Serial Number is 16E3-8DA9
C:.
No subdirectories exist
```

So you'll probably want to type

```
C:\VERY\DEEP\PATH>tree \
```

Since this generates a lot of output, you'll probably want to send it either through MORE, so you can see one screenful at a time, or to your printer:

```
C:\VERY\DEEP\PATH>tree \ | more
```

This last example lists all the files in each directory and uses text, rather than graphics, line-drawing characters so you can print it on any printer:

```
C:\>tree \ /a/f >prn
```

See also

CHDIR	Changes between directories.
CHKDSK	The /V option on CHKDSK also allows you to display all the files and directories on your disk.
DELTREE	This command deletes a directory, including all its files and subdirectories.
MKDIR	This command allows you to create subdirectories.
RMDIR	Removes an empty directory from your disk.

TYPE
All DOS, Internal

Display text file on-screen
This command allows you to see the contents of text files on the screen.

When and why
If you're using the DOS Shell or a third-party program such as the Norton Commander, you probably won't want to use this command except for short files. The TYPE command doesn't allow you to browse backwards and forwards through the file, which you often want to do when you're viewing a file on the screen.

Syntax
type *filespec*
Displays a file on the screen.

Parameters
filespec
The name of the file that you want to see on the screen. This can include a drive and/or path, but you can't use wildcard characters.

Notes
Binary files
Many programs don't save their files as text files. For example, spreadsheets and graphics programs obviously don't save their files as text files. But even word processors store binary information with the text, which tells your word processor how to format the text. TYPE often does a poor job of showing these files. Some programs, such as the commercial version of the Norton Commander, can actually display the contents of binary files as if you were running the program that created them.

Example
You'll probably want to use the TYPE command in conjunction with the MORE command most of the time. MORE allows you to see the output of TYPE one screenful at a time:

```
C:\>type readme.txt | more
```

See also
EDIT   You can also use the EDIT command to view a file, which will allow you to move forward and backward through the file and search for text. Be careful not to modify the file unless you intend to.

MORE   Allows you to view files or the output of other programs one page at a time.

UNDELETE   DOS 5 and later, External

Restore deleted files
This command allows you to recover files that you deleted by accident. How well UNDELETE performs depends on how you've set up your computer (see "Notes").

When and why
If you ever delete a file by accident, you can use this command to recover it. But you must try using the command as quickly as possible. If you write any new files to your disk, they may use the space freed when you deleted the file.

In DOS 5, you should also use the MIRROR /T deletion-tracking program, which will improve your chances of recovering deleted files.

Syntax
The first two commands are the DOS 5 and DOS 6 commands that recover files you deleted by accident.

undelete [/**list** | /**all** | [*filespec*] /**dt** | [*filespec*] /**ds** | [*filespec*] /**dos**]   (DOS 6 and later)
Undeletes the files *filespec* or asks you which files you want to delete if you don't tell it what to recover.

undelete [*filespec*] [/**list**] [/**all**] [/**dos** | /**dt**]   (DOS 5)
Undeletes the files *filespec* or all the files in the current directory if you don't tell it what to recover.

All the following commands allow you to load and control the delete protection part of UNDELETE in DOS 6. In DOS 5, delete protection was provided by MIRROR.

undelete /**load** | /**t***drive*[-*entries*] | /**s**[*drive*]   (DOS 6 and later)
Loads the memory-resident delete protection. This function in DOS 5 was provided by MIRROR.

undelete /**status**   (DOS 6 and later)
Tells you whether any type of delete protection is loaded and what drives are being protected.

undelete /**unload**   (DOS 6 and later)
Disables delete protection and unloads it from memory.

undelete /**purge**[*drive*]   (DOS 6 and later)
Deletes all of the hidden files that the Delete Sentry option keeps in the hidden SENTRY directory.

Parameters
filespec
The name of the file you want to undelete (you can supply a drive letter, a path, or both in front of the name). You can use DOS wildcard characters. If you don't supply a *filespec*, UNDELETE recovers all deleted files in the current directory.

Switches

The first set of switches applies to recovering files that you deleted by accident.

/list

List deleted files. Lists the files that can be undeleted, without actually recovering any of the files. If you've deleted files while Delete Tracker (MIRROR /T in DOS 5) or Delete Sentry were active, UNDELETE won't show you all your files. Instead, it will only show you files that you deleted with the highest level of protection (Delete Sentry is the highest, followed by Delete Tracker, with DOS at the bottom). However, it will always tell you how many files you can undelete that were protected by the other levels. You can control which files UNDELETE will actually list by using the /DOS, /DT, and /DS switches.

/all

Undelete all. Recovers all the deleted files without asking you to confirm each file. This option uses the best possible undeletion method (in order of decreasing protection: sentry, tracker, and DOS). If no Sentry directory is available, UNDELETE uses the deletion-tracking file (assuming one was created by loading UNDELETE with the /T option) if it's available. Otherwise, it uses the directory method (described under /DOS) and assigns a new first letter to make the filename unique (it starts with # and then uses letters in this order %&0123456789AB...). You'll probably want to use this switch only if you've installed some type of delete protection. You can control which level of undelete protection UNDELETE will use to recover files, using the /DOS, /DT, and /DS switches.

/dos

Directory undelete. Recovers files using the DOS directory information (this is the brute-force method) rather than the deletion-tracking file. This is the least reliable way to recover deleted files. (By default, UNDELETE uses the highest level of deletion tracking available, and the directory information otherwise.) You can supply a *filespec* to undelete a specific file, or group of files if you use wildcard characters (UNDELETE will ignore the first character in *filespec* and ask you to provide the first character for each file you undelete). Otherwise, UNDELETE will ask you if you want to undelete each file that it found deleted without protection.

/dt

Deletion tracking undelete. Uses the delete-tracking file to recover deleted files. (The delete-tracking file is created by MIRROR /T in DOS 5 and UNDELETE /T in DOS 6 and later.) This switch will keep UNDELETE from using the less reliable method of recovering deleted files (which uses the directory information). (By default, UNDELETE uses deletion tracking if present, and the directory information otherwise.) You can supply a *filespec* to undelete a specific file, or group of files if you use wildcard characters. Otherwise, UNDELETE will ask you if you want to undelete each file that it found deleted with delete tracking turned on.

/ds

Deletion sentry undelete (DOS 6 and later). Uses the information saved by Delete Sentry (UNDELETE /S) to recover deleted files. Since Delete Sentry moves the files rather than saves information about where the file was, this method of recovering a file will be 100 percent accurate as long as Delete Sentry hasn't purged your file. You can supply a *filespec* to undelete a specific file, or group of files if you use wildcard characters. Otherwise, UNDELETE will ask you if you want to undelete each file that it found deleted with delete tracking turned on.

This next set of switches controls the delete tracking of options in UNDELETE that were added in DOS 6. When you use any of these options, UNDELETE installs some code in memory to keep track of the files that you deleted, which makes it much easier and more reliable for UNDELETE to recover a file that you deleted by accident.

/s[*drive*]
Sentry protection (DOS 6 and later). Delete Sentry provides the highest level of protection. UNDELETE uses uses a small amount of memory (13.5K) and disk space (approximately 7 percent of the total size) to provide the Delete Sentry monitoring. To change which drives are protected, you'll need to unload UNDELETE. If you don't supply a drive letter, and you've used Sentry before, UNDELETE will protect the same set of drive letters (this uses the UNDELETE.INI file). Otherwise protects the current drive. You can use multiple /S switches if you want to protect more than one drive, and you can only use this switch when you first load UNDELETE.

/t*drive*[-*entries*]
Tracker protection (DOS 6 and later). The next level of protection is Delete Tracker (which was provided by MIRROR /T in DOS 5) and requires about 9.5K of memory but minimal disk space. The undelete information is stored in a hidden file called \PCTRACKR.DEL. The *entries* option specifies how many files UNDELETE should keep track of (it only keeps track of the last *entries* files you deleted on each drive). The default *entries* depends on the size of the disk (see "Notes" section). You can use multiple /T switches if you want to protect more than one drive, and you can only use this switch when you first load UNDELETE. Valid range for *entries* is 1 to 999. (Default depends on size of disk.)

/load
Load UNDELETE.INI protection (DOS 6 and later). UNDELETE.INI is an initialization file that contains configuration information for installing UNDELETE protection. UNDELETE updates this file whenever you use the /T or /S switches or whenever you use the MWUNDEL program to reconfigure protection. Using UNDELETE /LOAD in your AUTOEXEC.BAT file is the easiest way to provide consistent protection against accidentally deleting files.

/status
Protection status (DOS 6 and later). UNDELETE will report which method of deletion protection is loaded, if any, and which drives it's protecting.

/unload
Removed undelete protection (DOS 6 and later). Disables the UNDELETE command. The sentry and tracking information will still be around since they're stored in files on your disk.

/purge
Purge the Sentry directory (DOS 6 and later). Purges any entries in the Sentry directory. This can be used to ensure that a file cannot be recovered or if you want to recover the disk space currently being used by the deleted files in the hidden \SENTRY directory.

Notes

When not to use UNDELETE

Warning! Don't use UNDELETE if you're running under Microsoft Windows (use the Windows Undelete utility), the MS-DOS Task Swapper, or when any other program is active that might have files open. Some of the commercial utilities don't have this restriction and even have their own versions of UNDELETE that run as a native Windows program. You can, however, use the Windows MWUNDEL program to undelete files in Windows.

When UNDELETE doesn't work

There are two cases when UNDELETE may not work correctly: when you're recovering fragmented files that were deleted without any type of protection (see note on how UNDELETE works) and when other files have written over some of the areas used by the file you're trying to recover. See notes on setting up for UNDELETE. There isn't much you can do to prevent other files from using the space freed up by files you delete (except to use a deletion-tracking program like UNDELETE /S that puts the files into a special directory rather than deleting them right away).

Delete Tracker. Another case when UNDELETE won't work is when you've used the Delete Tracker or Delete Sentry options and you want to recover a file that you deleted a long time ago. In this case the information on that file may have been purged. Delete Tracker keeps track of the last *entries* files that you deleted on an entire disk. This number can be between 1 and 999 (see note about default size later). If you deleted more than this number of files since you deleted the file you want to recover, you won't be able to recover the file you deleted.

Delete Sentry (DOS 6 and later). Similarly, Delete Sentry periodically purges deleted files from its hidden directory. After a file's been purged, you won't be able to recover it. Files are purged either when they've been undeleted for too long (the default is 7 days) or when disk space becomes low. By default, Delete Sentry will never use more than 20 percent of your disk space to keep track of deleted files. When the deleted files use more than this amount of disk, UNDELETE will purge the files that have been deleted the longest until it reduces its use of disk space down to this maximum. If your hard disk is very full, UNDELETE will be able to keep even fewer files. It will purge the oldest file whenever another program requests disk space and there isn't any left on the disk, except for the space occupied by deleted files.

Using UNDELETE after DEFRAG

If you've used DEFRAG to defragment your hard disk, you may not be able to recover files that you deleted unless you were using Delete Sentry. Because DEFRAG moves all your files around on your hard disk, it tends to write over allocation units that had been used by files you deleted. Once other files take over these allocation units, there's no way you can recover your deleted file. This is a good reason for using the Delete Sentry option, which works even if you've used DEFRAG on your disk.

Undeleting directories

The DOS UNDELETE program provides no way to recover a directory that you deleted by accident unless you had Delete Sentry active when you deleted all the

UNDELETE

files in the directory. In this case you can recover the files in your deleted directory by creating a new directory with exactly the same name as the directory that you just deleted. You can then change to this directory and use UNDELETE /DS /ALL to recover all the files that were in this directory.

You can also use the MWUNDEL program to recover directories that you deleted by accident if you're not using Delete Sentry, although the reliability of this feature varies considerably. If you want to be able to recover deleted directories, we strongly recommend that you use the Delete Sentry option of UNDELETE to protect all of your files.

You might also try one of the commercial disk recovery programs (Norton Utilities, Mace Utilities, PC Tools). These programs tend to do a much better job of recovering deleted directories.

Setting up for UNDELETE for DOS 6 and later

It's a good idea to use the UNDELETE /T or /S switch to set up deletion tracking on your hard disk. Without this, UNDELETE may not be able to correctly recover a fragmented file; even though UNDELETE reports it's recovered a fragmented file, it may not have recovered the correct information.

How well UNDELETE performs its work depends on how you set up your computer before you delete a file. Here are the two possibilities:

- **Delete Sentry with UNDELETE /S.** If you're using Delete Sentry, you'll be able to recover the file exactly as long as the file hasn't been purged. Delete Sentry purges files either because they've been undeleted too long (the default is purge after seven days) or because you're running out of space on your hard disk, in which case Delete Sentry will start to purge the files that have been deleted the longest.

- **Delete Tracker with UNDELETE /T.** If you're using Delete Tracker, you'll be able to recover the file exactly as long as the space used by the file hasn't been overwritten and as long as UNDELETE still has information on the file. UNDELETE keeps track only of the most recent files you deleted (you can set the limit using the *entries* parameter of the /T switch).

- **Brute force.** In the absence of the other two pieces of information, UNDELETE can usually do a fairly good job of recovering a deleted file.

We recommend you always use the MIRROR /T command if you have 6K of memory to spare. This is the amount of memory used by deletion tracking.

Setting up for UNDELETE for DOS 5

It's a good idea to use the MIRROR /T switch to set up deletion tracking on your hard disk. Without this, UNDELETE may not be able to correctly recover a fragmented file; even though UNDELETE reports it's recovered a fragmented file, it may not have recovered the correct information.

How well UNDELETE performs its work depends on how you set up your computer before you delete a file. Here are the two possibilities:

- Deletion tracking with MIRROR /T. If you're using deletion tracking, you'll be able to recover the file exactly as long as the space used by the file hasn't been overwritten and as long as MIRROR still has information on the file. MIRROR keeps track only of the most recent files you deleted.

♦ Brute force. In the absence of the other two pieces of information, UNDELETE can usually do a fairly good job of recovering a deleted file.

We recommend you always use the MIRROR /T command if you have 6K of memory to spare. This is the amount of memory used by deletion tracking.

How UNDELETE works

There are three (two in DOS 5) ways UNDELETE can determine which files can be recovered. The first method uses the Delete Sentry files and directory created with the UNDELETE /S option (this isn't available in DOS 5). This directory keeps files that you've deleted recently, so you will be able to recover your files completely as long as they haven't been purged. Files will be purged if they've been deleted too long (the default is purge after seven days) or if your disk is running low on disk space. Delete Sentry is the most reliable method for recovering deleted files.

The second method uses the deletion-tracking file created by the UNDELETE /T (MIRROR /T in DOS 5) option. This file keeps track of the names and locations (including all fragments) of the most recent file you've deleted. Deletion tracking is the second most reliable method for recovering deleted files.

The final method uses a side-effect of the way DOS works with directories. Whenever you delete a file, DOS doesn't remove its directory entry. Instead, it changes the first letter of the filename to a special character that indicates that the file's been deleted. This last method keeps all the information on the file except for the first letter of the name and except for information on where all the pieces (beyond the first) of a fragmented file are stored. As a result, UNDELETE may not do a good job of recovering a fragmented file that was deleted unless you've installed deletion tracking.

Here's a quick look at how UNDELETE recovers a fragmented file when you're not using deletion tracking. DOS divides your hard disk into allocation units, which are the smallest disk chunk that DOS works with (usually 2,048 bytes, but it can be larger or smaller). A file larger than this minimum size requires more than one allocation unit to store the entire file. In some cases DOS creates large files using several groups of allocation units, on different parts of your hard disk.

UNDELETE only knows a file's size and the first allocation unit used by the file — it doesn't know anything about fragments. So UNDELETE assigns the first allocation unit to the file and then looks for enough additional free allocation units on a first-free, first-used basis. If you've deleted other files since you created a fragmented file, you may have larger gaps where the file you're trying to recover used to be. In this case, UNDELETE will end up assigning some allocation units to your recovered file that really belong to other files you deleted.

Networks

UNDELETE does not work on network drives, unless you use the Delete Sentry option in DOS 6 and later. To use Delete Sentry on a network drive, you must have read, write, create, and delete file access rights for the root directory of the network drive.

If you need to recover deleted files, some commercial utilities programs, such as the Norton Utilities, also have programs that move deleted files to other directories and therefore will work on a network.

UNDELETE

The default number of Delete Tracker entries

When you use the /T switch without providing a value for *entries*, UNDELETE uses the following number of entries in the hidden PCTRACKR.DEL file:

Disk size	Num entries	Size of PCTRACKR.DEL file
360K	25	5K
720K	50	9K
1.2 MB	75	14K
1.44 MB	75	14K
20 MB	101	18K
32 MB	202	36K
Above 32 MB	303	55K

Creating or Editing UNDELETE.INI

(DOS 6 and later.) Any time you load UNDELETE into memory using the /T or the /S switches, UNDELETE updates (or creates) the UNDELETE.INI file. Whenever you run UNDELETE /LOAD, UNDELETE uses the settings in this INI file to determine what it will protect and how it will protect your files.

There are several ways you can make changes to this file. First, you can let UNDELETE make all the changes for you. Just bear in mind that you'll need to unload UNDELETE before you can make any changes using the /S or /T switches. You can also use MWUNDEL to configure delete protection, which will change the UNDELETE.INI file for you. Again, however, you'll need to unload UNDELETE (using the /U switch) and then load it again with UNDELETE /LOAD before these changes will take effect.

Finally, you can use any ASCII text editor (such as EDIT) to edit the individual entries in the UNDELETE.INI file. This INI file has five sections in it: [configuration], [sentry.drives], [mirror.drives], [sentry.files], and [defaults]. Here is a brief description of each of these sections.

[configuration] This section can contain three lines, which control some options for Delete Sentry. You can set these options whenever you turn on Delete Sentry in the Windows MWUNDEL program. The three lines are as follows:

archive	TRUE or FALSE	Controls whether Delete Sentry will save files with the archive attribute turned on. FALSE means that it won't save such files. FALSE is a good setting if you're using a backup program to save your files.
days	*number*	UNDELETE will automatically purge files after they've been deleted for *number* of days. UNDELETE initially sets this to 7.
percentage	*percent*	This sets the maximum amount of space that Delete Sentry files will use on your disk. UNDELETE will automatically purge the files that have been deleted the longest when you delete a lot of files or when other programs need this disk space.

[sentry.drives] This section lists the drives that Delete Sentry will protect. Each drive must be on a line by itself, followed by an equal sign (=).

[mirror.drives] This section lists the drives that Delete Tracker will protect. Each drive must be on a line by itself, followed by an equal sign (=). After the equal sign you can add a number, which is the *entries* value after the /T switch and controls how many deleted files UNDELETE will keep track of on that drive. Valid range for *entries* is 1 to 999. The default depends on the size of your disk.

[sentry.files] This section controls which files Delete Sentry will track. Because some programs create and delete a lot of temporary files while they work, you won't want to fill up your Sentry directory with these files. This section allows you to control which files Sentry will keep track of when you delete them. By default, this is set to all files, except for files with the extensions TMP, VM?, WOA, SWP, SPL, RMG, IMG, THM, and DOV. You exclude files by putting a minus sign in front of a full filespec.

[defaults] This section contains two lines, which control which type of tracking you have on. The values can be either TRUE or FALSE, and here is what they mean:

d.sentry	d.tracker	Meaning
FALSE	FALSE	No delete protection (except DOS)
TRUE	FALSE	Protect with Delete Sentry
FALSE	TRUE	Protect with Delete Tracker
TRUE	TRUE	*Not allowed.* UNDELETE will set to Delete Tracker

Messages

```
Cannot operate on a SUBST drive.
```
You can't use UNDELETE with virtual drive letters created with the SUBST command. This is because UNDELETE needs to work with the actual disk. The solution is to use the SUBST command to find out what directory the virtual drive refers to and then use UNDELETE on that real drive and directory.

```
Cannot operate on specified drive (x).
It may be a network drive.
```
UNDELETE can't work on network drives, unless you've used the /S option (DOS 6 and later). You'll either need to use the network's equivalent of the UNDELETE command (if it exists) or use a commercial deletion-tracking program that works on networks (we know of one such program, EraseProtect, which is part of the Norton Utilities).

```
Cannot specify both /DT and /DOS.
```
(DOS 5 message.) If you want UNDELETE to use both of these methods, don't use any switches.

```
/DS was specified. Because there is no Delete Centry control file
for this drive, the UNDELETE command cannot continue.
```
The /DS switch tells UNDELETE to use only the Delete Sentry method for recovering files. If this information doesn't exist, you'll have to use UNDELETE without this switch or with the /DT or /DOS switches to recover deleted files using a different method.

```
/DT was specified. Because there is no delete-tracking file for
this drive, the UNDELETE command cannot continue.
```
The /DT switch tells UNDELETE to use only the deletion-tracking file method for recovering files. If this file doesn't exist, you'll have to use UNDELETE without this switch or with the /DS or /DOS switches to recover deleted files using a different method.

UNDELETE

```
None of the clusters for this file are available.
The file cannot be recovered. Press any key to continue.
```
Another file has completely overwritten the file you've asked to recover. There is no way you can recover it.

```
Only some of the clusters for this file are available. Do you want
to recover this file with only the available clusters? (Y/N)_
```
You'll see this message when you're using the deletion-tracking file. This message indicates that another file has used some of the clusters (allocation units) needed to recover this file. You can respond Y to have UNDELETE recover all the clusters that are still available (which might be useful for a text or word processing file but not for most other types of files).

```
Starting cluster is unavailable. This file cannot be recovered
with the UNDELETE command. Press any key to continue.
```
You'll see this message when another file has used the space that was reserved for the first part of the file you want to recover. There's not much you can do once you see this message, as your data's already been overwritten.

```
This file cannot be automatically recovered because
not all of the clusters are available.
```
You'll see this message when you're using the deletion-tracking file and the /ALL switch to automatically recover deleted files. This message indicates that another file has used some of the clusters needed to recover this file. You can use UNDELETE without /ALL to attempt to recover part of this file.

Examples

Listing deleted files

The following command lists all the files that have been deleted from the current directory using the highest level of protection:

```
C:\>undelete /list
```

This is a good way to see what deleted files are there before you try to undelete a file. You can also see which files you deleted without any protection active by using the /DOS switch:

```
C:\>undelete /list /dos
```

Recovering from DEL *.*

If you just deleted all the files in a directory using DEL *.*, you can bring them back using this command:

```
C:\>undelete *.* /all
```

If you're using deletion tracking, you'll want to make sure you've set the number of entries high enough to cover deleting all the files in the directory (which can have several hundred files or more).

Undeleting a file

If you're using deletion tracking, undeleting a file is very simple because the deletion-tracking file contains the full file and location information. Just type **UNDELETE** followed by the filename:

```
C:\>undelete file.txt
```

If, on the other hand, you're not using deletion tracking, you'll need to supply the first letter for the filename (since DOS changes the first letter to indicate that the file's been deleted):

```
C:\>undelete

UNDELETE - A delete protection facility
Copyright (C) 1987-1993 Central Point Software, Inc.
All rights reserved.

Directory: C:\TEST
File specifications: *.*

    Delete Sentry control file not found.

    Deletion-tracking file not found.

    MS-DOS directory contains    7 deleted files.
    Of these,    4 files may be recovered.
Using the MS-DOS directory method.
    ?ONFIG   SYS     288  3-12-93  8:59a  ...A  Undelete (Y/N)?y
    Please type the first character for ?ONFIG   .SYS: c

File successfully undeleted.
```

This file used to be called CONFIG.SYS, so you should answer Y to say that you'd like to recover the deleted file and then C to tell UNDELETE that the first letter used to be C.

Removing Delete Sentry files

When you're using the Delete Sentry feature of UNDELETE, you won't need to worry about removing files that it keeps around. UNDELETE will automatically purge files as you need more space. But if you turn off the Delete Sentry feature, UNDELETE won't purge these files automatically. In this case you may need to remove them yourself. The easiest way to remove these files is to use the /PURGE switch of UNDELETE. For example, to purge the files on drive C, you would type

```
C:\>undelete /purgec
```

The last letter is the drive letter on which you want UNDELETE to remove all your sentry files. You can only purge the files from one drive at a time.

When you run this command, UNDELETE will also delete the hidden \SENTRY directory.

See also

MIRROR /T   (DOS 5 only.) You'll probably want to load deletion tracking when you start your computer. This command does that.

MWUNDEL   The Windows version of UNDELETE. UNDELETE provides the delete protection part for both the DOS and the Windows Undelete programs.

UNFORMAT

DOS 5 and later, External

Restore an accidentally formatted disk
This command allows you to restore the contents of a disk after you've formatted it.

When and why
Hopefully, you'll never have to use this command. But chances are if you're reading this, you need to recover your hard disk after accidentally formatting it or after some other problem that wiped out its root directory or partition table. UNFORMAT fixes both problems quite easily if you've used the MIRROR command ahead of time or if you used the DOS 5 or later FORMAT command, which saves unformat information on the disk.

If, on the other hand, some other program destroyed your hard disk and you haven't used the MIRROR command to save disk information, UNFORMAT can still recover most of the files on your hard disk, although it may not be able to recover any files in the root directory.

You might also want to use a commercial utilities package, such as the Norton Utilities, PC Tools, or the Mace Utilities, to recover your disk because they're easier to use, faster, and do a better job.

Note: Back up your disk frequently. Don't rely on MIRROR and UNFORMAT to protect your data.

Note on MIRROR: Even though the MIRROR command has been dropped in DOS 6, the description of UNFORMAT makes many references to MIRROR because UNFORMAT still uses this word and the file created by MIRROR (which FORMAT also creates). If you upgraded from DOS 5, you can still use your MIRROR command. If you didn't upgrade from DOS 5, you can contact Microsoft to obtain a supplemental disk that contains an updated version of MIRROR, as well as updated versions of other files that were dropped from DOS 6.

Syntax
unformat *drive*:
Attempts to unformat the disk drive *drive:*. UNFORMAT will use the MIRROR.FIL file created by MIRROR and/or FORMAT to restore the contents of your disk. If it doesn't find this file, it will attempt to restore your hard disk by searching for directories.

unformat *drive:* /j
Checks to see if there is a file created by MIRROR (or FORMAT) that contains the disk information and reports if it matches the system area of the hard disk. This command will not make any changes to your disk.

unformat *drive*: [/u] [/l] [/test] [/p]
Unformats a hard disk without using the information saved by MIRROR (or FORMAT). It does this by searching your disk for directories. *Note:* You must use at least one of these switches to tell UNFORMAT that you don't want to use the information saved by MIRROR.

unformat *drive*: **/partn** [/l]
Restores a hard disk's partition table using a copy saved to a floppy disk by the MIRROR /PARTN command.

Parameters
drive
The disk drive that you want to unformat. This can be any hard or floppy disk drive.

Switches
/j
Check MIRROR file. Searches for the disk information file created by MIRROR (or FORMAT) and reports whether or not the information in this file agrees with the current information on the disk. (It won't if you've modified any files or directories.) This switch does not make any changes to your disk.

/u
Unformat without using MIRROR file. Unformats the disk without using the disk information file created by MIRROR. This works by searching your disk for subdirectories, which is a very slow, and not entirely reliable, process.

Note: This switch won't recover any files in the root directory.

/l
List recoverable files without MIRROR (the letter L).
(Without /PARTN switch.) Searches the disk for subdirectories (rather than using the MIRROR file) and lists all the files and subdirectories found (normally UNFORMAT lists only directories and files that are fragmented). *Note:* No files will be displayed until UNFORMAT finishes searching the entire disk. You'll probably want to use the /P switch to send this output to a printer. This process is very slow.

(With the /PARTN switch.) Displays the partition table for the current hard disk.

/test
Test UNFORMAT without changing. Reports what UNFORMAT will recover without making any of the changes to the disk. UNFORMAT does a search for files and subdirectories without using the disk information file created by MIRROR or FORMAT.

/p
Print output. Sends the output of this command to the printer connected to LPT1.

/partn
Restore partition table. Restores a hard disk's partition table. This command uses the PARTNSAV.FIL file created by the MIRROR /PARTN command, if available. You should save this information to a floppy disk stored in a safe location so that you can use this switch to recover your hard disk's partition information.

Notes

UNFORMAT, MIRROR, and DOS 6
Even though the MIRROR has been dropped from DOS 6, UNFORMAT still mentions the MIRROR command and the MIRROR file all over the place. In fact, the DOS 6 FORMAT command also mentions that it's saving the MIRROR file when you reformat a disk that doesn't have enough space free for the MIRROR file. In

UNFORMAT

fact, if you upgraded from DOS 5 to 6, you can still use the MIRROR command as mentioned here. In fact, the MIRROR command is the only way you can create the file used by UNFORMAT's /PARTN switch.

Unformatting using the MIRROR file

The disk information file created by MIRROR is also created by FORMAT, so if you use UNFORMAT immediately after running FORMAT, you'll be able to recover 100 percent of the files on your hard disk.

If, on the other hand, some other program damaged the root directory of your hard disk, UNFORMAT will restore the file allocation table (which describes which parts of your disk are being used by files) and root directory to the state most recently recorded by MIRROR. It won't recover files in the root directory that you changed or added since the last time you ran MIRROR. And it may not properly recover files that you've changed or added in other directories. For this reason, it's best to run MIRROR at least once a day by putting it in your AUTOEXEC.BAT file. You should also run MIRROR before you turn your computer off.

After you run UNFORMAT, you should check for lost clusters using CHKDSK (or better yet, a commercial utilities package).

Unformatting without the MIRROR file

You'll probably UNFORMAT a disk without using the MIRROR file in only two cases: You didn't use MIRROR or FORMAT to create the disk information file, or you created the MIRROR file a long time ago and the information isn't current. In both cases, you'll need to let UNFORMAT search your hard disk for subdirectories and the files in those subdirectories. It will not be able to recover any files that were in the root directory.

Restoring a partition table

If you get the following message whenever you try to switch to your hard disk, there may be a problem with your hard disk's partition table:

```
Invalid drive specification
```

You can view the current partition table using the UNFORMAT /PARTN /L command. If the information doesn't look correct, try using UNFORMAT /PARTN to restore your hard disk's partition table. UNFORMAT will prompt you to insert the floppy disk that contains the PARTNSAV.FIL file created by MIRROR /PARTN. Follow the prompts, and you should be able to use your hard disk again.

Note: If you didn't save a copy of your partition table, you'll need to use a commercial utilities program to repair your partition table.

FORMAT's /U switch

UNFORMAT won't be able to restore a floppy disk formatted with the /U switch, which writes over all the data on your floppy disk.

Networks

This command doesn't work with network drives. Network software has its own, proprietary operating system that uses a disk structure quite different from DOS's. Networks also don't provide the type of low-level access that UNFORMAT needs to do its job.

Examples

Normal recovery

The best way to use this command is to start with the /J switch:

`C:\>`**`unformat c: /j`**

This command will check to see if there is a disk information file on your disk. It also reports whether or not this file agrees with the current disk information (chances are that it doesn't, or you wouldn't be using UNFORMAT). This switch doesn't make any changes to your disk, so it's a good way to do a trial run.

Next, you'll want to actually unformat your disk with this command:

`C:\>`**`unformat c:`**

Search recovery

If you don't have a recent disk information file, UNFORMAT will have to search for subdirectories and all the files in those subdirectories. This method is slower and less reliable than using the disk information file. Before you actually unformat your hard disk, you should do a trial run and send the output to your printer:

`C:\>`**`unformat c: /test /p`**

Once you've checked this over and you decide to unformat your hard disk, use this command:

`C:\>`**`unformat c: /u`**

This command unformats your hard disk by searching for subdirectories instead of using the disk information file created by MIRROR or FORMAT.

See also

FORMAT   The FORMAT command will save MIRROR.FIL to a disk before it formats the disk, so you can use UNFORMAT to recover from an accidental FORMAT. *Note:* The /U switch will erase all the information on your floppy disk so that UNFORMAT won't be able to recover the information.

MIRROR   You'll want to run the MIRROR command often to save the MIRROR.FIL file, which is the information UNFORMAT uses to recover an accidentally formatted disk.

VER
All DOS, Internal

Display DOS version information

This command allows you to display the version number for the DOS that you're currently running. It can also tell you if you're running a version of DOS that was tailored for a specific company's computers.

Syntax
ver
Displays current version information. It displays it as *n.nn*, which shows the major version number, followed by the sub-version number.

Examples
If you're running Microsoft DOS 6, you'll see this message:
```
MS-DOS Version 6.00
```
One of our computers is running a version of DOS that was modified for Compaq computers, and its VER command displays this message:
```
COMPAQ Personal Computer DOS Version 3.31
```

VERIFY   All DOS, Internal

Verify disk writes
Sets the system's internal flag that controls whether or not disk writes are verified by reading the same sector.

Write-verification checks to see if the data can be read again, but it doesn't compare the data to see if it's the same (see "Notes").

When and why
Turning VERIFY on provides limited error checking for DOS commands that write to the disk. You may want to turn this option on to detect disk errors that can be caught by seeing if DOS can read sectors it just wrote. VERIFY may slow down writing to the disk somewhat, but it's often worth the extra time to ensure that your data is safe. We run our computers with VERIFY turned on (using a VERIFY ON command in our AUTOEXEC.BAT startup file).

Syntax
verify
Without any parameters, this command reports the current setting of the VERIFY option. It reports either "verify is off" or "verify is on."

verify on
Turns disk write-verification on. With this option turned on, DOS will read each block of data after it writes it to make sure the data can be read.

verify off
Turns disk write-verification off. (You can turn it on during a copy using COPY's /V switch.) With this option turned off, DOS won't check data just written to make sure it's readable. (Default setting when DOS first starts.)

Notes

Mysterious changes

It is possible for applications to change the setting of the VERIFY flag. Some applications turn this flag on or off while they're running and don't restore the previous setting. So if you find that VERIFY is mysteriously changed after running a program, you might want to create a batch file to launch that program so you can reset the VERIFY flag after the program finishes.

Networks

VERIFY has no effect on network drives. This is because networks provide their own form of verification that is much more sophisticated than DOS's write verification.

Speed

The VERIFY option slows down writing to the disk a little because DOS has to read back each block that it writes to make sure the block was readable. The amount by which writes will slow down depends on the disk drive and the speed of your computer. Typically, you won't be able to read a block until the disk makes an entire rotation (and that block appears again under the read head). This means that your write speed will be limited by the latency of your hard disk (how long it takes the block to appear again under the read head). With VERIFY turned off, your computer can write without having to read each block, which may mean that you can write one sector after another without waiting for the disk to make an entire rotation. We usually see about a 30 percent drop in speed on our computers when we turn VERIFY on.

Messages

```
Must specify ON or OFF
```
On and off are the only parameters you can specify to VERIFY. Enter the command again using one of these two parameters.

```
VERIFY is on
```
or
```
VERIFY is off
```
Tells you whether or not disk write-verification is currently on or off.

Technical Notes

Secret DOS: The disk controller keeps some error-checking information called the CRC in the header of each sector it writes. The CRC is a number calculated from the actual data in the sector. If the data isn't read correctly, the CRC calculated from this data won't match the CRC stored in the sector's header. The VERIFY function checks to make sure these two CRC values match.

Note: The VERIFY function is provided by the disk controller and device driver rather than DOS.

Example

This command turns disk write verification on:

```
C:\>verify on
```

See also
COPY   You can use the COPY command's /V switch to turn on write-verification during a copy.

VOL
All DOS, Internal

Display disk volume label
This command displays the current volume label, if there is one, for a disk.

Syntax
vol [*drive*:]
Displays volume label for a disk.

Parameters
drive:
The drive for which you want to know the volume label.

Notes
Volume serial numbers
The volume serial number is a unique number assigned to each disk you format. DOS uses this number to keep track of which disk is in a disk drive, which allows DOS to deal with cases where you change the floppy disk in a drive when DOS doesn't expect it. Without DOS serial numbers, it's possible for DOS to write information to the wrong disk.

Volume serial numbers are created (and changed) only when you format a disk. Only DOS 4.0 and later create and use volume serial numbers. Any disks you formatted with earlier versions of DOS won't contain a volume serial number, unless you reformat the disk with DOS 4.0 or later.

Messages
```
Volume in drive D has no label
```
You'll see this message when a disk doesn't have a volume label. You can use the LABEL command to create one.

Examples
When we run VOL on our laptop computer, it displays this information:

```
Volume in drive C is 386 LAPTOP
Volume Serial Number is 16E3-8Da9
```

See also
CHKDSK   This command displays more information about a disk. It also checks the disk for problems.

FORMAT   The FORMAT command asks you for a volume label after it finishes formatting a disk.

LABEL   The LABEL command allows you to change the volume label on a disk.

Part II: Command Reference

VSAFE
DOS 6 and later, External

Memory-resident virus protection

VSAFE is a memory-resident program that provides on going protection against viruses invading your system. If VSAFE finds a virus, it will inform you. With VSAFE installed, however, some programs may cause warning messages that do not necessarily indicate the presence of a virus.

When and why

Computer viruses are like human viruses—they can make your computer sick, which could mean losing some of your files and data. Fortunately, there are anti-virus programs like VSAFE that can help keep your computer safe from most viruses. This program keeps new viruses from invading your computer, but it doesn't look for dormant viruses that are already on your computer. To scan your computer for dormant viruses, use either MSAV or MWAV.

To ensure the maximum protection against computer viruses, you should install VSAFE in your AUTOEXEC.BAT file. Viruses are computer programs that are able to duplicate themselves onto your system. Although the intent may not be necessarily destructive, damage is often caused by careless program or other flaws within the virus. And, unfortunately, some viruses have been developed to deliberately create problems on your computer. By using a program such as VSAFE, you can protect your system from many types of viral infection. It is also important that you only run programs that come from reputable sources and that you scan your system using the Microsoft Anti-Virus utility.

Syntax

vsafe [/*option*[+ | -] ...] [/**ne**] [/**n***x*] [/**a***x* | /**c***x*] [/**n**] [/**d**]
Installs the memory-resident virus monitor.

vsafe /u
Deactivates VSAFE and removes it from memory.

Switches

/options
These switches control what types of actions VSAFE will monitor and prevent. Each option switch must consist of a number followed by a plus or a minus (the + or - is not optional). The VSAFE options are

1 (HD Low-level format)
   Warns of formatting that could completely erase your hard disk. (Default: on)

2 (Resident)
   Warns of an attempt by a program to stay in memory. (Default: off)
   Note: There are many programs, including DOS programs like DOSKEY, that will trigger this message when there isn't a problem. For such reasons, you may either want to keep this message off or load VSAFE after you've loaded all other memory-resident programs.

- 3 (General write-protect)
  Prevents programs from writing any of your disks. See "Notes" below for warning about using this feature. (Default: off)

- 4 (Check executable files)
  Checks executable files that MS-DOS opens. When this option is on, VSAFE checks programs for viruses any time you run a program (this can slow down your computer if you run a lot of different programs). (Default: on)

- 5 (Boot sector viruses)
  Checks all disks for boot sector viruses. This is a safe option to keep on. (Default: on)

- 6 (Protect HD boot sector)
  Warns of attempts to write to the boot sector or partition table of the hard disk. This is a very good option to keep on. You'll almost never run a legitimate program that would need to write to either part of your hard disk. (Default: on)

- 7 (Protect FD boot sector)
  Warns of attempts to write to the boot sector of a floppy disk. This is a good option to keep on. The only time a program should write to the boot sector of a floppy disk is when you format a disk. (Default: off)
  Note: Generates a warning when you format a floppy disk. If you have this option on when you format a floppy disk, simply select Continue (press C) when VSAFE asks you if it should allow a write to the boot sector.

- 8 (Protect executable files)
  Warns of attempts to modify executable files. You can probably turn this option on (unless you're a programmer). If you use this option, keep in mind that some programs write setup information back into their own code, which could trigger VSAFE if you turn on this option. (Default: off)

/n
Network. Enables VSAFE to check network drives.

/d
Disable Checksums. Normally, VSAFE uses what's known as a checksum to determine whether an executable file has been altered. But some legitimate actions (particularly programming) change the value of the checksum. If you know that what you are about to do will change a series of checksum values, you may want to disable the checksum feature until you are finished.

/u
Unload. Disables and removes VSAFE from memory.

/ne
No Extended. Prevents VSAFE from loading part of itself into extended memory.

/nx
No Expanded. Prevents VSAFE from loading part of itself into expanded memory.

/a*x*
Hot key using Alt. Sets the hot key used to activate the program to Alt plus the letter (in place of the *x*). (Default is Alt-V.)

/cx
Hot key using Ctrl. Sets the hot key used to activate the program to Ctrl plus the letter (in place of the *x*). (Default is Alt-V.)

Notes

For information on how to update VSAFE to detect new viruses, see your Microsoft manual.

Memory used by VSAFE

VSAFE normally uses about 23K of conventional memory and about 23K of extended or expanded memory. If you use the /NX switch and/or the /NE switch, VSAFE uses about 44K of conventional memory. Also, VSAFE will not load itself into upper memory, even if you use LOADHIGH to load it into upper memory.

Changing options while VSAFE is loaded

While VSAFE is loaded in memory, there are only two ways you can change VSAFE's options: either you can press VSAFE's hot key to display its window (the default hot key is Alt-V) and then type numbers to change options, or if you're using Windows, you can use the MWAVTSR program to change VSAFE's options. You can only use VSAFE's command-line switch to set options when you first load VSAFE into memory.

Using the write-protect option

Be very, very careful using the write-protect option (the /3+ switch) with VSAFE. This option will prevent every and all programs from writing to any of your disks, which could prevent some of your programs from working properly. When one of your programs does try to write to a disk, VSAFE will display a dialog box asking if you really want to write to the disk, and it will give you three options: Stop, Continue, and Boot. If you select Stop, VSAFE will keep asking you if you want to write to the disk. Your only real choices, then, are to allow VSAFE to write to your disk or to reboot your computer.

Note: Do not use this option inside Windows because it can cause Windows itself to stop running properly.

VSAFE and speed

On some computers (particularly 80286 computers with DoubleSpace), you might notice that your computer slows down significantly whenever you have VSAFE installed in memory. This is especially noticeable when you're running a number of different programs, rather than a single program, from within a shell program like the Norton Commander.

Using VSAFE with Windows

If you are running Windows 3.1, you should add the MWAVTSR to your startup group when using VSafe (use the LOAD= line in WIN.INI for Windows 3.0). MWAVTSR lets you configure the protection levels of VSAFE from within Windows and to control the display of messages.

VSAFE and installation programs

Many installation programs, including the one for Windows 3.1, are incompatible with the types of protection provided by VSAFE. You must unload VSAFE before running an incompatible installation program. In general, it is easiest to always unload VSAFE before installing new software. Otherwise, VSAFE will generate messages as the installation proceeds. The bottom line is: If you can't trust your software vendor, who can you trust?

Protection philosophies

There are two primary philosophies for protecting your system from computer viruses. Both start with a complete scan of your system using an Anti-Virus utility. Both also include cautions against running programs from questionable sources. Be very careful of anyone offering to "give" you a copy of a program. Reputable shareware developers always include a way for you to get in touch with them and most are members of the ASP. (For more information on the ASP, see Appendix D.)

Where the strategies differ is in how you should ensure on going protection. The TSR approach is to load VSAFE from your AUTOEXEC.BAT file. The advantage to this method is that no thought is required to maintain your system's integrity. Your system is constantly protected. The disadvantage is the number of warning messages that can be generated by harmless actions.

The scanning approach requires you to remember to check each floppy disk when you first use it. If the floppy has been used on another computer, you should check it before you use it. You can scan a disk using either the DOS MSAV or the Windows MWAV programs. In DOS, you must remember to run the MSAV command to check each floppy. In Windows, you can drag the icon representing the floppy disk in File Manager onto the MWAV icon. This will automatically scan the new disk. The advantage to this method is that it doesn't get in your way when working on your system (except that it takes a little extra time and discipline).

Whichever method you choose, DOS 6 provides the basic tools for protecting your computer.

Examples

Installing VSAFE

You can install VSAFE each time you start your computer by including the line

```
C:\>vsafe /cv /7+
```

The switch selects Ctrl-V as the hot key for displaying the configuration menu and tells VSAFE to warn you whenever a program tries to write to the boot sector on floppy disks.

See also

MSAV	The Microsoft Anti-Virus utility for DOS.
MWAV	The Microsoft Anti-Virus utility for Windows.
MWAVTSR	The TSR manager for Windows.

XCOPY

DOS 3.2 and later, External

Copy files and directories

This command is a souped-up version of COPY; it is faster and allows you to copy entire directories, including all the subdirectories. XCOPY can also copy files based on their modification date or archive bit (which is set whenever you modify a file).

When and why

XCOPY is a useful if somewhat intimidating command upon first look. If you want to copy a directory and all its subdirectories, you'll want to use XCOPY. Using COPY with MKDIR to copy an entire directory is a lot more work.

You might also want to use XCOPY if you need to copy a group of files that were created after a certain date.

Starting in DOS 6.2, the XCOPY command is a little safer because it now asks you before it writes over files that already exist (however, this feature doesn't work if you use the XCOPY command from within any type of DOS shell program).

Syntax

xcopy *source* [*destination*] [/y|/-y] [/a|/m] [/d:*date*] [/p] [/s [/e]] [/v] [/w]

Parameters

source
File to copy. The name of the file(s) that you want to copy. The name can include the DOS * and ? wildcard characters. If you provide a path without a name, DOS assumes *.* for the name.

destination
Where you want the files written. This can be a drive letter, a pathname, a filename, or any combination. If you add a \ to the end of *destination*, this tells XCOPY that this is the name of a directory.

Switches

/a
Archive bit. Copies only files that have their archive bit set, which means they've been modified since the last time you backed up your computer. XCOPY doesn't change the archive bit (unless you use the /M switch).

/m
Archive bit backup. This switch is identical to the /A switch, except that XCOPY turns off the archive bit for each file it copies. You can use this command in place of BACKUP to back up your files.

/d:*date*
On or after. Only copies files that have been modified on or after the date you provide. You can use the DATE command to see what format to use for the date.

/p
Prompt. Asks before copying each file. This allows you to selectively copy files when you can't describe the group with a wildcard pattern (using * and ?).

/s
Subdirectories. Copies all files in subdirectories as well as the directory you specify.

/e
Copy empty directories. Tells XCOPY to copy subdirectories even if they contain no files that match *source*. You'll need to use the /S switch with this switch.

/v
Verify. Verifies that each file is copied correctly. This is the same as using the VERIFY command to turn on write-verification.

/-y
Prompt before copying over files (DOS 6.2 and later). Tells XCOPY that it should ask before it overwrites a file that already exists. This is the default setting when you use XCOPY from the DOS command line. *Note:* You *do not* get an overwrite prompt if you run XCOPY from within a DOS shell, such as the Norton Commander, or from within a batch file. In these two cases, you need to use the /-Y switch if you want to confirm the overwriting of existing files. You can change the default setting using the COPYCMD environment variable. Default: /-Y from DOS prompt, /Y from DOS shells or batch files.

/y
Overwrite without prompting (DOS 6.2 and later). Tells XCOPY to copy over existing files without asking first. This switch overrides a /-Y switch in the COPYCMD environment variable. Default: /-Y from DOS prompt, /Y from DOS shells or batch files.

/w
Wait prompt. Waits for you to type a key before starting the copy. This allows you to insert a floppy disk into the drive. The message `Press any key to begin copying file(s)` is displayed.

Notes

COPY vs. XCOPY

XCOPY is basically a souped-up version of COPY. It is both faster at copying multiple files and can do more (such as copying subdirectories).

ERRORLEVEL returned

XCOPY returns information that batch files can test with the IF ERRORLEVEL command. Here are the exit codes that XCOPY returns:

0   All the files were copied.

1   XCOPY didn't find any files to copy.

2   You pressed Ctrl-C or Ctrl-Break to exit XCOPY before it finished.

4   There was not enough memory or disk space, the drive letter wasn't valid, or some of your switches or parameters aren't valid.

5   Disk write error.

Messages

```
Access denied
```
You'll see this message when XCOPY tries to write over a file that has the read-only attribute set. Use ATTRIB to turn off the read-only attribute and try again.

```
Cannot perform a cyclic copy
```
You'll see this message when you use the /S switch and the destination directory is a subdirectory of the source directory (or any of its subdirectories). For example, typing **XCOPY C:\WRITING C:\WRITING\BOOKS\DOS /S** will generate this message.

```
Cannot XCOPY from a reserved device
```
You probably provided a device name, such as CON, AUX, COMn, or LPTn for the source of the copy. The source must be the name of a file or directory, not a device.

```
Cannot XCOPY to a reserved device
```
You probably provided a device name, such as CON, AUX, COMn, or LPTn for the destination of the copy. The destination must be the name of a file or directory, not a device.

```
Does name specify a file name
or directory name on the target
(F = file, D = directory)?_
```
You'll see this message when the name you provided doesn't exist and XCOPY doesn't know if *destination* is the name of a file or a directory. Answering D tells XCOPY to create a directory with this name.

```
File cannot be copied onto itself
```
You've tried to copy a file onto itself. Make sure you provide a different name for the destination and try again.

```
Lock violation
```
You'll see this message if another program has a file open when you try to copy it. This will happen mostly when you're running a task-switching environment, such as DesqView, the DOS Task Swapper, or Microsoft Windows. Make sure no other program is trying to use the file and try again.

```
Path too long
```
Pathnames are limited to 64 characters, including the \ at the start of the path but not a drive letter. You'll see this message when you try to copy an entire branch of your directory structure to a deeper location, which causes one of the paths to be too long.

```
Sharing violation
```
You'll see this message if another program already has a file open when you try to copy it. This will happen mostly when you're running a task-switching environment, such as DesqView, the DOS Task Swapper, or Microsoft Windows. Make sure no other program is trying to use the file and try again.

```
Too many open files
```
You'll see this message when XCOPY runs out of file handles, which it needs to open files. Increase the number in the FILES= command in your CONFIG.SYS file.

XCOPY

```
Unable to create directory
```
You'll probably see this message when XCOPY tries to create a directory that has the same name as a file. You'll need to rename the file, or directory, and try again.

Examples

Let's say you just got a new hard disk, and you want to move part of your directory structure (say C:\WRITING and all its subdirectories) to your new hard disk D:. This command will allow you to do that:

C:\>xcopy c:\writing d:\writing\ /s /e

This will create an exact copy of the \WRITING directory and all its subdirectories (including subdirectories that have no files in them). XCOPY will create the D:\WRITING directory if it doesn't exist.

If you instead type

C:\>xcopy c:\writing d:

XCOPY will copy all the files in C:\WRITING to the root directory of D:, and all the directories in C:\WRITING will appear on drive D: as subdirectories D:\.

Confirming copying over existing files

Often, you may want XCOPY to ask before it copies files on top of existing files. To always do this (even from within a batch file), use the /-Y switch, as in the following:

C:\>copy file.txt d:\writing\books\newfile.txt

```
...
Overwrite d:\writing\books\newfile.txt (Yes/No/All)?
```

At this point you can press Y, N, or A followed by Enter. All means that XCOPY copies any other files that match wildcard characters in a name without asking whether you want to overwrite existing files.

Using the COPYCMD environment variable

You can set the COPYCMD environment variable so that XCOPY always asks you before it overwrites existing files (this environment variable also affects the COPY and MOVE commands). Here is the SET command you can place in your AUTOEXEC.BAT file to set up such an environment variable:

```
set copycmd=/-y
```

After you have this switch set, you can have XCOPY copy a file without asking for confirmation by using the /Y switch, as in the following:

C:\>xcopy /y file.txt d:\writing\books\newfile.txt

See also

ATTRIB   You can use this command to control the archive bit on files.

BACKUP   Your BACKUP command allows you to back up files that have their archive bit set.

Part II: Command Reference

COPY — If you don't need all the power of XCOPY, the COPY command is easier to learn and use.

COUNTRY — The COUNTRY setting controls the current format you'll need to use for date input. You can run the DATE command to see how it's currently set.

DATE — You can use the DATE command to show you the format you need to use for dates.

VERIFY — This command allows you to turn on write-verification, which does some additional tests on the data you write.

INDEX

Symbols

% (percent sign), 100–102
   with environment variables (%name%), 101, 102
      examples, 102
      syntax, 102
   with replacement variables (%n), 100–101, 102, 446
      examples, 101
      syntax, 101
   using, 101
* wildcard character, 91–92
   all files, 92
   matching names without extensions, 92
   in one character names, 91
   one extension, any name, 92
: (colon)name, 102–103, 287
   example, 103
   syntax, 102
; (semi-colon), 95, 160, 417
   in CONFIG.SYS file, 95
   syntax, 95
< (less than sign), 96, 99–100, 365, 459
   batch programs and, 99
   examples, 100
   parameters, 99
   spaces and, 99
   syntax, 99
> (greater than sign), 96, 97–98, 100, 459
   examples, 98
   parameters, 97
   spaces between, 98
   syntax, 97
? (question mark), 160
   as CONFIG.SYS prompt, 93–94
      examples, 94
      syntax, 93
   with SET command, 93
   as wildcard character, 91
@ (at sign), 92–93, 255
   with ECHO OFF command, 92, 93
   examples, 92–93
   syntax, 92
| (pipe character), 95–96, 99, 100, 365, 459
   in CALL command, 96
   examples, 96
   syntax, 96
   See also piping

A

/A switch
   BACKUP command, 117
   COMP command, 153
   COPY command, 161, 164
   DIR command, 232

FC command, 271
MSAV command, 374
REPLACE command, 420
RESTORE command, 423
SMARTDRV command, 450
TREE command, 471
XCOPY command, 494
allocation units, 44, 139
ANSI escape codes, 104–105
   cursor positioning, 104–105
   erasing, 105
   text colors, 105
ANSI.SYS device driver, 103–106, 146, 360, 411, 466
   DISPLAY.SYS and, 240
   for displaying status line, 410–411
   parameters, 104
   in prompts, 105–106
   switches, 104
   syntax, 103
   uses, 103
   See also device drivers
Anti-Virus program, 14, 82–84
   for DOS, 373–377
   non running, 83–84
   Prompt While Detect option, 83
   upgrade software, 83–84
   Verify Integrity option, 83
   Warning Options screen, 84
   for Windows, 387–389
   See also viral signatures; viruses
APPEND command, 106–110, 399
   ASSIGN command and, 108
   DOS function modifications, 109
   loading, 107
   messages, 108
   search path, 107
   shells and, 108
   switched, 107–108
   syntax, 107
   uses, 106
Argus Financial Software, 60
ASSIGN command, 108, 110–112, 317, 465
   DOS functions and, 111
   DOS interrupts and, 112
   example, 112
   incompatibilities, 111
   messages, 111
   switches, 110
   syntax, 110
   in TSR program, 111
   uses, 110
ATTRIB command, 48, 59, 113–115, 120, 380, 392, 422, 497
   attributes, 114
      multiple changes of, 115

examples, 115
parameters, 113–114
switches, 114
syntax, 113
uses, 113
AUTOEXEC.BAT file, 2, 9, 11
  /L switch, 67
  /S switch, 67
  APPEND /X in, 109
  batch file execution within, 74
  bypass, 24, 25, 94
  code pages and, 129
  command line, 23–24
  commands, 30–34
  communicating choices to, 343
  DATE command and, 171
  device driver in, 21
  DR DOS commands in, 20
  interacting with, 26
  MEMMAKER command in, 75
  MIRROR command in, 349
  multiple configurations in, 73, 345
  problems in, 21
    tracking down, 25, 26
  screen saver programs and, 54
  SHARE in, 442
  SMARTDRV in, 71
  time and, 469
  See also CONFIG.SYS file

B

/B switch
  COPY command, 161, 164
  DEFRAG command, 216
  DELOLDOS command, 222
  DIR command, 232
  DOSSHELL command, 249
  EDIT command, 256
  FC command, 272
  FORMAT command, 282
  GRAPHICS command, 289
  HELP command, 291
  INTERSVR command, 313
  MEMMAKER command, 335
  MSD command, 384
  PRINT command, 405
  QBASIC command, 411
  RESTORE command, 423
  SETUP command, 436
  SMARTDRV command, 448
BACKUP command, 14, 18, 57, 115, 116–120, 424, 497
  with ASSIGN, JOIN, SUBST commands, 118
  DOS versions and, 118
  ERRORLEVEL command and, 119
  examples, 119
  files created by, 118
  parameters, 116
  switches, 117–118
  syntax, 116
  SYS files and, 118
  uses, 116
Backup program, 14
  compatibility test, 78–80
    failure, 78–79, 80
    manual, 80
    with Windows 386 Enhanced Mode, 79–80
  component file, 82
  Compress Backup Data option, 81
  DoubleSpace disks with, 81
  file copy reliability, 81–82
  questions concerning, 78–82
  Three Little Things checklist, 78–79
  Use Error Correction on Diskettes option, 82
  Verify Backup Data option, 82
  See also BACKUP command
batch files, 100–102
  directory, 33
  environment variable in, 102
  FOR command and, 280
  friendly, 299
  labels in, 102–103
  loops, 298–299
  replaceable parameters in, 100–101
  single step, 147
  stopping, 399
  See also files
batch programs, 96
  > (greater than sign) and, 98
  > (less than sign) and, 99
  hiding output of, 98
  running second, 125–126
Binary files, TYPE command and, 472
BIOS (Basic Input Output System), 23
  AMI, 71
  ROM, 205
bit bucket, 11
blocks, noncontiguous, 139
booting, 2
Break, 120–122
  Ctrl-C break, 120–122
  syntax, 121
buffers, 32, 122–124
  allocation of, 32–33
  DMA, 81
  double, 39
  normal, 124
  parameter, 122
  read-ahead, 123
  setting disk, 122–124
  settings, 33
  size of, 123–124
BUFFERS command, 32, 66, 79, 122–124, 270, 456
  examples, 124
  parameters, 122–123
  SMARTDRV command and, 123
  switches, 123
  syntax, 122

Index

C

/C switch
  CHOICE command, 141
  COMMAND command, 125, 126, 147, 149
  COMP command, 153
  DIR command, 178, 204, 232
  DRIVER.SYS, 250
  DRIVPARM command, 252
  FC command, 271
  FIND command, 277
  FORMAT command, 282–283
  GRAPHICS command, 289
  MEM command, 331
  MSAV command, 374
  PRINT command, 404
  SMARTDRV command, 37, 448
caching
  controlling, options, 454
  directory information, 267–270
  disk, 35–36
  Read Only, 36
  status, 38
  write, 35–36
  write-behind, 36
    Windows and, 451
  See also disk cache
CALL command, 125–126, 151, 280, 300
  | (pipe character) in, 96
  /C switch vs., 125–126
  COMMAND command /C vs., 149
  emulating, 150
  examples, 126
  parameters, 125
  syntax, 125
CD command. *See* CHDIR command
CD-ROM
  DoubleSpace and, 48
  drive letter assignment, 381–383
  NEC-CDR-74, 383
  SmartDrive and, 2, 382–383, 450
  using, device, 383
character sets. *See* code pages
CHCP command, 126–129, 165, 168, 241, 288, 322, 358, 396, 408
  examples, 128–129
  messages, 128
  MODE CP vs., 357
  parameters, 127
  syntax, 127
  uses, 127
CHDIR command, 129–131, 351, 471
  examples, 131
  messages, 131
  parameters, 130
  syntax, 130
  uses, 129
CHKDSK command, 2, 14, 132–140, 177, 180, 334, 438, 471
  /F switch, 56, 132
  /V switch, 132

alternatives, 134
ASSIGN, JOIN, SUBST commands and, 134
DOS versions and, 135
with DoubleSpace, 134
errors reported by, 133, 138
examples, 138–139
information reported by, 139
messages, 135–138
networks and, 134
open files and, 134–135
parameters, 132
SCANDISK and, 429
syntax, 132
uses, 132
Windows and, 134–135
CHKLIST.MS, 376, 388
  deleting, 376, 388
CHKSTATE.SYS, 140
  See also MemMaker
CHOICE command, 140–145, 300
  default, 143
  with DOS 4 and 5, 142
  error conditions, 142
  examples, 143–144
  GOTO command with, 144
  IF ERRORLEVEL statements and, 142, 143
  messages, 142
  parameters, 141
  switches, 141–142
  syntax, 141
  uses, 140–141
clock, 170
  forgets date and time, 469
  ticks, 405
  See also date; time
CLS command, 29, 105, 145–146
  EGA/VGA modes and, 145
  escape sequence, 145
  screen colors and, 145
  syntax, 145
  uses, 145
CMOS
  MemMaker and, 76
  settings, 54
code pages, 126–129, 166
  CGA/monochrome displays and, 127
  commands related to, 168
  CON, 358
  device driver, 239–241
  in GRAFTABL, 288
  hardware, 240
  MODE CP command and, 355–358
  other programs and, 127
  using, 128, 356
Color Graphics Adapter (CGA), 287
colors
  laptop control of, 360
  screen, 145
  start-up menu, 28, 337–339
  text, 105
COMMAND.COM, 12, 67

COMMAND command, 102, 146–151, 169, 280, 301, 435, 444
  /C switch, 125, 126
  /P switch warning, 149, 264
  CALL command and, 149
  environment variables and, 148–149
  examples, 150–151
  leaving, 146
  messages, 149–150
  parameters, 147
  reloading, 148
    from RAM disk, 151
  switches, 147–148
  syntax, 146
  uses, 146
command-line
  editing, 246
  interpreter, 443–444
commands, 4
  AUTOEXEC.BAT, 30–34
  bypassing, 94
  code page, 168
  CONFIG.SYS, 30–34
  multiple, 248
  recalling, 245
  replacing internal, 247
  run, 147
  shared blocks of, 345
  syntax for, 266–267
  typing multiple, 245
  undocumented, 267
  See also DOSKEY; *specific commands*
COMP command, 152–155, 236, 274
  examples, 155
  hexadecimal numbers and, 154
  messages, 154–155
  parameters, 152–153
  prompts and, 153
  switches, 153
  syntax, 152
  uses, 152
  wildcard characters and, 153–154
Complete Communicator, 61
compressed volume file (CVF), 43, 45–46, 175
  adding new files to, 50
  adjusting size of, 52–53
  copying, to null device, 54
  creating, 46–47
  to drive letter, 49
compression program, 12–13
  conversion to DoubleSpace, 57–58
  on-the-fly compression and, 44
  See also disk compression; DoubleSpace
CONFIG.SYS file, 9, 11, 156–160, 227, 274, 302, 337, 346, 444, 462, 466
  8088, 159
  80286, 159
  80386, 159–160
  ? (question mark) in, 93–94
  /L switch, 67
  /S switch, 67
  absent, 156
  alt and, 156
  breaking in, 121
  bypass, 24, 25, 94
  CHKSTATE.SYS line, 75
  code pages and, 128
  command line, 23–24
  commands, 30–34
  commenting, 95
  comment lines, 94
  COUNTRY= command, 129
  device driver in, 21
  disabling commands in, 95
  DOS=HIGH, 93
  DOS processing of, 93, 157–158
  DoubleSpace and, 30
  DR DOS commands in, 20
  EMM386 command line, 60
  examples, 159–160
  FASTOPEN in, 270
  FILES line, 30–31
  INCLUDE command and, 301–302
  INSTALL= and, 157, 158–159
  interacting with, 25–26
  LASTDRIVE=, 175
  line order in, 157
  for loading EMM386, 263
  memory and, 65
  messages, 159
  multiple configurations and, 73
  NLSFUNC in, 395
  problems in, 21
    tracking down, 25–26
  REM in, 94, 95
  remark line, 416–417
  screen saver programs and, 54
  SHARE in, 442
  skipping, 158
  SMARTDRV from, 31
  Stacker and, 158
  stepping through, 158
  SUBMENU in, 461–462
  syntax, 156
  uses, 156
  See also AUTOEXEC.BAT file
configuration blocks
  defining, 341
  empty, 341
configurations, multiple. *See* multiple configurations
COPY command, 57, 111, 120, 160–165, 239, 373, 380, 392, 418, 422, 489, 498
  archive attribute and, 162
  DOS 6.2 upgrade, 2
  end-of-file mark and, 162
  examples, 163–164
  file combining and, 162–163
  file date/time and, 162
  messages, 163
  parameters, 161
  switches, 161, 164
    option, 162

Index

uses, 160
XCOPY vs., 495
zero-length files and, 163
COPYCMD environment variable, 164, 373, 497
countries, 166
   list of, 167
COUNTRY command, 165–168, 171, 234, 396, 424, 470, 498
   code pages and, 166, 167
   DOS commands affected by, 166
   examples, 167
   languages and, 166
   parameters, 165–166
   settings, 166
   syntax, 165
Ctrl-Break, 120–122
   return value, 142
Ctrl-C, 120–122
   return value, 142
CTTY command, 151, 168–169
   example, 169
   full-screen programs and, 169
   parameters, 168
   syntax, 168

D

/D switch
   BACKUP command, 117
   COMP command, 153
   DRIVER.SYS, 250
   DRIVPARM command, 252
   JOIN command, 316
   MEM command, 331
   PRINT command, 405
   RESTORE command, 423
   SETVER command, 439
   SUBST command, 463
   VSAFE command, 491
   XCOPY command, 494
date, 169–171
   clock forgets, 170
   format, 233
   in prompts, 409
   setting new, 171
   See also clock; time
DATE command, 120, 169–171, 424, 470, 498
   AUTOEXEC.BAT and, 171
   examples, 171
   IBM PC and, 170
   messages, 171
   parameters, 170
   prompting, 171
   syntax, 169
DBLSPACE /AUTOMOUNT command, 173, 178–179, 183, 212
   parameters, 179
   syntax, 178
DBLSPACE.BIN file, 24, 30, 49, 50, 176, 189
DBLSPACE /CHKDSK command, 172, 177, 179–180
   messages, 180
   parameters, 180
   switches, 180
   syntax, 180
   uses, 179
DBLSPACE command, 160, 171–178, 180, 438
   compressed volume size and, 174–175
   drive letter specification and, 176
   existing disk compression and, 174
   floppy disk compression and, 175
   messages, 177
   Ratio switch, 51
   running, 174
   switches, 172–173
   syntax, 172
   uses, 171–172
DBLSPACE /COMPRESS command, 172, 177, 180–183
   DBLSPACE.000 hidden file and, 182
   examples, 182–183
   parameters, 181–182
   switches, 181
   syntax, 181
   uses, 180–181
DBLSPACE /CREATE command, 172, 178, 183, 183–185, 198, 199, 211
   DBLSPACE.nnn hidden file and, 184
   examples, 185
   floppy disks and, 184
   messages, 185
   parameters, 184
   switches, 184
   syntax, 184
   uses, 183
DBLSPACE /DEFRAGMENT command, 53, 172, 178, 185–187, 208, 218
   DFRAG vs., 186
   examples, 187
   messages, 187
   parameters, 186
   stopping, 186
   switches, 186
   syntax, 186
   uses, 185–186
DBLSPACE /DELETE command, 172, 178, 188–189, 191
   examples, 189
   function of, 188–189
   parameters, 188
   syntax, 188
DBLSPACE /DOUBLEGUARD command, 173, 189–190
   parameters, 190
   syntax, 189
   uses, 189
DBLSPACE /FORMAT command, 173, 178, 189, 190–191, 285
   examples, 191
   messages, 191
   parameters, 191
   syntax, 190
   uses, 190

DBLSPACE /HOST command, 173, 191–193, 195
  examples, 193
  messages, 193
  parameters, 192
  syntax, 192
  uses, 191–192
DBLSPACE /INFO command
  examples, 194
  switches, 194
  syntax, 194
  uses, 193–194
DBLSPACE.INI file, 48, 49, 50, 176
  switches, 173–174
DBLSPACE /LASTDRIVE command, 173, 193, 195
  examples, 195
  parameters, 195
  syntax, 195
DBLSPACE /LIST command, 56, 58, 173, 178, 180, 193, 194, 196–197
  examples, 196
  syntax, 196
DBLSPACE /MAXFILEFRAGMENTS command, 173, 197–198
  parameters, 197
  syntax, 197
DBLSPACE /MAXREMOVABLEDRIVES command, 174, 198–199, 202
  examples, 199
  parameters, 198
  syntax, 198
DBLSPACE /MOUNT command, 173, 178, 183, 199–202
  examples, 202
  messages, 201
  parameters, 200
  switches, 200
  syntax, 200
  uses, 199
DBLSPACE /RATIO command, 173, 178, 202–204
  examples, 204
  parameters, 203
  switches, 203
  syntax, 203
  uses, 202–203
DBLSPACE /ROMSERVER command, 174, 205
  parameters, 205
  syntax, 205
DBLSPACE /SIZE command, 173, 178, 187, 195, 197, 204, 206–208
  examples, 207–208
  parameters, 207
  switches, 206–207
  syntax, 206
  uses, 206
DBLSPACE /SWITCHES command, 160, 174, 208–209
  Ctrl-F5/Ctrl-F8 and, 209
  examples, 209
  messages, 209
  parameters, 208
  syntax, 208

turning off, 209
  uses, 208
DBLSPACE.SYS device driver, 30, 178, 213–214
  conflicts with other device drivers, 214
  switches, 213
  syntax, 213
  uses, 213
  See also device drivers
DBLSPACE /UNCOMPRESS command, 173, 178, 210–211
  examples, 210
  parameters, 210
  syntax, 210
  uses, 210
DBLSPACE /UNMOUNT command, 173, 202, 211–213
  examples, 212
  messages, 212
  parameters, 211
  switches, 211
  syntax, 211
  uses, 211
DEBUG command, 214
DEFRAG command, 2, 53, 187, 198, 214–218
  /Q switch, 53
  on compressed volumes, 187
  DBLSPACE /DEFRAGMENT vs., 186
  DOS 6.2 improvements, 217
  DOS Task Swapper and, 217
  examples, 218
  exit codes, 218
  functioning of, 217–218
  parameters, 215
  SmartDrive and, 217
  switches, 215–216
  syntax, 215
  uses, 214–215
  using, 53
  Windows and, 217
defragmenting
  hidden volume files, 187
  maximum, 186–187
DEL command, 219–221, 224, 418
  ERASE vs., 220
  examples, 221
  functioning of, 219–220
  messages, 220–221
  parameters, 219
  switches, 219
  syntax, 219
  using, 220
  wildcard characters and, 220
DELOLDOS command, 9, 221–222, 438
  switches, 222
  syntax, 222
  uses, 221–222
DELTREE command, 9, 222–224, 351, 426, 471
  attributes and, 223
  examples, 223–224
  relative paths and, 223
  switches, 223

Index

syntax, 222
uses, 222
DEVICE command, 224–227, 230, 304, 337, 414, 441
    examples, 227
    messages, 226–227
    parameters, 225
    syntax, 224–225
    uses, 224
device drivers
    ANSI.SYS, 103–106
    code page, 239–241
    compressed drives and, 213–214
    conflicting, 94
    console, 225
    DBLSPACE.SYS, 213–214
        conflicts with other device drivers, 214
    DISPLAY.SYS, 239–241
    DOS, 225–226
    DRIVER.SYS, 250–252
    EGA.SYS, 257
    EMM386.EXE, 258–263
    extensions, 225
    installing, 224–227
    INTERLNK.EXE, 308–312
    load, in upper memory, 227
    list of, 230
    POWER.EXE, 401, 402–403
    PRINTER.SYS, 407–408
    prompting for, 94
    RAMDRIVE.SYS, 412–415
    See also HIMEM.SYS
DEVICEHIGH command, 66, 67, 70, 227–228, 241, 243, 310, 330, 334, 337, 358, 408, 414, 441
    DOS=UMB, 229
    examples, 230–231
    messages, 230
    parameters, 228
    size parameter, 229–230
    SMARTDRV and, 452
    switches, 228
    syntax, 228
    uses, 227
DIR command, 2, 139, 231–234, 436
    /C switch, 178, 204
    to check wildcards, 220
    default, options, 233–234
    DIRCMD environment variable, 234, 435
    examples, 234
    FIND and, 278–279
    parameters, 231
    switches, 231–233
    syntax, 231
direct memory access (DMA), 81
directories, 233
    absolute names and, 351
    changing, 131
    comparing, 155
    copying, 494–498
        files to, 164
    creating, 350–351
    deleting, 222–224, 425
        current, 223
    drive letter assignments to, 463–464
    hiding, 114
    printing, 98
    size of, 233
    structure display, 470–471
    undeleting, 86–87, 394, 476–477
disk
    accessing, 66
    comparing, 155
    compression, 180
    copying files to, 163
    defective, 11
    formatting, 281–285
    fragmented, 53
    RAM, 66
    scanning, 426–433
    structures, 133
    uncompression, 176
        system, 177
    upgrade, 10–11
    virtual, 66
    volume label, 322–324
    write verification, 487–488
    See also disk cache; disk drive; disk space; floppy disks; hard disks
disk cache, 35–36
    advantages, 32
    creating, 446–456
    effectiveness, 39
    flushing, 37
    RAM for, 32
    size, 40–41
    See also caching
disk compression, 1
    of current drive, 46
        uncompressed space and, 47
    defined, 43–46
    DR DOS, 20
    storage management, 44–46
    See also DoubleSpace
disk drive
    characteristic definition, 250–252
    compressed, missing, 48–49
        DBLSPACE.SYS and, 213–214
    connecting, 308
    installing foreign, 251
    joining, 317
    letter assignments, 47, 176, 251, 252
        ASSIGN command and, 110–112
        changing, 48
        DoubleSpace and, 192–193
        swapping, 112
    releasing, 308
    SCANDISK and, 430–431
    See also disk
disk space
    increasing with DoubleSpace, 14
    problems, 12–19
    requirement, 12

utility program requirements, 14
See also disk
disk-caching program, 11
  REM command and, 18
DISKCOMP command, 155, 234–236, 239, 274
  examples, 236
  exit codes, 235
  incompatibilities, 235
  messages, 236
  parameters, 235
  switches, 235
  syntax, 235
  uses, 234–235
DISKCOPY command, 120, 165, 236–239
  examples, 239
  exit codes, 238
  incompatibilities, 238
  messages, 238–239
  parameters, 237
  switches, 237
  syntax, 237
  temporary storage and, 2
  uses, 236–237
DISPLAY.SYS, 129, 168, 225, 239–241, 322, 358, 396, 408
  ANSI.SYS and, 240
  CGA/monochrome displays and, 240
  examples, 241
  memory usage, 240
  parameters, 239–240
  syntax, 239
  See also device drivers
DOS 6
  compressed floppy disks and, 49
  disk space, taking less, 14–16
  DR DOS conversion, 20
  on IBM PS/1, 19
  installing, 9–21
    disk space problem and, 12–14
    individual program files, 15–16
    manually, 12
  running problems, 21
  SmartDrive precautions with, 37
  on Tandy, 19
  uninstalling, 9, 438
DOS 6.2 upgrade, 2
  AutoMount feature, 48
  commas and, 2
  SmartDrive and, 37–38
DOS command, 241–244, 263, 334
  examples, 243
  messages, 243
  parameters, 242
  syntax, 242
  uses, 241–242
DOS=HIGH, 124, 241, 296, 297
DOS=UMB, 229, 231, 241, 330
DOS shells
  4.0, 249
  APPEND command and, 108
  DOSKEY and, 245

FASTOPEN command and, 269
SET within, 435
SHELL command and, 443–444
starting, 248–249
DOS Task Swapper
  DEFRAG command and, 217
  INTERSVR with, 314
  SCANDISK and, 430
DOSKEY, 244–248
  command-line editing, 246
  creating macros with, 246–247
  DOS shells and, 245
  examples, 247–248
  memory usage, 245
  messages, 247
  multiple commands and, 245
  parameters, 244
  recalling commands, 245
  switches, 244–245
  syntax, 244
  uses, 244
DOSSHELL command, 248–249, 444
  parameters, 249
  screen resolution, 249
  switches, 249
  syntax, 249
DOUBLE_BUFFER, 39
DoubleGuard, 2, 59
DoubleSpace, 1, 43–61, 311
  accessing, 171
  advantages of, 46
  allocation units, 44
  AutoMount option, 2
  with Backup program, 81
  bypassing disabled, 208–209
  Change Compression Ratio, 50
    dialog box, 51
  Change Size command, 52
  CHKDSK with, 134
  CVF, 43, 45–46, 47, 49
    adding files to, 50
    adjusting size of, 52–53
    copying, to null device, 54
  compression illustration, 45
  compression ratio, 46, 50
    actual, 51
    adjusting, 50–51
    changing, 203–204
    checking, 203
    free space, 51
    setting, 203
    for small files, 176, 177
    synchronizing, 204
  CONFIG.SYS file and, 30
  converting to, 57–58
  Custom Setup option, 47
  dangers, 1
  Defragment command, 52
  Delete command, 59
  DoubleGuard feature, 2
  drive C repair, 438

Index

drive caching, 42
drive info, 193
drive letter assignments, 47, 192–193
drives, 23
existing disk compression, 174
Express option, 47
files, defragmenting, 217
financial/spreadsheet programs and, 60
floppy disk use installation, 185
free disk space
    needed, 182
    predicting ratio, 202–204
    specifying, 207
functioning of, 43–50
games and, 60
incompatibilities, 59–61, 174
for increasing disk space, 14
LASTDRIVE and, 175
memory use, 1
MOUNT command, 48, 49
Novell Netware and, 47
optimizing, 50–57
Ratio switch, 51
removing, 58–59
SCANDISK and, 431–432
Setup program, 49
SmartDrive and, 451
Uncompress option, 2
uncompressed free space, 52
UNMOUNT command, 48
using, with floppy disk, 182
volume
    accessing, 182
    bad sectors in, 54–55
    creating, 183–185
    defragmenting, 185–187
    deleting, 188–189
    emptying, 190–191
    reducing to minimum size, 208
    repairing bad sectors in, 55
    size reduction, 207
    unmounted, checking, 433
Windows swapfiles and, 56–57
See also disk compression
DR DOS, DOS 6 conversion, 20
DRIVER.SYS, 250–252, 253
    switches, 250–251
        common settings for, 251
    syntax, 250
    See also device drivers
DRIVPARM command, 252–254
    switches, 252–253
    syntax, 252

E

/E switch
    APPEND command, 107
    COMMAND command, 147
    KEYB command, 318
    MSCDEX command, 382
    RESTORE command, 423

SETUP command, 77, 436
SMARTDRV command, 448
XCOPY command, 495
ECHO command, 92–93, 254–255, 400
    batch file output and, 254–255
    disallowed characters with, 255
    in DOS prompt, 254
    examples, 255
    message, 93
    OFF, 254
    state, 255
    syntax, 254
    uses, 254
ECHO OFF command, 92, 93
EDIT command, 255–256, 257, 472
    parameters, 256
    switches, 256
    syntax, 256
    uses, 255
Edit menu, 20
EDLIN command, 256–257
    uses, 256–257
EGA.SYS, 257
    mouse and, 257
    See also device drivers
EMM386.EXE, 231, 243, 258–263, 270, 330, 334, 337, 414, 456
    EMS page options, 260–261
    examples, 263
    messages, 262–263
    options, 261
        changing, 262
    parameters, 258–260
    syntax, 258
    uses, 258
    See also device drivers
EMM386 memory manager, 21, 297
    advanced options, 261
        changing, 262
    driver, 65
    expanded memory and, 64–65
    functions, 64
    MemMaker and, 73
    NOEMS parameter, 64, 67
    NOVCPI parameter, 64–65
    page options, 260–261
    Windows and, 262
    See also EMM386.EXE
EMS memory, 64, 333
    LIM 4.0, 333
    page frame, 64
    See also expanded memory
environment variables
    %name%, 101, 102
    in batch files, 102, 435
    COMMAND command, 148–149
    COPYCMD, 164, 373, 497
    DIRCMD, 234, 435
    DOS, 434–435
    INSTALL command, 304
    MOUSE command, 368

ERASE command, 219–220, 263, 426
    DEL vs., 220
    See also DEL command
error messages. *See* messages
ERRORLEVEL command, 119, 372
    SCANDISK and, 432
    to test for no errors, 299–300
    to test for specific values, 300
    testing, 143
EXE2BIN, 263
EXIT command, 151, 264
EXPAND command, 15, 264–266, 438
    example, 266
    extensions and, 265–266
    hard disks and, 265
    messages, 266
    parameters, 265
    syntax, 264–265
    uses, 264
expanded memory, 31, 64, 123, 332
    EMS, 64
    extended vs., 332
    RAMDRIVE.SYS and, 413
    SMARTDRV and, 455
    trouble accessing, 65
    See also EMS memory; memory
extended memory, 31, 64, 332
    BUFFERS command and, 124
    as expanded memory, 67
    expanded vs., 332
    freeing up, 67
    moving DOS to, 65–66
    RAMDRIVE.SYS and, 413
    SMARTDRV and, 453
    trouble accessing, 65
    See also memory; XMS memory

F

/F switch
    BACKUP command, 117
    CHKDSK command, 56, 132
    DBLSPACE /CHKDSK command, 180
    DBLSPACE /COMPRESS command, 181
    DBLSPACE /DEFRAGMENT command, 186
    DEFRAG command, 215
    DRIVER.SYS, 250–251
    DRIVPARM command, 253
    FORMAT command, 281–282
    GRAPHICS command, 289
    MEM command, 331
    MSAV command, 374
    MSD command, 384
    SETUP command, 436
    SHARE command, 442
    SMARTDRV command, 448–449
    SWITCHES command, 466
    TREE command, 471
FASTHELP command, 266–267
    examples, 267
    parameters, 267
    syntax, 267

    undocumented commands and, 267
    uses, 266–267
FASTOPEN command, 124, 267–270, 456
    disk optimization programs and, 269
    examples, 270
    installing, 269
        in CONFIG.SYS, 270
    memory used, 269
    messages, 269
    multiple drives and, 270
    networks and, 268–269
    parameters, 268
    switches, 268
    syntax, 268
    uses, 267–268
FAT (file allocation table), 45, 46, 133
    CHKDSK and, 138
FC command, 155, 236, 270–274
    examples, 273
    messages, 273
    parameters, 271
    switches, 271–272
    syntax, 271
    uses, 270–271
    wildcard characters, 272
FCB functions, 111
FCBs command, 76, 274
    memory used, 274
    parameters, 274
    syntax, 274
FDISK command, 17, 275
    Options screen, 17–18
    repartitioning hard disk with, 17–18
    switches, 275
    syntax, 275
File Manager (Windows)
    MWUNDEL with, 393
    Tools menu, 388, 390
filenames
    extensions of, 16, 265–266
    wildcard characters and, 91–92
files
    adding, 419–422
    BACKUP created, 118
    batch, 100–102
    changing name of, 164
    combining, 162–163
    comparing, 152–155, 270–274
    compressed, 12
        expanding, 264–266
    compression ratio, 203
    copying, 160–165, 494–498
    corruption prevention, 36–38
    creating, quick text, 163
    date/time of, 162
    Delete Sentry, 482
    deleted, listing, 481
    deleting, 219–221, 223
    edit, 255–256
    end-of-file mark, 162
    finding, 265

Index

fragmented, 53
hidden, 139
hiding, 114
multiple, searching, 278
open, number of, 275–277
printing, 163
protecting, 115
recovering, 415–416
restoring, 422–424
Setup Disk, 15
sharing, 441–443
startup, 25
swap, 56–57, 66
temporary, 96
undeleting, 85–86, 481–482
updating, 419–422
zero-length, 163
See also batch files; filenames
FILES command, 30–31, 66, 79, 124, 275–277
   example, 276–277
   memory used by, 276
   parameters, 276
   syntax, 276
   TSR programs and, 276
   uses, 276
   Windows and, 276
filters, 96, 100
   input redirection with, 99
   for sorting lines, 457–459
FIND command, 97, 100, 277–279
   DIR and, 278–279
   examples, 278
   messages, 278
   for multiple word strings, 278
   parameters, 277
   switches, 277–278
   syntax, 277
floppy disks
   comparing, 234–236
   compressed, 49, 175
      automatic mounting of, 178–179
   copying, 236–239
   DBLSPACE /CREATE and, 184
   during installation, 9
   formatting, 119
   uncompressing, 210
   unmounting, 212
   See also disk; disk drive
floppy drives
   change line and, 251, 253
   during installation, 9
   See also disk drive; floppy disks
flush the cache, 36
FOR command, 101, 279–280, 446
   batch files with, 280
   examples, 280
   lists and, 280
   parameters, 279
   syntax, 279
   uses, 279

FORMAT command, 2, 17, 18, 79, 80, 100, 281–285, 350, 468, 486
   examples, 284
   exit codes, 283
   incompatibilities, 283
   messages, 283–284
   parameters, 281
   switches, 281–283
   syntax, 281
   test, 299–300
   uses, 281
formatting, 281–285
   bad sectors and, 283
   drive incompatibilities and, 283
   floppies, 119
   lower capacity drive, 284
   reformatting, 284
   restore accidental, 483–486
   See also unformatting

G

/G switch
   DOSSHELL command, 249
   EDIT command, 256
   HELP command, 291
   QBASIC command, 412
   SETUP command, 437
GOTO command, 102–103, 285–287, 301, 346
   case and, 285
   CHOICE command with, 144
   examples, 286
   messages, 285
   with multiple configurations, 286
   replaceable parameters, 286
   syntax, 285
GRAFTABL command, 287–288
   display adapters, 288
   parameters, 287
   switches, 288
   syntax, 287
   text mode and, 288
   uses, 287
GRAPHICS command, 288–290
   memory used, 290
   parameters, 288–289
   printer and, 290
   STACKS and, 460
   switches, 289–290
   syntax, 288

H

/H switch
   DEFRAG command, 216
   DOSKEY command, 245
   DRIVER.SYS, 251
   DRIVPARM command, 253
   EDIT command, 256
   HELP command, 291
   QBASIC command, 412
   SETUP command, 437

hard disks
    configuring, 275
    EXPAND command and, 265
    repartitioning, 17–18
    See also disk drive
hardware, 19–20
HELP command, 267, 290–293
    examples, 292–293
    parameters, 291
    switches, 291
    syntax, 290–291
    uses, 290
    XCOPY command and, 292–293
Help program, 290
    Help file, 292
    moving through, 291–292
hexadecimal numbers, 154, 272
    binary differences in, 272
high memory area (HMA), 32, 34, 64, 65, 242, 333
    conflicts with other programs, 243
    DOS loading into, 242, 243, 296
    insufficient memory for, 71
    placing DOS in, 94
    UMB and, 243
    usage of, 241–244
    See also UMBs (upper memory blocks)
HIMEM.SYS, 2, 30, 34, 65, 71, 124, 231, 242, 244, 263, 293–297, 330, 334, 337, 414, 456
    DOS can't load into high memory and, 296
    examples, 297
    loading DOS in HMA and, 296
    messages, 296
    switches, 293–296
        advanced, 295–296
    syntax, 293
    uses, 293
    See also device drivers
hit rate, 41
host drive, 57

I

/I switch
    DRIVPARM command, 253
    FIND command, 278
    MSD command, 384
    SETUP command, 437
IBM PS/1, 19
icons, in this book, 5
IF command, 101, 145, 287, 297–301, 346
    examples, 298–300
    multiple configurations and, 299
    parameters, 298
    syntax, 297–298
    uses, 297
INCLUDE command, 301–302, 346
    common devices, 302
    examples, 302
    parameters, 301
    syntax, 301
    uses, 301

INSTALL= command, 157, 158–159, 303–305, 337, 443
    environmental variable and, 304
    example, 304
    lines run, 303–304
    LOADHIGH and, 329
    loading into upper memory and, 303
    messages, 304
    parameters, 303
    uses, 303
installing
    DOS 6, 9–21
        manually, 12
    individual program files, 15–16
    Setup from hard drive, 11–12
    utility programs, 77
    VSAFE, 493
interactive start-up, 2, 23
    disabling, 466
    method display, 26
    methods, 24
    with multiple configurations, 26
    restarting and, 26
    techniques, 23–27
    See also start-up
Interlnk, 311
    copying files, 314
    displaying status of, 308
    drives, 306
    starting server portion of, 312–315
    See also INTERLNK command; INTERLNK.EXE
INTERLNK command, 305–308, 315
    drive letters and, 306, 310–311
    LASTDRIVE and, 306–307, 311
    load in upper memory, 310
    with non-DOS 6 computer, 306
    parallel cables, 307
    parameters, 306
    redirection with Windows, 310
    serial cables, 307
    syntax, 305–306
    uses, 305
    volume labels and, 306
INTERLNK.EXE, 308–312, 315
    examples, 311–312
    incompatibilities, 311
    parameters, 309
    switches, 309–310
    syntax, 309
    uses, 308–309
    See also device drivers
INTERSVR command, 308, 312–315
    with DOS Task Swapper, 314
    examples, 314–315
    parameters, 313
    switches, 313–314
    syntax, 312–313
    uses, 312
    with Windows, 314

Index

J

/J switch, UNFORMAT command, 484
JOIN command, 112, 315–317
    canceling, 317
    examples, 317
    incompatibilities, 316
    messages, 316
    networks and, 316
    parameters, 316
    switches, 316
    syntax, 315
    uses, 315

K

/K switch
    ANSI.SYS, 104
    COMMAND command, 148
    MSCDEX command, 382
    SWITCHES command, 465, 466
KEYB.COM files, 318
KEYB command, 167, 241, 317–322, 358, 396, 408
    examples, 321
    exit codes, 320
    messages, 320–321
    parameters, 318
    switches, 318
    syntax, 318
    in upper memory, 318
    uses, 317
keyboard
    codes, 319–320
    dead keys and, 319
    input, 100
        redirecting, 99–100
    layout, 317–321
        changing, 321
        Italian, 321
        switching, 318
    single keystrokes from, 140
    See also KEYB command
KEYBOARD.SYS files, 318

L

/L switch
    BACKUP command, 118
    COMP command, 153
    CONFIG.SYS/AUTOEXEC.BAT and, 67
    DEVICEHIGH command, 228
    DIR command, 232
    DISKCOMP command, 235
    DISKCOPY command, 237
    FC command, 271
    FORMAT command, 282
    LOADHIGH command, 328
    MIRROR command, 347
    MSAV command, 374
    MSCDEX command, 382
    RESTORE command, 423
    SHARE command, 442

    SMARTDRV command, 449
    UNFORMAT command, 484
LABEL command, 140, 202, 285, 322–324, 418
    examples, 323–324
    incompatibilities, 323
    messages, 323
    networks and, 323
    parameters, 322–323
    syntax, 322
    uses, 322
labels
    in batch file, 102–103
    changing, 322–324
    deleting, 324
    GOTO and, 285
    repeated, 103
    setting, 323
    valid, 103
        characters, 323
    volume, 139, 201, 489
    See also LABEL command
LASTDRIVE command, 178, 324–326, 383, 465
    DoubleSpace, Interlnk, RAMDrive and, 325
    examples, 326
    hard drives and, 325
    Interlnk and, 306–307, 311
    memory used, 325
    messages, 325
    Netware and, 325
    parameters, 324
    syntax, 324
    uses, 324
LH command. *See* LOADHIGH command
LOADFIX command, 326–327
    examples, 327
    functioning of, 326–327
    parameters, 326
    syntax, 326
    uses, 326
LOADHIGH command, 66, 67, 70, 231, 244, 303,
        305, 322, 327–330, 334, 396, 443
    DOS programs and, 328
    examples, 330
    incompatibilities, 329
    INSTALL= and, 329
    parameters, 328
    switches, 328
    syntax, 328
    UMB memory and, 329
    uses, 327
Lotus 1–2–3, 60

M

/M switch
    BACKUP command, 117
    DISKCOPY command, 237
    DOSKEY command, 245
    MEM command, 331
    MSCDEX command, 382
    MWBACKUP command, 390
    PRINT command, 405

RESTORE command, 423
SETUP command, 15, 436–437
XCOPY command, 494
macros
    can't use, 245
    creating, 246–247
    define, 244
    deleting, 248
    reloading, 248
MD command. *See* MKDIR command
MDS (Microsoft Diagnostics program), 9
MEM command, 2, 64, 140, 231, 244, 263, 270, 297, 330–334, 337, 387, 414, 456
    /CLASSIFY switch, 67
        output, 68
    examples, 333–334
    /FREE switch, 70
    messages, 333
    output, 333–334
    switches, 331–332
    syntax, 331
    uses, 330–331
    See also MemMaker; memory
MemMaker, 67
    aborted, 75
    CMOS setup and, 76
    device drivers and, 336
    diskless workstations and, 72
    EMM386 and, 73
    FCB line and, 76
    fine-tuning, 336
    function of, 71
    memory adjustments, 73
    with multiple configurations, 72–73, 336
    optimization process, 73–74
    restart failure, 74
    restrictions on using, 72
    reversing changes, 337
    running, 71–76
        unattended, 337
    SCSI hard drive and, 75–76
    SIZER program, 74, 446
    STACKS and, 460
    stalling, 73–74
    system monitoring, 140
    UMB and, 229
    undoing changes, 74–75
    use decision on, 71–72
    See also memory
MEMMAKER command, 231, 244, 263, 297, 330, 334, 335–337
    examples, 337
    switches, 335–336
    syntax, 335
    uses, 335
    See also MemMaker
MEMMAKER.STS file, 68, 73
    sample, 68–69
memory, 139
    conventional. *See* RAM
    displaying info on, 330–334
    management, 63–76

drivers, 65
managers, 229
    See also specific memory managers
maximizing, 65–71
types, 63–65, 332
    See also MEM command; MemMaker; *specific types of memory*
memory-resident programs, 11
menu blocks, 27
MENUCOLOR command, 27, 337–339, 340, 346, 462
    examples, 338–339
    parameters, 338
    syntax, 338
    uses, 337, 338
MENUDEFAULT command, 27, 339–340, 346, 463
    examples, 340
    with no timer, 340
    switches, 339
    syntax, 339
    uses, 339, 340
MENUITEM command, 27, 28, 29, 93, 94, 145, 160, 302, 339, 340–346, 383, 463
    examples, 343–345
    INCLUDE command and, 301
    parameters, 341
    syntax, 341
    uses, 340
messages
    "10 mismatches - ending compare," 154
    "Access denied," 220, 421, 496
    "Active code page not available from CON device," 320
    "All specified file(s) are contiguous," 135, 432
    "Allocation error, size adjusted," 135
    "ANSI.SYS must be installed to perform requested function," 360
    "APPEND/ASSIGN conflict," 108
    "Bad command or file name," 149–150
    "Bad command or parameters," 325
    "Bad or missing command interpreter," 444
    "Bad or missing filespec," 226, 304
    "Bad or missing keyboard definition file," 320
    "Beep," 142
    "Cancel Defragment of drive H?" 187
    "Cannot change BUFSIZE," 247
    "Cannot CHDIR to pathname," 135
    "Cannot CHDIR to root," 136
    "Cannot CHKDSK a network drive, a SUBSTed or ASSIGNed drive," 136
    "Cannot do binary reads from a device," 163
    "Cannot find the file D:," 201
    "Cannot format an ASSIGNed or SUBSTed drive," 283
    "Cannot JOIN a network drive," 316
    "Cannot label a JOINed, SUBSTed or ASSIGNed drive," 323
    "Cannot label a network drive," 323
    "Cannot make a directory entry," 323
    "Cannot move test1 - No such file or directory," 371
    "Cannot operate on a SUBST drive," 480
    "Cannot operate on specific drive (x)," 480

Index

"Cannot perform a cyclic copy," 496
"Cannot recover..entry," 136
"Cannot specify both /DT and /DOS," 480
"Cannot SUBST a network drive," 464
"Cannot unload resident deletion-tracking software," 349
"Cannot use FASTOPEN for drive x:," 269
"Cannot XCOPY from/to a reserved device," 496
"Can't read file:," 154
"CHDIR .. failed, try alternate method," 136
"CHOICE:...," 142
"Code page nnn not prepared for all devices," 128
"Code page not prepared," 357
"Code page operation not supported on this device," 357
"Code page requested (nnn) is not valid for given keyboard code," 320
"Code page specified had not been prepared," 320
"Code page specified is inconsistent with the selected code page," 320
"Compare error on side 1, track 3," 236
"Compare more files (Y/N)?," 155
"Content of destination lost before copy," 163
"Could not expand second filename so as to match first," 155, 273
"Current keyboard does not support this code page," 357
"data error reading drive X," 54
"Destination directory does not exist," 266
"Device error during prepare," 320
"Device error during refresh," 357
"Device error during select," 357
"Device or code page missing from font file," 357
"Directory is totally empty," 136
"Directory not empty," 316
"Disk error reading/writing FAT n," 136
"Disk unsuitable for system disk," 284
"DMA Buffer Size Too Small," 81
"Does name specify a file name or directory name on the target," 496
"DoubleSpace cannot defragment because an unknown error occurred," 54
"Drive A is a removable, so you cannot create a compressed drive on it," 185
"Drive already SUBSTed," 464
"Drive assignment syntax error," 307
"Drive C is your startup disk drive and should not be mounted," 212
"Drive d is not a compressed drive," 180
"Drive types or diskette types not compatible," 236, 238
"/DS was specified. Because there is no Delete Sentry control file for this drive..," 480
"/DT was specified. Because there is no delete-tracking file for this drive..," 480
"Duplicate file name or file not found," 418
"EMM386 not installed," 262
"ERROR: An extended memory manager is already installed," 296
"Error: Unable to control A20 line?," 34
"Error: Unknown command "/1:0;1"," 67

"ERROR: VDISK memory allocator already installed," 296
"Error during read of font file," 357
"ERROR" HIMEM.SYS requires an 80X86-base machine," 296
"Error in CONFIG.SYS line n," 159
"Errors found. F parameter not specified," 137
"Errors on list device indicate that it may be off-line," 406
"Exception error 12," 460
"Expanded memory manager not present," 414
"Extended memory manager not present," 414
"Failure to access code page font file," 357
"FASTOPEN already installed," 269
"FASTOPEN EMS entry count exceeded. Use fewer entries," 269
"File allocation table bad, drive X:," 137
"File cannot be copied onto itself," 163, 421, 496
"File not found - name," 220, 278
"filename is cross-linked on allocation unit n," 133, 135
"Files are different sizes," 155
"Files compare OK," 155
"filespec contains n noncontiguous blocks," 438
"filespec is not a valid name for a DoubleSpace volume file," 438
"First allocation unit is invalid, entry truncated," 137
"Font file contents invalid," 358
"Formatting drive D will permanently erase all the files it contains," 191
"Has invalid allocation unit, file truncated," 137
"HMA not available : loading DOS low," 243
"Illegal device name," 353
"Incompatible disk partition detected," 454
"Incompatible hard disk or device driver," 18
"Incompatible partition," 19
"Incompatible switches," 273
"Incorrect DOS version," 108
"Insufficient memory," 414
"Insufficient memory to store macro," 247
"Insufficient room in root directory," 137
"Internal stack overflow," 460
"Invalid characters in volume label," 323
"Invalid code page," 128
"Invalid code page specified," 321
"Invalid current directory," 137
"Invalid date," 171
"Invalid directory," 163
"Invalid drive specification," 236, 238
"Invalid keyboard ID specified," 321
"Invalid keyword," 351
"Invalid macro definition," 247
"Invalid media or track) bad - disk unusable," 284
"Invalid number of parameters," 358
"Invalid parameter(s) specified," 349
"Invalid parameter," 316, 353, 355, 464
"Invalid path, not directory, or directory not empty," 425
"Invalid STACK parameters," 460
"Invalid subdirectory entry," 137
"Invalid time," 469

"Invalid unit reading drive F," 307
"Invalid Volume ID," 284
"KEYB has not been installed," 321
"Lock violation," 496
"LPTn: not redirected," 362
"Missing value - /new," 201
"Must specify ON or OFF," 488
"n lost allocation units found in i chains," 135
"NLSFUNC already installed," 395
"nnnnnn bytes disk space freed," 135
"No APPEND," 108
"No extended memory available," 414
"No files found," 421
"No files replaced," 421
"No free file handles," 150
"No hard drives on system," 454
"None of the clusters for this file are available," 481
"Not ready reading drive F," 307
"One of more device code pages invalid for given keyboard code," 321
"Only some of the clusters for this file are available..," 481
"Optimize upper memory for use with Windows?," 72
"Out of environment space," 108, 435
"Out of memory," 67
"Parameter format not correct," 351
"Parameter value not in allowed range," 150
"Parameters not supported by drive," 284
"Path not found," 221
"Path too long," 496
"Pathname too long," 406
"Power Manager (POWER.EXE) not installed," 401
"PRINT queue is empty," 406
"Printer error," 362
"Probable non-DOS disk," 137
"Rate and delay must be specified together," 355
"Required parameter missing," 150, 418
"Resident portion of MODE loaded," 362
"Resync failed. Files are too different," 273
"Sector not found reading drive X," 54, 266
"Sharing violation," 496
"SORT: Too many parameters," 458
"Source path required," 421
"Specified entry was not found in the version table," 440
"Starting cluster is unavailable. This file cannot be recovered..," 481
"Target diskette may be unusable," 239
"The drive letter D is not available for DoubleSpace's use," 193
"The entire drive will be reconstructed, directory structures will be destroyed," 416
"There are no more drive letters reserved for DoubleSpace to use," 50, 201
"There is no more deleted directory data on this disk," 394
"There is no more space in the version table new entries," 440
"This file cannot be automatically recovered..," 481

"Too many block devices," 308
"Too many bytes per track on hard drive," 454
"Too many characters in volume label," 323
"Too many drive entries," 269
"Too many file/directory entries," 269
"Too many open files," 496
"Too Many Primary Partitions or Incompatible Primary DOS Partition," 17
"Too much of memory fragmentation; MEM /C cannot be done," 333
"Unable to control A20," 296
"Unable to create directory," 351, 497
"Unable to create KEYB table in resident memory," 321
"Unable to deactivate EMM386 as UMBs are being provided," 262
"Unable to open component file," 82
"[Unable to open source]," 371
"Unable to perform refresh operation," 358
"Unable to write BOOT," 284
"[Unable to write destination]," 372
"Unrecognized command in CONFIG.SYS," 227
"Unrecoverable error in directory," 137
"Version table is corrupt," 440
"Volume in drive D has no label," 489
"Warning: Option ROM or RAM detected within page frame," 262–263
"WARNING: SMARTDrive will not check for incompatible disk partitions," 454
"WARNING: The A20 line was already enabled," 296
"Write protect error," 239, 284
"You are running the MS-DOS Shell. To run DoubleSpace you must quit the MS-DOS Shell," 177
"You are running Windows. To run DoubleSpace you must quit Windows," 177
"You must specify the host drive for a DoubleSpace drive," 454
"You must use "DBLSPACE /FORMAT d:" to format that drive," 284
"You pressed CTRL+F5 or CTRL+F8 to bypass DBLSPACE.BIN," 209
"Your computer uses a disk compression program," 16
"Your computer uses SuperStor disk compression," 17
Microsoft bulletin board, 93
Microsoft System Diagnostics, 384–387
MIRROR command, 221, 346–350, 482, 486
  in AUTOEXEC.BAT, 349
  for controlling deletion tracking, 349
  disk size and, 349
  DOS 6 and, 484–485
  examples, 349–350
  file created, 348
  messages, 349
  networks and, 348
  parameters, 347
  partition information, 348
    table, 349–350

Index

size in memory, 347
switches, 347
syntax, 347
UNFORMAT and, 485–486
uses, 346–347
what's restored with, 348
MKDIR command, 131, 350–351, 426, 471
   examples, 351
   long paths and, 351
   messages, 351
   multipart paths and, 351
   parameters, 350
   syntax, 350
   uses, 350
MODE COM command, 352–354, 363, 406
   examples, 353–354
   messages, 353
   P retry option, 353
   syntax, 352, 352–353
   use, 352
MODE command, 103, 146, 165, 169, 315, 359–360
   examples, 360
   messages, 360
   parameters, 359–360
   syntax, 359
   uses, 359
MODE CON command, 354–355
   examples, 355
   messages, 355
   nonrepeating keys and, 354
   parameters, 354
   syntax, 354
   unsupported keyboards, 355
   use, 354
MODE CP command, 168, 241, 322, 355–358, 363, 396, 408
   CHCP vs., 357
   example, 358
   messages, 357–358
   parameters, 356
   PREP= command, 129
   SELECT= command, 129
   status information, 356–357
   syntax, 355–356
   use, 355
MODE LPT command, 354, 361–363
   COLS/LINES and, 362
   examples, 363
   messages, 362
   P retry option, 362
   parameters, 361–362
   syntax, 361
   uses, 361
MODE STATUS command, 363–364
   example, 364
   parameters, 363
   switch, 364
   syntax, 363
   use, 363
MORE command, 97, 100, 364–365, 472
   examples, 365

long lines and, 365
next page and, 364
SORT and, 458–459
stopping, 364
syntax, 364
uses, 364
mounting
   second volume, 201
   volume labels and, 201
mouse, 365–366
   acceleration, 369
   activating, support, 369
   MSAV switches, 375
   with Windows, 367
MOUSE.COM, 367
   recent version of, 367
MOUSE command, 365–369
   environment variable, 368
   examples, 369
   messages in different languages, 369
   switches, 366–367
   syntax, 365–366
   uses, 365
   See also mouse
MOUSE.INI file, 367–368
   line descriptions, 368
MOUSE.SYS, 367
MOVE command, 369–373, 419
   changing file name/location and, 371
   COPYCMD environment variable, 373
   DOS 6.2 upgrade, 2
   examples, 372–373
   exit codes, 372
   functioning of, 371
   messages, 371–372
   parameters, 370
   relative paths and, 371
   switches, 370
   syntax, 370
   uses, 369–370
moving
   confirming, over existing files, 372
   file and changing name, 372
   files to floppy disk, 372
   See also MOVE command
MSAV command, 373–377, 388, 493
   CHKLIST.MS, 376
   error codes, 376
   examples, 377
   files checked by, 376
   MWAV and, 376
   parameters, 374
   switches, 374–375
      mouse, 375
   syntax, 373–374
   uses, 373
   See also MWAV command
MSAV.INI file, 376
MSBACKUP command, 57, 80, 116, 377–381, 392, 424
   ATTRIB command and, 115
   backup catalogs, 379

backup types, 378–379
catalog file naming, 380
examples, 380
MWBACKUP and, 378
parameters, 378
setup files and, 378
switches, 378
syntax, 377
uses, 377
See also MWBACKUP command
MSBACKUP.INI file, 379
MSCDEX command, 381–383
drive letter availability and, 382
examples, 383
parameters, 381
switches, 382
syntax, 381
uses, 381
version, 382
MSD command, 71, 384–387
buttons, 385–386
examples, 386
menus, 385
parameters, 384
quitting, 385
switches, 384–385
syntax, 384
uses, 384
MS-DOS Editor, 48, 49
MSHERC command, 387
switches, 387
syntax, 387
MultiMate, 60
multiple configurations, 27–29
in AUTOEXEC.BAT, 345
designing, 341–342
menus, 27–28
blank lines and, 29
optimizing, 341
realistic, 344
submenus, 28–29
MWAV command, 373, 377, 387–388, 493
CHKLIST.MS, 388
files checked, 388
MSAV and, 376
syntax, 387
Tool menu, 388
uses, 387–388
See also MSAV command
MWAVTSR program, 389, 493
MWBACKUP command, 80, 116, 424
backup catalogs, 391
backup types, 390–391
catalog file naming, 391–392
File Manager Tools menu and, 390
parameters, 390
setup files and, 390
switches, 390
syntax, 390
uses, 389
See also MSBACKUP command

MWBACKUP.INI file, 391
MWUNDEL command, 392–395, 482
delete protection type, 393
with File Manager, 393
messages, 394
sentry files, 393
undeleting directories, 394
uses, 392–393

N

/N switch
CHOICE command, 141
COMP command, 153
DRIVPARM command, 253
FC command, 271
FIND command, 277
FORMAT command, 282
MSAV command, 374
RESTORE command, 423
SMARTDRV command, 449
SWITCHES command, 466
VSAFE command, 491
NLSFUNC command, 129, 168, 241, 322, 358, 395–396, 408
examples, 395
in high memory, 395
messages, 395
parameters, 395
syntax, 395
use, 395
Norton Utilities Version 7, 61
null test, 11, 54
NUMLOCK command, 346, 396–397
syntax, 396–397
use, 396

O

/O switch, DIR command, 233
OLD_DOS_1 directory, 9, 14

P

/P switch
COMMAND command, 147, 149
DEL command, 219, 220
DIR command, 231
MEM command, 331–332
MSAV command, 374
MSD command, 385
PRINT command, 404
REPLACE command, 420
RESTORE command, 423
UNFORMAT command, 484
XCOPY command, 495
partition table, restoring, 485
partitions
creating new, 17–18
Everex, 18
incompatible, 19
Novell, 18
Priam, 18

Index

problems with, 12–19
UNIX, 18
XENIX, 18
PATH command, 25, 106, 110, 151, 397–399, 436
   complex, 399
   maximum length, 398
   minimum, 398
   parameters, 397
   prompts, 409–410
   search order, 397–398
   syntax, 397
   uses, 397
pathnames, 131
paths, 33
   absolute, 397
   defining, 397–399
   drive letters and, 397
   multipart, 425
   relative, 464
   See also PATH command
PAUSE command, 255, 399–400
   examples, 400
   syntax, 399
   use, 399
PC World DOS 6 Handbook, 18
PIF Editor, 33
piping, 95–96
   CALL command and, 125
   limitations on, 96
   uses, 96
   See also | (pipe character)
PKZIP, 44
POWER command, 400–402, 403
   examples, 401–402
   messages, 401
   parameters, 401
   syntax, 400
   uses, 400
POWER.EXE, 401, 402–403
   examples, 403
   parameters, 402–403
   switches, 403
   syntax, 402
   uses, 402
   See also device drivers
power management, 401
   device driver. *See* POWER.EXE
   features installation, 403
   maximum level of, 403
   temporarily suspending, 402
PRINT command, 404–406
   clock ticks and, 405
   examples, 406
   memory used, 405
   messages, 406
   parameters, 404
   switches, 404–405
   syntax, 404
   time slices and, 406
   uses, 404

PRINTER.SYS, 129, 168, 241, 322, 358, 396, 407–408
   examples, 408
   memory usage, 408
   parameters, 407
   syntax, 407
   uses, 407
   See also device drivers
printers
   controlling output of, 361–363
   GRAPHICS command and, 290
   network, 362
   redirection, 362
   Windows redirection, 310
   See also PRINTER.SYS
printing, files, 163
PROMPT command, 408–411, 436
   examples, 410–411
   parameters, 409
      special $, 409
   syntax, 409
   uses, 408
prompts
   $ parameters, 409
   command-line, 408–411
   comparing, 153
   date/time into, 409
   path, 409–410
      standard, 410
   in Windows 3.1, 410

Q

/Q switch
   DEFRAG command, 53, 216
   FORMAT command, 281
   PRINT command, 405
   SETUP command, 437
   SMARTDRV command, 449
QBASIC command, 256, 411–412
   parameters, 411
   switches, 411–412
   syntax, 411
   use, 411
Quick Basic programming system, 411–412
Quicken, 60

R

/R switch
   GRAPHICS command, 289
   MSAV command, 374
   REPLACE command, 420
   SMARTDRV command, 448
   SORT command, 458
RAM, 50, 63, 332
   device driver, 412–415
   disk, 66
   for disk cache, 32
   DoubleSpace use of, 50
   drive, 48
RAMDrive, 311
RAMDRIVE command, 30, 311

RAMDRIVE.SYS, 412–415, 456
    drive letters and, 413
    examples, 414
    expanded memory and, 413
    extended memory and, 413
    messages, 414
    parameters, 413
    switches, 413
    syntax, 412
    in upper memory, 414
    uses, 412
    See also device drivers
RD command. *See* RMDIR command
RECOVER command, 415–416
    functioning of, 416
    limitations, 416
    messages, 416
    parameters, 416
    syntax, 415
    uses, 415
redirection
    CALL command and, 125
    keyboard input, 99–100
        limitations on, 100
    screen output, 97–98
        limitations on, 98
        TSRs and, 98
REM command, 11, 160, 227, 416–417
    disk caching program and, 18
    examples, 417
    syntax, 416
    use, 416
REN command. *See* RENAME command
RENAME command, 373, 417–419
    directory renaming and, 418
    examples, 418
    file renaming and, 418
    messages, 418
    parameters, 417
    syntax, 417
    uses, 417
REPLACE command, 165, 381, 392, 419–422
    examples, 421–422
    exit codes, 420
    hidden/system files and, 420
    messages, 421
    parameters, 419
    switches, 419–420
    syntax, 419
    uses, 419
RESTORE command, 17, 18, 115, 120, 422–424
    ASSIGN, JOIN, SUBST and, 423
    examples, 424
    exit codes, 424
    parameters, 422
    previous versions, 424
    switches, 423
    syntax, 422
    system files and, 424
    uses, 422

RMDIR command, 131, 221, 224, 351, 425–426, 471
    deleting directories with, 425
    examples, 426
    messages, 425–426
    multipart paths and, 425
    parameters, 425
    syntax, 425
    uses, 425
ROM (read-only memory), 63
    BIOS compression, 205
ROMDOS, 19

S

/S switch
    ATTRIB command, 114
    BACKUP command, 117
    CHOICE command, 141
    CONFIG.SYS/AUTOEXEC.BAT and, 67
    DEFRAG command, 216
    DEVICEHIGH command, 228
    DIR command, 232
    DRIVER.SYS, 251
    DRIVPARM command, 253
    FORMAT command, 282
    LOADHIGH command, 328
    MSAV command, 374
    MSCDEX command, 382
    MSD command, 385
    PRINT command, 405
    REPLACE command, 420
    RESTORE command, 423
    SMARTDRV command, 39, 449
    UNDELETE command, 475
    XCOPY command, 495
scan utilities, 56
    See also ScanDisk
ScanDisk, 2, 55, 132, 134, 180
    using, 55
SCANDISK command, 140, 189, 426–433
    CHKDSK vs., 429
    DOS Task Swapper and, 430
    DoubleSpace volumes and, 431–432
    examples, 433
    exit codes, 432
    functioning of, 430
    marginal sectors and, 429
    messages, 432–433
    nonfunctioning drives, 429–430
    parameters, 428
    physical disk drive checks and, 430–431
    Stacker and, 430
    switches, 427–428
    syntax, 426–427
    /UNDO warning, 428
    uses, 426
    Windows and, 430
screen
    colors, 145
    graphics print, 288–290
    more lines on, 360

Index

resolution, 249
savers, 54
summary report to, 386
SCSI hard drive, MemMaker and, 75–76
sectors, bad, 139
serial port, parameters, 352–354
SET command, 102, 234, 399, 411, 434–436
   ? (question mark) and, 93
   DOS environment variables, 434–435
      in batch files, 435
   examples, 435
   messages, 435
   parameters, 434
   syntax, 434
   uses, 434
   within DOS shells, 435
SETUP command, 9, 436–438
   /E switch, 77, 436
   /M switch, 15, 436–437
   /U switch, 18, 437
   for installation, 13
   not enough free space and, 437
   switches, 9–10, 436–437
   syntax, 436
   uninstalling DOS and, 438
   uses, 436
Setup Disk, 10, 12
   filename extensions, 16
   files, 15
Setup program, 9
   from drive C, 10
   installing from hard drive, 11–12
   memory resident programs and, 11
   problems with, 10–12
   running, 9, 12
SETVER command, 438–441
   adding programs and, 441
   examples, 441
   exit codes, 440
   memory used, 439
   messages, 440
   parameters, 439
   removing programs and, 441
   switches, 439
   syntax, 439
   uses, 438–439
   version table and, 440
SETVER.EXE, 440
SHARE command, 441–443
   in AUTOEXEC.BAT, 442
   in CONFIG.SYS, 442
   DOS 4.0 and, 442
   examples, 442
   memory used, 442
   switches, 442
   syntax, 442
   uses, 441
SHELL command, 149, 151, 436, 443–444
   DOS shell and, 443–444
   examples, 444
   messages, 444

   parameters, 443
   syntax, 443
   uses, 443
   warning, 443
SHIFT command, 101, 444–446
   examples, 445–446
   function of, 445
   syntax, 445
   uses, 444–445
SmartDrive, 1, 35–42, 66
   caches, 35–36
   CD-ROM drives and, 382–383, 450
   from CONFIG.SYS file, 31
   current status of, 38–39
   default cache sizes, 451
   default settings, 2
   DEFRAG command and, 217
   Disk Caching Status chart, 38–39, 42
   DOS 6 data loss and, 450–451
   DOUBLE_BUFFER, 39
   double-buffering, 31
   DoubleSpace and, 451
   DoubleSpace drives and, 42
   ElementSize switch, 41
   file corruption prevention, 36–38
   Options button, 41
   performance increase of, 40
   questions about, 38–42
   Read Only option, 37
   sampling frequency, 41
   switches, 38
   versions of, 36–37
   Windows and, 451
   See also disk cache
SMARTDRV command, 31, 36, 38, 124, 446–456
   /C switch, 37
   /S switch, 39
   BUFFERS command vs., 32, 123
   caches, 452
   DEVICEHIGH and, 452
   DOS 4 and 5, 452
   double-buffering and, 453–454, 455
   examples, 454–456
   expanded memory and, 455
   extended memory and, 453
   installing, 455
   messages, 454
   networks and, 453
   parameter sequence, 41
   parameters, 447–448
   switches, 448–450
   syntax, 447
   uses, 446–447
   Windows and, 455–456
   writing cache to disk and, 452
   See also SmartDrive
SMARTDRV.EXE, 415
SMARTMON command, 456–457
SmartMonitor program, 39, 456–457
   hit rate, 41
software, third-party, 19–20

SORT command, 97, 100, 457–459
    case and, 458
    collating sequence, 458
    examples, 458–459
    maximum size, 458
    messages, 458
    MORE and, 458–459
    parameters, 458
    switches, 458
    syntax, 457
    uses, 457
sorting, 457–459
    list, 458
Stacker, 44, 57
    CONFIG.SYS and, 158
    Conversion disk, 58
    SCANDISK and, 430
    See also compression program
STACKS command, 459–460
    example, 460
    explained, 460
    MemMaker and, 460
    memory usage, 460
    messages, 460
    parameters, 459
    syntax, 459
    uses, 459
    Zenith computers GRAPHICS command and, 460
start-up, 23–34
    files, 25
    menu colors, 28, 337–339
        color table, 338
        side effect of, 338
    menu item
        create, 340–346
        default, 339–340
    options, 465–467
    See also interactive start-up
Startup menu, 27
    blank lines in, 29
    bypass of, 28
    colors, 28
Storage management, 44–46
STTY command, 315
SUBMENU command, 27, 28, 341, 346, 461–463
    examples, 461–462
    parameters, 461
    syntax, 461
    uses, 461
submenus
    create, 461–463
    defining, 461–462
SUBST command, 112, 317, 326, 463–465
    examples, 464
    incompatibilities, 464
    messages, 464
    parameters, 463
    relative paths and, 464
    switches, 463
    syntax, 463
    uses, 463

SuperStor disk, 17
switches. *See specific switches*
SWITCHES command, 160, 209, 465–466
    /K switch, 465, 466
    examples, 466
    switches, 465–466
    syntax, 465
    uses, 465
syntax lines, 4
SyQuest drive, 18
SYS command, 10, 12, 15, 120, 285, 424, 438, 467–468
    ASSIGN, JOIN, SUBST and, 468
    DOS 3.3 and earlier, 467
    DOS 4.0 and earlier, 468
    examples, 468
    parameters, 467
    syntax, 467
    uses, 467
system debugger, 214
System menu, 19
SYSTEM program, 333

T

/T switch
    ANSI.SYS, 104
    BACKUP command, 117–118
    CHOICE command, 142
    DOSSHELL command, 249
    DRIVER.SYS, 251
    DRIVPARM command, 253
    FC command, 271
    FORMAT command, 282
    MEMMAKER command, 336
    PRINT command, 404
Tandy, 19
temporary files, 96
time
    AUTOEXEC.BAT and, 469
    clock forgets, 170
    format, 233
    IBM PC and, 469
    in prompts, 409
    reporting, 468–469
    setting, 468–469
        new, 469–470
    slices, 406
    See also clock; date
TIME command, 120, 171, 424, 468–470
    examples, 469–470
    messages, 469
    parameters, 468–469
    prompt, 470
    syntax, 468
    uses, 468
TREE command, 131, 351, 470–471
    examples, 471
    messages, 471
    parameters, 470
    switches, 471
    syntax, 470

Index

uses, 470
TSRs
   FILES= command and, 276
   loading, 67–70
   programs, 328
   redirection and, 98
TYPE command, 472
   binary files and, 472
   example, 472
   parameters, 472
   syntax, 472

U

/U switch
   DBLSPACE /UNMOUNT command, 211
   DEFRAG command, 215
   FORMAT command, 281, 283
   PRINT command, 405
   REPLACE command, 420
   SETUP command, 18, 437
   SMARTDRV command, 449
   UNFORMAT command, 484
   VSAFE command, 491
UMBs (upper memory blocks), 64, 227, 229, 329, 333
   conflicts, 243
   DOS management of, 66
   effective use of, 67–70
   HMA and, 243
   insufficient memory for, 71
   MemMaker and, 229
   not enough, 329
   provider, 242
   See also high memory area (HMA)
UNDELETE command, 189, 221, 350, 395, 473–482
   /T switch, 479
   after DEFRAG, 476
   Delete Sentry, 482
   for DOS 6 and later, 477
   for DOS 5, 477–478
   examples, 481–482
   functioning of, 478
   messages, 480–481
   networks and, 478
   not working, 476
   parameters, 473
   switches, 474–475
   syntax, 473
   uses, 473
   when not to use, 476
   See also Undelete program
UNDELETE.INI, 479–480
Undelete program, 14, 84–87
   configuration section, 86
   defaults section, 86
   deleted file conditions, 85
   sentry.drives section, 86
   sentry.files section, 86
   Sentry protection, 85–86, 87
   Tracker level, 85, 86
   Windows version, 85
   See also UNDELETE command

UNFORMAT command, 285, 350, 395, 483–486
   /U switch, 485
   after FORMAT command, 485
   DOS 6 and, 484–485
   examples, 486
   MIRROR and, 484–485
   networks and, 485
   parameters, 484
   switches, 484
   syntax, 483–484
   uses, 483
unformatting, 483–486
   using MIRROR file, 485
   without MIRROR file, 485
   See also formatting
Uninstall disk, 9
   bypassing, 10
   incorrect, 11–12
UNMOUNT command, 56
Utility programs, 77–87
   DOS and Windows versions, 78
   installing, 77
   running, 77
   selection screen, 13
   space requirements, 14
   See also specific programs

V

/V switch
   CHKDSK command, 132
   COPY command, 162
   DISKCOPY command, 237
   FIND command, 277
   FORMAT command, 281
   HIMEM.SYS, 295
   INTERLNK.EXE, 310
   INTERSVR command, 313
   MSCDEX command, 382
   SMARTDRV command, 449
   XCOPY command, 495
VER command, 486–487
   examples, 487
   syntax, 487
   uses, 486
VERIFY command, 120, 165, 487–489, 498
   example, 488
   messages, 488
   mysterious changes with, 488
   networks and, 488
   speed, 488
   syntax, 487
   uses, 487
Video display, 10
Viral signatures, 82–83
   file update, 83
   See also Anti-Virus program
Viruses, 82
   curing, 83
   deletion of, 83–84
   detection of, 83
   protection against, 490–493

scanning for, 377
See also Anti-Virus program
VOL command, 140, 285, 489
    examples, 489
    messages, 489
    parameters, 489
    syntax, 489
volume
    compressed
        checking, 179–180
        deleting, 188
        host drives, 175
        size, 174–175
    creation, 47
    DoubleSpace. *See* DoubleSpace, volume
    label, 139
        changing, 322–324
        display, 489
        INTERLNK and, 306
        mounting and, 201
    serial numbers, 139, 238
    unmounting, secondary, 212
    See also disk drive
VSafe, 84, 388, 490–493
    manager, 389
    protection philosophies, 493
VSAFE command, 377, 490–493
    changing options and, 492
    installation programs and, 493
    installing, 493
    memory used, 492
    speed and, 492
    switches, 490–492
    syntax, 490
    uses, 490
    with Windows, 492
    write-protect option, 492

W

/W switch
    DIR command, 232
    FC command, 272
    MEMMAKER command, 336
    REPLACE command, 420
    SWITCHES command, 465
    XCOPY command, 495
wildcard characters, 91–92
    COMP command and, 153–154
    DEL command and, 220
    DELTREE command and, 223
    DIR command to check, 220
    FC command and, 272
Windows
    386 Enhanced Control Panel, 48
    Anti-Virus program for, 387–389
    Backup program and, 79–80
    CHKDSK and, 134–135
    DEFRAG command and, 217
    DOS program in, 33
    DoubleSpace volumes and, 175

    EMM386 and, 262
    FASTOPEN command and, 269
    FILES= command and, 276
    INTERSVR with, 314
    item, 340
    Microsoft backup for, 389–392
    mouse with, 367
    printer redirection, 310
    SCANDISK command and, 430
    SmartDrive and, 451
    SMARTDRV command and, 455–456
    swapfiles, 56–57
    undelete for, 392–395
    Undelete program, 85
    upper memory and, 72
    Utility programs and, 78
    VSAFE with, 492
    write-behind caching and, 451
    See also File Manager (Windows); SmartMonitor
        program
write caching, 35–36

X

/X switch
    ANSI.SYS, 104
    APPEND command, 108
    BUFFERS command, 123
    FASTOPEN command, 268
    INTERSVR command, 313
    SMARTDRV command, 448
XCOPY command, 115, 120, 165, 351, 373, 381,
        392, 419, 422, 494–498
    for confirming copying over existing files, 497
    COPY vs., 495
    COPYCMD environment variable, 497
    DOS 6.2 upgrade, 2
    examples, 497
    exit codes, 495
    HELP and, 292–293
    messages, 496–497
    parameters, 494
    switches, 494–495
    syntax, 494
    uses, 494
XMS memory, 64, 333
    missing, 71
    provider, 242
    See also extended memory

Y

/Y switch
    COMMAND command, 147
    COPY command, 162
    MOUSE command, 367
    MOVE command, 370
    XCOPY command, 495

Z

/Z switch, MOUSE command, 366

IDG Books

...*For Dummies* Beginners' Series

COMPUTER BOOK SERIES FROM IDG

Back by popular demand: author Dan Gookin shows "the rest of us" how to feel at ease with DOS. Covers all versions through DOS 6.

DOS For Dummies,® 2nd Edition

by Dan Gookin

"A godsend...*DOS For Dummies* saved my sanity." — Susan Darby, Rocky River, OH

Lighthearted but not lightweight, *DOS For Dummies, 2nd Edition* makes it easy to get what you want out of your PC — and nothing else. Says author Dan Gookin, "If all you need is to find the answer to that one tiny question and be on with your life, then this is the book you're looking for."

This completely revised and updated 2nd Edition covers DOS versions 2 through 6, and is organized so you can flip right to the section that pertains to the question at hand, get the answer fast, and get to lunch. Humorous icons and a glossary help clarify details. You'll learn the easy way to manage files, the low-anxiety way to change drives and disks; how to track down that lost file. Find out how to avoid being spooked by DOS error messages. See what to do when "bad things happen."

DOS For Dummies is arranged in modules, so you can start reading at any section. It includes a FREE keyboard template and bookmark as well as a tear-out "cheat sheet" with over 30 instant tips. Presented in Dan Gookin's friendly, irreverent style, and spiced with Richard Tennant's droll cartoons, this is the one book every smart "DOS Dummy" should have. 316 pages.

Book   **ISBN: 1-878058-75-4**   **$16.95 US/$21.95 Canada**

*I*llustrated Computer Dictionary For Dummies by three of today's most popular computer authors.

by Dan Gookin, Wally Wang, and Chris Van Buren

At last — translated into plain, hilarious English — the computerese that technojocks use to keep the rest of us off balance and in the dark. Over 200 illustrations help demystify the most arcane hardware and software terms. Plus you'll find full descriptions of commonly-used expressions like nerd and geek, along with a guide to effective usage. A handy phonetic pronunciation guide includes popular computer terms and acronyms. The perfect gift for every PC user.

Book   **ISBN: 1-56884-004-7**   **$12.95 US/$16.95 Canada**

For More Information Or To Order By Mail, Call 1-800-762-2974. Call For A Free Catalog!
For volume discounts and special orders, please call Tony Real, Special Sales, at 415-312-0644.

IDG Books

...For Dummies Beginners' Series

COMPUTER BOOK SERIES FROM IDG

OVER 5,008,476 DUMMIES BOOKS IN PRINT!

Presenting the ...For Dummies™ books, guaranteed to build your computer confidence and let you laugh while you learn to deal with your PC.

"Wonderful, informative, entertaining, and cheap, too!" — Sally J. Reed, Jacksonville, FL

"Cuts through the baloney and gets right to the source." — Alan V. Roat, Indianapolis, IN

- Newly expanded series of bestsellers covers today's most popular operating systems and business software.
- Entertaining yet informative, ...For Dummies' easy-to-follow format makes learning how to deal with your computer fun and easy.
- Every book in the series is written in plain English, with a clear, down-to-earth style that lets beginners feel at ease.
- Basic tasks and boring technicalities are logically presented and organized for quick reference.
- The books have enough detail so everyone (even friends who think they know it all) can learn plenty of new tricks.

OPERATING SYSTEMS

Windows For Dummies
$16.95 US/$21.95 Canada
ISBN: 1-878058-61-4   *Bestseller*

OS/2 For Dummies
$19.95 US/$26.95 Canada
ISBN: 1-878058-76-2   *NEW*

UNIX For Dummies
$19.95 US/$26.95 Canada
ISBN: 1-878058-58-4   *NEW*

SPREADSHEET/FINANCE

Excel For Dummies
$16.95 US/$21.95 Canada
ISBN: 1-878058-63-0   *Bestseller*

1-2-3 For Dummies
$16.95 US/$21.95 Canada
ISBN: 1-878058-60-6   *Bestseller*

For More Information Or To Order By Mail, Call 1-800-762-2974. Call For A Free Catalog!
For volume discounts and special orders, please call Tony Real, Special Sales, at 415-312-0644.

IDG Books

...For Dummies Beginners' Series

COMPUTER BOOK SERIES FROM IDG

WORD PROCESSING

WordPerfect For Dummies
$16.95 US/$21.95 Canada
ISBN: 1-878058-52-5
Bestseller

WordPerfect 6 For Dummies
$16.95 US/$21.95 Canada
ISBN: 1-878058-77-0
NEW

Word 6 for DOS For Dummies
$16.95 US/$21.95 Canada
ISBN: 1-56884-000-4
NEW

Word for Windows For Dummies
$16.95 US/$21.95 Canada
ISBN: 1-878058-86-X
NEW

HARDWARE

PCs For Dummies
$16.95 US/$21.95 Canada
ISBN: 1-878058-51-7

VIII FINALIST
Eighth Annual Computer Press Awards 1992

Bestseller

Macs For Dummies
$16.95 US/$21.95 Canada
ISBN: 1-878058-53-5
Bestseller

**For More Information Or To Order By Mail, Call 1-800-762-2974. Call For A Free Catalog!
For volume discounts and special orders, please call Tony Real, Special Sales, at 415-312-0644.**

IDG Books   ...For Dummies Quick Reference Series

COMPUTER BOOK SERIES FROM IDG

...*For* Dummies Quick Reference books are the smart way to keep the vital computer information you need always close at hand.

They're fun, they're fast and they're cheap! Here, in a concise, useful format, are quick reference books no computer user can afford to be without. All are written in clear, non-technical language, by bestselling authors and experts on the subject at hand. And each is cross-referenced to its main *...For Dummies* counterpart. They're great memory refreshers to have close by your PC.

Every book in the series guides you through complex commands keystroke by keystroke, to give users of all skill levels easy access to solutions. They're loaded with helpful icons throughout, to highlight tips and point out special features. Humorous icons are interspersed to indicate suitability and the general safety of the task being described.

DOS For Dummies™ Quick Reference
by Greg Harvey

Explains every DOS command. Special section lists and explains batch commands and configuration commands. Covers all versions, including DOS 6. 44 illustrations, 132 pages.

ISBN: 1-56884-007-1   **$8.95 USA/$11.95 Canada**

Windows For Dummies™ Quick Reference
by Greg Harvey

Includes all major Windows functions. Covers File Manager and Print Manager basics; Windows modes and Windows Help. Covers Windows 3.1. 48 illustrations, 175 pages.

ISBN: 1-56884-008-X   **$8.95 USA/$11.95 Canada**

WordPerfect for DOS For Dummies™ Quick Reference
by Greg Harvey

Explains WordPerfect's menus and tools, manipulating documents, text blocks; formatting and printing. Covers all versions of WordPerfect through 6. 49 illustrations.

ISBN: 1-56884-009-8   **$8.95 USA/$11.95**

For More Information Or To Order By Mail, Call 1-800-762-2974. Call For A Free Catalog!
For volume discounts and special orders, please call Tony Real, Special Sales, at 415-312-0644.

IDG Books

...For Dummies Quick Reference Series

COMPUTER BOOK SERIES FROM IDG

Excel For Dummies™ Quick Reference
by John Walkenbach

Includes comprehensive guides to @functions. Explains all menu commands including those for WYSIWYG add-ins. Covers Excel 4 for Windows. 63 illustrations, 132 pages.

ISBN: 1-56884-028-4   **$8.95 USA/$11.95 Canada**

1-2-3 For Dummies™ Quick Reference
by John Walkenbach

Provides an overview of 1-2-3 for DOS basics; includes all essential menu commands, plus a guide to 1-2-3's functions and macro commands. 59 illustrations, 175 pages.

ISBN: 1-56884-027-6   **$8.95 USA/$11.95 Canada**

Word for Windows For Dummies™ Quick Reference
by George Lynch

Strong graphics enhance coverage of features; includes formatting, macros, merge printing, importing spreadsheets. Covers Word 2 for Windows. 47 illustrations, 175 pages.

ISBN: 1-56884-029-2   **$8.95 USA/$11.95 Canada**

For More Information Or To Order By Mail, Call 1-800-762-2974. Call For A Free Catalog!
For volume discounts and special orders, please call Tony Real, Special Sales, at 415-312-0644.

IDG BOOKS

Order Form

Order Center: (800) 762-2974 (8 a.m.-5 p.m., PST, weekdays) or (415) 312-0650
For Fastest Service: Photocopy This Order Form and FAX it to : (415) 358-1260

Quantity	ISBN	Title	Price	Total

Shipping & Handling Charges

Subtotal	U.S.	Canada & International	International Air Mail
Up to $20.00	Add $3.00	Add $4.00	Add $10.00
$20.01-40.00	$4.00	$5.00	$20.00
$40.01-60.00	$5.00	$6.00	$25.00
$60.01-80.00	$6.00	$8.00	$35.00
Over $80.00	$7.00	$10.00	$50.00

In U.S. and Canada, shipping is UPS ground or equivalent.
For Rush shipping call (800) 762-2974.

Subtotal _____
CA residents add applicable sales tax _____
IN residents add 5% sales tax _____
Canadian residents add 7% GST tax _____
Shipping _____
TOTAL _____

Ship to:
Name _____
Company _____
Address _____
City/State/Zip _____
Daytime Phone _____

Payment: ❑ Check to IDG Books (US Funds Only)   ❑ Visa   ❑ MasterCard   ❑ American Express
Card # _____ Exp. _____ Signature _____

Please send this order form to: IDG Books, 155 Bovet Road, Suite 310, San Mateo, CA 94402.
Allow up to 3 weeks for delivery. Thank you!

BOBFD

IDG BOOKS WORLDWIDE REGISTRATION CARD

RETURN THIS REGISTRATION CARD FOR FREE CATALOG

Title of this book: DOS 6 Command Reference And Problem Solver

My overall rating of this book: ❏ Very good [1] ❏ Good [2] ❏ Satisfactory [3] ❏ Fair [4] ❏ Poor [5]

How I first heard about this book:
❏ Found in bookstore; name: [6]
❏ Book review: [7]
❏ Advertisement: [8]
❏ Catalog: [9]
❏ Word of mouth; heard about book from friend, co-worker, etc.: [10]
❏ Other: [11]

What I liked most about this book:

What I would change, add, delete, etc., in future editions of this book:

Other comments:

Number of computer books I purchase in a year: ❏ 1 [12] ❏ 2-5 [13] ❏ 6-10 [14] ❏ More than 10 [15]

I would characterize my computer skills as: ❏ Beginner [16] ❏ Intermediate [17] ❏ Advanced [18] ❏ Professional [19]

I use ❏ DOS [20] ❏ Windows [21] ❏ OS/2 [22] ❏ Unix [23] ❏ Macintosh [24] ❏ Other: [25] _____ (please specify)

I would be interested in new books on the following subjects:
(please check all that apply, and use the spaces provided to identify specific software)

❏ Word processing: [26]
❏ Spreadsheets: [27]
❏ Data bases: [28]
❏ Desktop publishing: [29]
❏ File Utilities: [30]
❏ Money management: [31]
❏ Networking: [32]
❏ Programming languages: [33]
❏ Other: [34]

I use a PC at (please check all that apply): ❏ home [35] ❏ work [36] ❏ school [37] ❏ other: [38] _____

The disks I prefer to use are ❏ 5.25 [39] ❏ 3.5 [40] ❏ other: [41] _____

I have a CD ROM: ❏ yes [42] ❏ no [43]

I plan to buy or upgrade computer hardware this year: ❏ yes [44] ❏ no [45]

I plan to buy or upgrade computer software this year: ❏ yes [46] ❏ no [47]

Name: _____ Business title: [48] _____ Type of Business: [49] _____

Address (❏ home [50] ❏ work [51] /Company name: _____)

Street/Suite#

City [52] /State [53] /Zipcode [54]: _____ Country [55] _____

❏ **I liked this book!** You may quote me by name in future IDG Books Worldwide promotional materials.

My daytime phone number is _____

IDG BOOKS
THE WORLD OF COMPUTER KNOWLEDGE

❏ **YES!**
Please keep me informed about IDG's World of Computer Knowledge.
Send me the latest IDG Books catalog.

BUSINESS REPLY MAIL
FIRST CLASS MAIL   PERMIT NO. 2605   SAN MATEO, CALIFORNIA

NO POSTAGE
NECESSARY
IF MAILED
IN THE
UNITED STATES

**IDG Books Worldwide
155 Bovet Road
San Mateo, CA 94402-9833**